Recent Titles in the
Children's and Young Adult Literature Reference Series
Catherine Barr, Series Editor

Best Books for Middle School and Junior High Readers: Grades 6–9. Supplement
to the First Edition
John T. Gillespie and Catherine Barr

Best Books for High School Readers: Grades 9–12. Supplement to the First
Edition
John T. Gillespie and Catherine Barr

War and Peace: A Guide to Literature and New Media, Grades 4–8
Virginia A. Walter

Across Cultures: A Guide to Multicultural Literature for Children
Kathy East and Rebecca L. Thomas

Best Books for Children, Supplement to the 8th Edition: Preschool
through Grade 6
Catherine Barr and John T. Gillespie

Best Books for Boys: A Resource for Educators
Matthew D. Zbaracki

Beyond Picture Books: Subject Access to Best Books for Beginning Readers
Barbara Barstow, Judith Riggle, and Leslie Molnar

A to Zoo: Subject Access to Children's Picture Books. Supplement to the 7th
Edition
Carolyn W. Lima and Rebecca L. Thomas

Gentle Reads: Great Books to Warm Hearts and Lift Spirits, Grades 5–9
Deanna J. McDaniel

Best New Media, K–12: A Guide to Movies, Subscription Web Sites, and
Educational Software and Games
Catherine Barr

Historical Fiction for Young Readers (Grades 4–8): An Introduction
John T. Gillespie

Twice Upon a Time: A Guide to Fractured, Altered, and Retold Folk and Fairy Tales
Catharine Bomhold and Terri E. Elder

POPULAR SERIES FICTION FOR MIDDLE SCHOOL AND TEEN READERS

POPULAR SERIES FICTION FOR MIDDLE SCHOOL AND TEEN READERS

A READING AND SELECTION GUIDE

2ND EDITION

Rebecca L. Thomas and Catherine Barr

Children's and Young Adult Literature Reference
Catherine Barr, Series Editor

A Member of the Greenwood Publishing Group

Westport, Connecticut • London

Library of Congress Cataloging-in-Publication Data

Thomas, Rebecca L.
  Popular series fiction for middle school and teen readers : a reading and
selection guide / Rebecca L. Thomas and Catherine Barr. — 2nd ed.
      p. cm. — (Children's and young adult literature reference)
  Includes bibliographical references and index.
  ISBN 978-1-59158-660-9 (alk. paper)
  1. Children's literature in series—Bibliography. 2. Children's stories—
Bibliography. 3. Young adult fiction—Bibliography. 4. Children—Books
and reading—United States. 5. Teenagers—Books and reading—United
States. 6. Children's libraries—Book selection. 7. Young adults'
libraries—Book selection. I. Barr, Catherine, 1951– II. Title.
  Z1037.T4655   2009
  011.62—dc22   2008038125

British Library Cataloguing in Publication Data is available.

Library of Congress Catalog Card Number: 2008038125
ISBN: 978-1-59158-660-9

First published in 2009

Libraries Unlimited, 88 Post Road West, Westport, CT 06881
A Member of the Greenwood Publishing Group, Inc.
www.lu.com

Printed in the United States of America

The paper used in this book complies with the
Permanent Paper Standard issued by the National
Information Standards Organization (Z39.48–1984).

10   9   8   7   6   5   4   3   2   1

CONTENTS

PREFACE

Series fiction is more popular than ever—in the first edition of *Popular Series Fiction* (2004), we had more than 1,500 series; now there are nearly 2,200—and the YA market continues to be hot. Clearly, staying current with popular books is crucial if libraries want to attract and serve teen readers.

Series books with media tie-ins (such as Princess Diaries and all the Star Wars entries) or about dating and school (A-List and Gossip Girl) and even fashion (The Fashion-Forward Adventures of Imogene, Flirt) are all the rage. Fantasy books are also extremely popular thanks in part to Harry Potter and The Lord of the Rings and a renewed fascination with all things vampire. Many established authors—Laurence Yep, Phyllis Reynolds Naylor, and Todd Strasser, to name just a few—have contributed series books that focus on issues and topics that are of interest to teens.

Graphic novels, manga, cine-manga, and other illustrated novels have greatly increased in availability and popularity. *Popular Series Fiction for Middle School and Teen Readers: A Reading and Selection Guide* includes a selection of these materials, chosen with the help of professional reference sources. Publishers' catalogs and Web sites were also examined, although these were often more hype then help. Assigning a grade level was problematic as sources varied widely on what was suitable for younger readers. A sentence is included in the annotation to alert users to any concerns about content. As these materials become more established, more selection information should be available.

Series for tweens—such as Zoey 101, How I Survived Middle School, and High School Musical—have continued to thrive. The books for this group focus on preparation for their upcoming independence. Chick lit remains very popular, with new series including Nannies, Celebutantes, the Ashleys, and Talent. And a new category has developed—urban lit—seen in Platinum Teen, Hotlanta, and Bluford High.

Keeping up with these materials is a challenge. *Popular Series Fiction for Middle School and Teen Readers* provides guidance for professionals— and for parents—seeking to encourage young people to read. Teachers work to find series books that meet the needs of the variety of readers in their classrooms. Librarians frequently hear questions such as "Do you know any mystery books that will attract reluctant readers?" and "What fantasy books do you recommend for middle school students?" With this book, librarians and teachers will find it easier to keep tabs on new titles in existing series and to evaluate new series (and each re-packaging).

Popular Series Fiction for Middle School and Teen Readers is a companion to *Popular Series Fiction for K–6 Readers*. These books evolved from *Reading in Series* (Bowker, 1999).

RESEARCH AND SELECTION

One of our first considerations was how to identify the series. To create our initial listing, we looked at current reviewing sources such as *Booklist* and *School Library Journal* and at reference compilations including *Best Books for Middle School and Junior High Readers* and *Best Books for High School Readers* (both from Libraries Unlimited) and Wilson's *Middle and Junior High School Library Catalog* and *Senior High School Library Catalog*. In addition, we made use of online sources including publisher and author Web sites, teen sites (http://www.teenreads.com, in particular), booksellers amazon.com and barnesandnoble.com, series sites such as those at Mid-Continent Public Library (http://www.mcpl.lib.mo.us) and Bettendorf Public Library (http://www.bettendorflibrary.com/teens/), and other specialized library sites.

As we search libraries and bookstores for the books themselves, the following criteria are applied:

1. The series we select are content-based groupings of books with a consistent theme, setting, or group of characters.

2. A series generally needs three or more books. However, we include some developing series that promise to become popular. Some "future titles" are included in an effort to be as current as possible. Titles for 2009 books may end up being changed, but their inclusion will alert librarians that additions to the series are forthcoming.

3. The grade range of the books in this volume is 6 through 12. A selection of adult books read by young adults are included. And some series that might seem more appropriate for a younger audience, such as Captain Underpants, have been included as possible choices for reluctant readers. Decisions about grade levels are based on knowledge of the audience, examination of the books, consultation of professional resources, and library experience.

4. As we annotate each series, every effort is made to examine several books, hoping to offer better insight to librarians making purchasing decisions or recommending these books to readers.

5. Older series are included too, especially those considered "classics." In selecting the "older" series to include, we rely on our judgment, on the judgment of our contributors, and on our ability to find copies of several titles in libraries and bookstores.

6. We focus on including series with some of the titles still in print. This can be a problem, especially for paperback series. Some

very popular books that were published only a few years ago are no longer available, but we decided to include these series because they can still be found in many libraries. Librarians and teachers who want to update their collections can use the Genre/Subject Index to find newer, similar books.

We scour libraries, bookstores, publishers' catalogs, and Web sites looking for new series and the newest titles in existing series. But this is not a comprehensive listing. Many of these series have spawned a number of offshoots—Star Wars is a prime example—often spanning generations of characters. We have attempted to include a sampling of some of the most important. *Popular Series Fiction for Middle School and Teen Readers* is a work in progress and we anticipate that each successive edition will grow.

ANATOMY OF AN ENTRY

Each entry provides the following information:

Series title: Cross-referenced as needed

Author: If individual books within a series have different authors, they are listed with the books.

Publisher: Many series have had several publishers over the years. The publisher shown is the most recent publisher. In some cases both hardback and paperback publishers are listed.

Grade level: This volume covers series for grades 6–YA (grades K–6 are covered in the companion volume). There is some overlap between the two volumes, particularly focusing on books that might be appropriate for reluctant readers.

Genres: These are broad thematic areas that will help link similar series. The genres included are: Adventure, Animal Fantasy, Family Life, Fantasy, Historical, Horror, Humor, Mystery, Real Life, Recreation, Science Fiction, and Values.

Accelerated Reader: The notation A/R indicates that Accelerated Reader resources are available for some or all of the titles in the series.

Annotation: This descriptive examination of the series provides information about important characters, plots, themes, and issues in the series. Specific books are often described in detail.

List of titles in the series: This list was compiled using the books themselves and the selection sources mentioned above, as well as Books in Print (R. R. Bowker), the CLEVNET database (which serves a large number of member libraries in northeast Ohio including the Cleveland Public Library), and literature sites including NoveList. These resources (along with the publisher catalogs and Web sites) often provided conflicting information about exact titles and copyright dates, so there may be some inconsistencies; however, every effort has been made to be as complete and accurate as possible. Book titles are shown in chronological order by year of publication. Numbered series are shown in number order, which is usually also chronological. Where series include prequels or alternative reading orders, this is mentioned in the annotation.

APPENDIXES AND INDEXES

Author and Title indexes will help the user who is searching for new series by a given author or who knows only one title in a series. The Genre/Subject Index gives access by genre and by more specific topics. Thus, the fan of horror can easily find more series in that genre; and readers can quickly identify series about horses. The addition of grade levels after the series titles allows users to pinpoint grade-appropriate series quickly. To make access easier, real animals and fantasy animals (mice that wear clothes and go to school, for example) are listed together.

In addition, there are lists of series of special interest to boys or girls and for reluctant readers. These are not comprehensive lists; series were selected for their current appeal to readers. The books for boys often feature as the main characters a group of boys who are involved in mysteries, sports, school problems, friendship, and the supernatural. The books for girls often feature one or more girls involved in mysteries, sports (horseback riding and skating, in particular), school problems, friendship, and growing up. The books for reluctant readers were chosen for their popular appeal, and often feature media tie-ins, monsters, and creatures.

There are many ways for librarians and teachers to use *Popular Series Fiction*. The Genre/Subject Index points the way to series on topics of interest. The genre Fantasy, for example, makes it easy to identify series of interest. For readers who want legends of King Arthur and Merlin, consult the subject Arthurian Legends to find T. A. Barron's Merlin and The Great Tree of Avalon as well as the classic series from T. H. White and the Arthur Trilogy by Kevin Crossley-Holland.

Popular Series Fiction is also a selection guide. Librarians may want to add new series or update titles in series that have already been purchased. If your students like mysteries, look at the P.C. Hawke Mysteries. For sports, there is Dream Series. For adventure, there is Alex Rider. Add the newer titles to existing series or fill in titles you may have missed. The annotations allow you to compare series and make decisions about which will best fit your needs.

Popular Series Fiction builds on the earlier *Reading in Series*. Compilation of that book involved the efforts of librarians and teachers who are well qualified in fiction for children:

Connie Parker	Cuyahoga County (Ohio) Public Library
Deanna McDaniel	Westerville (Ohio) City Schools
Jacqueline Albers	Cuyahoga County (Ohio) Public Library
Karen Breen	Program Officer, New Visions for Public Schools, New York, NY
Doris Gebel	Northport (NY) Public Library
Debbie Gold	Cuyahoga County (Ohio) Public Library

We would like to thank Barbara Ittner of Libraries Unlimited for her encouragement and support and Julie Miller, Christine Weisel McNaull, and Kris Aparicio for their work on the database, design and composition, editing, and research.

SERIES A–Z

A-LIST

Dean, Zoey

LITTLE, BROWN ◆ GRADES 9–12 ◆ A/R

REAL LIFE

Anna Percy adjusts to moving from Manhattan to Los Angeles. She hooks up with a privileged crowd that takes risks with drugs, boys, and other indulgences. Readers who enjoy this series are sure to like Gossip Girl books as well as The Ashleys and Clique.

1. The A-List ◆ 2003
2. Girls on Film: An A-List Novel ◆ 2004
3. Blonde Ambition: An A-List Novel ◆ 2004
4. Tall Cool One: An A-List Novel ◆ 2005
5. Back in Black: An A-List Novel ◆ 2005
6. Some Like It Hot: An A-List Novel ◆ 2006
7. American Beauty: An A-List Novel ◆ 2006
8. Heart of Glass: An A-List Novel ◆ 2007
9. Beautiful Stranger: An A-List Novel ◆ 2007
10. California Dreaming: An A-List Novel ◆ 2008

ABBY'S SOUTH SEAS ADVENTURES

Walls, Pamela

TYNDALE HOUSE ◆ GRADES 5–8 ◆ A/R

ADVENTURE | VALUES

In Hawaii in the mid-1800s, Abby and her family face many challenges to their safety and to their values. One adventure features Abby and her friend Luke searching for an arsonist before there is another fire. Their faith and their willingness to love and forgive sustain them.

1. Lost at Sea ◆ 2000
2. Quest for Treasure ◆ 2000
3. California Gold ◆ 2001
4. Secret at Cutter Grove ◆ 2001
5. King's Ransom ◆ 2001
6. Into the Dragon's Den ◆ 2001
7. Trouble in Tahiti ◆ 2002
8. Maui Mystery ◆ 2002

ABHORSEN

Nix, Garth

HARPERCOLLINS ◆ GRADES 7–12 ◆ A/R

FANTASY

This trilogy features a classic confrontation between good and evil. Characters include Lirael, formerly Second Assistant Librarian and now Abhorsen-in-Waiting, Prince Sam, and Disreputable Dog in a struggle to save the Old Kingdom.

1. Sabriel ◆ 1996
2. Lirael: Daughter of the Clayr ◆ 2001
3. Abhorsen ◆ 2003

ABRACADABRA

Becker, Eve

BANTAM ◆ GRADES 5–7

FANTASY

Dawn, 13, can make things happen simply by arching her left eyebrow. Despite her grandmother's warnings, she uses this talent to great effect, making herself popular and generally getting everything she wants . . . until her powers wane and she has to rely on her own resources, which she discovers are sufficient after all.

1. Thirteen Means Magic ◆ 1989
2. The Love Potion ◆ 1989
3. The Magic Mix-Up ◆ 1989
4. The Sneezing Spell ◆ 1989
5. The Popularity Potion ◆ 1990
6. Too Much Magic ◆ 1990

ACORNA

McCaffrey, Anne

HARPERCOLLINS ◆ GRADES 10–12 ◆ A/R

FANTASY | SCIENCE FICTION

The orphan Acorna, a pretty child with a horn on her forehead and other odd features, is discovered drifting in an escape pod. With the help of her rescuers, she grows into a strong, independent young woman who cares for the downtrodden. In *Acorna's Quest* and *Acorna's People,* she searches for—and finds—her own people. But, as always, there are dangers and challenges that test Acorna's powers and resolve.

1. Acorna: The Unicorn Girl ◆ 1997
2. Acorna's Quest ◆ 1998
3. Acorna's People ◆ 1999
4. Acorna's World ◆ 2000
5. Acorna's Search ◆ 2002
6. Acorna's Rebels ◆ 2003
7. Acorna's Triumph ◆ 2004

ACORNA'S CHILDREN

McCaffrey, Anne, and Elizabeth Ann Scarborough
EOS ◆ GRADES 10–12
FANTASY | SCIENCE FICTION

Khorii, daughter of the famous Acorna and her lifemate Aari, must fight a deadly plague that is spreading across the universe in this intricate fantasy.

1. First Warning ◆ 2005
2. Second Wave ◆ 2006
3. Third Watch ◆ 2007

ACROSS THE STEEL RIVER

Stenhouse, Ted
KIDS CAN ◆ GRADES 5–8 ◆ A/R
HISTORICAL | MYSTERY

In 1950s Canada, Will and Arthur, a white boy and an Indian boy who are friends despite local prejudices, are determined to find out what happened to an Indian they found barely alive near the railroad tracks. They later discover secrets about town residents and investigate a World War I mystery, all the while learning about racism and friendship.

1. Across the Steel River ◆ 2001
2. A Dirty Deed ◆ 2003
3. Murder on the Ridge ◆ 2005

ADAM PELKO

Mazer, Harry
SIMON & SCHUSTER ◆ GRADES 6–10 ◆ A/R
ADVENTURE

Fourteen-year-old Adam Pelko, newly arrived in Hawaii and proud of his father's position as a lieutenant on the battleship *Arizona,* is fishing with his Japanese American friend Davi when the attack on Pearl Harbor takes place before their eyes. In the second book, Adam—now living in California with his mother and sister—must deal with the loss of his father, his new surroundings, and his friend Davi's plea for help in finding his own father, who has been interned. In *Heroes Don't Run,* Adam joins the Marines at the age of 17 and faces combat on Okinawa.

1. A Boy at War: A Novel of Pearl Harbor ◆ 2001
2. A Boy No More ◆ 2004
3. Heroes Don't Run: A Novel of the Pacific War ◆ 2005

THE ADEPT

Kurtz, Katherine, and Deborah Turner Harris

ACE BOOKS ◆ GRADES 10–12

FANTASY | MYSTERY

Sir Adam Sinclair, a physician who assists the police with some of their more mysterious crimes, is a man of many talents. His interest in magic and the occult gives him an insight into the unknown. Set in present-day Scotland, these books are filled with evil groups seeking to release dangerous, forbidden powers. Druids, the Knights Templar, and occult experiences make for exciting, fast-paced reading. This series was reissued in the early 2000s.

1. The Adept ◆ 1991
2. The Lodge of the Lynx ◆ 1992
3. The Templar Treasure ◆ 1993
4. Dagger Magic ◆ 1995
5. Death of an Adept ◆ 1996

ADVENTURES IN ODYSSEY: PASSAGES *see* Passages

ADVENTURES OF A YOUNG SAILOR

Dowswell, Paul

BLOOMSBURY ◆ GRADES 5–8 ◆ A/R

ADVENTURE | HISTORICAL

At the beginning of the 19th century, 13-year-old Sam Witchall finds himself a powder monkey—supplying the gunpowder to the cannon crew—on the *HMS Miranda,* and his love of the sea is subdued by the conditions and the violent fighting of the Napoleonic Wars. In *Prison Ship,* Sam and his friend Richard have been falsely accused of cowardice. They are sent to Australia, where they face a wide variety of challenges. By the end of the third book, Sam is back in England, in the Navy, and preparing for the famous Battle of Trafalgar. These books are historically accurate and full of action.

1. Powder Monkey ◆ 2005
2. Prison Ship ◆ 2006
3. Battle Fleet ◆ 2008

THE ADVENTURES OF BEATRICE BAILEY

Forrester, Sandra

BARRON'S ◆ GRADES 5–8 ◆ A/R

FANTASY

In the first book, 11-year-old Beatrice is assigned a quest before receiving her final witch classification. She and her friends must rescue a famous sorcerer and his daughters, who have been seized by a rival wizard and are being guarded by monsters. In following books, she learns about her family as she frees the captives one by one, facing peril at every turn. This series has many elements of the Harry Potter stories.

1. The Everyday Witch ◆ 2002
2. The Witches of Friar's Lantern ◆ 2003
3. The Witches of Sea-Dragon Bay ◆ 2003
4. The Witches of Winged-Horse Mountain ◆ 2004
5. The Witches of Bailiwick ◆ 2005
6. The Witches of Widdershins Academy ◆ 2007

ADVENTURES OF DANIEL BOOM AKA LOUD BOY

Steinberg, D. J.

GROSSET & DUNLAP ◆ GRADES 4–7 ◆ A/R

HUMOR

Daniel Boom has a problem . . . actually, several problems. First, he is new in town. Second, he is loud. Third, the Kid-Rid corporation has invented the Soundsucker LX—a machine that will silence the world. This sounds like a job for Loud Boy, Daniel's inner superhero. In the second book, Kid-Rid invades the school cafeteria and makes a mind controlling mac and cheese. The graphic novel format will be a winner with reluctant readers.

1. Sound Off! ◆ 2008
2. Mac Attack! ◆ 2008
3. Game On! ◆ 2009

ADVENTURES OF MARY-KATE AND ASHLEY *see* Mary-Kate and Ashley: Adventures of Mary-Kate and Ashley

THE ADVENTURES OF UNCLE STINKY

Rumble, Chris

TRICYCLE PRESS ◆ GRADES 4–7 ◆ A/R

HUMOR

Hold your nose, here comes a smelly superhero—Uncle Stinky. In *Stink Trek,* Uncle Stinky outwits Theo Durzindapance at the 319th Annual Hootenhollerama and then is captured by intergalactic clowns. There is plenty of foolishness, as when Mayor Naise is beamed into the City Hall outhouse and the door is sealed with super glue, making it a "poo-poo prison." And there is an abundance of cartoon-style illustrations. At times, the text is totally replaced by action displayed in cartoon panels. Consider this for fans of Captain Underpants.

1. The Good, the Bad, and the Smelly ◆ 2004
2. Stink Trek ◆ 2004
3. Moby Stink ◆ 2005

ADVENTURES WITH THE PARKERS

Graf, Mike

FULCRUM ◆ GRADES 5–8 ◆ A/R

ADVENTURE

Ten-year-old twin brother and sister James and Morgan Parker learn about nature and ecology and have adventures as they explore the national parks with their parents. For example, in *Bryce and Zion,* the twins help to rescue an injured woman, encounter a rattlesnake, and play important roles when their father slips and falls in a rainstorm. Sketches and photographs bring the locations to life, and maps and diagrams add background material.

1. Bryce and Zion: Danger in the Narrows ◆ 2006
2. Grand Canyon: The Tail of the Scorpion ◆ 2006
3. Yosemite: Harrowing Ascent of Half Dome ◆ 2007
4. Yellowstone: Eye of the Grizzly ◆ 2007
5. Olympic National Park: Touch of the Tide Pool, Crack of the Glacier ◆ 2009
6. The Great Smoky Mountains: Ridge Runner Rescue ◆ 2009

AERIEL TRILOGY *see* Darkangel Trilogy

AGAINST THE ODDS

Strasser, Todd

ALADDIN ◆ GRADES 6–9 ◆ A/R

ADVENTURE

In *Gator Prey,* a small plane crashes in the Everglades and the two teen characters, Justin and Rachel, are the ones whose actions save the group. Along with Justin's mom and Rachel's dad, they face dangers from alligators and fire. In *Grizzly Attack,* Tyler runs away to Alaska, where he faces his own problems and a dangerous bear.

1. Shark Bite ◆ 1998
2. Grizzly Attack ◆ 1998
3. Buzzard's Feast ◆ 1999
4. Gator Prey ◆ 1999

AGE OF BRONZE

Shanower, Eric

IMAGE ◆ GRADES 9–12

HISTORICAL

This graphic novel retelling (in seven projected volumes) of the Trojan War has won much praise. The black-and-white cartoon illustrations bring to life the stories of Paris, Helen, Achilles, and other characters, and introduce many architectural and mythological details. Appended material (charts, glossary, and so forth) provides useful background information.

1. A Thousand Ships ◆ 2001
2. Sacrifice ◆ 2001
3. Betrayal: Part One ◆ 2007

AGE OF DISCOVERY TRILOGY

Stackpole, Michael A.

BANTAM ◆ GRADES 10–12 ◆ A/R

FANTASY

In Nalenyr (a fantasy world), the Royal Cartographers possess knowledge and power—controlling information as they explore, chart, and map the world. Keles and Jorim, grandsons of the Royal Cartographer, begin their exploration to chart the unknown and encounter ancient magical threats. At home, their sister Nirati deals with intrigues and danger. As the forces build to invade Nalenyr, the three take separate paths to save their world, even awakening old heroes trapped in a magical wasteland.

1. A Secret Atlas ◆ 2004
2. Cartomancy ◆ 2006
3. The New World ◆ 2007

AGE OF MAGIC TRILOGY

McGowen, Tom

LODESTAR/DUTTON ◆ GRADES 5–9 ◆ A/R

FANTASY

The troll wizard Gwolchmig foresees an invasion from beyond the sky and the destruction of Earth. He puts aside lifelong animosities to unite the five races of Earth: trolls, humans, little people, Alfar (elves), and dragons. Twelve-year-old Lithim faces fierce opposition from the Atlan domain and devises a plan that will save the planet.

1. The Magical Fellowship ◆ 1991
2. The Trial of Magic ◆ 1992
3. The Question of Magic ◆ 1993

THE AGE OF UNREASON

Keyes, J. Gregory

BALLANTINE DEL REY ◆ GRADES 10–12

FANTASY | HISTORICAL

History and fantasy are intertwined in these alternate views of 18th-century Europe and America featuring well-known individuals including Benjamin Franklin and Isaac Newton working with fictionalized characters to save society from the threat of destruction. These threats come both from ruthless individuals and from an invisible world.

1. Newton's Cannon ◆ 1998
2. A Calculus of Angels ◆ 1999
3. Empire of Unreason ◆ 2000
4. The Shadows of God ◆ 2001

AKIKO

Crilley, Mark

DELACORTE ◆ GRADES 4–7 ◆ A/R

FANTASY

Akiko, 10, is in fourth grade on Earth when she is asked to help rescue a kidnapped prince. Assisted by aliens, she goes on an intergalactic mission searching for the kidnapper, Alia Rellapor.

1. Akiko on the Planet Smoo ◆ 2000
2. Akiko in the Sprubly Islands ◆ 2000
3. Akiko and the Great Wall of Trudd ◆ 2001
4. Akiko in the Castle of Alia Rellapor ◆ 2001
5. Akiko and the Intergalactic Zoo ◆ 2002
6. Akiko and the Alpha Centauri 5000 ◆ 2003
7. Akiko and the Journey to Toog ◆ 2003
8. Akiko: The Training Master ◆ 2005
9. Akiko: Pieces of Gax ◆ 2006
10. Akiko and the Missing Misp ◆ 2008

AKIKO GRAPHIC NOVELS

Crilley, Mark
SIRIUS ENTERTAINMENT ◆ GRADES 4–7
FANTASY

In the opening trilogy, Akiko is on summer vacation when she is sent to the Planet Smoo to the castle of Alia Rellapor. She battles a dragon but then she and her colleagues are captured by Loza Throck. They escape . . . only to be confronted by Alia Rellapor herself. How will they rescue the prince? The adventures of Akiko were originally released as a monthly series and are gathered into this collection.

1. Menace of Alia Rellapor, Part 1 ◆ 2001
2. Menace of Alia Rellapor, Part 2 ◆ 2001
3. Menace of Alia Rellapor, Part 3 ◆ 2001
4. The Story Tree ◆ 2001
5. Bornstone's Elixir ◆ 2001
6. Stranded in Komura/Moonshopping ◆ 2003
7. The Battle of Boach's Keep ◆ 2004

AKIRA

Otomo, Katsuhiro
DARK HORSE ◆ GRADES 8–12
FANTASY

In post-apocalyptic Tokyo in 2019, two teenagers—Tetsuo and Kaneda—may hold the future of the world in their hands. They develop their paranormal skills to confront an unknown power known as Akira. This series reproduces the stunning black-and-white art of the original classic series.

1. Volume 1 ◆ 2000
2. Volume 2 ◆ 2001
3. Volume 3 ◆ 2001
4. Volume 4 ◆ 2001
5. Volume 5 ◆ 2001
6. Volume 6 ◆ 2002

AKSUM *see* Arthurian-Aksumite Cycle

AL (ALEXANDRA)

Greene, Constance C.

VIKING; PUFFIN ◆ GRADES 5–8 ◆ A/R

FAMILY LIFE │ REAL LIFE

Al is the new kid, "a little on the fat side," with glasses and pigtails, and a self-proclaimed nonconformist. She becomes the best friend of the unnamed seventh-grade narrator. Their friendship grows and helps them deal with the problems they face. Al's mother, divorced for several years, begins to date; her father visits for the first time in years; and Al sacrifices a summer visit at her father's farm to take care of her sick mother. Together, the friends face life's ups and downs with humor.

1. A Girl Called Al ◆ 1969
2. I Know You, Al ◆ 1975
3. Your Old Pal, Al ◆ 1979
4. Alexandra the Great ◆ 1982
5. Just Plain Al ◆ 1986
6. Al's Blind Date ◆ 1989

ALBRIGHT FAMILY *see* Sterling Family

ALDEN ALL STARS

Hallowell, Tommy, and David Halecroft

PENGUIN ◆ GRADES 4–8 ◆ A/R

REAL LIFE │ RECREATION

Soccer, baseball, basketball, and football are all featured in this sports series. Three seventh- and eighth-grade boys star in separate books. Nick is the wise guy; Dennis is the leader and captain of the basketball team. Justin's sport is soccer, but Alden Junior High doesn't have a team, so he goes to a camp and stands out there. All of the books in the series are loaded with sports details, but there are also some points made about relationships and the importance of studying. Fans of Matt Christopher's books will enjoy this series.

1. Duel on the Diamond ◆ 1990

2. Jester in the Back Cover ◆ 1990
3. Shot from Midfield ◆ 1990
4. Last Chance Quarterback ◆ 1990
5. Blindside Blitz ◆ 1991
6. Breaking Loose ◆ 1991
7. Championship Summer ◆ 1991
8. Hotshot on Ice ◆ 1991
9. Power Play ◆ 1991
10. Setting the Pace ◆ 1991
11. Wild Pitch ◆ 1991
12. Benched! ◆ 1991

ALEX BALFOUR

Appel, Allen

BANTAM DOUBLEDAY DELL ◆ GRADES 10–12

FANTASY

Alex Balfour, a time-traveling young history professor, has exciting adventures in 1917 Russia and 1876 Philadelphia, among other destinations, in this series for mature teens.

1. Time After Time ◆ 1985
2. Twice Upon a Time ◆ 1988
3. Till the End of Time ◆ 1990
4. In Time of War ◆ 2003

ALEX MACK *see* Secret World of Alex Mack

ALEX RIDER

Horowitz, Anthony

PHILOMEL/PENGUIN ◆ GRADES 6–10 ◆ A/R

ADVENTURE

Alex Rider is a teenager who has been recruited to be a spy. The British espionage agency, MI6, contacts him for special assignments, such as saving the world from a nuclear attack (*Skeleton Key*). In *Eagle Strike*, Air Force One has been hijacked in a plot to steal the President's fingerprints and access top security files. Alex uses many gadgets and technological innovations that will fascinate readers. These thrillers are packed with adventure and cliffhangers. *Alex Rider: The Gadgets* (2006) looks at the various gadgets used in the first five mysteries—including such wonders as a radio mouth brace, exploding ear stud, and pizza delivery assassin kit—with diagrams and details of how they were used. Graphic novel versions of the first two books were published in 2008.

1. Stormbreaker ◆ 2001
2. Point Blank ◆ 2002
3. Skeleton Key ◆ 2003
4. Eagle Strike ◆ 2003
5. Scorpia ◆ 2005
6. Ark Angel ◆ 2005
7. Snakehead ◆ 2005

ALEXANDER COLD AND NADIA SANTOS

Allende, Isabel

HARPERCOLLINS ◆ GRADES 6–10 ◆ A/R

ADVENTURE

In the first book, Alexander Cold, 15, and Nadia Santos, 12, are on an expedition in the Amazon rain forest where Alex's grandmother, Kate, is looking for a mysterious "beast." They encounter snakes, poison, and the murderous beast itself. The next book takes them to the Himalayas where they become involved with thieves who are looking for the Golden Dragon. One review compared these books to Indiana Jones adventures. Teen readers will be caught up in these exciting stories.

1. City of the Beasts ◆ 2002
2. Kingdom of the Golden Dragon ◆ 2004
3. Forest of the Pygmies ◆ 2005

ALIAS

Various authors

BANTAM ◆ GRADES 8–12

ADVENTURE

Sydney Bristow is uncertain about her future. A recruiter offers her a job with a secret government agency, SD-6, but things are not what they seem. Sydney takes the job knowing there is no way out if she changes her mind. Having a secret life takes its toll as Sydney becomes more distant from her friends and everyday activities. As the series progresses, she leaves her normal life behind and faces more secretive and dangerous assignments. These books are based on the popular television program. *Authorized Personnel Only* (2005; by Paul Ruditis and J. J. Abrams) is a guide to the series, providing mission-by-mission analysis; the agents' personal histories and psychological profiles; descriptions of the high-tech gadgets used; and so forth.

1. Recruited: An Alias Prequel (Mason, Lynn) ◆ 2002
2. A Secret Life (Roberts, Laura Peyton) ◆ 2003
3. Disappeared (Mason, Lynn) ◆ 2003

4. Sister Spy (Roberts, Laura Peyton) ◆ 2003
5. The Pursuit (Skurnick, Elizabeth) ◆ 2003
6. Close Quarters (Harrison, Emma) ◆ 2003
7. Father Figure (Roberts, Laura Peyton) ◆ 2003
8. Free Fall (Roberts, Christa) ◆ 2004
9. Infiltration (Frazier, Breen) ◆ 2004
10. Vanishing Act (Gerace, Sean) ◆ 2004
11. Skin Deep (Hapka, Cathy) ◆ 2004
12. Shadowed (Skurnick, Elizabeth) ◆ 2004
13. Faina (Gaborno, Rudy, Chris Hollier, and J. J. Abrams) ◆ 2005
14. Two of a Kind (Cox, Greg, and J. J. Abrams) ◆ 2005
15. Collateral Damage (Askegren, Pierce, and J. J. Abrams) ◆ 2005
16. Replaced (Harrison, Emma, and J. J. Abrams) ◆ 2005
17. The Road Not Taken (Cox, Greg, and J. J. Abrams) ◆ 2005
18. Vigilance (Ruditis, Paul, and J. J. Abrams) ◆ 2005
19. Strategic Reserve (York, Christina F., and J. J. Abrams) ◆ 2006
20. Once Lost (Beyer, Kirsten, and J. J. Abrams) ◆ 2006
21. Namesakes (Cox, Greg, and J. J. Abrams) ◆ 2006
22. Old Friends (Abrams, J. J., and Steven Hanna) ◆ 2006

ALICE

Naylor, Phyllis Reynolds
ATHENEUM; DELL ◆ GRADES 5–8 ◆ A/R
FAMILY LIFE | HUMOR

Affectionate and humorous, these stories feature Alice getting into all kinds of funny scrapes, mostly because of her good intentions. Putting up with the boys at school, getting her first boyfriend, making and keeping friends, and dealing with her father and older brother Lester are all part of the fun. As Alice matures (from sixth grade in the first book to eleventh grade in *Almost Alice*), the books deal with more mature topics, such as her questions about sexuality and intimacy. The prequels follow Alice from third grade, when she has just moved to Takoma Park and faces many changes, to fifth grade, a time of discovery.

1. The Agony of Alice ◆ 1985
2. Alice in Rapture, Sort of ◆ 1989
3. Reluctantly Alice ◆ 1991
4. All But Alice ◆ 1992
5. Alice in April ◆ 1993
6. Alice In-Between ◆ 1994
7. Alice the Brave ◆ 1995
8. Alice in Lace ◆ 1996
9. Outrageously Alice ◆ 1997
10. Achingly Alice ◆ 1998
11. Alice on the Outside ◆ 2000
12. The Grooming of Alice ◆ 2000

13. Alice Alone ◆ 2001
14. Simply Alice ◆ 2002
15. Patiently Alice ◆ 2003
16. Including Alice ◆ 2004
17. Alice on Her Way ◆ 2005
18. Alice in the Know ◆ 2006
19. Dangerously Alice ◆ 2007
20. Almost Alice ◆ 2008

ALICE PREQUELS

1. Starting with Alice ◆ 2002
2. Alice in Blunderland ◆ 2003
3. Lovingly Alice ◆ 2005

ALIEN ADVENTURES

Coville, Bruce

POCKET BOOKS ◆ GRADES 4–7 ◆ A/R

HUMOR | SCIENCE FICTION

Rod Allbright's science project has just been invaded! Tiny aliens have landed there and they want Rod's help. First they need to capture an interstellar criminal, then Rod is taken to another dimension. Rod's troubles continue when he and the aliens go through space to the home of the Mental Masters. But the worst is yet to come; Rod's body is stolen by a fiend and his personality must share space with Seymour, a blue alien. Like Coville's My Teacher books, this series combines science fiction and humor as Rod and the aliens stumble their way through intergalactic adventures.

1. Aliens Ate My Homework ◆ 1993
2. I Left My Sneakers in Dimension X ◆ 1994
3. The Search for Snout ◆ 1995
4. Aliens Stole My Body ◆ 1998

ALL ABOUT US NOVELS

Adina, Shelley

FAITHWORDS ◆ GRADES 8–10

VALUES

Lissa Mansfield wants to be accepted by the popular girls at the Spencer Academy, a boarding school in San Francisco. She decides to keep her devout Christian beliefs to herself, at least until she is "in." After she starts dating Callum, Lissa's values are tested.

1. It's All About Us ◆ 2008

2. The Fruit of My Lipstick ◆ 2008
3. Be Strong and Curvaceous ◆ 2009

ALLIANCE-UNION

Cherryh, C. J.
WARNER ◆ GRADES 10–12
SCIENCE FICTION

Earth loses control over its colonies, partly through failures in judgment and partly through sheer distance. The colonies grow more independent, some choosing to remain allied with Earth. But Cyteen rebels and founds a runaway colony. When faster-than-light travel is discovered, the tensions between Earth and the colonies increase. These novels are complex and show strong characters trying to resolve typical human problems with lots of action and intrigue.

1. Serpent's Reach ◆ 1980
2. Downbelow Station ◆ 1981
3. Merchanter's Luck ◆ 1982
4. Forty Thousand in Gehenna ◆ 1983
5. Voyager in Night ◆ 1984
6. Angel with the Sword ◆ 1985
7. Cyteen ◆ 1988
8. Rimrunners ◆ 1989
9. Heavy Time ◆ 1991
10. Hellburner ◆ 1992
11. Tripoint ◆ 1994
12. Finity's End ◆ 1997

ALLIE'S GHOST HUNTER

Jinks, Catherine
ALLEN & UNWIN ◆ GRADES 6–8 ◆ A/R
FANTASY

After moving into an old house, Allie Gebhardt, 11, shares her room with two others. One is her brother Bethan. The other is a ghost, Eglantine, who died in the old house. After psychic experts fail to remove Eglantine, Allie takes on the task. She becomes a "ghost hunter" and deals with various hauntings around Australia.

1. Eglantine ◆ 2007
2. Eustace ◆ 2007
3. Eloise ◆ 2007
4. Elysium ◆ 2007

ALOHA COVE

Kelly, Theresa

CONCORDIA HOUSE ◆ GRADES 7–10 ◆ A/R

FAMILY LIFE | REAL LIFE | VALUES

Cass, 17, is upset by the upheaval in her life. Her mother has remarried and Cass has a stepfather and a stepsister her own age—Tabitha. Now her mother is pregnant. At first, Cass and Tabitha have a strained relationship, but their faith brings them together. As they become closer, Cass and Tabitha reach out to others, including a friend with a violent boyfriend and another friend with anorexia. They follow God's way as they face each problem.

1. Living on Nothing Atoll ◆ 1999
2. Seaside High ◆ 1999
3. Tomorrow I'll Miss You ◆ 1999
4. Stand by Me ◆ 1999
5. Forget Me Not ◆ 2000
6. A Place in the Heart ◆ 2000
7. Dream a Little Dream ◆ 2000
8. Good-Bye Is Not Forever ◆ 2000

THE ALPHABETICAL HOOKUP LIST TRILOGY

McPhee, Phoebe

MTV/POCKET ◆ GRADES 9–12

REAL LIFE

College freshmen Jodi, Celeste, and Ali share a dorm room. In an effort to boost their social life, they dare themselves to kiss 26 boys—boys whose names begin with each letter of the alphabet. They even continue the dare in Paris.

1. The Alphabetical Hookup List A–J ◆ 2002
2. The Alphabetical Hookup List K–Q ◆ 2002
3. The Alphabetical Hookup List R–Z ◆ 2002

AL'S WORLD

Leonard, Elise

ALADDIN ◆ GRADES 4–8 ◆ A/R

HUMOR

Al is an ordinary kid who likes to pal around with his friend Keith. One Monday morning he becomes involved in a CIA chase when an agent bumps into Al and slides a flash drive into Al's pocket. The preposterous situations and Al's regular-guy goofiness should appeal to middle school readers, even reluctant ones.

1. Monday Morning Blitz ◆ 2007
2. Killer Lunch Lady ◆ 2007
3. Scared Stiff ◆ 2007
4. Monkey Business ◆ 2008

ALTERNAMORPHS *see* Animorphs: Alternamorphs

ALY AND AJ'S ROCK 'N' ROLL MYSTERIES

Noll, Katherine

GROSSET & DUNLAP ◆ GRADES 6–9

REAL LIFE | MYSTERY

Sisters Aly and AJ are in New York City rehearsing for their next tour. On a visit to the Girls Rock Academy they investigate the theft of the school's musical equipment. In *Mayhem in Miami,* the sisters are supposed to be models in a benefit fashion show. There is a saboteur at work—can Aly and AJ save the show?

1. First Stop, New York ◆ 2008
2. Mayhem in Miami ◆ 2008
3. Singing in Seattle ◆ 2008
4. Nashville Nights ◆ 2008

AMELIA

Moss, Marissa

TRICYCLE PRESS; PLEASANT CO.; SIMON & SCHUSTER ◆ GRADES 4–8 ◆

A/R

REAL LIFE

Amelia's notebooks (the covers of these books look like actual composition books) are actually top-secret journals chronicling the ups and downs of this young girl's life. Amelia is 9 at the beginning of the series; as she grows older and enters middle school, the books deal with issues of that age group. The scrapbook-like design is a large part of the appeal of these books. *My Notebook (With Help from Amelia)* invites kids to begin their own journal keeping. Related titles are *Amelia's School Survival Guide* (2002) and *Amelia's Card Game: The Game of Silly Sentences* (2001). There are Amelia guide books on such topics as babysitting, bullies, resolutions, and gossip.

1. Amelia's Notebook ◆ 1995
2. Amelia Writes Again ◆ 1996
3. Amelia Hits the Road ◆ 1997
4. Amelia Takes Command ◆ 1998
5. Dr. Amelia's Boredom Survival Guide ◆ 1999
6. The All-New Amelia ◆ 1999
7. Luv, Amelia Luv, Nadia ◆ 1999
8. Amelia's Family Ties ◆ 2000
9. Amelia's Easy-As-Pie Drawing Guide ◆ 2000
10. Amelia Works it Out ◆ 2000
11. Oh Boy, Amelia ◆ 2001
12. Madame Amelia Tells All ◆ 2001
13. Amelia Lends a Hand ◆ 2002
14. Amelia's Best Year Ever ◆ 2003
15. Amelia's 6th-Grade Notebook ◆ 2005
16. Amelia's Most Unforgettable Embarrassing Moments ◆ 2005
17. Amelia's Book of Notes and Note Passing ◆ 2006
18. Amelia's Longest, Biggest, Most-Fights-Ever Family Reunion ◆ 2006
19. Amelia's 5th-Grade Notebook ◆ 2006
20. Amelia's Are-We-There-Yet Longest Ever Car Trip ◆ 2006
21. Amelia's Bully Survival Guide ◆ 2006
22. The All-New Amelia ◆ 2007
23. Amelia's 7th-Grade Notebook ◆ 2007
24. Vote 4 Amelia ◆ 2007
25. Amelia's Itchy-Twitchy, Lovey-Dovey Summer at Camp Mosquito ◆ 2008

AMERICAN ADVENTURE

Roddy, Lee

BETHANY HOUSE ◆ GRADES 5–8 ◆ A/R

HISTORICAL | VALUES

Hildy Corrigan faces many challenges during the Great Depression as she and her family move, hoping for a better life. The different locations of this series put Hildy in situations that test her faith. Searching for a thief, adjusting to a new home, helping a girl whose father is a thief, and being accused of stealing a watch give Hildy opportunities to realize God's strength, love, and power of forgiveness. Readers looking for books in which characters struggle to be true to their values will want to read this series and other books by Lee Roddy.

1. The Overland Escape ◆ 1989
2. The Desperate Search ◆ 1989
3. Danger on Thunder Mountain ◆ 1989
4. The Secret of the Howling Cave ◆ 1990
5. The Flaming Trap ◆ 1990
6. Terror in the Sky ◆ 1991

7. Mystery of the Phantom Gold ◆ 1991
8. The Gold Train Bandits ◆ 1992
9. High Country Ambush ◆ 1992

AMERICAN DREAMS

Various authors

ALADDIN ◆ GRADES 8–10

REAL LIFE

The first two books in this series parallel the opening episodes of the television program. Meg Pryor is a teenager in the turbulent 1960s. There are civil rights marches, riots, and protests against the Vietnam War. Meg's life, however, is focused on music and her friends. One friend, Roxanne, is on *American Bandstand* and she helps Meg get on too. Popular music of the era is featured. Fans of the television series of the same name will enjoy these books.

1. End of Summer (Tigelaar, Liz) ◆ 2004
2. Dance with Me (Oz, Emily) ◆ 2004
3. Count on Me (Beechen, Adam) ◆ 2004
4. Star Maps (Tigelaar, Liz) ◆ 2004
5. Fair Play (Shaw, Deirdre) ◆ 2005
6. What Matters Most (Gallagher, Diana G.) ◆ 2005

AMERICAN DREAMS

Various authors

AVON ◆ GRADES 9–12

HISTORICAL

These books feature young women who are spirited and adventurous and destined to fall in love. In the first book, Sarah is on a ship to Jamestown Colony in 1620. When she arrives there, she tutors children. Her unhappiness leads her to plant tobacco with the hope of earning enough money to return to England. Her plans change when she finds love and marries. Fans of historical romance will enjoy the action in this series.

1. Sarah on Her Own (Coombs, Karen M.) ◆ 1996
2. Plainsong for Caitlin (Rees, Elizabeth M.) ◆ 1996
3. Into the Wind (Ferris, Jean) ◆ 1996
4. Song of the Sea (Ferris, Jean) ◆ 1996
5. Weather the Storm (Ferris, Jean) ◆ 1996
6. The Innkeeper's Daughter (Kassem, Lou) ◆ 1996
7. Reyna's Reward (Dionne, Wanda) ◆ 1996
8. Sofia's Heart (Cadwallader, Sharon) ◆ 1996
9. Heart of the Hills (Ritthaler, Shelly) ◆ 1996

    10. With Love, Amanda (Ritthaler, Shelly) ◆ 1997
    11. Carrie's Gold (Zach, Cheryl) ◆ 1997

AMERICAN EMPIRE *see* The Great War

AMERICAN GIRLS: GIRLS OF MANY LANDS

Various authors

PLEASANT COMPANY ◆ GRADES 4–8 ◆ A/R

HISTORICAL | REAL LIFE

This historical series features 12-year-old girls during times of change. Cecile is a servant in the French court of Louis XIV. What begins as an opportunity becomes a challenge. Neela lives in India during the independence movement (1939). In 1846, Saba is kidnapped from her home in Ethiopia and taken to the court of the emperor. Girls who like books about female characters facing challenges will enjoy this series. As with other books from this publisher, historical facts follow each story.

    1. Cecile: Gates of Gold, 1711 (Casanova, Mary) ◆ 2002
    2. Isabel: Taking Wing, 1592 (Dalton, Annie) ◆ 2002
    3. Minuk: Ashes in the Pathway, 1890 (Hill, Kirkpatrick) ◆ 2002
    4. Neela: Victory Song, 1939 (Divakaruni, Chitra Banerjee) ◆ 2002
    5. Spring Pearl: The Last Flower, 1857 (Yep, Laurence) ◆ 2002
    6. Saba: Under the Hyena's Foot, 1846 (Kurtz, Jane) ◆ 2003
    7. Kathleen: The Celtic Knot, 1937 (Parkinson, Siobhan) ◆ 2003
    8. Leyla: The Black Tulip, 1720 (Croutier, Alev Lytle) ◆ 2003

AMERICAN GIRLS: HISTORY MYSTERIES

Various authors

PLEASANT COMPANY ◆ GRADES 4–7 ◆ A/R

HISTORICAL | MYSTERY

Louisiana during the War of 1812; the Pony Express trail in 1860 Nebraska; San Francisco after the 1906 earthquake. These are just some of the places and times presented in this series. In each book, a girl who is around 12 years old becomes involved in a mysterious situation. There are concerns about spies, pirates, the Ku Klux Klan, and kidnappers. The intrepid behavior of the main characters saves the day. Historical information follows each novel. This is a good choice for girls who enjoy action.

    1. The Smuggler's Treasure (Buckey, Sarah Masters) ◆ 1999
    2. Hoofbeats of Danger (Hughes, Holly) ◆ 1999

3. The Night Fliers (Jones, Elizabeth McDavid) ◆ 1999
4. Voices at Whisper Bend (Ayres, Katherine) ◆ 1999
5. Secrets on 26th Street (Jones, Elizabeth McDavid) ◆ 1999
6. Mystery of the Dark Tower (Coleman, Evelyn) ◆ 2000
7. Trouble at Fort La Pointe (Ernst, Kathleen) ◆ 2000
8. Under Copp's Hill (Ayres, Katherine) ◆ 2000
9. Watcher in the Piney Woods (Jones, Elizabeth McDavid) ◆ 2000
10. Shadows in the Glasshouse (McDonald, Megan) ◆ 2000
11. The Minstrel's Melody (Tate, Eleanora E.) ◆ 2001
12. Riddle of the Prairie Bride (Reiss, Kathryn) ◆ 2001
13. Enemy in the Fort (Buckey, Sarah Masters) ◆ 2001
14. Circle of Fire (Coleman, Evelyn) ◆ 2001
15. Mystery on Skull Island (Jones, Elizabeth McDavid) ◆ 2001
16. Whistler in the Dark (Ernst, Kathleen) ◆ 2002
17. Mystery at Chilkoot Pass (Steiner, Barbara) ◆ 2002
18. The Strange Case of Baby H (Reiss, Kathryn) ◆ 2002
19. Danger at the Wild West Show (Hart, Alison) ◆ 2003
20. Gangsters at the Grand Atlantic (Buckey, Sarah Masters) ◆ 2003
21. Ghost Light on Graveyard Shoal (Jones, Elizabeth McDavid) ◆ 2003
22. Betrayal at Cross Creek (Ernst, Kathleen) ◆ 2004

AMERICAN GOLD GYMNASTS

Charbonnet, Gabrielle

BANTAM ◆ GRADES 4–7

RECREATION

Kelly Reynolds, 12, loves gymnastics. After her mother remarries, Kelly has a stepsister her own age who is also a gymnast—from Russia. At first the girls are wary of each other, but they become supportive friends. They even work together to deal with a difficult coach.

1. Competition Fever ◆ 1996
2. Balancing Act ◆ 1996
3. Split Decision ◆ 1996
4. The Bully Coach ◆ 1996

AMERICAN GOLD SWIMMERS

Wyeth, Sharon Dennis

BANTAM ◆ GRADES 4–7

RECREATION

The focus here is on swimming—practice, training, and competition. In one book, Kristy's interest in video games may keep her away from her swimming event. In another book, Kristy is older and is embarrassed about her appearance. She avoids swimming until she is needed for an important competition.

1. Winning Stroke ◆ 1996
2. The Human Shark ◆ 1996
3. Splash Party ◆ 1996
4. In Deep Water ◆ 1996

AMONG THE . . . *see* Shadow Children

ANGEL

Various authors

SIMON & SCHUSTER ◆ GRADES 7–12

HORROR

This popular spin-off from Buffy the Vampire Slayer features Angel, a troubled young vampire whose love for Buffy seems doomed. He moves to Los Angeles, where he seeks to right wrongs and seek redemption. The two volumes of *Angel: The Casefiles* (2002 and 2004) are official companions to the television show. *Angel: The Longest Night, Volume 1* (2002) is a collection of short stories.

1. City of Angel (Holder, Nancy) ◆ 1999
2. Not Forgotten (Holder, Nancy) ◆ 2000
3. Redemption (Odom, Mel) ◆ 2000
4. Close to the Ground (Mariotte, Jeff) ◆ 2000
5. Shakedown (DeBrandt, Don) ◆ 2000
6. Hollywood Noir (Mariotte, Jeff) ◆ 2001
7. Avatar (Passarella, John) ◆ 2001
8. Soul Trade (Sniegoski, Thomas E.) ◆ 2001
9. Bruja (Odom, Mel) ◆ 2001
10. The Summoned (Dokey, Cameron) ◆ 2001
11. Haunted (Mariotte, Jeff) ◆ 2002
12. Image (Odom, Mel) ◆ 2002
13. Stranger to the Sun (Mariotte, Jeff) ◆ 2002
14. Vengeance (Ciencin, Scott, and Dan Jolley) ◆ 2002
15. Endangered Species (Holder, Nancy, and Jeff Mariotte) ◆ 2002
16. Impressions (Durgin, Doranna) ◆ 2003
17. Sanctuary (Mariotte, Jeff) ◆ 2003
18. Fearless (Durgin, Doranna) ◆ 2003
19. Solitary Man (Mariotte, Jeff) ◆ 2003
20. Nemesis (Ciencin, Denise, and Scott Ciencin) ◆ 2004
21. Dark Mirror (Gardner, Craig Shaw) ◆ 2004
22. Monolith (Passarella, John) ◆ 2004

23. Book of the Dead (McConnell, Ashley) ◆ 2004
24. Love and Death (Mariotte, Jeff) ◆ 2004

ANGEL (GRAPHIC NOVELS)

Various authors

DARK HORSE ◆ GRADES 8–12

HORROR

This popular spin-off from Buffy the Vampire Slayer follows the adventures of Angel, a vampire with a soul. After he leaves Sunnydale (and Buffy) and heads to Los Angeles, Angel seeks to overcome his past and confront the evil demons that threaten society.

1. The Hollower (Golden, Christopher, Hector Gomez, and Sandu Florea) ◆ 2000
2. Surrogates (Golden, Christopher, Thomas E. Sniegoski, et al.) ◆ 2000
3. Earthly Possessions (Golden, Christopher, Thomas E. Sniegoski, et al.) ◆ 2001
4. Hunting Ground (Golden, Christopher, Thomas E. Sniegoski, et al.) ◆ 2001
5. Strange Bedfellows and Other Stories (Golden, Christopher, Thomas E. Sniegoski, et al.) ◆ 2002
6. Autumnal (Golden, Christopher, Thomas E. Sniegoski, et al.) ◆ 2002
7. Long Night's Journey (Matthews, Brett, Joss Whedon, et al.) ◆ 2002

ANGEL ON THE SQUARE

Whelan, Gloria

HARPERCOLLINS ◆ GRADES 6–9

HISTORICAL

The Russian Revolution brings changes for 12-year-old Katya, daughter of a lady-in-waiting to the Empress of Russia. She leaves the palace and lives with her cousin, Misha, a revolutionary who helps Katya see beyond her childish, romanticized view of royalty. Katya's children continue the story in the second book, which takes place after the Revolution. Marya, 13, and her younger brother try to reunite with their mother, who has been exiled to Siberia. The third book features Marya's younger brother Georgi, 14, as the family faces a German invasion in World War II and struggles to survive with little to eat and bitterly cold weather.

1. Angel on the Square ◆ 2001
2. The Impossible Journey ◆ 2003
3. Burying the Sun ◆ 2004

ANGELS UNLIMITED

Dalton, Annie

HARPERCOLLINS ◆ GRADES 4–7 ◆ A/R

FANTASY

Mel Beeby is 13 when she dies and enters the Angel Academy. Mel and her schoolmates, including Orlando and Lola, travel to Earth to help with problems, arriving in different regions and centuries. These kids still party and gossip even as they face dangers from the Opposition. These books first appeared in the early 2000s and were then repackaged under the name Mel Beeby: Agent Angel.

1. Winging It ◆ 2001
2. Losing the Plot ◆ 2001
3. Flying High ◆ 2001
4. Calling the Shots ◆ 2002
5. Fighting Fit ◆ 2003
6. Fogging Over ◆ 2003
7. Making Waves ◆ 2003
8. Budding Star ◆ 2004
9. Keeping It Real ◆ 2005

ANIKA SCOTT

Rispin, Karen

TYNDALE HOUSE ◆ GRADES 5–8

ADVENTURE | REAL LIFE | VALUES

When Anika Scott, 12, and her mother, father, and sister Sandy are involved in an adventure, they look to their Christian faith to guide them. On a trip to Africa, Anika finds that the elephants are in danger from poachers. Anika disobeys her parents when she leaves the camp and goes out into the Amboseli Game Preserve on her own. The strength of Anika's beliefs is tested as she faces danger and deals with the recent appearance of her half-brother Rick.

1. The Impossible Lisa Barnes ◆ 1992
2. Tianna the Terrible ◆ 1992
3. Anika's Mountain ◆ 1994
4. Ambush at Amboseli ◆ 1994
5. Sabrina the Schemer ◆ 1994

ANIMORPHS

Applegate, K. A.

SCHOLASTIC ◆ GRADES 4–8 ◆ A/R

ADVENTURE | SCIENCE FICTION

This fast-paced series involves the Yeerk—who have infected the brains of humans to control them—and the Animorphs, who have been given special powers by a dying Andalite. A special group of five friends find satisfaction in fighting the evil Yeerk. The Animorphs are able to "thought speak" and morph (for a period of two hours) into any animal they touch. A detailed discussion of the change process will hook readers as will the eye-catching covers. Short sentences plus continuous drama will keep readers involved. An *Animorph* television series and videos helped make this popular.

1. The Invasion ◆ 1996
2. The Visitor ◆ 1996
3. The Encounter ◆ 1996
4. The Message ◆ 1996
5. The Predator ◆ 1996
6. The Capture ◆ 1997
7. The Stranger ◆ 1997
8. The Alien ◆ 1997
9. The Secret ◆ 1997
10. The Android ◆ 1997
11. The Forgotten ◆ 1997
12. The Reaction ◆ 1997
13. The Change ◆ 1997
14. The Unknown ◆ 1998
15. The Escape ◆ 1998
16. The Warning ◆ 1998
17. The Underground ◆ 1998
18. The Decision ◆ 1998
19. The Departure ◆ 1998
20. The Discovery ◆ 1998
21. The Threat ◆ 1998
22. The Solution ◆ 1998
23. The Pretender ◆ 1998
24. The Suspicion ◆ 1998
25. The Extreme ◆ 1999
26. The Attack ◆ 1999
27. The Exposed ◆ 1999
28. The Experiment ◆ 1999
29. The Sickness ◆ 1999
30. The Reunion ◆ 1999
31. The Conspiracy ◆ 1999
32. The Separation ◆ 1999
33. The Illusion ◆ 1999
34. The Prophecy ◆ 1999
35. The Proposal ◆ 1999
36. The Mutation ◆ 1999
37. The Weakness ◆ 2000
38. The Arrival ◆ 2000
39. The Hidden ◆ 2000
40. The Other ◆ 2000
41. The Familiar ◆ 2000

42. The Journey ◆ 2000
43. The Test ◆ 2000
44. The Unexpected ◆ 2000
45. The Revelation ◆ 2000
46. The Deception ◆ 2000
47. The Resistance ◆ 2000
48. The Return ◆ 2000
49. The Diversion ◆ 2001
50. The Ultimate ◆ 2001
51. The Absolute ◆ 2001
52. The Sacrifice ◆ 2001
53. The Answer ◆ 2001
54. The Beginning ◆ 2001

ANIMORPHS: ALTERNAMORPHS

Applegate, K. A.
SCHOLASTIC ◆ GRADES 4–8 ◆ A/R
ADVENTURE | SCIENCE FICTION

Choose your own adventure in these related Animorphs books.

1. The First Journey ◆ 1999
2. The Next Passage ◆ 2000

ANIMORPHS: ANIMORPH CHRONICLES

Applegate, K. A.
SCHOLASTIC ◆ GRADES 4–8 ◆ A/R
ADVENTURE | SCIENCE FICTION

This is a prequel series to the Animorphs. It describes how Elfangor, an Andalite war-prince, gave five young humans the ability to morph into any animal they touch. Readers learn about other adventures of the Andalites.

1. The Andalite Chronicles ◆ 1997
2. The Hork-Bajir Chronicles ◆ 1998
3. Visser ◆ 1999
4. The Ellimist Chronicles ◆ 2000

ANIMORPHS: MEGAMORPHS

Applegate, K. A.
SCHOLASTIC ◆ GRADES 5–8 ◆ A/R
ADVENTURE | SCIENCE FICTION

Animorphs can morph into any animal, present-day or extinct, which can be a challenge if you choose to be a dinosaur. In these books, the Animorphs battle the Yeerk. In the fourth book, a decision is made to undo the creation of the Animorphs by traveling back in time and changing the original decision.

1. The Andalite's Gift ◆ 1997
2. In the Time of Dinosaurs ◆ 1998
3. Elfangor's Secret ◆ 1999
4. Back to Before ◆ 2000

ANNA

Kerr, Judith

BANTAM DOUBLEDAY DELL ◆ GRADES 4–8 ◆ A/R

HISTORICAL

Anna, aged 9, flees Berlin with her family when Hitler is elected. Anna must leave behind most of her possessions, including her beloved pink rabbit. The family travels through Switzerland and France eventually to reach England. These stories of a Jewish refugee family trying to stay together with dignity and pride in the face of anti-Semitism and depression are based on the author's own childhood.

1. When Hitler Stole Pink Rabbit ◆ 1971
2. The Other Way Round ◆ 1975
3. A Small Person Far Away ◆ 1978

ANNABEL ANDREWS

Rogers, Mary

HARPERCOLLINS ◆ GRADES 5–7 ◆ A/R

FANTASY | HUMOR

Annabel wakes up one morning to find she has turned into her mother. Annabel and her mother reverse roles for a day, and each gains a more sympathetic understanding of the other's life. Annabel blunders her way through the day and comes to appreciate her mother's daily trials, while her mother experiences life from her 13-year-old daughter's perspective. In the sequel, *A Billion for Boris,* Annabel and her 15-year-old boyfriend Boris discover a TV set that broadcasts tomorrow's news. And in *Summer Switch* it is brother Ben's turn to switch bodies with his father.

1. Freaky Friday ◆ 1972
2. A Billion for Boris ◆ 1974
3. Summer Switch ◆ 1982

ANNALS OF THE WESTERN SHORE

Le Guin, Ursula K.
HARCOURT ◆ GRADES 7–10 ◆ A/R
FANTASY

Imagine you have a gift, a special skill or ability. This gift could be that you can control animals or that you can "undo" or "unmake" others, meaning you destroy them. Two teens from the Uplands struggle with their gifts. Gry refuses to use her power over animals to call them to be hunted. Orrec tries to control his gift of "undoing," even wearing a blindfold so he will not look at others and destroy them. *Gifts* is a thought-provoking book about power and responsibility. *Voices* and *Powers* are companion volumes exploring similar issues. Orrec and Gry appear in both books but are not the featured characters.

1. Gifts ◆ 2004
2. Voices ◆ 2006
3. Powers ◆ 2007

ANNE SHIRLEY *see* Avonlea

ANNISA GOBROWSKI *see* Non-Blonde Cheerleader

ANTHONY MONDAY

Bellairs, John
DIAL ◆ GRADES 5–7 ◆ A/R
ADVENTURE | MYSTERY

Fourteen-year-old Anthony and his friend, librarian Miss Eells, search for a treasure rumored to have been hidden by wealthy eccentric Alpheus Winterborn. Anthony follows the clues to the Winterborn mansion and then back to the public library, where he outwits the efforts of another person who is seeking the treasure. In *The Lamp from the Warlock's Tomb,* Miss Eells buys an antique lamp and mysterious events begin to occur. There are strange voices, odd behavior, and an encounter with a ghost. These are suspenseful stories featuring supernatural events and puzzling mysteries.

1. The Treasure of Alpheus Winterborn ◆ 1978
2. The Dark Secret of Weatherend ◆ 1984
3. The Lamp from the Warlock's Tomb ◆ 1988
4. The Mansion in the Mist ◆ 1992

ANTRIAN

Wisler, G. Clifton

DUTTON ◆ GRADES 6–8 ◆ A/R

SCIENCE FICTION

Scott looks like an ordinary teenager, but he is not. Scott is an alien with the ability to see into the future. In these books, he discovers his powers and learns their limits. He also struggles to adapt to living on Earth and to keep his abilities a secret, especially from those who would exploit him. Readers who like the Animorphs series should enjoy this series too.

1. The Antrian Messenger ◆ 1986
2. The Seer ◆ 1988
3. The Mind Trap ◆ 1990

THE ANYBODIES

Bode, N. E.

HARPERCOLLINS ◆ GRADES 5–8 ◆ A/R

FANTASY

Fern Drudger has been growing up with the wrong family. A mistake at the hospital sent her home with the dull, boring Drudgers instead of her magical shape-shifting family. She is reunited with her widowed father and begins an adventure to restore his lost powers. As the series progresses, Fern and her grandmother defeat the evil Blue Queen and Fern discovers she is a Royal Anybody (shape shifter). As in the Series of Unfortunate Events books, there are fast-paced cliffhanging moments along with comments from the author to the reader throughout.

1. The Anybodies ◆ 2004
2. The Nobodies ◆ 2005
3. The Somebodies ◆ 2006

ARABUS FAMILY SAGA

Collier, James Lincoln, and Christopher Collier

DELL; DELACORTE ◆ GRADES 5–8 ◆ A/R

HISTORICAL

Daniel Arabus struggles to be free during the uncertain times of the Revolutionary War. Daniel's late father was granted freedom for his service to the Continental Army, but unscrupulous men want to deny that freedom to Daniel and his mother. Two related books feature young African American women—Willy Freeman and Carrie—who are involved in the conflicts of the war and their desire for personal freedom. The lives of

Daniel and his family intersect with each young woman. Entertaining reading that aptly describes the plight of African Americans during this period.

1. Jump Ship to Freedom ◆ 1981
2. War Comes to Willy Freeman ◆ 1983
3. Who Is Carrie? ◆ 1984

THE ARCHIVES OF ANTHROPOS

White, John

INTERVARSITY ◆ GRADES 4–8 ◆ A/R

FANTASY

The strange land of Anthropos is the setting for much of the action of these stories. Cousins Mary, Wesley, Lisa, and Kurt magically travel to Anthropos—a land of kings, sorcerers, and magic—to assist in the High Emperor's fight against evil. This series is modeled after the Chronicles of Narnia series and will appeal to children who enjoy allegorical fantasy stories.

1. The Tower of Geburah ◆ 1978
2. The Iron Sceptre ◆ 1981
3. The Sword Bearer ◆ 1986
4. Gaal the Conqueror ◆ 1989
5. Quest for the King ◆ 1995
6. The Dark Lord's Demise ◆ 2001

ARE YOU AFRAID OF THE DARK?

Various authors

MINSTREL/POCKET BOOKS ◆ GRADES 5–8

HORROR

Based on the Nickelodeon television series, these books are similar to Goosebumps and other books in the scary-stories genre. In one book, Duncan Evans is given three wishes and finds that the adage "be careful what you wish for" is very true. Another book features Glynis Barrons, who makes a rash statement that she lives to regret. There are sinister statues, ghost riders, secret mirrors, and a virtual nightmare. This is sure to be a hit with fans of horror books.

1. The Tale of the Sinister Statues (Peel, John) ◆ 1995
2. The Tale of Cutter's Treasure (Seidman, David L.) ◆ 1995
3. The Tale of the Restless House (Peel, John) ◆ 1995
4. The Tale of the Nightly Neighbors (MacHale, D. J., and Kathleen Derby) ◆ 1995
5. The Tale of the Secret Mirror (Strickland, Brad) ◆ 1995

6. The Tale of the Phantom School Bus (Strickland, Brad) ◆ 1996
7. The Tale of the Ghost Riders (Vornholt, John) ◆ 1996
8. The Tale of the Deadly Diary (Strickland, Brad) ◆ 1996
9. The Tale of the Virtual Nightmare (Pedersen, Ted) ◆ 1996
10. The Tale of the Curious Cat (Gallagher, Diana G.) ◆ 1996
11. The Tale of the Zero Hour (Peel, John) ◆ 1997
12. The Tale of the Shimmering Shell (Weiss, David Cody, and Bobbi J. G. Weiss) ◆ 1997
13. The Tale of the Three Wishes (Peel, John) ◆ 1997
14. The Tale of the Campfire Vampires (Emery, Clayton) ◆ 1997
15. The Tale of the Bad-Tempered Ghost (Mitchell, V. E.) ◆ 1997
16. The Tale of the Souvenir Shop (Cohen, Alice E.) ◆ 1997
17. The Tale of the Ghost Cruise (Weiss, David Cody, and Bobbi J. G. Weiss) ◆ 1998
18. The Tale of the Pulsating Gate (Gallagher, Diana G.) ◆ 1998
19. The Tale of the Stalking Shadow (Weiss, Bobbi J. G., and David Cody Weiss) ◆ 1998
20. The Tale of the Egyptian Mummies (Mitchell, Mark) ◆ 1998
21. The Tale of the Terrible Toys (Byers, Richard Lee) ◆ 1998
22. The Tale of the Mogul Monster (Weiss, David Cody, and Bobbi J. G. Weiss) ◆ 1998
23. The Tale of the Horrifying Hockey Team (Rodriguez, K. S.) ◆ 1999

ART ENCOUNTERS

Various authors
WATSON-GUPTILL ◆ GRADES 7–12 ◆ A/R
FANTASY | HISTORICAL

Each of these books features a young person interacting with a famous artist and in the process learning about art and history. In *The Spirit Catchers,* 15-year-old Parker, a Dust Bowl refugee, finds himself on Georgia O'Keeffe's New Mexico ranch and becomes her assistant. In *The Wedding,* set in 15th-century Bruges and channeling a van Eyck portrait, 14-year-old Giovanna falls in love with a troubadour called Angelo even as her father plans her marriage to a wealthy man.

1. The Spirit Catchers: An Encounter with Georgia O'Keeffe (Kudlinski, Kathleen) ◆ 2004
2. Casa Azul: An Encounter with Frida Kahlo (Hill, Laban Carrick) ◆ 2005
3. Lady with an Alien: An Encounter with Leonardo da Vinci (Resnick, Michael D.) ◆ 2005
4. Smoking Mirror: An Encounter with Paul Gauguin (Rees, Douglas) ◆ 2005
5. The Wedding: An Encounter with Jan van Eyck (Rees, Elizabeth M.) ◆ 2005

6. Jackal in the Garden: An Encounter with Bihzad (Ellis, Deborah) ◆ 2006
7. The Janus Gate: An Encounter with John Singer Sargent (Rees, Douglas) ◆ 2006
8. A Brush with Napoleon: An Encounter with Jacques-Louis David (Hill, Laban Carrick) ◆ 2006
9. A Club in Montmartre: An Encounter with Henri Toulouse-Lautrec (Resnick, Michael D.) ◆ 2006
10. World Behind the Door: An Encounter with Salvador Dali (Resnick, Michael D.) ◆ 2007
11. Deep in the Mountains: An Encounter with Zhu Qizhan (Cheng, Terrence) ◆ 2007

ARTEMIS FOWL

Colfer, Eoin

MIRAMAX/HYPERION ◆ GRADES 5–8 ◆ A/R

FANTASY

Artemis Fowl, 12, comes from a criminal family, so his larcenous talents are not surprising. He captures an elf and demands a ransom only to be confronted by the fairy police force. Later, Artemis takes action to find his father but he needs help from the fairies. Once his father is home, Artemis commits to a life without crime . . . after one more caper. A graphic novel version of the first book was published in 2007.

1. Artemis Fowl ◆ 2001
2. The Arctic Incident ◆ 2002
3. The Eternity Code ◆ 2003
4. The Opal Deception ◆ 2005
5. The Lost Colony ◆ 2006
6. The Time Paradox ◆ 2008

ARTHUR TRILOGY

Crossley-Holland, Kevin

SCHOLASTIC ◆ GRADES 6–9 ◆ A/R

FANTASY

Arthur de Caldicot, 13, lives in 12th-century England. His life is linked with the ancient Arthur (of Camelot fame), especially after he receives a "seeing stone." The stone gives him insight into the life of his namesake. In the second book, Arthur is now 14 and eager to participate in the Crusades.

1. The Seeing Stone ◆ 2001
2. At the Crossing Places ◆ 2002

3. King of the Middle March ◆ 2004

ARTHURIAN-AKSUMITE CYCLE

Wein, Elizabeth

VIKING ◆ GRADES 7–12 ◆ A/R

FANTASY

As this cycle begins, Lleu is the heir to King Artos's throne in 6th-century Britain. His illegitimate brother, Medraut, is jealous and plots against him. Their relationship is complicated by the sorcery of Medraut's mother, Morgause, who is also Artos's sister. The second book follows King Artos's daughter, Princess Goewin, to Aksum (a region in Africa that is now Ethiopia), where she uses her power to protect her young nephew Telemakos. In *The Sunbird,* Telemakos attempts to spy for the emperor on the salt smugglers of the Aksumite Empire, but is captured and enslaved in the salt mines.

1. The Winter Prince ◆ 1993
2. The Coalition of Lions ◆ 2003
3. The Sunbird ◆ 2004

THE MARK OF SOLOMON

While Telemakos is still recovering from his experiences in the desert, he and his sister are sent to live with Abreha, the ruler of Himyar. Here they should be safe but Telemakos soon learns that he must use all his talents to save himself and his people.

1. The Lion Hunter ◆ 2007
2. The Empty Kingdom ◆ 2008

ARTHURIAN KNIGHTS

Sutcliff, Rosemary

DUTTON ◆ GRADES 6–8 ◆ A/R

FANTASY | HISTORICAL

The well-known legend of King Arthur—from the intrigue surrounding Arthur's conception to the quest for the Holy Grail—is dramatically retold in this series. Based on history, ballads, and Malory's *Le Morte d'Arthur,* these books explain what happens to Arthur, Lancelot, Guinevere, and the others. Vivid detail describes feats of valor along with grave errors in judgment.

1. The Light Beyond the Forest: The Quest for the Holy Grail ◆ 1980
2. The Sword and the Circle: King Arthur and the Knights of the Round Table ◆ 1981
3. The Road to Camlann: The Death of King Arthur ◆ 1982

THE ASHLEYS

de la Cruz, Melissa

SIMON & SCHUSTER ♦ GRADES 8–10

REAL LIFE

At Miss Gamble's Preparatory School for Girls, three rich, fashionable, beautiful girls—all named Ashley—run the school. They are popular and hold all the power. Lauren Page wants to change that. She's tired of being an outsider, bullied by the Ashleys. Now that she is entering seventh grade, she is no longer a gawky loser. She is stylish and, thanks to her father's business success, she is as wealthy as the Ashleys. She thinks she wants to undermine the power of the Ashleys but will she be seduced by their power and position? Fans of the Celebutantes and the Au Pairs will enjoy these too.

1. There's a New Name at School ♦ 2008
2. Jealous? ♦ 2008
3. Birthday Vicious ♦ 2008

ASTEROID WARS

Bova, Ben

TOR ♦ GRADES 10–12 ♦ A/R

SCIENCE FICTION

Commerce plays an unusually strong role in this engrossing saga of a race to save Earth from environmental disaster.

1. The Precipice ♦ 2001
2. The Rock Rats ♦ 2002
3. The Silent War ♦ 2004
4. The Aftermath ♦ 2007

ASTRO BOY

Tezuka, Osamu

DARK HORSE ♦ GRADES 8–12

FANTASY

Astro Boy is an incredible super hero created by the late Osamu Tezuka, who has been considered the Walt Disney of Japan. This classic manga series is full of exciting adventures.

1. Volume 1 ◆ 2002
2. Volume 2 ◆ 2002
3. Volume 3 ◆ 2002
4. Volume 4 ◆ 2002
5. Volume 5 ◆ 2002
6. Volume 6 ◆ 2002
7. Volume 7 ◆ 2002
8. Volume 8 ◆ 2002
9. Volume 9 ◆ 2002
10. Volume 10 ◆ 2002
11. Volume 11 ◆ 2003
12. Volume 12 ◆ 2003
13. Volume 13 ◆ 2003
14. Volume 14 ◆ 2003
15. Volume 15 ◆ 2003
16. Volume 16 ◆ 2003
17. Volume 17 ◆ 2003
18. Volume 18 ◆ 2003
19. Volume 19 ◆ 2003
20. Volume 20 ◆ 2003
21. Volume 21 ◆ 2003
22. Volume 22 ◆ 2003
23. Volume 23 ◆ 2004

ATTOLIA

Turner, Megan Whelan

HARPERCOLLINS ◆ GRADES 5–10

FANTASY

In an ancient time a talented thief named Gen (Eugenides) is asked to steal a legendary jewel from the queen of Attolia. In exchange Gen will get his freedom. As the series progresses, Gen's right hand is cut off for his theft but he nonetheless falls in love with the queen, and in the third book they are married but Gen must cope with resentment and political intrigue. The first of these well-written and intricately plotted volumes was a Newbery Honor book in 1997.

1. The Thief ◆ 1996
2. The Queen of Attolia ◆ 2000
3. The King of Attolia ◆ 2006

AU PAIRS

de la Cruz, Melissa

SIMON & SCHUSTER ◆ GRADES 9–12 ◆ A/R

REAL LIFE

Three girls work as au pairs for a wealthy family in the Hamptons. Mara is from a small town and wants money for college while she enjoys the exciting social life. Eliza's father's financial mistakes caused her family to lose their summer home in the Hamptons and she wants to reconnect with that luxurious lifestyle. Jacqui is from Brazil and her beauty attracts a lot of attention, but she wants more. Sexuality, drinking, drugs, gossip, and name-dropping are part of this series, which should appeal to fans of Gossip Girl, the Nannies, and other chick lit books.

1. The Au Pairs ◆ 2004
2. Skinny Dipping ◆ 2005
3. Sun-Kissed ◆ 2006
4. Crazy Hot ◆ 2007

AUSTIN FAMILY *see* Vicky Austin

AVALON 1: WEB OF MAGIC

Roberts, Rachel

SCHOLASTIC; TOR/SEVEN SEAS ◆ GRADES 4–7 ◆ A/R

FANTASY

Three girls—Emily, Kara, and Adriane—explore deep into the woods. There they find a passage to another world. While some who travel through the passage come in peace, others have sinister plans. The girls face trials by earth, water, air, and fire as they confront the evil. The entire series was reissued by Tor/Seven Seas in trade paperback in late 2008 with new manga-style covers and interior illustrations. The first volume was initially published under the authorship of Shelly Roberts.

1. Circles in the Stream ◆ 2001
2. All that Glitters ◆ 2001
3. Cry of the Wolf ◆ 2001
4. Secret of the Unicorn ◆ 2002
5. Spellsinger ◆ 2002
6. Trial by Fire ◆ 2002

AVALON 2: QUEST FOR MAGIC

Roberts, Rachel

CDS BOOKS ◆ GRADES 4–7 ◆ A/R

FANTASY

The adventures continue for the three girls who have found Ravenswood—Emily, Kara, and Adriane. In one book, Adriane faces the Spider Witch that is threatening the woods. In another, Kara finds a mysterious portal. Fans of the Avalon: Web of Magic series may want to continue with these books. The entire series was being reissued by Macmillan in trade paperback in late 2008 with new manga-style covers and interior illustrations.

1. Song of the Unicorns ◆ 2003
2. All's Fairy in Love and War ◆ 2003
3. Ghost Wolf ◆ 2004
4. Heart of Avalon ◆ 2004
5. The Dark Mage ◆ 2004

AVATAR: THE EARTH KINGDOM CHRONICLES

Teitelbaum, Michael

SIMON SPOTLIGHT ◆ GRADES 4–7

FANTASY

Meet the main characters of the popular Nickelodeon cartoon series *Avatar,* including Aang, his earthbending teacher Toph, and Azula and Zuko of the Fire Nation. Each book features a different character, providing readers with plenty of background information about their skills and destiny.

1. The Tale of Aang ◆ 2007
2. The Tale of Azula ◆ 2007
3. The Tale of Toph ◆ 2007
4. The Tale of Sokka ◆ 2007
5. The Tale of Zuko ◆ 2008
6. The Tale of Katara ◆ 2008

AVATAR: THE LAST AIRBENDER

Various authors

SIMON SPOTLIGHT ◆ GRADES 4–7 ◆ A/R

FANTASY

Each of the "scrolls" presented here describes one of the four nations: Water Tribes, Earth Kingdom, Air Nomads, and Fire Nation. Aang is reluctant to accept his role as an airbender, one who can bend all four elements. As he begins his travels, he encounters challenges that lead him to his destiny. Fans of the Nickelodeon cartoon series will enjoy these books that feature Aang and his friends Katara and Sokka as they save the world from war with the Fire Nation.

1. The Lost Scrolls: Water (Teitelbaum, Michael) ◆ 2006
2. The Lost Scrolls: Fire (Mason, Tom, and Dan Danko) ◆ 2006
3. The Lost Scrolls: Air (Mason, Tom, and Dan Danko) ◆ 2007
4. The Lost Scrolls: Earth (Teitelbaum, Michael) ◆ 2007

AVATAR GRAPHIC NOVELS

DiMartino, Michael Dante

TOKYOPOP ◆ GRADES 4–7

FANTASY

Vivid illustrations by Bryan Konietzko are a highlight in this cine-manga adaptation of the cartoon series seen on Nickelodeon. Aang and his companions Sokka, Katara, and Toph face threats from the Fire Nation. In Volume 4, the group flies to the island of Kyoshi. While Aang is distracted by the adulation of the people on the island, the Fire Nation attacks.

1. Vol. 1–3: Boxed Set ◆ 2006
2. Vol. 4 ◆ 2007
3. Vol. 5 ◆ 2007
4. Vol. 6 ◆ 2007
5. Vol. 7 ◆ 2008
6. Vol. 8 ◆ 2008

AVONLEA

Montgomery, Lucy Maud

RANDOM HOUSE ◆ GRADES 5–8 ◆ A/R

FAMILY LIFE | HISTORICAL | REAL LIFE

Red-haired, imaginative Anne Shirley is mistakenly sent from an orphanage to live with the Cuthberts, who requested a boy to help on their farm. This series details the results. Montgomery tells Anne's life story from age 11 until well into her married years. Readers watch Anne blossom from an impetuous child into a mature woman, gaining not only physical beauty but a sense of self. Though the setting of these books is small-town Canada in the early 20th century, the themes of maturity, community, and friendship will surely resonate with today's readers. Girls who enjoy imagination and creativity will become fast friends with Anne.

1. Anne of Green Gables ◆ 1908
2. Anne of Avonlea ◆ 1909
3. Chronicles of Avonlea ◆ 1912
4. Anne of the Island ◆ 1915
5. Anne's House of Dreams ◆ 1917
6. Rainbow Valley ◆ 1919
7. Further Chronicles of Avonlea ◆ 1920
8. Rilla of Ingleside ◆ 1921
9. Anne of Windy Poplars ◆ 1936
10. Anne of Ingleside ◆ 1939

BABES

Dhami, Narinder

DELACORTE ◆ GRADES 5–7

REAL LIFE

Amber, Jazz, and Gina Dhillon are sisters who live with their father in England. They miss their mother, who died recently. The girls enjoy a lot of freedom and are indulged by their father even though he is distant and busy. They are surprised and a bit put out when their father's sister comes from India to stay with them. Their plan is to find a way to get rid of Auntie—perhaps by marrying her off. In the second book, the sisters become involved with a fading Bollywood movie star. And in the third book, they are looking forward to Auntie's marriage to the head of their school. The Indian heritage of the family adds to the flavor of the books.

1. Bindi Babes ◆ 2004
2. Bollywood Babes ◆ 2005
3. Bhangra Babes ◆ 2006
4. Superstar Babes ◆ 2008

BABY-SITTER

Stine, R. L.

SCHOLASTIC ◆ GRADES 6–8

HORROR

Mr. Hagen hates babysitters. He tries to kill Jenny when she is babysitting for him, but she kills him instead. The experience overwhelms her. Just as she is starting to recover, she takes another babysitting job in a haunted house. This time she confronts her fears and exorcises the ghosts. Stine's characteristic chapter endings range from the absurd to the really terrifying, and his fans will find just what they expect in this series.

1. The Baby-Sitter ◆ 1989
2. The Baby-Sitter II ◆ 1991
3. The Baby-Sitter III ◆ 1993
4. The Baby-Sitter IV ◆ 1995

BABY-SITTERS CLUB

Martin, Ann M.

SCHOLASTIC ◆ GRADES 4–7 ◆ A/R

REAL LIFE

The Baby-Sitters Club of Stoneybrook, Connecticut, is a group of five eighth-grade girls who are best friends and meet three times a week to take calls from parents who need sitters. Hardworking Kristy formed the club and tries to keep everyone in line. Quiet, sensitive Mary Anne is the secretary and sets up appointments. Stacey is the sophisticated one and has a great sense of style because she comes from New York City. The club's meetings are held at Claudia's house because she has a private phone in her room. She is the artistic member of the group and a junk-food addict. Each book in the series focuses on a different girl, and as the series goes on, Dawn moves to California, divorced parents remarry (two of the girls become stepsisters), and the girls deal with problems. Stacey is diabetic, Mary Anne's father won't let her grow up, and they all occasionally have difficulty getting along with the children they babysit or the parents they work for. In every story, they work together to resolve problems with good will and humor.

1. Kristy's Great Idea ◆ 1986
2. Claudia and the Phantom Phone Calls ◆ 1986
3. The Truth About Stacey ◆ 1986
4. Mary Anne Saves the Day ◆ 1987
5. Dawn and the Impossible Three ◆ 1987
6. Kristy's Big Day ◆ 1987
7. Claudia and Mean Janine ◆ 1987
8. Boy-Crazy Stacey ◆ 1987
9. The Ghost at Dawn's House ◆ 1988
10. Logan Likes Mary Anne! ◆ 1988
11. Kristy and the Snobs ◆ 1988
12. Claudia and the New Girl ◆ 1988
13. Good-bye Stacey, Good-bye ◆ 1988
14. Hello, Mallory ◆ 1988
15. Little Miss Stoneybrook . . . and Dawn ◆ 1988
16. Jessi's Secret Language ◆ 1988
17. Mary Anne's Bad Luck Mystery ◆ 1988
18. Stacey's Mistake ◆ 1988
19. Claudia and the Bad Joke ◆ 1988
20. Kristy and the Walking Disaster ◆ 1989
21. Mallory and the Trouble with the Twins ◆ 1989
22. Jessi Ramsey, Pet-Sitter ◆ 1989
23. Dawn on the Coast ◆ 1989
24. Kristy and the Mother's Day Surprise ◆ 1989
25. Mary Anne and the Search for Tigger ◆ 1989
26. Claudia and the Sad Good-bye ◆ 1989
27. Jessi and the Superbrat ◆ 1989
28. Welcome Back, Stacey! ◆ 1989
29. Mallory and the Secret Diary ◆ 1989
30. Mary Anne and the Great Romance ◆ 1990
31. Dawn's Wicked Stepsister ◆ 1990
32. Kristy and the Secret of Susan ◆ 1990
33. Claudia and the Great Search ◆ 1990
34. Mary Anne and Too Many Boys ◆ 1990
35. Stacey and the Mystery of Stoneybrook ◆ 1990
36. Jessi's Baby-Sitter ◆ 1990
37. Dawn and the Older Boy ◆ 1990
38. Kristy's Mystery Admirer ◆ 1990
39. Poor Mallory! ◆ 1990
40. Claudia and the Middle School Mystery ◆ 1991
41. Mary Anne vs. Logan ◆ 1991
42. Jessi and the Dance School Phantom ◆ 1991
43. Stacey's Emergency ◆ 1991

44. Dawn and the Big Sleepover ◆ 1991
45. Kristy and the Baby Parade ◆ 1991
46. Mary Anne Misses Logan ◆ 1991
47. Mallory on Strike ◆ 1991
48. Jessi's Wish ◆ 1991
49. Claudia and the Genius of Elm Street ◆ 1991
50. Dawn's Big Date ◆ 1992
51. Stacey's Ex-Best Friend ◆ 1992
52. Mary Anne + 2 Many Babies ◆ 1992
53. Kristy for President ◆ 1992
54. Mallory and the Dream Horse ◆ 1992
55. Jessi's Gold Medal ◆ 1992
56. Keep Out, Claudia! ◆ 1992
57. Dawn Saves the Planet ◆ 1992
58. Stacey's Choice ◆ 1992
59. Mallory Hates Boys (and Gym) ◆ 1992
60. Mary Anne's Makeover ◆ 1993
61. Jessi and the Awful Secret ◆ 1993
62. Kristy and the Worst Kid Ever ◆ 1993
63. Claudia's—Freind—Friend ◆ 1993
64. Dawn's Family Feud ◆ 1993
65. Stacey's Big Crush ◆ 1993
66. Maid Mary Anne ◆ 1993
67. Dawn's Big Move ◆ 1993
68. Jessi and the Bad Baby-Sitter ◆ 1993
69. Get Well Soon, Mallory! ◆ 1993
70. Stacey and the Cheerleaders ◆ 1993
71. Claudia and the Perfect Boy ◆ 1994
72. Dawn and the We Love Kids Club ◆ 1994
73. Mary Anne and Miss Priss ◆ 1994
74. Kristy and the Copycat ◆ 1994
75. Jessi's Horrible Prank ◆ 1994
76. Stacey's Lie ◆ 1994
77. Dawn and Whitney, Friends Forever ◆ 1994
78. Claudia and Crazy Peaches ◆ 1994
79. Mary Anne Breaks the Rules ◆ 1994
80. Mallory Pike, #1 Fan ◆ 1994
81. Kristy and Mr. Mom ◆ 1995
82. Jessi and the Troublemaker ◆ 1995
83. Stacey vs. the BSC ◆ 1995
84. Dawn and the School Spirit War ◆ 1995
85. Claudia Kishi, Live from WSTO! ◆ 1995
86. Mary Anne and Camp BSC ◆ 1995
87. Stacey and the Bad Girl ◆ 1995
88. Farewell, Dawn ◆ 1995
89. Kristy and the Dirty Diapers ◆ 1995
90. Welcome to BSC, Abby ◆ 1995
91. Claudia and the First Thanksgiving ◆ 1995
92. Mallory's Christmas Wish ◆ 1995

93. Mary Anne and the Memory Garden ◆ 1996
94. Stacey McGill, Super Sitter ◆ 1996
95. Kristy + Bart = ? ◆ 1996
96. Abby's Lucky Thirteen ◆ 1996
97. Claudia and the World's Cutest Baby ◆ 1996
98. Dawn and Too Many Baby-Sitters ◆ 1996
99. Stacey's Broken Heart ◆ 1996
100. Kristy's Worst Idea ◆ 1996
101. Claudia Kishi, Middle School Dropout ◆ 1996
102. Mary Anne and the Little Princess ◆ 1996
103. Happy Holidays, Jessi ◆ 1996
104. Abby's Twin ◆ 1997
105. Stacey the Math Whiz ◆ 1997
106. Claudia, Queen of the Seventh Grade ◆ 1997
107. Mind Your Own Business, Kristy! ◆ 1997
108. Don't Give Up, Mallory ◆ 1997
109. Mary Anne to the Rescue ◆ 1997
110. Abby the Bad Sport ◆ 1997
111. Stacey's Secret Friend ◆ 1997
112. Kristy and the Sister War ◆ 1997
113. Claudia Makes Up Her Mind ◆ 1997
114. The Secret Life of Mary Anne Spier ◆ 1998
115. Jessi's Big Break ◆ 1998
116. Abby and the Best Kid Ever ◆ 1998
117. Claudia and the Terrible Truth ◆ 1998
118. Kristy Thomas, Dog Trainer ◆ 1998
119. Stacey's Ex-Boyfriend ◆ 1998
120. Mary Anne and the Playground Fight ◆ 1998
121. Abby in Wonderland ◆ 1998
122. Kristy in Charge ◆ 1998
123. Claudia's Big Party ◆ 1998
124. Stacey McGill . . . Matchmaker? ◆ 1998
125. Mary Anne in the Middle ◆ 1998
126. The All-New Mallory Pike ◆ 1999
127. Abby's Un-Valentine ◆ 1999
128. Claudia and the Little Liar ◆ 1999
129. Kristy at Bat ◆ 1999
130. Stacey's Movie ◆ 1999
131. The Fire at Mary Anne's House ◆ 1999

BABY-SITTERS CLUB FRIENDS FOREVER

Martin, Ann M.
SCHOLASTIC ◆ GRADES 4–7 ◆ A/R
REAL LIFE

The girls have more babysitting adventures.

1. Kristy's Big News ◆ 1999
2. Stacey vs. Claudia ◆ 1999
3. Mary Anne's Big Breakup ◆ 1999
4. Claudia and the Friendship Feud ◆ 1999
5. Kristy Power! ◆ 2000
6. Stacey and the Boyfriend Trap ◆ 2000
7. Claudia Gets Her Guy ◆ 2000
8. Mary Anne's Revenge ◆ 2000
9. Kristy and the Kidnapper ◆ 2000
10. Stacey's Problem ◆ 2000
11. Welcome Home, Mary Anne ◆ 2000
12. Claudia and the Disaster Date ◆ 2000

BABY-SITTERS CLUB FRIENDS FOREVER SPECIAL
EDITIONS

1. Everything Changes ◆ 1999
2. Graduation Day ◆ 2000

BABY-SITTERS CLUB GRAPHIC NOVELS

Martin, Ann M.

SCHOLASTIC/GRAPHIX ◆ GRADES 4–7 ◆ A/R

REAL LIFE

Adapted from some of the very first Baby-sitters Club books, these graphic novels are a great way to capitalize on the popular series and discuss the graphic novel format. In the first book, Kristy has the idea for the club. Raina Telgemeier illustrated these books and adapted the story.

1. Kristy's Great Idea ◆ 2006
2. The Truth About Stacey ◆ 2006
3. Mary Anne Saves the Day ◆ 2007

BABY-SITTERS CLUB MYSTERIES

Martin, Ann M.

SCHOLASTIC ◆ GRADES 4–7 ◆ A/R

MYSTERY | REAL LIFE

The five girls from Stoneybrook, Connecticut, who formed the Baby-Sitters Club have their own mystery series. Kristy, founder and president of the group, Dawn the Californian, sophisticated Stacey, shy Mary Anne, and artistic Claudia run into mysteries involving empty houses that aren't really empty, missing rings, counterfeit money, and more—mysteries that they try to solve Nancy Drew style.

1. Stacey and the Missing Ring ◆ 1991

2. Beware Dawn! ◆ 1991
3. Mallory and the Ghost Cat ◆ 1992
4. Kristy and the Missing Child ◆ 1992
5. Mary Anne and the Secret in the Attic ◆ 1992
6. The Mystery at Claudia's House ◆ 1992
7. Dawn and the Disappearing Dogs ◆ 1993
8. Jessi and the Jewel Thieves ◆ 1993
9. Kristy and the Haunted Mansion ◆ 1993
10. Stacey and the Mystery Money ◆ 1993
11. Claudia and the Mystery at the Museum ◆ 1993
12. Dawn and the Surfer Ghost ◆ 1993
13. Mary Anne and the Library Mystery ◆ 1994
14. Stacey and the Mystery at the Mall ◆ 1994
15. Kristy and the Vampires ◆ 1994
16. Claudia and the Clue in the Photograph ◆ 1994
17. Dawn and the Halloween Mystery ◆ 1994
18. Stacey and the Mystery at the Empty House ◆ 1994
19. Kristy and the Missing Fortune ◆ 1995
20. Mary Anne and the Zoo Mystery ◆ 1995
21. Claudia and the Recipe for Danger ◆ 1995
22. Stacey and the Haunted Masquerade ◆ 1995
23. Abby and the Secret Society ◆ 1996
24. Mary Anne and the Silent Witness ◆ 1996
25. Kristy and the Middle School Vandal ◆ 1996
26. Dawn Schafer, Undercover Babysitter ◆ 1996
27. Claudia and the Lighthouse Ghost ◆ 1996
28. Abby and the Mystery Baby ◆ 1997
29. Stacey and the Fashion Victim ◆ 1997
30. Kristy and the Mystery Train ◆ 1997
31. Mary Anne and the Music Box Secret ◆ 1997
32. Claudia and the Mystery in the Painting ◆ 1997
33. Stacey and the Stolen Hearts ◆ 1998
34. Mary Anne and the Haunted Bookstore ◆ 1998
35. Abby and the Notorious Neighbor ◆ 1998
36. Kristy and the Cat Burglar ◆ 1998

SUPER MYSTERIES

1. Baby-Sitters' Haunted House ◆ 1995
2. Baby-Sitters Beware ◆ 1995
3. Baby-Sitters' Fright Night ◆ 1996
4. Baby-Sitters' Christmas Chiller ◆ 1997

BABY-SITTERS CLUB PORTRAIT COLLECTION

Martin, Ann M.

SCHOLASTIC ◆ GRADES 4–7 ◆ A/R

REAL LIFE

Vignettes from other books provide insight into the personality and behavior of each girl.

1. Stacey's Book ◆ 1994
2. Claudia's Book ◆ 1995
3. Dawn's Book ◆ 1995
4. Kristy's Book ◆ 1996
5. Mary Anne's Book ◆ 1996
6. Abby's Book ◆ 1997

BABY-SITTERS CLUB SUPER SPECIALS

Martin, Ann M.

SCHOLASTIC ◆ GRADES 4–7 ◆ A/R

REAL LIFE

The Super Specials are about twice as long as the regular Baby-Sitters Club books and deal with events such as weddings or a group visit to see Dawn when she moves to California. The books are narrated by all five girls, taking different chapters in turn. There are also special Super Chillers books.

1. Baby-Sitters on Board! ◆ 1988
2. Baby-Sitters' Summer Vacation ◆ 1989
3. Baby-Sitters' Winter Vacation ◆ 1989
4. Baby-Sitters' Island Adventure ◆ 1990
5. California Girls! ◆ 1990
6. New York, New York! ◆ 1991
7. Snowbound ◆ 1991
8. Baby-Sitters at Shadow Lake ◆ 1992
9. Starring the Baby-Sitters Club ◆ 1992
10. Sea City, Here We Come! ◆ 1993
11. The Baby-Sitters Remember ◆ 1994
12. Here Come the Bridesmaids ◆ 1994
13. Aloha, Baby-Sitters! ◆ 1996
14. BSC in the USA ◆ 1997
15. Baby-Sitters' European Vacation ◆ 1998

BAD GIRLS

Voigt, Cynthia

SCHOLASTIC; ATHENEUM ◆ GRADES 6–9 ◆ A/R

HUMOR | REAL LIFE

When this series starts, Michelle and Margalo are in fifth grade. They are both new and feel like outsiders. They team up and get a reputation for being aggressive. They are high-spirited girls whose humorous antics will appeal to many readers. By the time the girls are 14 and in the eighth grade (in *Bad Girls in Love*), they are still best friends and still outsiders. Then, they each fall in love. These books capture the pace, language, issues, and emotions of early adolescents.

1. Bad Girls ◆ 1996
2. Bad, Badder, Baddest ◆ 1999
3. It's Not Easy Being Bad ◆ 2000
4. Bad Girls in Love ◆ 2002
5. Bad Girls, Bad Girls, Whatcha Gonna Do? ◆ 2006

BAKER STREET IRREGULARS

Dicks, Terrance

DUTTON ◆ GRADES 4–7

MYSTERY

Four London youngsters recover a lost painting and become known as "The Baker Street Irregulars" after Sherlock Holmes's gang of street kids. The youngest, Mickey, welcomes all the attention and publicity and wants to solve another crime. Dan, the leader of the group, and Jeff, the one with the most common sense, are reluctant to get involved again. When a crime wave hits their neighborhood, Dan, Jeff, and Mickey, along with their friend Liz, find themselves drawn in almost in spite of themselves. Dan is capable of drawing conclusions by intuitive leaps, Jeff sometimes plays the Dr. Watson role, and Liz and Mickey are fearless in dangerous situations. Don, a young police detective, comes to rely on their expertise as the young quartet takes on more cases. Lots of action and fairly complex clues for young mystery fans.

1. The Case of the Missing Masterpiece ◆ 1978
2. The Case of the Fagin File ◆ 1978
3. The Case of the Blackmail Boys ◆ 1979
4. The Case of the Cinema Swindle ◆ 1980
5. The Case of the Ghost Grabbers ◆ 1981
6. The Case of the Cop Catchers ◆ 1981
7. The Case of the Disappearing Diplomat ◆ 1986
8. The Case of the Comic Crooks ◆ 1986
9. The Case of the Haunted Holiday ◆ 1987
10. The Case of the Criminal Computer ◆ 1987

BALEFIRE

Tiernan, Cate

RAZORBILL ◆ GRADES 8–11 ◆ A/R

FANTASY

Twin sisters Thais and Clio, 17, have been separated since birth, neither knowing of the other's existence. When they both end up at the same high school in New Orleans, they begin to unravel the mystery behind their separation. Both have magical powers. Now that they are together they are being pursued by a coven of witches who want to use their powers.

1. A Chalice of Wind ◆ 2005
2. A Circle of Ashes ◆ 2005
3. A Feather of Stone ◆ 2006
4. A Necklace of Water ◆ 2007

BALLAD

McCrumb, Sharyn
DUTTON ◆ GRADES 10–12 ◆ A/R

MYSTERY

Appalachia and County Sheriff Arrowwood are central characters in this series of mysteries that are rich in atmosphere and suspense. In the first book, a famous 1960s folksinger comes home to Hamelin, Tennessee, 20 years later in search of peace and inspiration. Instead she is threatened and a young woman who bears a resemblance to her younger self is murdered. A 20-year high school reunion taking place in the background and echoes of Vietnam add to the story. In the second book, the sheriff investigates the murder of four members of a single family and suicide of a fifth.

1. If Ever I Return, Pretty Peggy-O ◆ 1990
2. The Hangman's Beautiful Daughter ◆ 1993
3. She Walks These Hills ◆ 1994
4. The Rosewood Casket ◆ 1996
5. The Ballad of Frankie Silver ◆ 1998
6. The Songcatcher ◆ 2001
7. Ghost Riders ◆ 2003

BALLET FRIENDS

Michaels, Kitty
BOOKSURGE PUBLISHING ◆ GRADES 4–7

REAL LIFE

Jessie Garrett, 12, is a tomboy turned ballerina. Because of her competitive nature she pushes herself to be the best. Bianca has been taking ballet for years and she is used to being on top. Instead of confronting each other, Bianca helps Jessie and the two girls become best friends. Performances, a trip to Lincoln Center, injuries, and a fire at the dance studio are among the events that Jessie, Bianca, and their friends face. Royal Ballet School would be another series for readers who like these books.

1. Toe-tally Fabulous ◆ 2008
2. Barred from Ballet ◆ 2008
3. Birthday at the Ballet ◆ 2008
4. Nowhere to Turn ◆ 2008
5. Waiting in the Wings ◆ 2008

BARDIC VOICES

Lackey, Mercedes

BAEN ◆ GRADES 10–12

FANTASY

Music and magic are at the core of this series. In the first book, Rune is an outsider with a musical gift. The Bardic Guild offers her a way out of the poverty of life in her village. Supernatural elements including ghosts, mages, and elves are apparent as the characters cope with medieval life. *Free Bards* is a compilation of the first three books.

1. The Lark and the Wren ◆ 1991
2. The Robin and the Kestrel ◆ 1993
3. The Eagle and the Nightingales ◆ 1995
4. Four and Twenty Blackbirds ◆ 1997

THE BARTIMAEUS TRILOGY

Stroud, Jonathan

HYPERION/MIRAMAX KIDS ◆ GRADES 5–9 ◆ A/R

FANTASY

Bartimaeus is a djinn (genie) called forth by a 10-year-old magician, Nathaniel. Nathaniel orders Bartimaeus to steal the Amulet of Samarkand from Simon Lovelace. In the second book, Nathaniel is 14 and is responsible for capturing members of the Resistance. Readers will be intrigued by this magical fantasy series.

1. The Amulet of Samarkand ◆ 2003
2. The Golem's Eye ◆ 2004
3. Ptolemy's Gate ◆ 2006

BASEBALL CARD ADVENTURES

Gutman, Dan

HARPERCOLLINS ◆ GRADES 4–8 ◆ A/R

FANTASY | RECREATION

Joe Stoshack, 12, travels back through time to meet star baseball players of the past. The first adventure happens when Joe finds a valuable Honus Wagner card. That night, Honus Wagner appears in Joe's bedroom and they time-travel to the 1909 World Series. In the Babe Ruth story, Joe's dad comes too. They plan to have Babe Ruth autograph items to take back to the present and sell, but their plans hit a snag.

1. Honus and Me ◆ 1997
2. Jackie and Me ◆ 1999
3. Babe and Me ◆ 2000
4. Shoeless Joe and Me ◆ 2002
5. Mickey and Me ◆ 2003
6. Abner and Me ◆ 2005
7. Satch and Me ◆ 2005
8. Jim and Me ◆ 2008
9. Ray and Me ◆ 2009

BEACON STREET GIRLS

Bryant, Annie

B'TWEEN PRODUCTIONS ◆ GRADES 6–9 ◆ A/R

REAL LIFE

Char is just feeling settled in seventh grade. She has a new group of friends who call themselves the Beacon Street Girls. But now Char's father may move the family to England.

1. Worst Enemies/Best Friends ◆ 2004
2. Bad News/Good News ◆ 2004
3. Letters from the Heart ◆ 2004
4. Out of Bounds ◆ 2004
5. Promises, Promises ◆ 2005
6. Lake Rescue ◆ 2005
7. Freaked Out ◆ 2006
8. Lucky Charm ◆ 2006
9. Fashion Frenzy ◆ 2006

10. Just Kidding ◆ 2006
11. Ghost Town ◆ 2007
12. Time's Up ◆ 2008
13. Green Algae and Bubblegum Wars ◆ 2008

SPECIAL ADVENTURE

1. Charlotte in Paris ◆ 2006
2. Maeve on the Red Carpet ◆ 2007
3. Freestyle with Avery ◆ 2007
4. Kitani's Jamaican Holiday ◆ 2008
5. Isabel's Texas Two-Step ◆ 2008

BEATRICE BAILEY *see* The Adventures of Beatrice Bailey

BEKA COOPER

Pierce, Tamora
RANDOM HOUSE ◆ GRADES 7–10 ◆ A/R
FANTASY

In the Tortall Realms, Beka Cooper, 16, is being trained by the Provost's Guards, who are called Dogs. As a "Puppy," Beka uses her magical powers to solve crimes and help those in need. In the first book, Beka confronts the Shadow Snake, a mysterious creature that is kidnapping and murdering children. The story is told through Beka's journals entries, and readers will connect with this strong female main character.

1. Terrier ◆ 2006
2. Bloodhound ◆ 2009
3. Elkhound ◆ TBA

THE BELGARIAD

Eddings, David
BALLANTINE ◆ GRADES 10–12 ◆ A/R
FANTASY

Garion's journey from farm boy to sorcerer is explored in this series set in a mythical land. Garion disdains magic and sorcery. On a quest for the stolen Orb, he begins to realize his powers. Belgarath, a sorcerer, and his daughter Polgara also search for the Orb. As the series continues, Garion becomes king and must face the evil God Torak. The Malloreon series continues the story of Garion. There is a prequel to both series, *Belgarath the Sorcerer* (1995), and a final volume to both, *Polgara the Sorceress* (1997).

1. Pawn of Prophecy ◆ 1982
2. Queen of Sorcery ◆ 1982
3. Magician's Gambit ◆ 1983
4. Castle of Wizardry ◆ 1984
5. Enchanters' End Game ◆ 1984

BELLES OF LORDSBURG

Bly, Stephen

CROSSWAY BOOKS ◆ GRADES 9–12

HISTORICAL | VALUES

This is a Christian western series. In the first book, Grace Denison runs away from her senator father's home and finds adventure and romance in a New Mexico town. In *The Outlaw's Twin Sister,* friends of a renegade try to persuade his twin sister to help him escape from jail.

1. The Senator's Other Daughter ◆ 2001
2. The General's Notorious Widow ◆ 2001
3. The Outlaw's Twin Sister ◆ 2002

BELLTOWN MYSTERY

Murphy, T. M.

J. N. TOWNSEND PUBLISHING ◆ GRADES 6–9

MYSTERY

Orville Jacques, 16, is a teen detective who becomes involved in mysteries on Cape Cod. In one book, Orville wonders if one elderly woman's death was really an accident. In another book, he travels to Ireland and finds clues that may lead to a missing treasure. There are some romantic moments as well as detailed crime descriptions. The books listed here are reissues.

1. The Secrets of Belltown ◆ 2001
2. The Secrets of Cranberry Beach ◆ 2001
3. The Secrets of Cain's Castle ◆ 2001
4. The Secrets of Pilgrim Pond ◆ 2001
5. The Secrets of Code Z ◆ 2001
6. The Secrets of the Twisted Cross ◆ 2002

BERNIE MAGRUDER *see* Bessledorf Hotel

Berserker

Saberhagen, Fred
BALLANTINE ◆ GRADES 9–12
SCIENCE FICTION

Berserkers are life-destroying machines that are found throughout the galaxy. In *Berserker Prime,* these robots arrive just as the ruler of the Twin Planets of Prairie and Timber is deciding the fate of Huvean hostages. But do these hostages hold the secret to defeating the Berserkers? *Berserkers: The Beginning* (1994) collects *Berserker* and *The Ultimate Enemy* in one volume.

1. Berserker ◆ 1967
2. Brother Assassin ◆ 1969
3. Berserker's Planet ◆ 1975
4. Berserker Man ◆ 1979
5. The Ultimate Enemy ◆ 1979
6. Berserker Wars ◆ 1981
7. Berserker Base ◆ 1985
8. The Berserker Throne ◆ 1985
9. Berserker: Blue Death ◆ 1985
10. The Berserker Attack ◆ 1987
11. Berserker Lies ◆ 1991
12. Berserker Kill ◆ 1993
13. Berserkers: The Beginning ◆ 1998
14. Berserker's Star ◆ 2003
15. Berserker Prime ◆ 2004
16. Rogue Berserker ◆ 2005

Bessledorf Hotel

Naylor, Phyllis Reynolds
SIMON & SCHUSTER ◆ GRADES 5–7 ◆ A/R
FAMILY LIFE | HUMOR | MYSTERY

The Magruder family lives in an apartment at the Bessledorf Hotel. The father, Theodore, manages the hotel. Alma helps out, but she dreams of writing romance novels. Son Joseph goes to veterinary college, and daughter Delores works at a parachute factory. Bernie likes to solve mysteries, and the old hotel provides plenty of them to solve. A ghost appears to Bernie in one book and he must figure out what it wants so that it will rest in peace. The Magruder family's exploits have also been repackaged and reissued in the Bernie Magruder series.

1. The Mad Gasser of Bessledorf Street ◆ 1983
2. The Bodies in the Bessledorf Hotel ◆ 1986
3. Bernie and the Bessledorf Ghost ◆ 1990

4. The Face in the Bessledorf Funeral Parlor ◆ 1993
5. The Bomb in the Bessledorf Bus Depot ◆ 1996
6. The Treasure of Bessledorf Hill ◆ 1997
7. Peril in the Bessledorf Parachute Factory ◆ 1999

BERNIE MAGRUDER

1. Bernie Magruder and the Haunted Hotel ◆ 2001
2. Bernie Magruder and the Case of the Big Stink ◆ 2001
3. Bernie Magruder and the Disappearing Bodies ◆ 2001
4. Bernie Magruder and the Bus Station Blow Up ◆ 2001
5. Bernie Magruder and the Pirate's Treasure ◆ 2001
6. Bernie Magruder and the Parachute Peril ◆ 2001
7. Bernie Magruder and the Drive-Thru Funeral Parlor ◆ 2003
8. Bernie Magruder and the Bats in the Belfry ◆ 2003

BEST FRIENDS

Smith, Susan

POCKET BOOKS ◆ GRADES 4–7

REAL LIFE

Sonya moves back to California after living with her father in New York for two years. She renews her friendship with Terri, Angela, and Dawn, her best friends from fourth grade. Celia, a pretty and popular girl, takes an interest in her, and Sonya starts seeing faults in her old friends. Sonya decides to stick with them, though, after Celia asks her to cheat on a test. The rest of the series sees the friends through their middle-school years. Celia remains the "enemy," and she and her friends are a rival crowd. A fifth girl, Linda, becomes one of the Best Friends. There are boyfriends and school activities as the girls pursue their various interests.

1. Sonya Begonia and the Eleventh Birthday Blues ◆ 1988
2. Angela and the King-Size Crusade ◆ 1988
3. Dawn Selby, Super Sleuth ◆ 1988
4. Terri the Great ◆ 1989
5. Sonya and the Chain Letter Gang ◆ 1989
6. Angela and the Greatest Guy in the World ◆ 1989
7. One Hundred Thousand Dollar Dawn ◆ 1990
8. The Terrible Terri Rumors ◆ 1990
9. Linda and the Little White Lies ◆ 1990
10. Sonya and the Haunting of Room 16A ◆ 1990
11. Angela and the Great Book Battle ◆ 1990
12. Dynamite Dawn vs. Terrific Terri ◆ 1991
13. Who's Out to Get Linda ◆ 1991
14. Terri and the Shopping Mall Disaster ◆ 1991
15. The Sonya and Howard Wars ◆ 1991
16. Angela and the Accidental-on-Purpose Romance ◆ 1991

BEVERLY HILLS, 90210

Various authors

HARPERCOLLINS ◆ GRADES 7–10

REAL LIFE

Beverly Hills, 90210 was a popular 1990s television series that focused on teen problems. The show is still seen on cable channels, which keeps teens interested in these books.

1. Beverly Hills, 90210 (Gilden, Mel) ◆ 1991
2. Exposed! (Mills, Bart) ◆ 1991
3. No Secrets (Gilden, Mel) ◆ 1992
4. Which Way to the Beach? (Gilden, Mel) ◆ 1992
5. Fantasies (Smith, K. T.) ◆ 1992
6. 'Tis the Season (Gilden, Mel) ◆ 1992
7. Two Hearts (Gilden, Mel) ◆ 1993
8. Where the Boys Are (Gilden, Mel) ◆ 1993
9. More than Words (Gilden, Mel) ◆ 1993
10. Summer Love (Gilden, Mel) ◆ 1993
11. Senior Year (Gilden, Mel) ◆ 1993
12. Graduation Day (Gilden, Mel) ◆ 1994
13. College Bound (Gilden, Mel) ◆ 1994

THE BIG EMPTY

Stephens, J. B.

RAZORBILL ◆ GRADES 7–10 ◆ A/R

SCIENCE FICTION

A deadly virus has killed half the population of the world. The United States is being controlled by the military, who are relocating the survivors to the coasts. Seven teens who stayed in the central region of the country, the Big Empty, reach a secret community of Novo Mundum only to realize that they are in great danger.

1. The Big Empty ◆ 2004
2. Paradise City ◆ 2004
3. Desolation Angels ◆ 2004
4. No Exit ◆ 2005

BINGO BROWN

Byars, Betsy

VIKING ◆ GRADES 4–7 ◆ A/R

HUMOR | REAL LIFE

Bingo Brown is in sixth grade at the beginning of this series and is just discovering "mixed-sex conversations." He falls in and out of love many times but ends up being in love with Melissa. He is devastated when she moves to Oklahoma. That summer, he racks up a huge phone bill calling her and is pursued by her best friend. His parents go through a crisis of their own when his mother discovers she is pregnant. As Bingo enters seventh grade, he has a new baby brother, and is an acknowledged authority on romance among his friends.

1. The Burning Questions of Bingo Brown ◆ 1988
2. Bingo Brown and the Language of Love ◆ 1989
3. Bingo Brown, Gypsy Lover ◆ 1990
4. Bingo Brown's Guide to Romance ◆ 1992

BIONICLE ADVENTURES

Farshtey, Greg
SCHOLASTIC ◆ GRADES 4–7 ◆ A/R
FANTASY

Six Toa guard the city of Metru Nui. These warriors protect the Matoran. When the city is attacked, the Toa face unexpected dangers. There are related items including a sticker book, an *Official Guide to Bionicles,* and comic books. These stories are based on LEGO action figures.

1. Mystery of Metru Nui ◆ 2004
2. Trial by Fire ◆ 2004
3. Darkness Below ◆ 2004
4. Legends of Metru Nui ◆ 2004
5. Voyage of Fear ◆ 2004
6. Maze of Shadows ◆ 2004

BIONICLE CHRONICLES

Various authors
SCHOLASTIC ◆ GRADES 4–7 ◆ A/R
FANTASY

Mata Nui is an ancient land that has been peaceful until Makuta brings fear and darkness. Who will face the darkness? Six Toa, mighty warriors, are destined to rescue the land of Mata Nui. The Bionicle Chronicles describe the arrival of the Toa and their battles. Related items include a sticker book, an *Official Guide to Bionicles,* and comic books. These stories are based on LEGO action figures.

1. Tale of the Toa (Hapka, C. A.) ◆ 2003
2. Beware the Bohrok (Hapka, C. A.) ◆ 2003

3. Makuta's Revenge (Hapka, C. A.) ◆ 2003
4. Tales of the Masks (Farshtey, Greg) ◆ 2003

BIONICLE LEGENDS

Farshtey, Greg

SCHOLASTIC ◆ GRADES 4–7 ◆ A/R

FANTASY

This series features legends of the Toa's exploits. Facing the evil Piraka, retrieving the Mask of Life, and awakening the Great Spirit of Mata Nui are among the stories featured in these books.

1. Island of Doom ◆ 2006
2. Dark Destiny ◆ 2006
3. Power Play ◆ 2006
4. Legacy of Evil ◆ 2006
5. Inferno ◆ 2006
6. City of the Lost ◆ 2007
7. Prisoners of the Pit ◆ 2007
8. Downfall ◆ 2008
9. Shadows in the Sky ◆ 2008

THE BIRCHBARK HOUSE *see* Omakayas

THE BITTERBYNDE

Dart-Thornton, Cecilia

WARNER ◆ GRADES 10–12

FANTASY

A poor mute child named Imrhein escapes from a miserable life inside the Isse Tower, learns handspeech, and sets out to learn about her origins. In the second book, she regains the power of speech and her beauty even as she uncovers secrets and is pursued by dark forces. This is a rich fantasy full of folklore and tall tales.

1. The Ill-Made Mute ◆ 2001
2. The Lady of the Sorrows ◆ 2002
3. The Battle of Evernight ◆ 2003

BLACK BOOK (DIARY OF A TEENAGE STUD)

Black, Jonah

AVON ◆ GRADES 8–12

HUMOR | REAL LIFE

Jonah Black is repeating eleventh grade and living with his mother in Pompano Beach, Florida. (That boarding school in Pennsylvania just didn't work out.) Through his journal, Jonah describes his life. His mother is a sex expert who has written a popular book. The girl he has a crush on is attracted to a jerk. Jonah's reflections are regularly interrupted by fantasies, often sexual imaginings about Sophie, a girlfriend he left in Pennsylvania.

1. Volume 1: Girls, Girls, Girls ◆ 2001
2. Volume 2: Stop, Don't Stop ◆ 2001
3. Volume 3: Run, Jonah, Run ◆ 2001
4. Volume 4: Faster, Faster, Faster ◆ 2002

THE BLACK MAGICIAN TRILOGY

Canavan, Trudi

EOS ◆ GRADES 10–12

FANTASY

The magicians of Imardin assemble yearly to cleanse the city of undesirable elements. Sonea stands up to them and discovers her own magical powers. She is taken to the magicians' guild to improve her skills. At the guild, she is a novice, but she gets support from High Lord Akkarin, who has his own secret.

1. The Magicians' Guild ◆ 2004
2. The Novice ◆ 2004
3. The High Lord ◆ 2004

BLACK STALLION

Farley, Walter

RANDOM HOUSE ◆ GRADES 5–8 ◆ A/R

ADVENTURE

On his way home from visiting his missionary uncle, Alec is shipwrecked along with a wild black stallion. They are rescued, and Alec takes the horse back to New York and boards him at a nearby farm to be trained by Henry Dailey. Because there are no official papers on "the Black," Alec cannot enter him in races. However, in a special race for the fastest horse in the country, Alec and "the Black" earn the respect they deserve. In another book, Alec travels to Arabia to research the claim of a man who is trying to take away his horse. The series continues as the stallion sires foals that Alec and Henry train and race. Walter Farley wrote the early books in the series. Walter and Steven Farley wrote *The Young Black Stallion,* and Steven Farley is continuing the series. The Island Stallion series features another young man and a horse; the Young Black Stallion series by Steven Farley also features Alec Ramsay.

1. The Black Stallion ◆ 1941
2. The Black Stallion Returns ◆ 1945
3. Son of the Black Stallion ◆ 1947
4. The Black Stallion and Satan ◆ 1949
5. The Blood Bay Colt (retitled The Black Stallion's Blood Bay Colt) ◆ 1950
6. The Black Stallion's Filly ◆ 1952
7. The Black Stallion Revolts ◆ 1953
8. The Black Stallion's Sulky Colt ◆ 1954
9. The Black Stallion's Courage ◆ 1956
10. The Black Stallion Mystery ◆ 1957
11. The Black Stallion and Flame ◆ 1960
12. The Black Stallion Challenged ◆ 1964
13. The Black Stallion's Ghost ◆ 1969
14. The Black Stallion and the Girl ◆ 1971
15. The Black Stallion Legend ◆ 1983
16. The Young Black Stallion (Farley, Walter, and Steven Farley) ◆ 1989
17. The Black Stallion's Shadow (Farley, Steven) ◆ 1996

BLACK STALLION: YOUNG BLACK STALLION

Farley, Steven

RANDOM HOUSE ◆ GRADES 5–8 ◆ A/R

REAL LIFE

Danielle Connor, 13, is upset that Alec Ramsay has turned her family's farm into a Thoroughbred training center. Her own horse, Redman, has been sold and Danielle now works in the stables that her family owned.

1. The Promise ◆ 1998
2. A Horse Called Raven ◆ 1998
3. The Homecoming ◆ 1999
4. Wild Spirit ◆ 1999
5. The Yearling ◆ 1999
6. Hard Lessons ◆ 1999

BLOOD OF THE GODDESS

Dalkey, Kara

TOR ◆ GRADES 10–12

FANTASY

A historical fantasy in which a 16th-century English apothecary named Thomas Chinnery discovers in the Portuguese colony of Goa, in India, a powder that can revive the dead. In the sequel, Chinnery takes a dangerous journey deep into the interior in search of the source of this powder. Fact, lore, magic, and religious tenets are interwoven in these books.

1. Goa ◆ 1996
2. Bijapur ◆ 1997
3. Bhagavati ◆ 1998

BLOODWATER MYSTERIES

Hautman, Pete, and Mary Logue

PUTNAM ◆ GRADES 5–9 ◆ A/R

MYSTERY

Roni Delicata is the crime reporter for the high school newspaper. Brian Bain, 13, is a freshman with a specialty in science. Together they investigate mysteries in the town of Bloodwater. In *Doppelganger,* Roni sees a picture of a missing child that has been age-progressed. It looks a lot like Brian, who was born in Korea and adopted. As they look into Brian's past, they encounter other mysterious activities. There are kidnappings, schemes, and dangerous attacks that keep the reader involved. A good choice for reluctant readers.

1. Snatched ◆ 2006
2. Skullduggery ◆ 2007
3. Doppelganger ◆ 2008

BLOODY JACK ADVENTURES

Meyer, L. A.

HARCOURT ◆ GRADES 7–10 ◆ A/R

ADVENTURE

After her family is killed by the plague in London in 1797, Mary Faber disguises herself as a boy and becomes Jacky Faber, a ship's boy on the *HMS Dolphin*. Her bravery during an encounter with pirates wins her the title of "Bloody Jack." In the second book, her disguise is undone and Mary/Jacky is sent to an elite girls' school in Boston where she rebels against the constraints of society. Unable to conform, she resumes her disguise and signs on to work on a boat returning to England. As the series continues, Mary/Jacky becomes involved in more-adult intrigues and by the sixth book she fights in Napoleon's army and uses her seductive powers to trick a French general.

1. Bloody Jack: Being an Account of the Curious Adventures of Mary "Jacky" Faber, Ship's Boy ◆ 2002
2. Curse of the Blue Tattoo: Being an Account of the Misadventures of Jacky Faber, Midshipman and Fine Lady ◆ 2004
3. Under the Jolly Roger: Being an Account of the Further Nautical Adventures of Jacky Faber ◆ 2005
4. In the Belly of the Bloodhound: Being an Account of the Particularly Peculiar Adventure in the Life of Jacky Faber ◆ 2006
5. Mississippi Jack: Being an Account of the Further Waterborne Adventures of Jacky Faber, Midshipman, Fine Lady, and the Lily of the West ◆ 2007
6. My Bonny Light Horseman: Being an Account of the Further Adventures of Jacky Faber, in Love and War ◆ 2008

BLOSSOM CULP

Peck, Richard

DELL ◆ GRADES 5–7 ◆ A/R

FANTASY | MYSTERY

Blossom Culp lives on the wrong side of the tracks in a small midwestern town at the turn of the century. Her mother is a fortune teller, who is jealous when it seems that Blossom has "the gift." Alexander, the son of a wealthy and prominent family, lives right across the tracks, and his barn is right in Blossom's back yard. The barn is inhabited by a ghost that Blossom can see. Alexander is reluctantly drawn into this adventure, only the first of many inspired by Blossom's gift. Blossom's contacts with the dead bring her fame and a certain social standing in the town. She moves into her high school years and has more encounters with the beyond, including an Egyptian princess and time travel 70 years into the future.

1. The Ghost Belonged to Me ◆ 1975
2. Ghosts I Have Been ◆ 1977
3. The Dreadful Future of Blossom Culp ◆ 1983
4. Blossom Culp and the Sleep of Death ◆ 1986

THE BLOSSOM FAMILY

Byars, Betsy

DELL ◆ GRADES 4–7 ◆ A/R

FAMILY LIFE | HUMOR

Maggie, Junior, and Vern Blossom live with their mother, Vicki, and their grandfather, Pap. Their father, Cotton, was killed riding a bull in the rodeo when the children were small. Vicki is a trick rider and goes out on the rodeo circuit, leaving the children behind with Pap in a rural section of the eastern United States. They make friends with a lady who lives a hermit's life in a cave. One of the boys almost drowns making a raft to float on the river. Two of the children break into prison when Pap is arrested, and Maggie makes her debut in trick riding. In each book, the stories of all the family members intersect.

1. The Not-Just-Anybody Family ◆ 1986
2. The Blossoms Meet the Vulture Lady ◆ 1986
3. The Blossoms and the Green Phantom ◆ 1987
4. A Blossom Promise ◆ 1987
5. Wanted—Mud Blossom ◆ 1991

BLUE AVENGER

Howe, Norma

HOLT ◆ GRADES 7–10 ◆ A/R

REAL LIFE

David Schumacher likes to draw superhero comics. On his sixteenth birthday, he decides to stop drawing and take action. He creates a costume and names himself the Blue Avenger—and he really does bring about changes. Teens frustrated by social inequities will appreciate the way David tries to make a difference in the world.

1. The Adventures of the Blue Avenger ◆ 1999
2. Blue Avenger Cracks the Code ◆ 2000
3. Blue Avenger and the Theory of Everything ◆ 2002

BLUE BLOODS

de la Cruz, Melissa

HYPERION ◆ GRADES 9–12 ◆ A/R

FANTASY

At a private school in Manhattan a group of privileged teens has a secret. They are Blue Bloods—vampires. At age 15, Schuyler Van Alen and her friend Bliss begin to develop their vampire traits. At school, some of the Blue Bloods are dying—even though they are immortal. A group of Silver Bloods have found a way to destroy them. Merging teen topics such as dating, drinking, and sexuality with vampires, this series should resonate with readers of the Twilight books.

1. Blue Bloods ◆ 2006

2. Masquerade ◆ 2007
3. Revelations ◆ 2008

BLUE-EYED SON TRILOGY

Lynch, Chris
HARPERCOLLINS ◆ GRADES 7–10 ◆ A/R
REAL LIFE

Living on the mean streets of Boston's Irish American community, Mick, 15, faces a world of alcoholism, abuse, and violence. He feels alienated in his dysfunctional family. His father is aggressive, his mother is weak, and his older brother is a brutally cruel bully.

1. Mick ◆ 1996
2. Blood Relations ◆ 1996
3. Dog Eat Dog ◆ 1996

BLUE IS FOR NIGHTMARES

Stolarz, Laurie Faria
LLEWELLYN ◆ GRADES 7–10 ◆ A/R
FANTASY

Stacey Brown, 16, is a witch. In *Blue Is for Nightmares,* Stacey dreams that her best friend Drea is in danger. This is even more upsetting because Stacey's dreams are usually prophetic. Can Stacey use her magic to prevent Drea's murder?

1. Blue Is for Nightmares ◆ 2003
2. White Is for Magic ◆ 2004
3. Silver Is for Secrets ◆ 2005
4. Red Is for Remembrance ◆ 2005

BLUFORD HIGH

Various authors
TOWNSEND / SCHOLASTIC ◆ GRADES 9–12 ◆ A/R
REAL LIFE

Urban teens, primarily African American, cope with realistic situations in this series set in California. In the first book, the return of their long absent father causes problems for Darcy and her sister Jamee. In *Payback,* Tyray is used to being the bully. When he is taken down by Darrell, Tyray wants to get even, and that may involve using a gun. Like the Del Rio Bay Clique, Drama High, and Kimani Tru books, this series is

"Urban Lit" for teens. Originally published by Townsend, many of the books have been reissued by Scholastic and there is a *Teacher's Guide to the Bluford Series* by Eliza A. Comodromos (Townsend, 2004).

1. Lost and Found (Schraff, Anne) ◆ 2002
2. A Matter of Trust (Schraff, Anne) ◆ 2002
3. Secrets in the Shadows (Schraff, Anne) ◆ 2002
4. Someone to Love Me (Schraff, Anne) ◆ 2002
5. The Bully (Langan, Paul) ◆ 2002
6. The Gun (Langan, Paul) ◆ 2002
7. Until We Meet Again (Schraff, Anne) ◆ 2002
8. Blood Is Thicker (Langan, Paul, and D. M. Blackwell) ◆ 2004
9. Brothers in Arms (Langan, Paul, and Ben Alirez) ◆ 2004
10. Summer of Secrets (Langan, Paul) ◆ 2004
11. The Fallen (Langan, Paul) ◆ 2007
12. Shattered (Langan, Paul) ◆ 2007
13. Search for Safety (Langan, Paul) ◆ 2007

BODY OF EVIDENCE

Various authors

SIMON & SCHUSTER ◆ GRADES 9–12 ◆ A/R

MYSTERY

Jenna Blake is attending Somerset University near Boston. Her interests in medicine (her mother is a doctor) and in crime (her father is a criminologist) lead her to take a job in the medical examiner's office. This job puts her in danger. Mysteries include a dead congressional aide whose diseased brain contains insect larvae, a series of ritual killings, and "zombie crimes."

1. Body Bags (Golden, Christopher) ◆ 1999
2. Thief of Hearts (Golden, Christopher) ◆ 1999
3. Soul Survivor (Golden, Christopher) ◆ 1999
4. Meets the Eye (Golden, Christopher) ◆ 2000
5. Head Games (Golden, Christopher) ◆ 2000
6. Skin Deep (Golden, Christopher) ◆ 2000
7. Burning Bones (Golden, Christopher, and Rick Hautala) ◆ 2001
8. Brain Trust (Golden, Christopher, and Rick Hautala) ◆ 2001
9. Last Breath (Golden, Christopher, and Rick Hautala) ◆ 2004
10. Throat Culture (Golden, Christopher, and Rick Hautala) ◆ 2005

BONE

Smith, Jeff

CARTOON BOOKS ◆ GRADES 6–10 ◆ A/R

FANTASY

This graphic novel series describes the antics of the three Bone cousins. Fone Bone is the hero, Phoney Bone is a schemer, and Smiley Bone is silly. After they are run out of Boneville, they enter a world of dragons and monsters. They meet the beautiful Thorn and begin adventures to find their destiny. The nine books listed are three trilogies.

1. Out from Boneville ◆ 1996
2. The Great Cow Race ◆ 1996
3. Eyes of the Storm ◆ 1997
4. The Dragonslayer ◆ 1998
5. Rock Jaw, Master of the Eastern Border ◆ 1998
6. Old Man's Cave ◆ 1999
7. Ghost Circles ◆ 2001
8. Treasure Hunters ◆ 2004
9. Crown of Horns ◆ 2004

BONE CHILLERS

Haynes, Betsy

HarperCollins ◆ Grades 5–8 ◆ A/R

Horror | Humor

The covers of these books make statements like "Bone Chillers: They'll make your skin crawl!" and "Bone Chillers: They'll scare the words right out of your mouth!" With spooky situations and creepy creatures, this series is similar to others in the horror genre. The books feature different characters. Azie Appleton always tells lies until one day her claim about giant termites comes true. Isabella Richmond thinks that gargoyles are kidnapping neighborhood kids. Some books are not just spooky but gross: Jeremy Wilson sneezes and his mucus becomes a slimy green glob. Readers who want horror and humor will devour this series.

1. Beware the Shopping Mall! ◆ 1994
2. Little Pet Shop of Horrors ◆ 1994
3. Back to School ◆ 1994
4. Frankenturkey ◆ 1994
5. Strange Brew ◆ 1995
6. Teacher Creature ◆ 1995
7. Welcome to Alien Inn ◆ 1995
8. Attack of the Killer Ants ◆ 1996
9. Slime Time ◆ 1996
10. Toilet Terror ◆ 1996
11. Night of the Living Clay ◆ 1996
12. The Thing Under the Bed ◆ 1997
13. A Terminal Case of the Uglies ◆ 1997
14. Tiki Doll of Doom ◆ 1997
15. The Queen of the Gargoyles ◆ 1997
16. Why I Quit the Baby-Sitter's Club ◆ 1997
17. blowtorch@psycho.com ◆ 1997

18. The Night Squawker ◆ 1997
19. Scare Bear ◆ 1997
20. The Dog Ate My Homework ◆ 1997
21. Killer Clown of Kings County ◆ 1998
22. Romeo and Ghouliette ◆ 1998

THE BONEMENDER

Bennett, Holly

ORCA ◆ GRADES 7–10 ◆ A/R

FANTASY | ADVENTURE

Gabrielle, daughter of the king of Verdeau, is a healer—a bonemender. She uses her talents to heal a stranger whose companion is Feolan, an Elf who has come to warn her father of an invasion. Gabrielle's growing attraction to Feolan seems doomed (as an Elf, he will live for hundreds of years) until her mother reveals a secret—Gabrielle is half Elf. By the third book, Gabrielle and Feolan are married and begin an adventure to find Gabrielle's niece and nephew, who have been kidnapped by pirates.

1. The Bonemender ◆ 2005
2. The Bonemender's Oath ◆ 2006
3. The Bonemender's Choice ◆ 2007

BONNETS AND BUGLES

Morris, Gilbert

MOODY PRESS ◆ GRADES 5–7 ◆ A/R

HISTORICAL | VALUES

The Civil War splits neighbors and friends and provides opportunities for spiritual growth for five young people and their families. Tom and Jeff and their parents decide to move to Virginia and fight for the Confederacy, leaving Leah and Sarah and their parents in Kentucky as Union sympathizers. Mrs. Majors dies giving birth to Esther, and, with all the men off to war, there is no one to care for the baby. They turn to the Carters, who take her in to raise as their own. Throughout the course of the war, Jeff is a drummer boy and the other two boys are soldiers seeing action in major battles. They manage to get back to the girls often as Jeff courts Leah and Tom and Sarah become engaged. Tom loses his leg in Gettysburg and comes close to losing his faith in God, but the others help him back to spiritual health.

1. Drummer Boy at Bull Run ◆ 1995
2. Yankee Belles in Dixie ◆ 1995
3. The Secret of Richmond Manor ◆ 1995
4. The Soldier Boy's Discovery ◆ 1996

5. Blockade Runner ◆ 1996
6. The Gallant Boys of Gettysburg ◆ 1996
7. The Battle of Lookout Mountain ◆ 1996
8. Encounter at Cold Harbor ◆ 1997
9. Fire over Atlanta ◆ 1997
10. Bring the Boys Home ◆ 1997

BOOK OF EMBER *see* City of Ember

BOOK OF THE GODS

Saberhagen, Fred

TOR ◆ GRADES 10–12

FANTASY

Characters from Greek and Norse (*Gods of Fire and Thunder*) mythology are revisited in these action-packed books written for adults.

1. The Face of Apollo ◆ 1998
2. Ariadne's Web ◆ 2000
3. The Arms of Hercules ◆ 2000
4. God of the Golden Fleece ◆ 2001
5. Gods of Fire and Thunder ◆ 2002

THE BOOK OF THE LION

Cadnum, Michael

VIKING ◆ GRADES 6–9 ◆ A/R

HISTORICAL FICTION

Set during the Crusades, these books follow Edmund, an apprentice to a coin maker who becomes a knight's squire. Details about his daily life reveal the hardships and challenges, including the boredom of waiting for the battles to begin. Edmund hopes to become a knight but his past association with the coin maker puts him in danger.

1. The Book of the Lion ◆ 2000
2. The Leopard Sword ◆ 2002
3. The Dragon Throne ◆ 2005

BOOK OF WORDS

Jones, J. V.

WARNER ◆ GRADES 10–12

FANTASY

Melliandra, a young noblewoman rejecting an evil prince's offer of marriage, and a baker's apprentice named Jack who has magical powers run away from Castle Harvell. When the prince seizes power, these two become the only hope for the people of the land and Jack must test the strength of his magic.

1. The Baker's Boy ◆ 1995
2. A Man Betrayed ◆ 1996
3. Master and Fool ◆ 1996

BOOKS OF MAGIC

Jablonski, Carla

HARPERCOLLINS ◆ GRADES 9–12 ◆ A/R

FANTASY

Tim Hunter, 13, seems like a regular teenager but he is not. Four strangers lead him toward his destiny as a wizard, perhaps the greatest wizard ever. These books are based on the graphic novel series developed by Neil Gaiman and John Bolton.

1. The Invitation ◆ 2003
2. Bindings ◆ 2003
3. The Children's Crusade ◆ 2003
4. Consequences ◆ 2004
5. Lost Places ◆ 2004
6. Reckonings ◆ 2004

BOSTON JANE

Holm, Jennifer L.

HARPERCOLLINS ◆ GRADES 7–10 ◆ A/R

HISTORICAL

Jane Peck, 16, finds that her lessons in manners and polite society in Boston have not prepared her for a long sea voyage or life on the frontier in 1854. She is traveling to Washington Territory to marry William, her father's former apprentice. That relationship becomes strained by William's attitudes toward the native people and by Jane's growing independence.

1. Boston Jane: An Adventure ◆ 2001
2. Boston Jane: Wilderness Days ◆ 2002
3. Boston Jane: The Claim ◆ 2004

THE BOY SHERLOCK HOLMES

Peacock, Shane

TUNDRA ◆ GRADES 9–12 ◆ A/R

MYSTERY

At 13, Sherlock Holmes is an outsider. His aristocratic mother and his poor Jewish father defied tradition when they married and have been ostracized by 1860s London society. Alone and often bullied, Sherlock develops his observation skills. In the first book, he investigates the stabbing death of a woman. Other Holmes-related books like the Enola Holmes series are natural companions to this series.

1. Eye of the Crow ◆ 2007
2. Death in the Air ◆ 2008
3. The Vanishing Girl ◆ 2009

BRATZ

Various authors

GROSSET & DUNLAP ◆ GRADES 4–7 ◆ A/R

HUMOR | REAL LIFE

Tweens will enjoy the activities of Yasmin, Cloe, Jade and Sasha. The girls love fashion, dancing, parties, and fun. Sometimes, they even focus on school. In one book, the Homecoming Dance is coming and the girls are trapped in the mall. In another book, Cloe's artistic talent brings her some special attention. There are related materials with stickers and activities, like a guide to slumber party ideas. These are breezy books with lots of attitude.

1. Keepin' It Real: Bratz, the Video (O'Connor, Charles) ◆ 2004
2. Model Friendship (Krulik, Nancy) ◆ 2004
3. All-Night Mall Party! (O'Connor, Charles) ◆ 2004
4. Will Work for Fashion (Krulik, Nancy) ◆ 2004

BRATZ: CLUED IN!

Various authors

GROSSET & DUNLAP ◆ GRADES 4–7 ◆ A/R

HUMOR | REAL LIFE

The Bratz girls solve mysteries in these books. In *Behind-the-Scenes Secrets,* the girls are in a fashion show but first they have to find out who is causing the backstage problems that may ruin the show. Bratz fans will rush to read these.

1. Behind-the-Scenes Secrets (Goldman, Leslie) ◆ 2005
2. Seeing Double (Roberts, Christine N.) ◆ 2005
3. Breaking News (Burns, Laura J.) ◆ 2006
4. Accessory to the Crime (Fishman, Zoe) ◆ 2006

BRATZ: LIL' BRATZ

GROSSET & DUNLAP ◆ GRADES 4–7

HUMOR | REAL LIFE

Meet the Lil' Bratz: Nazalia, Zada, Ailani, and Talia. Like the older Bratz, these girls love fashion and fun. In *Hangin' with the Lil' Bratz,* you can read diary entries for each girl. In *Catwalk Cuties,* the girls plan a fashion show to raise money for an animal shelter. There are coloring books and other novelties that go with this series. Tween girls will love the nail polish and emery board that come with *Sweet Lil' Nails!*

1. Friends 4-Ever! ◆ 2004
2. Hangin' with the Lil' Bratz! ◆ 2004
3. Makin' It Up! ◆ 2004
4. School Time Style ◆ 2004
5. Dancin' Divas ◆ 2004
6. Beauty Sleepover Bash! ◆ 2005
7. Sweet Lil' Nails! ◆ 2005
8. Fashion Funk ◆ 2005
9. The Fabulous Style Swap ◆ 2005
10. Lights, Camera, Star! ◆ 2005
11. Funkhouse Adventure ◆ 2006
12. Around the World with the Lil' Bratz ◆ 2006
13. Catwalk Cuties ◆ 2006
14. Stylin' in the Sun ◆ 2007

THE BREADWINNER TRILOGY

Ellis, Deborah

GROUNDWOOD BOOKS ◆ GRADES 6–9 ◆ A/R

REAL LIFE

Set in Afghanistan during the rule of the Taliban, these books describe the experiences of a young girl, Parvana. Beginning when she is 11, Parvana watches as her father is arrested. To earn money for her family, she disguises herself as a boy. Her family moves away and Parvana is reunited with her father, only to have him die. With another girl who has been disguised, Shauzia, Parvana goes on a quest to find her family. The third book in the trilogy focuses on Shauzia, 14, and her experiences in an Afghan refugee camp.

1. The Breadwinner ◆ 2001

2. Parvana's Journey ◆ 2002
3. Mud City ◆ 2003

BRIAN ROBESON

Paulsen, Gary

DELACORTE ◆ GRADES 4–8 ◆ A/R

ADVENTURE | REAL LIFE

In *Hatchet,* 13-year-old Brian Robeson is stranded in the Canadian wilderness after a plane crash. He struggles to survive before being rescued just as winter approaches. *The River* features Brian returning to the site of his adventure with a psychologist, Derek Holtzer, who plans to observe and record the experience. Their trip turns into another struggle to survive. *Brian's Winter* is a continuation of *Hatchet,* but with the premise that Brian is not rescued before winter arrives and must struggle to survive even harsher circumstances. Fast-paced action—told in short, direct sentences—could appeal to reluctant readers. A related book is *Guts: The True Stories Behind Hatchet and the Brian Books* (2001).

1. Hatchet ◆ 1987
2. Brian's Return ◆ 1989
3. The River ◆ 1991
4. Brian's Winter ◆ 1996
5. Brian's Hunt ◆ 2004

BRIDES OF WILDCAT COUNTY

Watson, Jude

SIMON/ALADDIN ◆ GRADES 7–10

REAL LIFE

This series features women who take chances to find love and independence. One woman leaves an unhappy arranged marriage. In *Audacious,* Ivy escapes from her father's misfortunes in Maine and becomes a teacher in a frontier school in Wildcat County, California. These books combine romance with a Wild West setting.

1. Dangerous: Savannah's Story ◆ 1995
2. Scandalous: Eden's Story ◆ 1996
3. Audacious: Ivy's Story ◆ 1995
4. Impetuous: Mattie's Story ◆ 1995
5. Tempestuous: Opal's Story ◆ 1996

THE BRIMSTONE NETWORK

Sniegoski, Tom

ALADDIN ◆ GRADES 6–9

FANTASY

Elijah Stone is the leader of the Brimstone Network, warriors dedicated to stopping evil paranormal forces. His son Bram, 13, trains with monks in the Himalayan Mountains, who teach him ways to fight against supernatural beings. A strange visitor, Mr. Stitch, arrives at the monastery with shocking news. Bram's father and all of his followers have been killed. Bram must rebuild the Brimstone Network and stop the evil forces that are gathering to destroy humanity.

1. The Brimstone Network ◆ 2008
2. The Shrouds of A'Ranka ◆ 2008
3. Specter Rising ◆ 2009

BRIO GIRLS

Johnson, Lissa Halls

BETHANY HOUSE ◆ GRADES 6–10 ◆ A/R

REAL LIFE | VALUES

Jacie, Solana, Hannah, and Becca are in high school in Colorado. Three of the girls are Christian and their faith plays an important part in their dealings with family and friends. In *Fast Forward to Normal,* Becca is not happy that her parents plan to adopt a Guatemalan boy. In *Croutons for Breakfast,* Hannah and Jacie are on a mission trip to Venezuela and question God's plans for them.

1. Stuck in the Sky ◆ 2001
2. Fast Forward to Normal ◆ 2001
3. Opportunity Knocks Twice ◆ 2002
4. Double Exposure ◆ 2002
5. Good-Bye to All That ◆ 2002
6. Grasping at Moonbeams ◆ 2002
7. Croutons for Breakfast ◆ 2003
8. No Lifeguard on Duty ◆ 2003
9. Dragonfly on My Shoulder ◆ 2003
10. Going Crazy Till Wednesday ◆ 2003
11. When Stars Fall ◆ 2005
12. Bad Girl Days ◆ 2005

THE BROADWAY BALLPLAYERS

Holohan, Maureen

ALADDIN ◆ GRADES 4–7 ◆ A/R

RECREATION

Five girls who live on Broadway Avenue participate in a variety of sports. As in the Matt Christopher books, there are many dramatic moments involving injuries, family issues, jealousy, and "making the team." Each book features a different girl—Molly, Penny, Rosie, Wil, and Angel. In one book, Angel's feet are hurting but she won't tell anyone because she does not want to be left out of the big race. Sports fans will enjoy the action.

1. Friday Nights, by Molly ◆ 1998
2. Everybody's Favorite, by Penny ◆ 1998
3. Left Out, by Rosie ◆ 1998
4. Sideline Blues, by Wil ◆ 1998
5. Don't Stop, by Angel ◆ 1998
6. Ice Cold, by Molly ◆ 1999
7. Catch Shorty, by Rosie ◆ 1999

BROKEN SKY

Wooding, Chris

SCHOLASTIC ◆ GRADES 6–9

FANTASY

Ryushi is a prisoner. The Fane Aracq are trying to get him to reveal a secret that will allow Princess Aurin to defeat his people.

1. Broken Sky # 1 ◆ 2001
2. Broken Sky # 2 ◆ 2001
3. Broken Sky # 3 ◆ 2001
4. Broken Sky # 4 ◆ 2001
5. Broken Sky # 5 ◆ 2001
6. Broken Sky # 6 ◆ 2001
7. Broken Sky # 7 ◆ 2001

BROMELIAD

Pratchett, Terry

DELACORTE ◆ GRADES 6–9 ◆ A/R

FANTASY

A tiny race of beings called nomes came from outer space to earth centuries ago and showed man how to use metal. Then they forgot everything they knew. Some of them ended up living in the floorboards of a department store and developed a religion based on the founders of the store. "Outside" is a myth, they believe, and the whole universe is the store. Then one day everything changes, when nomes from the Outside show up carrying the Thing, the on-board computer from the spaceship. Fans of all kinds of fantasy will love the satire and inventiveness of this series.

1. Truckers ◆ 1989
2. Diggers: The Second Book of the Bromeliad ◆ 1992
3. Wings: The Last Book of the Bromeliad ◆ 1991

BRUNO AND BOOTS

Korman, Gordon

SCHOLASTIC ◆ GRADES 6–8 ◆ A/R

HUMOR

Bruno and Boots are pranksters at an exclusive boys' boarding school in Canada. They replace the Canadian flag with the flag of Malbonia and steal a rival school's mascot. The school's headmaster, Mr. Sturgeon ("The Fish"), knows they are the culprits and decides to separate them. But when they manage to rescue the son of the Malbonian ambassador, who is stuck in a tree in a hot-air balloon, the boys are allowed to room together again. In their further adventures, they drive "The Fish" crazy, delight their classmates, and plan mayhem with the girls from the finishing school across the street.

1. This Can't Be Happening at Macdonald Hall! ◆ 1990
2. Beware the Fish! ◆ 1991
3. The Zucchini Warriors ◆ 1991
4. Go Jump in the Pool ◆ 1991
5. Macdonald Hall Goes Hollywood ◆ 1991
6. Something Fishy at Macdonald Hall ◆ 1995

BUFFY THE VAMPIRE SLAYER

Various authors

ARCHWAY/POCKET BOOKS ◆ GRADES 6–10

ADVENTURE | HORROR

Buffy the Vampire Slayer has an intensely loyal following among preteens and adolescents who enjoy violent encounters involving vampires and their victims. Buffy Summers leads a group of high school friends to try to destroy the creatures that have targeted Sunnydale. These books parallel some of the episodes from the television series by the same name. The teens, aided by Giles, the school librarian, try to stop the zombies, vampires, and other ghouls. This is not for the faint-hearted. Buffy uses her wits and her physical skills to protect her friends and the world.

BUFFY THE VAMPIRE SLAYER—NUMBERED TITLES

1. The Harvest (Cusick, Richie Tankersley) ◆ 1997
2. Halloween Rain (Golden, Christopher, and Nancy Holder) ◆ 1997
3. Coyote Moon (Vornholt, John) ◆ 1998
4. The Night of the Living Rerun (Cover, Arthur) ◆ 1998
5. Blooded (Golden, Christopher, and Nancy Holder) ◆ 1998
6. Visitors (Gilman, Laura Anne, and Josepha Sherman) ◆ 1999
7. Unnatural Selection (Odom, Mel) ◆ 1999
8. Power of Persuasion (Massie, Elizabeth) ◆ 1999
9. Deep Water (Gilman, Laura Anne, and Josepha Sherman) ◆ 2000
10. Here Be Monsters (Dokey, Cameron) ◆ 2000
11. Ghoul Trouble (Passarella, John) ◆ 2000
12. Doomsday Deck (Gallagher, Diana G.) ◆ 2000
13. Sweet Sixteen (Ciencin, Scott) ◆ 2002
14. Crossings (Odom, Mel) ◆ 2002
15. Little Things (Moesta, Rebecca) ◆ 2002

BUFFY THE VAMPIRE SLAYER—ADDITIONAL TITLES

1. Child of the Hunt (Golden, Christopher, and Nancy Holder) ◆ 1998
2. Return to Chaos (Gardner, Craig Shaw) ◆ 1998
3. Obsidian Fate (Gallagher, Diana G.) ◆ 1999
4. Immortal (Golden, Christopher, and Nancy Holder) ◆ 2000
5. Sins of the Father (Golden, Christopher, and Nancy Holder) ◆ 2000
6. Resurrecting Ravana (Garton, Ray) ◆ 2000
7. Prime Evil (Gallagher, Diana G.) ◆ 2000
8. The Evil that Men Do (Holder, Nancy) ◆ 2000
9. How I Survived My Summer Vacation, Volume 1 (Holder, Nancy, Yvonne Navarro, et al.) ◆ 2000
10. Paleo (Navarro, Yvonne) ◆ 2000
11. Spike and Dru: Pretty Maids All in a Row (Golden, Christopher) ◆ 2001
12. The Faith Trials, Volume 1 (Laurence, James) ◆ 2001
13. Revenant (Odom, Mel) ◆ 2001
14. The Book of Fours (Holder, Nancy) ◆ 2002
15. Tempted Champions (Navarro, Yvonne) ◆ 2002
16. Oz (Golden, Christopher, and Logan Lubera) ◆ 2002
17. The Wisdom of War (Golden, Christopher) ◆ 2002
18. These Our Actors (Koogler, Dori, and Ashley McConnell) ◆ 2002
19. Blood and Fog (Holder, Nancy) ◆ 2003
20. Chaos Bleeds (Moore, James A.) ◆ 2003
21. Mortal Fear (Ciencin, Scott, and Denise Ciencin) ◆ 2003
22. Apocalypse Memories (Metz, Melinda, and Laura J. Burns) ◆ 2004

BUFFY THE VAMPIRE SLAYER

Various authors

DARK HORSE ◆ GRADES 6–10

ADVENTURE | HORROR

The popularity of the television program about Buffy the Vampire Slayer and her friends has led to many spinoffs, including these graphic novels.

1. The Dust Waltz (Brereton, Dan, and Rick Ketcham) ◆ 1998
2. Uninvited Guests (Watson, Andi, and Dan Brereton) ◆ 1999
3. The Origin (Golden, Christopher, et al.) ◆ 1999
4. Ring of Fire (Petrie, Doug, and Ryan Sook) ◆ 2000
5. Bad Blood (Watson, Andi, et al.) ◆ 2000
6. Crash Test Demons (Watson, Andi, et al.) ◆ 2000
7. Pale Reflections (Watson, Andi, et al.) ◆ 2000
8. Food Chain (Petrie, Doug, et al.) ◆ 2001
9. Blood of Carthage (Golden, Christopher, et al.) ◆ 2001
10. Autumnal (Boal, Chris, et al.) ◆ 2001
11. Past Lives (Golden, Christopher, et al.) ◆ 2001
12. Tales of the Slayers (Whedon, Joss, et al.) ◆ 2002
13. Haunted (Espenson, Jane, et al.) ◆ 2002
14. Oz (Golden, Christopher, and Logan Lubera) ◆ 2002
15. Out of the Woodwork (Fassbender, Tom, et al.) ◆ 2002
16. False Memories (Fassbender, Tom, et al.) ◆ 2002
17. Ugly Little Monsters (Fassbender, Tom, et al.) ◆ 2002
18. The Death of Buffy (Nicieza, Fabian, et al.) ◆ 2002
19. Night of a Thousand Vampires, and Ugly Little Monsters (Fassbender, Tom, and Jim Pascoe) ◆ 2002
20. Creatures of Habit (Fassbender, Tom, et al.) ◆ 2002
21. Note from the Underground (Lobdell, Scott, et al.) ◆ 2003
22. Slayer, Interrupted (Lobdell, Scott, et al.) ◆ 2003
23. Viva Las Buffy (Lobdell, Scott, et al.) ◆ 2003
24. A Stake to the Heart (Nicieza, Fabian) ◆ 2004
25. The Long Way Home (Whedon, Josh, et al.) ◆ 2007
26. No Future for You (Vaughan, Brian K.) ◆ 2008
27. Wolves at the Gate (Goddard, Drew) ◆ 2008

BUFFY THE VAMPIRE SLAYER OMNIBUS COLLECTIONS

1. Volume 1 ◆ 2007
2. Volume 2 ◆ 2007
3. Volume 3 ◆ 2008
4. Volume 4 ◆ 2008
5. Volume 5 ◆ 2008

BUFFY THE VAMPIRE SLAYER: BUFFY AND ANGEL

ARCHWAY/POCKET BOOKS ◆ GRADES 6–10

ADVENTURE | HORROR

These books feature Buffy and Angel confronting vampires and other demons.

1. Cursed (Odom, Mel) ◆ 2003
2. Seven Crows (Vornholt, John) ◆ 2003
3. Heat (Holder, Nancy) ◆ 2004
4. Monster Island (Golden, Christopher, and Thomas E. Sniegoski) ◆ 2004

BUFFY THE VAMPIRE SLAYER: BUFFY AND ANGEL: THE UNSEEN TRILOGY

Holder, Nancy, and Jeff Mariotte

ARCHWAY/POCKET BOOKS ◆ GRADES 6–10

ADVENTURE | HORROR

Buffy and Angel are in another reality ruled by monsters and they must find the portal to return to Sunnydale.

1. The Burning: The Unseen Trilogy Book 1 (Holder, Nancy, and Jeff Mariotte) ◆ 2001
2. Door to Alternity: The Unseen Trilogy Book 2 (Holder, Nancy, and Jeff Mariotte) ◆ 2001
3. Long Way Home: The Unseen Trilogy Book 3 (Holder, Nancy, and Jeff Mariotte) ◆ 2001

BUFFY THE VAMPIRE SLAYER: STAKE YOUR DESTINY

Various authors

SIMON SPOTLIGHT ◆ GRADES 6–10

ADVENTURE | HORROR

This series lets you decide the plot. Buffy is in high school and a demon ant creature, Belakane, is luring teens into her *Colony*. In *Night Terrors,* an evil being is stealing souls and it wants Buffy. The only person who can stop it is . . . YOU!

1. Colony (Metz, Melinda) ◆ 2005
2. Keep Me in Mind (Holder, Nancy) ◆ 2005
3. Night Terrors (Henderson, Alice) ◆ 2005
4. The Suicide King (Levy, Robert Joseph) ◆ 2005

BUFFY THE VAMPIRE SLAYER: THE ANGEL CHRONICLES

Various authors

ARCHWAY/POCKET BOOKS ◆ GRADES 6–10

ADVENTURE | HORROR

This trilogy explores Buffy's relationship with Angel. She is a vampire slayer; he is a vampire. Their passion for each other is doomed.

1. The Angel Chronicles, Volume 1 (Holder, Nancy) ◆ 1998
2. The Angel Chronicles, Volume 2 (Tankersley, Rick) ◆ 1998
3. The Angel Chronicles, Volume 3 (Holder, Nancy) ◆ 1999

BUFFY THE VAMPIRE SLAYER: THE GATEKEEPER TRILOGY

Golden, Christopher, and Nancy Holder

ARCHWAY/POCKET BOOKS ◆ GRADES 6–10

ADVENTURE | HORROR

New demons are arriving in Sunnydale. Buffy and her friends must destroy the creatures and close the time/space Gatehouse. But first, Buffy must rescue her mother, Joyce, from the demons.

1. Out of the Madhouse: The Gatekeeper Trilogy Book 1 (Golden, Christopher, and Nancy Holder) ◆ 1999
2. Ghost Roads: The Gatekeeper Trilogy Book 2 (Golden, Christopher, and Nancy Holder) ◆ 1999
3. Sons of Entropy: The Gatekeeper Trilogy Book 3 (Golden, Christopher, and Nancy Holder) ◆ 1999

BUFFY THE VAMPIRE SLAYER: THE LOST SLAYER SERIAL NOVEL

Golden, Christopher

ARCHWAY/POCKET BOOKS ◆ GRADES 6–10

ADVENTURE | HORROR

Buffy's mother Joyce has been killed and her corpse is controlled by evil forces. Spike and Faith are also gone. Buffy created this grim future and she must retrace her actions to find the way to undo the horror.

1. Part 1: Prophecies (Golden, Christopher) ◆ 2001
2. Part 2: The Dark Times (Golden, Christopher) ◆ 2001
3. Part 3: King of the Dead (Golden, Christopher) ◆ 2001
4. Part 4: Original Sins (Golden, Christopher) ◆ 2001

BUFFY THE VAMPIRE SLAYER: THE WILLOW FILES

Navarro, Yvonne

ARCHWAY/POCKET BOOKS ◆ GRADES 6–10

ADVENTURE │ HORROR

Willow's role has expanded during the Buffy series. Now she stands on her own and begins a romance with Oz while dealing with a witch hunt in Sunnydale.

1. The Willow Files, Volume 1 (Navarro, Yvonne) ◆ 1999
2. The Willow Files, Volume 2 (Navarro, Yvonne) ◆ 2001

BUFFY THE VAMPIRE SLAYER: THE XANDER YEARS

Mariotte, Jeff

ARCHWAY/POCKET BOOKS ◆ GRADES 6–10

ADVENTURE │ HORROR

Xander Harris has never been popular at school or with girls but he has played an important role with the Slayers and seemed to be content. After a field trip to the zoo, he begins to behave strangely.

1. The Xander Years, Volume 1 (Mariotte, Jeff) ◆ 2000
2. The Xander Years, Volume 2 (Mariotte, Jeff) ◆ 2000

BUFFY THE VAMPIRE SLAYER: WICKED WILLOW

Navarro, Yvonne

ARCHWAY/POCKET BOOKS ◆ GRADES 6–10

ADVENTURE │ HORROR

Willow has decided to practice magic on her own, forming her own coven. She has been working on a resurrection spell for her friend, the Ghost of Tara. Willow is upset when the Ghost disappears and she discovers that Buffy and the old gang are responsible.

1. Volume 1: The Darkening (Navarro, Yvonne) ◆ 2004
2. Volume 2: Shattered Twilight (Navarro, Yvonne) ◆ 2004
3. Volume 3: Broken Sunrise (Navarro, Yvonne) ◆ 2004

BUTT WARS

Griffiths, Andy

SCHOLASTIC ◆ GRADES 5–8 ◆ A/R

HUMOR

Twelve-year-old Zack Freeman's butt takes off for its own adventures. Yes, his butt runs away! There are battles with other butts, numerous butt wordplays, and lots of gross humor. Head butts, butt kicking, cluster butts, alien butts, even Great White Butts—you get the picture. This Australian import (which has been Americanized with butt for bum) is sure to be a hit with fans of Captain Underpants and the Riot Brothers.

   1. The Day My Butt Went Psycho! Based on a True Story ◆ 2003
   2. Zombie Butts from Uranus! ◆ 2004
   3. Butt Wars! The Final Conflict ◆ 2005

B.Y. TIMES

Klein, Leah

TARGUM/FELDHEIM ◆ GRADES 4–8

REAL LIFE

A group of girls attend the same middle school, Bais Yaakov, and work on their school newspaper, the *B.Y. Times*. The staff of the paper changes as students leave the school. In an early book, Shani Baum is the editor-in-chief; in a later book, Chani Kaufman has that job. There are references to school events and to Jewish events and holidays. An issue of the *B.Y. Times* is printed at the end of each book.

   1. Shani's Scoop ◆ 1991
   2. Batya's Search ◆ 1991
   3. Twins in Trouble ◆ 1991
   4. War! ◆ 1991
   5. Spring Fever ◆ 1992
   6. Party Time ◆ 1992
   7. Changing Times ◆ 1992
   8. Summer Daze ◆ 1992
   9. Here We Go Again ◆ 1992
  10. The New Kids ◆ 1992
  11. Dollars and Sense ◆ 1993
  12. Talking It Over ◆ 1993
  13. Flying High ◆ 1993
  14. Nechama on Strike ◆ 1993
  15. Secrets! ◆ 1993
  16. Babysitting Blues ◆ 1994

17. Jen Starts Over ◆ 1994
18. Who's Who ◆ 1994

@CAFE

Craft, Elizabeth

SIMON & SCHUSTER ◆ GRADES 7–10

REAL LIFE

The Internet cafe serves up coffee, computers, and romance. Six teens, three boys and three girls, work there. The friendships become complicated when two of the guys, Sam and Dylan, like the same girl, Natalie.

1. Love Bytes ◆ 1997
2. I'll Have What He's Having ◆ 1997
3. Make Mine to Go ◆ 1998
4. Flavor of the Day ◆ 1998

CALDER AND PETRA *see* Petra and Calder

CALIBAN *see* Isaac Asimov's Caliban

CALIFORNIA DIARIES

Martin, Ann M.

SCHOLASTIC ◆ GRADES 6–8

REAL LIFE

These books feature various girls who are facing problems that will be familiar to young teens. Sunny's family is struggling to cope with her mother's cancer. Even with this trauma, Sunny must deal with issues involving school, boys, and friends. Maggie wants to weigh 90 pounds. That means she must lose 13 pounds. She also must face her mother's drinking problem and her father's frequent absence from home. The girls mention each other in their diaries, and the format, which sometimes includes hand-printed words, may attract reluctant readers.

1. Dawn ◆ 1997
2. Sunny ◆ 1997
3. Maggie ◆ 1997
4. Amalia ◆ 1997
5. Ducky ◆ 1998
6. Sunny, Diary Two ◆ 1998
7. Dawn, Diary Two ◆ 1998
8. Maggie, Diary Two ◆ 1998

9. Amalia, Diary Two ◆ 1998
10. Ducky, Diary Two ◆ 1998
11. Dawn, Diary Three ◆ 1999
12. Sunny, Diary Three ◆ 1999
13. Maggy, Diary Three ◆ 1999
14. Amalia, Diary Three ◆ 2000
15. Ducky, Diary Three ◆ 2000

CALYPSO CHRONICLES

O'Connell, Tyne

BLOOMSBURY ◆ GRADES 7–10 ◆ A/R

REAL LIFE

Calypso Kelly,14, from Los Angeles, wants to fit in and be popular at her posh English boarding school. By pretending she has a boyfriend in the States, she gets a lot of attention—even attracting the interest of Prince Freddy, who attends the nearby boys' school. Calypso makes new friends and some enemies, like Honey who has her own plans for the prince. English teens and terminology are reminiscent of Louise Rennison's Confessions of Georgia Nicolson books. Other teen chick lit series would relate to this, including the Princess Diary books and the Girl/Jess Jordan books by Sue Limb.

1. Pulling Princes ◆ 2004
2. Stealing Princes ◆ 2005
3. Dueling Princes ◆ 2005
4. Dumping Princes ◆ 2006

CAMP CONFIDENTIAL

Morgan, Melissa

GROSSET & DUNLAP ◆ GRADES 4–7 ◆ A/R

REAL LIFE

When the series begins, the girls featured in each book are 11 and they are worried about being new at camp and making friends. For example, in *Jenna's Dilemma* Jenna is trying to cope with her parents' separation. Then, in *A Fair to Remember,* Jenna is 13 and upset that her twin brother has invited her old boyfriend to a family activity. At first, there is a core group of friends. They visit each other during the year after camp (when they are in sixth grade) and return to the camp the next summer. As the series continues, different girls are featured and their concerns reflect their growing maturity. In *Suddenly Last Summer,* Camp Lakeview is closed.

1. Natalie's Secret ◆ 2006

2. Jenna's Dilemma ◆ 2006
3. Grace's Twist ◆ 2006
4. Alex's Challenge ◆ 2006
5. TTYL ◆ 2006
6. RSVP ◆ 2006
7. Second Time's the Charm ◆ 2006
8. Wish You Weren't Here ◆ 2006
9. Best (Boy)friend Forever ◆ 2006
10. Over & Out ◆ 2006
11. Falling In Like ◆ 2006
12. Winter Games ◆ 2006
13. A Fair to Remember ◆ 2007
14. Hide and Shriek ◆ 2007
15. Reality Bites ◆ 2007
16. Golden Girls ◆ 2007
17. Freaky Tuesday ◆ 2007
18. And the Winner Is . . . ◆ 2007
19. Charmed Forces ◆ 2008
20. Suddenly Last Summer ◆ 2008

CAMP SUNNYSIDE

Kaye, Marilyn

AVON ◆ GRADES 4–7

REAL LIFE

Five girls from different parts of the country and with very different personalities meet every summer at Camp Sunnyside. Katie is a born leader and always has a scheme up her sleeve. Trina is more mature and thoughtful, while Erin is the sophisticated one of the group. Rounding out the complement of characters are Sarah, the intellectual, and Megan, the daydreamer. In *No Boys Allowed,* a neighboring boys camp has been destroyed by fire, and plans are made for the campers to stay at Camp Sunnyside temporarily. Katie, who has obnoxious older brothers, is vehemently opposed to the idea, and plans to let the boys know they are not welcome. She recruits the other girls to join her, but one by one they meet boys they like who share their interests. Eventually even Katie succumbs to a boy's advance. The series continues for several summers until the girls are in junior high.

1. No Boys Allowed ◆ 1989
2. Cabin Six Plays Cupid ◆ 1989
3. Color War! ◆ 1989
4. New Girl in Cabin Six ◆ 1989
5. Looking for Trouble ◆ 1990
6. Katie Steals the Show ◆ 1990
7. A Witch in Cabin Six ◆ 1990
8. Too Many Counselors ◆ 1990

9. The New and Improved Sarah ◆ 1990
10. Erin and the Movie Star ◆ 1991
11. The Problem with Parents ◆ 1991
12. The Tennis Trap ◆ 1991
13. Big Sister Blues ◆ 1991
14. Megan's Ghost ◆ 1991
15. Christmas Break ◆ 1991
16. Happily Ever After ◆ 1992
17. Camp Spaghetti ◆ 1992
18. Balancing Act ◆ 1992

CAMP ZOMBIE

Stine, Megan, and H. William Stine
RANDOM HOUSE ◆ GRADES 5–7
HORROR

Five people once drowned in the lake at Camp Harvest Moon in Maine. Years later, the camp reopens and Corey and his sister Amanda are among the first new campers. But something very strange is going on. Amanda, an excellent swimmer, is almost drowned, and she is sure something grabbed her. Corey and Amanda and some other campers confront the five zombies from the lake and a new zombie—a dead camp counselor. The next summer, their cousin Griffen is sent to the same camp! And the next summer, on a trip with their grandparents, the cousins meet the zombies again. There are plot twists and dramatic moments when the zombies are just inches away that will provide readers with moments of spine-tingling suspense.

1. Camp Zombie ◆ 1994
2. Camp Zombie: The Second Summer ◆ 1995
3. Camp Zombie: The Lake's Revenge ◆ 1996

CAPTAIN UNDERPANTS

Pilkey, Dav
SCHOLASTIC ◆ GRADES 3–8 ◆ A/R
HUMOR

Kids love these irreverent comic-book-style stories. They are gross, rude, and hilarious. George and Harold are the troublemakers. Adults are the dupes—the "butt" of the jokes. Just look at some of their names—Professor Poopypants and Stinky Jingleberry. Spanish editions and two activity books are also available. The Riot Brothers (Amato) and Butt Wars (Griffiths) are equally irreverent series.

1. The Adventures of Captain Underpants ◆ 1997

2. Captain Underpants and the Attack of the Talking Toilets ◆ 1999
3. Captain Underpants and the Invasion of the Incredibly Naughty Cafeteria Ladies from Outer Space ◆ 1999
4. Captain Underpants and the Perilous Plot of Professor Poopypants ◆ 2000
5. Captain Underpants and the Wrath of the Wicked Wedgie Woman ◆ 2001
6. Captain Underpants and the Big, Bad Battle of the Bionic Booger Boy, Part 1: The Night of the Nasty Nostril Nuggets ◆ 2003
7. Captain Underpants and the Big, Bad Battle of the Bionic Booger Boy, Part 2: The Revenge of the Ridiculous Robo-Boogers ◆ 2003
8. Captain Underpants and the Preposterous Plight of the Purple Potty People ◆ 2006

CARTER HOUSE GIRLS

Carlson, Melody

ZONDERKIDZ ◆ GRADES 8–10 ◆ A/R

REAL LIFE | VALUES

Katherine Carter, who was a fashion model in the 1960s, opens a boarding house for six teen girls, including her granddaughter DJ. Like other teens, the girls are interested in dances, dating, and clothes. In *Stealing Bradford,* Taylor shows an interest in Rhiannon's boyfriend. As the girls deal with their feelings of anger and betrayal, they also learn about forgiveness. Some see the importance of accepting God while others still struggle with their choices.

1. Mixed Bags ◆ 2008
2. Stealing Bradford ◆ 2008
3. Homecoming Queen ◆ 2008
4. Viva Vermont! ◆ 2008

CASSIE PERKINS

Hunt, Angela Elwell

TYNDALE HOUSE ◆ GRADES 4–7

REAL LIFE | VALUES

Cassie Perkins thinks she has the perfect life until her father walks out on her family. Later, her parents tell Cassie and her beloved little brother Max that he is going to live with their father. Cassie lands the lead in her school's production of *Oklahoma.* This makes her friend Andrea envious because she has a crush on Chip, the male lead. He becomes a good friend to Cassie, and leads her to faith in Christ. Her music teacher recommends her to a performing arts high school, but her mother doesn't think they can afford it. Cassie learns to trust in God for this and everything else.

1. No More Broken Promises ◆ 1991
2. A Forever Friend ◆ 1991
3. A Basket of Roses ◆ 1991
4. A Dream to Cherish ◆ 1992
5. The Much-Adored Sandy Shore ◆ 1992
6. Love Burning Bright ◆ 1992
7. Star Light, Star Bright ◆ 1993
8. The Chance of a Lifetime ◆ 1993
9. The Glory of Love ◆ 1993

CASSON FAMILY

McKay, Hilary

MARGARET K. MCELDERRY BOOKS ◆ GRADES 6–9 ◆ A/R

FAMILY LIFE

The first volume in this fast-paced series about an eccentric, artistic British family — parents Bill and Eve and children Cadmium, Saffron, Indigo and Rose — tells the story of 13-year-old Saffy's discovery that she was adopted. Subsequent volumes focus on other crises (12-year-old Indigo and his American friend Tom stand up to bullies, the parents have marital problems, Caddy questions her choice of future husband) while also portraying a loving, welcoming family.

1. Saffy's Angel ◆ 2002
2. Indigo's Star ◆ 2004
3. Permanent Rose ◆ 2005
4. Caddy Ever After ◆ 2006
5. Forever Rose ◆ 2008

CASTAWAYS OF THE FLYING DUTCHMAN

Jacques, Brian

PHILOMEL ◆ GRADES 5–8 ◆ A/R

FANTASY

Neb and his dog Ned stowed away on the *Flying Dutchman*. After falling into the sea during a storm, they were rescued by an angel and granted immortality. Now they roam the earth bringing aid to those in need. In the first book, it is 1896 and Neb—who is now called Ben—saves a village from being overrun by a shady businessman's plans for industrial development.

1. Castaways of the Flying Dutchman ◆ 2001

2. The Angel's Command ◆ 2003
3. Voyage of Slaves ◆ 2006

THE CAT PACK *see* Club of Mysteries

CAT ROYAL ADVENTURES

Golding, Julia
ROARING BROOK ◆ GRADES 6–8
MYSTERY | HISTORICAL

Catherine "Cat" Royal is an orphan in 1790s London. As an infant, she was abandoned in the Theatre Royal at Drury Lane. Mr. Sheridan, the theatre's owner, took her in and raised her. In the first book, Cat searches for a diamond that may be hidden in the theatre. Cat's friend Pedro, a freed slave who is a violin prodigy, joins her in the search.

1. The Diamond of Drury Lane ◆ 2008
2. Cat Among the Pigeons ◆ 2008
3. Den of Thieves ◆ 2009

CATHERINE MARSHALL'S CHRISTY *see* Christy

CAT'S EYE CORNER

Griggs, Terry
RAINCOAST BOOKS ◆ GRADES 4–7 ◆ A/R
FANTASY

Oliver is invited to visit his eccentric grandfather for the summer. Grandfather's third wife, Sylvia de Whosit of Whatsit, seems quite eccentric; however, she starts Oliver off on a scavenger hunt that becomes a fantastic adventure. Oliver is befriended by a fountain pen and a dragonfly. They, along with other items Oliver finds, help him succeed on a dangerous mission. Lots of wordplay and creative situations will remind readers of Juster's *The Phantom Tollbooth*.

1. Cat's Eye Corner ◆ 2003
2. The Silver Door ◆ 2004
3. Invisible Ink ◆ 2006

CELEBUTANTES

Pagliarulo, Antonio
DELACORTE ◆ GRADES 7–10 ◆ A/R
REAL LIFE | MYSTERY

Triplet sisters Lexington, Park, and Madison Hamilton live among the beautiful people in New York City. Although they are only 15, they plan parties, design clothess, and are chased by the paparazzi. In each book, they also get involved in a murder mystery. In *On the Avenue,* a fashion editor is found dead at the girls' party and Lexington is a suspect. Teen behaviors—boyfriends, drinking, partying, etc.—are included in the books.

1. On the Avenue ◆ 2007
2. In the Club ◆ 2008
3. To the Penthouse ◆ 2008

CELIA REES SUPERNATURAL TRILOGY

Rees, Celia
HODDER ◆ GRADES 6–8
FANTASY

Eleven-year-old Davey, his sister, and twin cousins Tom and Elinor visit historic ruins in their English town and find themselves transported into a parallel world of good and evil ghosts. In the final suspenseful installment, they work to save their ghost friends from a ghostbusting machine.

1. City of Shadows ◆ 2002
2. A Trap in Time ◆ 2002
3. The Host Rides Out ◆ 2002

CHANTERS OF TREMARIS TRILOGY

Constable, Kate
SCHOLASTIC ◆ GRADES 6–10 ◆ A/R
FANTASY

Calwyn sings magic. Along with the other Chanters, she uses her skills to protect their world, Tremaris. Samis is a dangerous sorcerer who is seeking to expand his power by learning the nine powers of chantment. Calwyn's destiny is to be a priestess in Antaris, but she longs for adventure outside the walls of her kingdom.

1. The Singer of All Songs ◆ 2004
2. The Waterless Sea ◆ 2005
3. The Tenth Power ◆ 2005

CHARLIE BONE *see* Children of the Red King

CHARMED

Various authors

SIMON & SCHUSTER ◆ GRADES 7–12

FANTASY

Once the Halliwell sisters—Prue, Piper, and Phoebe—discover their powers, they are in danger. Creatures want to steal their strength or kill them. As the series evolves, the witches continue to defend themselves from supernatural attacks on their power. The books parallel many episodes from the television shows. In later books, Prue has left and Paige becomes one of the Charmed Ones. *Seasons of the Witch* (2003) is a special book that features a story for each woman.

1. The Power of Three (Burge, Constance M.) ◆ 1999
2. Kiss of Darkness (Alexandra, Belinda) ◆ 2000
3. The Crimson Spell (Dokey, Cameron) ◆ 2000
4. Whispers from the Past (Noonan, Rosalind) ◆ 2000
5. Voodoo Moon (Burge, Constance M.) ◆ 2000
6. Haunted by Desire (Burge, Constance M.) ◆ 2000
7. The Gypsy Enchantment (Jablonski, Carla) ◆ 2001
8. The Legend of Merlin (Flood, E. L.) ◆ 2001
9. Soul of the Bride (Lenhard, Elizabeth) ◆ 2001
10. Beware What You Wish (Burge, Constance M.) ◆ 2001
11. Charmed Again (Lenhard, Elizabeth) ◆ 2002
12. Spirit of the Wolf (Gallagher, Diana G.) ◆ 2002
13. Garden of Evil (Harrison, Emma) ◆ 2002
14. Date with Death (Lenhard, Elizabeth) ◆ 2002
15. Dark Vengeance (Gallagher, Diana G.) ◆ 2002
16. Shadow of the Sphinx (Jablonski, Carla) ◆ 2003
17. Something Wiccan This Way Comes (Harrison, Emma) ◆ 2003
18. Mist and Stone (Gallagher, Diana G.) ◆ 2003
19. Mirror Image (Mariotte, Jeff) ◆ 2003
20. Between Worlds (Weiss, Bobbi J. G., and Jacklyn Weiss) ◆ 2003
21. Truth and Consequences (Dokey, Cameron) ◆ 2003
22. Luck Be a Lady (Ciencin, Scott) ◆ 2004
23. Inherit the Witch (Burns, Laura J.) ◆ 2004
24. The Book of Three (Gallagher, Diana G., and Paul Ruditis) ◆ 2004
25. A Tale of Two Pipers (Harrison, Emma) ◆ 2004
26. The Brewing Storm (Ruditis, Paul) ◆ 2004
27. Survival of the Fittest (Mariotte, Jeff) ◆ 2004

28. Pied Piper (Viguie, Debbie) ◆ 2004
29. Mystic Knoll (Gallagher, Diana G.) ◆ 2005
30. Changeling Places (Ostow, Mikol) ◆ 2005
31. The Queen's Curse (Harrison, Emma) ◆ 2005
32. Picture Perfect (Dokey, Cameron) ◆ 2005
33. Demon Doppelgangers (Elliott, Greg) ◆ 2005
34. As Puck Would Have It (Ruditis, Paul) ◆ 2006
35. Hurricane Hex (Gallagher, Diana G.) ◆ 2006
36. Sweet Talkin' Demon (Burns, Laura J.) ◆ 2006
37. Light of the World (Ciencin, Scott) ◆ 2006
38. House of Shards (Ostow, Mikol) ◆ 2006
39. Phoebe Who? (Harrison, Emma) ◆ 2006
40. High Spirits (Ciencin, Scott) ◆ 2007
41. Leo Rising (Ruditis, Paul) ◆ 2006
42. Trickery Treat (Gallagher, Diana G.) ◆ 2008

CHEER SQUAD

Singleton, Linda Joy

AVON CAMELOT ◆ GRADES 6–8

REAL LIFE | RECREATION

Oh, no! Darlene and her megapopular friends have been chosen to be seventh-grade cheerleaders. Will Wendi and Tabby always be popularity rejects? Not when a new cheer squad is formed for the basketball team. Now Wendi and Tabby and their classmates Krystal, Anna, Celine, and Rachel have a chance. Girls who like to read about regular girls who succeed against the "in" crowd will enjoy this series. There is even a bit of budding romance when boys join the cheer squad.

1. Crazy for Cartwheels ◆ 1996
2. Spirit Song ◆ 1996
3. Stand Up and Cheer ◆ 1996
4. Boys Are Bad News ◆ 1997
5. Spring to Stardom ◆ 1997
6. Camp Confessions ◆ 1997

CHEER USA!

Betancourt, Jeanne

SCHOLASTIC ◆ GRADES 6–9

REAL LIFE | RECREATION

At Claymore Middle School in Florida, making the cheer squad is a big deal. Four girls try out successfully and show lots of school spirit. They get involved in pre-game pranks and then go out and cheer their team to victory. They even compete in the regional cheering competition.

1. Go, Girl, Go ◆ 1999
2. Fight, Bulldogs, Fight! ◆ 1999
3. Ready, Shoot, Score! ◆ 1999
4. We've Got Spirit! ◆ 1999

CHEERLEADERS

Various authors

SCHOLASTIC ◆ GRADES 7–9

RECREATION

Who will win the big game? Can the cheer team win the state competition? How will the varsity captain confront the rumor that she is shoplifting? These questions and more are explored in this series. Dating, jealousy, clothes, body image, and more will delight readers. Fans of the Sweet Valley books will enjoy these.

1. Trying Out (Cooney, Caroline B.) ◆ 1984
2. Getting Even (Pike, Christopher) ◆ 1984
3. Rumors (Cooney, Caroline B.) ◆ 1984
4. Feuding (Norby, Lisa) ◆ 1984
5. All the Way (Cooney, Caroline B.) ◆ 1985
6. Splitting (Sarasin, Jennifer) ◆ 1985
7. Flirting (Hoh, Diane) ◆ 1985
8. Forgetting (Norby, Lisa) ◆ 1985
9. Playing Games (Sorenson, Jody) ◆ 1985
10. Betrayed (Hoh, Diane) ◆ 1985
11. Cheating (Sarasin, Jennifer) ◆ 1985
12. Staying Together (Hoh, Diane) ◆ 1985
13. Hurting (Norby, Lisa) ◆ 1986
14. Living It Up (Sarasin, Jennifer) ◆ 1986
15. Waiting (Sorenson, Jody) ◆ 1986
16. In Love (Stanley, Carol) ◆ 1986
17. Taking Risks (Reynolds, Anne) ◆ 1986
18. Looking Good (Ellis, Carol) ◆ 1986
19. Making It (Blake, Susan) ◆ 1986
20. Starting Over (Aks, Patricia) ◆ 1986
21. Pulling Together (Hoh, Diane) ◆ 1986
22. Rivals (Steinke, Ann E.) ◆ 1986
23. Proving It (Hoh, Diane) ◆ 1986
24. Going Strong (Ellis, Carol) ◆ 1986
25. Stealing Secrets (Steinke, Ann E.) ◆ 1987
26. Taking Over (Sarasin, Jennifer) ◆ 1987
27. Spring Fever (Hoh, Diane) ◆ 1987
28. Scheming (Norby, Lisa) ◆ 1987
29. Falling in Love (Steinke, Ann E.) ◆ 1987

30. Saying Yes (Cooney, Caroline B.) ◆ 1987
31. Showing Off (Ellis, Carol) ◆ 1987
32. Together Again (Sarasin, Jennifer) ◆ 1987
33. Saying No (Steinke, Ann E.) ◆ 1987
34. Coming Back (Norby, Lisa) ◆ 1987
35. Moving Up (Davis, Leslie) ◆ 1987
36. Changing Loves (Weber, Judith) ◆ 1987
37. Acting Up (Sarasin, Jennifer) ◆ 1988
38. Talking Back (Norby, Lisa) ◆ 1988
39. All or Nothing (Davis, Leslie) ◆ 1988
40. Getting Serious (Sarasin, Jennifer) ◆ 1988
41. Having It All (Steinke, Ann E.) ◆ 1988
42. Fighting Back (Ellis, Carol) ◆ 1988
43. Telling Lies (Norby, Lisa) ◆ 1988
44. Pretending (Davis, Leslie) ◆ 1988
45. Here to Stay (Sarasin, Jennifer) ◆ 1988
46. Overboard (Schurfranz, Vivian) ◆ 1988
47. Dating (Weber, Judith) ◆ 1989

CHEETAH GIRLS

Gregory, Deborah

HYPERION/JUMP AT THE SUN ◆ GRADES 6–9 ◆ A/R

REAL LIFE

Galleria Garibaldi, 14, is from a multicultural home—African American and Italian American. Her friend Chanel has a mixed Caribbean heritage. The two girls are headed for the Fashion Industries High School in Manhattan. They form a musical group with three other friends (Dorinda, Anginette, and Aquanette) and begin a search for fame. Related materials include videos.

1. Wishing on a Star ◆ 1999
2. Shop in the Name of Love ◆ 1999
3. Who's 'Bout to Bounce? ◆ 1999
4. Hey, Ho, Hollywood! ◆ 1999
5. Woof, There It Is ◆ 2000
6. It's Raining Benjamins ◆ 2000
7. Dorinda's Secret ◆ 2000
8. Growl Power ◆ 2000
9. Showdown at the Okie-Dokie ◆ 2001
10. Cuchifrita, Ballerina ◆ 2001
11. Dorinda Gets a Groove ◆ 2001
12. In the House with Mouse! ◆ 2001
13. Oops, Doggy, Dog! ◆ 2002

CHERUB

Muchamore, Robert

SIMON PULSE ◆ GRADES 6–10 ◆ A/R

ADVENTURE

CHERUB is a top-secret division of British intelligence. All of the agents are 17 years old and under. In *The Recruit,* James Choke and his sister are orphans. James is talented at math but has been causing problems at school and at home, making him a perfect candidate for CHERUB. James becomes James Adams He endures 100 days of rigorous training and is sent on his first mission. Terrorists, drug dealers, and religious cults are among the targets of the teens of CHERUB. This series would be a good choice for fans of the Alex Rider books.

1. The Recruit ◆ 2005
2. The Dealer (issued as Class A in Britain) ◆ 2005
3. Maximum Security ◆ 2006
4. The Killing ◆ 2006
5. Divine Madness ◆ 2006
6. Man vs. Beast ◆ 2007
7. The Fall ◆ 2007
8. Mad Dogs ◆ 2007
9. The Sleepwalker ◆ 2008
10. The General ◆ 2008

CHESTNUT HILL

Brooke, Lauren

SCHOLASTIC ◆ GRADES 4–7 ◆ A/R

REAL LIFE

This series focuses on five girls at Chestnut Hill, a boarding school in Virginia that features classes, horses, and competition. Dylan, Malory, Lani, Honey, and Razina are given individual stories. In *All or Nothing,* for example, Malory wonders about making the summer riding team, and in *Playing for Keeps* Lani must convince her parents to allow her to stay at Chestnut Hill. The Heartland series, also by Lauren Brooke, would be another choice for girls who like horses as would the Thoroughbred books and the Saddle Club series.

1. New Class ◆ 2005
2. Making Strides ◆ 2005
3. Heart of Gold ◆ 2006
4. Playing for Keeps ◆ 2006
5. Scheme Team ◆ 2006
6. All or Nothing ◆ 2007

CHET GECKO MYSTERIES

Hale, Bruce

HARCOURT ◆ GRADES 4–7 ◆ A/R

ANIMAL FANTASY | MYSTERY

Chet Gecko, fourth-grade lizard detective, and his partner, Natalie Attired, solve mysteries. The first case involves finding Sally Chameleon's missing brother. In *Give My Regrets . . .* , Chet searches for an actor missing from a school musical. There are nasty mice, tough hamsters, and bad bats in this wise-cracking series. All the books are subtitled *From the Tattered Casebook of Chet Gecko, Private Eye. Chet Gecko's Detective Handbook (and Cookbook): Tips for Private Eyes and Snack Food Lovers* (2005) is a spiral-bound companion to the series.

1. The Chameleon Wore Chartreuse ◆ 2000
2. The Mystery of Mr. Nice ◆ 2000
3. Farewell, My Lunchbag! ◆ 2001
4. The Big Nap ◆ 2001
5. The Hamster of the Baskervilles ◆ 2002
6. This Gum for Hire ◆ 2002
7. The Malted Falcoln ◆ 2003
8. Trouble Is My Beeswax ◆ 2003
9. Give My Regrets to Broadway ◆ 2004
10. Murder, My Tweet ◆ 2004
11. The Possum Always Rings Twice ◆ 2006
12. Key Lardo ◆ 2006
13. Hiss Me Deadly ◆ 2007

CHICKS WITH STICKS

Lenhard, Elizabeth

DUTTON ◆ GRADES 7–10 ◆ A/R

REAL LIFE

After Scottie, 15, learns to knit, she develops a friendship with other girls who knit at her school: Amanda, Bella, and Tay. As they knit, they discuss adolescent concerns including friends, boys, family, and future expectations. In the second book, Scottie branches out a bit and begins to date Beck. Scottie struggles to reconcile her loyalty to her friends and her desire to spend time with Beck. In the third book, the girls are finishing high school and applying to colleges.

1. Chicks with Sticks: It's a Purl Thing ◆ 2005
2. Chicks with Sticks: Knit Two Together ◆ 2006
3. Chicks with Sticks: Knitwise ◆ 2007

CHILDREN OF THE LAMP

Kerr, P. B.

ORCHARD ◆ GRADES 5–8 ◆ A/R

FANTASY

Having their wisdom teeth removed starts the adventure for 12-year-old twins John and Philippa Gaunt. They begin to have strange experiences and when they visit their Uncle Nimrod in London, they learn of their djinn (genie) heritage. They receive training in Egypt where they search for the lost tomb of Akhenaten. In subsequent books they travel around the world confronting evil djinns, curses, and cults.

1. The Akhenaten Adventure ◆ 2004
2. The Blue Djinn of Babylon ◆ 2006
3. The Cobra King of Kathmandu ◆ 2007
4. The Day of the Djinn Warriors ◆ 2008

CHILDREN OF THE RED KING

Nimmo, Jenny

SCHOLASTIC ◆ GRADES 4–7 ◆ A/R

FANTASY

Charlie Bone, 10, is from a seemingly ordinary family. When he begins to hear the people in photographs speaking to him, he is identified as having the Yewbeam gift. He is sent to Bloor's Academy to develop and to meet other gifted children. In the second book, Charlie encounters Henry Yewbeam, a young ancestor who disappeared in 1916. By the fifth book, Charlie has turned 12 is searching for his father while facing an ancient threat. These books are popular with Harry Potter fans.

1. Midnight for Charlie Bone ◆ 2003
2. Charlie Bone and the Time Twister ◆ 2003
3. Charlie Bone and the Invisible Boy ◆ 2004
4. Charlie Bone and the Castle of Mirrors ◆ 2005
5. Charlie Bone and the Hidden King ◆ 2006
6. Charlie Bone and the Beast ◆ 2007
7. Charlie Bone and the Shadow ◆ 2008

CHINA BAYLES MYSTERY

Albert, Susan Wittig

BERKLEY ◆ GRADES 9–12

MYSTERY

China Bayles is a former high-powered Houston attorney who has embraced a quieter life. Even as the owner of Thyme and Seasons Herbs in Pecan Springs, Texas, however, she cannot escape mysteries. In one book, her best friend Ruby Wilcox disappears. During the course of the series, China meets and marries Mike McQuaid, who joins her in solving some mysteries. This is an adult series that is recommended for young adults.

1. Thyme of Death ◆ 1992
2. Witches' Bane ◆ 1994
3. Hangman's Root ◆ 1994
4. Rosemary Remembered ◆ 1995
5. Rueful Death ◆ 1996
6. Love Lies Bleeding ◆ 1997
7. Chile Death ◆ 1998
8. Lavender Lies ◆ 1999
9. Mistletoe Man ◆ 2000
10. Bloodroot ◆ 2001
11. Indigo Dying ◆ 2003
12. A Dilly of a Death ◆ 2004
13. Dead Man's Bones ◆ 2006
14. Bleeding Hearts ◆ 2007
15. Spanish Dagger ◆ 2008
16. Nightshade ◆ 2008

CHINA TATE

Johnson, Lissa Halls

FOCUS ON THE FAMILY ◆ GRADES 5–8

REAL LIFE | VALUES

At Camp Crazy Bear, China Tate and her best friend Deedee Kiersey have adventures involving bear cubs, a lost dog, and the beginning of romance. China is the daughter of missionaries and many of her actions are guided by her faith in God. In one book, China befriends a charismatic young man and her interest in him makes her question the importance of her beliefs. In another book, China and Deedee learn a lesson about disobedience after they feed some wild bear cubs. Values and Christian beliefs are incorporated into each story.

1. Sliced Heather on Toast ◆ 1994
2. The Secret in the Kitchen ◆ 1994
3. Project Black Bear ◆ 1994
4. Wishing Upon a Star ◆ 1995
5. Comedy of Errors ◆ 1995
6. The Ice Queen ◆ 1996
7. The Never-Ending Day ◆ 1997

CHINATOWN MYSTERY

Yep, Laurence

HARPERCOLLINS ◆ GRADES 5–8 ◆ A/R

MYSTERY

Lily Lew's great aunt is a former movie star who appeared as "Tiger Lil." On the set of a television show, the two work as a team to help an actor under suspicion of using real bullets in a prop gun. In an earlier book, they team up to find out who is trying to sabotage a new restaurant. Details about their Chinese heritage are incorporated into these books.

1. The Case of the Goblin Pearls ◆ 1997
2. The Case of the Lion Dance ◆ 1998
3. The Case of the Firecrackers ◆ 1999

CHIP HILTON SPORTS SERIES

Bee, Coach Clair

BOARDMAN & HOLMAN ◆ GRADES 5–8 ◆ A/R

RECREATION

This series, which began in the 1940s, has been updated and reissued. A new title, *Fiery Fullback,* has also been released. Cynthia Bee Farley, the author's daughter, writes that the values and honesty of these books have connected with generations of readers. Like the Matt Christopher books, these cover a variety of sports and feature athletes in conflicts both on and off the field.

1. Touchdown Pass ◆ 1998
2. Championship Ball ◆ 1998
3. Strike Three! ◆ 1998
4. Clutch Hitter! ◆ 1998
5. A Pass and a Prayer ◆ 1999
6. Hoop Crazy ◆ 1999
7. Pitchers' Duel ◆ 1999
8. Dugout Jinx ◆ 1999
9. Freshman Quarterback ◆ 1999
10. Backboard Fever ◆ 1999
11. Fence Busters ◆ 1999
12. Ten Seconds to Play! ◆ 1999
13. Fourth Down Showdown ◆ 2000
14. Tournament Crisis ◆ 2000
15. Hardcourt Upset ◆ 2000
16. Pay-Off Pitch ◆ 2000
17. No-Hitter ◆ 2001
18. Triple-Threat Trouble ◆ 2001
19. Backcourt Ace ◆ 2001

20. Buzzer Basket ◆ 2001
21. Comeback Cagers ◆ 2001
22. Home Run Feud ◆ 2002
23. Hungry Hurler ◆ 2002
24. Fiery Fullback ◆ 2002

CHOOSE YOUR DESTINY *see* What If . . .

CHOOSE YOUR OWN ADVENTURE

Various authors

BANTAM ◆ GRADES 4–8

ADVENTURE | MYSTERY

With nearly 200 titles, this series has attracted a large audience. The format allows readers to make choices at key moments in the plot. Should you go left? Go right? Should you turn around? Each choice leads to a different page, more choices, and your own story. Then you can go back to an earlier choice, make different selections, and create a different story. Newer adventures feature ninjas, computers, aliens, cyberhacking, and mutant spider ants. This is a popular series with a fairly accessible reading level. See also the Choose Your Own Nightmare series.

1. Journey Under the Sea (Mountain, Robert) ◆ 1977
2. Deadwood City (Packard, Edward) ◆ 1978
3. The Cave of Time (Packard, Edward) ◆ 1979
4. By Balloon to the Sahara (Terman, Douglas) ◆ 1979
5. Your Code Name Is Jonah (Packard, Edward) ◆ 1979
6. Third Planet from Altair (Packard, Edward) ◆ 1979
7. Space and Beyond (Montgomery, Raymond) ◆ 1980
8. Mystery of Chimney Rock (Packard, Edward) ◆ 1980
9. Who Killed Harlowe Thrombey? (Packard, Edward) ◆ 1981
10. Lost Jewels of Nabooti (Montgomery, Raymond) ◆ 1981
11. Mystery of the Maya (Montgomery, Raymond) ◆ 1981
12. Inside UFO 54-40 (Packard, Edward) ◆ 1982
13. Abominable Snowman (Montgomery, Raymond) ◆ 1982
14. Forbidden Castle (Packard, Edward) ◆ 1982
15. House of Danger (Montgomery, Raymond) ◆ 1982
16. Survival at Sea (Packard, Edward) ◆ 1983
17. Race Forever (Montgomery, Raymond) ◆ 1983
18. Underground Kingdom (Packard, Edward) ◆ 1983
19. Secret of the Pyramids (Brightfield, Richard) ◆ 1983
20. Escape (Montgomery, Raymond) ◆ 1983
21. Hyperspace (Packard, Edward) ◆ 1983
22. Space Patrol (Goodman, Julius) ◆ 1983
23. Lost Tribe (Foley, Louise Munro) ◆ 1983
24. Lost on the Amazon (Montgomery, Raymond) ◆ 1983

25. Prisoner of the Ant People (Montgomery, Raymond) ◆ 1983
26. Phantom Submarine (Brightfield, Richard) ◆ 1983
27. Horror of High Ridge (Goodman, Julius) ◆ 1983
28. Mountain Survival (Packard, Edward) ◆ 1984
29. Trouble on Planet Earth (Montgomery, Raymond) ◆ 1984
30. Curse of Batterslea Hall (Brightfield, Richard) ◆ 1984
31. Vampire Express (Koltz, Tony) ◆ 1984
32. Treasure Diver (Goodman, Julius) ◆ 1984
33. Dragons' Den (Brightfield, Richard) ◆ 1984
34. Mystery of the Highland Crest (Foley, Louise Munro) ◆ 1984
35. Journey to Stonehenge (Graver, Fred) ◆ 1984
36. Secret Treasure of Tibet (Brightfield, Richard) ◆ 1984
37. War with the Evil Power Master (Montgomery, Raymond) ◆ 1984
38. Sabotage (Liebold, Jay) ◆ 1984
39. Supercomputer (Packard, Edward) ◆ 1984
40. Throne of Zeus (Goodman, Deborah Lerne) ◆ 1985
41. Search for the Mountain Gorillas (Wallace, Jim) ◆ 1985
42. Mystery of Echo Lodge (Foley, Louise Munro) ◆ 1985
43. Grand Canyon Odyssey (Liebold, Jay) ◆ 1985
44. Mystery of Ura Senke (Gilligan, Shannon) ◆ 1985
45. You Are a Shark (Packard, Edward) ◆ 1985
46. Deadly Shadow (Brightfield, Richard) ◆ 1985
47. Outlaws of Sherwood Forest (Kushner, Ellen) ◆ 1985
48. Spy for George Washington (Liebold, Jay) ◆ 1985
49. Danger at Anchor Mine (Foley, Louise Munro) ◆ 1985
50. Return to the Cave of Time (Packard, Edward) ◆ 1985
51. Magic of the Unicorn (Goodman, Deborah Lerne) ◆ 1985
52. Ghost Hunter (Packard, Edward) ◆ 1986
53. The Case of the Silk King (Gilligan, Shannon) ◆ 1986
54. Forest of Fear (Foley, Louise Munro) ◆ 1986
55. Trumpet of Terror (Goodman, Deborah Lerne) ◆ 1986
56. Enchanted Kingdom (Kushner, Ellen) ◆ 1986
57. Antimatter Formula (Liebold, Jay) ◆ 1986
58. Statue of Liberty Adventure (Kushner, Ellen) ◆ 1986
59. Terror Island (Koltz, Tony) ◆ 1986
60. Vanished! (Goodman, Deborah Lerne) ◆ 1986
61. Beyond Escape! (Montgomery, Raymond) ◆ 1986
62. Sugarcane Island (Packard, Edward) ◆ 1986
63. Mystery of the Secret Room (Kushner, Ellen) ◆ 1986
64. Volcano! (Siegman, Meryl) ◆ 1987
65. Mardi Gras Mystery (Foley, Louise Munro) ◆ 1987
66. Secret of the Ninja (Liebold, Jay) ◆ 1987
67. Seaside Mystery (Hodgman, Ann) ◆ 1987
68. Secret of the Sun God (Packard, Andrea) ◆ 1987
69. Rock and Roll Mystery (Wallace, Jim) ◆ 1987
70. Invaders of Planet Earth (Brightfield, Richard) ◆ 1987
71. Space Vampire (Packard, Edward) ◆ 1987
72. Brilliant Doctor Wogan (Montgomery, Raymond) ◆ 1987
73. Beyond the Great Wall (Liebold, Jay) ◆ 1987

74. Longhorn Territory (Newman, Marc) ◆ 1987
75. Planet of the Dragons (Brightfield, Richard) ◆ 1988
76. Mona Lisa Is Missing (Montgomery, Raymond) ◆ 1988
77. First Olympics (Baglio, Ben M.) ◆ 1988
78. Return to Atlantis (Montgomery, Raymond) ◆ 1988
79. Mystery of the Sacred Stones (Foley, Louise Munro) ◆ 1988
80. Perfect Planet (Packard, Edward) ◆ 1988
81. Terror in Australia (Gilligan, Shannon) ◆ 1988
82. Hurricane! (Brightfield, Richard) ◆ 1988
83. Track of the Bear (Montgomery, Raymond) ◆ 1988
84. You Are a Monster (Packard, Edward) ◆ 1988
85. Inca Gold (Beckett, Jim) ◆ 1988
86. Knights of the Round Table (Kushner, Ellen) ◆ 1988
87. Exiled to Earth (Montgomery, Richard) ◆ 1989
88. Master of Kung Fu (Brightfield, Richard) ◆ 1989
89. South Pole Sabotage (Johnson, Seddon) ◆ 1989
90. Mutiny in Space (Packard, Edward) ◆ 1989
91. You Are a Superstar (Packard, Edward) ◆ 1989
92. Return of the Ninja (Liebold, Jay) ◆ 1989
93. Captive! (Hampton, Bill) ◆ 1989
94. Blood on the Handle (Montgomery, Raymond) ◆ 1989
95. You Are a Genius (Packard, Edward) ◆ 1989
96. Stock Car Champion (Montgomery, Raymond) ◆ 1989
97. Through the Black Hole (Packard, Edward) ◆ 1990
98. You Are a Millionaire (Liebold, Jay) ◆ 1990
99. Revenge of the Russian Ghost (Liebold, Jay) ◆ 1990
100. Worst Day of Your Life (Packard, Edward) ◆ 1990
101. Alien, Go Home! (Johnson, Seddon) ◆ 1990
102. Master of Tae Kwon Do (Brightfield, Richard) ◆ 1990
103. Grave Robbers (Montgomery, Raymond) ◆ 1990
104. Cobra Connection (Foley, Louise Munro) ◆ 1990
105. Treasure of the Onyx Dragon (Gilligan, Alison) ◆ 1990
106. Hijacked! (Brightfield, Richard) ◆ 1990
107. Fight for Freedom (Liebold, Jay) ◆ 1990
108. Master of Karate (Brightfield, Richard) ◆ 1990
109. Chinese Dragons (Montgomery, Raymond) ◆ 1991
110. Invaders from Within (Packard, Edward) ◆ 1991
111. Smoke Jumper (Montgomery, Raymond) ◆ 1991
112. Skateboard Champion (Packard, Edward) ◆ 1991
113. Lost Ninja (Liebold, Jay) ◆ 1991
114. Daredevil Park (Compton, Sara) ◆ 1991
115. Island of Time (Montgomery, Raymond) ◆ 1991
116. Kidnapped! (Packard, Edward) ◆ 1991
117. Search for Aladdin's Lamp (Liebold, Jay) ◆ 1991
118. Vampire Invaders (Packard, Edward) ◆ 1991
119. Terrorist Trap (Gilligan, Shannon) ◆ 1991
120. Ghost Train (Foley, Louise Munro) ◆ 1992
121. Behind the Wheel (Montgomery, R. A.) ◆ 1992
122. Magic Master (Packard, Edward) ◆ 1992

123. Silver Wings (Montgomery, Raymond) ♦ 1992
124. Superbike (Packard, Edward) ♦ 1992
125. Outlaw Gulch (Montgomery, Ramsey) ♦ 1992
126. Master of Martial Arts (Brightfield, Richard) ♦ 1992
127. Showdown (Brightfield, Richard) ♦ 1992
128. Viking Raiders (Packard, Edward) ♦ 1992
129. Earthquake! (Gilligan, Alison) ♦ 1992
130. You Are Microscopic (Packard, Edward) ♦ 1992
131. Surf Monkeys (Liebold, Jay) ♦ 1993
132. Luckiest Day of Your Life (Packard, Edward) ♦ 1993
133. The Forgotten Planet (Wilhelm, Doug) ♦ 1993
134. Secret of the Dolphins (Packard, Edward) ♦ 1993
135. Playoff Champion (Von Moschzisker, Felix) ♦ 1993
136. Roller Star (Packard, Edward) ♦ 1993
137. Scene of the Crime (Wilhelm, Doug) ♦ 1993
138. Dinosaur Island (Packard, Edward) ♦ 1993
139. Motocross Mania (Montgomery, R. A.) ♦ 1993
140. Horror House (Packard, Edward) ♦ 1993
141. The Secret of Mystery Hill (Wilhelm, Doug) ♦ 1993
142. The Reality Machine (Packard, Edward) ♦ 1993
143. Project UFO (Montgomery, R. A.) ♦ 1994
144. Comet Crash (Packard, Edward) ♦ 1994
145. Everest Adventure (Montgomery, Anson) ♦ 1994
146. Soccer Star (Packard, Edward) ♦ 1994
147. The Antimatter Universe (Mueller, Kate) ♦ 1994
148. Master of Judo (Brightfield, Richard) ♦ 1994
149. Search the Amazon! (Wilhelm, Doug) ♦ 1994
150. Who Are You? (Packard, Edward) ♦ 1994
151. Gunfire at Gettysburg (Wilhelm, Doug) ♦ 1994
152. War with the Mutant Spider Ants (Packard, Edward) ♦ 1994
153. Last Run (Montgomery, R. A.) ♦ 1994
154. Cyberspace Warrior (Packard, Edward) ♦ 1994
155. Ninja Cyborg (Liebold, Jay) ♦ 1995
156. You Are an Alien (Packard, Edward) ♦ 1995
157. U.N. Adventure (Brightfield, Richard) ♦ 1995
158. Sky-jam! (Packard, Edward) ♦ 1995
159. Tattoo of Death (Montgomery, R. A.) ♦ 1995
160. The Computer Takeover (Packard, Edward) ♦ 1995
161. Possessed! (Montgomery, R. A.) ♦ 1995
162. Typhoon! (Packard, Edward) ♦ 1995
163. Shadow of the Swastika (Wilhelm, Doug) ♦ 1995
164. Fright Night (Packard, Edward) ♦ 1995
165. Snowboard Racer (Montgomery, Anson) ♦ 1995
166. Master of Aikido (Brightfield, Richard) ♦ 1995
167. Moon Quest (Montgomery, Anson) ♦ 1996
168. Hostage! (Packard, Edward) ♦ 1996
169. Terror on the Titanic (Brightfield, Richard) ♦ 1996
170. Greed, Guns, and Gold (Packard, Edward) ♦ 1996

171. Death in the Dorm (Montgomery, R. A.) ◆ 1996
172. Mountain Biker (Packard, Edward) ◆ 1996
173. The Gold Medal Secret (Wilhelm, Doug) ◆ 1996
174. The Power Dome (Packard, Edward) ◆ 1996
175. The Underground Railroad (Wilhelm, Doug) ◆ 1996
176. Master of Kendo (Brightfield, Richard) ◆ 1997
177. Killer Virus (Montgomery, Raymond) ◆ 1997
178. River of No Return (Lahey, Vince) ◆ 1997
179. Ninja Avenger (Liebold, Jay) ◆ 1997
180. Stampede! (Hill, Laban C.) ◆ 1997
181. Fire on Ice (Packard, Edward) ◆ 1998
182. Fugitive (Packard, Edward) ◆ 1998
183. CyberHacker (Montgomery, Anson) ◆ 1998
184. Mayday! (Packard, Edward, and Andrea Packard) ◆ 1998

Choose Your Own Nightmare

Various authors

BANTAM ◆ GRADES 4–8

ADVENTURE | HORROR

A spin-off of the Choose Your Own Adventure series, these books capitalize on the popularity of horror fiction. From *Night of the Werewolf* on, they are filled with venomous snakes, killer insects, mummies, and haunted babies. With twists and turns, doom and demons, they are sure to appeal to the scary-story crowd.

1. Night of the Werewolf (Packard, Edward) ◆ 1995
2. Beware the Snake's Venom (McMurtry, Ken) ◆ 1995
3. Island of Doom (Brightfield, Richard) ◆ 1995
4. Castle of Darkness (Montgomery, R. A.) ◆ 1995
5. The Halloween Party (Jakab, E. A. M.) ◆ 1995
6. Risk Your Life Arcade (McMurtry, Ken) ◆ 1995
7. Biting for Blood (Packard, Edward) ◆ 1996
8. Bugged Out! (Hill, Laban C.) ◆ 1996
9. The Mummy Who Wouldn't Die (Jakab, E. A. M.) ◆ 1996
10. It Happened at Camp Pine Tree (Montgomery, R. A., and Janet Hubbard-Brown) ◆ 1996
11. Watch Out for Room 13 (Hill, Laban C.) ◆ 1996
12. Something's in the Woods (Brightfield, Richard) ◆ 1996
13. The Haunted Baby (Packard, Edward) ◆ 1997
14. The Evil Pen Pal (Hill, Laban C.) ◆ 1997
15. How I Became a Freak (Brightfield, Richard) ◆ 1997
16. Welcome to Horror Hospital (Hill, Laban C.) ◆ 1997
17. Attack of the Living Mask (Hirschfeld, Robert) ◆ 1997
18. The Toy Shop of Terror (Hill, Laban C.) ◆ 1997

CHOOSE YOUR OWN STAR WARS ADVENTURES

Golden, Christopher

BANTAM ◆ GRADES 4–8

ADVENTURE | SCIENCE FICTION

This series links two popular items: the *Star Wars* movies, plots, and characters and the Choose Your Own Adventure format. The familiar characters—Luke Skywalker, Princess Leia, Han Solo, and Darth Vader—are embroiled in more intergalactic intrigues, and the reader gets to make choices about which direction the plot will take. Will there be rebellion or destruction? Will you be loyal to the Jedi or embrace the dark side? The 3-D hologram on the cover of each book will attract many readers. This is sure to be a great choice for fans of movies and participatory fiction.

1. Star Wars: A New Hope ◆ 1998
2. Star Wars: The Empire Strikes Back ◆ 1998
3. Star Wars: Return of the Jedi ◆ 1998

CHRESTOMANCI

Jones, Diana Wynne

BEECH TREE ◆ GRADES 6–9 ◆ A/R

FANTASY

This series begins with several characters with the promise of magical powers. They are sent to further their skills at Chrestomanci Castle. Gwendolyn is a young witch who shakes things up at the castle. Christopher Chant comes from a family that is skilled at sorcery and enchantment. When he finally realizes his own powers. he goes to the castle and develops into a powerful leader. The other books are filled with magical feuds and threats to those with supernatural powers. This series was first released in the 1970s and 1980s and has been reissued. *Mixed Magics: Four Tales of Chrestomanci* is a collection of short stories.

1. Charmed Life ◆ 1998
2. The Lives of Christopher Chant ◆ 1998
3. The Magicians of Caprona ◆ 1999
4. Witch Week ◆ 2001
5. Conrad's Fate ◆ 2005
6. The Pinhoe Egg ◆ 2006

CHRISTIE & COMPANY

Page, Katherine Hall

AVON ◆ GRADES 5–7

MYSTERY

Three girls—Christie, Maggie, and Vicky—meet at the boarding school where they begin eighth grade. They are from different backgrounds but they share an in interest in mysteries. Christie Montgomery is the main character and she directs the trio's activities, solving thefts at school, finding those responsible for the sabotage of an inn owned by Maggie's parents, and helping a family being threatened by a Chinese gang. While seeking solutions to these mysteries, the girls continue to grow and mature. There is lots of dialogue, making this fairly accessible. Children who enjoy mystery and adventure books featuring girls will like this series.

1. Christie & Company ◆ 1996
2. Christie & Company Down East ◆ 1997
3. Christie & Company in the Year of the Dragon ◆ 1998
4. Bon Voyage, Christie & Company ◆ 1999

CHRISTY

Marshall, Catherine

TOMMY NELSON WORDKIDS ◆ GRADES 5–8

HISTORICAL | REAL LIFE | VALUES

Christy Huddleston, 19, goes to teach in the Great Smoky Mountains, where she finds hardships, heartache, and hope. Christy's idealism and energy often put her in conflict with people in the community, but she has the ongoing support of Dr. Neil MacNeill and the admiration of David Grantland. Christy meets Miss Alice, a veteran missionary who understands the mountain people and helps her adjust to their ways. The stories have an element of romance and are filled with Christy's commitment to her religion and her values. The series follows the format of the popular television series. Catherine Marshall based these stories on the real life of her mother around the turn of the century.

1. The Bridge to Cutter Gap ◆ 1995
2. Silent Superstitions ◆ 1995
3. The Angry Intruder ◆ 1995
4. Midnight Rescue ◆ 1995
5. The Proposal ◆ 1995
6. Christy's Choice ◆ 1996
7. The Princess Club ◆ 1996

8. Family Secrets ◆ 1996
9. Mountain Madness ◆ 1997
10. Stage Fright ◆ 1997
11. Goodbye, Sweet Prince ◆ 1997
12. Brotherly Love ◆ 1997

CHRISTY MILLER

Gunn, Robin Jones
FOCUS ON THE FAMILY ◆ GRADES 6–8 ◆ A/R

REAL LIFE | VALUES

Christy Miller's faith in God and the support of her family help her deal with many teenage traumas. Making new friends in California, expressing her interest in Todd, being attracted by another boy (Rick), and almost losing her best friend Katie are some of Christy's concerns. Christy seeks guidance from the Lord as she tries to reconcile her personal wants with the needs of her faith. Opportunities for Biblical explications are provided as the characters attend study groups and seek guidance. Christy's romantic dilemmas will appeal to many girls. This series will connect with other values-related books. It was reissued in the late 1990s with new covers. *From the Secret Place in My Heart (Christy Miller's Diary)* (Bethany House, 1999) describes Christy's adjustment to a new life in California and her relationship with Todd.

1. A Summer Promise ◆ 1988
2. A Whisper and a Wish ◆ 1989
3. Yours Forever ◆ 1990
4. Surprise Endings ◆ 1991
5. Island Dreamer ◆ 1992
6. A Heart Full of Hope ◆ 1992
7. True Friends ◆ 1993
8. Starry Night ◆ 1993
9. Seventeen Wishes ◆ 1993
10. A Time to Cherish ◆ 1993
11. Sweet Dreams ◆ 1994
12. A Promise Is Forever ◆ 1994

CHRISTY MILLER: CHRISTY AND TODD: THE COLLEGE YEARS

Gunn, Robin Jones
BETHANY HOUSE ◆ GRADES 9–12 ◆ A/R

REAL LIFE

Christy is studying in Switzerland in the first book; Katie and Todd, Christy's boyfriend, come to visit but things don't go as well as expected.

In the second book, Christy is back in California and dating Todd. But she is also attracted to an old friend. In *I Promise,* Christy and Todd are planning their wedding.

1. Until Tomorrow ◆ 2000
2. As You Wish ◆ 2000
3. I Promise ◆ 2001

CHRONICLES OF ANCIENT DARKNESS

Paver, Michelle

HARPERCOLLINS ◆ GRADES 5–9 ◆ A/R

FANTASY | HISTORICAL | ADVENTURE

This series first published in Britain combines fantasy and adventure with a faithful re-creation of the culture of New Stone Age people in northern Europe. It features a 12-year-old Stone Age boy named Torak, part of the Wolf Clan; a girl named Renn who comes from the Raven Clan; and a wolf cub that Torak adopts and names Wolf. In *Wolf Brother,* Torak, Renn, and Wolf travel to the World of the Mountain Spirit in an effort to rid the clans of a dangerous, demon-possessed bear. Wolf disappears at the end of the book. In the second book, Torak is living with the Raven Clan but feels alone without Wolf. When a mysterious illness hits the clan, Torak sets off on a dangerous quest to find a cure. In *Soul Eater,* Wolf is kidnapped by the Soul Eaters and Torak and Renn must travel to the Arctic to rescue him. The books are thoroughly researched and present lots of details on Stone Age life—food, tools, housing, clothing, religious rites, and so forth. There is a site for fans at www.torak.info.

1. Wolf Brother ◆ 2005
2. Spirit Walker ◆ 2006
3. Soul Eater ◆ 2007
4. Outcast ◆ 2008
5. Oathbreaker ◆ 2008
6. Ghost Hunter ◆ 2009

CHRONICLES OF CHAOS

Wright, John C.

TOR ◆ GRADES 10–12

FANTASY

Five teens with special powers are the only students attending a boarding school in England. As their superhuman powers develop, they discover they are really prisoners. Their challenge is to find out why and to escape from the creatures that seek to control them.

1. Orphans of Chaos ◆ 2005

2. Fugitives of Chaos ◆ 2006
3. Titans of Chaos ◆ 2007

CHRONICLES OF CONAN

Various authors

DARK HORSE ◆ GRADES 9–12

FANTASY

This graphic novel series collects the adventures of Conan the Barbarian, a popular comic series from the 1970s.

1. Tower of the Elephant and Other Stories (Thomas, Roy, and Barry Windsor) ◆ 2003
2. Rogues in the House and Other Stories (Thomas, Roy, and Barry Windsor) ◆ 2003
3. The Monster of the Monoliths and Other Stories (Thomas, Roy, Barry Windsor, and Gil Kane Smith) ◆ 2004
4. The Song of Red Sonja and Other Stories (Thomas, Roy) ◆ 2004
5. The Shadow in the Tomb and Other Stories (Thomas, Roy) ◆ 2004
6. The Curse of the Golden Skull and Other Stories (Thomas, Roy) ◆ 2004
7. The Dweller in the Pool and Other Stories (Thomas, Roy, and Robert E. Howard) ◆ 2005
8. Brothers of the Blade and Other Stories (Thomas, Roy, and Mike Ploog) ◆ 2005
9. Riders of the River-Dragons and Other Stories (Thomas, Roy) ◆ 2005
10. When Giants Walk the Earth and Other Stories (Thomas, Roy) ◆ 2008
11. The Dance of the Skull and Other Stories (Thomas, Roy, and Howard Chaykin) ◆ 2007
12. The Beast King of Abombi and Other Stories (Thomas, Roy, and Robert E. Howard) ◆ 2007

CHRONICLES OF COURAGE

Torrey, Michele

KNOPF; DELL ◆ GRADES 6–9 ◆ A/R

HISTORICAL | ADVENTURE

Teenage boys face hardship and danger at sea in this trilogy of historical novels. In the first, set in the mid-19th century, 15-year-old Nick and his older brother experience life aboard a whaling ship and a shipwreck in the Arctic. In *Voyage of Plunder,* 14-year-old Daniel faces a new world in 1696 when his father is murdered and he finds himself the captive of pirates. And in *Voyage of Midnight,* orphaned Philip is happy to find work on his uncle's ship until he discovers his uncle is a slave trader.

1. Voyage of Ice ◆ 2004
2. Voyage of Plunder ◆ 2005
3. Voyage of Midnight ◆ 2006

CHRONICLES OF DERYNI

Kurtz, Katherine

BALLANTINE; ACE ◆ GRADES 9–12

FANTASY

Kelson, 14, lives in the kingdom of Gwynedd. He is destined to be king but his heritage may block his succession. Kelson is half Deryni, a magical people who have been forced into hiding. Yet the Eleven Kingdoms are being threatened and only Kelson's powers as a sorcerer and the help of the Deryni can meet this danger. Later, Kelson is King and his power is again in jeopardy. There are many spin-off Deryni sagas and a guidebook to the land of Deryni: *The Eleven Kingdoms: A Map of the Deryni World*. This series has been read for more than thirty years and was recently reissued in both hardcover and paperback.

1. Deryni Rising ◆ 1970
2. Deryni Checkmate ◆ 1972
3. High Deryni ◆ 1973

CHRONICLES OF ELANTRA

Sagara, Michelle

LUNA ◆ GRADES 10–12

FANTASY | ADVENTURE

In the first book, children are dying and Kaylin has been ordered to return to Nightshade to investigate the deaths. As a Hawk, her duty is to protect the city of Elantra. Kaylin uses her powers to find the killer. In the second book, Kaylin's magical powers increase, making her a threat to others in the High Court.

1. Cast in Shadow ◆ 2006
2. Cast in Courtlight ◆ 2008
3. Cast in Secret ◆ 2008
4. Cast in Fury ◆ 2008

CHRONICLES OF FAERIE

Melling, O. R.

AMULET ◆ GRADES 8–12 ◆ A/R

FANTASY

Each book in this series weaves myths, legends, and lore of Ireland with the activities of contemporary girls. In *The Hunter's Moon,* two cousins—Findabhair, who is Irish, and Gwen from America—are backpacking in Ireland when Finn is kidnapped by the King of Faeries. Gwen must search for her and save her from being sacrificed. In the second book, Laurel, 18, travels to her grandparents' home in Ireland to recover from the death of her twin sister. There she becomes involved in a quest to save the Faerie realm. In the third book, Dana, 12, accepts a dangerous task, hoping to be reunited with her mother.

1. The Hunter's Moon ◆ 2006
2. The Summer King ◆ 2006
3. The Light-Bearer's Daughter ◆ 2007

CHRONICLES OF NARNIA

Lewis, C. S.

MACMILLAN ◆ GRADES 4–8 ◆ A/R

FANTASY

Lucy, Peter, Susan, and Edmund are British schoolchildren during World War II in this series of fantasy adventures. Entering a mirrored wardrobe, they find a magical world called Narnia peopled by fauns, witches, nymphs, dwarves, and talking animals. The children fight many battles against evil and eventually become rulers of the land. Quirks in the chronicles include the facts that Narnia's inhabitants have always supposed humans to be mythical creatures and that the adventures that seem to last forever in Narnia only fill a split second at home. There is debate about the best order in which to read these books. Many prefer the order in which they were published, but boxed sets now present the books in chronological sequence: *The Magician's Nephew; The Lion, the Witch, and the Wardrobe; The Horse and His Boy; Prince Caspian, The Voyage of the Dawn Treader; The Silver Chair; and The Last Battle.*

1. The Lion, the Witch, and the Wardrobe ◆ 1950
2. Prince Caspian ◆ 1951
3. The Voyage of the Dawn Treader ◆ 1952
4. The Silver Chair ◆ 1953
5. The Horse and His Boy ◆ 1954
6. The Magician's Nephew ◆ 1955
7. The Last Battle ◆ 1956

CHRONICLES OF THE IMAGINARIUM GEOGRAPHICA

Owen, James A.

SIMON & SCHUSTER ◆ GRADES 8–12 ◆ A/R

FANTASY

After being questioned about the murder of an Oxford professor, three strangers find that they are the Caretakers of the Imaginarium Geographica. They struggle to restore the rightful king to the Archipelago of Dreams. Elements of classic fantasies are woven into the books and help the reader realize the true identity of each of the Caretakers.

1. Here, There Be Dragons ◆ 2006
2. The Search for the Red Dawn ◆ 2008
3. The Indigo King ◆ 2008

CIRCLE OF MAGIC

Pierce, Tamora

SCHOLASTIC ◆ GRADES 6–9 ◆ A/R

FANTASY

Four children are gifted with magical talents. They are unaware of their heritage but others are interested in their development. Niko, a powerful mage, brings them to Discipline Cottage to develop their powers. As they train, their special skills are enhanced. Sandry is interested in weaving; Daja in metal; Briar in plants; and Tris in the weather. Each young mage is featured in a book in the series.

1. Sandry's Book ◆ 1997
2. Tris's Book ◆ 1998
3. Daja's Book ◆ 1998
4. Briar's Book ◆ 2000

CIRCLE OF MAGIC: THE CIRCLE OPENS

Pierce, Tamora

SCHOLASTIC ◆ GRADES 6–9 ◆ A/R

FANTASY

The characters from the Circle of Magic series are now older and facing new adventures as they assist young mages. Sandry, 14, realizes that the magical skills of a young boy may be the key to stopping a murderer. Briar, 14, befriends a child from the streets of Chammur. He helps her develop her magical gift with stones. Daja's apprentices are twins whose magical specialties must be discovered. Tris assists Keth, a glassblower whose magical powers are needed to seek The Ghost.

1. Magic Steps ◆ 2000
2. Street Magic ◆ 2002
3. Cold Fire ◆ 2002
4. Shatterglass ◆ 2003

CIRCLE OF THREE

Bird, Isobel

AVON ◆ GRADES 7–10 ◆ A/R

FANTASY

Kate Morgan is a sophomore at Beecher Falls High School. While researching the Salem Witch Trials, she finds a book on spells and charms. She casts a spell to get a date to the dance and gets more than she bargained for. In additional adventures, Kate is joined by her friends Annie and Cooper.

1. So Mote It Be ◆ 2001
2. Merry Meet ◆ 2001
3. Second Sight ◆ 2001
4. What the Cards Said ◆ 2001
5. In the Dreaming ◆ 2001
6. Ring of Light ◆ 2001
7. Blue Moon ◆ 2001
8. The Five Paths ◆ 2001
9. Through the Veil ◆ 2001
10. Making the Saint ◆ 2001
11. House of Winter ◆ 2001
12. Written in the Stars ◆ 2001
13. And It Harm None ◆ 2002
14. The Challenge Box ◆ 2002
15. Initiation ◆ 2002

CIRQUE DU FREAK

Shan, Darren

LITTLE, BROWN ◆ GRADES 6–9 ◆ A/R

FANTASY

When Darren Shan and two friends get tickets to Cirque du Freak, they find that this is no ordinary circus. These freaks are really freaky, including a vampire who lures Darren into a dangerous deal. Darren becomes the vampire's assistant and faces numerous trials as the series progresses. Book 1, *Cirque du Freak,* has been reprinted with the title *A Living Nightmare.*

1. Cirque du Freak ◆ 2000
2. The Vampire's Assistant ◆ 2002
3. Tunnels of Blood ◆ 2002
4. Vampire Mountain ◆ 2002
5. Trials of Death ◆ 2003
6. The Vampire Prince ◆ 2003

7. Hunters of the Dusk ◆ 2004
8. Allies of the Night ◆ 2004
9. Killers of the Dawn ◆ 2005
10. The Lake of Souls ◆ 2005
11. Lord of the Shadows ◆ 2006
12. Sons of Destiny ◆ 2006

CITY OF EMBER

DuPrau, Jeanne

RANDOM HOUSE ◆ GRADES 6–8 ◆ A/R

SCIENCE FICTION

The underground city of Ember was built to offer protection from a disaster on the surface. More than 200 years later the city structures are deteriorating. Lina and Doon, both 12, have received their job assignments and they begin to see the extent of the damage and the danger it portends. They search for a way out of Ember. When they find the secret path, they lead 400 residents to the surface where they discover another community, Sparks. At first, the newcomers are welcomed, but conflict develops between the agrarian people of Sparks and the technological people of Ember. *The Prophet of Yonwood* is a prequel set 50 years before the settlement of the city of Ember and foreshadows the coming disaster.

1. The City of Ember ◆ 2003
2. The People of Sparks ◆ 2004
3. The Prophet of Yonwood ◆ 2006
4. Diamond of Darkhold ◆ 2008

CLAIDI JOURNALS

Lee, Tanith

DUTTON ◆ GRADES 6–9 ◆ A/R

FANTASY

Claidi, 16, records her adventures in her journals. Stifled by her life as a maid in the House, she helps a prisoner escape and travels with him to his home in the Waste. There, she rebels against the oppressive Rules and is rescued by the bandit Argul. Their adventures together continue and they marry in the fourth book.

1. Wolf Tower ◆ 2000
2. Wolf Star ◆ 2001
3. Wolf Queen ◆ 2001
4. Wolf Wing ◆ 2003

CLAMP SCHOOL DETECTIVES

Ohkawa, Ageha, team leader

TOKYOPOP ◆ **GRADES 4–8**

FANTASY

CLAMP School is a school for geniuses. Three teens at the school create an investigative agency to protect their fellow students, especially the girls. Nokoru, a sixth-grader, founded the group and is joined by his friends Akira and Suoh. They look into unusual situations including a ghost in the art department.

1. Volume 1 ◆ 2004
2. Volume 2 ◆ 2004
3. Volume 3 ◆ 2004

CLASS SECRETS

Baker, Jennifer

SIMON & SCHUSTER ◆ **GRADES 6–10**

REAL LIFE

This series features Hillcrest High in suburban Connecticut. Suzanne is new and feels left out, so she takes an audacious risk. Nikki is having problems with her boyfriend, Luke. Victoria wants to get her way and doesn't care who she hurts.

1. Most Likely to Deceive ◆ 1995
2. Just like Sisters ◆ 1995
3. Sworn to Silence ◆ 1995
4. The Lying Game ◆ 1996

CLEARWATER CROSSING

Roberts, Laura Peyton

BANTAM DOUBLEDAY DELL ◆ **GRADES 6–9** ◆ **A/R**

REAL LIFE | VALUES

In this series, good friends Melanie, Peter, Jenna, Jesse, Nicole, Miguel, Ben, and Leah face high school with the support of each other and their faith in God. Concerns including boyfriends, sports, school events— even hardship and tragedy—are resolved through the guidance of Christian friends and family. Modern photographic covers give these books an appeal similar to that of the Sweet Valley series.

1. Get a Life ◆ 1998
2. Reality Check ◆ 1998
3. Heart and Soul ◆ 1998

4. Promises, Promises ◆ 1998
5. Just Friends ◆ 1998
6. Keep the Faith ◆ 1998
7. New Beginnings ◆ 1998
8. One Real Thing ◆ 1999
9. Skin Deep ◆ 1999
10. No Doubt ◆ 1999
11. More Than This ◆ 1999
12. Hope Happens ◆ 2000
13. Dream On ◆ 2000
14. Love Hurts ◆ 2000
15. What Goes Around ◆ 2000
16. Tried and True ◆ 2000
17. Just Say Yes ◆ 2001
18. Prime Time ◆ 2001
19. Now and Always ◆ 2001
20. Don't Look Back ◆ 2001

CLEARWATER CROSSING DIARY SPECIAL

1. The Diaries ◆ 2000

CLIQUE

Harrison, Lisi

LITTLE, BROWN ◆ GRADES 6–9 ◆ A/R

REAL LIFE

Clair Lynons, a seventh-grader, is a victim of The Clique. Massie Block and the other popular girls at Octavian Country Day School decide to ostracize the new girl from Florida. They verbally abuse her and take every opportunity to embarrass her. This series focuses on teen issues such as body image, clothes, boys, school, and, of course, cliques.

1. The Clique ◆ 2004
2. Best Friends for Never ◆ 2004
3. Revenge of the Wannabes ◆ 2005
4. Invasion of the Boy Snatchers ◆ 2005
5. The Pretty Committee Strikes Back ◆ 2006
6. Dial L for Loser ◆ 2006
7. It's Not Easy Being Mean ◆ 2007
8. Sealed with a Diss ◆ 2007
9. Bratfest at Tiffany's ◆ 2008
10. P.S. I Loathe You ◆ 2009

SUMMER COLLECTION

1. Massie ◆ 2008
2. Dylan ◆ 2008
3. Alicia ◆ 2008

4. Kristen ◆ 2008
5. Claire ◆ 2008

CLUB OF MYSTERIES

Naylor, Phyllis Reynolds

MACMILLAN ◆ GRADES 4–7 ◆ A/R

ANIMAL FANTASY | MYSTERY

House cats Marco and Polo are ready for mystery and adventure. They make a *Grand Escape* and soon come across the leader of a cat Club of Mysteries. They must pass a test in order to join this group. In the second book, they must convince the others that they are suitable to succeed their longtime leader.

1. The Grand Escape ◆ 1993
2. The Healing of Texas Jake ◆ 1997
3. Carlotta's Kittens and the Club of Mysteries ◆ 2000
4. Polo's Mother ◆ 2005

CLUELESS

Various authors

ARCHWAY ◆ GRADES 6–9

REAL LIFE

This series is based on the movie that evolved into a television program. Cher was named for the famous singer and actress. She is the ultimate princess, daughter of an indulgent and busy father. Her goals while in high school include dressing appropriately in designer fashions, hanging out at the mall, and keeping up with popular friends. The plots change a little from title to title, but the theme remains the same.

1. Cher Negotiates New York (Baker, Jennifer) ◆ 1995
2. Cher's Guide to . . . Whatever (Gilmour, H. B., and Amy Heckerling) ◆ 1995
3. Clueless: A Novel (Gilmour, H. B.) ◆ 1995
4. Achieving Personal Perfection (Gilmour, H. B.) ◆ 1996
5. An American Betty in Paris (Reisfeld, Randi) ◆ 1996
6. Cher Goes Enviro-Mental (Reisfeld, Randi) ◆ 1996
7. Cher's Furiously Fit Workout (Reisfeld, Randi) ◆ 1996
8. Friend or Faux (Gilmour, H. B.) ◆ 1996
9. Baldwin from Another Planet (Gilmour, H. B.) ◆ 1996
10. Cher and Cher Alike (Gilmour, H. B.) ◆ 1997
11. Romantically Correct (Gilmour, H. B.) ◆ 1997
12. Too Hottie to Handle (Reisfeld, Randi) ◆ 1997

13. True Blue Hawaii (Reisfeld, Randi) ◆ 1997
14. Babes in Boyland (Gilmour, H. B.) ◆ 1998
15. Cher's Frantically Romantic Assignment (Gilmour, H. B.) ◆ 1998
16. Chronically Crushed (Reisfeld, Randi) ◆ 1998
17. Dude with a 'Tude (Reisfeld, Randi) ◆ 1998
18. A Totally Cher Affair (Gilmour, H. B.) ◆ 1998
19. Extreme Sisterhood (Reisfeld, Randi) ◆ 1999
20. Bettypalooza (Lenhard, Elizabeth) ◆ 1999
21. Southern Fried Makeover (Jablonski, Carla) ◆ 1999

COLONIAL CAPTIVES

Hunt, Angela Elwell
TYNDALE HOUSE ◆ GRADES 6–8
HISTORICAL

In 1627, Kimberly Hollis is traveling with her mother on a ship to Jamestown Colony. There, they will rejoin Kimberly's father. The other passengers on the boat include children who are to become indentured servants. Dangers on the voyage include pirates and bad weather. Kimberly's faith in God helps her deal with the difficulties.

1. Kimberly and the Captives ◆ 1996
2. The Deadly Chase ◆ 1996
3. Pirate's Revenge ◆ 1996
4. Lost in the Fog ◆ 1996

COLONIZATION

Turtledove, Harry
BALLANTINE DEL REY ◆ GRADES 9–12
SCIENCE FICTION

An alternate history of post-World War II Earth, set in the turbulent 1960s. It is 20 years since the first aliens arrived but they have failed to take control. So when their colonization fleet turns up, they meet unexpected resistance. The series is full of historical characters and anecdotes. In *Homeward Bound*, the aliens must decide whether humanity can be allowed to survive. This series is linked to Turtledove's earlier alternate World War II saga, in which the alien lizards make their debut.

1. Colonization: Second Contact ◆ 1999
2. Colonization: Down to Earth ◆ 2000
3. Colonization: Aftershocks ◆ 2001
4. Colonization: Homeward Bound ◆ 2004

THE COMPANIONS QUARTET

Golding, Julia

MARSHALL CAVENDISH ◆ GRADES 5–8

FANTASY

Connie Lionheart, 11, has always been different. Besides having mismatched eyes, she is often in the middle of unusual events involving animals. While visiting her aunt in England, Connie discovers she can communicate with all creatures. Aunt Evelyn is a member of a secret group dedicated to protecting mythical creatures and she needs Connie's skills when the sirens are threatened by a evil spirit. As in the Percy Jackson books, mythology and folklore are important elements in this series.

1. Secret of the Sirens ◆ 2007
2. The Gorgon's Gaze ◆ 2007
3. Mines of the Minotaur ◆ 2008
4. The Chimera's Curse ◆ 2008

THE COMPLICATED LIFE OF CLAUDIA CRISTINA CORTEZ

Gallagher , Diana G.

STONE ARCH ◆ GRADES 5–7

REAL LIFE

Claudia, 13, and her girlfriends hang out together as the "Whatever" club. When another good friend, Adam, wants to join them, they have to decide whether or not to let him. In *Dance,* Claudia is on the committee for the seventh-grade dance and she wants it to be casual and fun, but Anna, a popular girl, wants it to be more formal. These books are designed with different fonts and drawings that will attract many readers, including fans of Amelia (Moss).

1. Camp Can't ◆ 2007
2. Dance Trap ◆ 2007
3. Guilty! ◆ 2007
4. Whatever! ◆ 2007
5. Beach Blues ◆ 2008
6. Friends Forever? ◆ 2008
7. Party! ◆ 2008
8. Vote! ◆ 2008

CONCRETE

Chadwick, Paul

DARK HORSE ◆ **GRADES 7–10**

FANTASY

Ron Lithgow is a speechwriter trapped in an alien body made of stone. Despite his bulk, Concrete is able to help his friends and protect the world. In one graphic novel, a film crew hires Concrete to be like a special effect come to life. When accidents begin to happen, Concrete intervenes. This is a new series collecting these Dark Horse comic books. It replaces a series published in the 1990s, and some of the volumes have new titles.

1. Depths ◆ 2005
2. Heights ◆ 2005
3. Fragile Creatures ◆ 2006
4. Killer Smile ◆ 2006
5. Think Like a Mountain ◆ 2006
6. Strange Armor ◆ 2006
7. The Huge Dilemma ◆ 2006

CONFESSIONS OF A TEEN NANNY

Ashton, Victoria

HARPERCOLLINS ◆ **GRADES 8–12**

REAL LIFE

Adrienne, 16, is a nanny for Emma Warner, 8, whose rich socialite family lives in New York City. Emma's half-sister Cameron (Cam) is Adrienne's age and pretends to be her friend. Instead, Cam gets Adrienne to arrange secret parties, puts her in a compromising position, and steals her boyfriend. In the second book, Adrienne and her friend Liz (who is a nanny in the same NYC apartment building) team up to get even.

1. Confessions of a Teen Nanny ◆ 2005
2. Rich Girls ◆ 2006
3. Juicy Secrets ◆ 2006

CONFESSIONS OF A TEENAGE DRAMA QUEEN

Sheldon, Dyan
CANDLEWICK ◆ GRADES 7–10 ◆ A/R
REAL LIFE

Mary Elizabeth Cep must adjust to her family's move from New York City to New Jersey. To do so, she reinvents herself, becoming Lola and devising a plan to shake up suburbia. Her classmates are not interested. They already have a "drama queen" to worship—Carla Santini. Lola and Carla become rivals and the games begin.

1. Confessions of a Teenage Drama Queen ◆ 1999
2. My Perfect Life ◆ 2002
3. Confessions of a Teenage Hollywood Star ◆ 2006

CONFESSIONS OF GEORGIA NICOLSON

Rennison, Louise
HARPERCOLLINS ◆ GRADES 7–10
HUMOR | REAL LIFE

In her diary, Georgia Nicolson reflects on her teenage anxieties. She writes about her bra and about kissing. She dates a "Sex God" until he tells her she should date a younger boy. Set in England, the novels contain British terms and phrases but American teens have connected with this irreverent series. The first book received a Michael L. Printz Award for young adult literature.

1. Angus, Thongs and Full Frontal Snogging: Confessions of Georgia Nicolson ◆ 2000
2. On the Bright Side, I'm Now the Girlfriend of a Sex God: Further Confessions of Georgia Nicolson ◆ 2001
3. Knocked Out by My Nunga-Nungas: Further, Further Confessions of Georgia Nicolson ◆ 2002
4. Dancing in My Nuddy Pants: Even Further Confessions of Georgia Nicolson ◆ 2003
5. Away Laughing on a Fast Camel: Even More Confessions of Georgia Nicolson ◆ 2004
6. Then He Ate My Boy Entrancers: More Mad, Marvy Confessions of Georgia Nicolson ◆ 2005
7. Startled by His Furry Shorts: Confessions of Georgia Nicolson ◆ 2006
8. Love Is a Many Trousered Thing: Confessions of Georgia Nicolson ◆ 2007
9. Stop in the Name of Pants: Confessions of Georgia Nicolson ◆ 2008

THE CONTENDER

Lipsyte, Robert
HARPERCOLLINS ◆ **GRADES 6–8** ◆ **A/R**
REAL LIFE

Alfred is an orphaned inner-city boy who lives with his aunt and three cousins. When the series opens, he has dropped out of school and works in a grocery store. His best friend has fallen in with a crowd of punks and gets arrested for robbing a store. Alfred decides to start working out at Donatelli's Gym to become a boxer. Donatelli convinces him to try to become a contender. As the series continues, Alfred succeeds as a boxer, becomes a policeman, and teaches a young Native American, Sonny, the lessons he learned from Donatelli.

1. The Contender ◆ 1967
2. The Brave ◆ 1991
3. The Chief ◆ 1998

COOPER KIDS

Peretti, Frank
TOMMY NELSON WORDKIDS ◆ **GRADES 5–7** ◆ **A/R**
ADVENTURE | VALUES

Dr. Cooper, a biblical archeologist, travels all over the world with his two children, getting in and out of all sorts of danger and solving mysteries. Smart and competent, Jay and Lila help him out. Lila, traveling back to the United States from an assignment in Japan, is trapped at the bottom of the ocean. Her rescue is hampered by a conflict with Communist guerrillas in the Philippines. A hint of the supernatural is introduced in an episode involving a space-time warp, where the children are trapped in an old Western town and solve a century-old murder mystery. The eighth volume has been reissued with the title *Mayday at Two Thousand Five Hundred*. This series features lots of excitement and Christian characters, for whom prayer and trust in God is a part of life.

1. The Door in the Dragon's Throat ◆ 1985
2. Escape from the Island of Aquarius ◆ 1986
3. The Tombs of Anak ◆ 1987
4. Trapped at the Bottom of the Sea ◆ 1988
5. The Secret of the Desert Stone ◆ 1996
6. The Deadly Curse of Toco-Rey ◆ 1996
7. The Legend of Annie Murphy ◆ 1997
8. Flying Blind ◆ 1997

COUNTDOWN

Parker, Daniel

ALADDIN ◆ GRADES 7–10

FANTASY

As the millennium approaches, a strange space phenomenon destroys the children and adults on Earth. Only young adults survive and some of them are now searching for the Chosen One. Each month brings new dangers, culminating in *December* when the Chosen One faces the Demon.

1. January ◆ 1998
2. February ◆ 1998
3. March ◆ 1999
4. April ◆ 1999
5. May ◆ 1999
6. June ◆ 1999
7. July ◆ 1999
8. August ◆ 1999
9. September ◆ 1999
10. October ◆ 1999
11. November ◆ 1999
12. December: Time's Up ◆ 1999

CRIME THROUGH TIME

Doyle, Bill

LITTLE, BROWN ◆ GRADES 4–8 ◆ A/R

MYSTERY

Generations of a family of famous detectives solve mysteries set during notable historical eras (and one future setting). Cyanide poisoning on a train, bootleggers and kidnapping, and a stolen Egyptian necklace are among the mysteries for the young sleuths. Sidebars, clues, maps, sketches, and more involve the reader in the action.

1. Swindled! The 1906 Journal of Fitz Morgan ◆ 2006
2. Nabbed! The 1925 Journal of G. Codd Fitzmorgan ◆ 2006
3. Silenced! The 1969 Journal of Malcolm Moorie ◆ 2006
4. Betrayed! The 1977 Journal of Zeke Moorie ◆ 2006
5. Iced! The 2007 Journal of Nick Fitzmorgan ◆ 2006
6. Trapped! The 2031 Journal of Otis Fitzmorgan ◆ 2006

THE CRIMSON SHADOW

Salvatore, R. A.

WARNER ◆ GRADES 7–12

FANTASY

When the land of Eriador is enslaved by the Wizard-King Greensparrow, a young nobleman named Luthien Bedwyr becomes an outlaw. He always leaves behind the crimson mark of his shadow. Aided by elves, dwarves, and other humans, Luthien battles the evil, magical army of Belsen Krieg.

1. The Sword of Bedwyr ◆ 1995
2. Luthien's Gamble ◆ 1996
3. The Dragon King ◆ 1996

THE CRONUS CHRONICLES

Ursu, Anne

ATHENEUM ◆ GRADES 5–9 ◆ A/R

FANTASY

There are plans to take over the Underworld and overthrow Hades. Philonecron, Poseidon's grandson, plans to steal the shadows of children and use them to restore life to the dead. Two cousins, Charlotte and Zee (a boy with a mysterious heritage), become involved in the fight against Philonecron. This is a natural series to pair with Percy Jackson and the Olympians.

1. The Shadow Thieves ◆ 2006
2. The Siren Song ◆ 2007
3. The Promethian Flame ◆ 2009

CROSSROADS TRILOGY

O'Donohoe, Nick

ACE ◆ GRADES 8–12 ◆ A/R

FANTASY

Medical detail, mythology, and fantasy are intertwined in these stories of the magical world of Crossroads where veterinarian B. J. Vaughn treats beasts of legend. In the second book, she becomes romantically involved with a faun and teaches centaurs about first aid and wellness. In the last book, B. J. must protect her animal friends from outside threats.

1. The Magic and the Healing ◆ 1994
2. Under the Healing Sign ◆ 1995
3. The Healing of Crossroads ◆ 1996

CRYSTAL DOORS

Moesta, Rebecca, and Kevin J. Anderson

LITTLE, BROWN ◆ GRADES 5–8

FANTASY

Gwen and Vic, 14, are cousins whose family background is filled with strange occurrences. Both of their mothers just "appeared" in the jungle where their fathers were working on an archeological dig. Now, with the mysterious death of Gwen's parents and the disappearance of Vic's mother, the cousins begin a dangerous journey. They enter a room filled with crystals and are transported to Elantya, an island kingdom being threatened by merlons (sea monsters).

1. Crystal Doors: Island Realm ◆ 2006
2. Crystal Doors: Ocean Realm ◆ 2007
3. Crystal Doors: Sky Realm ◆ 2008

THE CULTURE

Banks, Iain M.

POCKET ◆ GRADES 11–12

SCIENCE FICTION

Epic space adventures are the focus of this well-written adult series that will challenge and interest older teens. The Culture is a technologically advanced giant civilization (31 trillion inhabitants) that values its own freedoms but is careless with those of others. In the first book, the Idirans hire an alien shape changer to battle against the Culture. In *The Player of Games,* the Culture's star player will compete in a contest that holds the key to the future. *The State of the Art* (1991) is a collection whose title story is a novella about the Culture.

1. Consider Phlebas ◆ 1987
2. The Player of Games ◆ 1988
3. Use of Weapons ◆ 1990
4. Excession ◆ 1996
5. Look to Windward ◆ 2000
6. Matter ◆ 2008

THE CURSE OF THE JOLLY STONE TRILOGY

Lawrence, Iain
DELACORTE ◆ GRADES 7–10
ADVENTURE | HISTORICAL

In the early 19th century, young Tom Tin finds himself on a prison ship bound for Van Dieman's Land (Australia). Conditions are terrible and in the second book, Tom and his fellow convict Midgely plot to escape from the prison ship as it approaches Australia, ignoring warnings about cannibals. This is a good page-turning adventure story with a Dickensian flavor.

1. The Convicts ◆ 2005
2. The Cannibals ◆ 2005
3. The Castaways ◆ 2007

CYBERQUEST

Brouwer, Sigmund
THOMAS NELSON ◆ GRADES 5–8
FANTASY

Set in the future, this series depicts Earth as a dangerous place. The Technocrats are in control, Christianity has been outlawed, and the Welfaros of Old Newyork are facing destruction. A leader is needed. Mok is chosen by the Committee to face virtual reality trials through history. His final trial is in ancient Jerusalem at the time of the crucifixion.

1. Pharaoh's Tomb ◆ 1997
2. Knight's Honor ◆ 1997
3. Pirate's Cross ◆ 1997
4. Outlaw's Gold ◆ 1997
5. Soldier's Aim ◆ 1997
6. Galilee Man ◆ 1997

CYBERSURFERS

Pedersen, Ted, and Mel Gilden
PRICE STERN SLOAN ◆ GRADES 6–9
ADVENTURE

Mr. Madison, the computer lab teacher at Fort Benson High School, engages two young computer students to explore the Internet in a special program. Fourteen-year-old techno-wizard Athena Bergstrom and computer hacker Jason Kane share adventures both dangerous and exciting.

Internet notes plus a user-friendly glossary explain terms for "Newbies" to the technology. This series would have a particular appeal to kids with an interest in computers.

1. Pirates on the Internet ◆ 1995
2. Cyberspace Cowboy ◆ 1995
3. Ghost on the Net ◆ 1996
4. Cybercops and Flame Wars ◆ 1996

DALEMARK QUARTET

Jones, Diana Wynne

HARPERCOLLINS ◆ GRADES 6–9 ◆ A/R

FANTASY

Dalemark is a land divided. Each book in this quartet features a young person who confronts dangerous magic and evil. In *The Crown of Dalemark,* Maewen time travels to Dalemark where she impersonates Noreth, a teen who believes she is destined to unite her land. Books in this series were first published in the 1970s.

1. Cart and Cwidder ◆ 2001
2. Drowned Ammet ◆ 2001
3. The Spellcoats ◆ 2001
4. The Crown of Dalemark ◆ 2001

DAMAR CHRONICLES

McKinley, Robin

GREENWILLOW ◆ GRADES 6–10 ◆ A/R

ADVENTURE | FANTASY

Two of the three books in this wonderful fantasy series are Newbery-winning titles. *The Blue Sword* is the story of Harry Crewe, who travels to the Homelander empire when her father dies. She is kidnapped by a native king with mysterious powers. *The Hero and the Crown* is the prequel to *The Blue Sword,* and gives the reader historical background on the magical powers of the kingdom. Aerin, the main character of this story, wins her birthright with the help of a wizard and the blue sword. The third volume in the series is a collection of short stories set in the kingdom of Damar. Maddy, the main character of *The Stone Fey,* is as strong-willed and independent as the women in the earlier books. Maddy's fascination with the Fey threatens her future.

1. The Blue Sword ◆ 1982
2. The Hero and the Crown ◆ 1984
3. A Knot in the Grain and Other Stories ◆ 1994
4. The Stone Fey ◆ 1998

DANGER BOY

Williams, Mark London

CANDLEWICK ◆ GRADES 6–9 ◆ A/R

FANTASY

When scientific research on "spacetime spheres" results in the death of his mother, Eli, 12, and his father leave Princeton, New Jersey, and move to Sonoma, California. It is 2019, and Eli's father wants to abandon his research but is coerced into continuing and using Eli as his test subject. Eli's time travel adventures begin. Clyne, a dinosaur, and Thea, a librarian from ancient Egypt, join him. The second book was originally called *Dino Sword*.

1. Ancient Fire ◆ 2001
2. Dragon Sword ◆ 2001
3. Trail of Bones ◆ 2005
4. City of Ruins ◆ 2007

DANGER.COM

Cray, Jordan

ALADDIN ◆ GRADES 6–9 ◆ A/R

ADVENTURE | MYSTERY

These books use communication on the Internet to establish the plots and then have the characters solve the mystery. In one book, Annie and her brother Nick send messages to a cute girl who has stolen Annie's boyfriend. When the messages fall into the wrong hands, there is danger, and Annie and Nick must use their computer skills to prevent even more trouble. Annie and Nick return in another book to solve a murder while on vacation in Florida. Internet dating, cyber terrorists, chat rooms, and a web of lies enhance the action-packed stories in this series.

1. Gemini 7 ◆ 1997
2. Firestorm ◆ 1997
3. Shadow Man ◆ 1997
4. Hot Pursuit ◆ 1997
5. Stalker ◆ 1998
6. Bad Intent ◆ 1998
7. Most Wanted ◆ 1998
8. Dead Man's Hand ◆ 1998
9. Shiver ◆ 1998

DANIEL BOOM *see* Adventures of Daniel Boom AKA Loud Boy

DANNY WATTS

McNab, Andy, and Robert Rigby

PUTNAM ◆ GRADES 8–10 ◆ A/R

ADVENTURE | MYSTERY

Fergus Watts is a traitor . . . or is he? His teenaged grandson, Danny, has been rejected by the Army because of his grandfather's traitorous past. Now Danny wants to find his grandfather and punish him for ruining his life. When Danny finally tracks Fergus down, they both become targets. They join forces to clear their names and eventually go undercover to work for MI-5, the British secret service agency. Danny's friend Elena, a computer whiz, often helps in their missions. As in many adult spy novels, there are moral dilemmas, untrustworthy superiors, hidden agendas, and violent confrontations.

1. Traitor ◆ 2005
2. Payback ◆ 2006
3. Avenger ◆ 2007
4. Meltdown ◆ 2008

DARK FUSION

Shusterman, Neal

DUTTON ◆ GRADES 7–10 ◆ A/R

FANTASY

Folk tales and mythology provide the foundation for this series. In *Dread Locks,* Parker, 14, is fascinated with his new neighbor. With her golden spiral curls, Tara is beautiful. She always wears sunglasses, adding to her mystique. But anyone who gets close to Tara becomes ill and Parker comes to realize her Medusa-like powers. *Red Rider's Hood* features a modern setting with werewolves and granny as a werewolf hunter.

1. Dread Locks ◆ 2005
2. Red Rider's Hood ◆ 2006
3. Duckling Ugly ◆ 2007

DARK GROUND TRILOGY

Cross, Gillian

DUTTON ◆ GRADES 6–9 ◆ A/R

FANTASY

Teens who fall, faint, or collapse undergo strange transformations. When they awake, they are as small as mice and the familiar world becomes dangerous and distant. Robert finds himself in this parallel universe and manages to escape. But as winter nears, he worries about the fate of those he left behind and sets out to rescue them.

1. The Dark Ground ◆ 2004
2. The Black Room ◆ 2006
3. The Nightmare Game ◆ 2007

DARK IS RISING

Cooper, Susan

COLLIER ◆ GRADES 4–8 ◆ A/R

ADVENTURE | FANTASY

This is a classic fantasy series. Two of the five books are Newbery Medal winners. The story starts out with the three Drew children: Simon, Jane, and Barney. While on holiday, they discover an ancient manuscript that will reveal the true story of King Arthur. In the second book, Will Stanton, age 11, discovers that he is the last of the Old Ones who are able to triumph over the evil forces of the Dark. In *Greenwitch,* Jane and her brothers help the Old Ones uncover the grail. As the quest continues, Will and his companions must uncover the items necessary to vanquish the rising forces of the Dark. Fantasy lovers will be absorbed by this series and will also enjoy C. S. Lewis's Chronicles of Narnia and Tolkien's Lord of the Rings trilogy, which plunge readers into mysterious fantasy worlds.

1. Over Sea, Under Stone ◆ 1965
2. The Dark Is Rising ◆ 1973
3. Greenwitch ◆ 1974
4. The Grey King ◆ 1975
5. Silver on the Tree ◆ 1977

DARK REFLECTIONS TRILOGY

Meyer, Kai

SIMON & SCHUSTER ◆ GRADES 5–8 ◆ A/R

FANTASY

Merle, 14, and Junipa, 13, are orphans serving as apprentices to the magic mirror maker. The Egyptian army has besieged the city (an alternate Venice) for years but the Flowing Queen has protected Venice from destruction. Now the spirit of the Queen has been captured in a glass vial. To save the city, Merle drinks the water in the vial and becomes filled with the spirit of the Flowing Queen. Merle, Junipa, and Vermithrax the flying stone lion meet with the lord of Hell while Serafin, Merle's friend, stays to battle the Egyptians. In *The Glass Word,* the characters come together in Egypt to thwart Seth, the highest of the Horus priests, who is seeking revenge on the pharoah. Translated from German, this series will interest readers of Mary Hoffman's Stravaganza.

1. The Water Mirror ◆ 2005
2. The Stone Light ◆ 2006
3. The Glass Word ◆ 2008

DARK SECRETS

Chandler, Elizabeth

SIMON & SCHUSTER ◆ **GRADES 7–10** ◆ **A/R**

FANTASY

In the first book of the series, Megan, 16, visits her grandmother in Maryland. They have been estranged for years, but now Megan feels the need to reestablish contact. Once she is there, Megan knows she has been there before . . . in her dreams. Megan has visions of Avril, her grandmother's sister who died years ago at the age of 16. The other books feature other teens in mysterious, supernatural situations.

1. Legacy of Lies ◆ 2000
2. Don't Tell ◆ 2001
3. No Time to Die ◆ 2001
4. The Deep End of Fear ◆ 2003
5. The Back Door of Midnight ◆ 2004

DARK TOWER

King, Stephen

VIKING; SCRIBNER ◆ **GRADES 9–12** ◆ **A/R**

FANTASY

Roland of Gilead is a gunslinger. The world is a wasteland and Roland is on a quest for the Dark Tower. Along the way he meets murderers, drug dealers, and other dangerous humans. He also encounters nonhuman characters including a cyborg bear and a demonic woman from a parallel world. Time travel, horror, fantasy, and supernatural events will keep YA readers enthralled. This series has evolved over several decades and the first volume has been revised for the 2003 reissue. There is a related guide to the characters, places, and events in the series.

1. The Gunslinger ◆ 2003
2. The Drawing of the Three ◆ 2003
3. The Waste Lands ◆ 2003
4. Wizard and Glass ◆ 2003
5. Wolves of the Calla ◆ 2003
6. Song of Susannah ◆ 2004
7. The Dark Tower ◆ 2004

DARK VISIONS

Smith, L. J.

SIMON & SCHUSTER ◆ GRADES 9–12

FANTASY | HORROR

Kaitlyn Fairchild has psychic powers that have resulted in her receiving a scholarship to the Zetes Institute. Strange, threatening things are happening at the institute even as the students form romantic attachments. Kaitlyn teams up with four other teens to escape the dangerous experiment that has been devised for them.

1. The Strange Power ◆ 1994
2. The Possessed ◆ 1995
3. The Passion ◆ 1995

DARKANGEL TRILOGY

Pierce, Meredith Ann

LITTLE, BROWN ◆ GRADES 6–10 ◆ A/R

FANTASY

Aeriel sets out on a quest to destroy the vampyre Irrylath. However, she cannot resist the fatal allure of this creature and chooses to love him rather than destroy him. Though mortal again, Irrylath is still tormented by the witch through the pull of dreams, and once again Aeriel must fight the dark forces, gathering the gargoyles to do battle with the witch. It is with the aid of a shimmering pearl that Aeriel is able to wage the last battle with the powerful white witch and break the spell cast on her husband.

1. Darkangel ◆ 1982
2. Gathering of the Gargoyles ◆ 1984
3. Pearl of the Soul of the World ◆ 1990

THE DARKEST AGE

Lake, A. J.

BLOOMSBURY ◆ GRADES 5–8 ◆ A/R

FANTASY

Edmund and Elspeth, both 11, are the only two survivors of a shipwreck. The son of a king, Edmund has kept his identity secret. Elspeth, the shipmaster's daughter, used her knowledge of the sea to help them survive. As they struggle to reach their home, they find that evil forces have taken over. Edmund and Elspeth realize their destiny as they become involved in the struggle to overcome the darkness. In the third book, they face Loki, the mythical trickster.

1. The Coming of Dragons ◆ 2006
2. The Book of the Sword ◆ 2007
3. The Circle of Stone ◆ 2008

Date Him or Dump Him?

Busby, Cylin

Bloomsbury ◆ Grades 6–9

Real Life

In the first book, you are a junior camp counselor. There are lots of cute guys at the camp. Who will you pick? If you don't like your choice, you can start over. Other books feature a school dance and a ski trip. Many of the "plot-your-own story" books are adventure books that may appeal more to boys. Here's one for middle school girls.

1. The Campfire Crush ◆ 2007
2. The Dance Dilemma ◆ 2007
3. Ski Trip Trouble ◆ 2007

Daughter of Destiny

Solitaire, Jenna

Tor ◆ Grades 9–12 ◆ A/R

Fantasy

Jenna Solitaire, 19, is writing the story of her adventures. After the death of her grandfather, she is the last living member of her family. As she cleans out her grandfather's home, she finds an unusual decorated board. A disk moves around the board revealing secrets of Jenna's destiny. Jenna is a Keeper and this is the Board of Air. To save the world from destruction, Jenna must find the other elemental boards and master them. There are not many people she can trust; however, Simon Monk, a man with a mysterious past, accompanies Jenna on her search.

1. Keeper of the Winds ◆ 2006
2. Keeper of the Waters ◆ 2006
3. Keeper of the Flames ◆ 2006
4. Keeper of the Earth ◆ 2006

Daughters of the Moon

Ewing, Lynne

Hyperion ◆ Grades 9–12 ◆ A/R

Fantasy | Horror

A group of high school girls discover they have magical powers. Catty can travel through time. Serina is a mind reader. Vanessa can become invisible. They must battle the evil of Atrox and the Followers. The multicultural characters will expand the appeal of this series. The combination of mythology and horror should attract the fans of the Buffy books.

1. Goddess of the Night ◆ 2000
2. Into the Cold Fire ◆ 2000
3. Night Shade ◆ 2001
4. The Secret Scroll ◆ 2001
5. The Sacrifice ◆ 2001
6. The Lost One ◆ 2001
7. Moon Demon ◆ 2002
8. Possession ◆ 2002
9. The Choice ◆ 2003
10. The Talisman ◆ 2003
11. The Prophecy ◆ 2004
12. The Becoming ◆ 2004
13. The Final Eclipse ◆ 2007

DAVID BRIN'S OUT OF TIME

Various authors

AVON ◆ GRADES 6–8

FANTASY

In a future Utopian world, conflict and danger no longer exist. It is peaceful. The people are not equipped to deal with problems such as aliens who want to destroy them. Instead, they pull teens from the past to confront terrors. The three books in this series feature different teens who have been "yanked" into the future. In the third book, Adam O'Connor is summoned to face the K'lugu and Devlins, dangerous warlike creatures.

1. Yanked (Kress, Nancy) ◆ 1999
2. Tiger in the Sky (Finch, Sheila) ◆ 1999
3. The Game of Worlds (Allen, Roger MacBride) ◆ 1999

DAWSON'S CREEK

Various authors

SIMON & SCHUSTER ◆ GRADES 7–12

REAL LIFE

Dawson and his friends Joey, Jen, and Pacey share their fears and dreams in these spin-off books from the popular television show. In *Lighthouse Legend,* Joey believes she hears voices in the abandoned lighthouse. Another book follows the teens on a ski weekend. Jack and Andie appear in later books. These books are filled with suspense, romance, and teen anxieties. There are companion materials including a scrapbook, a fan book (with cast biographies and episode guides), and a book about the production of the show.

1. Long Hot Summer (Rodriguez, K. S.) ◆ 1998
2. Calm Before the Storm (Baker, Jennifer) ◆ 1998
3. Shifting into Overdrive (Anders, C. J.) ◆ 1998
4. Major Meltdown (Rodriguez, K. S.) ◆ 1999
5. Double Exposure (Anders, C. J.) ◆ 1999
6. Trouble in Paradise (Anders, C. J.) ◆ 1999
7. Too Hot to Handle (Anders, C. J.) ◆ 1999
8. Don't Scream (Anders, C. J.) ◆ 1999
9. Tough Enough (Anders, C. J.) ◆ 2000
10. Running on Empty (Anders, C. J.) ◆ 2000
11. A Capeside Christmas (Anders, C. J.) ◆ 2000
12. Lighthouse Legend (Teglaar, Liz, and Holly E. Henderson) ◆ 2001
13. Bayou Blues (Fricke, Anna, and Barbara Sieberetz) ◆ 2001
14. Mysterious Boarder (Henderson, Holly E., and Liz Teglaar) ◆ 2001
15. Playing for Keeps (Anders, C. J.) ◆ 2001

DAYSTAR VOYAGES

Morris, Gilbert, and Dan Meeks

MOODY PUBLISHERS ◆ GRADES 6–9 ◆ A/R

SCIENCE FICTION │ VALUES

Captain Edge commands the *Daystar,* a shabby starship with a crew of teens who are dubbed the Junior Space Rangers. As they travel across the galaxy, they work on secret assignments, visit a planet with only children as inhabitants, and defeat wizards who want to control planets. These characters struggle with good and evil; they also deal with circumstances that test their faith.

1. Secret of the Planet Makon ◆ 1998
2. Wizards of the Galaxy ◆ 1998
3. Escape From the Red Comet ◆ 1998
4. Dark Spell Over Morlandria ◆ 1998
5. Revenge of the Space Pirate ◆ 1998
6. Invasion of the Killer Locusts ◆ 1999
7. Dangers of the Rainbow Nebula ◆ 1999
8. The Frozen Space Pilot ◆ 1999
9. The White Dragon of Sharnu ◆ 1999
10. Attack of the Denebian Starship ◆ 2000

DAYWORLD

Farmer, Philip José

PUTNAM; TOM DOHERTY ASSOCIATES ◆ GRADES 10–12

SCIENCE FICTION

This futuristic series focuses on the New Era. To cope with overpopulation, suspended animation is used. There are seven groups of people and each group "lives" for one day each week and is suspended for the others. One man, who can transform his appearance, lives every day. When he is discovered, he escapes and finds there are secret groups organizing to rebel against the government.

1. Dayworld ◆ 1985
2. Dayworld Rebel ◆ 1987
3. Dayworld Breakup ◆ 1990

DE GRANVILLE TRILOGY

Grant, K. M.

WALKER & CO. ◆ GRADES 6–10 ◆ A/R

HISTORICAL

As the series begins, William de Granville, 13, and his older brother Gavin are in Jerusalem fighting in the Crusades. In the battles between the Christian and Muslim forces, Gavin is seriously injured. When the brothers return to England (in the second book), the political situation threatens their future and Gavin's bethrothed, Eleanor, is kidnapped by Constable de Scabious. By the third book, Gavin is dead. Eleanor and Will are realizing their feelings for each other. While taking the ransom to free King Richard, Will is betrayed by his Muslim friend Kamil. Throughout the books, Hosanna, a powerful blood red warhorse, plays a key role in the adventures.

1. Blood Red Horse ◆ 2005
2. Green Jasper ◆ 200
3. Blaze of Silver ◆ 2007

DEADTIME STORIES

Cascone, A. G.

TROLL ◆ GRADES 4–7

HORROR

What would you do if you encountered a man-eating spider? Has a ghost ever communicated with you through your cell phone? Have you ever wondered if your toys are planning a coup? These are some of the circumstances that occur in this series of books. Like others in the horror genre, this series features different characters in bizarre situations, often with spooky creatures. Applehead dolls that take the place of parents, magic tricks that can't be undone, and mutant sea creatures should capture the interest of horror fans.

1. Terror in Tiny Town ◆ 1996
2. Invasion of the Appleheads ◆ 1996
3. Along Came a Spider ◆ 1996
4. Ghost Knight ◆ 1996
5. Revenge of the Goblins ◆ 1996
6. Little Magic Shop of Horrors ◆ 1996
7. It Came from the Deep ◆ 1997
8. Grave Secrets ◆ 1997
9. Mirror Mirror ◆ 1997
10. Grandpa's Monster Movies ◆ 1997
11. Nightmare on Planet X ◆ 1997
12. Welcome to the Terror-Go-Round ◆ 1997
13. The Beast of Baskerville ◆ 1997
14. Trapped in Tiny Town ◆ 1997
15. Cyber Scare ◆ 1997
16. Night of the Pet Zombies ◆ 1997
17. Faerie Tale ◆ 1997

DEAR DIARY

Various authors

BERKLEY ◆ GRADES 7–12

REAL LIFE

In *Runaway,* Cassie is pregnant and Zach is the father. Cassie's father is outraged and sends her to a Home for Girls. Zach finds her and the two run away. Cassie's diary reveals her fears and hopes for her future and her baby. Other books use the diary format to focus on teens in trouble. Shoplifting, Internet "romance," and a girl's search for her biological mother are among the problems described.

1. Runaway (Zach, Cheryl) ◆ 1995
2. Remember Me (Lanham, Cheryl) ◆ 1996
3. Family Secrets (Zach, Cheryl) ◆ 1996
4. Secret Admirer (Zach, Cheryl) ◆ 2000
5. Dying Young (Lanham, Cheryl) ◆ 2000
6. Fighting Back (Lanham, Cheryl) ◆ 2000
7. Shadow Self (Zach, Cheryl) ◆ 2000

DEAR DUMB DIARY

Benton, Jim

SCHOLASTIC ◆ GRADES 5–8 ◆ A/R

REAL LIFE | HUMOR

In a diary format, Jamie Kelly of Mackeral Middle School describes her everyday experiences. Her comments about her life are supplemented by numerous cartoon-style illustrations. In the third book (*Am I the Princess or the Frog?*), Jamie describes the awful meat loaf served on Meat Loaf Day. Her comments are overheard by the lunch monitor, Miss Bruntford, who decides to teach Jamie a lesson. Jamie's best friend is Isabella and her nemesis is Angeline (aka Princess Turd of Turdsylvania). Fans of Captain Underpants will enjoy this series.

1. Let's Pretend This Never Happened ◆ 2004
2. My Pants Are Haunted ◆ 2004
3. Am I the Princess or the Frog? ◆ 2005
4. Never Do Anything, Ever ◆ 2005
5. Can Adults Become Human? ◆ 2006
6. The Problem with Here Is That It's Where I'm From ◆ 2007
7. Never Underestimate Your Dumbness ◆ 2008

DEAR MR. PRESIDENT

Various authors

WINSLOW PRESS ◆ GRADES 5–7 ◆ A/R

HISTORICAL

These books use historical documents—maps, timelines, archival sources—to illuminate a fictional correspondence between a young person and a famous historical figure. Through the letters, the reader learns about the events of the era: FDR and the Great Depression, Lincoln and slavery/the Civil War, and so forth. Readers who enjoy historical fiction books with a diary format, like the Dear America books, will connect with this series.

1. Thomas Jefferson: Letters from a Philadelphia Bookworm (Armstrong, Jennifer) ◆ 2000
2. Theodore Roosevelt: Letters from a Young Coal Miner (Armstrong, Jennifer) ◆ 2001
3. John Quincy Adams: Letters from a Southern Planter's Son (Kroll, Steven) ◆ 2001
4. Franklin Delano Roosevelt: Letters from a Mill Town Girl (Winthrop, Elizabeth) ◆ 2001

5. Abraham Lincoln: Letters from a Slave Girl (Pinkney, Andrea Davis) ◆ 2001

6. Dwight D. Eisenhower: Letters from a New Jersey Schoolgirl (Karr, Kathleen) ◆ 2003

DEEP SPACE NINE *see* Star Trek: Deep Space Nine

DEGREES OF BETRAYAL

Various authors

TYNDALE HOUSE ◆ GRADES 8–10 ◆ A/R

VALUES

Three perspectives of the same event—and three teens whose faith is being tested—are presented in this series. Following a car accident, Sierra is in the hospital. While there, she learns that her boyfriend, Ryun, and her best friend, Kenzie, have been secretly seeing each other. Sierra's feelings of betrayal lead her to reject God. Meanwhile, Ryun's conceited behavior and Kenzie's insecurities have led them to make choices that go against their values. Can these three friends make the choices that lead them back to God?

1. Sierra's Story (Mackall, Dandi Daley) ◆ 2004
2. Ryun's Story (Nesbit, Jeffrey Asher) ◆ 2004
3. Kenzie's Story (Carlson, Melody) ◆ 2004

DEGREES OF GUILT

Various authors

TYNDALE HOUSE ◆ GRADES 7–10 ◆ A/R

REAL LIFE

Three teens may be heading for destruction. Kyra, 17, struggles to cope with the pressures of school, the play, and preparing for college. She begins to abuse prescription drugs. Miranda is a senior who decides to be a "party girl." Tyrone, 18, wonders how he might have influenced a friend who overdosed.

1. Kyra's Story (Mackall, Dandi Daley) ◆ 2003
2. Miranda's Story (Carlson, Melody) ◆ 2003
3. Tyrone's Story (Brouwer, Sigmund) ◆ 2003

DEL RIO BAY CLIQUE

Chase, Paula

DAFINA ◆ GRADES 7–10

REAL LIFE

Mina Moore is used to being soooooo popular. As she starts high school, she wants to be in with the best crowd—a group of black girls who seem to have it all. As Mina, who is also African American, gets to know the girls, she sees their differences. Kelly is Puerto Rican, Jacinta is from the projects, and Jessica is spoiled and wealthy. Mina begins to move away from Lizzie, a white girl, but a school assignment on prejudice causes her to reflect on her own behavior. In *Don't Get It Twisted,* Mina writes for the school paper and gets invited out by a really hot boy. Mina and her friends instant-message their concerns to each other and use contemporary language, which should appeal to many teen readers.

1. So Not the Drama: A Del Rio Bay Clique Novel ◆ 2007
2. Don't Get It Twisted: A Del Rio Bay Clique Novel ◆ 2007
3. That's What's Up! A Del Rio Bay Clique Novel ◆ 2008
4. Who Are You Wit'? A Del Rio Bay Clique Novel ◆ 2008

DELTORA: DELTORA QUEST

Rodda, Emily

SCHOLASTIC ◆ GRADES 4–7 ◆ A/R

FANTASY

Deltora is being threatened by the evil Shadow Lord. The magic belt of Deltora could overcome the evil but only if all seven stones are in the belt. Lief, 16, Barda, and Jasmine seek the stones.

1. The Forests of Silence ◆ 2000
2. The Lake of Tears ◆ 2000
3. City of the Rats ◆ 2000
4. The Shifting Sands ◆ 2001
5. Dread Mountain ◆ 2001
6. The Maze of the Beast ◆ 2001
7. The Valley of the Lost ◆ 2001
8. Return to Del ◆ 2001

DELTORA: DELTORA SHADOWLANDS

Rodda, Emily

SCHOLASTIC ◆ GRADES 4–7 ◆ A/R

FANTASY

Even though the Shadow Lord has been defeated, his evil still reigns over Deltora captives in the Shadowlands. In this new quest, Lief, Barda, and Jasmine seek the Pirran Pipe. This trilogy follows the adventures in the Deltora Quest series.

1. Cavern of the Fear ◆ 2002
2. The Isle of Illusion ◆ 2002
3. The Shadowlands ◆ 2002

DELTORA: DRAGONS OF DELTORA

Rodda, Emily

SCHOLASTIC ◆ GRADES 4–7 ◆ A/R

FANTASY

Another series set in Deltora and again featuring Lief, Jasmine, and Barda. Now they must get help from seven dragons to save Deltora from the seeds of death that are controlled by the Four Sisters. If they fail, the Shadow Lord will return. Companion books to the Deltora series, also illustrated by Marc McBride, are *The Deltora Book of Monsters* (2002), *How to Draw Deltora Monsters* (2005), *Tales of Deltora* (2006)—a beautifully presented collection of Deltora stories about castles and dragons, magic and monsters.

1. Dragon's Nest ◆ 2004
2. Shadowgate ◆ 2004
3. Isle of the Dead ◆ 2004
4. Sister of the South ◆ 2005

DEMONATA

Shan, Darren

LITTLE, BROWN ◆ GRADES 9–12 ◆ A/R

HORROR

Three teens, each from a different era, face off against The Demonata. Lord Loss is the demon master who controls the evil forces that are threatening the world. The Shadow is an even stronger demon that must be stopped. In *Lord Loss,* Grubbs Grady has run away from home. When he hears that his family has been attacked, he returns and finds them not just dead but ripped to shreds by Lord Loss and his minions. There are graphic descriptions of the gore and destruction. Two other teens appear in other books: Kernel Fleck from the 1970s and Bec MacConn from around 350 A.D. Middle school fans of Shan's Cirque du Freak series may graduate to this more intense look at the pain and suffering brought on by The Demonata.

1. Lord Loss ◆ 2005

2. Demon Thief ◆ 2006
3. Slawter ◆ 2006
4. Bec ◆ 2007
5. Blood Beast ◆ 2007
6. Demon Apocalypse ◆ 2007
7. Death's Shadow ◆ 2008

THE DEMONWARS

Salvatore, R. A.
BANTAM DOUBLEDAY DELL ◆ GRADES 10–12 ◆ A/R

FANTASY

Elbryan Wyndon and Jilseponie (Pony) Ault, orphans in league with elves, find themselves in conflict with a variety of beings who seek to rule the world. *Mortalis* (2000), a related book, features Pony's efforts to combat a plague and forms a bridge between the two trilogies. The Second DemonWars Saga starts with *Ascendance* and continues Pony's story. *Highwayman* (2004) begins a new series set in Corona.

1. The Demon Awakens ◆ 1997
2. The Demon Spirit ◆ 1998
3. The Demon Apostle ◆ 1999

THE SECOND DEMONWARS SAGA

1. Ascendance ◆ 2002
2. Transcendence ◆ 2003
3. Immortalis ◆ 2004

DEN OF SHADOWS

Atwater-Rhodes, Amelia
DELACORTE ◆ GRADES 7–10 ◆ A/R

HORROR

More than 300 years ago, Risika was a human named Rachel Weatere. Then Aubrey and a group of vampires transformed her into one of them. Although she still remembers her human life, Risika has adjusted to being vampire; however, she has not forgiven Aubrey for killing her brother. As the series progresses, Aubrey uses his powers to attract a human teen, Jessica, to the power of vampires. The author began this series as a teenager.

1. In the Forests of the Night ◆ 2000
2. Demon in My View ◆ 2001
3. Shattered Mirror ◆ 2001
4. Midnight Predator ◆ 2003

THE DENIZENS OF CAMELOT

Morris, Gerald

HOUGHTON MIFFLIN ◆ GRADES 6–9 ◆ A/R

FANTASY

Tales of Camelot are told from the viewpoint of peripheral characters—
for example, Sir Tristram's younger brother Sir Dinadan, an 11-year-old
page to Sir Parsifal, and an aristocratic lady seeking aid for her sister.

1. The Squire's Tale ◆ 1998
2. The Squire, His Knight, and His Lady ◆ 1999
3. The Savage Damsel and the Dwarf ◆ 2000
4. Parsifal's Page ◆ 2001
5. The Ballad of Sir Dinadan ◆ 2003
6. The Princess, the Crone, and the Dung-Cart Knight ◆ 2004
7. The Lioness and Her Knight ◆ 2005
8. The Quest of the Fair Unknown ◆ 2006

DEPTFORD HISTORIES

Jarvis, Robin

SEASTAR/CHRONICLE ◆ GRADES 5–8 ◆ A/R

ANIMAL FANTASY

This series provides background information about the events in the
Deptford Mice trilogy. How did Jupiter the cat gain his power over the
sewer rats? What caused the wars between the bats and the squirrels?

1. The Alchemist's Cat ◆ 2003
2. The Oaken Throne ◆ 2005
3. Thomas ◆ 2006

DEPTFORD MICE

Jarvis, Robin

SEASTAR ◆ GRADES 5–8 ◆ A/R

ANIMAL FANTASY

Fans of the Redwall books by Brian Jacques will connect with this British
import about the mice of the London borough of Deptford. They are a
quiet group of mice who enjoy a simple life. But when Audrey Brown's
father goes missing, the young mouse searches for him in the dangerous
sewers. She is followed by her brother and some other brave young mice.
In the sewers, the evil cat Jupiter controls the rats with a mysterious
power. In the second book, the mice move to the country but the evil
follows them. There is a series of prequels called the Deptford Histories.

1. The Dark Portal ◆ 2000
2. The Crystal Prison ◆ 2001
3. The Final Reckoning ◆ 2002

DEPTFORD MICE HISTORIES *see* Deptford Histories

DERYNI *see* Chronicles of Deryni

DEVERRY

Kerr, Katharine
BANTAM ◆ GRADES 10–12 ◆ A/R
FANTASY

This fantasy based on Celtic mythology features a sorcerer named Nevyn and a long battle between good and evil. The first book introduces Nevyn's urge to atone for a wrong he committed. In the second book, Nevyn and companions Rhodry and Jill combat sorcerers who would introduce new vices to the humans of Deverry.

1. Daggerspell ◆ 1986
2. Darkspell ◆ 1987
3. The Bristling Wood ◆ 1989
4. The Dragon Revenant ◆ 1990
5. A Time of Exile ◆ 1991
6. A Time of Omens ◆ 1992
7. Days of Blood and Fire ◆ 1993
8. Days of Air and Darkness ◆ 1994
9. The Red Wyvern ◆ 1997
10. The Black Raven ◆ 1999
11. The Fire Dragon ◆ 2001

DIADEM

Peel, John
SCHOLASTIC ◆ GRADES 6–8 ◆ A/R
ADVENTURE | FANTASY

Three characters from diverse backgrounds and eras are drawn into adventures in another dimension. Score is an orphan from the streets of New York. Renald is a girl warrior from medieval times. Pixel exists in virtual reality. They are kidnapped by an unknown force and drawn toward the Diadem. To survive, they seek the help of magicians, both good and evil, and they try to understand the reason for their selection.

1. Book of Names ◆ 1997

    2. Book of Signs ◆ 1997
    3. Book of Magic ◆ 1997
    4. Book of Thunder ◆ 1997
    5. Book of Earth ◆ 1998
    6. Book of Nightmares ◆ 1998

THE DIAMOND BROTHERS

Horowitz, Anthony

PHILOMEL ◆ GRADES 5–8 ◆ A/R

HUMOR | MYSTERY

Tim and Nick are the Diamond Brothers. Tim is the older brother and he is not a very good detective. Nick, 13, manages to keep them both one step ahead of trouble and to solve the mystery too. In *The Falcon's Malteser,* Tim has been framed and is in jail for murder. Nick tries to deal with a mysterious package and find the real killer. These books have humorous moments that reflect on the genre of detective fiction.

    1. The Falcon's Malteser ◆ 2004
    2. Public Enemy, Number Two ◆ 2004
    3. Three of Diamonds: Three Diamond Brothers Mysteries ◆ 2005
    4. South by Southeast ◆ 2005
    5. The Greek Who Stole Christmas ◆ 2008

DIARY OF A CRUSH

Manning, Sarra

PUFFIN ◆ GRADES 8–11 ◆ A/R

REAL LIFE

In England, 16-year-old Edie is attracted to Dylan, an older boy in her art class, but he has a history of quick conquests. On a class trip to Paris, the two kiss and make out, then their relationship fizzles. So, on to Carter (in the second book) and then back to Dylan (in the third book). One reviewer called this "junior chick-lit."

    1. French Kiss ◆ 2006
    2. Kiss and Make Up ◆ 2006
    3. Sealed With a Kiss ◆ 2006

DIARY OF A TEENAGE GIRL

Carlson, Melody

MULTNOMAH ◆ GRADES 9–12 ◆ A/R

REAL LIFE | VALUES

The first five books in this series feature Caitlin O'Connor, who is 16 in the first book and getting married in the last. As she approaches adulthood, she searches to understand her place in the world. She struggles with her changing role with her family, her friends, and her boyfriend, Josh Miller. Her growing commitment to Christ provides a foundation for her decisions. Using her diary, Caitlin explores her feelings and the issues she faces. The next four books are told from the perspective of Chloe Miller, Josh's rebellious younger sister, and her Christian band, Redemption. Kim's books reveal how she deals with her mother's cancer, her faith, dating, and writing an advice column.

CAITLIN

1. Becoming Me ◆ 2000
2. It's My Life ◆ 2002
3. Who I Am ◆ 2002
4. On My Own ◆ 2002
5. I Do ◆ 2004

CHLOE

1. My Name Is Chloe ◆ 2002
2. Sold Out ◆ 2003
3. Road Trip ◆ 2004
4. Face the Music ◆ 2004

KIM

1. Just Ask ◆ 2005
2. Meant to Be ◆ 2005
3. Falling Up ◆ 2006
4. That Was Then ◆ 2006

MAYA

1. Not-So-Simple Life ◆ 2008

DIARY OF A WIMPY KID

Kinney, Jeff

AMULET ◆ GRADES 5–8

HUMOR | REAL LIFE

Greg Heffley is just starting middle school. As a sixth-grader, he feels small and insignificant among the older students. He and his friend Rowley just try to survive in their new situation. Greg's story is told in diary entries that are enhanced by numerous illustrations. While this is not a true graphic novel, the illustrated format will attract many graphic novel readers. *The Diary of a Wimpy Kid Do-It-Yourself Book* is a journal with

writing prompts and illustrations. This series began on the Web at
www.funbrain.com.

1. Diary of a Wimpy Kid: Greg Heffley's Journal ◆ 2007
2. Diary of a Wimpy Kid: Rodrick Rules ◆ 2008
3. Diary of a Wimpy Kid: The Last Straw ◆ 2009

DINOTOPIA

Various authors

RANDOM HOUSE ◆ GRADES 6–9 ◆ A/R

FANTASY

Dinotopia Island is a peaceful world where humans and dinosaurs exist as
friends. The first book is set in the 1860s and two boys, Raymond and
Hugh, are shipwrecked on the island and try to adjust. Subsequent books
feature other humans and dinosaurs facing a variety of problems such as a
threat to Waterfall City and a journey into the Rainy Basin jungles.

1. Windchaser (Ciencin, Scott) ◆ 1995
2. River Quest (Vornholt, John) ◆ 1995
3. Hatchling (Snyder, Midori) ◆ 1995
4. Lost City (Ciencin, Scott) ◆ 1995
5. Sabertooth Mountain (Vornholt, John) ◆ 1996
6. Thunder Falls (Ciencin, Scott) ◆ 1996
7. Firestorm (DeWeese, Gene) ◆ 1997
8. The Maze (David, Peter) ◆ 1999
9. Rescue Party (Garland, Mark A.) ◆ 1999
10. Sky Dance (Ciencin, Scott) ◆ 2000
11. Chomper (Glut, Don) ◆ 2000
12. Return to Lost City (Ciencin, Scott) ◆ 2000
13. Survive! (Strickland, Brad) ◆ 2001
14. The Explorers (Ciencin, Scott) ◆ 2001
15. Dolphin Watch (Vornholt, John) ◆ 2002
16. Oasis (Hapka, Cathy) ◆ 2002

DINOVERSE

Ciencin, Scott

RANDOM HOUSE ◆ GRADES 6–9 ◆ A/R

FANTASY

It all started when Bertram's science fair project went wacko. He and
three junior high classmates—Mike, Candayce, and Janine—travel back
to prehistoric times and become dinosaurs. They have to figure out how
to survive in their new environment. As the series progresses, other teens

have prehistoric adventures. And in one book, Bertram travels back in time while the dinosaurs come to our time. Talk about trouble!

1. I Was a Teenage T. Rex ◆ 2000
2. The Teens Time Forgot ◆ 2000
3. Raptor Without a Cause ◆ 2000
4. Please Don't Eat the Teacher! ◆ 2000
5. Beverly Hills Brontosaurus ◆ 2000
6. Dinosaurs Ate My Homework ◆ 2000

DISCWORLD

Pratchett, Terry
HARPERCOLLINS ◆ GRADES 6–12 ◆ A/R
FANTASY | HUMOR

The first four books—including *The Amazing Maurice and His Educated Rodents,* winner of the 2001 Carnegie Medal—listed here were written for readers in middle and junior high school. Older readers (grades 10 and up) will enjoy the many absorbing adult installments in this humorous fantasy set on a flat earth populated by everything from dragons to robots. *Where's My Cow?* (2005), a companion volume to *Thud!* for "people of all sizes," is a fully illustrated storybook.

1. The Amazing Maurice and His Educated Rodents ◆ 2001
2. The Wee Free Men ◆ 2003
3. A Hat Full of Sky: The Continuing Adventures of Tiffany Aching and the Wee Free Men ◆ 2004
4. Wintersmith ◆ 2006

ADULT DISCWORLD BOOKS

1. The Color of Magic ◆ 1983
2. The Light Fantastic ◆ 1986
3. Equal Rites ◆ 1987
4. Mort ◆ 1987
5. Wyrd Sisters ◆ 1988
6. Sourcery ◆ 1989
7. Pyramids ◆ 1989
8. Guards! Guards! ◆ 1989
9. Eric ◆ 1990
10. Moving Pictures ◆ 1990
11. Reaper Man ◆ 1991
12. Witches Abroad ◆ 1991
13. Lords and Ladies ◆ 1992
14. Small Gods ◆ 1992
15. Men at Arms ◆ 1993
16. Interesting Times ◆ 1994
17. Soul Music ◆ 1995

18. Maskerade ◆ 1995
19. Feet of Clay ◆ 1996
20. Hogfather ◆ 1996
21. Jingo ◆ 1997
22. The Last Continent ◆ 1998
23. Carpe Jugulum ◆ 1999
24. The Fifth Elephant ◆ 2000
25. The Truth ◆ 2000
26. Thief of Time ◆ 2001
27. The Last Hero ◆ 2001
28. Night Watch ◆ 2002
29. The Monstrous Regiment ◆ 2003
30. Going Postal ◆ 2004
31. Thud! ◆ 2005
32. Making Money ◆ 2007

DISH

Muldrow, Diane
GROSSET & DUNLAP ◆ GRADES 4–7 ◆ A/R
REAL LIFE

Amanda and Molly are 11-year-old twins who show an interest in cooking and are given cooking lessons. Later, they form a cooking club with
friends. The club becomes a business, DISH, and the children have to
deal with problems—too many customers, trying to balance school and
work, and so forth. The girls represent diverse backgrounds; for example,
Peichi helps with her family's celebration of Chinese New Year.

1. Stirring It Up ◆ 2002
2. Turning Up the Heat ◆ 2002
3. Boiling Point ◆ 2002
4. Into the Mix ◆ 2002
5. Truth Without the Trimmings ◆ 2002
6. On the Back Burner ◆ 2003
7. A Recipe for Trouble ◆ 2003
8. Lights, Camera, Cook ◆ 2003
9. Sweet-and-Sour Summer ◆ 2003
10. A Measure of Thanks ◆ 2003
11. Winner Takes the Cake ◆ 2003
12. Deep Freeze ◆ 2004
13. Working Lunch ◆ 2004

DISNEY HIGH SCHOOL MUSICAL STORIES FROM EAST HIGH *see* High School Musical Stories from East High

DISTRESS CALL 911

Carey, D. L.
SIMON & SCHUSTER ◆ GRADES 7–10
REAL LIFE

These books feature teenagers who have volunteered for emergency services. As "Yellowjackets," they end up in life-and-death situations. One volunteer is trapped in a basement during a flood. Another tries to distance himself from his former gang as they commit arson on Devil's Night. Readers who like adventure where the teens are right in the middle of the action will enjoy these books.

1. Twist of Fate ◆ 1996
2. Buried Alive ◆ 1996
3. Danger Zone ◆ 1996
4. Worth Dying For ◆ 1996
5. Million Dollar Mistake ◆ 1996
6. Roughing It ◆ 1996
7. Promise Me You'll Stop Me ◆ 1997

THE DIVAS

Murray, Victoria Christopher
POCKET ◆ GRADES 7–10
REAL LIFE | VALUES

Four friends—Diamond, India, Veronique, and Aaliyah—form a gospel music group called the Divine Divas. They are all around 15 years old and they enter the Glory 2 God Gospel Talent Search hoping to be selected as the hottest new gospel group. Each girl has a distinct personality and each is featured in one of the four books. Diamond, the leader, is also interested in fashion, while India is shy. Show this series to fans of Payton Skyy.

1. Diamond ◆ 2008
2. India ◆ 2008
3. Veronique ◆ 2009

DIVE

Korman, Gordon
SCHOLASTIC ◆ GRADES 7–10 ◆ A/R
ADVENTURE

On a summer expedition to study marine habitats, four teens find themselves in an exciting and dangerous adventure. Kaz, Star, Adriana, and

Dante find a shipwreck with a sunken treasure. Will they be able to recover the treasure? Will the sharks stop them or will human predators reach the treasure first?

1. The Discovery ◆ 2003
2. The Deep ◆ 2003
3. The Danger ◆ 2003

THE DIVIDE TRILOGY

Kay, Elizabeth

CHICKEN HOUSE ◆ GRADES 5–9 ◆ A/R

FANTASY

While on vacation on the Continental Divide in Costa Rica, Felix, 13, is transported to a magical world whose creatures consider humans to be mythical. Felix convinces Betony, an elf, that he is really a human and the two begin a quest for a magical cure for Felix's heart defect. Their search is disrupted by Snakeweed, an evil pixie. At the close of the first book, Felix is cured and returns home, but Snakeweed finds his way to our world too.

1. The Divide ◆ 2003
2. Back to the Divide ◆ 2004
3. Jinx on the Divide ◆ 2005

DOGTOWN GHETTO

Bonham, Frank

DELL ◆ GRADES 6–8 ◆ A/R

REAL LIFE

This series depicts the tough lives of children who grow up in housing projects. Keeny is proud of his Mexican heritage and wants to live up to his dead father's expectations, but he is often led astray by circumstances in his environment. The theme of feeling misunderstood will resonate with readers, and the near-journalistic depiction of street life is admirable, but readers may find much of the material dated. The first book was reissued in 1999.

1. Durango Street ◆ 1965
2. Mystery of the Fat Cat ◆ 1968
3. Golden Bees of Tulami ◆ 1974

DOLLANGANGER

Andrews, V. C.

SIMON & SCHUSTER ◆ GRADES 8–12 ◆ A/R

HORROR

Four children have been locked away. Their own mother has sinister plans for them. Now they will have their revenge. This series has had a following among teen fans of horror and violence. *Garden of Shadows* is a prequel.

1. Flowers in the Attic ◆ 1979
2. Petals on the Wind ◆ 1980
3. In There Be Thorns ◆ 1981
4. Seeds of Yesterday ◆ 1984
5. Garden of Shadows ◆ 1987

DON'T GET CAUGHT

Strasser, Todd

SCHOLASTIC ◆ GRADES 6–9 ◆ A/R

REAL LIFE

Three middle school boys—Kyle, Dusty, and Wilson—play pranks that put them in danger of being caught. Of course, they narrowly escape the attention of the bumbling adults in their school, which should add to the appeal of this series.

1. Don't Get Caught Driving the School Bus ◆ 2000
2. Don't Get Caught in the Girls' Locker Room ◆ 2001
3. Don't Get Caught in the Teachers' Lounge ◆ 2001
4. Don't Get Caught Wearing the Lunch Lady's Hairnet ◆ 2001

DON'T TOUCH THAT REMOTE!

Abbott, Tony

MINSTREL ◆ GRADES 5–7 ◆ A/R

REAL LIFE

Slapstick situations are commonplace when the middle school becomes the site for a sitcom. Spencer Babbitt and his friends must come up with enough action to keep the cameras rolling. They succeed with immature, even gross, antics that should appeal to tween readers.

1. Sitcom School ◆ 1999
2. The Fake Teacher ◆ 1999
3. Stinky Business ◆ 1999
4. Freak Week ◆ 1999

THE DOOR WITHIN TRILOGY

Batson, Wayne Thomas

THOMAS NELSON ◆ GRADES 6–9 ◆ A/R

FANTASY

After reading the ancient scrolls he found in his grandfather's basement, Aidan Thomas is transported through "The Door Within." He enters a fantasy medieval world of lords and knights in a classic battle between good and evil. Aidan begins training to be a knight in the King's Elder Guard and to protect the Realm from the warriors of Paragory. Like C. S. Lewis's Narnia books, this series has strong Christian overtones.

1. The Door Within ◆ 2005
2. The Rise of the Wyrm Lord ◆ 2006
3. The Final Storm ◆ 2006

THE DOUBLE DUTCH CLUB

Singletary, Mabel Elizabeth

LIFT EVERY VOICE ◆ GRADES 5–7

REAL LIFE | VALUES

In *Just Jump!,* Nancy Adjei watches the group of sixth-grade girls from Mrs. Richards's class jump rope on the playground. She wants to join them but she is the "new girl" whose family has just moved to the United States from Sierra Leone. When Rachel Carter asks Nancy to turn the ropes, Nancy is excited and scared, and her fear gets the best of her. She starts to turn the ropes but drops them and runs back into the school. As the book progresses, readers meet other members of this multicultural group including Tanya Gordon, who must learn to control her temper; Ming Li, whose family emigrated from China; and Carla Rodriquez. The books are filled with the importance of faith in the power of God.

1. Just Jump! ◆ 2007
2. Something to Jump About ◆ 2008
3. A Promise and a Rainbow ◆ 2008

Dragon

D'Lacey, Chris

SCHOLASTIC ◆ GRADES 7–10 ◆ A/R

FANTASY

In England, Liz Pennykettle lives with her daughter Lucy, 11. Liz makes unusual clay dragons that have special powers. When David Fain comes to room with Liz and Lucy, he receives his own dragon, Gadzooks, with the power to forecast the future. David tells stories about the dragons and, as the series progresses, he becomes involved in dragon lore. Eventually David realizes that his stories are becoming real. There is a dragon encased in an ice mountain and Gwilanna from the Fain plans to release it. This series was originally planned as a trilogy; David Fain reappears in *The Fire Eternal*.

1. The Fire Within ◆ 2005
2. Icefire ◆ 2006
3. Fire Star ◆ 2008
4. The Fire Eternal ◆ 2008

Dragon Ball

Toriyama, Akira

VIZ COMMUNICATIONS ◆ GRADES 7–10

FANTASY

Goku is a monkey-tailed boy who joins Bulma on a quest for seven Dragon Balls to give to the Eternal Dragon. This act will be rewarded with one wish. Goku and Bulma team up with Kuririn and face many enemies including ghouls, a robot, a giant octopus, Commander Blue, and the Great Demon King Piccolo. Related materials include drawing/tracing books and strategy guides.

1. Volume 1 ◆ 2003
2. Volume 2 ◆ 2003
3. Volume 3 ◆ 2003
4. Volume 4 ◆ 2003
5. Volume 5 ◆ 2003
6. Volume 6 ◆ 2003
7. Volume 7 ◆ 2003
8. Volume 8 ◆ 2003
9. Volume 9 ◆ 2003
10. Volume 10 ◆ 2003
11. Volume 11 ◆ 2003
12. Volume 12 ◆ 2003
13. Volume 13 ◆ 2003
14. Volume 14 ◆ 2004
15. Volume 15 ◆ 2004
16. Volume 16 ◆ 2004

DRAGON BALL Z

Toriyama, Akira

VIZ COMMUNICATIONS ◆ GRADES 7–10

FANTASY

Goku grows and faces many dangers in this manga series from Japan. He discovers that one enemy is his brother, Raditz. Another danger comes from Cell, a creature from the future that destroys cities and eats people. Throughout the adventures, there are time travels, special training, and magical maneuvers that help Goku and his colleagues. Related materials include drawing/tracing books and strategy guides.

1. Volume 1 ◆ 2003	14. Volume 14 ◆ 2003
2. Volume 2 ◆ 2003	15. Volume 15 ◆ 2004
3. Volume 3 ◆ 2003	16. Volume 16 ◆ 2004
4. Volume 4 ◆ 2003	17. Volume 17 ◆ 2004
5. Volume 5 ◆ 2003	18. Volume 18 ◆ 2005
6. Volume 6 ◆ 2003	19. Volume 19 ◆ 2005
7. Volume 7 ◆ 2003	20. Volume 20 ◆ 2005
8. Volume 8 ◆ 2003	21. Volume 21 ◆ 2005
9. Volume 9 ◆ 2003	22. Volume 22 ◆ 2005
10. Volume 10 ◆ 2003	23. Volume 23 ◆ 2005
11. Volume 11 ◆ 2003	24. Volume 24 ◆ 2006
12. Volume 12 ◆ 2003	25. Volume 25 ◆ 2006
13. Volume 13 ◆ 2003	26. Volume 26 ◆ 2006

DRAGON CHRONICLES

Fletcher, Susan

ATHENEUM ◆ GRADES 6–9 ◆ A/R

ADVENTURE | FANTASY

With her strange green eyes, Kaeldra, 15, is an outsider. The king of Elythian uses her ability to communicate with dragons to arrange for dragons to be killed. Kara is heartsick and runs away, joining a "Kyn" (family) of dragons. In a later book, the dragons are aided by Lyf, Kaeldra's foster sister. *Flight of the Dragon Kyn* is a prequel to *Dragon's Milk*.

1. Dragon's Milk ◆ 1989
2. Flight of the Dragon Kyn ◆ 1993
3. Sign of the Dove ◆ 1996

DRAGON KEEPER TRILOGY

Wilkinson, Carole

HYPERION ◆ GRADES 5–8 ◆ A/R

FANTASY

Ping is an orphan who is a slave serving the Emperor's Dragon Keeper, who neglects the two dragons in his care. One of the dragons dies and Ping escapes with remaining dragon Danzi and they begin a journey to the sea. Danzi, who is an aged dragon, is protecting a mysterious purple stone, which hatches into a baby purple dragon, Kai. Danzi dies, leaving Ping to protect Kai, the last of the Imperial dragons, and keep him safe from his enemies.

1. Dragon Keeper ◆ 2005
2. Garden of the Purple Dragon ◆ 2007
3. Dragon Moon ◆ 2008

DRAGON OF THE LOST SEA

Yep, Laurence

HARPERCOLLINS ◆ GRADES 6–9 ◆ A/R

FANTASY

Shimmer is able to leave the human world and transform herself into dragon form. In the first novel, she tries to redeem herself by capturing a witch with the help of Thorn, her human companion. In each book, there is a quest or adventure that Shimmer and her companions must experience.

1. Dragon of the Lost Sea ◆ 1982
2. Dragon Steel ◆ 1985
3. Dragon Cauldron ◆ 1991
4. Dragon War ◆ 1992

THE DRAGON QUARTET

Kellogg, Marjorie

DAW ◆ GRADES 7–12

FANTASY

Four dragons—Earth, Water, Fire, and Air—may hold the future of the world in their hands in this series with an environmental focus on a future America. In the third book, Fire rebels and in the last book Earth and Water struggle to rescue Air and to control Fire's dangerous actions.

1. The Book of Earth ◆ 1995
2. The Book of Water ◆ 1997
3. The Book of Fire ◆ 2000
4. The Book of Air ◆ 2003

DRAGONBACK

Zahn, Timothy

TOR; STARSCAPE ◆ GRADES 7–10

SCIENCE FICTION

Fourteen-year-old Jack Morgan, an orphan, has been accused of a crime he did not commit and hides out in his uncle's spaceship on a remote planet. There he meets up with Draycos, a dragonlike poet-warrior who depends on a symbiotic host. The two join forces to clear Jack's name and to track down mercenaries threatening Draycos's race. They have a series of dangerous adventures laced with humor.

1. Dragon and Thief ◆ 2003
2. Dragon and Soldier ◆ 2004
3. Dragon and Slave ◆ 2005
4. Dragon and Herdsman ◆ 2006
5. Dragon and Judge ◆ 2007
6. Dragon and Liberator ◆ 2008

DRAGONCROWN WAR CYCLE

Stackpole, Michael A.

BANTAM ◆ GRADES 10–12

FANTASY

An evil sorceress named Chytrine rules the city of Yslin. Will, a young thief, discovers to his surprise that he holds the key to overthrowing this brutal regime. In the second book, Will and a varied cast of rebels band together to resist Chytrine's renewed attacks in her search for pieces of the DragonCrown. This adult series is recommended for mature teens. *The Dark Glory War* (2000) is a prelude.

1. Fortress Draconis ◆ 2001
2. When Dragons Rage ◆ 2002
3. The Grand Crusade ◆ 2003

DRAGONFLIGHT

Various authors

SIMON & SCHUSTER ◆ GRADES 7–10 ◆ A/R

FANTASY

The books in this series all have a supernatural element that adds to the danger and mystery. Shape shifters, time travel, mind transfers, nightmares, spirit visions, encounters with a vampire, and more. Three of the books—*Black Unicorn, Gold Unicorn,* and *Red Unicorn*—feature a character named Tanaquil, who is the daughter of a sorceress.

1. Letters from Atlantis (Silverberg, Robert) ◆ 1990
2. Black Unicorn (Lee, Tanith) ◆ 1991
3. The Sleep of Stone (Cooper, Louise) ◆ 1991
4. Child of an Ancient City (Williams, Tad) ◆ 1992
5. Dragon's Plunder (Strickland, Brad) ◆ 1992
6. The Dreaming Place (De Lint, Charles) ◆ 1992
7. Wishing Season (Friesner, Esther M.) ◆ 1993
8. The Wizard's Apprentice (Somtow, S. P.) ◆ 1993
9. Gold Unicorn (Lee, Tanith) ◆ 1994
10. Born of Elven Blood (Anderson, Kevin J.) ◆ 1995
11. The Monster's Legacy (Norton, Andre) ◆ 1996
12. The Orphan's Tent (De Haven, Tom) ◆ 1996
13. Monet's Ghost (Yarbro, Chelsea Quinn) ◆ 1997
14. Red Unicorn (Lee, Tanith) ◆ 1997

DRAGONLANCE DEFENDERS OF MAGIC

Kirchoff, Mary L.

WIZARDS OF THE COAST ◆ GRADES 9–12

FANTASY

The land of Krynn has three moons. When they form a line in the sky, it is the Night of the Eye. On this night, Guerrand DiThon leaves his betrothed to begin a search for wizardly powers in the Tower of Wayreth. Eventually, he becomes the High Defender of Bastion, but evil forces seek to destroy him. There are many Dragonlance books connected with the role-playing games.

1. Night of the Eye ◆ 1994
2. The Medusa Plague ◆ 1994
3. The Seventh Sentinel ◆ 1995

DRAGONLANCE DWARVEN NATIONS TRILOGY

Parkinson, Dan

WIZARDS OF THE COAST ◆ GRADES 9–12

FANTASY

Fans of the Dragonlance role-playing games will read these books set in the land of Krynn. The dwarven clans come together to secure the survival of their race. There are many Dragonlance books connected with the role-playing games.

1. The Covenant of the Forge ◆ 1993
2. Hammer and Axe ◆ 1993
3. The Swordsheath Scroll ◆ 1994

DRAGONMASTER

Bunch, Chris

ORBIT ◆ GRADES 9–12

FANTASY

As this series begins, Hal Kailas, 13, is fascinated with dragons. Years pass and Hal becomes a Dragonmaster and joins the dragon fliers. His goal is to avenge the deaths of his comrades in the war against the Roche.

1. Storm of Wings ◆ 2003
2. Knighthood of the Dragon ◆ 2003
3. The Last Battle ◆ 2004

DRAGONS IN OUR MIDST

Davis, Bryan

LIVING INK BOOKS ◆ GRADES 6–10 ◆ A/R

FANTASY | VALUES

Two teens, Bonnie and Billy, realize that they have special skills. Billy's father is a dragon and as Billy matures, he develops more dragon-like behaviors. Billy is shocked when he learns of his heritage. Bonnie has known about her dragon side and she joins with Billy to face the evil forces that threaten their world. Throughout the series the characters rely on their faith to guide them and give them courage in the face of all obstacles.

1. Raising Dragons ◆ 2004

2. The Candlestone ◆ 2004
3. Circles of Seven ◆ 2005
4. Tears of a Dragon ◆ 2005

DRAGONS IN OUR MIDST: ORACLES OF FIRE

Davis, Bryan

AMG PUBLISHERS; LIVING INK BOOKS ◆ GRADES 6–10 ◆ A/R

FANTASY | VALUES

This prequel series explores the time before Dragons in Our Midst.

1. Eye of the Oracle ◆ 2006
2. Enoch's Ghost ◆ 2007
3. The Last of the Nephilim ◆ 2008

DRAGONS OF DELTORA *see* Deltora: Dragons of Deltora

DRAGONSBANE HORN TRILOGY *see* Knightscares

DRAGONSPAWN CYCLE

Garrison, Terie

FLUX ◆ GRADES 7–9

FANTASY

Donavah, 15, studies at the Roylinn Academy. When her brother Breyard finds and hatches a dragon egg, he is arrested by the Royal Guards and sentenced to death. It is the law that only King Erno may have dragons. Donavah is sent away and learns of a dragon prophecy that leads her to develop her maejic powers even though maejic has been outlawed too. As the series progresses, Donavah joins with the red dragon Xyla to try and fulfill the prophecy.

1. AutumnQuest ◆ 2006
2. WinterMaejic ◆ 2007
3. SpringFire ◆ 2007
4. SummerDanse ◆ 2007

DRAMA!

Ruditis, Paul
SIMON PULSE ◆ GRADES 10–12 ◆ A/R
REAL LIFE

At Orion Academy in Malibu, California, auditions for the school play are highly competitive. There is so much pressure to be the star that four girls are cast as Dorothy for *The Wizard of Oz*. Bryan is a boy on the outside who is observing the action; he is also struggling with his identity as a gay teen. He describes the rehearsals and the strange events that are threatening each Dorothy. In *Entrances and Exits*, Bryan is directing one of the student-written one-act plays. The action onstage is heating up between Sam (a girl) and Jason, which causes problems on the part of Sam's boyfriend, Eric. Fans of the Gossip Girl books will enjoy this series.

1. The Four Dorothys ◆ 2007
2. Everyone's a Critic ◆ 2007
3. Show, Don't Tell ◆ 2008
4. Entrances and Exits ◆ 2008

DRAMA CLUB

Lerangis, Peter
PUFFIN ◆ GRADES 9–12 ◆ A/R
REAL LIFE

In the first book, Casey Chang, a new student at Ridgeport High, gets involved in the school's Drama Club and experiences the everyday drama of being in high school. Subsequent books feature other students and their problems. There is a variety of characters, including divas, jocks, a homosexual teen, and technology geeks. The plots revolve around the club's productions, even touching on censorship when there is community reaction to one of the plays. With the popularity of the Disney High School Musical movies and the related Stories from East High books, this series should find an audience.

1. The Fall Musical ◆ 2007
2. The Big Production ◆ 2007
3. Too Hot! ◆ 2008
4. Summer Love ◆ 2008

DRAMA HIGH

Devine, L.
DAFINA ◆ GRADES 10–12
REAL LIFE

African American Jayd Jackson, 16, lives in a neighborhood where crack addicts and drive-by shootings are common. Along with some other kids from the 'hood, she attends a mostly white high school in a wealthy part of Los Angeles. This series follows Jayd through relationships and confrontations. Her former boyfriend, KJ, is now with Trecee, who wants to fight Jayd. Later Jayd begins an interracial romance with a wealthy white boy, Jeremy. The "drama" in this book is not connected to theater but to the everyday dramatic events in Jayd's life.

1. The Fight ◆ 2006
2. Second Chance ◆ 2006
3. Jayd's Legacy ◆ 2007
4. Frenemies ◆ 2008
5. Lady J ◆ 2008
6. Courtin' Jayd ◆ 2008

DREAM SERIES

Various authors

SCOBRE PRESS ◆ GRADES 6–12 ◆ A/R

RECREATION

Each of these books features characters involved in sports who are also trying to deal with problems in their own lives. In *The Highest Stand,* Dede is on the outside until he begins to run in hurdle races. He hopes to win the race and the acceptance of his peers. *Hoop City* features African American twins who confront a tragedy when Mike is paralyzed. His brother, Tony, is inspired to achieve. Different sports (including soccer, tennis, football, golf, and more) involving males and females provide the foundation for these inspiring stories. The grade level varies among the books from middle school through young adults.

1. The Road to the Majors (Blumenthal, Scott) ◆ 2001
2. Hoop City (Blumenthal, Scott) ◆ 2002
3. Keeper (Sloan, Holly Goldberg) ◆ 2002
4. Chasing the King (Stein, Joshua) ◆ 2003
5. The Green (Reichman, Justin) ◆ 2003
6. The Highest Stand (Campbell, Tonie) ◆ 2003
7. The Kid from Courage (Berman, Ron) ◆ 2003
8. Long Shot (Fowler, Marie) ◆ 2003
9. The Long Way Around (Hand, Jimmie) ◆ 2003

DREAMHOUSE KINGS

Liparulo, Robert

THOMAS NELSON ◆ GRADES 9–12

FANTASY

The King family has moved from Los Angeles into an old Victorian house in a small town and the kids are disappointed. Xander, 15, and his siblings David and Toria are not impressed with the new town, although they are fascinated as they explore the rooms in the old house. Then strange things begin to happen. The kids realize that the doors in the house are portals to other times and places. In *Watcher in the Woods,* their mother has been kidnapped and taken through one of the portals, but which one? The author has a contest for readers to suggest new locations for the portals to lead. Visit www.dreamhousekings.com.

1. House of Dark Shadows ◆ 2008
2. Watcher in the Woods ◆ 2008
3. Gatekeepers ◆ 2009

DRIFTX

Strasser, Todd

SIMON PULSE ◆ GRADES 9–12

REAL LIFE

Kennin, 17, and his older sister move to Las Vegas to be near their father, who is in prison. Kennin becomes involved in "drifitng," a fast and dangerous form of car racing. Because he is underage, he begins by racing *tsuios,* illegal races involving bets and money. His skill is amazing. Even though he is winning and making a lot of money, Kennin wants to enter legitimate races. An opportunity to fix a race for a big payoff leaves Kennin with a dilemma.

1. Slide or Die ◆ 2006
2. Battle Drift ◆ 2006
3. Sidewayz Glory ◆ 2006

DUNGEONS AND DRAGONS: ENDLESS QUEST

Various authors

TSR; WIZARDS OF THE COAST ◆ GRADES 9–12

FANTASY

You are Caric, a fighter lured into a dungeon of treasure; you are Landon, an elf . . . ; you are Jaimie, a villager . . . . These are some of the scenarios in these books that connect to the Dungeons and Dragons game worlds. Elves, goblins, ogres, and other creatures try to keep you from your mission. Readers make choices (as in Choose Your Own Adventure books). In the first series, most of the books use Dungeons and Dragons settings. In the second series, most of the settings are from Advanced

Dungeon and Dragons games. Both series contain books that link to other game worlds.

THE FIRST SERIES

1. Dungeon of Dread (Estes, Rose) ◆ 1982
2. Mountain of Mirrors (Estes, Rose) ◆ 1982
3. Pillars of Pentegarn (Estes, Rose) ◆ 1982
4. Return to Brookmere (Estes, Rose) ◆ 1982
5. Revolt of the Dwarves (Estes, Rose) ◆ 1983
6. Revenge of the Rainbow Dragons (Estes, Rose) ◆ 1983
7. Hero of Washington Square (Estes, Rose) ◆ 1983
8. Villains of Volturnus (Blashfield, Jean) ◆ 1983
9. Robbers and Robots (Carr, Mike) ◆ 1983
10. Circus of Fear (Estes, Rose) ◆ 1983
11. Spell of the Winter Wizard (Lowery, Linda) ◆ 1983
12. Light on Quests Mountain (Kirchoff, Mary L.) ◆ 1983
13. Dragon of Doom (Estes, Rose) ◆ 1983
14. Raid on Nightmare Castle (McGuire, Catherine) ◆ 1983
15. Under Dragon's Wing (Kendall, John) ◆ 1983
16. Dragon's Ransom (French, Laura) ◆ 1983
17. Captive Planet (Simon, Morris) ◆ 1984
18. King's Quest (McGowen, Tom) ◆ 1984
19. Conan the Undaunted (Ward, James Michael) ◆ 1984
20. Conan and the Prophecy (Moore, Roger E.) ◆ 1984
21. Duel of the Masters (Martindale, Chris) ◆ 1984
22. Endless Catacombs (Weis, Margaret Baldwin) ◆ 1984
23. Blade of the Young Samurai (Simon, Morris) ◆ 1984
24. Trouble on Artule (McGuire, Catherine) ◆ 1984
25. Conan the Outlaw (Moore, Roger E.) ◆ 1985
26. Tarzan and the Well of Slaves (Niles, Douglas) ◆ 1985
27. Lair of the Lich (Algozin, Bruce) ◆ 1985
28. Mystery of the Ancients (Simon, Morris) ◆ 1985
29. Tower of Darkness (Fultz, Regina Oehler) ◆ 1985
30. Fireseed (Simon, Morris) ◆ 1985
31. Tarzan and the Tower of Diamonds (Reinsmith, Richard) ◆ 1986
32. Prisoner of Elderwood (Algozin, Bruce) ◆ 1986
33. Knights of Illusion (Kirchoff, Mary L.) ◆ 1986
34. Claw of the Dragon (Algozin, Bruce) ◆ 1986
35. Vision of Doom (Kirchoff, Mary L.) ◆ 1987
36. Song of the Dark Druid (Sherman, Josepha) ◆ 1987

THE SECOND SERIES

1. Dungeon of Fear (Andrews, Michael) ◆ 1994
2. Castle of the Undead (Baron, Nick) ◆ 1994
3. Secret of the Djinn (Rabe, Jean) ◆ 1994
4. Siege of the Tower (Antilles, Kem) ◆ 1994
5. A Wild Ride (Anderson, Louis) ◆ 1994
6. Forest of Darkness (Andrews, Michael) ◆ 1994

7. American Knights (Pollotta, Nick) ◆ 1995
8. Night of the Tiger (Rabe, Jean) ◆ 1995
9. Galactic Challenge (Varney, Allen) ◆ 1995
10. Bigby's Curse (Brown, Anne) ◆ 1995
11. The 24-Hour War (Pollotta, Nick) ◆ 1995
12. The Test (Nicholson, Wes) ◆ 1996
13. Sands of Deception (Rabe, Jean) ◆ 1996

DUNGEONS AND DRAGONS: FORGOTTEN REALMS—THE LAST MYTHAL

Baker, Richard

WIZARDS OF THE COAST ◆ GRADES 9–12

FANTASY

A society of elves who have lived apart from the Forgotten Realms want to return to the mainstream. They face threats and danger as they try to complete their journey. Forgotten Realms is one of the original settings for Dungeons and Dragons.

1. Forsaken House ◆ 2004
2. Farthest Reach ◆ 2005
3. Final Gate ◆ 2006

DUNGEONS AND DRAGONS: KNIGHTS OF THE SILVER DRAGON

Various authors

WIZARDS OF THE COAST ◆ GRADES 5–8 ◆ A/R

FANTASY

Set in the world of Greyhawk, a fantasy world of Dungeons and Dragons, three kids solve mysteries and face magical forces and creatures. Kellach, 14, is an apprentice wizard who is smart but self-centered. His younger brother, Driskoll, 12, is always ready to stand up for what he believes is right. Moyra, 13, is a thief whose live has been a struggle and, as a result, she is resilient and brave. The three are unlikely partners protecting the city of Curston.

1. Secret of the Spiritkeeper (Forbeck, Matt) ◆ 2004
2. Riddle in Stone (Soesbee, Ree) ◆ 2004
3. Sign of the Shapeshifter (Donovan, Dale, and Linda Johns) ◆ 2004
4. Eye of Fortune (Graham, Denise R.) ◆ 2004
5. Figure in the Frost (Perez, Lana) ◆ 2005
6. Dagger of Doom (Roberts, Kerry Daniel) ◆ 2005
7. Hidden Dragon (Trumbauer, Lisa Trutkoff) ◆ 2005
8. The Silver Spell (Banerjee, Anjali) ◆ 2005

9. Key to the Griffon's Lair (Ransom, Candice) ◆ 2005
10. Curse of the Lost Grove (Graham, Denise R.) ◆ 2005
11. Mystery of the Wizard's Tomb (Plummer, Rachel) ◆ 2006
12. Mark of the Yuan-Ti (Roberts, Kerry Daniel) ◆ 2006
13. Revelations, Part 1: Prophecy of the Dragons (Forbeck, Matt) ◆ 2006
14. Revelations, Part 2: The Dragons Revealed (Forbeck, Matt) ◆ 2006

EAGER

Fox, Helen

WENDY LAMB BOOKS/HODDER BOOKS ◆ GRADES 6–9 ◆ A/R

SCIENCE FICTION

The Bell family's robot, Grumps, needs to be replaced. The family decides to get a new robot named Eager. Eager has been secretly programmed to learn about humans and their world. England in the late 21st century is technologically advanced but there is a problem. Some of the robots seem to be rebelling against their human owners. Eager and the Bell children have to rescue the head of LifeCorp, a technology conglomerate. In *Eager's Nephew,* Eager and some of the other robots have evolved to be more independent from humans and the government wants to destroy them.

1. Eager ◆ 2004
2. Eager's Nephew ◆ 2006
3. Eager and the Mermaid ◆ 2007

EARTHSEA

Le Guin, Ursula K.

ATHENEUM ◆ GRADES 7–8 ◆ A/R

FANTASY

Readers who enjoy Tolkien's Middle Earth books and the Narnia books by C. S. Lewis will enjoy this journey into the realm of wizards and dragons. This fantasy world is full of strong characters and powerful language and features Sparrowhawk, apprentice to a master wizard. As in many fantasies, there is a confrontation with the powers of darkness, and the realization that some of the most dangerous evils come from within. *Tales of Earthsea* (2001) is a collection of five Earthsea stories.

1. A Wizard of Earthsea ◆ 1968
2. The Tombs of Atuan ◆ 1971
3. The Farthest Shore ◆ 1972
4. Tehanu ◆ 1990
5. The Other Wind ◆ 2001

ECHO FALLS MYSTERY

Abrahams, Peter

HARPERCOLLINS ◆ **GRADES 6–9** ◆ **A/R**

MYSTERY

Mix Sherlock Holmes with theater acting, soccer, middle school, and mysteries and you have the makings of an exciting series. Ingrid Levin-Hill, 13, is in eighth grade when she becomes involved in the murder investigation of an eccentric woman. Ingrid loves reading Sherlock Holmes and she applies the detective's techniques to her own questions about the crime. In addition to attending middle school, Ingrid is starring as Alice in a production of "Alice in Wonderland" and Ingrid's own life takes on a surreal quality as she moves closer to solving the murder. Readers may want to read Enola Holmes, another Holmes-related series featuring Sherlock and Mycroft's younger sister.

1. Down the Rabbit Hole ◆ 2005
2. Behind the Curtain ◆ 2006
3. Into the Dark ◆ 2008

ECHORIUM SEQUENCE

Roberts, Katherine

CHICKEN HOUSE ◆ **GRADES 6–9** ◆ **A/R**

FANTASY

Echorium is the Land of Echoes. Three students—Rialle, Kherron, and Frenn—are learning to be Singers so their songs will influence the thoughts and feelings of other beings. The world is filled with strange creatures and conflicts. The events in the second and third books take place decades after those in the first.

1. Song Quest ◆ 2001
2. Crystal Mask ◆ 2001
3. Dark Quetzal ◆ 2003

EDGAR AND ELLEN

Ogden, Charles

TRICYCLE PRESS ◆ **GRADES 4–7** ◆ **A/R**

HUMOR

Edgar and Ellen are 12-year-old twins. They live in a dilapidated mansion and enjoy creating chaos. For example, they decorate the neighbor's pets and try to sell them as exotic animals. The *Edgar and Ellen Mischief*

Manual (2007) is a guide to planning and perpetrating pranks. This series might be a choice for the fans of Lemony Snicket.

1. Rare Beasts ◆ 2003
2. Tourist Trap ◆ 2004
3. Under Town ◆ 2004
4. Pet's Revenge ◆ 2005
5. High Wire ◆ 2006
6. Nod's Limbs ◆ 2007
7. Frost Bites ◆ 2008
8. Split Ends ◆ 2009

EDGAR FONT'S HUNT FOR A HOUSE TO HAUNT

Doyle, Patrick

ARMADILLO BOOKS ◆ GRADES 4–7

FANTASY

Eccentric, elderly Edgar Font is looking for just the right place to haunt. In the first book, joined by his grandchildren, Audrey and Garrett, he explores an abandoned lighthouse that is already being haunted by a spirit that wants to be free.

1. The Castle Tower Lighthouse ◆ 2006
2. The Fakersville Power Station ◆ 2007
3. The Flint Island Treehouse ◆ 2008

EDGE CHRONICLES

Stewart, Paul, and Chris Riddell

DAVID FICKLING ◆ GRADES 5–9 ◆ A/R

FANTASY

The first three books in the Edge Chronicles feature Twig, 13, whose mother, a wood troll, reveals that she found him when he was a baby. So begins Twig's quest for his true identity, eventually leading him to his father, Cloud Wolf, a captain of the sky pirates. Twig assists his father in the search for stormphrax, a substance necessary to keep the floating city of Sanctaphrax from drifting away. The fourth book, *The Curse of the Gloamglozer,* is a prequel and describes the early lives of Twig's parents. The fifth book, *The Last of the Sky Pirates,* begins the Rook Barkwater sequence, featuring a knight librarian who challenges Vox Verlix plans to take over Edgeworld. Books 8 and 9 return to the early exploits of Twig's father. This British import has all the elements of a classic fantasy: a clearly defined setting—the Edge with the Deepwoods and a floating city, Sanctaphrax; a character on a quest—Twig searching for his identity and his destiny; and encounters with unusual creatures—sky pirates, spindlebugs, and gloamglozers. This should appeal to fans of Tolkein and other intricate fantasies.

1. Beyond the Deepwoods ◆ 2004
2. Stormchaser ◆ 2004
3. Midnight Over Sanctaphrax ◆ 2004
4. The Curse of the Gloamglozer ◆ 2005
5. The Last of the Sky Pirates ◆ 2005
6. Vox ◆ 2005
7. Freeglader ◆ 2006
8. The Winter Knights ◆ 2007
9. Clash of the Sky Galleons ◆ 2007

EERIE INDIANA

Various authors

AVON CAMELOT ◆ GRADES 5–8

HORROR | MYSTERY

Marshall Teller and his family have left the crowded, noisy, crime-filled streets of a New Jersey city to live the bucolic small-town life in Eerie, Indiana. What a mistake! This town is not normal. Weird things happen here, like the release of characters from a cryogenic store—including Jesse James. Then, there is a dollhouse that looks like a real house and a doll that looks like a real girl and Marshall seems to be getting smaller. This series mixes the horror genre with bizarre situations that many readers will find amusing.

1. Return to Foreverware (Ford, Mike) ◆ 1997
2. Bureau of Lost (Peel, John) ◆ 1997
3. The Eerie Triangle (Ford, Mike) ◆ 1997
4. Simon and Marshall's Excellent Adventure (Peel, John) ◆ 1997
5. Have Yourself an Eerie Little Christmas (Ford, Mike) ◆ 1997
6. Fountain of Weird (Shahan, Sherry) ◆ 1998
7. Attack of the Two-Ton Tomatoes (Ford, Mike) ◆ 1998
8. Who Framed Alice Prophet? (Ford, Mike) ◆ 1998
9. Bring Me a Dream (James, Robert) ◆ 1998
10. Finger-Lickin' Strange (Roberts, Jeremy) ◆ 1998
11. The Dollhouse that Time Forgot (Ford, Mike) ◆ 1998
12. They Say (Ford, Mike) ◆ 1998
13. Switching Channels (Ford, Mike) ◆ 1998
14. The Incredible Shrinking Stanley (James, Robert) ◆ 1998
15. Halloweird (Ford, Mike) ◆ 1998
16. Eerie in the Mirror (James, Robert) ◆ 1998
17. We Wish You an Eerie Christmas (James, Robert) ◆ 1998

EGERTON HALL NOVELS

Geras, Adèle

HARCOURT ◆ GRADES 9–12 ◆ A/R

REAL LIFE

Megan, Bella, and Alice become friends at an exclusive British girls' school in the early 1960s. The clash between their secluded school surroundings and the often harsh nature of the outside world provides the basis for many of the plots. The girls confront jealous stepmothers, family curses, and first loves over the course of the series, which uses fairy tales as a foundation. *Pictures of the Night*, for example, is based on the story of Snow White.

1. The Tower Room ◆ 1990
2. Watching the Roses ◆ 1991
3. Pictures of the Night ◆ 1992

ELFQUEST

Pini, Wendy, and Richard Pini

DC COMICS ◆ GRADES 9–12

FANTASY

This graphic novel fantasy series first appeared in the 1970s and has been reissued in small, manga-sized paperbacks. The series focuses on Chief Cutter, a tribal leader whose mythological heritage provides guidance for his people. The elves have been isolated and secure. The problems begin when humans move too close to the elves.

1. EflQuest: Wolfrider: Vol. 1 ◆ 2003
2. ElfQuest: Archives: Vol. 1 ◆ 2003
3. ElfQuest: The Grand Quest: Vol. 1 ◆ 2004
4. ElfQuest: The Grand Quest: Vol. 2 ◆ 2004
5. ElfQuest: The Grand Quest: Vol. 3 ◆ 2004
6. ElfQuest: The Grand Quest: Vol. 4 ◆ 2004
7. ElfQuest: The Grand Quest: Vol. 5 ◆ 2004
8. ElfQuest: The Grand Quest: Vol. 6 ◆ 2004
9. ElfQuest: The Grand Quest: Vol. 7 ◆ 2004
10. ElfQuest: The Grand Quest: Vol. 8 ◆ 2004
11. ElfQuest: The Searcher and the Sword ◆ 2004
12. ElfQuest: Archives: Vol. 2 ◆ 2005
13. ElfQuest: The Grand Quest: Vol. 9 ◆ 2005
14. ElfQuest: The Grand Quest: Vol. 10 ◆ 2005
15. ElfQuest: The Grand Quest: Vol. 11 ◆ 2005
16. ElfQuest: The Grand Quest: Vol. 12 ◆ 2005
17. ElfQuest: The Grand Quest: Vol. 13 ◆ 2006

ELLEN FREMEDON

Givner, Joan
GROUNDWOOD ◆ GRADES 5–7
REAL LIFE

Ellen, 11, expects to spend a quiet summer in Partridge Cove writing a
novel but things heat up when her family protests a new housing development and threats are made against Ellen and her twin brothers. In the
second book, Ellen uncovers some shocking stories when she starts a
newspaper with her best friend Jenny. These are thoughtful books, with
the first-person narrative revealing Ellen's emotions and growing maturity as the series progresses.

1. Ellen Fremedon ◆ 2004
2. Ellen Fremedon, Journalist ◆ 2005
3. Ellen Fremedon, Volunteer ◆ 2007

THE ELLIE CHRONICLES

Marsden, John
SCHOLASTIC ◆ GRADES 8–12
ADVENTURE

Ellie Linton, 16, last seen in Marsden's Tomorrow series, is featured in
these books. The war is over, but there is still looting and violence. Her
parents have been killed by marauders and Ellie faces decisions about her
future. She decides to keep her family's farm even though it will be a
struggle. Her friend Homer is involved with a vigilante group. When
Homer is captured by terrorists, Ellie is involved in his rescue.

1. While I Live ◆ 2007
2. Incurable ◆ 2008
3. Circle of Flight ◆ 2009

THE ELLIOTT COUSINS

Thesman, Jean
AVON ◆ GRADES 7–8
REAL LIFE

Jamie, Meredith, and Teresa are cousins and very close friends. They
meet at an annual family reunion and help each other with problems,
especially those with boys. Teresa is shy and her mother is overprotective,
so when she meets a new boy named Ian her insecurities almost keep her
from making friends with him and getting her first kiss. Jamie is afraid to

tell her boyfriend that she wants to see other people. Meredith is still getting over being betrayed by her boyfriend and her (former) best friend. These are romances that will appeal to junior high girls.

1. Jamie ◆ 1998
2. Meredith ◆ 1998
3. Teresa ◆ 1998

ELSIE EDWARDS

DeClements, Barthe

VIKING ◆ GRADES 4–8 ◆ A/R

REAL LIFE

Elsie Edwards and Jenny Sawyer become friends in fifth grade. This series chronicles their progress through the awkward middle school years. Elsie grows from an overweight fifth-grader to a slim ninth-grader, gaining self-confidence along the way. The girls in this series have typical concerns—school, family, and "fitting in"—and the books reinforce the importance of self-esteem and the value of friendship. Elsie and Jenny make cameo appearances in *Sixth Grade Can Really Kill You* (1985), which may attract readers to that book, too.

1. Nothing's Fair in Fifth Grade ◆ 1981
2. How Do You Lose Those Ninth Grade Blues? ◆ 1983
3. Seventeen and In-Between ◆ 1984

EMILY WILLIAMS

Maxwell, Katie

DORCHESTER PUBLISHING ◆ GRADES 10–12

REAL LIFE

Emily Williams, 16, has moved with her family from Seattle to a small town in England. She is appalled and writes her observations in emails to her best friend. Yet, even as Emily disses her provincial surroundings, she is really not ready for the drinking and sexual activity (aka snogging) of her new friends. In the second book, Emily is spending a month on a sheep farm in Scotland. In the third book, she spends spring break in Paris. Show this series to readers of Louise Rennison's Confessions of Georgia Nicolson series.

1. The Year My Life Went Down the Loo ◆ 2003
2. They Wear What Under Their Kilts ◆ 2004
3. What's French for "EW"? ◆ 2004
4. The Taming of the Dru ◆ 2004

EMILY WINDSNAP

Kessler, Liz

CANDLEWICK ◆ GRADES 4–7

FANTASY

When 12-year-old Emily Windsnap's mother finally lets her take swimming lessons, Emily realizes she is half mermaid and longs to meet her father. In the second book, Liz, reunited with her father and now living on an island where humans and mer-people coexist, endangers the community by waking a sleeping monster. Details of life underwater and the appealing illustrations will draw readers in.

1. The Tail of Emily Windsnap ◆ 2004
2. Emily Windsnap and the Monster from the Deep ◆ 2006
3. Emily Windsnap and the Castle in the Mist ◆ 2007

EMORTALITY

Stableford, Brian

ST. MARTIN'S PRESS ◆ GRADES 9–12

SCIENCE FICTION

In a 22nd-century world of plenty, Damon Hart, son of the inventor of the artificial womb, is under attack from those who accuse his father of wrongdoing. This series, written for adults, looks at biotechnology, longevity, and the spread of the human race. In *Dark Ararat,* colonists arriving on a supposedly habitable planet tackle a number of challenges.

1. Inherit the Earth ◆ 1998
2. Architects of Emortality ◆ 1999
3. The Fountains of Youth ◆ 2000
4. The Cassandra Complex ◆ 2001
5. Dark Ararat ◆ 2002
6. The Omega Expedition ◆ 2002

ENCHANTED FOREST CHRONICLES

Wrede, Patricia C.

HARCOURT; SCHOLASTIC ◆ GRADES 4–7 ◆ A/R

FANTASY

Sensing the boredom that awaits her if she marries Prince Therandil as her parents require, reluctant princess Cimorene escapes to the Enchanted Forest to meet Kazul, King of the Dragons. With the dragons, Cimorene finally experiences the adventure she craves. Throughout the series, Cimorene and Kazul confront wicked wizards to save the forest.

1. Dealing with Dragons ◆ 1990
2. Searching for Dragons ◆ 1991
3. Calling on Dragons ◆ 1993
4. Talking to Dragons ◆ 1993

ENCHANTED HEARTS

Various authors

AVON ◆ GRADES 7–12 ◆ A/R

FANTASY

Romance with a touch of the supernatural is the focus of these books. Gina realizes her family's house is haunted. Emily gets some help with a witch. Colleen must choose between Kevin and Luke—will hypnosis help?

1. The Haunted Heart (Bennett, Cherie) ◆ 1999
2. Eternally Yours (Baker, Jennifer) ◆ 1999
3. Lost and Found (Dokey, Cameron) ◆ 1999
4. Love Potion (Quin-Harkin, Janet) ◆ 1999
5. Spellbound (Karas, Phyllis) ◆ 1999
6. Love Him Forever (Bennett, Cherie) ◆ 1999

ENDER WIGGIN

Card, Orson Scott

TOM DOHERTY ASSOCIATES; TOR ◆ GRADES 9–12 ◆ A/R

SCIENCE FICTION

Ender Wiggin is selected to attend a special school that will hone his computer talents. Although he is just a child, he has the skills to command the Earth fleet that is the last defense against an alien race. After these experiences, Ender tries to prevent war from starting in *Speaker for the Dead*. *First Meetings in the Enderverse* (Tor, 2003) includes *Ender's Game* and three novellas about Ender.

1. Ender's Game ◆ 1985
2. Speaker for the Dead ◆ 1986
3. Xenocide ◆ 1991
4. Children of the Mind ◆ 1996
5. Ender's Shadow ◆ 1999
6. Shadow of the Hegemon ◆ 2001
7. Shadow Puppets ◆ 2002
8. Shadow of the Giant ◆ 2005
9. A War of Gifts: An Ender Story ◆ 2007
10. Ender in Exile ◆ 2008

ENDLESS QUEST *see* Dungeons and Dragons: Endless Quest

ENOLA HOLMES

Springer, Nancy

PHILOMEL ◆ GRADES 5–8 ◆ A/R

MYSTERY | HISTORICAL

Meet Enola Holmes, 14, is the much younger sister of Sherlock and Mycroft Holmes. When Enola's mother disappears, her brothers arrive at the estate determined to solve the mystery. Enola thwarts their plan to send her to boarding school and sets off for London. Life in Victorian England is difficult for women and Enola faces many challenges and another mystery—the disappearance of a young marquess. Readers will relate to Enola's independent spirit and will enjoy solving the clues throughout the books.

1. The Case of the Missing Marquess: An Enola Holmes Mystery ◆ 2006
2. The Case of the Left-handed Lady: An Enola Holmes Mystery ◆ 2007
3. The Case of the Bizarre Bouquets: An Enola Holmes Mystery ◆ 2008
4. The Case of the Peculiar Pink Fan: An Enola Holmes Mystery ◆ 2008

EVEREST

Korman, Gordon

SCHOLASTIC ◆ GRADES 6–9 ◆ A/R

ADVENTURE

Climbing Mount Everest. It's dangerous. It's deadly. Especially if you are one of four teens hoping to be the youngest to reach the summit. It's even more difficult when one member of the expedition is a saboteur.

1. The Contest ◆ 2002
2. The Climb ◆ 2002
3. The Summit ◆ 2002

EVERWOOD

Various authors

SIMON & SCHUSTER ◆ GRADES 7–12

REAL LIFE

Ephram Brown is a teenager whose life seems normal. He's close to his mom and distant from his dad, a neurosurgeon who is busy with work.

When his mom dies in an accident, Ephram's father moves the family to Everwood, Colorado. After living in New York City, this small town seems dull . . . until he meets Amy. But Amy has a boyfriend who is in a coma and Dr. Brown is going to operate on him. This series parallels the popular television series.

1. First Impressions (Burns, Laura J., and Melinda Metz) ◆ 2004
2. Moving On (Harrison, Emma) ◆ 2004
3. Love Under Wraps (Harrison, Emma) ◆ 2004
4. Making Choices (Burns, Laura J., and Melinda Metz) ◆ 2004
5. Slipping Away (Harrison, Emma) ◆ 2005
6. Worlds Apart (Burns, Laura J., and Melinda Metz) ◆ 2006
7. Under Pressure (Mericle, Wendy) ◆ 2007
8. Change of Plans (Burns, Laura J., and Melinda Metz) ◆ 2007

EVERWORLD

Applegate, K. A.
SCHOLASTIC ◆ GRADES 7–12 ◆ A/R

FANTASY

Five high schoolers are drawn into adventures in a parallel universe. They encounter monsters, mythological characters, and magic. In the first book, Senna has been captured by a wolflike creature. David and his friends enter a strange and dangerous place to try to rescue her.

1. Search for Senna ◆ 1999
2. Land of Loss ◆ 1999
3. Enter the Enchanted ◆ 1999
4. Realm of the Reaper ◆ 1999
5. Discover the Destroyer ◆ 2000
6. Fear the Fantastic ◆ 2000
7. Gateway to the Gods ◆ 2000
8. Brave the Betrayal ◆ 2000
9. Inside the Illusion ◆ 2000
10. Understand the Unknown ◆ 2000
11. Mystify the Magician ◆ 2001
12. Entertain the End ◆ 2001

THE EXTRAORDINARY ADVENTURES OF ORDINARY BOY

Boniface, William
HARPERCOLLINS ◆ GRADES 4–7 ◆ A/R

FANTASY | HUMOR

In a town of superheros, Ordinary Boy is ordinary. His friends in the fifth grade at Watson Elementary have superpowers, although they are a bit problematic; for example, whenever Stench uses his super strength, he creates a super stink. In the first book, super villain and evil genius Professor Brain Drain has a scheme involving collectible cards featuring the Amazing Indestructo. As Ordinary Boy investigates, he realizes that the professor is not really behind the scheme. The Amazing Indestructo, who has his own television show, is building on his endorsements and creating a shortage of his merchandise. In the second book, Ordinary Boy looks into the disappearance of Meteor Boy. Numerous cartoon illustrations by Stephen Gilpin add to the appeal.

1. The Hero Revealed ◆ 2006
2. The Return of Meteor Boy? ◆ 2008
3. The Great Powers Outage ◆ 2008

EXTREME TEAM

Christopher, Matt

LITTLE, BROWN ◆ GRADES 4–7 ◆ A/R

RECREATION

Mark Goldstein and his friends enjoy skateboarding and doing kickflips and ollies. But Mark is embarrassed because he is not as coordinated as the others. Taking kung fu classes helps improve his control and gives him insights into his feelings. In all the books, there is a nice mix of sports and character interaction.

1. One Smooth Move ◆ 2004
2. Day of the Dragon ◆ 2004
3. Roller Hockey Rumble ◆ 2004
4. On Thin Ice ◆ 2004
5. Rock On ◆ 2004
6. Into the Danger Zone ◆ 2004
7. Wild Ride ◆ 2005
8. Head to Head ◆ 2005

EXTREME ZONE

Sumner, M. C.

SIMON & SCHUSTER ◆ GRADES 7–12 ◆ A/R

HORROR

Kathleen "Harley" Davisidaro got her nickname because she rides a Harley. With her friend, Noah Templer, she investigates a mysterious research facility. They end up in the Extreme Zone—a creepy world where they can trust no one.

1. Night Terrors ◆ 1997
2. Dark Lies ◆ 1997
3. Unseen Powers ◆ 1997
4. Deadly Secrets ◆ 1997
5. Common Enemy ◆ 1997
6. Inhuman Fury ◆ 1997
7. Lost Soul ◆ 1997
8. Dead End ◆ 1998

FAB 5

Rushton, Rosie

HYPERION ◆ GRADES 7–10 ◆ A/R

REAL LIFE

Chelsea, Laura, Jemma, Jon, and Sumitha are five British teens who want to establish their independence. In one book, Sumitha lies to her father, who adheres to his Bengali traditions. Will she be found out? Jemma's mother is overly protective. The friends struggle with serious issues such as anorexia and depression along with more usual concerns about dating and romance.

1. Just Don't Make a Scene, Mum! ◆ 1999
2. Think I'll Just Curl Up and Die ◆ 1999
3. How Could You Do This to Me, Mum? ◆ 1999
4. Where Do We Go From Here? ◆ 1999
5. Poppy ◆ 2000
6. Olivia ◆ 2000
7. Sophie ◆ 2000
8. Melissa ◆ 2000

FABLEHAVEN

Mull, Brandon

SHADOW MOUNTAIN/ALADDIN ◆ GRADES 5–8 ◆ A/R

FANTASY | ADVENTURE

As the series begins, Kendra, 13, and Seth, 11, visit their grandparents and discover that Grandfather Sorenson is the caretaker of Fablehaven, a sanctuary for magical creatures. Fablehaven is being threatened by the evil Society of the Evening Star. Kendra and Seth must rely on their own skills and powers to face this evil and protect Fablehaven.

1. Fablehaven ◆ 2006
2. Rise of the Evening Star ◆ 2007
3. Grip of the Shadow Plague ◆ 2008

FABULOUS FIVE

Haynes, Betsy

BANTAM ◆ GRADES 6–9

REAL LIFE

Five junior high girls experience ups and downs in relationships with boys, school activities, other groups, and in their friendships with each other. Each book features one of the girls, who all excel in different areas. This is the same group that united in elementary school against the snobby Taffy Sinclair in the series by that name.

1. Seventh Grade Rumors ◆ 1988
2. The Trouble with Flirting ◆ 1988
3. The Popularity Trap ◆ 1988
4. Her Honor, Katie Shannon ◆ 1988
5. The Bragging War ◆ 1989
6. Parent Game ◆ 1989
7. The Kissing Disaster ◆ 1989
8. The Runaway Crisis ◆ 1989
9. The Boyfriend Dilemma ◆ 1989
10. Playing the Part ◆ 1989
11. Hit and Run ◆ 1989
12. Katie's Dating Tips ◆ 1989
13. The Christmas Countdown ◆ 1989
14. Seventh-Grade Menace ◆ 1989
15. Melanie's Identity Crisis ◆ 1990
16. The Hot-line Emergency ◆ 1990
17. Celebrity Auction ◆ 1990
18. Teen Taxi ◆ 1990
19. Boys Only Club ◆ 1990
20. The Witches of Wakeman ◆ 1990
21. Jana to the Rescue ◆ 1990
22. Melanie's Valentine ◆ 1991
23. Mall Mania ◆ 1991
24. The Great TV Turnoff ◆ 1991
25. Fabulous Five Minus One ◆ 1991
26. Laura's Secret ◆ 1991
27. The Scapegoat ◆ 1991
28. Breaking Up ◆ 1991
29. Melanie Edwards, Super Kisser ◆ 1992
30. Sibling Rivalry ◆ 1992
31. The Fabulous Five Together Again ◆ 1992
32. Class Trip Calamity ◆ 1992

THE FACE ON THE MILK CARTON *see* Janie

FAERIE PATH

Jones, Frewin

EOS ◆ GRADES 7–10 ◆ A/R

FANTASY

In modern-day London, Anita is preparing to celebrate her sixteenth birthday. Suddenly, she is transported to Faerie where she is hailed as Princess Tania who has been missing for 500 years. Her parents are King Oberon and Queen Titania and she has six sisters—each with magical powers. Anita's boyfriend from London, Evan, is in Faerie, too, as Edric. As the series develops, Anita/Tania faces threats to Faerie. She discovers and embraces her magical powers, ultimately confronting the Sorcerer King of Lyonesse.

1. The Faerie Path ◆ 2007
2. The Lost Queen ◆ 2007
3. The Sorcerer King ◆ 2008

THE FAERIE WARS CHRONICLES

Brennan, Herbie

BLOOMSBURY ◆ GRADES 7–10 ◆ A/R

FANTASY

In England, Henry, a teenager, helps elderly physicist Mr. Fogarty. In Faerie Realm, Prince Pyrgus Malvae is sent by his father (the Purple Emperor) to our world, arriving through a portal that brings him to Mr. Fogarty's home. As the heir to the Faeries of the Light, Pyrgus is escaping from those who want to harm him—the Faeries of the Night. As the series progresses, the three characters journey to Faerie Realm, becoming embroiled in the conflict there.

1. Faerie Wars ◆ 2003
2. The Purple Emperor ◆ 2004
3. Ruler of the Realm ◆ 2006
4. Faerie Lord ◆ 2007

THE FAIRY GODMOTHER

Scarborough, Elizabeth Ann

BERKLEY/ACE ◆ GRADES 7–12

FANTASY | HUMOR

In Seattle, Rosalie gets what she wants: a fairy godmother. Although this godmother's abilities are somewhat limited, she succeeds in some of her goals and provides entertainment and a review of some classic fairy tales in the process. In *The Godmother's Apprentice,* Snohomish Quantrill ("Sno"—or Snow White) travels to Ireland to learn from Dame Felicity Fortune.

1. The Godmother ◆ 1994
2. The Godmother's Apprentice ◆ 1995
3. The Godmother's Web ◆ 1998

FAITHGIRLZ: BLOG ON

Mackall, Dandi Daley

ZONDERKIDZ ◆ GRADES 7–10 ◆ A/R

REAL LIFE | VALUES

Instead of making friends, Gracie observes her high school classmates and records her observations on her online journal—her blog. After learning about Gracie's blog, three girls—Annie, Jazz, and Storm—join her, each contributing a different element to the online journal. For example, Annie writes an advice column. Their friendship and their blogging is guided by their faith. The faithgirlz.com Web site has activities and discussion suggestions.

1. Grace Notes ◆ 2006
2. Love, Annie ◆ 2006
3. Just Jazz ◆ 2006
4. Storm Rising ◆ 2006
5. Grace Under Pressure ◆ 2007
6. Upsetting Annie ◆ 2007
7. Jazz Off-Key ◆ 2007
8. Storm Warning ◆ 2007

FAITHGIRLZ: GIRLS OF 622 HARBOR VIEW

Carlson, Melody

ZONDERKIDZ ◆ GRADES 5–7 ◆ A/R

VALUES | REAL LIFE

Four girls live in a trailer park in Oregon. Their friendship is strengthened by their commitment to being good neighbors, helping others, and loving God. There is information for discussion at faithgirlz.com.

1. Project: Girl Power ◆ 2007
2. Project: Mystery Bus ◆ 2007
3. Project: Rescue Chelsea ◆ 2007
4. Project: Take Charge ◆ 2007
5. Project: Raising Faith ◆ 2008

6. Project: Runaway ◆ 2008
7. Project: Ski Trip ◆ 2008
8. Project: Secret Admirer ◆ 2008

FALCON

Gray, Luli

HOUGHTON MIFFLIN ◆ GRADES 4–7 ◆ A/R

FANTASY

Falcon, 11, finds an unusual red egg in Central Park and takes it home to hatch. Since her parents' divorce, Falcon has felt alienated. Her mother is focused on her own career while her father is often traveling. As she waits for the egg to hatch, Falcon reaches out to her neighbor Ardene, her great-great-aunt Emily, and an ornithologist. This group, called Friends of Egg, also provide Falcon with support and friendship. When the egg hatches, it is a dragon that they name Egg, who eventually leaves to find other dragons. In subsequent books, Falcon is reunited with Egg.

1. Falcon's Egg ◆ 1993
2. Falcon and the Charles Street Witch ◆ 2002
3. Falcon and the Carousel of Time ◆ 2005

THE FALLEN

Sniegoski, Thomas E.

SIMON & SCHUSTER ◆ GRADES 8–12

FANTASY

Aaron Corbet, 18, discovers he has special powers. He wonders why and learns he is a Nephilim—an offspring of an angel and an earth woman. Aaron must face "the Powers" that want to kill him. The series follows Aaron's encounters with those who want to keep him from fulfilling the prophecy that he is the one who will reunite the fallen angels with Heaven.

1. The Fallen ◆ 2003
2. Leviathan ◆ 2003
3. Aerie ◆ 2003
4. Reckoning ◆ 2004

FAME SCHOOL

Jefferies, Cindy

PUFFIN ◆ GRADES 6–8 ◆ A/R

REAL LIFE

The students at Rockley Park School for the Performing Arts are learning what it takes to be a star. Singing, dancing, musical instruments—each book features a different teen's dream and dilemma. In *Tara's Triumph,* Tara's dream is to play bass guitar in a rock band. She wants the fame and recognition. When two classmates tell her about a school for orphans in Africa, Tara decides to help raise money for the school. Her ambitious plans turn out to be almost overwhelming.

1. Reach for the Stars ◆ 2007
2. Rising Star ◆ 2007
3. Secret Ambition ◆ 2007
4. Rivals! ◆ 2007
5. Tara's Triumph ◆ 2007
6. Lucky Break ◆ 2008
7. Solo Star ◆ 2008

FARSALA TRILOGY

Bell, Hilari

SIMON & SCHUSTER ◆ GRADES 6–10 ◆ A/R

FANTASY

This intricate fantasy is set in Farsala, a Persia-like culture that is under threat of attack. The Hrum army, which has characteristics of the ancient Roman military, plans to take over the country and add it to the Hrum empire. Three teens play pivotal roles in the conflict: Jiaan, the illegitimate son of the High Commander of the Farsala Army; Soraya, the High Commander's daughter; and Kavi, a traveling merchant. The first volume was originally published under the title *Flame* and the series name Book of Sorahb (2003).

1. Fall of a Kingdom ◆ 2005
2. Rise of a Hero ◆ 2005
3. Forging the Sword ◆ 2006

THE FASHION-FORWARD ADVENTURES OF IMOGENE

Barham, Lisa

SIMON PULSE ◆ GRADES 6–10 ◆ A/R

REAL LIFE

Imogene spends all her money on fashion. Really—ALL her money. Now her summer trip to Paris with her best friend Evie may be doomed unless Imogene gets some funds. That means a job! Lucky Imogene. She finds the perfect job working at a fashion agency in New York City. In

Project Paris, it's off to the City of Lights for Imogene and Evie. Readers who enjoyed Project Fashion books will relate to this series.

1. A Girl Like Moi ◆ 2006
2. Project Paris ◆ 2007
3. Accidentally Fabulous ◆ 2008

FAT GLENDA

Perl, Lila

CLARION ◆ GRADES 4–8

REAL LIFE

Overweight Glenda struggles with her weight over the course of the series. She loses pounds and finds a boyfriend, only to gain the weight back when he doesn't call. Later, she meets an even more obese teen who interests her in plus-size modeling, Throughout, her mother makes things more difficult for her by denying that she has a problem.

1. Me and Fat Glenda ◆ 1972
2. Hey, Remember Fat Glenda? ◆ 1981
3. Fat Glenda's Summer Romance ◆ 1986
4. Fat Glenda Turns Fourteen ◆ 1991

FEAR STREET

Stine, R. L.

SIMON & SCHUSTER ◆ GRADES 7–10 ◆ A/R

HORROR

Evil, danger, creatures, murders, and more are featured in these books from the master of horror. In *Into the Dark,* Paulette Fox is blind and in love with Brad Jones. But her friends are sure he committed a horrible crime. Can Paulette trust her heart? In *Trapped,* there is a sinister red mist in the tunnels under Shadyside High School. When a group of teens explore the tunnels, their escape is blocked by the skeletons of teens who died there years ago.

1. The New Girl ◆ 1989
2. The Surprise Party ◆ 1989
3. The Overnight ◆ 1989
4. Missing ◆ 1989
5. The Wrong Number ◆ 1990
6. The Sleepwalker ◆ 1990
7. Haunted ◆ 1990
8. Halloween Party ◆ 1990
9. The Stepsister ◆ 1990
10. Ski Weekend ◆ 1990

11. The Fire Game ◆ 1990
12. Lights Out ◆ 1991
13. The Secret Bedroom ◆ 1992
14. The Knife ◆ 1992
15. Prom Queen ◆ 1992
16. First Date ◆ 1992
17. The Best Friend ◆ 1992
18. The Cheater ◆ 1993
19. Sunburn ◆ 1993
20. The New Boy ◆ 1993
21. The Dare ◆ 1994
22. Bad Dreams ◆ 1994
23. Double Date ◆ 1994
24. The Thrill Club ◆ 1994
25. One Evil Summer ◆ 1994
26. The Mind Reader ◆ 1994
27. Wrong Number 2 ◆ 1994
28. Truth or Dare ◆ 1994
29. Dead End ◆ 1995
30. Final Grade ◆ 1995
31. Switched ◆ 1995
32. College Weekend ◆ 1995
33. The Stepsister 2 ◆ 1995
34. What Holly Heard ◆ 1995
35. The Face ◆ 1995
36. Secret Admirer ◆ 1996
37. The Perfect Date ◆ 1996
38. The Confession ◆ 1996
39. The Boy Next Door ◆ 1996
40. Night Games ◆ 1996
41. The Runaway ◆ 1996
42. Killer's Kiss ◆ 1997
43. All-Night Party ◆ 1997
44. The Rich Girl ◆ 1997
45. Cat ◆ 1996
46. Who Killed the Homecoming Queen ◆ 1997
47. Into the Dark ◆ 1997
48. The Best Friend 2 ◆ 1997
49. Midnight Diary ◆ 1997
50. Trapped ◆ 1997
51. The Stepbrother ◆ 1998
52. Camp Out ◆ 1998
53. Let's All Kill Jennifer ◆ 1998

FEAR STREET: FEAR STREET CHEERLEADERS

Stine, R. L.

SIMON & SCHUSTER ◆ **GRADES 7–10** ◆ **A/R**

HORROR

An evil spirit is lurking, waiting to take control of unsuspecting teens and make them kill. Corky Corcoran thought she destroyed the spirit (and she died in the process). Will Amanda open the wooden box that Corky left behind?

1. First Evil ◆ 1992
2. Second Evil ◆ 1992
3. Third Evil ◆ 1992
4. The New Evil ◆ 1994

FEAR STREET: FEAR STREET SAGAS

Stine, R. L.

SIMON & SCHUSTER ◆ **GRADES 7–10** ◆ **A/R**

HORROR

The town of Shadyside is controlled by the evil power of the curse of the Fear family. In *A New Fear*, Nora Goode married Daniel Fear, hoping to escape the curse. But the pair died in a fire on their wedding day and their son was the only survivor. Will he follow the evil of the Fears?

1. A New Fear ◆ 1996
2. House of Whispers ◆ 1996
3. Forbidden Secrets ◆ 1996
4. The Sign of Fear ◆ 1996
5. The Hidden Evil ◆ 1997
6. Daughters of Silence ◆ 1997
7. Children of Fear ◆ 1997
8. Dance of Death ◆ 1997
9. Heart of the Hunter ◆ 1997
10. The Awakening Evil ◆ 1997
11. Circle of Fire ◆ 1998
12. Chamber of Fear ◆ 1998
13. Faces of Terror ◆ 1998
14. One Last Kiss ◆ 1998
15. Door of Death ◆ 1998
16. Hand of Power ◆ 1998

FEAR STREET SAGAS TRILOGY

1. The Betrayal ◆ 1993
2. The Secret ◆ 1993
3. The Burning ◆ 1993

FEAR STREET: FEAR STREET SENIORS

Stine, R. L.

GOLDEN BOOKS ◆ GRADES 7–10

HORROR

Trisha's party turns sinister when she has a premonition that her classmates will not survive their senior year.

1. Let's Party ◆ 1998
2. In Too Deep ◆ 1998
3. The Thirst ◆ 1998
4. No Answer ◆ 1998
5. Last Chance ◆ 1998
6. The Gift ◆ 1998
7. Fight, Team, Fight ◆ 1999
8. Sweetheart, Evil Heart ◆ 1999
9. Spring Break ◆ 1999
10. Wicked ◆ 1999
11. Prom Date ◆ 1999
12. Graduation Day ◆ 1999

FEAR STREET: FEAR STREET SUPER CHILLERS

Stine, R. L.

SIMON & SCHUSTER ◆ GRADES 7–10 ◆ A/R

HORROR

Teens face more danger in this series. Josie is receiving threatening Valentines. Billy is chasing vampires. And one by one, the lifeguards are disappearing. There are many cliff-hanging moments in these fast-paced thrillers.

1. Party Summer ◆ 1991
2. Silent Night ◆ 1991
3. Goodnight Kiss ◆ 1992
4. Broken Hearts ◆ 1993
5. Silent Night 2 ◆ 1993
6. The Dead Lifeguard ◆ 1993
7. The New Evil: Cheerleaders ◆ 1994
8. Bad Moonlight ◆ 1995

9. The New Year's Party ◆ 1995
10. Goodnight Kiss 2 ◆ 1996
11. Silent Night 3 ◆ 1996
12. High Tide ◆ 1997
13. The Evil Lives! Cheerleaders ◆ 1997

FEAR STREET: GHOSTS OF FEAR STREET

Stine, R. L.

POCKET BOOKS ◆ GRADES 4–8 ◆ A/R

HORROR

Shadow people, ooze, the bugman, the werecat, ghouls, ghosts, and other creatures populate these horror books. The unsuspecting characters experience nightmares; they encounter body switchers and screaming jokers; they have frightening Christmas celebrations and are attacked by aqua apes. There are many cliff-hangers—chapters ending with a scream or with fingers grabbing the character's neck—so readers enjoy lots of scary moments.

1. Hide and Shriek ◆ 1995
2. Who's Been Sleeping in My Grave? ◆ 1995
3. The Attack of the Aqua Apes ◆ 1995
4. Nightmare in 3-D ◆ 1996
5. Stay Away from the Treehouse ◆ 1996
6. The Eye of the Fortuneteller ◆ 1996
7. Fright Knight ◆ 1996
8. The Ooze ◆ 1996
9. The Revenge of the Shadow People ◆ 1996
10. The Bugman Lives! ◆ 1996
11. The Boy Who Ate Fear Street ◆ 1996
12. Night of the Werecat ◆ 1996
13. How to Be a Vampire ◆ 1996
14. Body Switchers from Outer Space ◆ 1996
15. Fright Christmas ◆ 1996
16. Don't Ever Get Sick at Granny's ◆ 1997
17. House of a Thousand Screams ◆ 1997
18. Camp Fear Ghouls ◆ 1997
19. Three Evil Wishes ◆ 1997
20. Spell of the Screaming Jokers ◆ 1997
21. The Creature from Club Lagoona ◆ 1997
22. Field of Screams ◆ 1997
23. Why I'm Not Afraid of Ghosts ◆ 1997
24. Monster Dog ◆ 1997
25. Halloween Bugs Me! ◆ 1997
26. Go to Your Tomb—Right Now! ◆ 1997
27. Parents from the 13th Dimension ◆ 1997

28. Hide and Shriek II ◆ 1998
29. The Tale of the Blue Monkey ◆ 1998
30. I Was a Sixth-Grade Zombie ◆ 1998
31. Escape of the He-Beast ◆ 1998
32. Caution: Aliens at Work ◆ 1998
33. Attack of the Vampire Worms ◆ 1998
34. Horror Hotel: The Vampire Checks In ◆ 1998
35. Horror Hotel: Ghost in the Guest Room ◆ 1998
36. Funhouse of Dr. Freek ◆ 1998

GHOSTS OF FEAR STREET CREEPY COLLECTION

1. Happy Hauntings ◆ 1998
2. Beastly Tales ◆ 1998
3. The Scream Tea ◆ 1998
4. Big Bad Bugs ◆ 1998
5. Ghoul Friends ◆ 1998
6. Weird Science ◆ 1998

FEAR STREET: 99 FEAR STREET

Stine, R. L.

SIMON & SCHUSTER ◆ GRADES 6–9 ◆ A/R

HORROR

Don't move into any house on Fear Street! Ever! Especially not 99 Fear Street. Cally and Kody Frasier moved there and faced the evil in the house. Then Cally's ghost threatened the next inhabitant. Finally, Kody returns to make a movie of her life, which quickly becomes a horror-filled experience.

1. The First Horror ◆ 1994
2. The Second Horror ◆ 1994
3. The Third Horror ◆ 1994

FEARLESS

Pascal, Francine

SIMON & SCHUSTER ◆ GRADES 8–12 ◆ A/R

ADVENTURE

Gaia Moore, 17, is different from other high school seniors. She has a black belt in karate and she has no "fear gene." She faces dangerous situations, including terrorists and drug dealers. As the series progresses, Gaia becomes disenchanted with her situation.

1. Fearless ◆ 1999
2. Sam ◆ 1999

3. Run ◆ 1999
4. Twisted ◆ 2000
5. Kiss ◆ 2000
6. Payback ◆ 2000
7. Rebel ◆ 2000
8. Heat ◆ 2000
9. Blood ◆ 2000
10. Liar ◆ 2000
11. Trust ◆ 2000
12. Killer ◆ 2000
13. Bad ◆ 2001
14. Missing ◆ 2001
15. Tears ◆ 2001
16. Naked ◆ 2001
17. Flee ◆ 2001
18. Love ◆ 2001
19. Twins ◆ 2002
20. Sex ◆ 2002
21. Blind ◆ 2002
22. Alone ◆ 2002
23. Fear ◆ 2002
24. Betrayed ◆ 2002
25. Lost ◆ 2003
26. Escape ◆ 2003
27. Shock ◆ 2003
28. Chase ◆ 2003
29. Lust ◆ 2003
30. Freak ◆ 2003
31. Normal ◆ 2004
32. Terror ◆ 2004
33. Wired ◆ 2004
34. Fake ◆ 2004
35. Exposed ◆ 2004
36. Gone ◆ 2004

SUPER EDITIONS

1. Before Gaia ◆ 2002
2. Gaia Abducted ◆ 2003
3. The Silent Hand ◆ 2004
4. The Screaming Heart ◆ 2004

FEARLESS FBI

Pascal, Francine
SIMON & SCHUSTER ◆ GRADES 8–12 ◆ A/R

ADVENTURE

Gaia Moore is back in this series in which she joins the FBI. Her amazing eyesight, reflexes, and strength get her through boot camp despite her inclination to ignore rules. This tendency gets her in trouble in the second volume and in the third, she has gone AWOL and is being chased by FBI agents. These are fast-paced books that present the story using a mix of narrative and official reports.

1. Kill Game ◆ 2005
2. Live Bait ◆ 2005
3. Agent Out ◆ 2006
4. Naked Eye ◆ 2006

FEATHER AND BONE: THE CROW CHRONICLES

Martini, Clem

KIDS CAN PRESS ◆ GRADES 5–8 ◆ A/R

ANIMAL FANTASY

In *The Mob,* the birds of the Crow clans have convened at the Gathering Tree. One crow, Kyp, endangers the flock and is banished. He returns to rescue the Family. Each book uses the device of an elder telling the stories of plagues, dangerous encounters with humans, and the search for a safe home.

1. The Mob ◆ 2004
2. The Plague ◆ 2005
3. The Judgment ◆ 2006

FERRET CHRONICLES

Bach, Richard

SCRIBNER ◆ GRADES 7–10 ◆ A/R

FANTASY

The human race is in trouble, and riding to the rescue are ferrets. They have left their own perfect world on another planet to deal with the chaos on Earth. In *Rescue Ferrets at Sea,* Bethany Ferret achieves her dream of becoming part of the sea rescue ferrets. In *The Last Wars,* two ferrets search for a future-changing object that may help them contact their home planet.

1. Air Ferrets Aloft ◆ 2002
2. Rescue Ferrets at Sea ◆ 2002
3. Writer Ferrets Chasing the Muse ◆ 2002
4. Rancher Ferrets on the Range ◆ 2003
5. The Last Wars: Detective Ferrets and the Case of the Golden Deed ◆ 2003

FIENDLY CORNERS

Leroe, Ellen W.

HYPERION ◆ GRADES 5–8

HORROR

In this small town, strange things happen. Like when the pizza parlor sends out toy robots with each pizza. The robots turn the residents into *Pizza Zombies* and Bryan Hartley must try to undo the damage and save the town. Another book features Jamie, who receives the contact lenses of a dead magician and is haunted by his ghost. A werewolf and an evil snowman cause problems in other books. Action, suspense, horror, and creatures make these a choice for the Goosebumps and Fear Street fans.

1. Monster Vision ◆ 1996
2. Pizza Zombies ◆ 1996
3. Revenge of the Hairy Horror ◆ 1996
4. Nasty the Snowman ◆ 1996

FINGERPRINTS

Metz, Melinda

AVON ◆ GRADES 7–10 ◆ A/R

FANTASY

Rae is hospitalized for having delusions. She realizes that her "visions" come from touching objects. She uses this ability to investigate a mysterious bombing. As the series progresses, Rae develops her power, touching fingerprints to find out the inner thoughts of others.

1. Gifted Touch ◆ 2001
2. Haunted ◆ 2001
3. Trust Me ◆ 2001
4. Secrets ◆ 2001
5. Betrayed ◆ 2001
6. Revelations ◆ 2001
7. Payback ◆ 2002

FINNEGAN ZWAKE

Dahl, Michael

SIMON & SCHUSTER ◆ GRADES 6–9 ◆ A/R

ADVENTURE | MYSTERY

Finnegan Zwake, 13, encounters mysteries and adventure. His parents disappeared in Iceland but they could be anywhere. With his Uncle Stoppard, a mystery writer, Finnegan travels the world searching for them.

They come across pirates in Australia and mysterious events in Iceland. There are humorous moments in these books and readers of A Series of Unfortunate Events will enjoy them.

1. The Horizontal Man ◆ 1999
2. The Worm Tunnel ◆ 1999
3. The Ruby Raven ◆ 1999
4. The Viking Claw ◆ 2001
5. The Coral Coffin ◆ 2002

FIRE-US TRILOGY

Armstrong, Jennifer, and Nancy Butcher

HARPERCOLLINS ◆ GRADES 6–12 ◆ A/R

FANTASY

This post-apocalyptic trilogy describes the survivors of a virus ("fire-us") that seems to have destroyed the adult population. A group of children in Florida band together to become the Family and take on roles of protectors, nurturers, and needy. As they learn to survive, they decide to travel and discover that they are not alone. Eventually, they realize that there are dangerous adults at the Crossroads. These adults survived by going underground before the virus hit and they are led by a power-hungry madman.

1. The Kindling ◆ 2002
2. The Keepers of the Flame ◆ 2002
3. The Kiln ◆ 2003

FIREBALL

Christopher, John

DUTTON ◆ GRADES 5–7

FANTASY

Two cousins encounter a "fireball," which proves to be an entry into a parallel, "what-if" world in which the Roman Empire has endured and European society has been static for two thousand years. In our hemisphere, without interference from the white man, the Aztecs have conquered the Incas and taken over North and South America. Brad and Simon travel all over this world having one adventure after another. They provoke a revolution against the Empire in Britain, but then are victims of persecution by the new regime. They flee to the New World and become the heroes of an Aztec game. Then they run into a Chinese civilization that has also remained static. In all their adventures, they use their superior technical knowledge to come out on top. In the end, given the opportunity to go home, they decide to explore other possible worlds.

1. Fireball ◆ 1981
2. New Found Land ◆ 1983
3. Dragon Dance ◆ 1986

FIREBRINGER TRILOGY

Pierce, Meredith Ann

FIREBIRD ◆ GRADES 7–10 ◆ A/R

FANTASY

The world of unicorns is the setting for this series. Aljan, a unicorn whose name means "Dark Moon," is the son of Prince Korr. Jan's destiny is to become a Firebringer. To achieve this, he must face dangers, overcome his own reckless nature, and confront the dark secret that haunts his father.

1. Birth of the Firebringer ◆ 1985
2. Dark Moon ◆ 1992
3. The Son of Summer Stars ◆ 2003

FIRST PERSON FICTION

Various authors

SCHOLASTIC ◆ GRADES 6–10 ◆ A/R

REAL LIFE

This series looks at the difficulties of leaving homelands and coming to America. Early books describe the experiences of characters from Korea, Cambodia, Cuba, and Haiti. The stories take place in different eras. Yara and her family are from 1967 Cuba (*Flight to Freedom*). Nakri and her family leave Cambodia in the 1970s. In *Call Me Maria,* Maria tries to adjust to life in New York City. She misses her mother, who is still in Puerto Rico. Her father is busy as the super in their apartment building. Out of her sense of loneliness, Maria finds a voice through poetry.

1. Finding My Hat (Son, John) ◆ 2003
2. The Stone Goddess (Ho, Minfong) ◆ 2003
3. Flight to Freedom (Veciana-Suarez, Ana) ◆ 2004
4. Behind the Mountains (Danticat, Edwidge) ◆ 2004
5. Call Me María (Cofer, Judith Ortiz) ◆ 2004

FIVE ANCESTORS

Stone, Jeff

RANDOM HOUSE ◆ GRADES 6–9 ◆ A/R

HISTORICAL | ADVENTURE

Ying attacks the temple where he was once a student and he thinks all have been destroyed. The Grandmaster has hidden five students—orphans who have been raised as brothers and trained in the martial arts to become warrior monks. In *Tiger,* Fu seeks to reclaim the ancient scrolls that Ying has stolen. As the series progresses, each of the "Five Ancestors" takes a turn at confronting Ying and also overcoming aspects of their own personalities that may block their success. The martial arts action of this series set in 17th-century China makes it an exciting choice for middle school readers.

1. Tiger ◆ 2005
2. Monkey ◆ 2005
3. Snake ◆ 2006
4. Crane ◆ 2007
5. Eagle ◆ 2008

FLAMBARDS

Peyton, K. M.

PHILOMEL ◆ GRADES 7–8

FAMILY LIFE | HISTORICAL

This saga of the Russell family and Flambards, their historic mansion in rural England, begins in 1908. Christina comes to the family as an orphan, sent to live at Flambards with her uncle and two cousins. The series is filled with historical details and provides a glimpse into social conventions of the era. This saga is still popular with many readers, especially those who enjoy English historical fiction.

1. Flambards ◆ 1967
2. The Edge of the Cloud ◆ 1969
3. Flambards in Summer ◆ 1969
4. Flambards Divided ◆ 1981

FLICKA

O'Hara, Mary

HARPERCOLLINS ◆ GRADES 5–8 ◆ A/R

REAL LIFE

A dreamy young boy living on a ranch in Wyoming has trouble getting along with his practical father. His mother persuades his father to let him have a colt, hoping this will change things for him. Ken becomes devoted to the horse and is devastated when Flicka becomes seriously ill. His father is ready to shoot the ailing horse rather than see it suffer, but Ken persuades him to let her live. Kens wins his father's admiration in the end. The sequel, *Thunderhead,* is about Flicka's colt. Ken dreams of

Thunderhead being a racehorse. The 1940s setting provides historical interest, and the relationships between the family members are complex and emotional.

1. My Friend Flicka ◆ 1941
2. Thunderhead ◆ 1943
3. Green Grass of Wyoming ◆ 1946

FLIGHT 29 DOWN

Various authors

GROSSET & DUNLAP ◆ GRADES 7–10 ◆ A/R

ADVENTURE

Ten teens plus a plane crash on an island in the South Pacific lead to a survival series with action and adventure. After the crash, the pilot and three teens search the island for help. The remaining seven have to overcome their fear and petty jealousies to come up with a plan to survive. These books are novelizations of a television series. *Ten Rules* (2006) is a prequel.

1. Static (Sorrells, Walter) ◆ 2006
2. The Seven (Vornholt, John) ◆ 2006
3. The Return (Vornholt, John) ◆ 2006
4. The Storm (Strickland, Brad) ◆ 2006
5. Scratch (Sorrells, Walter) ◆ 2006
6. On Fire (Sorrells, Walter) ◆ 2007
7. Survival (Sorrells, Walter) ◆ 2007

FLIRT

Clarke, Nicole

GROSSET & DUNLAP ◆ GRADES 7–10 ◆ A/R

REAL LIFE

Four girls, all 16, are in Manhattan for their dream job—a summer internship at *Flirt* magazine. There is naive Mel, London socialite Olivia, party girl Kiyoko (whose father is a Japanese diplomat), and Alexa, a beautiful Latina. Fashionistas, trendsetters, Manhattan clubs, Fashion Week, and trips to Paris and London will keep teen readers turning pages. After the fourth book, the interns get to stay on for the fall semester. In later books, a new group of interns is introduced.

1. Write Here, Right Now ◆ 2006
2. Close Up and Personal ◆ 2006
3. High Fashion ◆ 2006
4. Spin City ◆ 2006
5. Issues ◆ 2006

6. VIP's ◆ 2006
7. French Twist ◆ 2007
8. London Calling ◆ 2007
9. Copycat ◆ 2007
10. Model Behavior ◆ 2007

THE FLOODS

Thompson, Colin

HARPERCOLLINS ◆ GRADES 5–7 ◆ A/R

FANTASY | HUMOR

The Floods are not your ordinary family. They are a family of witches and wizards. There are seven kids, each stranger than the one before—except for Betty who looks normal but isn't. Having remodeled their house, the Floods are dismayed when the rude, noisy Dent family moves in next door. Well, they will just have to disappear. Creepy events, like when one of the Dents is devoured by a creature buried in the Floods' yard, will appeal to many readers.

1. Good Neighbors ◆ 2008
2. School Plot ◆ 2008
3. Witch Friend ◆ 2008

FOG MOUND

Schade, Susan

SIMON & SCHUSTER ◆ GRADES 4–7 ◆ A/R

ANIMAL FANTASY

For Thelonious, a chipmunk, the existence of humans is a mysterious legend. After Thelonious is swept away from his home he arrives in the City of Ruins, a place of lawlessness filled with dangerous animals. He becomes friends with a bear, a porcupine, and a lizard. As they begin their journey to Fog Mound, they find clues about what happened to the humans. The chapters alternate between text and comic panels (illustrated by Joe Buller), which will appeal to fans of graphic novels.

1. Travels of Thelonious ◆ 2006
2. Faradawn ◆ 2007
3. Simon's Dream ◆ 2008

FORBIDDEN DOORS

Myers, Bill

TYNDALE HOUSE ◆ GRADES 7–9 ◆ A/R

HORROR | VALUES

After living in Brazil, Scott and Becka are back in school in the United States. They encounter many problems with supernatural events and the occult. In *The Society,* they discover a cult that is trying to entice students to participate. Scott and Becka intervene, getting guidance from the Bible and trusting their faith. Other books feature Scott and Becka and other students of faith coping with mysterious, supernatural situations.

1. The Society ◆ 2001
2. The Deceived ◆ 2001
3. The Spell ◆ 2001
4. The Haunting ◆ 2001
5. The Guardian ◆ 2001
6. The Encounter ◆ 2002
7. The Curse ◆ 2002
8. The Undead ◆ 2002
9. The Scream ◆ 2002
10. The Ancients ◆ 2003
11. The Wiccan ◆ 2003
12. The Cards ◆ 2003

FORBIDDEN GAME

Smith, L. J.

SIMON & SCHUSTER ◆ GRADES 7–10

HORROR

In the tradition of Buffy, the Vampire Slayer, this series pits teens against a demonic spirit named Julian. In the first book, Jenny and her friends are transported to Julian's mansion, where they face frightening events. In the second and third books, the Shadow Man appears, putting the teens in even greater danger.

1. The Hunter ◆ 1994
2. The Chase ◆ 1994
3. The Kill ◆ 1994

FOREIGNER

Cherryh, C. J.
DAW ◆ GRADES 10–12
SCIENCE FICTION

Mature readers of science fiction will enjoy this complex and well-written series about the colonization of an alien world. The occupants of this planet are the Atevi, a people who look like humans but have quite different characteristics. Bren Cameron is chosen to lead the humans in their efforts to befriend the Atevi and avoid further misunderstandings and violence.

1. Foreigner ◆ 1994
2. Invader ◆ 1995
3. Inheritor ◆ 1996
4. Precursor ◆ 1999
5. Defender ◆ 2001
6. Explorer ◆ 2002
7. Destroyer ◆ 2005
8. Pretender ◆ 2006
9. Deliverer ◆ 2007

FORENSIC MYSTERY

Ferguson, Alane
VIKING ◆ GRADES 9–12 ◆ A/R
MYSTERY

There is a serial killer on the loose who leaves a St. Christopher medal with the victims. Seventeen-year-old Cameryn Mahoney's interest in forensic pathology brings her into the investigation of the murder of a friend. Her father is the county coroner, so Cameryn has access to all of the autopsy records and medical clues. Fans of television programs like C.S.I. will be fascinated by this series.

1. The Christopher Killer ◆ 2006
2. The Angel of Death ◆ 2006
3. The Circle of Blood ◆ 2008

FOREVER ANGELS

Weyn, Suzanne
TROLL ◆ GRADES 4–7 ◆ A/R
FANTASY

Molly, Katie, Ashley, and Christina all have guardian angels. The books in this series generally feature one of the girls. In *An Angel for Molly,* for example, Molly finds her angel on a trip to Ireland. *Katie's Angel* describes Katie's loneliness after the death of her parents and how she finds and accepts her guardian angel. This is a series that will appeal to readers who like magic and who are reassured by the idea that someone is watching over them.

1. Ashley's Lost Angel ◆ 1995
2. The Baby Angel ◆ 1995
3. Christina's Dancing Angel ◆ 1995
4. Katie's Angel ◆ 1995
5. An Angel for Molly ◆ 1996
6. Ashley's Love Angel ◆ 1996
7. The Blossom Angel ◆ 1996
8. The Forgotten Angel ◆ 1996
9. The Golden Angel ◆ 1997
10. The Snow Angel ◆ 1997
11. The Movie Star Angel ◆ 1998

FORGOTTEN REALMS—THE LAST MYTHAL *see* Dungeons and Dragons: Forgotten Realms—The Last Mythal

FOUNDATION

Asimov, Isaac

HARPERCOLLINS ◆ GRADES 10–12 ◆ A/R

SCIENCE FICTION

Asimov first wrote in the 1940s about the collapse of a galactic empire and the establishment by a psychohistorian called Hari Seldon of a Foundation to limit the impact of the empire's demise. As the empire dies, the Foundation is left exposed to invading warlords. Asimov's early stories were collected in the first three volumes. *Prelude to Foundation* is a prequel that describes the birth of psychohistory. *Forward the Foundation* was published after Asimov's death. This series has been published in many editions.

1. Foundation ◆ 1951
2. Foundation and Empire ◆ 1952
3. Second Foundation ◆ 1953
4. Foundation's Edge ◆ 1982
5. Foundation and Earth ◆ 1986
6. Prelude to Foundation ◆ 1988
7. Forward the Foundation ◆ 1993

THE SECOND FOUNDATION TRILOGY

1. Foundation's Fear (Benford, Gregory) ◆ 1997
2. Foundation and Chaos (Bear, Greg) ◆ 1998
3. Foundation's Triumph (Brin, David) ◆ 1999

FOXFIRE *see* Golden Mountain Chronicles

THE FREAK

Matas, Carol

KEY PORTER BOOKS ◆ GRADES 8–10

FANTASY

After recovering from a serious illness, Jade, 16, discovers she has psychic powers. Her visions range from the mundane, the gossipy inner thoughts of her friends, to the frightening, the knowledge that a murder is about to be committed. Jade struggles to adjust to her insights and to decide what to do about them. In *Far,* Jade visits a university that specializes in psychic testing and she experiences a disturbing new vision. The first book was originally published in 1997 and reissued in 2007.

1. The Freak ◆ 1997
2. Visions ◆ 2007
3. Far ◆ 2007

FRIENDS FOR A SEASON

Byrd, Sandra

BETHANY HOUSE ◆ GRADES 5–8 ◆ A/R

REAL LIFE | VALUES

Faith plays a role in each of these stories about young teen girls facing new situations. In *Island Girl,* 13-year-old Meg—on vacation at her grandparents' farm in Oregon—makes friends with Tia, whose Hispanic father oversees the farm, and tries to decide whether to live with her father or with her mother and her new husband. In *Chopstick,* 13-year-olds Paige and Kate are competing in a worship-music contest, each so sure of winning that she has already promised the $500 prize to charity.

1. Island Girl ◆ 2005
2. Chopstick ◆ 2005
3. Red Velvet ◆ 2005
4. Daisy Chains ◆ 2006

THE FRIENDSHIP RING

Vail, Rachel

SCHOLASTIC ◆ GRADES 6–9 ◆ A/R

REAL LIFE

A group of seventh-grade friends are the focus of this series. Each story is told from one of the friends' perspectives and looks at family and social problems. The friends have very different backgrounds, very different talents, and very different likes and dislikes. Preteen and adolescent girls will particularly enjoy these stories about friendship and growing awareness of the differences between the sexes.

1. If You Only Knew ◆ 1998
2. Please, Please, Please ◆ 1998
3. Not That I Care ◆ 1998
4. What Are Friends For? ◆ 1999
5. Popularity Contest ◆ 2000
6. Fill in the Blank ◆ 2000

FROM THE FILES OF MADISON FINN

Dower, Laura

HYPERION ◆ GRADES 6–8 ◆ A/R

REAL LIFE

At Far Hills Junior High, Madison Finn and her friends Fiona and Aimee are looking forward to new activities. They enjoy their classes, friends, field trips, and concerts. In *Give Me a Break,* Maddie is going on a skiing trip with her dad and can only take one friend. How can she choose?

1. Only the Lonely ◆ 2001
2. Boy, Oh Boy! ◆ 2001
3. Play It Again ◆ 2001
4. Caught in the Web ◆ 2001
5. Thanks for Nothing ◆ 2001
6. Lost and Found ◆ 2001
7. Save the Date ◆ 2001
8. Picture Perfect ◆ 2002
9. Just Visiting ◆ 2002
10. Give and Take ◆ 2002
11. Heart to Heart ◆ 2003
12. Lights Out ◆ 2003
13. Sink or Swim ◆ 2003
14. Double Dare ◆ 2003
15. Off the Wall ◆ 2004
16. Three's a Crowd ◆ 2004

17. On the Case ◆ 2004
18. Give Me a Break ◆ 2005
19. Keep It Real ◆ 2005
20. All that Glitters ◆ 2005
21. Forget Me Not ◆ 2006
22. All Shook Up ◆ 2006

SUPER EDITIONS

1. To Have and to Hold ◆ 2004
2. Hit the Beach ◆ 2006
3. Friends Till the End ◆ 2007

GALAXY OF FEAR *see* Star Wars Galaxy of Fear

THE GATEKEEPERS

Horowitz, Anthony

SCHOLASTIC ◆ GRADES 5–9 ◆ A/R

ADVENTURE | FANTASY

Five teens are destined to save the world from the evil of the Old Ones. In *Raven's Gate,* Matt, 14, is sent to live in a village in Yorkshire with Mrs. Deverill, who turns out to be a witch. Raven's Gate, an ancient portal to the world of evil, is opening and it is up to Matt to stop it. In *Evil Star,* Matt travels to South America and meets Pedro, a Peruvian teen who joins in the efforts to fight evil. In *Nightrise,* two more teens join the struggle—Scott and Jamie, Native American twins with telepathic skills. Readers of Horowitz's Alex Rider books will enjoy the fast-paced, almost breathless action of this series.

1. Raven's Gate ◆ 2006
2. Evil Star ◆ 2006
3. Nightrise ◆ 2007

GEMMA DOYLE

Bray, Libba

DELACORTE ◆ GRADES 9–12 ◆ A/R

FANTASY

It is 1895 and Gemma Doyle, 16, has been sent from India to an exclusive boarding school in England. A mysterious diary and Gemma's own disturbing visions lead her to use her magical powers and travel into the Realms. There she realizes her destiny—to restore the power of the Order. Gemma is joined by two girls from school, Felicity and Ann, on her search for the lost Temple. Throughout the series Gemma and her friends travel between their real world in Victorian England, with its strict rules about behavior, and the magical world of the Realms, where they face mythical creatures and danger.

1. A Great and Terrible Beauty ◆ 2003
2. Rebel Angels ◆ 2005
3. The Sweet Far Thing ◆ 2007

GENERATION GIRL

Stewart, Melanie

GOLDEN BOOKS ◆ GRADES 7–10 ◆ A/R

REAL LIFE

Lara, Barbie, Chelsie, Tori, and Nichelle are some of the girls involved in the activities at International High in New York City. Barbie is featured in several books as she makes friends and finally gets a chance to do some acting.

1. New York, Here We Come ◆ 1999
2. Bending the Rules ◆ 1999
3. Pushing the Limits ◆ 1999
4. Singing Sensation ◆ 1999
5. Picture Perfect? ◆ 1999
6. Secrets of the Past ◆ 1999
7. Stage Fright ◆ 1999
8. Taking a Stand ◆ 1999
9. Hitting the Slopes ◆ 1999
10. Taking Charge! ◆ 1999
11. First Crush ◆ 2000
12. Campaign Chaos ◆ 2000

GHOST

Various authors

DARK HORSE ◆ GRADES 10–12

HORROR

Elisa Cameron is Ghost, the protector of Arcadia. She faces zombies, an evil villainess named Dr. October, and other demonic forces. As she faces these dark threats, she searches for those who killed her and tries to understand her special powers.

1. Nocturnes (Luke, Eric) ◆ 1996
2. Exhuming Elisa (Luke, Eric) ◆ 1997
3. Black October (Luke, Eric) ◆ 1999

4. Painful Music (Luke, Eric) ◆ 1999
5. No World So Dark (Warner, Chris) ◆ 2000

THE GHOST IN THE TOKAIDO INN

Hoobler, Dorothy, and Thomas Hoobler
PUTNAM ◆ GRADES 7–9 ◆ A/R
HISTORICAL | MYSTERY

In dramatic stories set in 18th-century Japan, 14-year-old Seikei, a resourceful boy who dreams of becoming a samurai, becomes involved in solving mysteries. In *The Demon in the Teahouse,* Seikei investigates murders and arson that are connected with popular geishas, and in the third book, he tangles with a ninja.

1. The Ghost in the Tokaido Inn ◆ 1999
2. The Demon in the Teahouse ◆ 2001
3. In Darkness, Death ◆ 2004
4. A Samurai Never Fears Death ◆ 2007

GHOST SQUAD

Hildick, E. W.
DUTTON ◆ GRADES 5–8
FANTASY | MYSTERY

Joe, Danny, Karen, and Carlos are ghosts who have learned how to communicate with living people using a computer. They make contact with Carlos and Danny's best friends, Buzz and Wacko, and together the four ghosts and two boys form the Ghost Squad to solve crimes. Joe, the group's leader, was murdered and wants to find out who did it and assure his wife that it was not a suicide. Karen and Danny also want to help their families, but Carlos's family has adjusted to his death. His concern is with computers, and he figures out how to use a ghost's "micro-micro energy" to operate a word processor. The Ghost Squad battles both living enemies and Malevs (ghosts who try to harm living people) in their adventures, which include plenty of action.

1. The Ghost Squad Breaks Through ◆ 1984
2. The Ghost Squad and the Halloween Conspiracy ◆ 1985
3. The Ghost Squad Flies Concorde ◆ 1985
4. The Ghost Squad and the Ghoul of Grunberg ◆ 1986
5. The Ghost Squad and the Prowling Hermits ◆ 1987
6. The Ghost Squad and the Menace of the Malevs ◆ 1988

GHOSTS OF FEAR STREET *see* Fear Street: Ghosts of Fear Street

GIDEON THE CUTPURSE

Buckley-Archer, Linda

SIMON & SCHUSTER ◆ GRADES 5–8 ◆ A/R

FANTASY

In England, Peter and Kate, 12, are transported from the 21st century to 1763. Kate's father has been working on an anti-gravity machine but it has been stolen by the Tar Man. The children are befriended by a thief, Gideon, who helps them adjust to the era and in their search for a way home. In *The Time Thief,* Kate has returned to the 21st century, but so has the Tar Man. Peter is stranded in the past. When Kate and her father return for Peter, they enter the wrong time and Peter is in his forties. Peter keeps his identity hidden, hoping that Kate and her father will find a way to the right time. The title of the first book was changed to *The Time Travelers* for the paperback edition.

1. Gideon the Cutpurse ◆ 2006
2. The Time Thief ◆ 2007
3. The Splintering of Time ◆ 2009

GILDA JOYCE

Allison, Jennifer

DUTTON ◆ GRADES 6–9 ◆ A/R

MYSTERY

Meet Gilda Joyce. Since the death of her father, Gilda, 13, has been developing her psychic abilities hoping to contact him. Also, as a fan of *Harriet the Spy,* Gilda wants to solve mysteries. For summer vacation, Gilda goes to San Francisco to visit a relative she has never met. The home is a gloomy Victorian mansion and Gilda is intrigued by the secrecy surrounding a death that occurred there. In *The Ladies of the Lake,* Gilda is attending a new school that seems to be haunted. There are humorous moments blended in with the mystery in this appealing series.

1. Gilda Joyce, Psychic Investigator ◆ 2005
2. The Ladies of the Lake ◆ 2006
3. The Ghost Sonata ◆ 2007

GILMORE GIRLS

Various authors

HARPERCOLLINS ◆ GRADES 7–10

FAMILY LIFE

Based on the popular television program, these books feature a mom, Lorelai, and daughter, Rory, who are best friends. Raising Rory as a single parent has not been easy for Lorelai. It has even led to estrangement from her parents. Now, Lorelai has borrowed money from her parents so that Rory can go to a private prep school. Fans of the television show will enjoy these books.

1. I Do, Don't I? (Clark, Catherine) ◆ 2002
2. I Love You, You Idiot (Dubowski, Cathy East) ◆ 2002
3. Like Mother, Like Daughter (Clark, Catherine) ◆ 2002
4. The Other Side of Summer (Pai, Helen) ◆ 2002

GINGERBREAD

Cohn, Rachel

SIMON & SCHUSTER ◆ GRADES 10–12 ◆ A/R

REAL LIFE

After being kicked out of boarding school, Cyd Charisse, 16, has been sent home to her mother and stepfather in San Francisco. Cyd continues her wild ways, breaking the rules and staying out all night with Shrimp, her surfer boyfriend. Cyd is sent to live with her biological father in New York City, where she bonds with a family she has never known. In *Shrimp,* Cyd, now going by CC, is 17 and back in San Francisco for her senior year.

1. Gingerbread ◆ 2002
2. Shrimp ◆ 2005
3. Cupcake ◆ 2007

GIRL

Limb, Sue

DELACORTE ◆ GRADES 7–10 ◆ A/R

REAL LIFE | HUMOR

Jess Jordan has the wrong combination of body parts—big butt, small boobs. Of course, her best friend, Flora, is a goddess. Jess's family is dysfunctional and her love life is hopeless. Set in England, this is similar in tone to Louise Rennison's Confessions of Georgia Nicolson books. *Girl, Barely 15, Flirting for England* is a prequel.

1. Girl, 15, Charming But Insane ◆ 2004
2. Girl, (Nearly) 16, Absolute Torture ◆ 2005
3. Girl, Going on 17, Pants on Fire ◆ 2006
4. Girl, Barely 15, Flirting for England ◆ 2008

GIRLS OF AVENUE Z

Pielichaty, Helena
ALADDIN ◆ GRADES 5–7 ◆ A/R
REAL LIFE

Originally published in England as the "After School Club" series, these books feature girls who are left on their own after school. They could become involved in problem situations. Instead, they attend the Avenue Z Club. Each book features a different girl and her problems. In *Starring Jolene,* Jolene has run away and goes with her aunt to the club. There, she notices a young boy with bruises and she decides to get involved.

1. Starring Sammie ◆ 2006
2. Starring Brody ◆ 2006
3. Starring Alex ◆ 2006
4. Starring Jolene ◆ 2007

GIRLS OF MANY LANDS *see* American Girls: Girls of Many Lands

THE GIRLS QUARTET

Wilson, Jacqueline
DELACORTE ◆ GRADES 6–9 ◆ A/R
REAL LIFE

Ellie feels like an ugly duckling. Her friends Magda and Nadine are stunning while Ellie is flabby. She diets and works out and begins to look fit, but she is cranky. Can she look great and be a good friend too? This series is set in England.

1. Girls in Love ◆ 2002
2. Girls Under Pressure ◆ 2002
3. Girls Out Late ◆ 2002
4. Girls in Tears ◆ 2003

GIRLS R.U.L.E.

Lowe, Kris

BERKLEY ◆ GRADES 6–8

ADVENTURE | REAL LIFE

Cayenga Park is adding a girls' division of junior rangers. The tryouts will be difficult, especially since the boys' division is not totally in favor of this new group. Five girls—Kayla Adams, Carson McDonald, Sophie Schultz, Becca Fisher, and Alex Loomis-Drake—tell their own stories about their lives and interest in the park program. The first book established the personality of each girl and her strengths, insecurities, and special needs. Sophie is stubborn and outspoken; Carson does not let her hearing disability limit her accomplishments; Becca's jokes and sarcasm sometimes cause problems. This adventure series will appeal to girls who like intrepid, strong-willed, female main characters.

1. Girls R.U.L.E. ◆ 1998
2. Trail of Terror ◆ 1998
3. Seal Island Scam ◆ 1998

THE GIVER

Lowry, Lois

HOUGHTON MIFFLIN ◆ GRADES 6–10 ◆ A/R

SCIENCE FICTION

These companion books may not be a true series but they are connected by the strength of the young main characters in worlds that have gone wrong. Jonas (in *The Giver*), Kira (in *Gathering Blue*), and Matty (in *Messenger*) face cruelty, oppression, and hostility. Each responds with creativity, independence, and courage. *The Giver* received the Newbery Medal for its depiction of Jonas's life in a society that has repressed emotions, colors, senses, and memory. Jonas's Assignment is to be the Receiver of Memories and he begins to uncover everything that has been hidden from him.

1. The Giver ◆ 1993
2. Gathering Blue ◆ 2000
3. Messenger ◆ 2004

GLORY

Lynn, Jodi

PUFFIN ◆ GRADES 6–9 ◆ A/R

REAL LIFE

Glory, 13, lives in Dogwood, West Virginia, in a strict religious sect that shuns modern ways. After becoming drunk with her friend Katie (who dies in an accident), Glory is cast out. She struggles to survive as she tries to reach Boston. But there is an added danger. She has been given a slow poison and she must return to Dogwood to confront her transgressions.

1. Glory ◆ 2003
2. Shadow Tree ◆ 2003
3. Blue Girl ◆ 2003
4. Forget Me Not ◆ 2003

GODDESSES

Hantman, Clea

HARPERCOLLINS ◆ GRADES 6–9 ◆ A/R

FANTASY | HUMOR

In a fit of temper, Zeus banishes his daughters—Polly, Era, and Thalia—but accidentally sends them to present-day Athens, Georgia. There the girls try to fit in at school and in their social life, learning about contemporary customs and language. The Furies are also there, in disguise, and Thalia's boyfriend Apollo turns up in *Three Girls and a God*. In the last book, the trio find themselves in Hades.

1. Heaven Sent ◆ 2002
2. Three Girls and a God ◆ 2002
3. Muses on the Move ◆ 2002
4. Love or Fate ◆ 2002

GOLDEN FILLY SERIES

Snelling, Lauraine

BETHANY HOUSE ◆ GRADES 6–9 ◆ A/R

REAL LIFE

Tricia Evanston wants to train and race horses. Her mother disapproves and her father is too ill to intervene (in *Shadow over San Mateo,* her father dies). When Tricia gets the horse Spitfire, she begins to succeed. Trish and Spitfire are the surprise winners of the Santa Anita Derby. What's next . . . the Kentucky Derby! The series follows Trish through high school where she deals with horse racing, dating, and a stalker.

1. The Race ◆ 1991
2. Eagle's Wing ◆ 1991
3. Go for the Glory ◆ 1991
4. Kentucky Dreamer ◆ 1992
5. Call for Courage ◆ 1992
6. Shadow over San Mateo ◆ 1993

7. Out of the Mist ◆ 1993
8. Second Wind ◆ 1994
9. Close Call ◆ 1994
10. The Winner's Circle ◆ 1995

GOLDEN MOUNTAIN CHRONICLES

Yep, Laurence

HARPERCOLLINS ◆ GRADES 7–8 ◆ A/R

HISTORICAL

Each of these books has a different main character, but they are all inter-twined by family ties. In the first book, *The Serpent's Children,* Foxfire and Cassia are a brother and sister in China whose father, Gallant, has gone to war against the British invaders. Cassia struggles to hold her family together. In the second novel, *Mountain Light,* another character, Squeaky, loses his home in one of the rebellions and goes off to America to seek his fortune. And in *Dragon's Gate,* Otter goes to join his Uncle Foxfire in America to become rich and then return to China and continue fighting against the Manchu. Instead, he discovers that Foxfire is not the man he thought he was and that the Chinese working on the railroad are little more than slaves. With much historical detail, these books make for great reads.

1. Dragonwings: 1903 ◆ 1975
2. Child of the Owl: 1965 ◆ 1977
3. Sea Glass: 1970 ◆ 1979
4. The Serpent's Children: 1849 ◆ 1984
5. Mountain Light: 1855 ◆ 1985
6. Dragon's Gate: 1867 ◆ 1993
7. Thief of Hearts: 1995 ◆ 1995
8. The Traitor: 1885 ◆ 2003
9. Dragon Road: 1939 ◆ 2008

GOLDSTONE TRILOGY

Lawson, Julie

STODDART ◆ GRADES 5–7 ◆ A/R

FANTASY | REAL LIFE

In early 20th-century British Columbia, 12-year-old Karin, a girl of Swedish descent, inherits a goldstone pendant when her mother is killed in an avalanche. This necklace allows Karin to dream of the future. In the first book, she foresees a second avalanche. In *Turns on a Dime,* set in the 1950s, lonely and uncertain 11-year-old Jo inherits the pendant and finds it gives her strength and self-confidence. In the final volume, Jo passes the pendant on to her niece Ashley, who is challenged by a ghost seeking to return the goldstone to its original home.

1. Goldstone ◆ 1998
2. Turns on a Dime ◆ 1999
3. The Ghost of Avalanche Mountain ◆ 2000

GOOSE GIRL

Hale, Shannon
BLOOMSBURY ◆ GRADES 6–9 ◆ A/R
FANTASY

Princess Anidori, who can speak to animals, is betrayed by her servants and guards. Disguising herself, she becomes a goose girl. She falls in love with a prince, marries, and takes her rightful place as queen. *Enna Burning* is a companion book featuring Enna, the best friend of Princess Anidori, while *River Secrets* features Razo, a friend of both girls. Fairy tale conventions permeate these books, which could be read along with the books of Gail Carson Levine, Robin McKinley, and Donna Jo Napoli.

1. The Goose Girl ◆ 2003
2. Enna Burning ◆ 2004
3. River Secrets ◆ 2007

GOOSEBUMPS

Stine, R. L.
SCHOLASTIC ◆ GRADES 4–8 ◆ A/R
HORROR

According to the publisher, more than 200 million copies of Goosebumps have been sold. There are spin-off series, television tie-ins, and a Web site (http://www.scholastic.com/goosebumps). The books are filled with creatures and gore, with implausible situations and frightening circumstances. The characters are often unsuspecting innocents—just like your neighbors and friends, or even yourself—caught in the clutches of gnomes, werewolves, monsters, vampires, and other creatures. The locations include a mummy's tomb, Camp Nightmare, Horrorland, and the Haunted School. This popular series brings the horror genre to a younger audience, giving them dripping blood, shrunken heads, and monsters awaiting their next victim.

1. Welcome to Dead House ◆ 1992
2. Stay Out of the Basement ◆ 1992
3. Monster Blood ◆ 1992
4. Say Cheese and Die! ◆ 1992
5. Curse of the Mummy's Tomb ◆ 1993

6. Let's Get Invisible! ◆ 1993
7. Night of the Living Dummy ◆ 1993
8. The Girl Who Cried Monster ◆ 1993
9. Welcome to Camp Nightmare ◆ 1993
10. The Ghost Next Door ◆ 1993
11. The Haunted Mask ◆ 1993
12. Be Careful What You Wish For ◆ 1993
13. Piano Lessons Can Be Murder ◆ 1993
14. The Werewolf of Fever Swamp ◆ 1993
15. You Can't Scare Me! ◆ 1994
16. One Day at Horrorland ◆ 1994
17. Why I'm Afraid of Bees ◆ 1994
18. Monster Blood II ◆ 1994
19. Deep Trouble ◆ 1994
20. The Scarecrow Walks at Midnight ◆ 1994
21. Go Eat Worms! ◆ 1994
22. Ghost Beach ◆ 1994
23. Return of the Mummy ◆ 1994
24. Phantom of the Auditorium ◆ 1994
25. Attack of the Mutant ◆ 1994
26. My Hairiest Adventure ◆ 1994
27. A Night in Terror Tower ◆ 1995
28. The Cuckoo Clock of Doom ◆ 1995
29. Monster Blood III ◆ 1995
30. It Came from Beneath the Sink! ◆ 1995
31. Night of the Living Dummy II ◆ 1995
32. The Barking Ghost ◆ 1995
33. The Horror at Camp Jellyjam ◆ 1995
34. Revenge of the Lawn Gnomes ◆ 1995
35. A Shocker on Shock Street ◆ 1995
36. The Haunted Mask II ◆ 1995
37. The Headless Ghost ◆ 1995
38. The Abominable Snowman of Pasadena ◆ 1995
39. How I Got My Shrunken Head ◆ 1996
40. Night of the Living Dummy III ◆ 1996
41. Bad Hare Day ◆ 1996
42. Egg Monsters from Mars ◆ 1996
43. The Beast from the East ◆ 1996
44. Say Cheese and Die—Again! ◆ 1996
45. Ghost Camp ◆ 1996
46. How to Kill a Monster ◆ 1996
47. Legend of the Lost Legend ◆ 1996
48. Attack of the Jack-O'-Lanterns ◆ 1996
49. Vampire Breath ◆ 1996
50. Calling All Creeps! ◆ 1996
51. Beware, the Snowman ◆ 1997
52. How I Learned to Fly ◆ 1997
53. Chicken Chicken ◆ 1997
54. Don't Go to Sleep! ◆ 1997

55. The Blob That Ate Everyone ◆ 1997
56. The Curse of Camp Cold Lake ◆ 1997
57. My Best Friend Is Invisible ◆ 1997
58. Deep Trouble II ◆ 1997
59. The Haunted School ◆ 1997
60. Werewolf Skin ◆ 1997
61. I Live in Your Basement! ◆ 1997
62. Monster Blood IV ◆ 1998

GOOSEBUMPS: GIVE YOURSELF GOOSEBUMPS

Stine, R. L.

SCHOLASTIC ◆ GRADES 4–8

HORROR | ADVENTURE

What do you get when you cross the incredibly popular horror stories of Goosebumps with the popular format of Choose Your Own Adventure? You get Give Yourself Goosebumps. The cover of each book announces "Choose from over 20 different scary endings," giving readers many different ways to direct the adventures. Like the basic Goosebumps books, these are scary stories where characters try to escape from weird creatures or are attacked by monsters or lost in a swamp. You meet werewolves, vampires, and terrible toys. You visit such places as the Carnival of Horrors and the Dead-End Hotel. Depending on the choices, the reader can triumph over the evil creatures, just barely escape, or be swallowed by a sea monster. The two popular genres represented in this series are sure to capture the interest of even the most reluctant readers.

1. Escape from the Carnival of Horrors ◆ 1995
2. Tick Tock, You're Dead! ◆ 1995
3. Trapped in Bat Wing Hall ◆ 1995
4. The Deadly Experiments of Dr. Eek ◆ 1996
5. Night in Werewolf Woods ◆ 1996
6. Beware of the Purple Peanut Butter ◆ 1996
7. Under the Magician's Spell ◆ 1996
8. The Curse of the Creeping Coffin ◆ 1996
9. The Knight in Screaming Armor ◆ 1996
10. Diary of a Mad Mummy ◆ 1996
11. Deep in the Jungle of Doom ◆ 1996
12. Welcome to the Wicked Wax Museum ◆ 1996
13. Scream of the Evil Genie ◆ 1997
14. The Creepy Creations of Professor Shock ◆ 1997
15. Please Don't Feed the Vampire! ◆ 1997
16. Secret Agent Grandma ◆ 1997
17. Little Comic Shop of Horrors ◆ 1997
18. Attack of the Beastly Baby-Sitter ◆ 1997
19. Escape from Camp Run-for-Your-Life ◆ 1997

20. Toy Terror: Batteries Included ◆ 1997
21. The Twisted Tale of Tiki Island ◆ 1997
22. Return to the Carnival of Horrors ◆ 1997
23. Zapped in Space ◆ 1997
24. Lost in Stinkeye Swamp ◆ 1997
25. Shop 'Til You Drop . . . Dead ◆ 1998
26. Alone in Snakebite Canyon ◆ 1998
27. Checkout Time at the Dead-End Hotel ◆ 1998
28. Night of a Thousand Claws ◆ 1998
29. Invaders from the Big Screen ◆ 1998
30. You're Plant Food! ◆ 1998
31. The Werewolf of Twisted Tree Lodge ◆ 1998
32. It's Only a Nightmare ◆ 1998
33. It Came from the Internet ◆ 1999
34. Elevator to Nowhere ◆ 1999
35. Hocus-Pocus Horror ◆ 1999
36. Ship of Ghouls ◆ 1999
37. Escape from Horror House ◆ 1999
38. Into the Twister of Terror ◆ 1999
39. Scary Birthday to You! ◆ 1999
40. Zombie School ◆ 2000
41. Danger Time ◆ 2000
42. All-Day Nightmare ◆ 2000

GIVE YOURSELF GOOSEBUMPS SPECIAL EDITIONS

1. Into the Jaws of Doom ◆ 1998
2. Return to Terror Tower: The Nightmare Continues ◆ 1998
3. Power Play: Trapped in the Circus of Fear ◆ 1998
4. The Ultimate Challenge: One Night in Payne House ◆ 1998
5. The Curse of the Cave Creatures ◆ 1999
6. Revenge of the Body Squeezers ◆ 1999
7. Trick or . . . Trapped ◆ 1999
8. Weekend at Poison Lake ◆ 1999

GOOSEBUMPS GRAPHIX

Stine, R. L.

GRAPHIX ◆ GRADES 4–8 ◆ A/R

HORROR

Familiar Goosebumps stories have been reformatted as graphic novels. As in the original stories, there are twists and turns that leave the reader breathless. Goosebumps books have always been popular; adding the graphic novel illustrations and format will reach many new fans, including reluctant readers.

1. Creepy Creatures ◆ 2006

2. Terror Trips ◆ 2007
3. Scary Summer ◆ 2007

GOOSEBUMPS HORRORLAND

Stine, R. L.

SCHOLASTIC ◆ GRADES 4–8 ◆ A/R

HORROR

Welcome to Horrorland! An amusement park that will thrill you . . . to death! In the first book, Britney, 12, has a frightening encounter with a ventriloquist's dummy. Then, on a trip to Horrorland, Britney discovers that the terror is just beginning. In *Creep from the Deep,* Billy and his sister Sheena are on an underwater ride of doom. Goosebumps fans will delight in this new series of books.

1. Revenge of the Living Dummy ◆ 2008
2. Creep from the Deep ◆ 2008
3. Monster Blood for Breakfast! ◆ 2008
4. The Scream of the Haunted Mask ◆ 2008
5. Dr. Maniac vs. Robby Schwartz ◆ 2008
6. Who's Your Mummy? ◆ 2009
7. My Friends Call Me Monster ◆ 2009

GOOSEBUMPS SERIES 2000

Stine, R. L.

SCHOLASTIC ◆ GRADES 4–8 ◆ A/R

HORROR

Advertised as having a "scarier edge," Goosebumps 2000 capitalizes on the popularity of the horror genre and the familiar name of Goosebumps. The danger in these books is a bit more intense and could appeal to an older audience and provide a transition to YA horror titles. As with the related series, there are weird creatures and slime, ghosts, and gore.

1. Cry of the Cat ◆ 1998
2. Bride of the Living Dummy ◆ 1998
3. Creature Teacher ◆ 1998
4. Invasion of the Body Squeezers, Part 1 ◆ 1998
5. Invasion of the Body Squeezers, Part 2 ◆ 1998
6. I Am Your Evil Twin ◆ 1998
7. Revenge R Us ◆ 1998
8. Fright Camp ◆ 1998
9. Are You Terrified Yet? ◆ 1998
10. Headless Halloween ◆ 1998
11. Attack of the Graveyard Ghouls ◆ 1998

12. Brain Juice ◆ 1998
13. Return to Horrorland ◆ 1999
14. Jekyll and Heidi ◆ 1999
15. Scream School ◆ 1999
16. The Mummy Walks ◆ 1999
17. The Werewolf in the Living Room ◆ 1999
18. Horrors of the Black Ring ◆ 1999
19. Return to Ghost Camp ◆ 1999
20. Be Afraid—Be Very Afraid! ◆ 1999
21. The Haunted Car ◆ 1999
22. Full Moon Fever ◆ 1999
23. Slappy's Nightmare ◆ 1999
24. Earth Geeks Must Go! ◆ 1999
25. Ghost in the Mirror ◆ 2000

GORDIANUS THE FINDER *see* Roma Sub Rosa

GORDY SMITH

Hahn, Mary Downing
CLARION ◆ GRADES 5–7 ◆ A/R
FAMILY LIFE | HISTORICAL

This series begins during World War II when best friends Elizabeth and Margaret spy on their sixth-grade classmate—a bully named Gordy Smith. They discover that he is hiding his brother Stu, who is an Army deserter. This is a grave moral dilemma for these patriotic friends. The sequels focus on Gordy as he is separated from his abusive family and sent to live with a grandmother in North Carolina. On her sudden death, Gordy returns to his hometown and the lingering perceptions that he is a bully from a "trashy" family. These are thoughtfully written books with realistic insights into the era and the characters.

1. Stepping on the Cracks ◆ 1991
2. Following My Own Footsteps ◆ 1996
3. As Ever, Gordy ◆ 1998

GOSSIP GIRL

von Ziegesar, Cecily
LITTLE, BROWN ◆ GRADES 9–12 ◆ A/R
REAL LIFE

These books narrated by an anonymous observer feature teens who have it all—money, good schools, and beauty. But they also have serious problems with alcohol, drugs, and sex. The core group of kids includes Blair, her ex-boyfriend Nate, Serena, Dan, and Vanessa. They attend posh prep schools in Manhattan and are sometimes friends and sometimes rivals. One review called these books "soap operalike," but they are among the most popular with teens right now. In the Carlyles subseries, wealthy triplets Avery, Baby, and Owen Carlyle are settling into a Manhattan penthouse but are still drawn to their Nantucket home. *It Had to Be You* (2007) is a prequel to the main series, covering the girls' sophomore year.

1. Gossip Girl ◆ 2002
2. You Know You Love Me ◆ 2002
3. All I Want Is Everything ◆ 2003
4. Because I'm Worth It ◆ 2003
5. I Like It Like That ◆ 2004
6. You're the One That I Want ◆ 2004
7. Nobody Does It Better ◆ 2005
8. Nothing Can Keep Us Together ◆ 2005
9. Only in Your Dreams ◆ 2006
10. Would I Lie to You ◆ 2006
11. Don't You Forget About Me ◆ 2007

GOSSIP GIRL: THE CARLYLES

1. The Carlyles ◆ 2008
2. You Just Can't Get Enough ◆ 2008

GRADUATION SUMMER *see* Mary-Kate and Ashley: Graduation Summer

GRAIL QUEST

Gilman, Laura Anne
HARPERCOLLINS ◆ GRADES 5–8
FANTASY

On the eve of King Arthur's quest for the Holy Grail, three young teens of different backgrounds — Gerard, Newt, and Ailias — must reverse a spell crippling all adults. This trilogy is suspenseful, with characters readers will recognize as well as fantastic creatures.

1. The Camelot Spell ◆ 2006
2. Morgain's Revenge ◆ 2006
3. The Shadow Companion ◆ 2006

GRAVEYARD SCHOOL

Stone, Tom B.

BANTAM ◆ GRADES 4–7 ◆ A/R

HORROR | MYSTERY

Grove School is right next to a graveyard. So naturally the kids call it Graveyard School. Park, who considers himself a detective, and his friend Stacey solve mysteries and get into some terrifying situations. At the beginning of their sixth-grade year, the principal, Dr. Morehouse, introduces a new lunch room supervisor who promises tasty meals at low cost. Soon after, pets start disappearing all over town. The series continues as the friends solve more scary mysteries at the school.

1. Don't Eat the Mystery Meat ◆ 1994
2. The Skeleton on the Skateboard ◆ 1994
3. The Headless Bicycle Rider ◆ 1994
4. Little Pet Werewolf ◆ 1995
5. Revenge of the Dinosaurs ◆ 1995
6. Camp Dracula ◆ 1995
7. Slime Lake ◆ 1995
8. Let's Scare the Teacher to Death ◆ 1995
9. The Abominable Snow Monster ◆ 1995
10. There's a Ghost in the Boy's Bathroom ◆ 1996
11. April Ghoul's Day ◆ 1996
12. Scream, Team! ◆ 1996
13. Tales Too Scary to Tell at Camp ◆ 1996
14. The Tragic School Bus ◆ 1996
15. The Fright Before Christmas ◆ 1996
16. Don't Tell Mummy ◆ 1997
17. Jack and the Beanstalker ◆ 1997
18. The Dead Sox ◆ 1997
19. The Gator Ate Her ◆ 1997
20. Creature Teacher ◆ 1997
21. The Skeleton's Revenge ◆ 1997
22. Boo Year's Eve ◆ 1998
23. The Easter Egg Haunt ◆ 1998
24. Scream Around the Campfire ◆ 1998
25. Escape from Vampire Park ◆ 1998
26. Little School of Horrors ◆ 1998
27. Here Comes Santa Claws ◆ 1998
28. The Spider Beside Her ◆ 1998

THE GREAT BRAIN

Fitzgerald, John D.

DIAL ◆ GRADES 5–7 ◆ A/R

HISTORICAL | HUMOR | REAL LIFE

Tom, Sweyn, and J.D. are three brothers growing up in a small Utah town in the late 1800s. Tom has a great brain and an insatiable love for money, a combination that leads him to concoct endless schemes for swindling his friends and family. One of his first enterprises is to charge the neighborhood kids to see his family's toilet, the first in town. Occasionally, he has fits of conscience and promises to reform, most notably when the neighborhood kids decide to stop speaking to him. Sweyn, the oldest brother, is amused by Tom's schemes, but J.D., the youngest brother and narrator, always seems to be taken in.

1. The Great Brain ◆ 1967
2. More Adventures of the Great Brain ◆ 1969
3. Me and My Little Brain ◆ 1971
4. The Great Brain at the Academy ◆ 1972
5. The Great Brain Reforms ◆ 1973
6. The Return of the Great Brain ◆ 1974
7. The Great Brain Does It Again ◆ 1975
8. The Great Brain Is Back ◆ 1995

THE GREAT GOOD THING *see* Sylvie Cycle

THE GREAT SKINNER

Tolan, Stephanie S.

MACMILLAN ◆ GRADES 4–7

FAMILY LIFE | HUMOR

Jennifer Skinner narrates the hilarious adventures of the not-quite-normal Skinner family. The slide from normalcy begins when her mother decides to go on strike to get her family to do more of the housework. The strike gains national attention, much to the disgust of Jennifer and her siblings. The strike is finally settled when everyone in the family agrees to do more around the house. But Mr. Skinner has been irrevocably changed by the whole business. He decides to quit his job and start a family business, which turns out to be too successful. Just as the family is hoping to settle down again, he buys a motor home and they start off on a trip across the country.

1. The Great Skinner Strike ◆ 1983
2. The Great Skinner Enterprise ◆ 1986
3. The Great Skinner Getaway ◆ 1987
4. The Great Skinner Homestead ◆ 1988

THE GREAT TREE OF AVALON

Barron, T. A.

PHILOMEL ◆ GRADES 7–12 ◆ A/R

FANTASY

The seven roots of a huge tree serve as separate realms of Avalon. During a drought, the realms enter into conflicts that could lead to their destruction. Tamwyn, 17, and his companions struggle to resolve the conflicts. Is Tamwyn the true heir of Merlin or the child of the Dark Prophecy? Barron's Lost Years of Merlin books would also interest readers of this series.

1. Child of the Dark Prophecy ◆ 2004
2. Shadows on the Stars ◆ 2005
3. The Eternal Flame ◆ 2006

THE GREAT WAR

Turtledove, Harry

BALLANTINE DEL REY ◆ GRADES 10–12

SCIENCE FICTION

Trench warfare reaches America in this alternate history that starts when the U.S. sides with Germany and the Confederate States of America sides with France and Great Britain. *How Few Remain* (1997), in which the Confederate States of America has won the Civil War but conflicts persist, serves as a prequel to this series and to American Empire, a trilogy of turmoil across the North American continent. Volumes in that series are *Blood and Iron* (2001), *The Center Cannot Hold* (2002), and *The Victorious Opposition* (2003).

1. American Front ◆ 1998
2. Walk in Hell ◆ 1999
3. Breakthroughs ◆ 2000

GREEN KNOWE

Boston, L. M.

HARCOURT ◆ **GRADES 4–8** ◆ **A/R**

FANTASY

An ancient house in Great Britain is rich with history and stories of the children who have lived there over the centuries. Lonely young Tolly goes to live there with his Great-Grandmother Oldknow in the early 1930s. Tolly soon discovers that his great-grandmother's stories about the children who used to live there literally come to life. We are not sure at first whether he is time-traveling or seeing the children's ghosts, but it soon becomes clear that all time blends together in this house. The series continues with more stories of children from different eras and with mysteries about the house itself, including hidden treasure.

1. The Children of Green Knowe ◆ 1954
2. The Treasure of Green Knowe ◆ 1958
3. The River at Green Knowe ◆ 1959
4. A Stranger at Green Knowe ◆ 1961
5. An Enemy at Green Knowe ◆ 1964
6. The Stones of Green Knowe ◆ 1976

THE GREEN RIDER

Britain, Kristen

DAW HARDCOVER ◆ **GRADES 10–12** ◆ **A/R**

FANTASY

After leaving her school following a disagreement, Karigan G'ladheon meets a dying Green Rider, a messenger for the King of Sacoridia. Karigan takes the message, a magic brooch, and his horse and delivers the message to King Zachary. Karigan becomes a Green Rider and, as the series continues, confronts the evil forces that are threatening Sacoridia. She uses her connection with the First Rider, a woman who has been dead for a thousand years, to aid her in her fight. Fans of Robin McKinley's *The Blue Sword* and *The Hero and the Crown* will enjoy the strong female main character in this series.

1. The Green Rider ◆ 1998
2. First Rider's Call ◆ 2003
3. The High King's Tomb ◆ 2007

GREY GRIFFINS

Benz, Derek, and J. S. Lewis

SCHOLASTIC ◆ GRADES 5–8 ◆ A/R

FANTASY

Max, Harley, Natalia, and Ernie enjoy playing a fantasy role playing game called Round Table. Using cards and dice, the game features witches, faeries, goblins, and other magical creatures. Mr. Iverson, the elderly owner of an antique shop, plays with them. When Max inadvertently releases one of the game card characters, other characters begin to leave the game and enter reality. Max and his friends, who call themselves the Grey Griffins, need to find a way to return the creatures to the game. They begin to realize that there is more to the game than they expected as Max is revealed to be a descendant of King Arthur and the Knights Templar.

1. The Revenge of the Shadow King ◆ 2006
2. The Rise of the Black Wolf ◆ 2007
3. The Fall of the Templar ◆ 2008

GRK

Doder, Joshua

RANDOM HOUSE; ANDERSEN PRESS ◆ GRADES 5–7 ◆ A/R

ADVENTURE

Tim Malt, a plucky British 12-year-old, discovers a dog that belongs to the Stanislavian ambassador's family. Only trouble is, the family is no longer in London. Tim sets off to Stanislavia with Grk in tow and plunges into an adventure full of fast-paced action. In the second book, Tim, Grk, and the Stanislavian children are off to Brazil on the trail of bank robbers.

1. A Dog Called Grk ◆ 2007
2. Grk: Operation Tortoise ◆ 2007
3. Grk and the Pelotti Gang ◆ 2007
4. Grk Smells a Rat ◆ 2008
5. Grk and the Hot Dog Trail ◆ 2008

THE GROO

Aragones, Sergio, and Mark Evanier

DARK HORSE ◆ GRADES 6–12

FANTASY | HUMOR

Groo is a barbarian swordsman with strength but little sense. With his dog, Rufferto, he wanders the world encountering magic, confronting

evil, and bumbling through adventures. Some of the books may be appropriate for a younger audience while others are more satirical. Reviewers tend to place these in YA collections.

1. The Groo: Most Intelligent Man in the World ◆ 1998
2. The Groo: Inferno ◆ 1999
3. The Groo: Houndbook ◆ 1999
4. The Groo: Jamboree ◆ 2000
5. Groo and Rufferto ◆ 2000
6. The Groo: Library ◆ 2001
7. The Groo: Mightier than the Sword ◆ 2001
8. The Groo: Kingdom ◆ 2001
9. The Groo: Death and Taxes ◆ 2002
10. The Groo: Nursery ◆ 2002
11. The Groo: Odyssey ◆ 2002
12. The Groo: Maiden ◆ 2002

THE GROSSE ADVENTURES

Auerbach, Annie

TOKYOPOP ◆ GRADES 4–7 ◆ A/R

HUMOR

Stinky and Stan Grosse are twin brothers with a smelly skill—passing gas. Their odor-producing ability is helpful when they encounter aliens. The brothers are always on the lookout for adventure. The stories are presented with graphic novel sections along with more traditional text. Show these to fans of the Riot Brothers and Captain Underpants.

1. The Good, the Bad & the Gassy ◆ 2006
2. Stinky & Stan Blast Off! ◆ 2007
3. Trouble at Twilight Cave ◆ 2007

GUARDIANS OF GA'HOOLE

Lasky, Kathryn

SCHOLASTIC ◆ GRADES 4–8 ◆ A/R

FANTASY

The Academy for Orphaned Owls is not a kind place. Soren, a barn owl, discovers this when he arrives and is given a number to replace his name. All the young owls are made to follow the very strict rules. With the help of an old owl, Soren and his friends subvert the rules. They learn to fly and to confront the evil that surrounds them. Fans of Avi's books about Poppy and Brian Jacques's Redwall should try this series.

1. The Capture ◆ 2003
2. The Journey ◆ 2003

3. The Rescue ◆ 2003
4. The Siege ◆ 2004
5. The Shattering ◆ 2004
6. The Burning ◆ 2004
7. The Hatchling ◆ 2005
8. The Outcast ◆ 2005
9. The First Collier ◆ 2006
10. The Coming of Hoole ◆ 2006
11. To Be a King ◆ 2006
12. The Golden Tree ◆ 2007
13. The River of Wind ◆ 2007
14. Exile ◆ 2008
15. The War of the Ember ◆ 2008

GUY STRANG

Weeks, Sarah

HARPERCOLLINS ◆ GRADES 5–8 ◆ A/R

REAL LIFE

Guy Strang, 12, wonders if he's in the right family. His parents are eccentric, often even embarrassing. For example, his father sucks oysters up his nose. When Guy and his friend Buzz find a classmate with the same birthday as Guy, they become convinced that Guy was switched at birth. In the second book, Guy's parents separate and Guy adjusts to his changing feelings about girls.

1. Regular Guy ◆ 1999
2. Guy Time ◆ 2000
3. My Guy ◆ 2001
4. Guy Wire ◆ 2003

GWYN GRIFFITHS TRILOGY

Nimmo, Jenny

SCHOLASTIC ◆ GRADES 4–7 ◆ A/R

FANTASY

Gwyn's sister has disappeared in the Welsh mountains. Gwyn's grandmother gives him five magic gifts to help him solve this mystery. In the second book, Gwyn and a girl called Nia save Gwyn's cousin Emlyn from the creatures that snatched Gwyn's sister. The series concludes as Gwyn uses his magical powers to capture an evil spirit. This series was reissued in 2006–2007 as the Magician Trilogy. The middle volume, *Orchard of the Crescent Moon,* was renamed *Emlyn's Moon.*

1. The Snow Spider ◆ 1987

2. Orchard of the Crescent Moon ◆ 1989
3. The Chestnut Soldier ◆ 1991

HAMILTON HIGH

Reynolds, Marilyn

MORNING GLORY PRESS ◆ GRADES 8–12

REAL LIFE

This series focuses on typical teen problems. In *Telling,* a 12-year-old girl confides to her teenage cousin about being sexually molested by the father of the children she is babysitting. Other books deal with teen sexuality, pregnancy, drug addiction, and more. *Beyond Dreams* is a collection of six short stories.

1. Detour for Emily ◆ 1993
2. Too Soon for Jeff ◆ 1994
3. Beyond Dreams ◆ 1995
4. But What About Me? ◆ 1996
5. Telling ◆ 1996
6. Baby Help ◆ 1997
7. If You Loved Me ◆ 1999
8. Love Rules ◆ 2001
9. No More Sad Goodbyes ◆ 2007
10. Shut Up ◆ 2008

HAMLET CHRONICLES

Maguire, Gregory

CLARION ◆ GRADES 4–7 ◆ A/R

FANTASY

In Hamlet, Vermont, problems arise when seven frozen prehistoric Siberian snow spiders thaw. Each imprints on a different girl in the Tattletale Club. Things are fine while the spiders are small. But when they begin to grow, they become mean and have plans for the boys in the Copycat Club and their teacher, Miss Earth. The same students return in other books as the Tattletales and Copycats continue their rivalry.

1. Seven Spiders Spinning ◆ 1994
2. Six Haunted Hairdos ◆ 1997
3. Five Alien Elves ◆ 1998
4. Four Stupid Cupids ◆ 2000
5. Three Rotten Eggs ◆ 2002
6. A Couple of April Fools ◆ 2004
7. One Final Firecracker ◆ 2005

A HANDFUL OF MEN

Duncan, David

BALLANTINE DEL REY ◆ GRADES 9–12

FANTASY

Readers of fantasy will be attracted to this lively, detailed series set in the world of Pandemia. Magic, trolls, gnomes, sorcerers, and battles against evil forces fill each book. In the concluding book, Zinixo, a dwarf, has enslaved many magicians. Rap, the faun king, struggles to confront Zinixo and free the magicians. Fans of the Fellowship of the Ring could follow up with these books. Duncan has a previous series about Pandemia, A Man of His Word.

1. The Cutting Edge ◆ 1992
2. Upland Outlaws ◆ 1993
3. The Stricken Field ◆ 1993
4. The Living God ◆ 1994

HAPPY BUNNY *see* It's Happy Bunny

HARD CASH

Cann, Kate

SIMON & SCHUSTER ◆ GRADES 9–12 ◆ A/R

REAL LIFE

Rich, 17, is obsessed with money. His life at home has been a struggle. Now he is on the way to financial success. His job at an ad agency pays incredibly well, although he has to use his art talent on banal accounts. With his new income status, Rich begins to buy the things he has dreamed about and goes beyond his resources. After he loses his job, he tries to go back to college and begins to date a vapid beauty, Portia, ignoring Bonny, who clearly would like to have his attention. This British series will be enjoyed by readers of Louise Rennison's books.

1. Hard Cash ◆ 2003
2. Shacked Up ◆ 2004
3. Speeding ◆ 2004

HARDY BOYS

Dixon, Franklin W.

SIMON & SCHUSTER ◆ GRADES 5–7 ◆ A/R

MYSTERY

Frank and Joe Hardy, the sons of famous detective Fenton Hardy, have
become well-known detectives in their own right, even though they are
still in their teens. In each book, the two boys are pursuing their various
interests when they are confronted with a crime or mystery. After much
action and adventure, the mystery is solved, the criminal caught, and all
is well again in Bayport. Frank is cast as the serious and thoughtful one,
while Joe is more athletic and impulsive. They are aided occasionally by
their friend Chet and their father's sister Gertrude.

1. The Tower Treasure ◆ 1927
2. The House on the Cliff ◆ 1927
3. The Secret of the Old Mill ◆ 1927
4. The Missing Chums ◆ 1928
5. Hunting for Hidden Gold ◆ 1928
6. The Shore Road Mystery ◆ 1928
7. Secret of the Caves ◆ 1929
8. Mystery of Cabin Island ◆ 1929
9. Great Airport Mystery ◆ 1930
10. What Happened at Midnight? ◆ 1931
11. While the Clock Ticked ◆ 1932
12. Footprints Under the Window ◆ 1933
13. The Mark on the Door ◆ 1934
14. The Hidden Harbor Mystery ◆ 1935
15. Sinister Signpost ◆ 1936
16. Figure in Hiding ◆ 1937
17. Secret Warning ◆ 1938
18. The Twisted Claw ◆ 1939
19. The Disappearing Floor ◆ 1940
20. Mystery of the Flying Express ◆ 1941
21. The Clue of the Broken Blade ◆ 1942
22. The Flickering Torch Mystery ◆ 1943
23. The Melted Coins ◆ 1944
24. Short-Wave Mystery ◆ 1945
25. The Secret Panel ◆ 1946
26. The Phantom Freighter ◆ 1947
27. The Secret of Skull Mountain ◆ 1948
28. The Sign of the Crooked Arrow ◆ 1949
29. The Secret of the Lost Tunnel ◆ 1950
30. The Wailing Siren Mystery ◆ 1951
31. The Secret of Wildcat Swamp ◆ 1952
32. The Yellow Feather Mystery ◆ 1953
33. The Crisscross Shadow ◆ 1953
34. The Hooded Hawk Mystery ◆ 1954
35. The Clue in the Embers ◆ 1955
36. The Secret of Pirates' Hill ◆ 1957
37. The Ghost at Skeleton Rock ◆ 1957
38. Mystery at Devil's Paw ◆ 1959
39. Mystery of the Chinese Junk ◆ 1960
40. Mystery of the Desert Giant ◆ 1961
41. Clue of the Screeching Owl ◆ 1962

42. The Viking Symbol Mystery ◆ 1963
43. Mystery of the Aztec Warrior ◆ 1964
44. The Haunted Fort ◆ 1965
45. Mystery of the Spiral Bridge ◆ 1966
46. Secret Agent on Flight 101 ◆ 1967
47. Mystery of the Whale Tattoo ◆ 1968
48. The Arctic Patrol Mystery ◆ 1969
49. Bombay Boomerang ◆ 1970
50. Danger on Vampire Trail ◆ 1971
51. The Masked Monkey ◆ 1972
52. The Shattered Helmet ◆ 1973
53. The Clue of the Hissing Serpent ◆ 1974
54. The Mysterious Caravan ◆ 1975
55. The Witchmaster's Key ◆ 1976
56. The Jungle Pyramid ◆ 1977
57. Firebird Rocket ◆ 1978
58. The Sting of the Scorpion ◆ 1979
59. Night of the Werewolf ◆ 1979
60. The Mystery of the Samurai Sword ◆ 1979
61. The Pentagon Spy ◆ 1980
62. The Apeman's Secret ◆ 1980
63. The Mummy Case ◆ 1980
64. Mystery of Smuggler's Cove ◆ 1980
65. The Stone Idol ◆ 1981
66. The Vanishing Thieves ◆ 1981
67. The Outlaw's Silver ◆ 1981
68. Deadly Chase ◆ 1981
69. The Four-Headed Dragon ◆ 1981
70. The Infinity Clue ◆ 1981
71. The Track of the Zombie ◆ 1982
72. The Voodoo Plot ◆ 1982
73. The Billion Dollar Ransom ◆ 1982
74. Tic-Tac Terror ◆ 1982
75. Trapped at Sea ◆ 1982
76. Game Plan for Disaster ◆ 1982
77. The Crimson Flame ◆ 1983
78. Cave-In! ◆ 1983
79. Sky Sabotage ◆ 1983
80. The Roaring River Mystery ◆ 1984
81. The Demon's Den ◆ 1984
82. The Blackwing Puzzle ◆ 1984
83. The Swamp Monster ◆ 1985
84. Revenge of the Desert Phantom ◆ 1985
85. The Skyfire Puzzle ◆ 1985
86. The Mystery of the Silver Star ◆ 1987
87. Program for Destruction ◆ 1987
88. Tricky Business ◆ 1988
89. Sky Blue Frame ◆ 1988
90. Danger on the Diamond ◆ 1988

91. Shield of Fear ◆ 1988
92. The Shadow Killers ◆ 1988
93. The Serpent's Tooth Mystery ◆ 1988
94. Breakdown in Axeblade ◆ 1989
95. Danger on the Air ◆ 1989
96. Wipeout ◆ 1989
97. Cast of Criminals ◆ 1989
98. Spark of Suspicion ◆ 1989
99. Dungeon of Doom ◆ 1989
100. The Secret of the Island Treasure ◆ 1990
101. The Money Hunt ◆ 1990
102. Terminal Shock ◆ 1990
103. The Million-Dollar Nightmare ◆ 1990
104. Tricks of the Trade ◆ 1990
105. The Smoke Screen Mystery ◆ 1990
106. Attack of the Video Villains ◆ 1991
107. Panic on Gull Island ◆ 1991
108. Fear on Wheels ◆ 1991
109. The Prime-Time Crime ◆ 1991
110. The Secret of Sigma Seven ◆ 1991
111. Three-Ring Terror ◆ 1991
112. The Demolition Mission ◆ 1992
113. Radical Moves ◆ 1992
114. The Case of the Counterfeit Criminals ◆ 1992
115. Sabotage at Sports City ◆ 1992
116. Rock 'n' Roll Renegades ◆ 1992
117. The Baseball Card Conspiracy ◆ 1992
118. Danger in the Fourth Dimension ◆ 1993
119. Trouble at Coyote Canyon ◆ 1993
120. The Case of the Cosmic Kidnapping ◆ 1993
121. The Mystery in the Old Mine ◆ 1993
122. Carnival of Crime ◆ 1993
123. The Robot's Revenge ◆ 1993
124. Mystery with a Dangerous Beat ◆ 1993
125. Mystery on Makatunk Island ◆ 1994
126. Racing with Disaster ◆ 1994
127. Reel Thrills ◆ 1994
128. Day of the Dinosaur ◆ 1994
129. The Treasure at Dolphin Bay ◆ 1994
130. Sidetracked to Danger ◆ 1995
131. Crusade of the Flaming Sword ◆ 1995
132. Maximum Challenge ◆ 1995
133. Crime in the Kennel ◆ 1995
134. Cross-Country Crime ◆ 1995
135. The Hypersonic Secret ◆ 1995
136. The Cold Cash Caper ◆ 1996
137. High-Speed Showdown ◆ 1996
138. The Alaskan Adventure ◆ 1996
139. The Search for the Snow Leopard ◆ 1996

140. Slam Dunk Sabotage ◆ 1996
141. The Desert Thieves ◆ 1996
142. Lost in the Gator Swamp ◆ 1997
143. The Giant Rat of Sumatra ◆ 1997
144. The Secret of Skeleton Reef ◆ 1997
145. Terror at High Tide ◆ 1997
146. The Mark of the Blue Tattoo ◆ 1997
147. Trial and Terror ◆ 1998
148. The Ice-Cold Case ◆ 1998
149. The Chase for the Mystery Twister ◆ 1998
150. The Crisscross Crime ◆ 1998
151. The Rocky Road to Revenge ◆ 1998
152. Danger in the Extreme ◆ 1998
153. Eye on Crime ◆ 1998
154. The Caribbean Cruise Caper ◆ 1999
155. The Hunt for the Four Brothers ◆ 1999
156. A Will to Survive ◆ 1999
157. The Lure of the Italian Treasure ◆ 1999
158. The London Deception ◆ 1999
159. Daredevils ◆ 1999
160. A Game Called Chaos ◆ 2000
161. Training for Trouble ◆ 2000
162. The End of the Trail ◆ 2000
163. The Spy that Never Lies ◆ 2000
164. Skin and Bones ◆ 2000
165. Crime in the Cards ◆ 2001
166. Past and Present Danger ◆ 2001
167. Trouble Times Two ◆ 2001
168. The Castle Conundrum ◆ 2001
169. Ghost of a Chance ◆ 2001
170. Kickoff to Danger ◆ 2001
171. The Test Case ◆ 2002
172. Trouble in Warp Space ◆ 2002
173. Speed Times Five ◆ 2002
174. Hide and Sneak ◆ 2002
175. Trick-or-Trouble ◆ 2002
176. In Plane Sight ◆ 2002
177. The Case of the Psychic's Vision ◆ 2003
178. The Mystery of the Black Rhino ◆ 2003
179. Passport to Danger ◆ 2003
180. Typhoon Island ◆ 2003
181. Double Jeopardy ◆ 2003
182. The Secret of the Soldier's Gold ◆ 2003
183. Warehouse Rumble ◆ 2004
184. The Dangerous Transmission ◆ 2004
185. Wreck and Roll ◆ 2004
186. Hidden Mountain ◆ 2004
187. No Way Out ◆ 2004
188. Farming Fear ◆ 2004

189. One False Step ◆ 2005
190. Motocross Madness ◆ 2005

HARDY BOYS CASEFILES

Dixon, Franklin W.

ARCHWAY ◆ GRADES 6–8 ◆ A/R

MYSTERY

The Hardy Boys Casefiles series is for an older audience of readers. Frank and Joe Hardy have girlfriends and face more serious crimes than in the original series. Corruption, organized crime, hired thugs, conspiracies, and even the threat of murder are included in the action. Even though Frank and Joe always succeed, the increased realism of the danger and violence make this a choice for middle school and older.

1. Dead on Target ◆ 1987
2. Evil, Inc. ◆ 1987
3. Cult of Crime ◆ 1987
4. The Lazarus Plot ◆ 1988
5. Edge of Destruction ◆ 1988
6. The Crowning Terror ◆ 1988
7. Deathgame ◆ 1988
8. See No Evil ◆ 1988
9. The Genius Thieves ◆ 1988
10. Hostages of Hate ◆ 1988
11. Brother Against Brother ◆ 1988
12. Perfect Getaway ◆ 1988
13. The Georgia Dagger ◆ 1989
14. Too Many Traitors ◆ 1989
15. Blood Relations ◆ 1989
16. Line of Fire ◆ 1989
17. The Number File ◆ 1989
18. A Killing in the Market ◆ 1989
19. Nightmare in Angel City ◆ 1989
20. Witness to Murder ◆ 1989
21. Street Spies ◆ 1989
22. Double Exposure ◆ 1989
23. Disaster for Hire ◆ 1989
24. Scene of the Crime ◆ 1989
25. The Borderline Case ◆ 1989
26. Trouble in the Pipeline ◆ 1989
27. Nowhere to Run ◆ 1989
28. Countdown to Terror ◆ 1989
29. Thick as Thieves ◆ 1989
30. The Deadliest Dare ◆ 1989
31. Without a Trace ◆ 1989
32. Blood Money ◆ 1989

33. Collision Course ◆ 1989
34. Final Cut ◆ 1989
35. The Dead Season ◆ 1990
36. Running on Empty ◆ 1990
37. Danger Zone ◆ 1990
38. Diplomatic Deceit ◆ 1990
39. Flesh and Blood ◆ 1991
40. Fright Wave ◆ 1991
41. Highway Robbery ◆ 1990
42. The Last Laugh ◆ 1990
43. Strategic Moves ◆ 1990
44. Castle Fear ◆ 1991
45. In Self-Defense ◆ 1990
46. Foul Play ◆ 1990
47. Flight into Danger ◆ 1991
48. Rock 'n' Revenge ◆ 1991
49. Dirty Deeds ◆ 1991
50. Power Play ◆ 1991
51. Choke Hold ◆ 1991
52. Uncivil War ◆ 1991
53. Web of Horror ◆ 1991
54. Deep Trouble ◆ 1991
55. Beyond the Law ◆ 1991
56. Height of Danger ◆ 1991
57. Terror on Track ◆ 1991
58. Spiked! ◆ 1991
59. Open Season ◆ 1992
60. Deadfall ◆ 1992
61. Grave Danger ◆ 1992
62. Final Gambit ◆ 1992
63. Cold Sweat ◆ 0992
64. Endangered Species ◆ 1992
65. No Mercy ◆ 1992
66. The Phoenix Equation ◆ 1992
67. Lethal Cargo ◆ 1992
68. Rough Riding ◆ 1992
69. Mayhem in Motion ◆ 1992
70. Rigged for Revenge ◆ 1992
71. Real Horror ◆ 1993
72. Screamers ◆ 1993
73. Bad Rap ◆ 1993
74. Road Pirates ◆ 1993
75. No Way Out ◆ 1993
76. Tagged for Terror ◆ 1993
77. Survival Run ◆ 1993
78. The Pacific Conspiracy ◆ 1993
79. Danger Unlimited ◆ 1993
80. Dead of Night ◆ 1993

81. Sheer Terror ◆ 1993
82. Poisoned Paradise ◆ 1993
83. Toxic Revenge ◆ 1994
84. False Alarm ◆ 1994
85. Winner Take All ◆ 1994
86. Virtual Villainy ◆ 1994
87. Dead Man in Deadwood ◆ 1994
88. Inferno of Fear ◆ 1994
89. Darkness Falls ◆ 1994
90. Deadly Engagement ◆ 1994
91. Hot Wheels ◆ 1994
92. Sabotage at Sea ◆ 1994
93. Mission: Mayhem ◆ 1994
94. A Taste for Terror ◆ 1994
95. Illegal Procedure ◆ 1995
96. Against All Odds ◆ 1995
97. Pure Evil ◆ 1995
98. Murder by Magic ◆ 1995
99. Frame-Up ◆ 1995
100. True Thriller ◆ 1995
101. Peak of Danger ◆ 1995
102. Wrong Side of the Law ◆ 1995
103. Campaign of Crime ◆ 1995
104. Wild Wheels ◆ 1995
105. Law of the Jungle ◆ 1995
106. Shock Jock ◆ 1995
107. Fast Break ◆ 1996
108. Blown Away ◆ 1996
109. Moment of Truth ◆ 1996
110. Bad Chemistry ◆ 1996
111. Competitive Edge ◆ 1996
112. Cliff-Hanger ◆ 1996
113. Sky High ◆ 1996
114. Clean Sweep ◆ 1996
115. Cave Trap ◆ 1996
116. Acting Up ◆ 1996
117. Blood Sport ◆ 1996
118. The Last Leap ◆ 1996
119. The Emperor's Shield ◆ 1997
120. Survival of the Fittest ◆ 1997
121. Absolute Zero ◆ 1997
122. River Rats ◆ 1997
123. High-Wire Act ◆ 1997
124. The Viking's Revenge ◆ 1997
125. Stress Point ◆ 1997
126. Fire in the Sky ◆ 1997
127. Dead in the Water ◆ 1998

HARDY BOYS, UNDERCOVER BROTHERS

Dixon, Franklin W.

ALADDIN ◆ GRADES 5–9 ◆ A/R

MYSTERY

In this updated Hardy Boys series, the brothers now work undercover for A.T.A.C.—American Teens Against Crime. They still overcome the odds to catch criminals. In the first book, extreme athletes are gathering in Philadelphia for the Big Air Games. It's up to Frank and Joe to prevent anything from disrupting the games. Short sentences and lots of action will attract reluctant readers.

1. Extreme Danger ◆ 2005
2. Running on Fumes ◆ 2005
3. Boardwalk Bust ◆ 2005
4. Thrill Ride ◆ 2005
5. Rocky Road ◆ 2005
6. Burned ◆ 2005
7. Operation: Survival ◆ 2005
8. Top Ten Ways to Die ◆ 2006
9. Martial Law ◆ 2006
10. Blown Away ◆ 2006
11. Hurricane Joe ◆ 2006
12. Trouble in Paradise ◆ 2006
13. The Mummy's Curse ◆ 2006
14. Hazed ◆ 2007
15. Death and Diamonds ◆ 2007
16. Bayport Buccaneers ◆ 2007
17. Murder at the Mall ◆ 2007
18. Pushed ◆ 2007
19. Foul Play ◆ 2007
20. Feeding Frenzy ◆ 2008
21. Comic Con Artist ◆ 2008
22. House Arrest ◆ 2008

HARDY BOYS, UNDERCOVER BROTHERS MURDER HOUSE TRILOGY

The brothers go undercover at a reality show house to find who is causing "accidents" to befall the teens on the show.

1. Deprivation House: Book One in the Murder House Trilogy ◆ 2008
2. House Arrest: Book Two in the Murder House Trilogy ◆ 2008
3. Murder House: Book Three in the Murder House Trilogy ◆ 2008

HARDY BOYS, UNDERCOVER BROTHERS SUPER MYSTERIES

1. Wanted ◆ 2006

2. Kidnapped at the Casino ◆ 2007
3. Haunted ◆ 2008

HARDY BOYS, UNDERCOVER BROTHERS: GRAPHIC NOVELS

Lobdell, Scott
PAPERCUTZ ◆ GRADES 5–9 ◆ A/R
MYSTERY

Mystery, action, suspense—all of the expected elements of a Hardy Boys book plus the added attraction of the graphic novel format. Various illustrators use bold lines and sharp angles to give these books a manga-inspired look. This could appeal to middle school/junior high reluctant readers.

1. The Ocean of Osyria ◆ 2005
2. Identity Theft ◆ 2005
3. Mad House ◆ 2005
4. Malled ◆ 2006
5. Sea You, Sea Me! ◆ 2006
6. Hyde and Shriek ◆ 2006
7. The Opposite Numbers . . . ◆ 2006
8. Board to Death ◆ 2007
9. To Die or Not to Die? ◆ 2007
10. A Hardy Day's Night ◆ 2007
11. Abracadeath ◆ 2008
12. Dude Ranch O'Death ◆ 2008
13. The Deadliest Stunt ◆ 2008
14. Haley Danelle's Top Eight ◆ 2008
15. Live Free, Die Hardy! ◆ 2008
16. Shhhhh! ◆ 2008

HARPER WINSLOW

Trembath, Don
ORCA ◆ GRADES 6–9 ◆ A/R
REAL LIFE

Harper Winslow, 15, tells his own stories in this series of books set in Canada, near Toronto. In *The Tuesday Cafe,* Harper describes his problems with his parents and his school, problems that have resulted in an appearance in juvenile court. He is assigned to write an essay about changing his life, so he enrolls in a writing class called "The Tuesday Cafe." Harper grows and changes as a character, developing insights into his personality and choices that will resonate with junior high school readers. The essay that he writes appears toward the end of the book and provides a wonderful look at a character's growth. Subsequent books allow Harper to continue to change by writing for the school newspaper and beginning a romantic friendship.

1. The Tuesday Cafe ◆ 1996
2. A Fly Named Alfred ◆ 1997
3. A Beautiful Place on Yonge Street ◆ 1998
4. The Popsicle Journal ◆ 2002

HARRY POTTER

Rowling, J. K.

SCHOLASTIC ◆ GRADES 3–9 ◆ A/R

FANTASY

Harry Potter's adventures at Hogwarts, a school for wizards and witches, are chronicled in this series. From his initial discovery of his magical past to his developing skills at spells and Quidditch to his realization that there are dark forces at work around him, these books have attracted the attention of readers around the world. Many younger children (in grades three and four) read the earlier books, especially after seeing the movies. They also have the books read to them or listen to them on audio. With each book, as Harry matures, the description of creatures, spells, and violence becomes more graphic and detailed. The optimum audience for the complete series is grades five and up. The books are available in many languages and the movies have been wildly successful. There are many related items including toys, games, books about Quidditch and Beasts, puzzles, computer programs, and more.

1. Harry Potter and the Sorcerer's Stone ◆ 1998
2. Harry Potter and the Chamber of Secrets ◆ 1999
3. Harry Potter and the Prisoner of Azkaban ◆ 1999
4. Harry Potter and the Goblet of Fire ◆ 2000
5. Harry Potter and the Order of the Phoenix ◆ 2003
6. Harry Potter and the Half-Blood Prince ◆ 2005
7. Harry Potter and the Deathly Hallows ◆ 2007

HARVEY ANGELL TRILOGY

Hendry, Diana

POCKET/MINSTREL ◆ GRADES 4–7 ◆ A/R

FANTASY | MYSTERY

Henry, an orphan living in a depressing boarding house with his miserly Aunt Agatha, is cheered by the arrival of new resident Harvey Angell, who brings music and a kit full of magical gadgets. Henry calls for Harvey's help with mysteries in subsequent books. In the third, Henry discovers an abandoned baby that has antennae. These entertaining stories were first published in Britain.

1. Harvey Angell ◆ 2001
2. Harvey Angell and the Ghost Child ◆ 2002
3. Harvey Angell Beats Time ◆ 2002

HATCHET *see* Brian Robeson

HAUNTING WITH LOUISA

Cates, Emily

BANTAM ◆ GRADES 5–8

MYSTERY

Dee Forest comes to Misty Island to live with her Aunt Winnifred after her mother dies and her father cannot cope with his grief. There she meets Louisa, a young ghost who must help four of her living relatives before she can go on to the next life. With Dee's help, and after many adventures, Louisa finds three of them. In the last book, they discover that Dee herself is Louisa's distant cousin, and Louisa saves her life. Meanwhile, Louisa is concerned that Dee doesn't have any living friends and urges her to make some. At the same time, Dee's father finds a new romance, which Dee comes to accept.

1. The Ghost in the Attic ◆ 1990
2. The Mystery of Misty Island Inn ◆ 1991
3. The Ghost Ferry ◆ 1991

HAVE A NICE LIFE

Macdougal, Scarlett

ALLOYBOOKS ◆ GRADES 9–12

FANTASY | HUMOR

On prom night, fairy godfather Clarence Terence shows four girls their dismal futures. One will be an unsuccessful model, one will have a failed marriage, one will continue to live with her mother. The girls immediately decide to improve themselves and the series follows their efforts to do so. In *Score,* a rival fairy godmother turns up and advises the girls to take a different course. Which godmother is giving the right advice?

1. Start Here ◆ 2000
2. Play ◆ 2000
3. Popover ◆ 2003
4. Score ◆ 2001

HAZELWOOD HIGH

Draper, Sharon M.
ATHENEUM ◆ GRADES 7–10 ◆ A/R
REAL LIFE

Sharon M. Draper has written a trilogy of books about African American teens who are connected by their participation on the Hazelwood High basketball team, the Tigers. These students deal with harsh issues including drug addiction, drunk driving, and abuse. In *Tears of a Tiger,* Robert Washington has been killed in an auto accident. The driver was his best friend, Andy Jackson, and all the kids in the car had been drinking. In *Darkness Before Dawn,* Keisha Montgomery tries to recover after her ex-boyfriend's suicide. That boyfriend was Andy Jackson. Draper received the Coretta Scott King Genesis Award for *Tears of a Tiger* and the Coretta Scott King Award for *Forged by Fire.* The reading order of the books is different from their chronological release.

1. Forged by Fire ◆ 1997
2. Tears of a Tiger ◆ 1994
3. Darkness Before Dawn ◆ 2001

HE-MAN WOMEN HATERS CLUB

Lynch, Chris
HARPERCOLLINS ◆ GRADES 6–9 ◆ A/R
REAL LIFE

Four adolescent boys take guidance from Spanky and Alfalfa and form their own He-Man Women Haters Club. They don't really hate women; they are just confused about their changing relationships. Steven, 13, starts out as the leader but makes a mess of things. The second book features Jerome; Wolfgang (who is in a wheelchair) is the leader in the third book; and Ling is in charge in the fourth book. The boys go camping, play in a band, and try to deal with their developing interest in girls. There is a lot here for male reluctant readers.

1. Johnny Chesthair ◆ 1997
2. Babes in the Woods ◆ 1997
3. Scratch and the Sniffs ◆ 1997
4. Ladies' Choice ◆ 1997
5. The Wolf Gang ◆ 1998

HEAR NO EVIL

Chester, Kate
SCHOLASTIC ◆ GRADES 9–12 ◆ A/R
MYSTERY

Most of Sara Howell's perceptions are heightened but she does not have "super powers." Sara is deaf. She uses her insights and intelligence to solve such mysteries as finding Kimberly Roth and investigating the murder of her friend Amy. The exciting action in these books should interest reluctant readers.

1. Death in the Afternoon ◆ 1996
2. Missing ◆ 1996
3. Time of Fear ◆ 1996
4. Dead and Buried ◆ 1996
5. Sudden Death ◆ 1997
6. Playing with Fire ◆ 1997

HEART BEATS

Rees, Elizabeth M.
ALADDIN ◆ GRADES 7–8 ◆ A/R
REAL LIFE

The students at Dance Tech dream of success in dancing. They are also devoted to their friends and boyfriends. Sophy likes having Carlos as her dance partner, but she is also interested in him romantically. Ray is worried about Daly's commitment to losing weight. Can he help her and still be her boyfriend? The dance school setting provides a background for stories of jealousy, both personal and professional.

1. Moving as One ◆ 1998
2. Body Lines ◆ 1998
3. In the Spotlight ◆ 1998
4. Latin Nights ◆ 1998
5. Face the Music ◆ 1999
6. Last Dance ◆ 1999

HEARTLAND

Brooke, Lauren
SCHOLASTIC ◆ GRADES 4–7 ◆ A/R
REAL LIFE

Heartland is a farm in Virginia that specializes in caring for horses that have been mistreated. Amy, 14, is developing her skills as a horse whisperer. Throughout the series as Amy works with horses, she also deals with different people and their problems. By the end of the series, Amy has finished high school and has a boyfriend, Ty. The Special Editions follow her progress at college, where she is in a pre-vet program.

1. Coming Home ◆ 2000
2. After the Storm ◆ 2000
3. Breaking Free ◆ 2000

4. Taking Chances ◆ 2001
5. Come What May ◆ 2001
6. One Day You'll Know ◆ 2001
7. Out of the Darkness ◆ 2002
8. Thicker than Water ◆ 2002
9. Every New Day ◆ 2002
10. Tomorrow's Promise ◆ 2002
11. True Enough ◆ 2003
12. Sooner or Later ◆ 2003
13. Darkest Hour ◆ 2003
14. Everything Changes ◆ 2003
15. Love Is a Gift ◆ 2004
16. Holding Fast ◆ 2004
17. A Season of Hope ◆ 2004
18. New Beginnings ◆ 2005
19. From This Day On ◆ 2005
20. Always There ◆ 2005

SPECIAL EDITIONS

1. A Holiday Memory ◆ 2004
2. A Winter's Gift ◆ 2007
3. Beyond the Horizon ◆ 2007
4. A Summer to Remember ◆ 2008

HEARTLIGHT

Barron, T. A.

PUTNAM ◆ GRADES 6–9 ◆ A/R

FANTASY | SCIENCE FICTION

Kate Gordon, 13, and her 80-year-old grandfather, Dr. Miles Prancer, have a special bond and an ability to journey through time and space. Dr. Prancer is an astrophysicist working on saving the planet Earth and its solar system from total destruction. In the third book, Kate and her father travel to California on a quest for a lost treasure. This fantasy with elements of science fiction includes conflicts between the forces of good and evil and features links to Arthurian legends that should appeal to many readers. Fans of L'Engle's Time Fantasy Series will enjoy these adventures, which are somewhat technical and a little more scientific.

1. Heartlight ◆ 1990
2. The Ancient One ◆ 1992
3. The Merlin Effect ◆ 1994

THE HEIR

Chima, Cinda Williams

HYPERION ◆ GRADES 8–12 ◆ A/R

FANTASY

In *The Warrior Heir,* Jack, 16, believes he is an ordinary human but he is not. When he was an infant, a warrior stone was secretly placed in his chest. The powers of the stone have been controlled with "medicine" that Jack forgets to take one day. Members of a mysterious group called the Weir appear to push a reluctant Jack toward his destiny. *The Wizard Heir* is a companion volume and expands the story of Seph McCauley, 16, who is to be trained in magic. In the third book, two more characters are featured as the wizard wars begin.

1. The Warrior Heir ◆ 2006
2. The Wizard Heir ◆ 2007
3. The Dragon Heir ◆ 2008

HELLBOY

Various authors

DARK HORSE ◆ GRADES 10–12

HORROR

This is one of the most popular horror comics with adults and older teenagers. Hellboy is a paranormal investigator determined to save the world from mystical forces of evil. In *Wake the Devil,* his search for a missing corpse leads him to an encounter with a vampire. In another book, he faces the conqueror worm. Hellboy has been released in a variety of formats, often with the same titles. The books listed below are Hellboy stories that have been released as trade paperbacks.

1. Seed of Destruction (Mignola, Mike, and John Byrne) ◆ 1994
2. Wake the Devil (Mignola, Mike) ◆ 1997
3. The Chained Coffin and Others (Mignola, Mike) ◆ 1998
4. The Right Hand of Doom (Mignola, Mike) ◆ 2000
5. Conqueror Worm (Mignola, Mike) ◆ 2002
6. Strange Places (Mignola, Mike) ◆ 2006
7. The Troll Witch and Others (Mignola, Mike) ◆ 2007
8. Darkness Calls (Mignola, Mike) ◆ 2008

HELLSING

Hirano, Kohta

DARK HORSE ◆ GRADES 10–12

HORROR

Based in England, the Hellsing Organization protects the world from vampires, ghouls, and other dark forces. The secret weapon of Hellsing is Arucard, a vampire! Talk about fighting fire with fire!

1. Volume 1 ◆ 2003
2. Volume 2 ◆ 2004
3. Volume 3 ◆ 2004
4. Volume 4 ◆ 2004
5. Volume 5 ◆ 2004
6. Volume 6 ◆ 2005
7. Volume 7 ◆ 2005
8. Volume 8 ◆ 2007
9. Volume 9 ◆ 2008

HELP, I'M TRAPPED

Strasser, Todd

SCHOLASTIC ◆ GRADES 5–8 ◆ A/R

FANTASY | HUMOR

Jake Sherman seems like an ordinary middle school student, but he has a secret. He can body switch. He has been trapped in his teacher's body, his sister's body, the President's body, and his gym teacher's body. He has even been trapped in a dog's body. In some of the books, he is trapped in repeating events. For example, he has to live through the first day of school until he makes the right choices that break the cycle. Readers will like the implausible situations and the ensuing confusion. These are entertaining books with lots of clever dialogue, albeit at the humor level of a junior high school audience.

1. Help! I'm Trapped in My Teacher's Body ◆ 1993
2. Help! I'm Trapped in the First Day of School ◆ 1994
3. Help! I'm Trapped in Obedience School ◆ 1995
4. Help! I'm Trapped in My Gym Teacher's Body ◆ 1996
5. Help! I'm Trapped in the President's Body ◆ 1996
6. Help! I'm Trapped in Obedience School Again ◆ 1997
7. Help! I'm Trapped in Santa's Body ◆ 1997
8. Help! I'm Trapped in My Sister's Body ◆ 1997
9. Help! I'm Trapped in the First Day of Summer Camp ◆ 1997
10. Help! I'm Trapped in an Alien's Body ◆ 1998
11. Help! I'm Trapped in a Movie Star's Body ◆ 1998
12. Help! I'm Trapped in My Principal's Body ◆ 1998
13. Help! I'm Trapped in My Lunch Lady's Body ◆ 1999
14. Help! I'm Trapped in a Professional Wrestler's Body ◆ 2000
15. Help! I'm Trapped in a Vampire's Body ◆ 2000
16. Help! I'm Trapped in a Supermodel's Body ◆ 2001

HERCULEAH JONES

Byars, Betsy

PENGUIN ◆ GRADES 5–7 ◆ A/R

HUMOR | MYSTERY

Herculeah Jones is the daughter of a divorced police detective and a private investigator, so mystery solving comes naturally to her. Her friend Meat appreciates being allowed to help out, and occasionally works on his own. In *Dead Letter,* Herculeah buys a coat at a thrift store and finds a note in its hem. A woman is trapped and someone is going to kill her. Meat and Herculeah trace the note to a wealthy older woman being cared for by her nephew. In and out of danger the whole time, they are eventually responsible for the culprit's arrest. Herculeah is proud of being strong, and her hair always stands on end when there is danger. Girls will appreciate tough, smart Herculeah, and the relationship between her and Meat provides some humor.

1. The Dark Stairs ◆ 1994
2. Tarot Says Beware ◆ 1995
3. Dead Letter ◆ 1996
4. Death's Door ◆ 1997
5. Disappearing Acts ◆ 1998
6. King of Murder ◆ 2006
7. The Black Tower ◆ 2006

HERE COMES HEAVENLY

Strasser, Todd

SIMON & SCHUSTER ◆ GRADES 6–8 ◆ A/R

FANTASY

Heavenly Litebody is no ordinary nanny. With her piercings, tattoos, and purple hair, she looks at situations creatively. There are five children in the Rand family, so there are lots of problems to solve. Especially when the family takes a trip to Rome. Kit, 14, is the narrator.

1. Here Comes Heavenly ◆ 1999
2. Dance Magic ◆ 1999
3. Pastabilities ◆ 2000
4. Spell Danger ◆ 2000

HERMUX TANTAMOQ ADVENTURES

Hoeye, Michael

PUTNAM ◆ GRADES 5–8 ◆ A/R

ANIMAL FANTASY | MYSTERY

Hermux Tantamoq, a mouse, is a watchmaker who enjoys a quiet and orderly life . . . until the intrepid aviatrix Linka Perflinger appears, dragging him into adventure and mystery in *Time Stops for No Mouse*. In the sequels, he continues to show courage while investigating such mysteries as the early relationship between mice and cats.

1. Time Stops for No Mouse ◆ 2002
2. The Sands of Time ◆ 2003
3. No Time Like Show Time ◆ 2004

HIGH HURDLES

Snelling, Lauraine

BETHANY HOUSE ◆ GRADES 4–7 ◆ A/R

FAMILY LIFE | REAL LIFE | VALUES

DJ Randall, 13 at the start of the series, loves horses. She lives with her mother and has never met her father. As the series progresses, her biological father makes contact for the first time in 14 years. Her mother remarries and DJ must adjust to a stepfather and stepsiblings. DJ spends a lot of time at the riding academy. Like many teens, she is busy with friends, family, and activities. She seeks God's guidance to help her with problems. As the series closes, DJ helps save the horses from a fire and is seriously burned. Her faith helps her face the challenges of her recovery.

1. Olympic Dreams ◆ 1995
2. DJ's Challenge ◆ 1995
3. Setting the Pace ◆ 1996
4. Out of the Blue ◆ 1996
5. Storm Clouds ◆ 1997
6. Close Quarters ◆ 1998
7. Moving Up ◆ 1998
8. Letting Go ◆ 1999
9. Raising the Bar ◆ 1999
10. Class Act ◆ 2000

HIGH SCHOOL MUSICAL STORIES FROM EAST HIGH

Various authors

DISNEY PRESS ◆ GRADES 4–8 ◆ A/R

REAL LIFE

Tween fans of the Disney High School Musical movies will be thrilled with these books. All of their favorite characters are featured, including Troy, Sharpay, Ryan, Chad, Taylor, and Gabriella. There are performances as well as familiar school activities such as pep rallies, sports, and

Spirit Week. Numerous other spin-off items are available from trivia books and calendars to a Super Special book, *Under the Stars* (2008).

1. Battle of the Bands (Grace, N. B) ◆ 2007
2. Wildcat Spirit (Hapka, Catherine) ◆ 2007
3. Poetry in Motion (Alfonsi, Alice) ◆ 2007
4. Crunch Time (Grace, N. B.) ◆ 2007
5. Broadway Dreams (Grace, N. B.) ◆ 2007
6. Heart to Heart (Perelman, Helen) ◆ 2007
7. Friends 4Ever (Hapka, Catherine) ◆ 2008
8. Get Your Vote On! (Grace, N. B., and Beth Beechwood) ◆ 2008
9. Ringin' It In (Grace, N. B.) ◆ 2008
10. Turn Up the Heat (Perelman, Helen) ◆ 2008
11. In the Spotlight (Hapka, Catherine) ◆ 2008
12. Bonjour, Wildcats (Grace, N. B.) ◆ 2008

HIGH SEAS TRILOGY

Lawrence, Iain

DELACORTE ◆ GRADES 6–9 ◆ A/R

ADVENTURE

As ships sail along the Cornish coast, villagers deliberately wreck them to loot the cargo. It is 1799. John Spencer, 14, is on his father's merchant ship and it crashes. The villagers want to plunder the ship and cannot allow any witnesses. John manages to escape them and find his father. Their second adventure involves piracy. In the final book, John is 17 and must deal with a dangerous stranger.

1. The Wreckers ◆ 1998
2. The Smugglers ◆ 1999
3. The Buccaneers ◆ 2001

HIGHLAND HEROES

Reding, Jaclyn

NAL ◆ GRADES 11–12

HISTORICAL

These entertaining historical romances feature women with independent spirits. In *The Pretender,* Lady Elizabeth Drayton rebels against an arranged marriage. The second book involves an enchanted stone that seems to guide Lady Isabella's introduction to an attractive adventurer. This adult romance series is recommended for mature teens.

1. The Pretender ◆ 2002
2. The Adventurer ◆ 2002
3. The Secret Gift ◆ 2003

HIS DARK MATERIALS

Pullman, Philip
KNOPF ◆ GRADES 7–12 ◆ A/R
FANTASY

With her *daemon,* an animal manifestation of her soul, Lyra intervenes in a dangerous scheme to kidnap children. Later, with her friend Will, she searches for Will's father and discovers the Subtle Knife, a tool that cuts into other worlds. Lyra is captured and Will must find her and rescue her. But he is not alone in his search. Fantasy readers will be challenged by the complexity of this series but will appreciate the classic battle between good and evil. *Once Upon a Time in the North* (2008) is a prequel, and *Lyra's Oxford* (2003) is a companion volume with a story about Lyra and some pieces of memorabilia, including a fold-out map of Lyra's Oxford.

1. The Golden Compass ◆ 1995
2. The Subtle Knife ◆ 1997
3. The Amber Spyglass ◆ 2000

HISTORY MYSTERIES *see* American Girls: History Mysteries

HITCHHIKER'S TRILOGY

Adams, Douglas
BALLANTINE ◆ GRADES 7–12 ◆ A/R
FANTASY

What began as a popular BBC radio program evolved into a "trilogy" of five books following the exploits of Ford Prefect and Arthur Dent. Ford is researching a new edition of a book—*The Hitchhiker's Guide to the Galaxy.* Just as Earth is being destroyed, Ford rescues his friend, Arthur Dent. The two start their trek through the galaxy on a Vogon constructor ship. After they are thrown off that ship, they continue to hitchhike through space, often saving the universe from destruction. In the fifth book, Arthur Dent's daughter, Random, investigates her heritage. *The Salmon of Doubt* (2002) includes letters, early writings, and part of an unfinished novel left by Adams on his death.

1. The Hitchhiker's Guide to the Galaxy ◆ 1980
2. The Restaurant at the End of the Universe ◆ 1980
3. Life, the Universe and Everything ◆ 1982
4. So Long, and Thanks for All the Fish ◆ 1984
5. Mostly Harmless ◆ 1992

HOLLOW

Golden, Christopher, and Ford Lytle Gilmore

RAZORBILL ◆ GRADES 7–10 ◆ A/R

HORROR

Evil forces are loose in Sleepy Hollow. Shane and his sister Aimee have moved from Boston to the small New York town. Their arrival has released a deadly curse, which the teens and their friends try to control. There are vicious attacks and murders (including the beheading of a librarian); demons and creatures; and a mysterious Horseman. Show these books to fans of R. L. Stine's many books.

1. Horseman ◆ 2005
2. Drowned ◆ 2005
3. Mischief ◆ 2006
4. Enemies ◆ 2006

HOLLOW KINGDOM

Dunkle, Clare B.

HOLT ◆ GRADES 6–9 ◆ A/R

FANTASY

Set in England in the 19th century, this series has magic and mystery. Two orphaned sisters, Kate and Emily, are sent to live at Hallow Hill. There they encounter goblins whose king, Marak, wants to marry Kate. To protect her sister, Kate agrees and she moves to Marak's underground kingdom, where she comes to appreciate Marak's attributes. The following volumes feature difficult romances between goblins, elves, and humans.

1. The Hollow Kingdom ◆ 2003
2. Close Kin ◆ 2004
3. In the Coils of the Snake ◆ 2005

HOLLY'S HEART

Lewis, Beverly

BETHANY HOUSE ◆ GRADES 6–9 ◆ A/R

REAL LIFE | VALUES

Romance and Christian faith play large roles in these stories of Holly Meredith and her friendships and romantic attachments at school. In *Best Friend, Worst Enemy,* Holly faints and is given mouth-to-mouth resuscitation. But her best friend won't tell her which boy was involved. In another book, Holly develops a crush on a teacher and wonders whether her affection is returned.

   1. Best Friend, Worst Enemy ◆ 2001
   2. Secret Summer Dreams ◆ 2001
   3. Sealed with a Kiss ◆ 2002
   4. The Trouble with Weddings ◆ 2002
   5. California Crazy ◆ 2002
   6. Second-Best Friend ◆ 2002
   7. Good-Bye, Dressel Hills ◆ 2002
   8. Straight-A Teacher ◆ 2003
   9. No Guys Pact ◆ 2003
  10. Little White Lies ◆ 2003
  11. Freshman Frenzy ◆ 2003
  12. Mystery Letters ◆ 2003
  13. Eight Is Enough ◆ 2003
  14. It's a Girl Thing ◆ 2003

HOLLYWOOD SISTERS

Wilcox, Mary

DELACORTE ◆ GRADES 5–8 ◆ A/R

MYSTERY | REAL LIFE

Jessica, 13, is shy while her older sister, Eva, is an outgoing actress who has a role in a television sitcom. As Jessica adjusts to their new home and her new school, she also solves a few light mysteries, such as who is planting stories about Eva in the tabloids and who is causing the pranks on the set. The Hollywood setting adds to the appeal of this series.

   1. Backstage Pass ◆ 2006
   2. On Location ◆ 2007
   3. Caught on Tape ◆ 2007
   4. Star Quality ◆ 2008
   5. Truth or Dare ◆ 2009

HOMECOMING SAGA

Card, Orson Scott

TOR ◆ GRADES 9–12 ◆ A/R

FANTASY | SCIENCE FICTION

On the planet Harmony, the Oversoul has kept the peace. Now the artificial intelligence system is failing. A group has been selected to leave Harmony and search for the planet Earth. Naifeh and his family are among those chosen. The journey is made even more difficult by the treachery of some of those on the starship. Eventually, they reach Earth and establish a colony there.

1. The Memory of Earth ◆ 1992
2. The Call of Earth ◆ 1993
3. The Ships of Earth ◆ 1994
4. Earthfall ◆ 1995
5. Earthborn ◆ 1995

HOMEROOM

Norton, Nancy

SCHOLASTIC ◆ GRADES 7–10

REAL LIFE

Piper is eager to begin high school. After fixing some scheduling problems, she makes new friends—Tamara and Judd. Grades, dating, friends,
and other high school concerns are featured in this series.

1. Strange Times at Fairwood High ◆ 1988
2. The Princess of Fairwood High ◆ 1988
3. Triple Trouble at Fairwood High ◆ 1988

HONOR HARRINGTON

Weber, David

BAEN ◆ GRADES 9–12 ◆ A/R

SCIENCE FICTION

Manticoran Navy Commander Honor Harrington manages to overcome
the deficiencies of her starship when attacked by the enemy. The series,
written for adults but enjoyed by teens, follows her exploits in pursuit of
foes and her ability to deal with political intrigues. In *Honor Among Enemies,* she is brought out of forced retirement to tackle intrepid space
pirates.

1. On Basilisk Station ◆ 1993
2. The Honor of the Queen ◆ 1993
3. The Short Victorious War ◆ 1994
4. Field of Dishonor ◆ 1994
5. Flag in Exile ◆ 1995
6. Honor Among Enemies ◆ 1996
7. In Enemy Hands ◆ 1997
8. Echoes of Honor ◆ 1998
9. Ashes of Victory ◆ 2000
10. War of Honor ◆ 2002
11. At All Costs ◆ 2005

HORSEFEATHERS

Mackall, Dandi Daley

CONCORDIA ◆ GRADES 7–10 ◆ A/R

REAL LIFE | VALUES

Scoop, 16, is good at caring for horses. Living with her aunt and her grandfather on a struggling horse farm, Scoop's life is difficult. Her love for her horse, Orphan, and her faith in God help sustain her.

1. Horsefeathers! ◆ 2000
2. Horse Cents ◆ 2000
3. Horse Whispers in the Air ◆ 2000
4. A Horse of a Different Color ◆ 2000
5. Horse Angels ◆ 2000
6. Home Is Where Your Horse Is ◆ 2001
7. Horsefeathers' Mystery ◆ 2001
8. All the King's Horses ◆ 2001

HORSESHOES

Leitch, Patricia

HARPERCOLLINS ◆ GRADES 5–7

REAL LIFE | RECREATION

Living in a manor in Scotland gives Sally Lorimer what she has always wanted: the chance to own a horse. After finding the right horse, Sally and her friend Thalia take riding lessons, participate in horse shows, and make the Pony Club team. In one book, Thalia is injured in a riding accident and Sally helps Thalia deal with her father's decision to take away her horse. Girls who enjoy the many horse and riding series set in America will enjoy the Scottish setting and riding details in these books.

1. The Perfect Horse ◆ 1992
2. Jumping Lessons ◆ 1992
3. Cross-Country Gallop ◆ 1996
4. Pony Club Rider ◆ 1996
5. Show Jumper Wanted ◆ 1997
6. Mystery Horse ◆ 1997

HOTLANTA

Millner, Denene, and Mitzi Miller

SCHOLASTIC POINT ◆ GRADES 7–10 ◆ A/R

REAL LIFE

Set in the upscale Buckhead neighborhood in Atlanta, this series focuses on twin sisters Sydney and Lauren Duke, who are African American. They are popular, wealthy, and beautiful, but they have a family secret— their father has been in prison and now is a suspect in an unsolved murder. The urban setting of this series will appeal to many readers. Girls who enjoy Gossip Girl and Clique will relate to these books. Also share other urban lit series such as Drama High, Kimani Tru, and Platinum Teen.

1. Hotlanta ◆ 2008
2. If Only You Knew ◆ 2008
3. What Goes Around ◆ 2009

"HOUR" BOOKS

Williams, Maiya

AMULET ◆ GRADES 5–8 ◆ A/R

FANTASY

After the death of their mother, 13-year-old Rowan and 11-year-old Nina Popplewell are sent to spend the summer with their great-aunts in Maine. They meet Xanthe and Xavier, 14-year-old African American twins, and begin to explore an abandoned resort. The resort offers a time-travel portal at "the golden hour" (right before sunset). In the first book, Nina disappears and the others follow her to Paris in 1789. Other adventures take place in ancient Egypt and in the Old West at the time of the gold rush. In addition to the historical and fantasy elements, the characters in this series deal with realistic present-day problems, such as the death of Rowan and Nina's mother in an accident involving a drunk driver. The stories have a lot to offer including action, history, and time travel, which make them a good choice for reluctant readers.

1. The Golden Hour ◆ 2004
2. The Hour of the Cobra ◆ 2006
3. The Hour of the Outlaw ◆ 2007

HOUSE OF HORRORS

Various authors

HARPERCOLLINS ◆ GRADES 5–7

HORROR

What would you do if a ghost were stalking your brother? And then, what if your Aunt Wendy came to visit and took off her head? How about if your dog turned into an angry beast and brought home a gross claw that wasn't quite dead? These are just some of the problems faced by

Sara and Michael Buckner in the House of Horrors series. There are oozing eggs and a scheming gargoyle. Readers who enjoy being scared and disgusted will want to read these creepy adventures.

1. My Brother, the Ghost (Weyn, Suzanne) ◆ 1994
2. Rest in Pieces (Weyn, Suzanne) ◆ 1994
3. Jeepers Creepers (Weyn, Suzanne) ◆ 1995
4. Aunt Weird (Lloyd, Alan) ◆ 1995
5. Knock, Knock . . . You're Dead (Stine, Megan) ◆ 1995
6. Night of the Gargoyle (Lloyd, Alan) ◆ 1995
7. Evil on Board (Moore, Leslie) ◆ 1995

HOUSE OF NIGHT

Cast, P. C., and Kristin Cast

ST. MARTIN'S GRIFFIN ◆ GRADES 9–12 ◆ A/R

HORROR | ADVENTURE

The House of Night is a school where those marked by vampyres go to fulfill their destiny or die. Zoey Redbird, 16, arrives at the school to begin her training only to discover that there are evil forces at work. Humans and vampyres are dying, threatening their coexistence. When Zoey is betrayed by those she trusts she understands that she must face these dangers alone. Other series that relate to House of Night include Buffy, Angel, and Twilight.

1. Marked ◆ 2007
2. Betrayed ◆ 2007
3. Chosen ◆ 2008
4. Untamed ◆ 2008

HOUSE ON CHERRY STREET

Philbrick, W. Rodman

SCHOLASTIC ◆ GRADES 5–8 ◆ A/R

FANTASY

Ghosts haunt the vacation cabin of Jason, 12, and his younger sister, Sally. These are not friendly, Casper-like ghosts. These are demons that victimize the children and their babysitter. They may even have caused the death of a former vacationer.

1. The Haunting ◆ 1995
2. The Horror ◆ 1995
3. The Final Nightmare ◆ 1995

HOVER CAR RACER

Reilly, Matthew

SIMON & SCHUSTER ◆ GRADES 6–9 ◆ A/R

SCIENCE FICTION

In the early 21st century, teenager Jason Chaser attends the International Race School learning to drive hover cars, super-fast vehicles that hover just above the ground. In *Crash Course,* Jason competes in a race in Italy, where he discovers danger behind the scenes. Will Jason earn enough points to compete in the big New York City race? The first book was originally published on the Internet (for free). TeenReads.com has an interview with the author, who is Australian.

1. Crash Course ◆ 2005
2. Full Throttle ◆ 2006
3. Photo Finish ◆ 2007

HOW I SURVIVED MIDDLE SCHOOL

Krulik, Nancy E.

SCHOLASTIC ◆ GRADES 4–7 ◆ A/R

REAL LIFE

Middle school is not easy and Jenny McAfee faces typical problems—making and keeping friends, quelching rumors, and suspecting others of cheating. Jenny and her friends do everything they can to stop the popular Pops from running the joint; Jenny even runs for class president!

1. Can You Get an F in Lunch? ◆ 2007
2. Madame President ◆ 2007
3. I Heard a Rumor ◆ 2007
4. The New Girl ◆ 2007
5. Cheat Sheet ◆ 2007
6. P.S. I Really Like You ◆ 2008
7. Who's Got Spirit? ◆ 2008
8. It's All Downhill from Here ◆ 2009

HOWL'S MOVING CASTLE

Jones, Diana Wynne

GREENWILLOW ◆ GRADES 6–10 ◆ A/R

FANTASY

Sophie expects to have a dull life working in her family's hat shop. After a witch turns Sophie into an old woman, Sophie goes to work for Wizard

Howl, whose castle magically moves throughout the kingdom. Hoping to become a young girl again, Sophie makes a bargain with Howl and his fire demon. At the conclusion of the book, Sophie and Howl realize they are in love and they marry. In the subsequent books, Sophie and other characters from the first book are in the story but often they are not in a recognizable form at first. For example, Sophie is first seen as a cat in *Castle in the Air*. This is a detailed, inventive series with many twists and turns. *Howl's Moving Castle* was adapted by Hayao Miyazaki into an award-winning animated film in 2004.

1. Howl's Moving Castle ◆ 1986
2. Castle in the Air ◆ 1990
3. House of Many Ways ◆ 2008

HOWL'S MOVING CASTLE (GRAPHIC NOVELS)

Miyazaki, Hayao

VIZ MEDIA ◆ GRADES 6–10

FANTASY

The screenplay of the 2004 animated film version of *Howl's Moving Castle* is presented in four volumes that are illustrated with art from the film.

1. Howl's Moving Castle, Vol. 1 ◆ 2005
2. Howl's Moving Castle, Vol. 2 ◆ 2005
3. Howl's Moving Castle, Vol. 3 ◆ 2005
4. Howl's Moving Castle, Vol. 4 ◆ 2005

THE HUNGRY CITY CHRONICLES

Reeve, Philip

HARPERCOLLINS ◆ GRADES 7–10 ◆ A/R

SCIENCE FICTION

Many years ago, the Sixty Minute War brought death and destruction. Now, cities move on huge tracks and consume smaller towns. Fifteen-year-old Tom is an orphan who is apprenticed to Valentine, a scavenger/historian. Tom saves Valentine from being stabbed but, inexplicably, Valentine pushes Tom off a bridge along with Hester, the disfigured girl who attacked Valentine. Tom and Hester find themselves in Out-Country and only at the beginning of their crusade to restore order to the world. In *Predator's Gold,* Tom and Hester become involved in Anchorage's effort to outrun its pursuers.

1. Mortal Engines ◆ 2003
2. Predator's Gold ◆ 2004

3. Infernal Devices ◆ 2005
4. A Darkling Plain ◆ 2007

I AM AMERICAN

Various authors

NATIONAL GEOGRAPHIC ◆ GRADES 4–7

HISTORICAL

A series of historical novels that blend fiction and fact, using a combination of fictional journals, letters, and narrative with background details and photographs. *Cowboys on the Western Trail* portrays the excitement of a cattle drive in 1887, using an appealing magazine format. In *Servant to Abigail Adams,* a teenage servant accompanies First Lady Abigail Adams to the Executive Mansion in Philadephia and later to the new presidential residence in Washington, D.C.

1. Yankee Blue or Rebel Grey? The Civil War Adventures of Sam Shaw (Connell, Kate) ◆ 2003
2. The Eve of Revolution: The Colonial Adventures of Benjamin Wilcox (Burt, Barbara) ◆ 2003
3. Servant to Abigail Adams: The Early American Adventures of Hannah Cooper (Connell, Kate) ◆ 2003
4. We Came Through Ellis Island: The Immigrant Adventures of Emma Markowitz (Thompson, Gare) ◆ 2003
5. Our Journey West: The Oregon Trail Adventures of Sarah Marshall (Thompson, Gare) ◆ 2003
6. When the Mission Padre Came to the Rancho: The Early California Adventures of Rosalinda and Simon Delgado (Thompson, Gare) ◆ 2004
7. Cowboys on the Western Trail: The Cattle Drive Adventures of Josh McNabb and Davy Bartlett (Oatman, Eric) ◆ 2004
8. Escape to Freedom: The Underground Railroad Adventures of Callie and William (Simon, Barbara Brooks) ◆ 2004
9. Hoping for Rain: The Dust Bowl Adventures of Patty and Earl Buckler (Connell, Kate) ◆ 2004

I "HEART" BIKINIS

Various authors

SCHOLASTIC ◆ GRADES 7–10

REAL LIFE

Relationships, romance, vacations, beaches, and boys are featured in this frothy series. In *He's With Me,* Lexie likes her brother's friend Jake but he treats her like a sister. Then Jake needs a plan to escape Bree McKennis's attentions and he agrees to pretend that Lexie is his girlfriend. Oh, how

Lexie hopes that the relationship becomes real! In *What's Hot,* Holly has a summer job at the country club's snack bar and is attracted to her coworker Paul. What should she do when her best friend says that she is interested in Paul? Light fun—perfect beach books for teens.

1. He's with Me (Summers, Tamara) ◆ 2007
2. Island Summer (Ny, Jeanine Le) ◆ 2007
3. What's Hot (Davis, Caitlyn) ◆ 2007

I, ROBOT

Asimov, Isaac

BANTAM DOUBLEDAY DELL ◆ GRADES 10–12 ◆ A/R

SCIENCE FICTION

Robots take on many human characteristics in these entertaining stories featuring Dr. Susan Calvin and her mechanical inventions.

1. I, Robot ◆ 1950
2. The Caves of Steel ◆ 1954
3. The Naked Sun ◆ 1957
4. The Robots of Dawn ◆ 1983
5. Robots and Empire ◆ 1985

THE ICEMARK CHRONICLES

Hill, Stuart

SCHOLASTIC ◆ GRADES 6–10 ◆ A/R

FANTASY

The king of the Icemark is dead and Thirrin, 13, is now the queen. To protect her country from the gathering enemies, Thirrin has formed alliances with the werewolves, the Vampire King and Queen, and the snow leopards. She relies on Oskan, a young warlock, for guidance and support. As the first book ends, there is an epic battle between the forces of the Icemark and the invaders. The second book focuses on the heroic exploits of Charlemagne, the youngest son of Queen Thirrin and Oskan.

1. The Cry of the Icemark ◆ 2005
2. Blade of Fire ◆ 2007
3. The Last Battle of the Icemark ◆ 2008

THE ILLMOOR CHRONICLES

Stone, David Lee

HYPERION ◆ GRADES 5–9 ◆ A/R

FANTASY | HUMOR

As in the Pied Piper of Hamlin, rats have overtaken the city of Dullitch and the Duke offers a reward to be rid of them. Diek Westapha, who possesses evil magic, accomplishes the task but is not given the reward. Again, as in the Pied Piper, he leads the children out of town. A motley collection of citizens (including an ex-wizard, a barbarian, a dwarf, and a thief) band together to try to rescue the children. In the second book, a new threat looms as the evil Yowler plans to change the people of Dullitch into rocks. A vampire, thief/gravedigger, and the Duke are among those who confront the Yowler. Puns and jokes throughout the text will keep readers interested.

1. The Ratastrophe Catastrophe ◆ 2004
2. The Yowler Foul-Up ◆ 2006
3. The Shadewell Shenanigans ◆ 2006

IMMORTALS

Pierce, Tamora

ATHENEUM ◆ GRADES 7–10 ◆ A/R

FANTASY

Daine, 13, is an orphan who has a way with animals. When the kingdom of Tortall is threatened by immortal beings, Daine's skills are needed. She works with an endangered pack of wolves and helps the emperor's dying birds. As the series progresses, Daine grows up and becomes attracted to the mage Numair.

1. Wild Magic ◆ 1992
2. Wolf-Speaker ◆ 1994
3. Emperor Mage ◆ 1995
4. The Realms of the Gods ◆ 1996

IMPACT ZONE

Strasser, Todd

SIMON & SCHUSTER ◆ GRADES 7–12 ◆ A/R

FAMILY LIFE | REAL LIFE | RECREATION

Kai, 15, has left his home in Hawaii to live with his father and stepbrother near New York City. His father is abusive, forcing Kai to work selling cheaply made T-shirts for outlandish prices. Kai finds peace when he is surfing. He begins to make friends, including a girlfriend, Shauna. Family problems, romance, and surfing should keep teen readers interested.

1. Take Off ◆ 2004
2. Cut Back ◆ 2004
3. Close Out ◆ 2004

IN OR OUT

Gabel, Claudia

SCHOLASTIC POINT ◆ GRADES 7–10 ◆ A/R

REAL LIFE

As best friends Nola and Marnie begin ninth grade they make choices that strain their friendship. Marnie follows Lizette and her mean girls while Nola is left out and lonely. By *Friends Close, Enemies Closer,* the girls are no longer friends; however, Nola is becoming more popular (especially with boys) and Marnie's fight with Lizette has left her out, out, out!

1. In or Out ◆ 2007
2. Loves Me, Loves Me Not ◆ 2007
3. Sweet and Vicious ◆ 2008
4. Friends Close, Enemies Closer ◆ 2008

IN THE CARDS

Fredericks, Mariah

ATHENEUM ◆ GRADES 5–8 ◆ A/R

REAL LIFE

Tarot cards, fortune-telling, and predictions are the twist in this series about eighth-grade girls. In *Love,* Anna's elderly neighbor dies leaving her a set of tarot cards. Anna and her friends Eve and Syd consult the cards about dating, school success, and the future. Anna's reading leads her to begin dating Declan Kelso. Eventually she realizes that her fantasy about Declan was not realistic. In *Fame,* Eve wants to be a musical star while *Life* focuses on Syd's family and fears.

1. Love ◆ 2007
2. Fame ◆ 2008
3. Life ◆ 2008

IN THE SHADOW OF THE BEAR

Randall, David

ATHENEUM ◆ GRADES 7–12 ◆ A/R

FANTASY

Clovermead, 12, lives with her father Waxmelt, an innkeeper. When a stranger comes to the inn, Clovermead and her father leave the inn and begin a journey that reveals secrets about Clovermead's past. She learns she is the daughter of Lady Cindertallow, the sovereign of Chandlefort and that her "father" stole her when she was a child. As Clovermead matures, her magical powers increase and she begins to train as a Yellow-jacket soldier. A bear-tooth talisman that she wears brings her a connection with Lord Ursus and the bear worshipers. This is a complex series with shape-shifting, jealousy, betrayal, and an epic struggle between the evil of Lord Ursus and the power of light of Lady Moon.

1. Clovermead ◆ 2004
2. Chandlefort ◆ 2006
3. Sorrel ◆ 2007

INDIGO

Cooper, Louise

TOR ◆ GRADES 7–12

FANTASY

Princess Indigo releases demons from the Tower of Regrets and she must struggle to undo this wrong in a life of continual wandering. By *Aisling,* she has destroyed six of the seven demons over a 50-year period but now she loses her memory.

1. Nemesis ◆ 1989
2. Inferno ◆ 1989
3. Infanta ◆ 1990
4. Nocturne ◆ 1990
5. Troika ◆ 1991
6. Avatar ◆ 1992
7. Revenant ◆ 1993
8. Aisling ◆ 1994

INHERITANCE

Paolini, Christopher

KNOPF ◆ GRADES 5–12 ◆ A/R

FANTASY

Eragon, 15, finds a dragon egg that hatches. Out comes a female dragon he names Saphira. The two of them have a strange psychic connection that comes to their aid as they face challenges. Eragon discovers his destiny as a Dragon Rider, a new generation of warriors who are rising against King Galbatorix. Filled with magic and epic battles, this series will attract fans of the Lord of the Rings (Tolkien) and McCaffrey's Pern/Dragonrider books. *Eragon* was made into a popular movie.

1. Eragon ◆ 2003
2. Eldest ◆ 2005
3. Brisingr ◆ 2008

THE INK DRINKER

Sanvoisin, Eric

DELACORTE ◆ GRADES 4–7 ◆ A/R

FANTASY

Draculink, an ink-drinking vampire bites Odilon, a boy who hates reading. Now Odilon sips the words out of the books in his father's bookstore, leaving them filled with empty pages. A new classmate, Camilla, is also an ink drinker and the two enjoy sharing books—until they are drawn into a Little Red Riding Hood story.

1. The Ink Drinker ◆ 1998
2. A Straw for Two ◆ 1999
3. The City of Ink Drinkers ◆ 2002
4. Little Red Ink Drinker ◆ 2003

INKHEART

Funke, Cornelia

SCHOLASTIC ◆ GRADES 5–12 ◆ A/R

FANTASY | ADVENTURE

As the series begins, Meggie, 12, discovers that her father, Mo, can bring book characters to life when he reads aloud. After reading a book called *Inkheart,* Mo has released some dangerous characters and Meggie must help her father escape from them. In the second book, Meggie enters Inkworld and with Farid, an apprentice, faces war and the possible execution of her father.

1. Inkheart ◆ 2003
2. Inkspell ◆ 2005
3. Inkdeath ◆ 2008

INSIDE GIRL

Minter, J.

BLOOMSBURY ◆ GRADES 9–12

REAL LIFE

Flan Flood, 14 (younger sister of one of the boys in the Insiders series), spins off into her own series. She has decided to leave her trendy private school and attend public school. Being a freshman in a new school is certainly a change, but it is also a challenge. Flan's new "normal" friends don't know about her cool celebrity friends and she wants to keep it that way. As the series progresses, Flan decides to return to private school—and now has to be the "new" kid all over again. Parties, dating, fashion, and relationships will keep teen readers hooked.

1. Inside Girl ◆ 2007
2. The Sweetest Thing ◆ 2007
3. Some Kind of Wonderful ◆ 2008
4. All That Glitters ◆ 2008
5. Perfect Match ◆ 2009

THE INSIDERS

Minter, J.

BLOOMSBURY ◆ GRADES 9–12 ◆ A/R

REAL LIFE

Five wealthy boys enjoy parties, dating, fashion, sex, and drinking in Manhattan. Focusing on Jonathan, these books follow the group from their junior year at private schools through their plans for college. Along the way the guys take a break from school on a luxury yacht in the Mediterranean. This series could be a choice for fans of Gossip Girl books along with newer series like Private. Inside Girl is a spinoff series.

1. The Insiders ◆ 2004
2. Pass It On ◆ 2004
3. Take It Off ◆ 2005
4. Break Every Rule ◆ 2005
5. Hold on Tight ◆ 2006
6. Girls We Love ◆ 2006

INTERNET GIRLS

Myracle, Lauren

AMULET ◆ GRADES 10–12 ◆ A/R

REAL LIFE

Zoe, Maddie, and Angela are sophomores in the first book of this series, *ttyl.* They constantly instant-message each other and the book is told through their messages and chat room discussions. They discuss relationships, drinking, and, as the series progresses, sexual encounters and drugs. In *l8r, g8r,* the three are seniors preparing for college and dealing with typical teen anxieties.

1. ttyl ◆ 2004
2. ttfn ◆ 2006
3. l8r, g8r ◆ 2007

INTERNS

Walsh, Chloe

HARPERTEEN ◆ GRADES 8–10

REAL LIFE

Fashion, parties, New York City, and four teen girls with the opportunity of a lifetime—that's the focus of the Interns. Callie, Nadine, Ava, and Aynsley have very different backgrounds, but they share a love of fashion. A summer internship at the premier fashion magazine *Couture* provides them with the chance to get the inside scoop on style. The Violet series by Melissa Walker is another fashion-based series.

1. Fashionistas ◆ 2008
2. Truth or Fashion ◆ 2008

INVISIBLE DETECTIVES

Richards, Justin

DUTTON/SLEUTH ◆ GRADES 5–9 ◆ A/R

MYSTERY | FANTASY

Who is the Invisible Detective? In London in 1936, four young people work as a team to help solve crimes. They keep their involvement and identities a secret, working as one. Art, 14, is part of the team helping Scotland Yard (where Art's father works) solve strange crimes. The crimes are not just robberies and kidnappings; they involve murderous puppets, an underground monster, and a zombie army. One arc of this series is the inclusion of a present-day teen, Arthur Drake, who reads about the crimes in a journal that seems to be written by him.

1. Double Life ◆ 2005
2. Shadow Beast ◆ 2005
3. Ghost Soldiers ◆ 2006

ISAAC ASIMOV'S CALIBAN

Allen, Roger MacBride

ORION ◆ GRADES 9–12

SCIENCE FICTION

This trilogy expands on Asimov's Three Laws of Robotics. Caliban is a no-law robot. He does not conform to the behavior code that keeps other robots from harming humans. As a result, he is a rogue who strives to establish his own identity in a world where robots are servants.

1. Isaac Asimov's Caliban ◆ 1994

2. Isaac Asimov's Inferno ◆ 1994
3. Isaac Asimov's Utopia ◆ 1996

ISLAND

Korman, Gordon
SCHOLASTIC ◆ GRADES 6–9 ◆ A/R
ADVENTURE

Six trouble-prone children are part of a program called "Charting a New Course." They will spend one month on a boat in the Pacific Ocean. It is expected to be tough and it gets tougher when the boat is shipwrecked. The captain and first mate disappear, but the children are not alone on the island.

1. Shipwreck ◆ 2001
2. Survival ◆ 2001
3. Escape ◆ 2001

ISLAND TRILOGY

Whelan, Gloria
HARPERCOLLINS ◆ GRADES 6–9 ◆ A/R
HISTORICAL

During the War of 1812, Mary O'Shea, 12, lives with her older brother and sister on Mackinac Island. Their father has left them and gone to fight against the British. Mary and her siblings are now in charge of the family farm. They face the dangers of war and the difficulty of managing the farm. There is a subplot with a Native American boy, Gavin, who has lived among the settlers. After the war, Mary travels to London, gets swept up in the social whirl, and finds romance. After she returns to Mackinac Island, she must choose between two paths for her future.

1. Once on This Island ◆ 1995
2. Farewell to the Island ◆ 1998
3. Return to the Island ◆ 2000

THE IT GIRL

Von Ziegesar, Cecily
LITTLE, BROWN ◆ GRADES 9–12 ◆ A/R
REAL LIFE

Jenny Humphrey, recently kicked out of prep school in New York City, is now attending an exclusive boarding school, Waverly Academy. She has not changed her wild ways, which include underage drinking, sexual encounters, and numerous disciplinary issues. Her new roommates, Callie and Brett, are equally headstrong. Jenny is on a mission—to be the It Girl at Waverly Academy. As a Gossip Girl spin-off, this series will be popular with those readers.

1. The It Girl ◆ 2005
2. Notorious ◆ 2006
3. Reckless ◆ 2006
4. Unforgettable ◆ 2007
5. Lucky ◆ 2007
6. Tempted ◆ 2008
7. Infamous ◆ 2008

IT'S HAPPY BUNNY

Benton, Jim
SCHOLASTIC ◆ GRADES 7–10
HUMOR

Having problems with your love life? Happy Bunny is here for you. Romance, breaking up, gifts, secrets, and dating disasters are presented with humor and attitude. There are puzzles, quizzes, games, and other activities. While not graphic novels, these books have numerous illustrations and limited text. The tongue-in-cheek comments are sure to attract teen readers.

1. Love Bites ◆ 2005
2. What's Your Sign? ◆ 2005
3. Life. Get One. ◆ 2006
4. The Good, the Bad, and the Bunny ◆ 2006

JACK HENRY

Gantos, Jack
FARRAR, STRAUS & GIROUX ◆ GRADES 5–8 ◆ A/R
HUMOR

It's the late 1960s. Jack's family moves a lot—he's lived in nine houses and he's only in the sixth grade. Jack feels confused and disoriented yet he strives to find his own identity. In the second book, the family has moved again. This time they are in Barbados and Jack keeps a journal of his year there. The books follow a sequence that is different from their chronological release dates: *Jack Adrift, Jack on the Tracks, Heads or Tails, Jack's New Power,* and *Jack's Black Book.*

1. Heads or Tails: Stories from the Sixth Grade ◆ 1994

2. Jack's New Power: Stories from a Caribbean Year ◆ 1995
3. Jack's Black Book ◆ 1997
4. Jack on the Tracks: Four Seasons of Fifth Grade ◆ 1999
5. Jack Adrift: Fourth Grade Without a Clue ◆ 2003

JACKIE CHAN ADVENTURES

Various authors

GROSSET & DUNLAP ◆ GRADES 4–8

ADVENTURE | FANTASY

When Jackie's talisman breaks in half, he becomes two people—Jackie Light and Jackie Dark. The two must team up to rescue Jackie's niece, Jade, from the dangers of the group called the Dark Hand. The Super Special book, *Day of the Dragon,* includes puzzles and a secret message from Jackie.

1. The Dark Hand (Willard, Eliza) ◆ 2001
2. Jade's Secret Power (West, Cathy) ◆ 2002
3. Sign of the Ox (Stine, Megan) ◆ 2002
4. Enter . . . the Viper (Carroll, Jacqueline) ◆ 2002
5. Shendu Escapes! (Slack, David) ◆ 2002
6. A New Enemy (Ashby, R. S.) ◆ 2002
7. Revenge of the Dark Hand (Willard, Eliza) ◆ 2002
8. The Power of the Rat (Stine, Megan) ◆ 2002
9. Stronger than Stone (Ashby, R. S.) ◆ 2002
10. Uncle's Big Surprise (Carroll, Jacqueline) ◆ 2002
11. The Jade Monkey (Katschke, Judy) ◆ 2002
12. The Strongest Evil (Carroll, Jacqueline) ◆ 2002
13. Day of the Dragon: Super Special (Willard, Eliza) ◆ 2003

JACKIE CHAN ADVENTURES (TOKYOPOP)

1. Enter the Dark Hand ◆ 2003
2. Legend of the Zodiac ◆ 2004
3. Jackie and Jade Save the Day ◆ 2004

JACKY FABER *see* Bloody Jack Adventures

JAMES BUDD

Carlson, Dale Bick

WESTERN PUBLISHING ◆ GRADES 7–10

MYSTERY

James Budd, 16, is a supersleuth who takes on difficult cases. A Vietnam vet accused of murder, a classmate who is being abused, and a mad scientist are among the challenges that he faces.

1. The Mystery of the Madman at Cornwall Crag ◆ 1984
2. The Secret of Operation Brain ◆ 1984
3. The Mystery of the Lost Princess ◆ 1984
4. The Mystery of Galaxy Games ◆ 1984

JAMESTOWN'S AMERICAN PORTRAITS

Various authors

GLENCOE/MCGRAW-HILL ◆ GRADES 5–8 ◆ A/R

HISTORICAL

An indentured servant in Virginia, an immigrant girl working in a New York City sweatshop, and a teen pilot in the Women's Airforce Service Pilots are among the characters featured in this series. In *All for Texas,* Thomas Jefferson "Jeff" Byrd, 13, moves to Texas with his family in the 1830s. Jeff faces hardships and loss as both his father and a young friend are killed in battles with Mexican soldiers. Show these books to readers who enjoyed the Survival series by Kathleen Duey and Karen A. Bale.

1. All For Texas: A Story of Texas Liberation (Wisler, G. Clifton) ◆ 2001
2. Corn Raid: A Story of the Jamestown Settlement (Collier, James Lincoln) ◆ 2001
3. Eye for an Eye: A Story of the Revolutionary War (Roop, Peter) ◆ 2001
4. Revenge of the Aztecs: A Story of 1920s Hollywood (Pfeffer, Susan Beth) ◆ 2001
5. The Road to Freedom: A Story of the Reconstruction (Asim, Jabari) ◆ 2001
6. Sweet America: An Immigrant's Story (Kroll, Steven) ◆ 2001
7. This Generation of Americans: A Story of the Civil Rights Movement (McKissack, Fredrick L.) ◆ 2001
8. To Touch the Stars: A Story of World War II (Zeinert, Karen) ◆ 2001
9. When I Dream of Heaven: Angelina's Story (Kroll, Steven) ◆ 2001
10. Wind on the River: A Story of the Civil War (Lawlor, Laurie) ◆ 2001
11. The Worst of Times: A Story of the Great Depression (Collier, James Lincoln) ◆ 2001

JANIE

Cooney, Caroline B.

DELACORTE ◆ GRADES 6–9 ◆ A/R

REAL LIFE

When Janie was 15, she saw her face on a milk carton as a missing child and began the search for her true identity. She discovers that she was kidnapped from her biological parents 12 years before. The couple who have raised her have their own secret. Janie is betrayed by her boyfriend when he reveals her family's secret. Ultimately, Janie discovers the mystery of her past.

1. The Face on the Milk Carton ◆ 1990
2. Whatever Happened to Janie? ◆ 1993
3. The Voice on the Radio ◆ 1996
4. What Janie Found ◆ 2000

JENNIE McGRADY MYSTERIES

Rushford, Patricia H.

BETHANY HOUSE ◆ GRADES 7–10 ◆ A/R

MYSTERY | VALUES

Like Nancy Drew, Jennie McGrady gets involved in mysterious situations. From finding her grandmother—who is missing along with a million dollars in stolen diamonds—to discovering a classmate's secret past to traveling to Ireland where she is threatened, Jennie's life is full of adventure. Her family, friends, and faith help her face each new challenge.

1. Too Many Secrets ◆ 1993
2. Silent Witness ◆ 1993
3. Pursued ◆ 1994
4. Deceived ◆ 1994
5. Without a Trace ◆ 1995
6. Dying to Win ◆ 1995
7. Betrayed ◆ 1996
8. In Too Deep ◆ 1996
9. Over the Edge ◆ 1997
10. From the Ashes ◆ 1997
11. Desperate Measures ◆ 1998
12. Abandoned ◆ 1999
13. Forgotten ◆ 2000
14. Stranded ◆ 2001
15. Grave Matters ◆ 2002

THE JERSEY

Various authors

DISNEY PRESS ◆ GRADES 4–7 ◆ A/R

FANTASY

A group of friends have a jersey with magical powers. When they use it, they connect with a well-known sports star. In *Fight for Your Right,* Morgan boxes with Laila Ali. Other famous sports figures who appear in these stories include skateboarder Tony Hawk, BMX star Dave Mirra, and track star Michael Johnson. Gordon Korman created the series for television and these books are adapted from several episodes.

1. It's Magic (Sinclair, Jay) ◆ 2000
2. No Girly Girls Allowed (Sinclair, Jay) ◆ 2000
3. Nick's a Chick (Selman, Matty) ◆ 2000
4. This Rocks! (Selman, Matty) ◆ 2000
5. Team Player (Mantell, Paul) ◆ 2001
6. Head over Heels (Mantell, Paul) ◆ 2001
7. Fight for Your Right (Mantell, Paul) ◆ 2001
8. Need for Speed (Rees, Elizabeth M.) ◆ 2001

JESS JORDAN *see* Girl

JESSICA DARLING

McCafferty, Megan
CROWN ◆ GRADES 10–12 ◆ A/R
FAMILY LIFE | HUMOR | REAL LIFE

When her best friend moves away, 16-year-old Jessica Darling struggles to deal alone with her feelings of isolation at home and at school. In the second book, Jessica is in her senior year and the poignant but humorous description of unrequited love and parental over-involvement continues. By the third book, she is in college, and in the fourth, she has graduated and is considering a proposal of marriage from on-again off-again boyfriend Marcus.

1. Sloppy Firsts ◆ 2001
2. Second Helpings ◆ 2003
3. Charmed Thirds ◆ 2006
4. Fourth Comings ◆ 2007

JIGGY MCCUE

Lawrence, Michael
DUTTON ◆ GRADES 4–7 ◆ A/R
FANTASY | HUMOR

In the first of these entertaining adventures imported from Britain, Jiggy and his friends investigate what is haunting his new house and suspect it's the ghost of a goose. In the second, Jiggy and his friend Angie end up switching bodies after playing a beta version of a computer game, causing much confusion.

1. The Poltergoose ◆ 2002
2. The Killer Underpants ◆ 2002
3. The Toilet of Doom ◆ 2002
4. The Snottle ◆ 2003
5. Maggot Pie ◆ 2004
6. Nudie Dudie ◆ 2004
7. Neville the Devil ◆ 2005
8. Ryan's Brain ◆ 2006
9. The Iron, the Switch and the Broom Cupboard ◆ 2007

JIMMY FINCHER SAGA

Dashner, James
BONNEVILLE BOOKS ◆ GRADES 7–10
SCIENCE FICTION

Jimmy Fincher is drawn into hidden worlds of villains and danger. There are Four Gifts that will help him face the Shadow Ka and the Stompers. Will he find the Gifts in time to prevent destruction?

1. A Door in the Woods ◆ 2003
2. A Gift of Ice ◆ 2004
3. The Tower of Air ◆ 2004
4. War of the Black Curtain ◆ 2005

JOE GREY MYSTERIES

Murphy, Shirley Rousseau
HARPERCOLLINS ◆ GRADES 9–12
ANIMAL FANTASY | MYSTERY

Joe Grey and Dulcie, intrepid and intelligent cat investigators, use their varied feline skills to solve intricately plotted crimes.

1. Cat on the Edge ◆ 1996
2. Cat Under Fire ◆ 1997
3. Cat Raise the Dead ◆ 1997
4. Cat in the Dark ◆ 1999
5. Cat to the Dogs ◆ 2000
6. Cat Spitting Mad ◆ 2001
7. Cat Laughing Last ◆ 2002
8. Cat Seeing Double ◆ 2003
9. Cat Fear No Evil ◆ 2004
10. Cat Cross Their Graves ◆ 2005
11. Cat Breaking Free ◆ 2005

12. Cat Pay the Devil ◆ 2007
13. Cat Deck the Halls ◆ 2007

JOEY PIGZA

Gantos, Jack

FARRAR, STRAUS & GIROUX ◆ GRADES 5–9 ◆ A/R
REAL LIFE

Joey Pigza is out of control. His hyperactivity causes him trouble at school. He can't pay attention; he can't sit still. His medication works for a while, but it wears off. He finally gets his meds balanced only to visit his father who wants him to try going without them. This series provides a revealing look at a special education student. The second book received a Newbery Honor award.

1. Joey Pigza Swallowed the Key ◆ 1998
2. Joey Pigza Loses Control ◆ 2000
3. What Would Joey Do? ◆ 2002
4. I Am Not Joey Pigza ◆ 2007

JOHNNY DIXON

Bellairs, John, and Brad Strickland

DIAL ◆ GRADES 5–8 ◆ A/R
FANTASY | MYSTERY

Johnny Dixon's mother is dead and his dad is fighting in the Korean War. He lives with his grandparents across the street from the eccentric but kindly Professor Childermass. The two strike up a strange friendship, and together with Johnny's friend Fergie they solve mysteries involving ghosts, demon possession, and even time travel. Johnny is a small, almost timid boy who seems an unlikely candidate for such adventures. The professor is knowledgeable in many areas and sometimes unwillingly draws the boys into things. Fergie is a bit of a smart aleck and adds humor to the situations. Edward Gorey's black-and-white drawings add to the air of mystery. *The Drum, the Doll, and the Zombie* was completed by Strickland after Bellairs's death. The last three books are by Strickland.

1. The Curse of the Blue Figurine ◆ 1983
2. The Mummy, the Will, and the Crypt ◆ 1983
3. The Spell of the Sorcerer's Skull ◆ 1984
4. The Revenge of the Wizard's Ghost ◆ 1985
5. The Eyes of the Killer Robot ◆ 1986
6. The Trolley to Yesterday ◆ 1989
7. The Chessmen of Doom ◆ 1989
8. The Secret of the Underground Room ◆ 1990

9. The Drum, the Doll, and the Zombie ◆ 1994
10. The Hand of the Necromancer ◆ 1996
11. The Bell, the Book, and the Spellbinder ◆ 1997
12. The Wrath of the Grinning Ghost ◆ 1999

JOHNNY MAXWELL

Pratchett, Terry

HARPERCOLLINS ◆ GRADES 5–8 ◆ A/R

HUMOR | FANTASY | SCIENCE FICTION

Johnny Maxwell is already facing enough problems—his parents' unhappy marriage and constant scenes of fighting in the 1991 Gulf War—when his new computer game, Only You Can Save Mankind, throws out a new challenge. In the second volume in this funny trilogy, ghosts of "post-senior citizens" seek Johnny's help when their cemetery is under threat. The final volume involves time travel as Johnny and friends seek to save his English village from a bomb that will fall on it in World War II. These books were first published in Britain in the 1990s.

1. Only You Can Save Mankind: If Not You, Who Else? ◆ 2005
2. Johnny and the Dead ◆ 2006
3. Johnny and the Bomb ◆ 2007

JOURNEY OF ALLEN STRANGE

Various authors

ALADDIN ◆ GRADES 4–7

SCIENCE FICTION

Allen Strange is an alien from Xela. He was left behind by his spaceship and he has adopted the appearance of an African American human boy. He needs Robbie Stevenson's help but Robbie does not believe he is an alien until Allen appears as he really looks. Allen and Robbie help prevent several alien invasions, including the arrival of the insect-like Arubii. This is fun for fans of science fiction.

1. The Arrival (Weiss, Bobbi J. G., and David Cody Weiss) ◆ 1999
2. Invasion (Gallagher, Diana G.) ◆ 1999
3. Split Image (Dubowski, Cathy East) ◆ 1999
4. Legacy (Odom, Mel) ◆ 1999
5. Depth Charge (Weiss, Bobbi J. G., and David Cody Weiss) ◆ 1999
6. Alien Vacation (Weiss, Bobbi J. G., and David Cody Weiss) ◆ 1999
7. Election Connection (Ponti, James) ◆ 1999
8. Changeling Diapers (Weiss, Bobbi J. G., and David Cody Weiss) ◆ 2000
9. Joyride (Vornholt, John) ◆ 2000

JULEP O'TOOLE

Trueit, Trudi
PENGUIN ◆ GRADES 4–7 ◆ A/R
FAMILY LIFE

In the first book, poor Julep, 11, is a middle child, stuck (and generally ignored) between a perfect older sister and an asthmatic and demanding younger brother. By the second book, the focus is more on her needs and her wish to be more independent, to choose her own clothes. Julep's diary entries, interspersed throughout the text, reveal her point of view.

1. Julep O'Toole: Confessions of a Middle Child ◆ 2005
2. Julep O'Toole: Miss Independent ◆ 2006
3. Julep O'Toole: What I Really Want To Do Is Direct ◆ 2007

JULI SCOTT SUPER SLEUTH

Reece, Colleen L.
BARBOUR PUBLISHING ◆ GRADES 5–8
MYSTERY | VALUES

Juli Scott imagines that she will be an author of Nancy Drew-style stories. Meanwhile, she solves some of her own mysteries, including the mysterious "death" of her own father. In *Mysterious Monday,* Juli's father, Gary, who is a policeman, loses his memory after an explosion. Trying to trick some drug dealers, the local police tell Juli and her mother, Anne, that Gary is dead. In other books, Juli tries to rescue her friend Shannon Riley from the influence of a spiritualist, and Juli and her boyfriend, Dave Gilmore, are in danger as witnesses to a robbery. Juli and her family incorporate Christian values into their daily lives and activities. Juli often writes in her journal, struggling with her conscience, beliefs, and spiritual questions.

1. Mysterious Monday ◆ 1997
2. Trouble on Tuesday ◆ 1997
3. Wednesday Witness ◆ 1998
4. Thursday Trials ◆ 1998
5. Friday Flight ◆ 1998
6. Saturday Scare ◆ 1998

JULIAN ESCOBAR

O'Dell, Scott
HOUGHTON MIFFLIN ◆ GRADES 6–8 ◆ A/R
HISTORICAL

Set in the 16th century, this series chronicles the adventures of Julian Escobar, a young seminarian from Spain who journeys to the Americas. He is captured by Mayan Indians and manages to convince them that he is Kukulcan, a god who had promised to return to them. He continues this charade in the second book when he leaves the Maya and encounters Cortez in the days when the Aztec king Moctezuma is conquered by a few hundred Spanish soldiers. In the third book, his fortunes change and he becomes a wanderer, but eventually he ends up with Francisco Pizarro in the land of the Incas.

1. The Captive ◆ 1979
2. The Feathered Serpent ◆ 1981
3. The Amethyst Ring ◆ 1983

JULIE OF THE WOLVES

George, Jean Craighead
HARPERCOLLINS ◆ GRADES 5–8 ◆ A/R

ADVENTURE

Beginning with the Newbery-winning *Julie of the Wolves,* George explores the experiences of people and animals in the Alaskan tundra. Julie's story follows her quest for her identity through her return to her father's home. *Julie's Wolf Pack* describes the hardships faced by Kapu, first seen as a pup in the first book. The wolves face famine, disease, rivalries, and other dangers. These are exciting, realistic adventure novels. Readers will also relate to George's series about Sam Gribley and the falcon called Frightful.

1. Julie of the Wolves ◆ 1972
2. Julie ◆ 1996
3. Julie's Wolf Pack ◆ 1997

JUMPER

Gould, Steven
TOR ◆ GRADES 10–12 ◆ A/R

SCIENCE FICTION

David Rice, 17, "jumps" to escape his abusive father. He learns to control his ability to jump—teleport—and he uses it to survive, even robbing a bank to get money. In *Reflex,* Davy is in his twenties, married, and working as an agent for a secret government organization. *Jumper: Griffin's Story* seems somewhat unrelated to the earlier books but connects to the movie adaptation of the novels.

1. Jumper ◆ 1992

2. Reflex ◆ 2004
3. Jumper: Griffin's Story ◆ 2007

JUNEBUG

Mead, Alice

FARRAR, STRAUS & GIROUX ◆ GRADES 4–7 ◆ A/R

REAL LIFE

These realistic novels begin when Reeve McClain, Jr., "Junebug," is 10 years old. His family lives in the projects, facing all the threats of urban life—drugs, gangs, and loneliness. In the second book, they have moved to a safer neighborhood where Junebug's mother is the supervisor of a home for the elderly. Junebug helps her and interacts with Reverend Ashford. The third book finds Junebug meeting up with his friend Robert, who still lives in the projects. Junebug faces his family problems (his father has been in jail) and makes choices about his future.

1. Junebug ◆ 1995
2. Junebug and the Reverend ◆ 1998
3. Junebug in Trouble ◆ 2003

JUNIOR JEDI KNIGHTS *see* Star Wars Junior Jedi Knights

JUNIPER *see* Wise Child

JURASSIC PARK ADVENTURES

Ciencin, Scott

RANDOM HOUSE ◆ GRADES 4–7

FANTASY

Here are three stories set in Jurassic Park. In the first book, Eric is 13 and he goes para-sailing with Ben (his mother's boyfriend) to observe the dinosaurs from a safe distance above. There is an accident and Ben is killed. Eric is trapped on the island of Jurassic Park. Fans of the movie will enjoy this series.

1. Survivor ◆ 2001
2. Prey ◆ 2001
3. Flyers ◆ 2001

JUST . . .

Griffiths, Andy

SCHOLASTIC ◆ GRADES 5–8

HUMOR

Barf, poop, flesh-eating zombies, and other outrageous topics are just right for many middle school readers. The humorous stories in these books are sure to attract fans of Griffiths's Butt Wars books.

1. Just Annoying! ◆ 2003
2. Just Joking! ◆ 2003
3. Just Wacky! ◆ 2004
4. Just Stupid! ◆ 2004
5. Just Disgusting! ◆ 2004
6. Just Shocking! ◆ 2008

JUSTICE TRILOGY

Hamilton, Virginia

GREENWILLOW ◆ GRADES 5–8 ◆ A/R

FANTASY | SCIENCE FICTION

Justice and her two brothers discover that they are the first of a new race with extraordinary powers. Together with their friend Dorian, they form a unit that is able to travel into the distant future. Among the beings they find there is Duster, the leader of a group of young people. He is hindered, as is all of this world, by the evil Mal. When the Mal is defeated, all the friends they have made are free to be themselves. When Justice and her brothers return to their own time, they find that they have lost some of their powers but have gained maturity.

1. Justice and Her Brothers ◆ 1978
2. Dustland ◆ 1980
3. The Gathering ◆ 1981

THE KARMIDEE

Haptie, Charlotte

HOLIDAY HOUSE ◆ GRADES 4–7 ◆ A/R

FANTASY

The City of Trees is an isolated place surrounded by mountains and magic. The Normals are in power and they make rules to control those with magical powers, the Karmidee. Otto believes he is a Normal and is surprised to learn that his father, a librarian, is actually the King of the Karmidee. Otto's life is totally upended and he faces dangers as he tries to protect the Karmidee from the prejudice of the Normals. In the third book, Otto and a young girl named Rhiannon who opposes magic find themselves thrown together in a quest to save Otto's people.

1. Otto and the Flying Twins: The First Book of the Karmidee ◆ 2004
2. Otto and the Bird Charmers: The Second Book of the Karmidee ◆ 2005
3. Otto in the Time of the Warrior ◆ 2006

KATE GORDON *see* Heartlight

KATIE JOHN

Calhoun, Mary
HARPERCOLLINS ◆ GRADES 4–8 ◆ A/R
FAMILY LIFE | REAL LIFE

Katie John's story begins when her parents inherit a huge, decrepit house in a small town. They decide to move there for the summer, but Katie is not happy about leaving her friends. Over the summer, she makes new friends and begins to appreciate the house and its family history. In the end, she convinces her parents to stay and make a living by renting out rooms. She agrees to help with all the work involved in such an endeavor. In subsequent books, she starts a "boy haters" club but later she becomes a romantic after reading *Wuthering Heights* and begins to look for her Heathcliff.

1. Katie John ◆ 1960
2. Depend on Katie John ◆ 1961
3. Honestly, Katie John! ◆ 1963
4. Katie John and Heathcliff ◆ 1980

THE KEEPER'S CHRONICLES

Huff, Tanya
DAW ◆ GRADES 7–12
FANTASY

Claire Hanson is a Keeper, a protector of the universe. Accompanied by her talking cat Austin, she tackles problems including a hole to Hell. In *The Second Summoning*, she must deal with an angel and a devil who appear as teenagers and face the usual teen problems. These are entertaining stories.

1. Summon the Keeper ◆ 1998
2. The Second Summoning ◆ 2001
3. Long Hot Summoning ◆ 2003

KEYS TO THE KINGDOM

Nix, Garth

SCHOLASTIC ♦ GRADES 5–8 ♦ A/R

FANTASY

Mister Monday wants to recover a mysterious key from Arthur Pen-haligon. It turns out that Arthur is the heir to "the Will" and there are seven keys that he must acquire. The Second Key brings him into contact with Grim Tuesday. Arthur battles to save not only the Earth but also the magical worlds that have been revealed to him.

1. Mister Monday ♦ 2003
2. Grim Tuesday ♦ 2004
3. Drowned Wednesday ♦ 2005
4. Sir Thursday ♦ 2006
5. Lady Friday ♦ 2007
6. Superior Saturday ♦ 2008

KEYSTONE STABLES

Hubler, Marsha

ZONDERKIDZ ♦ GRADES 5–8 ♦ A/R

REAL LIFE

After being in foster homes, Skye, 13, is difficult and belligerent. The juvenile court is ready to send her to a detention center until Mr. and Mrs. Chambers agree to become her new foster family. The Chambers own Keystone Stables and as Skye begins to connect with the horses, she begins to trust the people around her, too. Guided by her new family, Skye finds faith in God's love.

1. The Trouble with Skye ♦ 2004
2. A True Test for Skye ♦ 2004
3. Trouble Times Two ♦ 2005
4. Teamwork at Camp Tioga ♦ 2005
5. The Winning Summer ♦ 2005
6. Skye's Final Test ♦ 2005

KIDNAPPED

Korman, Gordon

SCHOLASTIC ♦ GRADES 5–8 ♦ A/R

ADVENTURE

Meg, 11, and Aiden, 15, have been fugitives from the FBI (see the On the Run series). Just as their lives begin to settle down, Meg is kidnapped. Although he still distrusts them, Aiden must cooperate with the FBI to find his sister. Meanwhile, Meg is trying to escape from her captors. This is an action-packed series with cliff-hanging moments and plot twists that leave the reader breathless.

1. Abduction ◆ 2006
2. Search ◆ 2006
3. Rescue ◆ 2006

KIDS FROM KENNEDY MIDDLE SCHOOL

Cooper, Ilene

MORROW ◆ **GRADES 5–7** ◆ **A/R**

REAL LIFE

Friends and foes at a middle school are the focus of this series. Robin and Veronica are friends but when Veronica creates an exclusive club, Robin is uneasy. If she speaks up, she'll be left out. Jon Rossi is a sixth-grader who plays basketball but dislikes his coach's negative approach. If he leaves the team, he'll disappoint his father. Gretchen, 12, loses weight, but she still remembers the way she was treated.

1. Queen of the Sixth Grade ◆ 1988
2. Choosing Sides ◆ 1990
3. Mean Streak ◆ 1991
4. The New, Improved Gretchen Hubbard ◆ 1992

KIESHA'RA

Atwater-Rhodes, Amelia

DELACORTE ◆ **GRADES 7–10** ◆ **A/R**

FANTASY

Hoping to end a long conflict, mediators propose that two royal leaders of different shapeshifters marry. At first, Danica, an avian shapeshifter, and Zane, a serpiente, reject the plan; however, the prospect of peace and their growing attraction lead them to reconsider. Subsequent books follow their adventures and those of their descendants at the Wyvern court.

1. Hawksong ◆ 2003
2. Snakecharm ◆ 2004
3. Falcondance ◆ 2005
4. Wolfcry ◆ 2006
5. Wyvernhail ◆ 2007

KIM POSSIBLE (CHAPTER BOOKS)

Various authors

HYPERION; DISNEY PRESS ♦ GRADES 4–7

FANTASY

Kim Possible will save the world. She faces the evil Drakken. She finds a kidnapped scientist. She stops DNAmy from creating a stuffed-animal army. All the while, she manages to stay involved with cheerleading, ski trips, and watching television. There are related items to this series including a puzzle book, *Code Word: Kim*.

1. Bueno Nacho (Thorpe, Kiki) ♦ 2003
2. The New Ron (Thorpe, Kiki) ♦ 2003
3. Showdown at Camp Wannaweep (Thorpe, Kiki) ♦ 2003
4. Downhill (Jones, Jasmine) ♦ 2003
5. Killigan's Island (Pascoe, Jim) ♦ 2004
6. Monkey Business (Cerasini, Marc) ♦ 2004
7. Attack of the Killer Bebes (Pascoe, Jim) ♦ 2004
8. Royal Pain (Jones, Jasmine) ♦ 2004
9. Extreme (unknown) ♦ 2004
10. Tweeb Trouble (unknown) ♦ 2004
11. Grudge Match (unknown) ♦ 2005
12. Cloned (Cling, Jacqueline) ♦ 2006

KIM POSSIBLE: PICK A VILLAIN

Various authors

DISNEY PRESS ♦ GRADES 4–7

FANTASY

Here's a Kim Possible series with a "Choose Your Own Adventure" format. You pick the villain and then you decide what Kim will do to save the world.

1. Game On! (Ciencin, Scott, and Mark McCorkle) ♦ 2005
2. Badical Battles (Schooley, Bob, and Mark McCorkle) ♦ 2005
3. Masters of Mayhem (Ciencin, Scott) ♦ 2005
4. So Not the Drama! (Schooley, Bob, and Mark McCorkle) ♦ 2005

KIM POSSIBLE (TOKYOPOP)

Schooley, Bob, and Mark McCorkle

TOKYOPOP ♦ GRADES 4–7

FANTASY

Kim Possible is a typical high school girl who saves the world from evil villains in her spare time.

1. Bueno Nacho and Tick Tick Tick ◆ 2003
2. Monkey Fist Strikes and Attack of the Killer Bebes ◆ 2003
3. The New Ron and Mind Games ◆ 2003
4. Royal Pain and Twin Factor ◆ 2003
5. Animal Attraction and All the News ◆ 2004
6. Sink or Swim and Number One ◆ 2004
7. Monkey Ninjas in Space and Crush ◆ 2004

KIM POSSIBLE CINE-MANGA

1. Vol. 1 ◆ 2003
2. Vol. 2 ◆ 2003
3. Vol. 3 ◆ 2004
4. Vol. 4 ◆ 2004
5. Vol. 5 ◆ 2004
6. Vol. 6 ◆ 2004
7. Vol. 7 ◆ 2004

KIMANI TRU

Various authors
HARLEQUIN ◆ GRADES 10–12
REAL LIFE

In *Indigo Summer,* Indigo is 15 and seems to be on the right track for popularity. Her boyfriend is on the football team and she is going to the homecoming dance. Then she gets dumped and reaches out to her neighbor, Marcus Carter, who suddenly could be more than a friend. Other books feature the growing relationship between Indigo and Marcus. In *If I Were Your Boyfriend,* Keysha's "friend" plants drugs on her and Keysha becomes an outcast until Wesley Morris, who has his own troubled past, reaches out to her. Featuring African American characters and contemporary issues, the Kimani Tru series is a good choice for reluctant readers.

1. Indigo Summer (McKayhan, Monica) ◆ 2007
2. The Edification of Sonya Crane (Guilford, J. D.) ◆ 2007
3. Can't Stop the Shine (Davis, Joyce) ◆ 2007
4. Keysha's Drama (Sewell, Earl) ◆ 2007
5. Spin It Like That (Taylor, Chandra Sparks) ◆ 2007
6. Fast Life (Carter, Cassandra) ◆ 2007
7. First Semester (Cross III, Cecil R.) ◆ 2007
8. Hallway Diaries: How To Be Down/Double Act/The Summer She Learned to Dance (Various authors) ◆ 2007
9. Pushing Pause (Norfleet, Celeste O.) ◆ 2007
10. Gettin' Hooked (Scott, Nyomi) ◆ 2007
11. Trouble Follows (McKayhan, Monica) ◆ 2007
12. How to Salsa in a Sari (Sarker, Dona) ◆ 2008
13. A Matter of Attitude (Hayden) ◆ 2008
14. 16 Isn't Always Sweet (Carter, Cassandra) ◆ 2008

15. She Said, She Said (Norfleet, Celeste O., and Jennifer Norfleet) ◆ 2008
16. If I Were Your Boyfriend (Sewell, Earl) ◆ 2008
17. The Pact (McKayhan, Monica) ◆ 2008
18. Dirty Jersey (Duck, Phillip Thomas) ◆ 2008
19. Shrink to Fit (Sarker, Dona) ◆ 2008

THE KIN

Dickinson, Peter

GROSSET & DUNLAP ◆ GRADES 6–9 ◆ A/R

FANTASY

In a prehistoric era, five children have been separated from the Moon-hawk clan. It is dangerous for them to be on their own without food, water, shelter, or protection. They encounter a man, Tor, who is unable to speak. He uses his skill with tools to help them survive. Mythology and mysticism pervade these novels. Noli is a character with a strong spirit connection. She seems able to communicate with the group's totem animal, a hawk. Po's character is involved in a struggle to prove his bravery.

1. Suth's Story ◆ 1998
2. Noli's Story ◆ 1998
3. Mana's Story ◆ 1998
4. Po's Story ◆ 1998

KING GARION *see* Malloreon

THE KINGDOM

Black, Chuck

MULTNOMAH ◆ GRADES 8–10 ◆ A/R

VALUES

Leinad is a farmer whose father also trained him to use swords and to be loyal to the King. Leinad wonders about the reason for his training until his father is killed. Then Leinad begins to fulfill his destiny, joining the Noble Knights who serve the King. His first mission is to free the slaves controlled by Lord Fairos. Throughout the series there are biblical parallels that might make it an attractive choice for readers of the Chronicles of Narnia.

1. Kingdom's Dawn ◆ 2006
2. Kingdom's Hope ◆ 2006
3. Kingdom's Edge ◆ 2006
4. Kingdom's Call ◆ 2007

5. Kingdom's Quest ◆ 2007
6. Kingdom's Reign ◆ 2007

THE KINGDOM

Voigt, Cynthia

ATHENEUM; SCHOLASTIC ◆ GRADES 6–10 ◆ A/R

FANTASY

The books in this series are all set in an imaginary world of the past. They feature strong characters who defy expectations and face unusual challenges and choices. In the first book, Gwyn is the daughter of an innkeeper. She hears the legend of Jackaroo and decides to masquerade as the Robin Hood-like character. She realizes that she is not the only one disguised as Jackaroo. There are dramatic encounters with the Wolfers, a dangerous group that threatens the Kingdom. Readers will appreciate the classic fantasy elements in these books.

1. Jackaroo ◆ 1985
2. On Fortune's Wheel ◆ 1990
3. The Wings of a Falcon ◆ 1993
4. Elske ◆ 1999

THE KINGDOMS AND THE ELVES OF THE REACHES *see* Ruin Mist: The Kingdoms and the Elves of the Reaches

KLOOZ

Banscherus, J.

STONE ARCH BOOKS ◆ GRADES 4–7 ◆ A/R

MYSTERY

Klooz is a young detective who investigates mysteries like a haunted school and sabotage at the carnival. He even checks on an attack by flying cows. Reluctant readers will find the format—spacious text layout and numerous illustrations—accessible.

1. After School Ghost Hunter ◆ 2007
2. Clues in the Car Wash ◆ 2007
3. Detective's Duel ◆ 2007
4. The Great Snake Swindle ◆ 2007
5. The Mysterious Mask ◆ 2007
6. Trouble Under the Big Top ◆ 2007
7. The Night of the Blue Heads ◆ 2008

8. The Puzzle of the Power Drain ◆ 2008
9. The Secret of the Flying Cows ◆ 2008
10. The Snarling Suspect ◆ 2008

KNIGHTS OF THE SILVER DRAGON *see*

Dungeons and Dragons: Knights of the Silver Dragon

A KNIGHT'S STORY

Stewart, Paul, and Chris Riddell
ATHENEUM ◆ GRADES 4–8 ◆ A/R
ADVENTURE

As an unbonded knight, "Free Lance" participates in a variety of adventures. In the first book, Lord Big Nose challenges him to recover a crown from the Lake of Skulls. Jousts, treachery, and damsels in distress contribute to the medieval setting. Battles and action along with exciting illustrations by Chris Riddell should attract readers.

1. Lake of Skulls ◆ 2004
2. Joust of Honor ◆ 2005
3. Dragon's Hoard ◆ 2005

KNIGHTSCARES

Anthony, David, and Charles David
SIGIL PUBLISHING ◆ GRADES 6–9
FANTASY

Josh and Jozlyn face witches, an ogre, and evil spells in *Cauldron Cooker's Night*. In an underground castle, Connor and Simon are surrounded by goblins and skeletons in *Skull in the Birdcage*. Each book in this series features young people overcoming dangerous, supernatural creatures. Books 4, 5, and 6 are linked together as the Dragonsbane Horn trilogy in which characters search for the pieces of a legendary, magical horn.

1. Cauldron Cooker's Night ◆ 2003
2. Skull in the Birdcage ◆ 2003
3. Early Winter's Orb ◆ 2003
4. Voyage to Silvermight ◆ 2004
5. Trek Through Tangleroot ◆ 2004
6. Hunt for Hollowdeep ◆ 2004
7. The Ninespire Experiment ◆ 2006
8. Aware of the Wolf ◆ 2007

KOBIE ROBERTS

Ransom, Candice F.

SCHOLASTIC ◆ GRADES 4–7

REAL LIFE

Kobie lives with her parents in the country. We first meet Kobie persuading her best friend, Gretchen, to help her build a roller coaster ride. She is 10 at the time, and the series follows her until she is 15. The series deals in some depth with her maturing process as she learns to get along better with her mother, with Gretchen, and with the other children in her class. A good artist, but a poor student, she learns to make the most of her abilities and to see things from others' points of view.

1. Thirteen ◆ 1986
2. Fourteen and Holding ◆ 1987
3. Fifteen at Last ◆ 1987
4. Going on Twelve ◆ 1988
5. Almost Ten and a Half ◆ 1990

KYLA MAY MISS. BEHAVES

May, Kyla

PRICE STERN SLOAN ◆ GRADES 4–7 ◆ A/R

REAL LIFE | HUMOR

"Hi, my name is Kyla May!! I am 11 years old & i live in Australia . . . and i have a very, very active *imagination*." This is the opening of the first Kyla May book but add in a lot of decorations—like a heart around "Hi," and a cloud around "May," and many different fonts, drawings, and colors (red, pink, purple, and black). Kyla can't help day-dreaming—especially when she is at school. Music class makes her think about being a pop-star! Kyla May has earned her nickname: Miss. Behaves. Fans of Marissa Moss's Amelia books will want to check these out.

1. Introducing Kyla May Miss. Behaves ◆ 2005
2. Kyla May Miss. Behaves Around the World ◆ 2005
3. Kyla May Miss. Behaves Live on Stage ◆ 2005
4. Kyla May Miss. Behaves as an International Superspy ◆ 2006

LADY GRACE MYSTERIES

Various authors

DELACORTE ◆ GRADES 7–10

HISTORICAL | MYSTERY

In the court of Elizabeth I, Lady Grace Cavendish is a favorite. She serves the Queen and enjoys the frivolity and intrigue of the court. One intrigue comes too close—Lady Grace's fiancé is accused of murder and Lady Grace decides to investigate. Writing in "daybookes," Lady Grace is smart and intrepid as she confronts counterfeiting, thieves, and poison.

1. Assassin: Lady Grace Mysteries, From the Daybookes of Lady Grace Cavendish; Book the First (Finney, Patricia) ◆ 2004
2. Betrayal: Lady Grace Mysteries, From the Daybookes of Lady Grace Cavendish; Book the Second (Finney, Patricia) ◆ 2004
3. Conspiracy: Lady Grace Mysteries, From the Daybookes of Lady Grace Cavendish; Book the Third (Finney, Patricia) ◆ 2005
4. Deception: Lady Grace Mysteries, From the Daybookes of Lady Grace Cavendish; Book the Fourth (Burchett, Jan, and Sara Vogler) ◆ 2005
5. Exile: Lady Grace Mysteries, From the Daybookes of Lady Grace Cavendish; Book the Fifth (Burchett, Jan, and Sara Vogler) ◆ 2006
6. Feud: Lady Grace Mysteries, From the Daybookes of Lady Grace Cavendish; Book the Sixth (Finney, Patricia) ◆ 2007

LANDON SNOW

Mortenson, R. K.
BARBOUR ◆ GRADES 5–8 ◆ A/R
FANTASY | VALUES

Landon Snow, 11, is an ordinary boy searching for meaning in life, a search which requires him to find extraordinary courage. In the first book, he enters the Book of meaning and finds a fantasy world. There he is challenged to solve riddles that eventually help him rescue his sister who has been under an enchantment. As the series continues, Landon travels to the Island of Arcanum to free the animals of Wonderwood. Christian values guide and support Landon on his journeys.

1. Landon Snow and the Auctor's Riddle ◆ 2005
2. Landon Snow and the Shadows of Malus Quidam ◆ 2006
3. Landon Snow and the Island of Arcanum ◆ 2006
4. Landon Snow and the Volucer Dragon ◆ 2007
5. Landon Snow and the Auctor's Kingdom ◆ 2007

LASSIE

Bray, Marian F., adapter
CHARIOT BOOKS ◆ GRADES 4–8
REAL LIFE | VALUES

These books feature the familiar characters of Lassie and the Harmon family. Jimmy and Lassie are more than owner and pet; they are best friends. In one book, Lassie is lost and Jimmy is devastated. His father, Reverend Harmon, reminds Jimmy of his faith in God and helps him accept the circumstances and trust God's judgment. When Lassie returns, Jimmy and his family are thankful, knowing that their prayers have been answered. Lessons about honesty, hope, courage, and faith pervade these books, supporting the Christian values of the publishers, a division of Cook Communications Ministries.

1. Under the Big Top ◆ 1995
2. Treasure at Eagle Mountain ◆ 1995
3. To the Rescue ◆ 1995
4. Hayloft Hideout ◆ 1996
5. Danger at Echo Cliffs ◆ 1996

LAST APPRENTICE

Delaney, Joseph

GREENWILLOW ◆ GRADES 5–8 ◆ A/R

HORROR

Old Gregory is the Spook who has protected the village from demons, creatures, and beasts. As he approaches the end of his life, he searches for an apprentice. Many have tried to serve as his apprentice, but all have failed. The only one left is Thomas Ward, 12, the seventh son of a seventh son. Thomas begins his apprenticeship with a huge challenge. While the Spook is away, Mother Malkin, an evil witch, escapes and it is up to Thomas to stop her attacks. As Thomas's apprenticeship continues, his challenges increase in danger and difficulty.

1. Revenge of the Witch ◆ 2005
2. Curse of the Bane ◆ 2006
3. Night of the Soul Stealer ◆ 2007
4. Attack of the Fiend ◆ 2008
5. Wrath of the Bloodeye ◆ 2008

THE LAST VAMPIRE

Pike, Christopher

POCKET BOOKS ◆ GRADES 9–12 ◆ A/R

HORROR

Alisa is a 5,000-year-old vampire. In the first book, she must enter high school in an effort to escape a threat. There she falls for a shy young man. In *Red Dice,* Alisa is the focus of a government manhunt; and in *Phantom,* Alisa becomes pregnant and the nature of her child is in question.

1. The Last Vampire ◆ 1994
2. Black Blood ◆ 1994
3. Red Dice ◆ 1995
4. The Phantom ◆ 1996
5. Evil Thirst ◆ 1996
6. Creatures of Forever ◆ 1996

LaVaughn *see* Make Lemonade Trilogy

LBD (Les Bambinos Dangereuses)

Dent, Grace

PUTNAM ◆ GRADES 7–10 ◆ A/R

REAL LIFE

Ronnie, Fleur, and Claudette, all 14, are girlfriends who call themselves LBD for "Les Bambinos Dangereuses." They have plans for fun and boys. Unfortunately, their parents often thwart these plans. In the first book, the girls are not allowed to attend a music festival so they decide to stage their own festival. In the third book, the girls are sixteen and have summer jobs at a seaside resort. The British setting and the attitudes of the girls are reminiscent of Louise Rennison's books.

1. LBD: It's a Girl Thing ◆ 2003
2. LBD: Live and Fabulous! ◆ 2004
3. LBD: Friends Forever! ◆ 2006

Lechow Family

Benary-Isbert, Margot

HARCOURT ◆ GRADES 5–8

FAMILY LIFE │ HISTORICAL

Set in postwar Germany, *The Ark* begins the trilogy of the Lechow family. Mrs. Lechow is trying to keep her family alive while her husband is in a Russian prison camp. The family fortunately finds its way to Rowan Farm and makes a home in the Ark, an old railroad car. The author was born in Germany, lived under Nazi rule, and arrived in the United States in 1957. The stories, translated from German, are based on the author's childhood.

1. The Ark ◆ 1948
2. Rowan Farm ◆ 1949
3. Castle on the Border ◆ 1956

LEFT BEHIND—THE KIDS

Jenkins, Jerry B., and Tim LaHaye

TYNDALE HOUSE ♦ GRADES 6–10 ♦ A/R

FANTASY | VALUES

Many thousands of people have disappeared. Those who are left behind are confused and frightened. They include four teens who try to understand what has happened. They come to realize that those who have disappeared experienced the Rapture, a time when God brings the truly faithful to be with Him. Judd, Vicki, Lionel, and Ryan have adventures that test their commitment to God. This is based on a popular religious series for adults.

1. The Vanishings ♦ 1998
2. Second Chance ♦ 1998
3. Through the Flames ♦ 1998
4. Facing the Future ♦ 1998
5. Nicolae High ♦ 1999
6. The Underground ♦ 1999
7. Busted! ♦ 2000
8. Death Strike ♦ 2000
9. The Search ♦ 2000
10. On the Run ♦ 2000
11. Into the Storm ♦ 2000
12. Earthquake! ♦ 2000
13. The Showdown ♦ 2001
14. Judgment Day ♦ 2001
15. Battling the Commander ♦ 2001
16. Fire from Heaven ♦ 2001
17. Terror in the Stadium ♦ 2001
18. Darkening Skies ♦ 2001
19. Attack of Apollyon ♦ 2002
20. A Dangerous Plan ♦ 2002
21. Secrets of New Babylon ♦ 2002
22. Escape from New Babylon ♦ 2002
23. Horsemen of Terror ♦ 2002
24. Uplink from the Underground ♦ 2002
25. Death at the Gala ♦ 2003
26. The Beast Arises ♦ 2003
27. Wildfire ♦ 2003
28. Mark of the Beast ♦ 2003
29. Breakout! ♦ 2003
30. Murder in the Holy Place ♦ 2003
31. Escape to Masada ♦ 2003
32. War of the Dragon ♦ 2003
33. Attack on Petra ♦ 2004
34. Bounty Hunters ♦ 2004
35. The Rise of the False Messiahs ♦ 2004

36. Ominous Choices ◆ 2004
37. Heat Wave ◆ 2004
38. Perils of Love ◆ 2004
39. The Road to War ◆ 2004
40. Triumphant Return ◆ 2004

LEVEN THUMPS

Skye, Obert

SHADOW MOUNTAIN ◆ GRADES 5–8 ◆ A/R

FANTASY

As this fantasy series begins there are two worlds—Reality and Foo, which is the land of dreams and hope. In Foo, the evil ruler Sabine is looking for a way to enter Reality and in so doing destroy both worlds. The fate of these worlds is in the hands of Leven Thumps, 14, from Burnt Culvert, Oklahoma. Lev discovers a gateway to Foo and with the help of three companions discovers his special powers and confronts the dangers that threaten the two worlds. These books are filled with humor; for example, Geth has been transformed into a toothpick. In the second book, Leven and his compatriots strive to free Geth, the rightful heir of Foo.

1. Leven Thumps and the Gateway to Foo ◆ 2005
2. Leven Thumps and the Whispered Secret ◆ 2006
3. Leven Thumps and the Eyes of the Want ◆ 2007
4. Leven Thumps and the Wrath of Ezra ◆ 2008

LEWIS BARNAVELT

Bellairs, John, and Brad Strickland

DIAL ◆ GRADES 5–8 ◆ A/R

FANTASY

Lewis is a 10-year-old orphan who goes to live with his Uncle Jonathan in the small town of New Zebedee. His uncle is a kind old man who practices "white magic," and his neighbor and best friend is Mrs. Zimmerman, who is a good witch. Jonathan lives in a big old house that was previously owned by an evil man who practiced black magic. Lewis makes a new friend toward the end of the first book in the series: Rose Rita, who loves baseball and lives in a nearby mansion. Some of the books in the series feature Rose Rita and Mrs. Zimmerman as they fight black magic together. The first three books were written by Bellairs; the fourth and fifth were completed by Strickland after Bellairs's death; and the remaining books were written by Strickland and are based on the characters of Bellairs.

1. The House with a Clock in its Walls ◆ 1973

2. The Figure in the Shadows ◆ 1975
3. The Letter, the Witch, and the Ring ◆ 1976
4. The Ghost in the Mirror ◆ 1993
5. The Vengeance of the Witch-Finder ◆ 1993
6. The Doom of the Haunted Opera ◆ 1995
7. The Specter from the Magician's Museum ◆ 1998
8. The Beast under the Wizard's Bridge ◆ 2000
9. The Tower at the End of the World ◆ 2001
10. The Whistle, the Grave and the Ghost ◆ 2003
11. The House Where Nobody Lived ◆ 2006

LIBERTY LETTERS

LeSourd, Nancy

ZONDERKIDZ ◆ GRADES 7–10

HISTORICAL

These books use a fictional correspondence between two teenage women to explore the impact of historical events on everyday life and faith. In the first book, Abigail Matthews has left England and settled in Virginia, first at Jamestown and then in Henricus. She writes to her friend in England, Elizabeth Walton, and describes her adventures.

1. The Personal Correspondence of Elizabeth Walton and Abigail Matthews: The Story of Pocahontas, 1613 ◆ 2003
2. The Personal Correspondence of Hannah Brown and Sarah Smith: The Underground Railroad, 1858 ◆ 2003
3. The Personal Correspondence of Emma Edmunds and Mollie Turner: Assignment: Civil War Spies, 1862 ◆ 2004
4. The Personal Correspondence of Catherine Clark and Meredith Lyons: Pearl Harbor, 1941 ◆ 2004

THE LIFE AND TIMES

Denenberg, Barry

SCHOLASTIC ◆ GRADES 4–7 ◆ A/R

ADVENTURE | HISTORICAL

This series begins with two adventures. One features the life of a slave in a wealthy home in the Roman Republic. Although his master is kind, Atticus becomes caught up in the intrigues and plots. The second book tells the story of a young girl, Pandora, who is dreading her 14th birthday. On that day, she will be old enough to marry. Her father has already arranged an engagement for her. Pandora chafes under the restrictions of life in ancient Athens.

1. Atticus of Rome, 30 B.C. ◆ 2004

2. Pandora of Athens, 399 B.C. ◆ 2004
3. Maia of Thebes, 1463 B.C. ◆ 2005

LIFE AT SIXTEEN

Various authors

BERKLEY ◆ GRADES 7–9

REAL LIFE

These books feature teens facing difficult situations. In *No Guarantees,* Courtney is used to having money and being a cheerleader. When her father loses his job, she must help out with the family and deal with how her friends now treat her. In *Good Intentions,* Chloe has been in a coma. As she recovers, she learns about how selfish she was in the past. Now she wants to try to change.

1. Silent Tears (Zach, Cheryl) ◆ 1997
2. Second Best (Lanham, Cheryl) ◆ 1997
3. Blue Moon (Kirby, Susan E.) ◆ 1997
4. No Guarantees (Lanham, Cheryl) ◆ 1997
5. Good Intentions (Lanham, Cheryl) ◆ 1998

THE LIGHTHOUSE TRILOGY

McKinty, Adrian

AMULET ◆ GRADES 6–9 ◆ A/R

SCIENCE FICTION

Living in a lighthouse on an island near Ireland is just one of the changes facing Jamie O'Neill, 13. He and his mother have moved from Harlem and Jamie, who recently lost an arm to cancer, is mute—communicating through a computer tablet. In Ireland, Jamie discovers he is descended from kings. With his friend Ramsay he travels through a portal to Altair, a distant planet fighting invaders. On Altair, Jamie's arm and voice are restored and he leads the battle to save the planet.

1. The Lighthouse Land ◆ 2006
2. The Lighthouse War ◆ 2007
3. The Lighthouse Keepers ◆ 2008

LIGHTNING ON ICE

Brouwer, Sigmund

THOMAS NELSON ◆ GRADES 8–10 ◆ A/R

RECREATION | VALUES

Ice hockey action provides a backdrop to these books that focus on teens struggling to succeed while maintaining their values. In the first book, B. T. McPhee, 17, wants to be a professional hockey player. A series of unusual accidents causes him to wonder if his team will even make the playoffs.

1. Rebel Glory ◆ 1995
2. All-Star Pride ◆ 1995
3. Thunderbird Spirit ◆ 1996
4. Winter Hawk Star ◆ 1996
5. Blazer Drive ◆ 1996
6. Chief Honor ◆ 1997

The Lily Adventures

Leppard, Lois Gladys

Random House ◆ Grades 8–10

Values

While visiting England with her young sister, Lily Masterson, 16, receives word that her father has died. It is 1901 and Lily does not have enough money to return home until a mysterious packet of money is given to her. Her Christian faith supports her as she returns to South Carolina to investigate her father's death.

1. Secret Money ◆ 1995
2. Suspicious Identity ◆ 1995
3. Accidental Dreams ◆ 1996

Lily B.

Kimmel, Elizabeth Cody

HarperCollins ◆ Grades 5–8 ◆ A/R

Real Life

With her best friend at summer camp, Lily Blennerhassett, 13, feels her summer is doomed. She enjoys writing in her journal but the details of her life are so boring! Then, at her cousin's wedding, she meets the super cool LeBlanc family. She is drawn into their activities, even defying her parents, only to discover they are taking advantage of her good nature. Readers will enjoy reading Lily B.'s insights in her diary.

1. Lily B. on the Brink of Cool ◆ 2003
2. Lily B. on the Brink of Love ◆ 2005
3. Lily B. on the Brink of Paris ◆ 2006

LILY DALE

Staub, Wendy Corsi
WALKER & CO. ◆ GRADES 8–10 ◆ A/R
FANTASY

After the death of her mother, Calla, 17, goes to live with her grandmother in Lily Dale, a spiritualist community. As she adjusts to her new
surroundings, she realizes that she has psychic abilities. Calla communes
with a spirit about her mother's death.

1. Awakening ◆ 2007
2. Believing ◆ 2008
3. Connecting ◆ 2008

LILY QUENCH

Prior, Natalie Jane
PUFFIN ◆ GRADES 4–7 ◆ A/R
FANTASY

Dragons, quests, magic, and a battle with dangers from the past are all
part of this fantasy series. Lily Quench has been paired with the Queen
Dragon to try to protect Ashby from Gordon, the Black Count, and his
army. One of their adventures helps them learn the secrets of the Eyes of
Time.

1. Lily Quench and the Dragon of Ashby ◆ 2004
2. Lily Quench and the Black Mountains ◆ 2004
3. Lily Quench and the Treasure of Mote Ely ◆ 2004
4. Lily Quench and the Lighthouse of Skellig Mor ◆ 2004
5. Lily Quench and the Magician's Pyramid ◆ 2004
6. Lily Quench and the Hand of Manuelo ◆ 2004
7. Lily Quench and the Search for King Dragon ◆ 2005

LIONBOY TRILOGY

Corder, Zizou
DIAL ◆ GRADES 4–8 ◆ A/R
FANTASY

Charlie Ashanti's parents have been kidnapped. With his special power to
communicate with cats, Charlie begins his search for them. His journey
takes him (and his lion friends) from London to various sites around the
world. This series is written by a mother and her young daughter using a
pseudonym.

1. Lionboy ◆ 2003
2. Lionboy: The Chase ◆ 2004
3. Lionboy: The Truth ◆ 2005

LIVE FROM BRENTWOOD HIGH

Baer, Judy

BETHANY HOUSE ◆ GRADES 6–9 ◆ A/R

REAL LIFE │ VALUES

The school's radio news is run by a group including Darby, Sarah, Jake, Molly, and Izzy. These teens cover stories about a range of problems in the community—for example, violence, discrimination, teen parents, and graffiti—while also indulging in fun and romance.

1. Risky Assignment ◆ 1994
2. Price of Silence ◆ 1994
3. Double Danger ◆ 1994
4. Sarah's Dilemma ◆ 1995
5. Undercover Artists ◆ 1996
6. Faded Dreams ◆ 1996

LIZZIE MCGUIRE

Various authors

DISNEY PRESS ◆ GRADES 4–7 ◆ A/R

FAMILY LIFE │ REAL LIFE

Lizzie McGuire was a popular character in a Disney television series. She was a live-action character with a cartoon alter ego. She would hang out with her friends at school talking about boys, family, and projects. In the first book, she is eager to go on a camping trip but is chagrined to discover her mom is a chaperone. In another book, she models in a fashion show. There is a lot of Lizzie McGuire merchandise for preteens.

1. When Moms Attack! (Ostrow, Kim) ◆ 2002
2. Totally Crushed! (Thorpe, Kiki) ◆ 2002
3. Lizzie Goes Wild (Larsen, Kirsten) ◆ 2002
4. The Rise and Fall of the Kate Empire (Larsen, Kirsten) ◆ 2002
5. Picture This (Jones, Jasmine) ◆ 2003
6. New Kid in School (Jones, Jasmine) ◆ 2003
7. Broken Hearts (Thorpe, Kiki) ◆ 2003
8. A Very Lizzie Christmas (Jones, Jasmine) ◆ 2003
9. Just like Lizzie (Jones, Jasmine) ◆ 2003
10. Lizzie Loves Ethan (Jones, Jasmine) ◆ 2003
11. On the Job (Goldman, Leslie) ◆ 2004
12. Head over Heels (Jones, Jasmine) ◆ 2004

13. Best Dressed (Jones, Jasmine) ◆ 2004
14. Mirror, Mirror (Jones, Jasmine) ◆ 2004
15. Freaked Out (Alfonsi, Alice) ◆ 2004
16. Lizzie for President (Alfonsi, Alice) ◆ 2004
17. Oh, Brother! (Jones, Jasmine) ◆ 2005
18. The Importance of Being Gordo (Jones, Jasmine) ◆ 2005
19. All Over It (Jones, Jasmine) ◆ 2005
20. The 'Rents (Alfonsi, Alice) ◆ 2005
21. High Five! (Alfonsi, Alice) ◆ 2006

LIZZIE MCGUIRE MYSTERIES

Banim, Lisa
DISNEY PRESS ◆ GRADES 4–7 ◆ A/R
MYSTERY | REAL LIFE

Lizzie and her friends are back in these light mysteries. In the first book, Lizzie sets out to prove she is not responsible for the creepy notes kids have been getting. In the third book, Lizzie has hurt Audrey's feelings and now Audrey is missing. Gordo and Miranda go with Lizzie to a science fiction convention looking for Audrey and find some really strange characters.

1. Get a Clue! ◆ 2004
2. Case at Camp Get-Me-Outie ◆ 2004
3. Case of the Missing She-Geek ◆ 2004
4. Hands Off My Crush-Boy! ◆ 2004
5. In the Doghouse ◆ 2005
6. Case of the Kate Haters ◆ 2005
7. Spring It On! ◆ 2006

LIZZIE MCGUIRE (TOKYOPOP)

Minsky, Terri
TOKYOPOP ◆ GRADES 4–7
REAL LIFE

Lizzie McGuire is in junior high and her life revolves around school. No! Her life revolves around boys and her friends! Lizzie is a live-action character with a cartoon alter ego. This cine-manga captures all the flair of this popular character.

1. Pool Party and Picture Day ◆ 2003
2. Rumors and I've Got Rhythmic ◆ 2003
3. When Moms Attack and Misadventures in Babysitting ◆ 2003
4. I Do, I Don't and Come Fly with Me ◆ 2003
5. Lizzie's Nightmare and Sibling Bonding ◆ 2004

6. Mom's Best Friend and Movin' On Up ◆ 2004
7. Over the Hill and Just Friends ◆ 2004
8. Gordo and the Girl and You're a Good Man Lizzie McGuire ◆ 2004
9. Magic Train and Grubby Longjohn's Olde Tyme Revue ◆ 2004
10. Inner Beauty and Best Dressed for Less ◆ 2005
11. In Miranda, Lizzie Does Not Trust and The Longest Yard ◆ 2005

LOGAN FAMILY

Taylor, Mildred D.

DIAL ◆ GRADES 4–7 ◆ A/R

HISTORICAL | REAL LIFE

Cassie tells the story of the African American Logan family, living in Mississippi during the Great Depression. High taxes and the mortgage on their house have forced her father to take a job away from home on the railroad. Mrs. Logan works as a schoolteacher. Although poor, the Logans are economically self-sufficient, which makes them more fortunate than their neighbors, who are all in debt to the local store. When Mrs. Logan is fired for teaching black history and Mr. Logan loses his job when he is injured by some angry white men, the family lives in fear that they will lose their land. *Roll of Thunder, Hear My Cry* is a Newbery Medal winner. *Song of the Trees* is written for younger readers. *The Land* is a prequel to *Roll of Thunder, Hear My Cry*. Members of the Logan family also appear in other books by this author.

1. Song of the Trees ◆ 1975
2. Roll of Thunder, Hear My Cry ◆ 1976
3. Let the Circle Be Unbroken ◆ 1981
4. The Road to Memphis ◆ 1990
5. The Well: David's Story ◆ 1995
6. The Land ◆ 2001

LONGLIGHT LEGACY

Foon, Dennis

ANNICK ◆ GRADES 6–10 ◆ A/R

FANTASY

Fifteen-year-old Roan survives a murderous attack on his village in this intricate fantasy set on a post-apocalyptic Earth. Roan is torn between the peaceful ways of his upbringing and a desire for revenge.

1. The Dirt Eaters ◆ 2003
2. Freewalker ◆ 2004
3. The Keeper's Shadow ◆ 2006

LORD OF THE RINGS

Tolkien, J. R. R.

HOUGHTON MIFFLIN ◆ **GRADES 5–12** ◆ **A/R**

FANTASY

When Hobbit Bilbo Baggins is visited by Gandalf the wizard, he finds himself tricked into being part of a dangerous quest. Together, they seek to recover a stolen treasure hidden in Lonely Mountain, guarded by Smaug the Dragon. *The Hobbit* (1937) is the introduction to Middle Earth and the Lord of the Rings trilogy, in which Bilbo names his cousin, Frodo Baggins, his heir. Frodo embarks on a journey to destroy the Ring of Power, a ring that would enable evil Sauron to destroy all that is good in Middle Earth. It is up to Frodo and his servant, Sam, to carry the Ring to the one place it can be destroyed. Author Tolkien was an eminent philologist and an authority on myths and sagas. *The Silmarillion* (1977) tells the story of the First Age, an ancient drama to which characters in the main trilogy look back. These books have been made into a popular series of movies.

1. The Fellowship of the Ring ◆ 1954
2. The Two Towers ◆ 1954
3. The Return of the King ◆ 1955

LOSERS, INC.

Mills, Claudia

FARRAR, STRAUS & GIROUX ◆ **GRADES 4–7** ◆ **A/R**

REAL LIFE

Ethan and Julius are both in sixth grade. They feel so left out that they form their own club—Losers, Inc. Ethan wants to be more like his smart, athletic older brother. Julius's mom tries to help him develop more confidence. Lizzie and Alex also feel like losers. These stories should give readers insights into kids on the outside.

1. Losers, Inc ◆ 1997
2. You're a Brave Man, Julius Zimmerman ◆ 1999
3. Lizzie at Last ◆ 2000
4. Alex Ryan, Stop That ◆ 2003
5. Makeovers by Marcia ◆ 2005

L.O.S.T.

Federici, Debbie, and Susan Vaught

LLEWELLYN ◆ **GRADES 8–10** ◆ **A/R**

FANTASY

While traveling, Brendan, 17, finds himself in L.O.S.T. (Live Oak Springs Township), a witch village where he meets Jasmina, 16, Queen of the Witches. Jazz is searching for the chosen one to help the witches in their fight against Nire, an ancient evil Shadowmancer.

1. L.O.S.T. ◆ 2004
2. ShadowQueen ◆ 2005
3. Witch Circle ◆ 2006

THE LOST YEARS OF MERLIN

Barron, T. A.

PHILOMEL ◆ GRADES 6–10 ◆ A/R

FANTASY

Using the well-known Arthurian legends about Merlin as a base, Barron speculates about the unknown details of the wizard's childhood. From when he is washed onto the shores of ancient Wales and raised by Branwen, to his journey to the isle of Fincayra and his challenge to solve the riddle of the Dance of the Giants, these books weave adventure and fantasy. Merlin encounters and battles mythic creatures—Balor the ogre and a sleeping dragon; he also grapples with his own evil, greed, and desires. This fantasy will connect with readers who have read Jane Yolen's Young Merlin books and who enjoy Arthurian legends.

1. The Lost Years of Merlin ◆ 1996
2. The Seven Songs of Merlin ◆ 1997
3. The Fires of Merlin ◆ 1998
4. The Mirror of Merlin ◆ 1999
5. The Wings of Merlin ◆ 2000

LOUD BOY *see* Adventures of Daniel Boom AKA Loud Boy

LOVE LETTERS

Malcolm, Jahnna N.

SIMON PULSE ◆ GRADES 7–10 ◆ A/R

REAL LIFE

In *Mixed Messages,* Jade writes a love letter to Zephyr but it is opened by Adam by mistake. But maybe it isn't really a mistake! In *The Write Stuff,* Rachel wants Dylan to notice her. Her friend, Hannah, writes an email for Rachel to send. Dylan is attracted by the email, but will he ever realize that Hannah is the author? Each book features correspondence that leads to romance.

1. Mixed Messages ◆ 2004

2. The Write Stuff ◆ 2005
3. Message in a Bottle ◆ 2005
4. Perfect Strangers ◆ 2005

LOVE STORIES

Various authors

BANTAM ◆ GRADES 7–10 ◆ A/R

REAL LIFE

Romance novels are extremely popular with teen girls. This series portrays teens involved in the difficulties of finding true love. In one book, it's hard enough to manage schoolwork and swimming, now Amy is also in love. Her romance with Chris complicates everything. Other books feature girls who are trying to attract boys and girls who can't choose between two boys.

1. My First Love (West, Callie) ◆ 1995
2. Sharing Sam (Applegate, K. A.) ◆ 1995
3. How to Kiss a Guy (Bernard, Elizabeth) ◆ 1995
4. The Boy Next Door (Quin-Harkin, Janet) ◆ 1995
5. The Day I Met Him (Clark, Catherine) ◆ 1995
6. Love Changes Everything (Presser, Arlynn) ◆ 1995
7. More than a Friend (Winfrey, Elizabeth) ◆ 1995
8. The Language of Love (Emburg, Kate) ◆ 1996
9. My So-Called Boyfriend (Winfrey, Elizabeth) ◆ 1996
10. It Had to Be You (Doyon, Stephanie) ◆ 1996
11. Some Girls Do (Kosinski, Dahlia) ◆ 1996
12. Hot Summer Nights (Chandler, Elizabeth) ◆ 1996
13. Who Do You Love? (Quin-Harkin, Janet) ◆ 1996
14. Three-Guy Weekend (Page, Alexis) ◆ 1996
15. Never Tell Ben (Namm, Diane) ◆ 1997
16. Together Forever (Dokey, Cameron) ◆ 1997
17. Up All Night (Michaels, Karen) ◆ 1997
18. 24/7 (Wilensky, Amy) ◆ 1997
19. It's a Prom Thing (Schwemm, Diane) ◆ 1997
20. The Guy I Left Behind (Brooke, Ali) ◆ 1997
21. He's Not What You Think (Reisfeld, Randi) ◆ 1997
22. A Kiss Between Friends (Haft, Erin) ◆ 1997
23. The Rumor About Julia (Sinclair, Stephanie) ◆ 1997
24. Don't Say Good-Bye (Schwemm, Diane) ◆ 1997
25. Crushing on You (Loggia, Wendy) ◆ 1998
26. Our Secret Love (Harry, Miranda) ◆ 1998
27. Trust Me (Scott, Kieran) ◆ 1998
28. He's the One (Alexander, Nina) ◆ 1998
29. Kiss and Tell (Scott, Kieran) ◆ 1998
30. Falling for Ryan (Taylor, Julie) ◆ 1998
31. Hard to Resist (Loggia, Wendy) ◆ 1998

32. At First Sight (Chandler, Elizabeth) ◆ 1998
33. What We Did Last Summer (Craft, Elizabeth) ◆ 1998
34. As I Am (Mason, Lynn) ◆ 1999
35. I Do (Chandler, Elizabeth) ◆ 1999
36. While You Were Gone (Scott, Kieran) ◆ 1999
37. Stolen Kisses (Abrams, Liesa) ◆ 1999
38. Torn Apart (Quin-Harkin, Janet) ◆ 1999
39. Behind His Back (Schwemm, Diane) ◆ 1999
40. Playing for Keeps (Alexander, Nina) ◆ 1999
41. How Do I Tell? (Scott, Kieran) ◆ 1999
42. His Other Girlfriend (Abrams, Liesa) ◆ 1999

LOVE STORIES: BROTHERS TRILOGY

Zimmerman, Zoe
BANTAM ◆ GRADES 7–10
REAL LIFE

Three summer stories featuring three teen boys. In one book, Kevin's summer job is at the Surf City Beach Resort. It's fun, and made even more interesting by the boss's beautiful daughter.

1. Danny ◆ 2000
2. Kevin ◆ 2000
3. Johnny ◆ 2000

LOVE STORIES: HIS. HERS. THEIRS

Various authors
BANTAM ◆ GRADES 7–10
REAL LIFE

Teen girls describe their romances in these first-person accounts. One girl gets a date with a senior. Another, Edie, turns down a date with a cool, popular guy. Another series for romance fans.

1. The Nine-Hour Date (Henry, Emma) ◆ 2001
2. Snag Him! (Greene, Gretchen) ◆ 2001
3. Nick and the Nerd (Hawthorne, Rachel) ◆ 2001
4. You're Dating Him? (Gersh, A.) ◆ 2001
5. The Popular One (Skurnick, Lizzie) ◆ 2001
6. The Older Guy (Hawthorne, Rachel) ◆ 2001

LOVE STORIES: PROM TRILOGY

Craft, Elizabeth

BANTAM ◆ GRADES 7–10

REAL LIFE

The Prom! Just thinking about it sends thrills through Jane. Will she get the attention of that special boy in time for him to invite her? These books are sure to appeal to teenage girls. The featured couples include an African American pair, Justin and Nicole.

1. Max and Jane ◆ 2000
2. Justin and Nicole ◆ 2000
3. Jake and Christy ◆ 2000

LOVE STORIES: SUPER EDITIONS

Various authors

BANTAM ◆ GRADES 7–10 ◆ A/R

REAL LIFE

More romance and heartache are featured in these books. Jeremy falls in love with Liv. That should be great, right? Wrong! Liv is Patrick's girlfriend and Patrick is Jeremy's best friend. In another book, Noah and Meg have been friends forever. Then Noah starts to feel more than friendship for Meg.

1. Listen to My Heart (Applegate, K. A.) ◆ 1996
2. Kissing Caroline (Zach, Cheryl) ◆ 1996
3. It's Different for Guys (Leighton, Stephanie) ◆ 1997
4. My Best Friend's Girlfriend (Loggia, Wendy) ◆ 1997
5. Love Happens (Chandler, Elizabeth) ◆ 1998
6. Out of My League (Owens, Everett) ◆ 1998
7. A Song for Caitlin (Bright, J. E.) ◆ 1998
8. The "L" Word (Mason, Lynn) ◆ 1998
9. Summer Love (Loggia, Wendy) ◆ 1999
10. All That (Mason, Lynn) ◆ 1999
11. The Dance (Hillman, Craig, Kieran Scott, and Elizabeth Skurnick) ◆ 1999
12. Andy and Andie (Vallik, Malle) ◆ 2000
13. Sweet Sixteen (Raine, Allison) ◆ 2000
14. Three Princes (Mason, Lynn) ◆ 2000

LOVE STORIES: YEAR ABROAD

Hawthorne, Rachel

BANTAM ◆ GRADES 7–10

REAL LIFE

Dana is spending her junior year in Paris and she only wants one thing—a French boyfriend. Why does she keep coming across Alex Turner, a boy from her hometown? Readers will enjoy the romantic settings for these love stories.

1. London: Kit and Robin ◆ 2000
2. Paris: Alex and Dana ◆ 2000
3. Rome: Antonio and Carrie ◆ 2000

LOVE TRILOGY

Cann, Kate

HARPERCOLLINS ◆ GRADES 10–12 ◆ A/R

REAL LIFE

Colette, 16, and Art meet and start dating in the first book. The series follows their up-and-down relationship, the pressure to become sexually active, and the toll this pressure takes on their initial friendship.

1. Ready? ◆ 2001
2. Sex? ◆ 2001
3. Go! ◆ 2001

LOWTHAR'S BLADE

LaFevers, R. L.

DUTTON ◆ GRADES 5–8 ◆ A/R

FANTASY

Lord Mordig has been kidnapping blacksmiths and forcing them to work on a powerful sword, one that will make him invincible. Kenric's father, a blacksmith, is being held by Lord Mordig. Kenric defeats Lord Mordig and returns the true king to power. As the series continues, Lord Mordig escapes and Kenric must unite with the goblins, the Fey folk, and other creatures to save Lowthar.

1. The Forging of the Blade ◆ 2004
2. The Secrets of Grim Woods ◆ 2005
3. The True Blade of Power ◆ 2005

LUDELL

Wilkinson, Brenda

HARPERCOLLINS ◆ GRADES 5–8

FAMILY LIFE | HISTORICAL

Ludell Wilson is an African American girl growing up in the rural town of Waycross, Georgia, in the mid-1950s. She is being raised by her loving, protective, but strict grandmother because her mother is living in New York City. *Ludell* depicts three years in a segregated southern school, Ludell's friends and family, and the people who affect her life. In *Ludell and Willie,* Ludell and her boyfriend are seniors in high school, frustrated by the standards of their small town. In *Ludell's New York Time,* Ludell moves to Harlem to plan her wedding. A strong portrait of growing up in the South in the 1950s and 1960s.

1. Ludell ◆ 1975
2. Ludell and Willie ◆ 1977
3. Ludell's New York Time ◆ 1980

LUKE HARDING, FORENSIC INVESTIGATOR *see* Traces: Luke Harding, Forensic Investigator

LULU BAKER

Dunbar, Fiona

ORCHARD ◆ GRADES 4–7 ◆ A/R

FANTASY

With her father's remarriage imminent, Lulu Baker, 13, finds a mysterious cookbook with a recipe for "truth" cookies. If her father's fiancée eats one, Lulu knows her father will realize the fiancée's duplicity. Readers will enjoy the combination of magic and cooking in these books.

1. The Truth Cookie ◆ 2005
2. Cupid Cakes ◆ 2005
3. Chocolate Wishes ◆ 2005

LUNA BAY

Various authors

HARPERCOLLINS ◆ GRADES 6–9 ◆ A/R

REAL LIFE

Five friends in Southern California are working as counselors at a surfing camp. Each girl deals with issues in her life. Luna wants to do her best in a surfing competition but is distracted by her interest in a new boy. Rae is worried that her parents are separating and she will have to move. In *Hawaii Five-Go!,* the girls are in Hawaii on a fashion shoot and Kanani decides to explore her heritage.

1. Pier Pressure: A Roxy Girl Series (Lantz, Francess) ◆ 2003
2. Wave Good-Bye: A Roxy Girl Series (Lantz, Francess) ◆ 2003
3. Weather or Not: A Roxy Girl Series (Lantz, Francess) ◆ 2003
4. Oh, Buoy! A Roxy Girl Series (Lantz, Francess) ◆ 2003
5. Hawaii Five-Go! A Roxy Girl Series (Lantz, Francess) ◆ 2003
6. Heart Breakers: A Roxy Girl Series (Lantz, Francess) ◆ 2004
7. Board Games: A Roxy Girl Series (Dubowski, Cathy East) ◆ 2004
8. Sea for Yourself: A Roxy Girl Series (Lantz, Francess) ◆ 2004

THE LURKER FILES

Ciencin, Scott

RANDOM HOUSE ◆ GRADES 6–10

FANTASY

The Lurker seems to control many students and teachers at Wintervale University. Using information from the university computer network, the Lurker manipulates people and situations.

1. Faceless ◆ 1996
2. Know Fear ◆ 1996
3. Nemesis ◆ 1997
4. Incarnate ◆ 1997

THE LUXE

Godbersen, Anna

HARPERCOLLINS ◆ GRADES 9–12 ◆ A/R

REAL LIFE | HISTORICAL FICTION

Although she is in love with someone else, wealthy, privileged Elizabeth Holland is betrothed to marry Henry Schoonmaker. Still, it is 1899 in New York City and Elizabeth's social standing dictates that she do her duty. Her younger sister, Diana, is in love with Henry even though he is an unscrupulous cad. When Elizabeth is presumed drowned after her carriage crashes into the Hudson River, the intrigues and deceptions continue. Think Gossip Girl and It Girl in 19th-century Manhattan.

1. The Luxe ◆ 2007
2. Rumors ◆ 2008
3. Envy ◆ 2009

LYON SAGA

Stainer, M. L.

CHICKEN SOUP PRESS ◆ GRADES 6–9 ◆ A/R

HISTORICAL

Jessabel, 14, describes her voyage from England to Roanoke Island. As a colony is established there, the settlers struggle to survive. Of course, the Roanoke Colony does not thrive and historians have speculated about what happened. In subsequent novels, readers follow Jess's fictional adventures as she lives with the Croatan tribe, eventually marrying a Native American and returning to England. Along the way, they encounter pirates whose violent actions destroy two Native women.

1. The Lyon's Roar ◆ 1997
2. The Lyon's Cub ◆ 1998
3. The Lyon's Pride ◆ 1998
4. The Lyon's Throne ◆ 1999
5. The Lyon's Crown ◆ 2004

M. T. ANDERSON'S THRILLING TALES

Anderson, M. T.

HARCOURT ◆ GRADES 4–7 ◆ A/R

HUMOR | MYSTERY

Lily's father works for a mad scientist named Larry who wants to take over the world using mind-controlled whales with laser beam eyes. Lily and her friends Kate and Jasper have to stop Larry and save the world. The wacky humor and kids vs. adults premise will appeal to tween audiences.

1. Whales on Stilts ◆ 2005
2. The Clue of the Linoleum Lederhosen ◆ 2006
3. Jasper Dash and the Flame-Pits of Delaware ◆ 2009

MacDONALD HALL *see* Bruno and Boots

MacGREGOR FAMILY ADVENTURE

Trout, Richard

PELICAN PUBLISHING COMPANY ◆ GRADES 5–8 ◆ A/R

ADVENTURE

The MacGregors are scientists who deal with environmental issues around the world. Dr. Jack MacGregor is a zoologist and his wife Mavis is a paleontologist. Their three teenaged children—Chris, Heather, and

Ryan—are often in the middle of these adventures. In *Sign of the Dragon,* the family is in China, where the teens expose poachers and the illegal distribution of dinosaur bones.

1. Cayman Gold: Lost Treasure of Devils Grotto ◆ 2005
2. Elephant Tears: Mask of the Elephant ◆ 2006
3. Falcon of Abydos: Oracle of the Nile ◆ 2006
4. Czar of Alaska: The Cross of Charlemagne ◆ 2006
5. Sign of the Dragon ◆ 2007
6. Devil's Breath Volcano ◆ 2008

MAGGIE QUINN: GIRL VS. EVIL

Clement-Moore, Rosemary

DELACORTE ◆ GRADES 9–12 ◆ A/R

HORROR

Something is threatening the high school "in" crowd and Maggie Quinn becomes involved in revealing and stopping the threat. Normally, Maggie just works on the school newspaper and avoids the cliques at her school. But when demons invade her dreams, she knows something is amiss. With the help of a college student from her father's paranormal studies class, Maggie has a showdown with the demons at the senior prom. Here's a new choice for fans of Buffy, Charmed, and the Mediator books.

1. Prom Dates from Hell ◆ 2008
2. Hell Week ◆ 2008
3. Highway to Hell ◆ 2009

MAGGIE VALLEY

Madden, Kerry

VIKING ◆ GRADES 5–8 ◆ A/R

FAMILY LIFE | HISTORICAL

Livy Two, 12, reads about the world but feels trapped in the struggles of her family in the hills of North Carolina in the 1960s. With eight siblings, including a little sister who is blind, Livy Two often shoulders adult responsibilities. A visit from Grandma seems a burden at first, but Grandma's strength helps sustain Livy Two through desperate circumstances.

1. Gentle's Holler ◆ 2005
2. Louisiana's Song ◆ 2007
3. Jessie's Mountain ◆ 2008

MAGIC: THE GATHERING SERIES OVERVIEW

Various authors

WIZARDS OF THE COAST ◆ GRADES 10–12

FANTASY

Magic: The Gathering is a card game using printed cards or virtual cards (for Internet play). Players also trade and collect cards. The role-playing games feature battles between wizards aka planeswalkers. The book series parallel different sets of cards; often a series of books is released along with a new expansion set of cards. Visit the web site at wizards.com.

MAGIC: THE GATHERING— ARTIFACTS CYCLE

WIZARDS OF THE COAST ◆ GRADES 9–12

FANTASY

Brothers Urza and Mishra battle each other for the control of Terisiare. Mishra is killed and Urza becomes a planeswalker.

1. The Brothers' War (Grubb, Jeff) ◆ 1998
2. Planeswalker (Abbey, Lynn) ◆ 1998
3. Time Streams (King, J. Robert) ◆ 1999
4. Bloodlines (Coleman, Loren) ◆ 1999

MAGIC: THE GATHERING— ICE AGE CYCLE

WIZARDS OF THE COAST ◆ GRADES 9–12

FANTASY

The enemy has defeated Terisiare; ice covers the world. The evil Lim Dul and his barbarians seek to destroy all who remain.

1. The Gathering Dark (Grubb, Jeff) ◆ 1999
2. The Eternal Ice (Grubb, Jeff) ◆ 2000
3. The Shattered Alliance (Grubb, Jeff) ◆ 2000

MAGIC: THE GATHERING— INVASION CYCLE

WIZARDS OF THE COAST ◆ GRADES 9–12

FANTASY

The Thran controlled Dominaria but the evil Phyrexia begin to grow, preparing to invade.

1. The Thran (King, J. Robert) ◆ 1999
2. Invasion (King, J. Robert) ◆ 2000
3. Planeshift (King, J. Robert) ◆ 2001
4. Apocalypse (King, J. Robert) ◆ 2001

MAGIC: THE GATHERING—KAMIGAWA CYCLE

WIZARDS OF THE COAST ◆ GRADES 9–12

FANTASY

Kamigawa, which means "Spirit River," is a new world in Magic: The Gathering. Here dragon spirits guard the regions of Kamigawa. These books are influenced by elements of Japanese fantasies.

1. Outlaw: Champions of Kamigawa (McGough, Scott) ◆ 2004
2. Heretic: Betrayers of Kamigawa (McGough, Scott) ◆ 2004
3. Guardian: Saviors of Kamigawa (McGough, Scott) ◆ 2004

MAGIC: THE GATHERING—LORWYN CYCLE

WIZARDS OF THE COAST ◆ GRADES 9–12

FANTASY

This new Magic: The Gathering world features elves, boggarts, faeries, and other magical creatures.

1. Lorwyn (Herndon, Cory J., and Scott McGough) ◆ 2007
2. Morningtide (Herndon, Cory J., and Scott McGough) ◆ 2008

MAGIC: THE GATHERING—MAGIC LEGENDS CYCLE

WIZARDS OF THE COAST ◆ GRADES 9–12

FANTASY

The focus in these books is on popular characters in the Magic: The Gathering sagas. Johan, Leader of Tirras, seeks to conquer Bryce, which is led by Hazezon Tamar.

1. Johan (Emery, Clayton) ◆ 2001
2. Jedit (Emery, Clayton) ◆ 2001
3. Hazezon (Emery, Clayton) ◆ 2002

MAGIC: THE GATHERING— MAGIC LEGENDS CYCLE TWO

WIZARDS OF THE COAST ◆ GRADES 9–12

FANTASY

Emperor Madarin's assassin is secretly building his own power.

1. Assassin's Blade (McGough, Scott) ◆ 2002
2. Emperor's Fist (McGough, Scott) ◆ 2003
3. Champion's Trial (McGough, Scott) ◆ 2003

MAGIC: THE GATHERING— MASQUERADE CYCLE

WIZARDS OF THE COAST ◆ GRADES 9–12

FANTASY

The crew of the *Weatherlight* defends Dominaria from the Dark Lord and his invaders from the Phyrexian empire.

1. Mercadian Masques (Lebaron, Francis) ◆ 1999
2. Nemesis (Thompson, Paul B.) ◆ 2000
3. Prophecy (Moore, Vance) ◆ 2000

MAGIC: THE GATHERING— MIRRODIN CYCLE

WIZARDS OF THE COAST ◆ GRADES 9–12

FANTASY

Mirrodin is a metal world. Glissa, an elf, and her followers confront the evil forces of Memnarch.

1. The Moons of Mirrodin (McDermott, Will) ◆ 2003
2. The Darksteel Eye (Lebow, Jess) ◆ 2003
3. The Fifth Dawn (Herndon, Cory J.) ◆ 2004

MAGIC: THE GATHERING— ODYSSEY CYCLE

WIZARDS OF THE COAST ◆ GRADES 9–12

FANTASY

Wizards, barbarians, and other fighters seek to attain the Mirari, an artifact that will bring them power.

1. Odyssey (Moore, Vance) ◆ 2001

2. Chainer's Torment (McGough, Scott) ◆ 2002

3. Judgment (McDermott, Will) ◆ 2002

MAGIC: THE GATHERING— ONSLAUGHT CYCLE

WIZARDS OF THE COAST ◆ GRADES 9–12

FANTASY

The focus in these books is on the epic battle between Akroma, an angel, and Phage, the sister of Kamahl the barbarian.

1. Onslaught (King, J. Robert) ◆ 2002

2. Legions (King, J. Robert) ◆ 2003

3. Scourge (King, J. Robert) ◆ 2003

MAGIC: THE GATHERING— RAVNICA CYCLE

WIZARDS OF THE COAST ◆ GRADES 9–12

FANTASY

The conflicts among the ten guilds of Ravinica are finally over, but will the Guildpact ensure the peace?

1. Ravinica: City of Guilds (Herndon, Cory J.) ◆ 2005

2. Guildpact (Herndon, Cory J.) ◆ 2006

3. Dissension (Herndon, Cory J.) ◆ 2006

MAGIC: THE GATHERING— SHADOWMOOR CYCLE

WIZARDS OF THE COAST ◆ GRADES 9–12

FANTASY

Set in Lorwyn, a world of elves, faeries, and magic, the Shadowmoor Cycle follows the struggles of the elves.

1. Shadowmoor (Morris, Susan J.) ◆ 2008

2. Eventide (Herndon, Cory J., and Scott McGough) ◆ 2008

MAGIC: THE GATHERING— TIME SPIRAL CYCLE

WIZARDS OF THE COAST ◆ GRADES 9–12

FANTASY

Teferi, a planeswalker, returns home to Dominaria only to find time is fracturing, bringing chaos and threatening destruction.

1. Time Spiral (McGough, Scott) ◆ 2006
2. Planar Chaos (McGough, Scott, and Timothy Sanders) ◆ 2007
3. Future Sight (McGough, Scott, and John Delaney) ◆ 2008

MAGIC IN MANHATTAN

Mlynowski, Sarah

DELACORTE ◆ GRADES 6–9 ◆ A/R

FANTASY

How would you feel if your mom and your younger sister were witches and you had no magical powers? That's one of the problems for Rachel Weinstein, 14. Rachel decides to have her younger sister, Mimi, use magic to help with popularity and dating but, of course, that backfires. And so does the plan to magically stop their father from remarrying. In the second book, Rachel's mom and sister overuse their magic. In the third book, Rachel discovers she is a witch. This is a fun series for girls and would go well with McClymer's Witch books.

1. Bras and Broomsticks ◆ 2006
2. Frogs and French Kisses ◆ 2007
3. Spells and Sleeping Bags ◆ 2007
4. Parties and Potions ◆ 2008

MAGIC OR MADNESS TRILOGY

Larbalestier, Justine

RAZORBILL ◆ GRADES 8–11 ◆ A/R

FANTASY

After her mother goes insane, Reason, 15, goes to stay with her grandmother, Esmeralda, who is a witch. Reason's mother taught her to value what is rational and real. When Reason passes through a magic door, she is transported from Australia to New York City. There she begins to accept magic and her own destiny. As the series progresses, Reason discovers that those who use their magic die young while those who do not use their magic go crazy.

1. Magic or Madness ◆ 2005
2. Magic Lessons ◆ 2006
3. Magic's Child ◆ 2007

MAGIC PICKLE GRAPHIC NOVELS

Morse, Scott

GRAPHIX ◆ GRADES 5–8 ◆ A/R

HUMOR

Born in a top secret U.S. Army lab, the Magic Pickle is a flying kosher dill superhero. His mission, to stop other remnants of the experiment from destroying the world. The rotten vegetables have formed an evil society, the Brotherhood of Evil Produce. After years in a cryogenic state, Magic Pickle is released and bursts through the floor of JoJo Wigman's bedroom. Together, they face the attacks of the Brotherhood. Share this with fans of humorous superheroes and graphic novels.

1. Magic Pickle ◆ 2008
2. Magic Pickle vs. the Egg Poacher ◆ 2008
3. Magic Pickle and the Planet of the Grapes ◆ 2008

MAGICIAN TRILOGY

McGowen, Tom

PENGUIN ◆ GRADES 4–7 ◆ A/R

FANTASY | SCIENCE FICTION

Far in the future, civilization has been destroyed by war, and the people look back at our era as the Age of Magic and call our inventions "spells." People who seek wisdom are called Sages, and they attempt to make sense of the ruins and find out what ancient objects were used for. The head of these Sages, Armindor, takes as an apprentice a boy named Tigg, who had been a pickpocket. Together they travel to the Wild Lands and find a tape recorder with a tape that they believe will help them find the key to the ancient language. First, they must fight a terrible threat from intelligent ratlike creatures bent on taking over the human race. With Jilla, an orphan girl, and Reepah, a "grubber," they travel to the city of Ingarron and lead a successful attack.

1. The Magician's Apprentice ◆ 1987
2. The Magician's Company ◆ 1988
3. The Magician's Challenge ◆ 1989

MAGICIAN TRILOGY (Nimmo) *see* Gwyn Griffiths Trilogy

MAGICIAN'S HOUSE QUARTET

Corlett, William

POCKET BOOKS ♦ GRADES 5–8 ♦ A/R

FANTASY

William Constant, 13, and his younger sisters, Mary and Alice, are spending Christmas in Wales with their Uncle Jack. As they investigate Uncle Jack's home, they discover a secret room in the chimney. There they meet a magician who warns them of the tests they will soon face. In subsequent books, they return to Golden House for more magical adventures. This series was originally published in England in the early 1990s.

1. The Steps Up the Chimney ♦ 2000
2. The Door in the Tree ♦ 2000
3. The Tunnel Behind the Waterfall ♦ 2001
4. The Bridge in the Clouds ♦ 2001

THE MAGICKERS

Drake, Emily

DAW ♦ GRADES 6–10 ♦ A/R

FANTASY

In the first book, 11-year-old Jason is invited to Camp Ravenwyng, where—to his surprise—he finds that he will be trained as a Magicker and will work against evil. In the second book, Jason realizes that the Dark Hand, whom he battled at the Camp, is present in his hometown.

1. The Magickers ♦ 2001
2. The Curse of Arkady ♦ 2002
3. The Dragon Guard ♦ 2003
4. The Gate of Bones ♦ 2004

MAIZON

Woodson, Jacqueline

DELACORTE; PUTNAM ♦ GRADES 6–8

FAMILY LIFE | REAL LIFE

Margaret and Maizon are best friends, but they are separated when Maizon goes to boarding school. At Blue Hill, Maizon adjusts to being one of only five African American students. She misses her grandmother and her friends. Returning home, she rebuilds her friendship with Margaret and makes some new friends. Maizon even meets her father, who left when she was a baby. This series follows a character from the end of her childhood into independence and young adulthood.

1. Last Summer with Maizon ◆ 1990
2. Maizon at Blue Hill ◆ 1992
3. Between Madison and Palmetto ◆ 1993

THE MAJIPOOR CYCLE

Silverberg, Robert
HARPERCOLLINS ◆ GRADES 10–12 ◆ A/R
FANTASY | SCIENCE FICTION

This is a rich saga—combining elements of fantasy and science fiction—about events on the planet of Majipoor, which has many medieval aspects. Valentine is an itinerant juggler until he realizes that he is in fact heir to the kingdom. Other books follow various characters as they deal with intrigue and dark forces.

1. Lord Valentine's Castle ◆ 1980
2. The Majipoor Chronicles ◆ 1982
3. Valentine Pontifex ◆ 1983
4. The Mountains of Majipoor ◆ 1995
5. Sorcerers of Majipoor ◆ 1996
6. Lord Prestimion ◆ 1999
7. The King of Dreams ◆ 2001

MAKE LEMONADE TRILOGY

Wolff, Virginia Euwer
HOLT; ATHENEUM ◆ GRADES 7–10 ◆ A/R
REAL LIFE

In *Make Lemonade,* LaVaughn, 14, describes the difficulties faced by Jolly, a 17-year-old dropout with two children from two different fathers. LaVaughn babysits for Jolly while Jolly looks for work. The free verse poetry of LaVaughn's observations is sparse and powerful. In *True Believer,* LaVaughn's poetic writing describes her own attraction to her childhood friend Jody and the impact it has on her efforts to get out of the projects.

1. Make Lemonade ◆ 1993
2. True Believer ◆ 2001
3. This Full House ◆ 2009

MAKING OUT

Applegate, K. A.
AVON ◆ GRADES 8–12
REAL LIFE

A group of teenagers—Zoey, Jake, Benjamin, Claire, Lucas, and Nina—grow up together on an island off the coast of Maine. They remain close while developing different relationships. In the first book, the status quo is rocked when Lucas returns to the island after two years in reform school. Originally published as the Boyfriends, Girlfriends series by HarperPaperbacks.

1. Zoey Fools Around ◆ 1998
2. Jake Finds Out ◆ 1998
3. Nina Won't Tell ◆ 1998
4. Ben's in Love ◆ 1998
5. Claire Gets Caught ◆ 1998
6. What Zoey Saw ◆ 1998
7. Lucas Gets Hurt ◆ 1998
8. Aisha Goes Wild ◆ 1999
9. Zoey Plays Games ◆ 1999
10. Nina Shapes Up ◆ 1999
11. Ben Takes a Chance ◆ 1999
12. Claire Can't Love ◆ 1999
13. Don't Tell Zoey ◆ 1999
14. Aaron Let's Go ◆ 1999
15. Who Loves Kate ◆ 1999
16. Lara Gets Even ◆ 1999
17. Two-Timing Aisha ◆ 1999
18. Zoey Speaks Out ◆ 1999
19. Kate Finds Love ◆ 1999
20. Never Trust Lara ◆ 2000
21. Trouble with Aaron ◆ 2000
22. Always Loving Zoey ◆ 2000
23. Lara Gets Lucky ◆ 2000
24. Now Zoey's Alone ◆ 2000
25. Don't Forget Lara ◆ 2000
26. Zoey's Broken Heart ◆ 2000
27. Falling for Claire ◆ 2000
28. Zoey Comes Home ◆ 2000

MAKING WAVES

Applegate, K. A.
17TH STREET PRESS ◆ GRADES 9–12
REAL LIFE

When their ex-boyfriends show up, dynamics change at the beach house that high school graduates Kate and Chelsea are sharing. Previously published by HarperCollins under the series title Ocean City.

1. Making Waves ◆ 2001
2. Tease ◆ 2001
3. Sweet ◆ 2001
4. Thrill ◆ 2001
5. Heat ◆ 2001
6. Secret ◆ 2001
7. Attitude ◆ 2001
8. Burn ◆ 2001
9. Wild ◆ 2001
10. Chill ◆ 2001
11. Last Splash ◆ 2001

MALLOREON

Eddings, David
BALLANTINE ◆ GRADES 10–12
FANTASY

Garion is now the King of Riva. The evil God Torak is dead. Garion must face demon worshippers and later, Zandramas, the Child of the Dark. Earlier events are described in the Belgariad. There is a prequel to both series, *Belgarath the Sorcerer* (1995), and a final volume to both, *Polgara the Sorceress* (1997).

1. Guardians of the West ◆ 1987
2. King of the Murgos ◆ 1987
3. Demon Lord of Karanda ◆ 1988
4. Sorceress of Darshiva ◆ 1989
5. The Seeress of Kell ◆ 1991

MAN OF HIS WORD

Duncan, David
BALLANTINE DEL REY ◆ GRADES 10–12
FANTASY

From the beginning, Inos, daughter of the King, and Rap, a stable boy, were friends. As they grow up, their paths diverge. Inos is destined to be married to nobility while Rap begins to realize his magical powers. Throughout this series, Rap is there for Inos, even after she marries the evil Sultan Azak.

1. Magic Casement ◆ 1990
2. Faery Lands Forlorn ◆ 1991

3. Perilous Seas ◆ 1991
4. Emperor and Clown ◆ 1997

MARS YEAR ONE

Strickland, Brad, and Thomas E. Fuller
SIMON & SCHUSTER ◆ GRADES 5–8 ◆ A/R
SCIENCE FICTION

It is 2085. Sean is leaving the turmoil on Earth to travel to Mars. There are only 20 teenagers in the colony and Sean must try to fit in and find a way to contribute.

1. Marooned! ◆ 2004
2. Missing! ◆ 2004
3. Marsquake! ◆ 2005

MARY-KATE AND ASHLEY: ADVENTURES OF MARY-KATE AND ASHLEY

Various authors
SCHOLASTIC ◆ GRADES 4–7 ◆ A/R
FAMILY LIFE | MYSTERY | REAL LIFE

The Olsen twins, Mary-Kate and Ashley, have achieved great popularity on television, video, and in movies. This series capitalizes on the popularity of these appealing twins.

1. The Case of the Christmas Caper (Waricha, Jean) ◆ 1996
2. The Case of the Mystery Cruise (Thompson, Carol) ◆ 1996
3. The Case of the Fun House Mystery (Scholastic staff) ◆ 1996
4. The Case of the U.S. Space Camp Mission (Scholastic staff and Bonnie Bader) ◆ 1996
5. The Case of the Sea World Adventure (Dubowski, Cathy East) ◆ 1996
6. The Case of the Shark Encounter (Krulik, Nancy E.) ◆ 1997
7. The Case of the Hotel Who-Done-It (O'Neil, Laura) ◆ 1997
8. The Case of the Volcano Mystery (Thompson, Carol) ◆ 1997
9. The Case of the U.S. Navy Adventure (Perlberg, Deborah) ◆ 1997
10. The Case of Thorn Mansion (Alexander, Nina) ◆ 1997

THE NEW ADVENTURES OF MARY-KATE AND ASHLEY

1. The Case of the 202 Clues (Alexander, Nina) ◆ 1998
2. The Case of the Ballet Bandit (O'Neil, Laura) ◆ 1998
3. The Case of the Blue-Ribbon Horse (Swobud, I. K) ◆ 1998
4. The Case of the Haunted Camp (Alexander, Nina) ◆ 1998
5. The Case of the Wild Wolf River (Katschke, Judy) ◆ 1998

6. The Case of the Rock and Roll Mystery (Eisenberg, Lisa) ◆ 1998
7. The Case of the Missing Mummy (Lantz, Francess) ◆ 1999
8. The Case of the Surprise Call (Metz, Melinda) ◆ 1999
9. The Case of the Disappearing Princess (Eisenberg, Lisa) ◆ 1999
10. The Case of the Great Elephant Escape (Doolittle, June) ◆ 1999
11. The Case of the Summer Camp Caper (Katschke, Judy) ◆ 1999
12. The Case of the Surfing Secret (Dubowski, Cathy East) ◆ 1999
13. The Case of the Green Ghost (Ellis, Carol) ◆ 1999
14. The Case of the Big Scare Mountain Mystery (Ellis, Carol) ◆ 1999
15. The Case of the Slam Dunk Mystery (Dubowski, Cathy East) ◆ 2000
16. The Case of the Rock Star's Secret (Metz, Melinda) ◆ 2000
17. The Case of the Cheerleading Camp Mystery (Fiedler, Lisa) ◆ 2000
18. The Case of the Flying Phantom (Metz, Melinda) ◆ 2000
19. The Case of the Creepy Castle (Katschke, Judy) ◆ 2000
20. The Case of the Golden Slipper (Metz, Melinda) ◆ 2000
21. The Case of the Flapper 'Napper (Katschke, Judy) ◆ 2001
22. The Case of the High Seas Secret (Leonhardt, Alice) ◆ 2001
23. The Case of the Logical I Ranch (Preiss, Pauline) ◆ 2001
24. The Case of the Dog Camp Mystery (Katschke, Judy) ◆ 2001
25. The Case of the Screaming Scarecrow (Katschke, Judy) ◆ 2001
26. The Case of the Jingle Bell Jinx (Leonhardt, Alice) ◆ 2001
27. The Case of the Game Show Mystery (Thomas, Jim) ◆ 2002
28. The Case of the Mall Mystery (Leonhardt, Alice) ◆ 2002
29. The Case of the Weird Science Mystery (Katschke, Judy) ◆ 2002
30. The Case of Camp Crooked Lake (Ellis, Carol) ◆ 2002
31. The Case of the Giggling Ghost (Metz, Melinda) ◆ 2002
32. The Case of the Candy Cane Clue (Katschke, Judy) ◆ 2002
33. The Case of the Hollywood Who-Done-It (Metz, Melinda) ◆ 2003
34. The Case of the Sundae Surprise (Metz, Melinda) ◆ 2003
35. The Case of Clue's Circus Caper (Katschke, Judy) ◆ 2003
36. The Case of Camp Pom-Pom (Alexander, Heather) ◆ 2003
37. The Case of the Tattooed Cat (Alexander, Heather) ◆ 2003
38. The Case of the Nutcracker Ballet (Stine, Megan) ◆ 2003
39. The Case of the Clue at the Zoo (Katschke, Judy) ◆ 2004
40. The Case of the Easter Egg Race (Alexander, Heather) ◆ 2004
41. The Case of the Dog Show Mystery (author not available) ◆ 2004
42. The Case of the Cheerleading Tattletale (author not available) ◆ 2004
43. The Case of the Haunted Maze (author not available) ◆ 2004
44. The Case of the Hidden Holiday Riddle (author not available) ◆ 2004
45. The Case of the Icy Igloo Inn (author not available) ◆ 2005
46. The Case of the Unicorn Mystery (author not available) ◆ 2005

MARY-KATE AND ASHLEY: GRADUATION SUMMER

Various authors

HARPERENTERTAINMENT ◆ GRADES 4–7 ◆ A/R

REAL LIFE

It's the end of the senior year of high school for Mary-Kate and Ashley. They are savoring the fun parties and prom even as they anticipate the start of college. In the third book, the girls begin college, meeting their roommates, making new friends, and meeting lots of cute boys.

1. We Can't Wait! (Harrison, Emma) ◆ 2004
2. Never Say Good-bye (Butcher, Nancy) ◆ 2004
3. Everything I Want (Dokey, Cameron) ◆ 2004

MARY-KATE AND ASHLEY: SO LITTLE TIME

Olsen, Mary-Kate, and Ashley Olsen
HARPERCOLLINS ◆ GRADES 4–7 ◆ A/R
FAMILY LIFE | REAL LIFE

Based on the television series *So Little Time,* in which Mary-Kate and Ashley Olsen play Chloe and Riley Carlson. The girls enjoy being in high school, paying some attention to books and studying but spending most of their time on boys and dating.

1. How to Train a Boy ◆ 2002
2. Instant Boyfriend ◆ 2002
3. Too Good to Be True ◆ 2002
4. Just Between Us ◆ 2002
5. Tell Me About It ◆ 2002
6. Secret Crush ◆ 2002
7. Girl Talk ◆ 2002
8. The Love Factor ◆ 2003
9. Dating Game ◆ 2003
10. A Girl's Guide to Guys ◆ 2003
11. Boy Crazy ◆ 2003
12. Best Friends Forever ◆ 2003
13. Love Is in the Air ◆ 2003
14. Spring Breakup ◆ 2004
15. Get Real ◆ 2004
16. Surf Holiday ◆ 2004
17. The Makeover Experiment ◆ 2005

MARY-KATE AND ASHLEY: TWO OF A KIND

Various authors
HARPERCOLLINS ◆ GRADES 4–7 ◆ A/R
FAMILY LIFE | REAL LIFE

In this series, Mary-Kate and Ashley are older and they love shopping and hanging out with their friends. They also have hopes about boys and dating. Tween girls will enjoy these books.

1. It's a Twin Thing (Katschke, Judy) ◆ 1999
2. How to Flunk Your First Date (Stine, Megan) ◆ 1999
3. The Sleepover Secret (Katschke, Judy) ◆ 1999
4. One Twin Too Many (Stine, Megan) ◆ 1999
5. To Snoop or Not to Snoop (Katschke, Judy) ◆ 1999
6. My Sister the Supermodel (Stine, Megan) ◆ 1999
7. Two's a Crowd (Katschke, Judy) ◆ 1999
8. Let's Party (Katschke, Judy) ◆ 1999
9. Calling All Boys (Katschke, Judy) ◆ 2000
10. Winner Take All (Banim, Lisa) ◆ 2000
11. P.S. Wish You Were Here (Stine, Megan) ◆ 2000
12. The Cool Club (Katschke, Judy) ◆ 2000
13. War of the Wardrobes (Stine, Megan) ◆ 2000
14. Bye-Bye-Boy Friend (Katschke, Judy) ◆ 2000
15. It's Snow Problem (Butcher, Nancy) ◆ 2001
16. Likes Me, Likes Me Not (Stine, Megan) ◆ 2001
17. Shore Thing (Katschke, Judy) ◆ 2001
18. Two for the Road (Butcher, Nancy) ◆ 2001
19. Surprise, Surprise! (Stine, Megan) ◆ 2001
20. Sealed with a Kiss (Katschke, Judy) ◆ 2001
21. Now You See Him, Now You Don't (Stine, Megan) ◆ 2002
22. April Fools' Rules (Katschke, Judy) ◆ 2002
23. Island Girls (Butcher, Nancy) ◆ 2002
24. Surf, Sand, and Secrets (Butcher, Nancy) ◆ 2002
25. Closer than Ever (Katschke, Judy) ◆ 2002
26. The Perfect Gift (Stine, Megan) ◆ 2002
27. The Facts About Flirting (Katschke, Judy) ◆ 2003
28. The Dream Date Debate (Stine, Megan) ◆ 2003
29. Love-Set-Match (Dubowski, Cathy East) ◆ 2003
30. Making a Splash (Stine, Megan) ◆ 2003
31. Dare to Scare (Katschke, Judy) ◆ 2003
32. Santa Girls (Gallagher, Diana G.) ◆ 2003
33. Heart to Heart (Katschke, Judy) ◆ 2004
34. Prom Princess (Gallagher, Diana G.) ◆ 2004
35. Camp Rock 'n' Roll (Katschke, Judy) ◆ 2004
36. Twist and Shout (Katschke, Judy) ◆ 2004
37. Hocus-Pocus (Gikow, Louise) ◆ 2004
38. Holiday Magic (Gallagher, Diana G.) ◆ 2004
39. Candles, Cake, Celebrate! (Katschke, Judy) ◆ 2005
40. Wish on a Star (Gikow, Louise) ◆ 2005

MARY-KATE AND ASHLEY IN ACTION

Olsen, Mary-Kate, and Ashley Olsen

HARPERCOLLINS ◆ GRADES 4–7 ◆ A/R

FAMILY LIFE | MYSTERY | REAL LIFE

There are mysteries to be solved. Mary-Kate and Ashley go undercover as secret agents Misty and Amber. They are on the spot when strange things happen and they investigate such mysteries as why a restaurant is too popular and why all the radio stations are playing the same song. There are lots of cartoon-style illustrations in these books, which add to the appeal.

1. Makeup Shake-Up ◆ 2002
2. The Dream Team ◆ 2002
3. Fubble Bubble Trouble ◆ 2002
4. Operation Evaporation ◆ 2003
5. Dog Gone Mess ◆ 2003
6. The Music Meltdown ◆ 2003
7. Password: Red Hot ◆ 2003
8. Fast Food Fight ◆ 2003

MARY-KATE AND ASHLEY STARRING IN
● ● ●

Various authors

HARPERCOLLINS ◆ GRADES 4–7 ◆ A/R

FAMILY LIFE | REAL LIFE

These books feature the Olsen twins in stories from their video series. In one book, the girls play twins who switch places. Emma is popular but her father gives more attention to her sister, Sam. Sam is athletic but wants to attract a cute guy. Emma and Sam switch and develop an understanding for each other. In another book, the Olsens play twins whose family has moved to Australia to escape the wrath of a jewel thief they helped to catch. Of course, the thief ends up in Australia, too.

1. Switching Goals (Fiedler, Lisa) ◆ 2000
2. Our Lips Are Sealed (Willard, Eliza) ◆ 2001
3. Winning London (Kruger, Elizabeth) ◆ 2001
4. School Dance Party (Willard, Eliza) ◆ 2001
5. Holiday in the Sun (Willard, Eliza) ◆ 2001
6. When in Rome (Stine, Megan) ◆ 2002
7. The Challenge (author not available) ◆ 2003

MARY-KATE AND ASHLEY SWEET 16

Olsen, Mary-Kate, and Ashley Olsen

HARPERCOLLINS ◆ GRADES 4–7 ◆ A/R

FAMILY LIFE | REAL LIFE

The Olsen twins turn 16! They can drive, go to parties, visit the mall, and enjoy their friends—including boyfriends.

1. Never Been Kissed ◆ 2002
2. Wishes and Dreams ◆ 2002
3. The Perfect Summer ◆ 2002
4. Getting There ◆ 2002
5. Starring You and Me ◆ 2002
6. My Best Friend's Boyfriend ◆ 2002
7. Playing Games ◆ 2003
8. Cross Our Hearts ◆ 2003
9. All That Glitters ◆ 2003
10. Keeping Secrets ◆ 2003
11. Little White Lies ◆ 2003
12. Dream Holiday ◆ 2003
13. Love and Kisses ◆ 2004
14. Spring into Style ◆ 2004
15. California Dreams ◆ 2004
16. Truth or Dare ◆ 2004
17. Forget Me Not ◆ 2005
18. I Want My Sister Back ◆ 2005

MATES, DATES, AND . . .

Hopkins, Cathy

SIMON & SCHUSTER ◆ GRADES 6–9 ◆ A/R

REAL LIFE

Three friends, all 14, live in London and describe their adolescent concerns. Lucy worries about her self-image. Izzie realizes that a relationship is not right for her. Nesta learns that telling the truth is better than living a lie. This series was originally published in England with different titles. *The Mates, Dates Guide to Life, Love, and Looking Luscious* (2005) is full of advice.

1. Mates, Dates, and Inflatable Bras ◆ 2003
2. Mates, Dates, and Cosmic Kisses ◆ 2003
3. Mates, Dates, and Designer Divas ◆ 2003
4. Mates, Dates, and Sleepover Secrets ◆ 2003
5. Mates, Dates, and Sole Survivors ◆ 2003
6. Mates, Dates, and Mad Mistakes ◆ 2004
7. Mates, Dates, and Sequin Smiles ◆ 2004

8. Mates, Dates, and Tempting Trouble ◆ 2005
9. Mates, Dates, and Great Escapes ◆ 2005
10. Mates, Dates, and Chocolate Cheats ◆ 2006
11. Mates, Dates, and Diamond Destiny ◆ 2006
12. Mates, Dates, and Sizzling Summers ◆ 2006

MATT CHRISTOPHER'S SPORTS STORIES

Various authors

LITTLE, BROWN ◆ GRADES 3–7 ◆ A/R

RECREATION

Generations of readers have enjoyed the action in these sports stories. Football, baseball, soccer, swimming, volleyball, snowboarding, swimming, and more are featured in this classic series. Many of the books have lessons about tolerance, teamwork, competition, and preparation. Matt Christopher died in 1997. Newer books are published under the "Matt Christopher" name, although they are written by various authors.

1. The Lucky Baseball Bat (Christopher, Matt) ◆ 1954
2. Baseball Pals (Christopher, Matt) ◆ 1956
3. Basketball Sparkplug (Christopher, Matt) ◆ 1957
4. Slide, Danny, Slide (Christopher, Matt) ◆ 1958
5. Two Strikes on Johnny (Christopher, Matt) ◆ 1958
6. Little Lefty (Christopher, Matt) ◆ 1959
7. Touchdown for Tommy (Christopher, Matt) ◆ 1959
8. Break for the Basket (Christopher, Matt) ◆ 1960
9. Long Stretch at First Base (Christopher, Matt) ◆ 1960
10. Tall Man in the Pivot (Christopher, Matt) ◆ 1961
11. Challenge at Second Base (Christopher, Matt) ◆ 1962
12. Crackerjack Halfback (Christopher, Matt) ◆ 1962
13. Baseball Flyhawk (Christopher, Matt) ◆ 1963
14. Shoot for the Hoop (Christopher, Matt) ◆ 1963
15. Sink It, Rusty (Christopher, Matt) ◆ 1963
16. Catcher With a Glass Arm (Christopher, Matt) ◆ 1964
17. Wingman on Ice (Christopher, Matt) ◆ 1964
18. The Counterfeit Tackle (Christopher, Matt) ◆ 1965
19. Too Hot to Handle (Christopher, Matt) ◆ 1965
20. Long Shot for Paul (Christopher, Matt) ◆ 1966
21. The Reluctant Pitcher (Christopher, Matt) ◆ 1966
22. Miracle at the Plate (Christopher, Matt) ◆ 1967
23. The Basket Counts (Christopher, Matt) ◆ 1968
24. The Year Mom Won the Pennant (Christopher, Matt) ◆ 1968
25. Catch That Pass! (Christopher, Matt) ◆ 1969
26. Hard Drive to Short (Christopher, Matt) ◆ 1969
27. Johnny Long Legs (Christopher, Matt) ◆ 1970
28. Shortstop from Tokyo (Christopher, Matt) ◆ 1970
29. Look Who's Playing First Base: 0 (Christopher, Matt) ◆ 1971

30. Tough to Tackle (Christopher, Matt) ◆ 1971
31. Face-Off (Christopher, Matt) ◆ 1972
32. The Kid Who Only Hit Homers (Christopher, Matt) ◆ 1972
33. Ice Magic (Christopher, Matt) ◆ 1973
34. Mystery Coach (Christopher, Matt) ◆ 1973
35. Front Court Hex (Christopher, Matt) ◆ 1974
36. Jinx Glove (Christopher, Matt) ◆ 1974
37. No Arm in Left Field (Christopher, Matt) ◆ 1974
38. Glue Fingers (Christopher, Matt) ◆ 1975
39. The Team That Stopped Moving (Christopher, Matt) ◆ 1975
40. Football Fugitive (Christopher, Matt) ◆ 1976
41. Power Play (Christopher, Matt) ◆ 1976
42. The Submarine Pitch (Christopher, Matt) ◆ 1976
43. The Diamond Champs (Christopher, Matt) ◆ 1977
44. Johnny No Hit (Christopher, Matt) ◆ 1977
45. The Fox Steals Home (Christopher, Matt) ◆ 1978
46. Jackrabbit Goalie (Christopher, Matt) ◆ 1978
47. Soccer Halfback (Christopher, Matt) ◆ 1978
48. Dirt Bike Racer (Christopher, Matt) ◆ 1979
49. Run, Billy, Run (Christopher, Matt) ◆ 1980
50. Wild Pitch (Christopher, Matt) ◆ 1980
51. Tight End (Christopher, Matt) ◆ 1981
52. Drag Strip Racer (Christopher, Matt) ◆ 1982
53. Dirt Bike Runaway (Christopher, Matt) ◆ 1983
54. The Great Quarterback Switch (Christopher, Matt) ◆ 1984
55. Supercharged Infield (Christopher, Matt) ◆ 1985
56. The Hockey Machine (Christopher, Matt) ◆ 1986
57. Red-Hot Hightops (Christopher, Matt) ◆ 1987
58. Tackle Without a Team (Christopher, Matt) ◆ 1989
59. Takedown (Christopher, Matt) ◆ 1990
60. Skateboard Tough (Christopher, Matt) ◆ 1991
61. Centerfield Ballhawk (Christopher, Matt) ◆ 1992
62. Return of the Home Run Kid (Christopher, Matt) ◆ 1992
63. Undercover Tailback (Christopher, Matt) ◆ 1992
64. Line Drive to Shore (Christopher, Matt) ◆ 1993
65. Pressure Play (Christopher, Matt) ◆ 1993
66. Top Wing (Christopher, Matt) ◆ 1994
67. The Winning Stroke (Christopher, Matt) ◆ 1994
68. Double Play at Short (Christopher, Matt) ◆ 1995
69. Fighting Tackle (Christopher, Matt) ◆ 1995
70. The Comeback Challenge (Christopher, Matt) ◆ 1996
71. Halfback Attack (Christopher, Matt) ◆ 1996
72. Olympic Dream (Christopher, Matt) ◆ 1996
73. Baseball Turnaround (Christopher, Matt) ◆ 1997
74. Penalty Shot (Christopher, Matt) ◆ 1997
75. Snowboard Maverick (Christopher, Matt) ◆ 1997
76. The Team That Couldn't Lose (Christopher, Matt) ◆ 1997
77. Center Court Sting (Christopher, Matt) ◆ 1998
78. Mountain Bike Mania (Christopher, Matt) ◆ 1998

79. Prime-Time Pitcher (Christopher, Matt) ◆ 1998
80. Roller Hockey Radicals (Christopher, Matt) ◆ 1998
81. Soccer Scoop (Christopher, Matt) ◆ 1998
82. Long-Arm Quarterback (Christopher, Matt) ◆ 1999
83. Snowboard Showdown (Christopher, Matt) ◆ 1999
84. Spike It! (Christopher, Matt) ◆ 1999
85. Tie Breaker (Christopher, Matt) ◆ 1999
86. Soccer Duel (Christopher, Matt) ◆ 2000
87. Tennis Ace (Christopher, Matt) ◆ 2000
88. Wheel Wizards (Christopher, Matt) ◆ 2000
89. Skateboard Renegades (Mantell, Paul) ◆ 2000
90. Cool as Ice (Mantell, Paul) ◆ 2001
91. Football Nightmare (Hirschfeld, Robert) ◆ 2001
92. Inline Skater (Hirschfeld, Robert) ◆ 2001
93. Dive Right In (Hirschfeld, Robert) ◆ 2002
94. Goalkeeper in Charge (Hirschfeld, Robert) ◆ 2002
95. Run for It (Hirschfeld, Robert) ◆ 2002
96. Windmill Windup (Mantell, Paul) ◆ 2002
97. Body Check (Hirschfeld, Robert) ◆ 2003
98. Fairway Phenom (Mantell, Paul) ◆ 2003
99. Nothin' But Net (Mantell, Paul) ◆ 2003
100. Slam Dunk (Hirschfeld, Robert) ◆ 2004
101. Snowboard Champ (Mantell, Paul) ◆ 2004
102. Stealing Home (Mantell, Paul) ◆ 2004
103. Comeback of the Home Run Kid (Peters, Stephanie True) ◆ 2006
104. Soccer Hero (Peters, Stephanie True) ◆ 2007
105. Football Double Threat (Peters, Stephanie True) ◆ 2008
106. Lacrosse Firestorm (Peters, Stephanie True) ◆ 2008

MAX REMY *see* Spy Force

MAXIMUM RIDE

Patterson, James
LITTLE, BROWN ◆ GRADES 7–10 ◆ A/R
SCIENCE FICTION

At the School, an experimental laboratory, kids are being genetically altered to possess special talents. Led by Max (aka Maximum Ride), 14, one group has escaped and are being pursued by the Erasers. When Angel, 6, is captured by the Erasers, Max uses all of her powers to rescue her. As the series continues, Max and her flock save the world from evil enemies.

1. The Angel Experiment ◆ 2005
2. School's Out—Forever ◆ 2006

    3. Saving the World and Other Extreme Sports ◆ 2007
    4. The Final Warning ◆ 2008

MAY BIRD

Anderson, Jodi Lynn

ATHENEUM ◆ GRADES 5–7 ◆ A/R

FANTASY

May Bird has lived in isolation with only her pet cat, Somber Kitty, for a companion. After she falls into the lake, she enters the world of Ever After and is transformed—she can see and communicate with ghosts. May Bird begins a quest in Ever After seeking her own destiny. In the third book, May Bird goes back home only to realize that she belongs in Ever After. She returns there only to find that everything has changed and it is up to her to restore this world.

    1. May Bird and the Ever After ◆ 2005
    2. May Bird Among the Stars ◆ 2006
    3. May Bird, Warrior Princess ◆ 2007

MEASLE

Ogilvy, Ian

HARPERCOLLINS ◆ GRADES 4–7 ◆ A/R

FANTASY

Ten-year-old Measle Stubbs is being raised by a mad guardian/wizard Basil Tramplebone. To punish Measle for playing with his miniature trains, Basil shrinks the boy and places him in the train set environment. Measle faces cockroaches and bats and must try to regain his proper size. As the series continues, Measle finds his parents and continues to battle magical dangers.

    1. Measle and the Wrathmonk ◆ 2004
    2. Measle and the Dragodon ◆ 2005
    3. Measle and the Mallockee ◆ 2006

MED CENTER

Hoh, Diane

SCHOLASTIC ◆ GRADES 6–8

REAL LIFE

Abby and Susannah are best friends who love their work as volunteers at the large Medical Center in Grant, Massachusetts. The two girls come from very different backgrounds. Susannah is the descendent of the town's founders and lives in the most lavish house in town. Abby comes from a more middle-class family. Each book deals with a disaster that strikes the small town and the reactions of the girls, their families, and friends.

1. Virus ◆ 1996
2. Flood ◆ 1996
3. Fire ◆ 1996
4. Blast ◆ 1996
5. Blizzard ◆ 1997
6. Poison ◆ 1997

THE MEDIATOR

Cabot, Meg

AVON; HARPERCOLLINS ◆ GRADES 7–10 ◆ A/R

FANTASY

Susannah Simon, 16, is eager to get settled in California with her mom, stepdad, and stepbrothers. Before she can feel at ease, she must deal with the ghost in her bedroom. Later, there is the ghost of a dead woman who gives Suze a message about her murder. Like Buffy the Vampire Slayer, Susannah deals with her supernatural powers. She also has a normal life as a sophomore and attractive boys are included in each book.

1. Shadowland ◆ 2001
2. Ninth Key ◆ 2001
3. Reunion ◆ 2001
4. Darkest Hour ◆ 2001
5. Haunted ◆ 2003
6. Twilight ◆ 2005

MEG MURRY *see* Time Fantasy Series

MEL BEEBY: AGENT ANGEL *see* Angels Unlimited

MENNYMS

Waugh, Sylvia

GREENWILLOW ◆ GRADES 5–8 ◆ A/R

FAMILY LIFE | FANTASY

This is a fantasy quintet set in England that older readers will enjoy. The Mennyms are a family of rag dolls that are able to pass quietly for human—that is to say, until various adventures happen to them. First there is the Australian owner of the house who comes to pay a visit. Then they discover that they are in the care of an antiques dealer, who, it seems, will shortly discover their secret. Readers will want to read all five books in the series.

1. The Mennyms ◆ 1994
2. Mennyms in the Wilderness ◆ 1995
3. Mennyms Under Siege ◆ 1996
4. Mennyms Alone ◆ 1996
5. Mennyms Alive ◆ 1997

MERLIN *see* The Lost Years of Merlin

MERLIN CODEX

Holdstock, Robert

TOR ◆ GRADES 9–12

FANTASY

The legend of Merlin is merged with elements of Greek mythology in this fascinating series. In *Celtika,* Merlin is a young man wandering the earth seeking enlightenment. He encounters Jason and joins him in the search for the Golden Fleece. When Medea kills Jason's sons, Jason sails away, consumed by his loss. Hundreds of years later, Merlin hears Jason's cries and uses magic to help reunite him with his sons.

1. Celtika ◆ 2003
2. The Iron Grail ◆ 2004
3. The Broken Kings ◆ 2007

THE MIDNIGHT LIBRARY

Graves, Damien

SCHOLASTIC ◆ GRADES 5–8 ◆ A/R

HORROR

Each book in this series features three scary stories. In *Voices,* Kate hears voices telling her about her future. What she hears may scare her to death! In *End Game,* when the computer game is over, so is your life. The format of these books—three short stories—and the high-interest content should make them popular with reluctant readers.

1. Voices ◆ 2006
2. Blood and Sand ◆ 2006

3. End Game ◆ 2006
4. The Cat Lady ◆ 2007
5. Liar ◆ 2007
6. Shut Your Mouth ◆ 2007
7. I Can See You ◆ 2007
8. The Deadly Catch ◆ 2008

MIDNIGHTERS

Westerfeld, Scott

EOS ◆ GRADES 6–10 ◆ A/R

SCIENCE FICTION | HORROR

After Jessica Day, 15, moves to Oklahoma, she discovers that she is a Midnighter. This group of teens, all born at midnight, have magical powers that allow them to confront the darklings, evil creatures that exist in a hidden hour that is accessible at midnight. The darklings are building their power, looking for ways to expand their access to the human world and in *Blue Noon* they may have found a way in.

1. The Secret Hour ◆ 2004
2. Touching Darkness ◆ 2004
3. Blue Noon ◆ 2005

MIKE PILLSBURY

Mackel, Kathy

HARPERCOLLINS ◆ GRADES 6–9 ◆ A/R

FANTASY

Mike is a geeky outsider who enjoys making up stories about encounters with aliens. As a joke, he sends a message into space asking for help and strange creatures come to rescue him. By the time they arrive, Mike does not want to be rescued. In the second book, Mike helps a friend, Scott, who has become involved in an intergalactic battle. The third book features Nick, Mike's sister Jill, and a time warp.

1. Can of Worms ◆ 1999
2. Eggs in One Basket ◆ 2000
3. From the Horse's Mouth ◆ 2002

MIKI FALLS

Crilley, Mark

HARPERTEEN ◆ GRADES 7–12 ◆ A/R

ROMANCE

Miki Yoshida, a Japanese high school senior, is falling in love with Hiro, a new boy at school who is also a Deliverer, a superhuman being who saves and protects love. There are rules about relationships between these beings and humans, so Miki's romance seems doomed. Yet Miki and Hiro cannot deny their feelings for each other, even when Reika, another Deliverer, tries to come between them. The graphic novel format of this series adds to the intensity of the story of star-crossed lovers.

1. Spring ◆ 2007
2. Summer ◆ 2007
3. Autumn ◆ 2007
4. Winter ◆ 2008

MIND OVER MATTER

Zach, Cheryl

AVON ◆ GRADES 4–8

ADVENTURE | MYSTERY

Quinn McMann lives with his cousin Jamie Anderson and her mother Maggie. Although they live in Los Angeles, Maggie's job as a television producer allows the group to travel for some of their adventures. The two 12-year-old cousins join forces to solve mysteries. Quinn has psychic powers, and Jamie is a genius and a computer whiz. These books combine supernatural elements with mysterious adventures. One book features a mummy that is stalking Quinn in his nightmares. When Quinn and Jamie get locked in a museum, they are able to find the hidden entrance to a vault filled with stolen treasures. In other books, they find out who is sabotaging a movie production and Quinn answers the call of an ancient skull.

1. The Mummy's Footsteps ◆ 1997
2. The Phantom of the Roxy ◆ 1997
3. The Curse of the Idol's Eye ◆ 1997
4. The Gypsy's Warning ◆ 1997

THE MINDS SERIES

Matas, Carol, and Perry Nodelman

SIMON & SCHUSTER ◆ GRADES 6–9 ◆ A/R

FANTASY

Princess Lenora and Prince Coren, who both have unusual powers, initially resist plans for their marriage. As the series progresses, they become engaged and together fight evil in a variety of situations including a mall in Winnipeg. These are entertaining and lively stories.

1. Of Two Minds ◆ 1998

2. More Minds ◆ 1998
3. Out of Their Minds ◆ 1998
4. A Meeting of Minds ◆ 1999

MINDWARP

Archer, Chris

MINSTREL/POCKET BOOKS ◆ GRADES 6–8 ◆ A/R

ADVENTURE | FANTASY | HORROR

A group of friends at Metier (Wisconsin) Junior High School seem to be the only ones who are aware that there are aliens among us. Ethan Rogers is a kind of a geek until an alien force invades him. Ethan knows that something is wrong but he can't seem to convince anyone else in town, including his father, the police chief. Can Ethan save the town from the *Alien Terror*? Ashley Rose is the next victim. The aliens take over her body, giving her special powers. In another adventure, Ashley and her friends try to escape the aliens in a UFO only to enter a future world that is worse than their own. This series will interest readers of Goosebumps and Ghosts of Fear Street.

1. Alien Terror ◆ 1997
2. Alien Blood ◆ 1997
3. Alien Scream ◆ 1997
4. Second Sight ◆ 1998
5. Shape-Shifter ◆ 1998
6. Aftershock ◆ 1998
7. Flash Forward ◆ 1998
8. Face the Fear ◆ 1998
9. Out of Time ◆ 1998
10. Meltdown ◆ 1999

MINERVA CLARK

Karbo, Karen, Karen

BLOOMSBURY ◆ GRADES 5–8 ◆ A/R

MYSTERY

Like many young teens, Minerva Clark, 13, is an insecure, self-conscious adolescent. Then she is zapped by lightning and her life and personality change. Minerva becomes confident and resourceful. She begins investigating local mysteries, like finding a missing red diamond and tracking a kidnapper. Fans of Sammy Keyes will enjoy these light mysteries.

1. Minerva Clark Gets a Clue ◆ 2005
2. Minerva Clark Goes to the Dogs ◆ 2006
3. Minerva Clark Gives Up the Ghost ◆ 2007

MIRROR IMAGE

Bennett, Cherie, and Jeff Gottesfeld

SIMON & SCHUSTER ◆ GRADES 7–10

FANTASY

In the first book, a mysterious rock gives Callie Bailey her every wish and she goes from being a geek to being popular. Along the way, though, she alienates her friends and hurts her sister, Laurel. Subsequent books show the impact of the magic rock on other teen girls.

1. Stranger in the Mirror ◆ 1999
2. Rich Girl in the Mirror ◆ 2000
3. Star in the Mirror ◆ 2000
4. Flirt in the Mirror ◆ 2000

MISERY GUTS

Gleitzman, Morris

HARCOURT ◆ GRADES 6–8

FAMILY LIFE | REAL LIFE

Keith worries that his parents aren't happy running a fish-and-chips shop in dreary London, so he invents all kinds of schemes to cheer them up. After convincing them to move to sunnier Australia, Keith plans to seek a fortune for his family in the opal mines. When his parents separate, Keith suggests ways for each of them to become better-looking to attract new mates. Throughout the series, Keith's humorous adventures border on the absurd.

1. Misery Guts ◆ 1991
2. Worry Warts ◆ 1991
3. Puppy Fat ◆ 1994

MISFITS, INC.

Delaney, Mark

PEACHTREE ◆ GRADES 5–9 ◆ A/R

MYSTERY

Four high school students who are outsiders band together to solve mysteries. Jake, Peter, Byte, and Mattie have individual skills that help with each mystery. In the first book, they clear a security guard and find the real thief of a powerful computer chip.

1. The Vanishing Chip ◆ 1998
2. Of Heroes and Villains ◆ 1999
3. Growler's Horn ◆ 2000
4. The Kingfisher's Tale ◆ 2000
5. The Protester's Song ◆ 2001
6. Hit and Run ◆ 2002

MISSING LINK TRILOGY

Thompson, Kate

BLOOMSBURY ◆ GRADES 6–9

SCIENCE FICTION

Danny, 15, and his stepbrother Christie, 13, are joined by a homeless girl, a talking dog, and a talking bird as they journey to Scotland. There they find Danny's mother, Maggie, and her experimental laboratory, which focuses on genetic engineering. Danny has always been different and, as the series progresses, the reader learns that he is part dolphin. The final book provides two parallel stories—one featuring diary entries from Christie describing the events leading to the end of humanity and the other taking place centuries in the future in a world that is facing a cataclysmic war.

1. Fourth World: Book One in the Missing Link Trilogy ◆ 2005
2. Only Human: Book Two in the Missing Link Trilogy ◆ 2006
3. Origins: Book Three in the Missing Link Trilogy ◆ 2007

MISSING PERSONS

Rabb, M. E.

SPEAK; PUFFIN ◆ GRADES 7–10 ◆ A/R

MYSTERY

Sophie and Sam Shattenberg are Jewish sisters from Queens, New York. Circumstances cause them to leave their home and go into hiding. They end up in Venice, Indiana, where Sophie goes to high school and Sam assists a private investigator. Their specialty is missing persons. In *The Chocolate Lover,* they help Professor Shattenberg (who may be their grandfather's missing cousin) find his missing sweetheart. These books are fast and fun and should attract reluctant readers.

1. The Rose Queen ◆ 2004
2. The Chocolate Lover ◆ 2004
3. The Venetian Policeman ◆ 2004
4. The Unsuspecting Gourmet ◆ 2004

MISTMANTLE CHRONICLES

McAllister, Margaret I.

MIRAMAX ◆ GRADES 4–7 ◆ A/R

ANIMAL FANTASY

On the island of Mistmantle, Urchin, an orphaned squirrel, has been raised by Crispin, another squirrel who serves King Brushen, a hedgehog. When the King's son is killed, Crispin is accused and banished. Urchin remains on Mistmantle, working for Padma the otter and determined to clear Crispin's name. As the series progresses, Crispin becomes King of Mistmantle while Urchin serves him as a captain. These books should appeal to fans of the Dimwood Forest books by Avi as well as the Redwall books by Brian Jacques.

1. Urchin of the Riding Stars ◆ 2005
2. Urchin and the Heartstone ◆ 2006
3. The Heir of Mistmantle ◆ 2007
4. Urchin and the Raven War ◆ 2008

MOB PRINCESS

Strasser, Todd

SIMON PULSE ◆ GRADES 9–12 ◆ A/R

REAL LIFE

Kate Blessing is a senior in high school with a great car, great clothes, and a great boyfriend. You would think she has it all. Everything begins to unravel when her mother leaves her father, a mob boss whose mistress is pregnant. Kate's boyfriend dumps her when she refuses to have sex with him. Her father is being threatened by a rival mob and Kate devises the plan to defeat them. (Her mother had been the strategist for her father's business.) Things get even more complicated when Kate becomes romantically involved with the son of the rival mobster.

1. For Money and Love ◆ 2007
2. Stolen Kisses, Secrets, and Lies ◆ 2007
3. Count Your Blessings ◆ 2007

MOESHA

Various authors

ARCHWAY ◆ GRADES 6–8

REAL LIFE

Based on the television series, these books feature Moesha Mitchell, a 15-year-old African American girl who experiences typical teen dilemmas.

Her family consists of a younger brother, father, and a new stepmother (her mother died several years ago), and there are realistic moments involving family adjustments and concerns. Moesha's friends often come to her aid with guidance and support, but they also get involved in minor scrapes and misunderstandings. With plots that are current, upbeat language, and a positive family model, this series provides solid reading that will be of special interest to girls.

1. Everybody Say Moesha! (Scott, Stefanie) ◆ 1997
2. Keeping It Real (Scott, Stefanie) ◆ 1997
3. Trippin' Out (Scott, Stefanie) ◆ 1997
4. Hollywood Hook-Up (Scott, Stefanie) ◆ 1998
5. What's Up, Brother? (Reed, Teresa) ◆ 1998
6. House Party! (Scott, Stefanie) ◆ 1998

MOLLY

Chaikin, Miriam
HARPERCOLLINS ◆ GRADES 4–7 ◆ A/R
FAMILY LIFE | HISTORICAL | REAL LIFE

A Jewish immigrant family living in Brooklyn during World War II struggles with staying true to its roots while at the same time becoming more American. Molly has an older brother, Joey; a younger sister, Rebecca; and Yaaki, the beautiful baby brother whom everyone adores. Molly's best friend is Tsippi, but she has other friends at school with whom she quarrels and makes up in typical schoolgirl fashion. One of them asks her to go to a restaurant that is not kosher, and she sneaks out and goes, only to get sick. As she talks to God about this (from a special window she reserves for this purpose), she realizes she was wrong. The series follows her to her upper elementary years, when many of her friends get their periods, causing her to feel left behind. Details of Jewish life are woven into all the books.

1. I Should Worry, I Should Care ◆ 1979
2. Finders Weepers ◆ 1980
3. Getting Even ◆ 1982
4. Lower! Higher! You're a Liar! ◆ 1984
5. Friends Forever ◆ 1988

MONTMORENCY

Updale, Eleanor
SCHOLASTIC/ORCHARD ◆ GRADES 7–10
HISTORICAL | MYSTERY

In Victorian London, a successful thief exploits his knowledge of the city and its residents, adopting two Jekyll-and-Hyde-style personas—that of a respectable gentleman named Montmorency and that of his corrupt servant Scarper. Montmorency becomes a government investigator and by the third book has shed his alter ego and is seeking revenge for the murder of his friend George Fox-Selwyn.

1. Montmorency: Thief, Liar, Gentleman? ◆ 2003
2. Montmorency on the Rocks: Doctor, Aristocrat, Murderer? ◆ 2004
3. Montmorency and the Assassins ◆ 2006
4. Montmorency's Revenge ◆ 2007

MOONDOG

Garfield, Henry

ST. MARTIN'S ◆ GRADES 10–12 ◆ A/R

HORROR

Three women . . . three dead bodies. The gruesome discoveries bring fear to the isolated town of Julian, California. Cyrus "Moondog" Nygerski thinks the murders may be connected. Each occurred during a full moon. Moondog believes there are supernatural elements at work, and he should know because he is a werewolf. The third book takes place in Boston during the 1967 pennant race by the Red Sox, which may attract sports fans to this series.

1. Moondog ◆ 1995
2. Room 13 ◆ 1997
3. Tartabull's Throw ◆ 2001

MRS. MURPHY

Brown, Rita Mae

BANTAM ◆ GRADES 10–12 ◆ A/R

MYSTERY

Mary Minor ("Harry") Haristeen is postmaster in a small southern town in these books coauthored by Brown and her cat, Sneaky Pie. With her sidekicks—Mrs. Murphy the cat and Welsh corgi Tee Tucker, both of whom converse and comment on human behavior in italics—Harry investigates and solves many mysteries. These range from dead bodies to computer viruses.

1. Wish You Were Here ◆ 1990
2. Rest in Pieces ◆ 1992
3. Murder at Monticello ◆ 1994
4. Pay Dirt ◆ 1995
5. Murder, She Meowed ◆ 1996

6. Murder on the Prowl ◆ 1998
7. Cat on the Scent ◆ 1999
8. Pawing Through the Past ◆ 2000
9. Claws and Effect ◆ 2001
10. Catch as Cat Can ◆ 2002
11. Tail of the Tip-off ◆ 2003
12. Whisker of Evil ◆ 2004
13. Cat's Eyewitness ◆ 2005
14. Sour Puss ◆ 2006
15. Puss 'n Cahoots ◆ 2007
16. The Purrfect Murder ◆ 2008

MUMMY CHRONICLES

Wolverton, Dave
SKYLARK ◆ GRADES 4–7 ◆ A/R
FANTASY

Alex O'Connell, 12, wants to be a Medjai—one who works against the forces of darkness. It is 1937 and Alex is in Egypt. He discovers that his amulet gives him special powers. Alex battles mummies and faces a special test. In the spirit of Young Indiana Jones, Alex rescues the world from evil powers.

1. Revenge of the Scorpion King ◆ 2001
2. Heart of the Pharaoh ◆ 2001
3. The Curse of the Nile ◆ 2001
4. Flight of the Phoenix ◆ 2001

MUSTANG MOUNTAIN

Siamon, Sharon
WALRUS BOOKS ◆ GRADES 5–8 ◆ A/R
REAL LIFE | ADVENTURE

Three girls, Meg, Alison, and Becky, face adventure and danger in the Rocky Mountains at Mustang Mountain Ranch. In *Sky Horse,* Meg and Alison come to visit the ranch and they are met by Becky and Jesse, the driver. On their trip from the airport to the ranch, they are caught in a snowstorm. Meg and Becky take the horses from the trailer they have been towing and search for help. Instead, they find a plane that has crashed. In *Night Horse,* the girls spend the night in the Rockies protecting a stallion from bounty hunters. Fans of horse books like Saddle Club and Thoroughbred will enjoy these books.

1. Sky Horse ◆ 2001
2. Fire Horse ◆ 2002

   3. Night Horse ◆ 2002
   4. Wild Horse ◆ 2003
   5. Rodeo Horse ◆ 2003
   6. Brave Horse ◆ 2004
   7. Free Horse ◆ 2004
   8. Swift Horse ◆ 2005
   9. Dark Horse ◆ 2005
   10. Stone Horse ◆ 2006

MY SIDE OF THE MOUNTAIN

George, Jean Craighead
DUTTON ◆ GRADES 4–8 ◆ A/R
REAL LIFE

Sam Gribley leaves his home in the city to spend a year in the Catskill Mountains. He survives and develops a relationship with a falcon he names Frightful. The third book is presented from Frightful's point of view. The fourth book is a picture book that focuses on Oksi, Frightful's daughter, as she grows from a hatchling to a young falcon. *My Side of the Mountain* was a Newbery Honor book.

   1. My Side of the Mountain ◆ 1959
   2. On the Far Side of the Mountain ◆ 1990
   3. Frightful's Mountain ◆ 1999
   4. Frightful's Daughter ◆ 2002

MY SIDE OF THE STORY

Various authors
KINGFISHER ◆ GRADES 4–8 ◆ A/R
HISTORICAL

Two perspectives of the same event are presented in this historical fiction series. In *The Brothers' War,* a family's loyalties are divided as Melody's family supports the Union while her cousin's family is siding with the Confederacy. In another book, Lizzy works in the mill where conditions are deplorable. Her childhood friendship with Josh, the mill owner's son, is threatened when she joins with fellow workers in a protest.

   1. The Brothers' War (Hermes, Patricia) ◆ 2005
   2. Escape from War (Riordan, James) ◆ 2005
   3. Journey to Jamestown (Ruby, Lois) ◆ 2005
   4. Trouble at the Mill (Wooderson, Philip) ◆ 2005
   5. The Plague (Wooderson, Philip) ◆ 2006
   6. Salem Witch (Hermes, Patricia) ◆ 2006

MY SISTER THE VAMPIRE

Mercer, Sienna

HarperCollins ◆ Grades 5–8 ◆ A/R

Fantasy

When Ivy and Olivia meet at Franklin Grove Middle School they discover they are twins who were separated at birth. They have very *very* different personalities—Olivia is an outgoing cheerleader while Ivy is a vampire. This series is not about blood lust and gore, instead it deals with tween concerns including friendship, identity, and dating.

1. Switched ◆ 2007
2. Fangtastic! ◆ 2007
3. Re-Vamped! ◆ 2007
4. Vampalicious! ◆ 2008

MYSTERIES IN OUR NATIONAL PARKS

Skurzynski, Gloria, and Alane Ferguson

National Geographic ◆ Grades 5–8 ◆ A/R

Adventure | Mystery

Jack, 12, and his younger sister, Ashley, travel with their parents to national parks. On these trips, they encounter mysteries that they try to solve. At Yellowstone, a pack of wolves may have killed a hunting dog. Jack and Ashley find out what is really happening. At Carlsbad Caverns National Park, Jack and Ashley search for a lost boy and become lost in the caverns. This series written by popular author Skurzynski and her daughter offers fast-paced adventure and brief information about each park.

1. Wolf Stalker: A Mystery in Yellowstone National Park ◆ 2001
2. Rage of Fire ◆ 2001
3. Cliff Hanger: A Mystery in Mesa Verde National Park ◆ 2001
4. Deadly Waters: A Mystery in Glacier National Park ◆ 2001
5. The Hunted: A Mystery in Virgin Islands National Park ◆ 2001
6. Ghost Horses: A Mystery in Zion National Park ◆ 2002
7. Over the Edge: A Mystery in Grand Canyon National Park ◆ 2002
8. Valley of Death: A Mystery in Death Valley National Park ◆ 2002
9. Escape from Fear: A Mystery in Virgin Islands National Park ◆ 2002
10. Out of the Deep: A Mystery in Acadia National Park ◆ 2002
11. Running Scared: A Mystery in Carlsbad Caverns National Park ◆ 2002
12. Buried Alive: A Mystery in Denali National Park ◆ 2003
13. Night of the Black Bear: A Mystery in Great Smoky Mountains National Park ◆ 2007

MYSTIC KNIGHTS OF TIR NA NOG

Various authors

HARPERCOLLINS ◆ **GRADES 5–8**

FANTASY

Ivan, Rohan, Deirdre, and Angus confront many dangers, including dragons and other creatures. They battle the forces of the evil queen Maeve and hope to earn their armor. The stories include references to Celtic heroes and legends. A television program featured these characters.

1. The Legend of the Ancient Scroll (Teitelbaum, Michael) ◆ 1999
2. Fire Within, Air Above! (Simpson, Robert) ◆ 1999
3. Water Around, Earth Below! (Brightfield, Richard) ◆ 1999
4. The Taming of the Pyre (Whitman, John) ◆ 1999
5. Dragata Revealed! (Teitelbaum, Michael) ◆ 1999

MYTH ADVENTURES

Asprin, Robert

ACE ◆ **GRADES 5–8** ◆ **A/R**

FANTASY

Skeeve, a magician's apprentice, begins a series of adventures. He jumps to different dimensions and confronts characters such as the evil wizard Isstvan. Skeeve and his companions, Aahz and Tanada, have humorous, fast-paced encounters with many strange creatures. There have been a variety of editions and reissues of this series.

1. Another Fine Myth ◆ 1985
2. Myth Conceptions ◆ 1985
3. Myth Directions ◆ 1985
4. Hit or Myth ◆ 1985
5. Myth-ing Persons ◆ 1986
6. Little Myth Marker ◆ 1986
7. M.Y.T.H. Inc. Link ◆ 1986
8. Myth-Nomers and Im-Pervections ◆ 1990
9. M.Y.T.H. Inc. in Action ◆ 1990
10. Sweet Myth-tery of Life ◆ 2000
11. Something M.Y.T.H. Inc. ◆ 2002
12. Myth-ion Improbable ◆ 2002
13. Myth-told Tales ◆ 2003
14. Myth Alliances ◆ 2003
15. Myth-taken Identity ◆ 2004

MYTH-O-MANIA

McMullan, Kate
HYPERION/VOLO ◆ GRADES 4–7 ◆ A/R

FANTASY | HUMOR

Everyone thinks they know the real Greek myths, but they are wrong. Hades, King of the Underworld, tells his side of the stories here. Like the one about Hercules. Do you really think he did the "XII Labors" by himself? No way! This series takes a creative look at some of the best-known stories.

1. Have a Hot Time, Hades! ◆ 2002
2. Phone Home, Persephone! ◆ 2002
3. Say Cheese, Medusa! ◆ 2002
4. Nice Shot, Cupid ◆ 2002
5. Stop that Bull, Theseus! ◆ 2003
6. Keep a Lid on It, Pandora! ◆ 2003
7. Get to Work, Hercules! ◆ 2003
8. Go for the Gold, Atalanta! ◆ 2003

MYTHIC MISADVENTURES

Hennesy, Carolyn
BLOOMSBURY ◆ GRADES 5–8

FANTASY

Building on the story of "Pandora's Box," this series features Pandora as a 13-year-old girl. Pandy finds a box that is supposed to be filled with ancient evils, so she takes it to school for her school project. She is not planning to open the box; however, the box gets opened and the evils are released. Zeus and Hera are not pleased. Pandy is given a year to collect all the evils. Along with her BFFs Alcie and Iole, she begins the search.

1. Pandora Gets Jealous ◆ 2007
2. Pandora Gets Vain ◆ 2008
3. Pandora Gets Lazy ◆ 2009

MYTHQUEST

Various authors
BANTAM BOOKS ◆ GRADES 4–8

FANTASY

In *The Minotaur,* Alex and Cleo Bellows want to find their father, an archaeologist whose computer research into ancient times opened a portal into the world of ancient myths. Alex is transported to ancient Crete where he faces the Minotaur. As the series continues, the teens travel to other myths. These novelizations were based on a PBS series.

1. The Minotaur ◆ 2002
2. Hammer of the Gods ◆ 2003
3. Red Wolf's Daughter ◆ 2003
4. Minokichi ◆ 2003

NADIA SANTOS *see* Alexander Cold and Nadia Santos

THE NAMED *see* Ratha Quartet

NANCY DREW

Keene, Carolyn

SIMON & SCHUSTER ◆ GRADES 4–7 ◆ A/R

MYSTERY

Nancy Drew is a teenage detective who solves crimes while her friends George and Bess tag along. In one book, Bess is working for a wedding consultant based in an old mansion on the outskirts of River Heights. During a busy week in June, she asks George and Nancy to help out. As the first wedding begins, it seems that someone is trying to sabotage it. Nancy suspects a cousin of the bride; but when a second wedding is sabotaged, suspicion shifts to the sister of the wedding manager. The history of the old house eventually helps to solve the mystery. Throughout the series, Nancy is thorough, methodical, and undistracted. Bess and George provide contrast, Bess being a food-loving flirt and George serious and athletic.

1. The Secret of the Old Clock ◆ 1930
2. The Hidden Staircase ◆ 1930
3. The Bungalow Mystery ◆ 1930
4. The Mystery at Lilac Inn ◆ 1930
5. The Secret of Shadow Ranch ◆ 1930
6. The Secret of Red Gate Farm ◆ 1931
7. The Clue in the Diary ◆ 1932
8. Nancy's Mysterious Letter ◆ 1932
9. The Sign of the Twisted Candles ◆ 1933
10. The Password to Larkspur Lane ◆ 1933
11. The Clue of the Broken Locket ◆ 1934
12. The Message in the Hollow Oak ◆ 1935
13. The Mystery of the Ivory Charm ◆ 1936

14. The Whispering Statue ◆ 1937
15. The Haunted Bridge ◆ 1937
16. The Clue of the Tapping Heels ◆ 1939
17. The Mystery of the Brass-Bound Trunk ◆ 1940
18. The Mystery of the Moss-Covered Mansion ◆ 1941
19. The Quest of the Missing Map ◆ 1942
20. The Clue in the Jewel Box ◆ 1943
21. The Secret in the Old Attic ◆ 1944
22. The Clue in the Crumbling Wall ◆ 1945
23. The Mystery of the Tolling Bell ◆ 1946
24. The Clue in the Old Album ◆ 1947
25. The Ghost of Blackwood Hall ◆ 1948
26. The Clue of the Leaning Chimney ◆ 1949
27. The Secret of the Wooden Lady ◆ 1950
28. The Clue of the Black Keys ◆ 1951
29. The Mystery at the Ski Jump ◆ 1952
30. The Clue of the Velvet Mask ◆ 1953
31. The Ringmaster's Secret ◆ 1953
32. The Scarlet Slipper Mystery ◆ 1954
33. The Witch Tree Symbol ◆ 1955
34. The Hidden Window Mystery ◆ 1957
35. The Haunted Showboat ◆ 1957
36. The Secret of the Golden Pavilion ◆ 1959
37. The Clue in the Old Stagecoach ◆ 1960
38. The Mystery of the Fire Dragon ◆ 1961
39. The Clue of the Dancing Puppet ◆ 1962
40. The Moonstone Castle Mystery ◆ 1963
41. The Clue of the Whistling Bagpipes ◆ 1964
42. The Phantom of Pine Hill ◆ 1965
43. The Mystery of the 99 Steps ◆ 1966
44. The Clue in the Crossword Cypher ◆ 1967
45. The Spider Sapphire Mystery ◆ 1968
46. The Invisible Intruder ◆ 1969
47. The Mysterious Mannequin ◆ 1970
48. The Crooked Bannister ◆ 1971
49. The Secret of Mirror Bay ◆ 1972
50. The Double Jinx Mystery ◆ 1974
51. The Mystery of the Glowing Eye ◆ 1974
52. The Secret of the Forgotten City ◆ 1975
53. The Sky Phantom ◆ 1976
54. Strange Message in the Parchment ◆ 1977
55. Mystery of Crocodile Island ◆ 1978
56. The Thirteenth Pearl ◆ 1979
57. Triple Hoax ◆ 1979
58. The Flying Saucer Mystery ◆ 1980
59. The Secret in the Old Lace ◆ 1980
60. The Greek Symbol Mystery ◆ 1981
61. The Swami's Ring ◆ 1981
62. The Kachina Doll Mystery ◆ 1981

63. The Twin Dilemma ◆ 1981
64. Captive Witness ◆ 1981
65. Mystery of the Winged Lion ◆ 1982
66. Race Against Time ◆ 1982
67. The Sinister Omen ◆ 1982
68. The Elusive Heiress ◆ 1982
69. Clue in the Ancient Disguise ◆ 1982
70. The Broken Anchor ◆ 1983
71. The Silver Cobweb ◆ 1983
72. The Haunted Carousel ◆ 1983
73. Enemy Match ◆ 1984
74. The Mysterious Image ◆ 1984
75. The Emerald-Eyed Cat ◆ 1984
76. The Eskimo's Secret ◆ 1985
77. The Bluebeard Room ◆ 1985
78. The Phantom of Venice ◆ 1985
79. The Double Horror of Fenley Place ◆ 1987
80. The Case of the Disappearing Diamonds ◆ 1987
81. Mardi Gras Mystery ◆ 1988
82. The Clue in the Camera ◆ 1988
83. The Case of the Vanishing Veil ◆ 1988
84. The Joker's Revenge ◆ 1988
85. The Secret of Shady Glen ◆ 1988
86. The Mystery of Misty Canyon ◆ 1988
87. The Case of the Rising Stars ◆ 1988
88. The Search for Cindy Austin ◆ 1988
89. The Case of the Disappearing Deejay ◆ 1989
90. The Puzzle at Pineview School ◆ 1989
91. The Girl Who Couldn't Remember ◆ 1989
92. The Ghost of Craven Cove ◆ 1989
93. The Case of the Safecracker's Secret ◆ 1990
94. The Picture-Perfect Mystery ◆ 1990
95. The Silent Suspect ◆ 1990
96. The Case of the Photo Finish ◆ 1990
97. The Mystery at Magnolia Mansion ◆ 1990
98. The Haunting of Horse Island ◆ 1990
99. The Secret at Seven Rocks ◆ 1991
100. The Secret in Time: Nancy Drew's 100th Anniversary Edition ◆ 1991
101. The Mystery of the Missing Millionaires ◆ 1991
102. The Secret in the Dark ◆ 1991
103. The Stranger in the Shadows ◆ 1991
104. The Mystery of the Jade Tiger ◆ 1991
105. The Clue in the Antique Trunk ◆ 1992
106. The Case of the Artful Crime ◆ 1992
107. The Legend of Miner's Creek ◆ 1992
108. The Secret of the Tibetan Treasure ◆ 1992
109. The Mystery of the Masked Rider ◆ 1992
110. The Nutcracker Ballet Mystery ◆ 1992
111. The Secret at Solitaire ◆ 1993

112. Crime in the Queen's Court ◆ 1993
113. The Secret Lost at Sea ◆ 1993
114. The Search for the Silver Persian ◆ 1993
115. The Suspect in the Smoke ◆ 1993
116. The Case of the Twin Teddy Bears ◆ 1993
117. Mystery on the Menu ◆ 1993
118. Trouble at Lake Tahoe ◆ 1994
119. The Mystery of the Missing Mascot ◆ 1994
120. The Case of the Floating Crime ◆ 1994
121. The Fortune-Teller's Secret ◆ 1994
122. The Message in the Haunted Mansion ◆ 1994
123. The Clue on the Silver Screen ◆ 1995
124. The Secret of the Scarlet Hand ◆ 1995
125. The Teen Model Mystery ◆ 1995
126. The Riddle in the Rare Book ◆ 1995
127. The Case of the Dangerous Solution ◆ 1995
128. The Treasure in the Royal Tower ◆ 1995
129. The Baby-Sitter Burglaries ◆ 1996
130. The Sign of the Falcon ◆ 1996
131. The Hidden Inheritance ◆ 1996
132. The Fox Hunt Mystery ◆ 1996
133. The Mystery at the Crystal Palace ◆ 1996
134. The Secret of the Forgotten Cave ◆ 1996
135. The Riddle of the Ruby Gazelle ◆ 1997
136. The Wedding Day Mystery ◆ 1997
137. In Search of the Black Rose ◆ 1997
138. Legend of the Lost Gold ◆ 1997
139. The Secret of Candlelight Inn ◆ 1997
140. The Door-to-Door Deception ◆ 1997
141. The Wild Cat Crime ◆ 1997
142. The Case of Capital Intrigue ◆ 1998
143. Mystery on Maui ◆ 1998
144. The E-Mail Mystery ◆ 1998
145. The Missing Horse Mystery ◆ 1998
146. The Ghost of the Lantern Lady ◆ 1998
147. The Case of the Captured Queen ◆ 1998
148. On the Trail of Trouble ◆ 1999
149. The Clue of the Gold Doubloons ◆ 1999
150. Mystery at Moorsea Manor ◆ 1999
151. The Chocolate-Covered Contest ◆ 1999
152. The Key in the Satin Pocket ◆ 1999
153. Whispers in the Fog ◆ 2000
154. The Legend of the Emerald Lady ◆ 2000
155. The Mystery in Tornado Alley ◆ 2000
156. The Secret in the Stars ◆ 2000
157. The Music Festival Mystery ◆ 2000
158. The Curse of the Black Cat ◆ 2001
159. The Secret of the Fiery Chamber ◆ 2001
160. The Clue on the Crystal Dove ◆ 2001

161. Lost in the Everglades ◆ 2001
162. The Case of the Lost Song ◆ 2001
163. The Clues Challenge ◆ 2001
164. The Mystery of the Mother Wolf ◆ 2002
165. The Crime Lab Case ◆ 2002
166. The Case of the Creative Crime ◆ 2002
167. Mystery By Moonlight ◆ 2002
168. The Bike Tour Mystery ◆ 2002
169. The Mistletoe Mystery ◆ 2002
170. No Strings Attached ◆ 2002
171. Intrigue at the Grand Opera ◆ 2003
172. The Riding Club Crime ◆ 2003
173. Danger on the Great Lakes ◆ 2003
174. A Taste of Danger ◆ 2003
175. Werewolf in a Winter Wonderland ◆ 2003

NANCY DREW: GIRL DETECTIVE

Keene, Carolyn

SIMON & SCHUSTER ◆ GRADES 4–7 ◆ A/R

MYSTERY

This updated series puts Nancy into more contemporary situations. She finds the money that is missing from the Bucks for Charity race. She is chosen to appear in a film and then ends the sabotage that is plaguing the production.

1. Without a Trace ◆ 2004
2. A Race Against Time ◆ 2004
3. False Notes ◆ 2004
4. High Risk ◆ 2004
5. Lights, Camera . . . ◆ 2004
6. Action! ◆ 2004
7. The Stolen Relic ◆ 2004
8. The Scarlet Macaw Scandal ◆ 2004
9. Secret of the Spa ◆ 2005
10. Uncivil Acts ◆ 2005
11. Riverboat Ruse ◆ 2005
12. Stop the Clock ◆ 2005
13. Trade Wind Danger ◆ 2005
14. Bad Times, Big Crimes ◆ 2005
15. Framed ◆ 2005
16. Dangerous Plays ◆ 2006
17. En Garde ◆ 2006
18. Pit of Vipers ◆ 2006
19. The Orchid Thief ◆ 2006
20. Getting Burned ◆ 2006
21. Close Encounters ◆ 2006

22. Dressed to Steal ◆ 2007
23. Troubled Waters ◆ 2007
24. Murder on the Set ◆ 2007
25. Trails of Treachery ◆ 2007
26. Fishing for Clues ◆ 2007
27. Intruder ◆ 2007
28. Mardi Gras Masquerade ◆ 2008
29. The Stolen Bones ◆ 2008
30. Pageant Perfect Crime ◆ 2008
31. Perfect Cover ◆ 2008
32. Perfect Escape ◆ 2008
33. Secret Identity ◆ 2008

NANCY DREW: GIRL DETECTIVE SUPER MYSTERIES

1. Where's Nancy ◆ 2005
2. Once Upon a Crime ◆ 2006
3. Real Fake ◆ 2007

NANCY DREW AND THE HARDY BOYS SUPER MYSTERIES

Keene, Carolyn

SIMON & SCHUSTER ◆ GRADES 7–9 ◆ A/R

MYSTERY

Nancy teams up with Frank and Joe Hardy for mysteries. In one book, they investigate sabotage directed at the site of the Winter Olympics in Salt Lake City.

1. Dangerous Games ◆ 1989
2. Shock Waves ◆ 1989
3. Buried in Time ◆ 1990
4. Last Resort ◆ 1990
5. Mystery Train ◆ 1990
6. Paris Connection ◆ 1990
7. Best of Enemies ◆ 1991
8. A Crime for Christmas ◆ 1991
9. Double Crossing ◆ 1991
10. High Survival ◆ 1991
11. New Year's Evil ◆ 1991
12. Spies and Lies ◆ 1992
13. Tour of Danger ◆ 1992
14. Tropic of Fear ◆ 1992
15. Courting Disaster ◆ 1993
16. Evil in Amsterdam ◆ 1993
17. Hits and Misses ◆ 1993
18. Copper Canyon Conspiracy ◆ 1994
19. Desperate Measures ◆ 1994

20. Hollywood Horror ◆ 1994
21. Passport to Danger ◆ 1994
22. Danger Down Under ◆ 1995
23. Dead on Arrival ◆ 1995
24. Secrets of the Nile ◆ 1995
25. Target for Terror ◆ 1995
26. High Stakes ◆ 1996
27. Islands of Intrigue ◆ 1996
28. Murder on the Fourth of July ◆ 1996
29. A Question of Guilt ◆ 1996
30. At All Costs ◆ 1997
31. Exhibition of Evil ◆ 1997
32. Nightmare in New Orleans ◆ 1997
33. Out of Control ◆ 1997
34. Royal Revenge ◆ 1997
35. Operation: Titanic ◆ 1998
36. Process of Elimination ◆ 1998

NANCY DREW FILES

Keene, Carolyn

ARCHWAY ◆ GRADES 6–9 ◆ A/R

MYSTERY

In the Nancy Drew Files, geared more for older readers, Nancy remains the same gutsy, smart, accomplished sleuth she has always been. In this series, Nancy goes undercover at a high school, solves a rock 'n' roll mystery and travels to exotic places, such as a ski resort or Ft. Lauderdale during spring break. A new character in this series is Brenda Carlton, an aspiring investigative reporter who thinks she can outsmart Nancy, and has the habit of messing up her investigations.

1. Secrets Can Kill ◆ 1986
2. Deadly Intent ◆ 1986
3. Murder on Ice ◆ 1986
4. Smile and Say Murder ◆ 1986
5. Hit and Run Holiday ◆ 1986
6. White Water Terror ◆ 1987
7. Deadly Doubles ◆ 1987
8. Two Points for Murder ◆ 1987
9. False Moves ◆ 1987
10. Buried Secrets ◆ 1987
11. Heart of Danger ◆ 1987
12. Fatal Ransom ◆ 1987
13. Wings of Fear ◆ 1987
14. This Side of Evil ◆ 1987
15. Trial by Fire ◆ 1987
16. Never Say Die ◆ 1987

17. Stay Tuned for Danger ◆ 1987
18. Circle of Evil ◆ 1987
19. Sisters in Crime ◆ 1988
20. Very Deadly Yours ◆ 1988
21. Recipe for Murder ◆ 1988
22. Fatal Attraction ◆ 1988
23. Sinister Parade ◆ 1988
24. Till Death Do Us Part ◆ 1988
25. Rich and Dangerous ◆ 1988
26. Playing with Fire ◆ 1988
27. Most Likely to Die ◆ 1988
28. The Black Widow ◆ 1988
29. Pure Poison ◆ 1988
30. Death by Design ◆ 1988
31. Trouble in Tahiti ◆ 1989
32. High Marks for Malice ◆ 1989
33. Danger in Disguise ◆ 1989
34. Vanishing Act ◆ 1989
35. Bad Medicine ◆ 1989
36. Over the Edge ◆ 1989
37. Last Dance ◆ 1989
38. The Final Scene ◆ 1989
39. The Suspect Next Door ◆ 1989
40. Shadow of a Doubt ◆ 1989
41. Something to Hide ◆ 1989
42. The Wrong Chemistry ◆ 1989
43. False Impressions ◆ 1990
44. Scent of Danger ◆ 1990
45. Out of Bounds ◆ 1990
46. Win, Place, or Die ◆ 1990
47. Flirting with Danger ◆ 1990
48. A Date with Deception ◆ 1990
49. Portrait in Crime ◆ 1990
50. Deep Secrets ◆ 1990
51. A Model Crime ◆ 1990
52. Danger for Hire ◆ 1990
53. Trail of Lies ◆ 1990
54. Cold as Ice ◆ 1990
55. Don't Look Twice ◆ 1991
56. Make No Mistake ◆ 1991
57. Into Thin Air ◆ 1991
58. Hot Pursuit ◆ 1991
59. High Risk ◆ 1991
60. Poison Pen ◆ 1991
61. Sweet Revenge ◆ 1991
62. Easy Marks ◆ 1991
63. Mixed Signals ◆ 1991
64. The Wrong Track ◆ 1991
65. Final Notes ◆ 1991

66. Tall, Dark, and Deadly ◆ 1991
67. Nobody's Business ◆ 1992
68. Crosscurrents ◆ 1992
69. Running Scared ◆ 1992
70. Cutting Edge ◆ 1992
71. Hot Tracks ◆ 1992
72. Swiss Secrets ◆ 1992
73. Rendezvous in Rome ◆ 1992
74. Greek Odyssey ◆ 1992
75. A Talent for Murder ◆ 1992
76. The Perfect Plot ◆ 1992
77. Danger on Parade ◆ 1992
78. Update in Crime ◆ 1992
79. No Laughing Matter ◆ 1993
80. Power of Suggestion ◆ 1993
81. Making Waves ◆ 1993
82. Dangerous Relations ◆ 1993
83. Diamond Deceit ◆ 1993
84. Choosing Sides ◆ 1993
85. Sea of Suspicion ◆ 1993
86. Let's Talk Terror ◆ 1993
87. Moving Target ◆ 1993
88. False Pretenses ◆ 1993
89. Designs in Crime ◆ 1993
90. Stage Fright ◆ 1993
91. If Looks Could Kill ◆ 1994
92. My Deadly Valentine ◆ 1994
93. Hotline to Danger ◆ 1994
94. Illusions of Evil ◆ 1994
95. An Instinct for Trouble ◆ 1994
96. The Runaway Bride ◆ 1994
97. Squeeze Play ◆ 1994
98. Island of Secrets ◆ 1994
99. The Cheating Heart ◆ 1994
100. Dance Till You Die ◆ 1994
101. The Picture of Guilt ◆ 1994
102. Counterfeit Christmas ◆ 1994
103. Heart of Ice ◆ 1995
104. Kiss and Tell ◆ 1995
105. Stolen Affections ◆ 1995
106. Flying Too High ◆ 1995
107. Anything for Love ◆ 1995
108. Captive Heart ◆ 1995
109. Love Notes ◆ 1995
110. Hidden Meanings ◆ 1995
111. The Stolen Kiss ◆ 1995
112. For Love or Money ◆ 1995
113. Wicked Ways ◆ 1996

114. Rehearsing for Romance ◆ 1996
115. Running into Trouble ◆ 1996
116. Under His Spell ◆ 1996
117. Skipping a Beat ◆ 1996
118. Betrayed By Love ◆ 1996
119. Against the Rules ◆ 1997
120. Dangerous Loves ◆ 1997
121. Natural Enemies ◆ 1997
122. Strange Memories ◆ 1997
123. Wicked for the Weekend ◆ 1997
124. Crime at the Ch@t Cafe ◆ 1997

NANCY DREW GRAPHIC NOVELS

Petrucha, Stefan
PAPERCUTZ ◆ GRADES 4–8 ◆ A/R
MYSTERY

Nancy and her friends face all-new mysteries in this graphic novel series from Papercutz. Mysterious strangers, evil plots, kidnapping, theft, and more—all solved by our intrepid sleuth. The illustrations have a manga feel with bold lines, sharp angles, and emphasized eyes. Reluctant readers will be attracted to these books.

1. The Demon of River Heights ◆ 2005
2. Writ in Stone ◆ 2005
3. The Haunted Dollhouse ◆ 2005
4. The Girl Who Wasn't There ◆ 2006
5. The Fake Heir ◆ 2006
6. Mr. Cheeters Is Missing ◆ 2006
7. The Charmed Bracelet ◆ 2006
8. Global Warning ◆ 2007
9. Ghost in the Machinery ◆ 2007
10. The Disoriented Express ◆ 2007
11. Monkey-Wrench Blues ◆ 2007
12. Dress Reversal ◆ 2008
13. Doggone Town ◆ 2008
14. Sleight of Dan ◆ 2008
15. Tiger Counter ◆ 2008
16. What Goes Up . . . ◆ 2008

NANCY DREW ON CAMPUS

Keene, Carolyn
SIMON & SCHUSTER ◆ GRADES 7–10
MYSTERY

Nancy is attending Wilder University. She lives in a co-ed dorm and still solves mysteries. She finds out why a fraternity prank went out of control. And investigates the mysterious death of a photographer. Nancy's job as the co-host of a campus television show keeps her right in the thick of things.

1. New Lives, New Loves ◆ 1995
2. On Her Own ◆ 1995
3. Don't Look Back ◆ 1995
4. Tell Me the Truth ◆ 1995
5. Secret Rules ◆ 1996
6. It's Your Move ◆ 1996
7. False Friends ◆ 1996
8. Getting Closer ◆ 1996
9. Broken Promises ◆ 1996
10. Party Weekend ◆ 1996
11. In the Name of Love ◆ 1996
12. Just the Two of Us ◆ 1996
13. Campus Exposures ◆ 1996
14. Hard to Get ◆ 1996
15. Loving and Losing ◆ 1996
16. Going Home ◆ 1996
17. New Beginnings ◆ 1997
18. Keeping Secrets ◆ 1997
19. Love On-Line ◆ 1997
20. Jealous Feelings ◆ 1997
21. Love and Betrayal ◆ 1997
22. In and Out of Love ◆ 1997
23. Otherwise Engaged ◆ 1997
24. In the Spotlight ◆ 1997
25. Snowbound ◆ 1998

NANNIES

Mayer, Melody

DELACORTE ◆ GRADES 9–12 ◆ A/R

REAL LIFE

In California, three teen girls work as nannies and, while their charges are busy with activities, the girls get to know each other and share secrets. Kiley is on a reality television show hoping to be chosen as the nanny for Platinum, a rock star. Lydia is working as a nanny for her aunt, while Esme, who speaks Spanish, is working with a wealthy family's adopted twins from Colombia. Dating, drinking, drugs, relationships, sex, money, and other teen issues are woven into these books. The Au Pairs series is a natural choice for readers who liked the Nannies.

1. The Nannies ◆ 2005
2. Friends with Benefits ◆ 2006

3. Have to Have It ◆ 2006
4. Tainted Love ◆ 2007
5. All Night Long ◆ 2008
6. Bad to the Bone ◆ 2009

NASCAR POLE POSITION ADVENTURES

Calhoun, T. B.

HARPERCOLLINS ◆ GRADES 5–8

REAL LIFE | RECREATION

This series should appeal to stock-car racing enthusiasts. Kin Travis is 15. Along with his sister Laura and his brother Laptop, Kin is involved in adventures involving cars, mysteries, and high-speed action. Throughout the books, there is information about stock cars and NASCAR racing events. The Travis kids are helped by their grandfather, Hotshoe Hunter, a famous stock-car racer. His knowledge about racing and his connections with other racers give Kin and his siblings an up-close look at these exciting events.

1. Rolling Thunder ◆ 1998
2. In the Groove ◆ 1998
3. Race Ready ◆ 1998
4. Speed Demon ◆ 1999
5. Spinout ◆ 1999
6. Hammer Down ◆ 1999

NATIONAL PARKS MYSTERY *see* Mysteries in Our National Parks

THE NAVIGATOR TRILOGY

McNamee, Eoin

RANDOM HOUSE ◆ GRADES 6–10 ◆ A/R

FANTASY

Teenager Owen enters a time vortex where time runs backward. The world he knows is gone as The Harsh, an ancient enemy of ice people, seek to destroy all humans. Owen realizes that he is the Navigator, chosen to save the world. Aided by Cati and other Resisters, Owen begins his fight against The Harsh.

1. The Navigator ◆ 2006
2. City of Time ◆ 2008
3. The Frost Child ◆ 2009

NEOTOPIA

Espinosa, Rod

ANTARCTIC PRESS ◆ GRADES 6–12

FANTASY

In the opening volume of this graphic novel series, Nalyn, a servant girl, takes over her spoiled mistress's responsibilities as grand duchess of Mathenia, but the going gets tough when the peaceful nation of Mathenia comes under attack from the evil empire of Krossos. Nalyn takes on the role of leader and proves her worth in the ensuing conflicts. The lush illustrations of the environmentally Mathenia will draw readers into this exciting story.

1. Neotopia: The Enlightened Age (Neotopia Color Manga No. 1) ◆ 2004
2. Neotopia: The Perilous Winds of Athanon (Neotopia Color Manga No. 2) ◆ 2004
3. Neotopia: The Kingdoms Beyond (Neotopia Color Manga No. 3) ◆ 2005

NEPTUNE ADVENTURES

Saunders, Susan

AVON ◆ GRADES 4–7

ADVENTURE | REAL LIFE

Dana Chapin and her cousin Tyler participate in Project Neptune, a resource designed to protect sea life from environmental threats. They also deal with the behavior of people whose greed or lack of knowledge puts sea creatures at risk. The two cousins help clean up after an oil spill; they come to the aid of a school of pilot whales; they protect a dolphin that has been released into the ocean. This series will appeal to readers who like to see characters like themselves taking action to help others and change the world.

1. Danger on Crab Island ◆ 1998
2. Disaster at Parson's Point ◆ 1998
3. The Dolphin Trap ◆ 1998
4. Stranding on Cedar Point ◆ 1998
5. Hurricane Rescue ◆ 1998
6. Red Tide Alert ◆ 1998

NET FORCE

Clancy, Tom, and Steve Pieczenik

BERKLEY JAM BOOKS ◆ GRADES 7–10 ◆ A/R

REAL LIFE

In this futuristic series, the Net Force Explorers track criminals who are making illegal use of computers and the Net. *Virtual Vandals* focuses on four teens who use assumed identities to create cyber chaos. Other books feature different teens investigating computer crimes.

1. Virtual Vandals ◆ 1999
2. The Deadliest Game ◆ 1999
3. One Is the Loneliest Number ◆ 1999
4. The Ultimate Escape ◆ 1999
5. The Great Race ◆ 1999
6. End Game ◆ 1999
7. Cyberspy ◆ 1999
8. Shadow of Honor ◆ 2000
9. Private Lives ◆ 2000
10. Safe House ◆ 2000
11. Gameprey ◆ 2000
12. Duel Identity ◆ 2000
13. Deathworld ◆ 2000
14. High Wire ◆ 2001
15. Cold Case ◆ 2001
16. Runaways ◆ 2001
17. Cloak and Dagger ◆ 2003
18. Death Match ◆ 2003

NEVER LAND

Barry, Dave, and Ridley Pearson
DISNEY ◆ GRADES 4–7
FANTASY | ADVENTURE

Considerably shorter than the Peter and the Starcatchers books, the adventures in these books happen while Peter is away but involve his Lost Boys, Captain Hook, and other familiar characters. In the first book, Princess Little Scallop of the Mollusk tribe goes exploring in the sea with her mermaid friends, Aqua and Surf. When they are quite far from Mollusk Island, Surf is captured by a gang of greedy men. The Lost Boys join in the rescue.

1. Escape from the Carnivale: A Never Land Book ◆ 2006
2. Cave of the Dark Wind: A Never Land Book ◆ 2007
3. Blood Tide: A Never Land Book ◆ 2008

NEXT GENERATION: STARFLEET ACADEMY *see* Star Trek: The Next Generation: Starfleet Academy

NFL MONDAY NIGHT FOOTBALL CLUB

Korman, Gordon

HYPERION ◆ GRADES 4–7 ◆ A/R

FANTASY | RECREATION

When Nick, 11, puts on an old football jersey, he is transported into the body of John Elway—right in the middle of a Monday Night Football game! Then, when Elliot tries on the jersey, he becomes Barry Sanders. Even Nick's sister Hilary puts on the jersey and is transformed—into Junior Seau. Football fans will like the action and humor of this series.

1. Quarterback Exchange: I Was John Elway ◆ 1997
2. Running Back Conversion: I Was Barry Sanders ◆ 1997
3. Super Brown Switch: I Was Dan Marino ◆ 1997
4. Heavy Artillery: I Was Junior Seau ◆ 1997
5. Ultimate Scoring Machine: I Was Jerry Rice ◆ 1998

NICKELODEON ARE YOU AFRAID OF THE DARK? *see* Are You Afraid of the Dark?

NIGHT WORLD

Smith, L. J.

POCKET BOOKS ◆ GRADES 9–12

HORROR

The lives of vampires and teen girls intersect in this series with a romantic twist. In *Soulmate,* Hannah is wary of approaching danger. Is Thierry, the Lord of the Night World, her friend or her foe? In *Black Dawn,* Maggie is tempted by the delights offered by a young vampire prince but fears that he killed her brother.

1. Secret Vampire ◆ 1996
2. Daughters of Darkness ◆ 1996
3. Spellbinder ◆ 1996
4. Dark Angel ◆ 1996
5. The Chosen ◆ 1996
6. Soulmate ◆ 1997
7. Huntress ◆ 1997
8. Black Dawn ◆ 1997
9. Witchlight ◆ 1997

NIGHTMARE HALL

Hoh, Diane

SCHOLASTIC ◆ GRADES 6–9

HORROR | MYSTERY

The Nightmare Hall series takes place in a dormitory where evil seems to lurk. A girl is found hanged in her bedroom, and her spirit tries to help incoming students find the truth about her murder. Jessica Vogt leads the group in discovering the clues. As the first novel ends, there is a sense of relief but not complete peace. This sets the mood for the sequels.

1. The Silent Scream ◆ 1993
2. The Roommate ◆ 1993
3. Deadly Attraction ◆ 1993
4. The Wish ◆ 1993
5. The Scream Team ◆ 1993
6. Guilty ◆ 1993
7. Pretty Please ◆ 1994
8. The Experiment ◆ 1994
9. The Night Walker ◆ 1994
10. Sorority Sister ◆ 1994
11. Last Date ◆ 1994
12. The Whisperer ◆ 1994
13. Monster ◆ 1994
14. The Initiation ◆ 1994
15. Truth or Die ◆ 1994
16. Book of Horrors ◆ 1994
17. Last Breath ◆ 1994
18. Win, Lose, or Die ◆ 1994
19. The Coffin ◆ 1995
20. Deadly Visions ◆ 1995
21. Student Body ◆ 1995
22. The Vampire's Kiss ◆ 1995
23. Dark Moon ◆ 1995
24. The Biker ◆ 1995
25. Captives ◆ 1995
26. Revenge ◆ 1995
27. Kidnapped ◆ 1995
28. The Dummy ◆ 1995
29. The Voice in the Mirror ◆ 1995

NIGHTMARE ROOM

Stine, R. L.

AVON ◆ GRADES 4–7 ◆ A/R

HORROR

These stories are somewhat scary, with elements of mystery, the supernatural, and aliens. In *Liar, Liar,* Ross Arthur goes to a party and sees his twin. One problem—he does not have a twin. In another book, Alex Smith's blank journal is being written in, but not by Alex. When Alex reads the journal, he realizes he is learning about the future. Fans of creepy stories will enjoy these.

1. Don't Forget Me! ◆ 2000
2. Locker 13 ◆ 2000
3. My Name Is Evil ◆ 2000
4. Liar, Liar ◆ 2000
5. Dear Diary, I'm Dead ◆ 2001
6. They Call Me Creature ◆ 2001
7. The Howler ◆ 2001
8. Shadow Girl ◆ 2001
9. Camp Nowhere ◆ 2001
10. Full Moon Halloween ◆ 2001
11. Scare School ◆ 2001
12. Visitors ◆ 2001

NIGHTMARE ROOM THRILLOGY

Stine, R. L.

AVON ◆ GRADES 4–7 ◆ A/R

HORROR

More chills and thrills in the Nightmare Room, where it is not safe to be alone.

1. Fear Games ◆ 2001
2. What Scares You the Most? ◆ 2001
3. No Survivors ◆ 2001

NIGHTMARES! HOW WILL YOURS END?

Wulffson, Don L.

PRICE STERN SLOAN ◆ GRADES 4–7

HORROR

Your father and brother are missing in the jungles of Malaysia—which way do you choose to go? Or, you are on Earth but it has been invaded by aliens—what will you do? Readers are given scary situations and make choices to create different endings.

1. Castle of Horror ◆ 1995
2. Cave of Fear ◆ 1995
3. Planet of Terror ◆ 1995
4. Valley of the Screaming Statues ◆ 1995

NIKKI SHERIDAN

Brinkerhoff, Shirley
BETHANY HOUSE ◆ GRADES 6–9 ◆ A/R
REAL LIFE | VALUES

Nikki becomes pregnant at the age of 16 and has to face difficult choices. As the series progresses and she finds religion, she struggles to accept her decision to give the baby up and she confronts differing views on adoption, abortion, and divorce.

1. Choice Summer ◆ 1996
2. Mysterious Love ◆ 1996
3. Narrow Walk ◆ 1998
4. Balancing Act ◆ 1998
5. Tangled Web ◆ 1999
6. Second Choices ◆ 2000

NINE CHARMS *see* Tales of the Nine Charms

THE NINE LIVES OF CHLOE KING

Thomson, Celia
SIMON & SCHUSTER ◆ GRADES 9–12 ◆ A/R
FANTASY

Chloe King is almost 16 when she falls from the top of a tower in San Francisco. While she appears to be unharmed, there are hints that something unusual has happened. Chloe has mysterious encounters with a supernatural society and comes to realize that she now has special cat-like powers.

1. The Fallen ◆ 2004
2. The Stolen ◆ 2004
3. The Chosen ◆ 2005

THE NINE LIVES OF ROMEO CRUMB

Rifkin, L.

STRATFORD ROAD PRESS ◆ GRADES 6–8 ◆ A/R

FANTASY

Conflicts in the world of cats are explored in this fantasy. Romeo Crumb thinks he has always been a pet cat, aka a "Stick." His neighbor, Queen Elizabeth, introduces him to the world of the "Alleys" led by the evil Fidel. Romeo trains at the Factory and learns about his heritage. Romeo leads the Sticks in their battle with the Alleys and he discovers his own heroic destiny. The Warriors books also feature cats in mythic battles.

1. The Nine Lives of Romeo Crumb: Life One ◆ 2004
2. The Nine Lives of Romeo Crumb: Life Two ◆ 2005
3. The Nine Lives of Romeo Crumb: Life Three ◆ 2006
4. The Nine Lives of Romeo Crumb: Life Four ◆ 2008

99 FEAR STREET *see* Fear Street: 99 Fear Street

NO SECRETS: THE STORY OF A GIRL BAND

Krulik, Nancy

GROSSET & DUNLAP ◆ GRADES 6–9

REAL LIFE

PCBS is the Professional Children's Boarding School and it's time for the Fall Showcase. This year, a talent agent, Eileen Kerr, is in the audience. Eight girls will make *The First Cut* but only four will be in the all-girl band.

1. The First Cut ◆ 2001
2. Sneaking Around ◆ 2001
3. Spring Fever ◆ 2001
4. In the Spotlight ◆ 2001

NOBLE WARRIORS

Nicholson, William

HARCOURT ◆ GRADES 7–10 ◆ A/R

FANTASY | ADVENTURE

Seeker After Truth, 16, is studying to be a scholar but longs to join the Nomana (Noble Warriors) and protect the All and Only god. Seeker and his two friends—Morning Star, who can interpret people's "colors," and The Wildman, an outlaw—discover the Nomana have dark, dangerous secrets. Each begins a journey encountering challenges that reveal their destiny and bring them back together. In *Noman,* the Nomana have disbanded and a new leader appears. Only Seeker questions the leader's true purpose.

1. Seeker ◆ 2006
2. Jango ◆ 2007
3. Noman ◆ 2008

NOMES *see* Bromeliad

NON-BLONDE CHEERLEADER

Scott, Kieran

PUTNAM ◆ GRADES 8–12 ◆ A/R

REAL LIFE

After moving from New Jersey to Florida, Annisa Gobrowski inadvertently alienates some of the most popular girls in her new school—the cheerleaders. When she makes the squad, her troubles intensify. The other girls are blonde and Annisa, a brunette, struggles to fit in. In *A Non-Blonde Cheerleader in Love,* boys join the cheer squad and Annisa is thrilled to be working with her boyfriend Daniel. This series is sure to be a hit with cheerleading fans.

1. I Was a Non-Blonde Cheerleader ◆ 2005
2. Brunettes Strike Back ◆ 2006
3. A Non-Blonde Cheerleader in Love ◆ 2007

NORBY

Asimov, Janet, and Isaac Asimov

WALKER & CO. ◆ GRADES 5–7 ◆ A/R

ADVENTURE | SCIENCE FICTION

Jeff Wells is a student at the Space Academy. He buys Norby as a teaching robot, but he soon discovers that Norby is unique. Norby has many useful abilities because he was fashioned from salvaged spaceship parts. In each novel, Jeff and Norby become involved in intergalactic intrigue. Often they must help Jeff's older, but not wiser, brother Fargo and save the galaxy. Science fiction, humor, and believable characters work well together in this entertaining series.

1. Norby, the Mixed-Up Robot ◆ 1983
2. Norby's Other Secret ◆ 1984

3. Norby and the Lost Princess ◆ 1985
4. Norby and the Invaders ◆ 1985
5. Norby and the Queen's Necklace ◆ 1986
6. Norby Finds a Villain ◆ 1987
7. Norby Down to Earth ◆ 1989
8. Norby and Yobo's Great Adventure ◆ 1989
9. Norby and the Oldest Dragon ◆ 1990
10. Norby and the Court Jester ◆ 1991
11. Norby and the Terrified Taxi ◆ 1997

NORTHERN FRIGHTS

Slade, Arthur G.

ORCA ◆ GRADES 5–8 ◆ A/R

FANTASY

Exciting adventures are interwoven with Norse mythology in this Canadian series. On Drang Island off the coast of British Columbia, Michael, 15, meets Fiona and together they encounter ghosts, spirits, and other dangers. This could be a good choice for R. L. Stine fans.

1. The Haunting of Drang Island ◆ 1998
2. Draugr ◆ 1998
3. The Loki Wolf ◆ 2000

NORY RYAN

Giff, Patricia Reilly

DELACORTE; RANDOM HOUSE ◆ GRADES 5–8 ◆ A/R

HISTORICAL

Strong, resourceful, heroic, determined, courageous. These are just a few of the words to describe Nory Ryan. As this series begins, Nory, 12, is coping with the impact of the failure of the potato crop in Ireland in 1845. With Da (her father) at sea trying to earn money, the family is hungry and facing eviction. Nory looks for ways to support them, showing resilience and ingenuity. In *Maggie's Door,* Nory is sailing to America to join her sister in Brooklyn. Details about the voyage—filthy conditions, inadequate food, abusive passengers—accurately portray the experiences of many immigrants. Nory's friend, Sean Red Mallon, helps her deal with the difficulties. The third book, *Water Street,* focuses on Bridget (Bird) Mallon, who is Nory and Sean's youngest daughter.

1. Nory Ryan's Song ◆ 2000
2. Maggie's Door ◆ 2003
3. Water Street ◆ 2006

NOSE

Scrimger, Richard

TUNDRA ◆ GRADES 6–8 ◆ A/R

FANTASY | HUMOR

Alan Dingwell is 13 and, like many middle school boys, he struggles with schoolwork and bullies. Then Norbert, an alien from Jupiter, comes to his rescue and takes up residence in his nose! Norbert is opinionated and funny and he gets Alan into and out of trouble. Reluctant readers will find these books accessible.

1. The Nose from Jupiter ◆ 1998
2. A Nose for Adventure ◆ 2000
3. Noses Are Red ◆ 2002
4. The Boy from Earth ◆ 2004

NOT JUST PROMS AND PARTIES

Penny, Patricia G.

LOBSTER PRESS ◆ GRADES 9–12 ◆ A/R

REAL LIFE

In *Chelsea's Ride,* Chelsea Davison's reckless behavior has gotten her into trouble and her parents have taken away her car keys. How can a popular girl survive without a car? Chelsea gets Danny, a boy who has always liked her, to be her driver, but Chelsea's selfishness leads to even more problems. This series features popular girls facing challenges—and learning lessons—that teens can relate to.

1. Chelsea's Ride ◆ 2006
2. Rica's Summer ◆ 2006
3. Belinda's Obsession ◆ 2007
4. Karin's Dilemma ◆ 2007
5. Emily's Rebellion ◆ 2008

NOTES FROM A SPINNING PLANET

Carlson, Melody

WATERBROOK PRESS ◆ GRADES 8–10

REAL LIFE | VALUES

In the first book, Maddie Chase, 19, travels to Ireland with her Aunt Sid and Sid's godson Ryan. Maddie and Ryan look into the IRA car bombing that killed Ryan's father. As the series progresses, Maddie is attracted to Ryan. On a trip to Mexico, Ryan's beautiful former girlfriend arrives and Maddie is jealous. Maddie reflects on her faith and values to overcome her negative feelings.

1. Notes From a Spinning Planet—Ireland ◆ 2006
2. Notes From a Spinning Planet—Papua New Guinea ◆ 2007
3. Notes From a Spinning Planet—Mexico ◆ 2007

OBSIDIAN CHRONICLES

Watt-Evans, Lawrence

TOR ◆ GRADES 10–12

FANTASY

Arlian is the only survivor of a dragon attack on his village. He has vowed vengeance and for 14 years has devoted himself to slaying dragons. When he returns to the walled city of Manfort, he finds that a wild magic has been released. His treatment of dragons may be responsible and Arlian must investigate the power of dragon venom.

1. Dragon Weather ◆ 1999
2. The Dragon Society ◆ 2001
3. Dragon Venom ◆ 2003

THE O.C.

Various authors

SCHOLASTIC ◆ GRADES 10–12

REAL LIFE

Fans of the television show will want to read these related books. Ryan Atwood, 16, goes to live with a wealthy family in Orange County, California (the O.C.). He feels out of place and has trouble relating to rich teens like Seth and Marissa Cooper. There are many related materials including cast biographies and calendars.

1. The Misfit (Wallington, Aury) ◆ 2004
2. The Outsider (Martin, Cory) ◆ 2004
3. The Way Back (Martin, Cory) ◆ 2004
4. Spring Break (Wallington, Aury) ◆ 2005
5. The Summer of Summer (Martin, Cory) ◆ 2005
6. Bait and Switch (Wallington, Aury) ◆ 2005
7. Cohen! (Wallington, Aury) ◆ 2006

OCEAN CITY *see* Making Waves

OH MY GODDESS!

Fujishima, Kosuke

DARK HORSE ◆ GRADES 10–12

FANTASY

So, you want to order a pizza. When you dial for delivery, you connect with a goddess, Belldandy, who grants you one wish. That's when the adventure begins for Keiichi Morisato, who wishes that Belldandy would stay with him forever. This is a classic manga adventure series with magic, more goddesses, and fun. The dates for this series vary as some volumes have been reworked or repackaged. (For example, the first three books are re-created from the 1996 title *1-555-Goddess*.) In 2008, the entire series was repackaged and reissued with no titles apart from volume numbers, from number 1 to number 31.

1. Wrong Number ◆ 2002
2. Leader of the Pack ◆ 2002
3. Final Exam ◆ 2002
4. Love Potion, No. 9 ◆ 1997
5. Sympathy for the Devil ◆ 1998
6. Terrible Master Urd ◆ 2001
7. The Queen of Vengeance ◆ 1999
8. Mara Strikes Back! ◆ 2000
9. Ninja Master! ◆ 2000
10. Miss Keiichi ◆ 2001
11. The Devil in Miss Urd ◆ 2001
12. The Fourth Goddess ◆ 2001
13. Childhood's End ◆ 2002
14. Queen Sayoko ◆ 2002
15. Hand in Hand ◆ 2003
16. Mystery Child ◆ 2003
17. Traveler ◆ 2003
18. Phantom Racer ◆ 2004

OMAKAYAS

Erdrich, Louise

HYPERION; HARPERCOLLINS ◆ GRADES 5–8

HISTORICAL

In the late 1840s, a young Ojibwa girl named Omakayas is living a contented life on an island on Lake Superior. Then smallpox hits the village and Omakayas, who was exposed as a baby, is the only one able to nurse the others but she cannot save them all. In the second book, the Ojibwa face eviction from their homes by white men, and the third book finds them searching for a home, facing a freezing winter and near-starvation. The details of Ojibwa life will appeal to fans of Laura Ingalls Wilder's books.

1. The Birchbark House ◆ 1999
2. The Game of Silence ◆ 2005
3. The Porcupine Year ◆ 2008

ON THE ROAD

Doyon, Stephanie

ALADDIN ◆ GRADES 6–10 ◆ A/R

REAL LIFE

Miranda, 18, is tired of the routine of her life. She is bored with always doing what is expected. She decides to delay going to college and to travel across the country with her friend Kirsten. Along the way, Miranda spends some time doing volunteer work with her brother in Virginia. And she develops a romantic attraction for a boy who helps her try rock climbing.

1. Leaving Home ◆ 1998
2. Buying Time ◆ 1999
3. Taking Chances ◆ 1999
4. Making Waves ◆ 1999

ON THE RUN

Korman, Gordon

SCHOLASTIC ◆ GRADES 5–8 ◆ A/R

ADVENTURE

After Frank Lindenaur, a CIA agent, disappeared, Meg and Aiden Falconer's parents were investigated and convicted of treason. Meg and Aiden are placed in a juvenile detention center, but they escape and begin their search for evidence to prove their parents' innocence. There are close calls and narrow escapes; Meg and Aiden are betrayed at every turn. They face danger not only from the FBI but also from a mysterious man who seems intent on stopping their search at any cost. Their adventure continues in the Kidnapped series.

1. Chasing the Falconers ◆ 2005
2. The Fugitive Factor ◆ 2005
3. Now You See Them, Now You Don't ◆ 2005
4. The Stowaway Solution ◆ 2005
5. Public Enemies ◆ 2005
6. Hunting the Hunter ◆ 2006

ON TIME'S WING

Various authors

ROUSSAN ◆ GRADES 5–8 ◆ A/R

HISTORICAL

This series features well-researched historical novels. In *Living Freight,* Emma has been orphaned and is waiting to go to the workhouse. Instead, she boards a ship sailing from England to Canada. Once in Canada, she tries to sell her mother's ring to fund her journey to British Columbia, where she hopes to look for gold. The ring brings Emma to the father she believed was dead. Each book features intrepid young teens who overcome obstacles.

1. Home Child (Haworth-Attard, Barbara) ◆ 1991
2. Candles (Kositsky, Lynne) ◆ 1996
3. Dark of the Moon (Haworth-Attard, Barbara) ◆ 1996
4. Living Freight (Campbell, Gaetz Dayle) ◆ 1998
5. Love-Lies-Bleeding (Haworth-Attard, Barbara) ◆ 1999
6. Rebecca's Flame (Kositsky, Lynne) ◆ 1999
7. Run for Your Life (Alexander, Wilma E.) ◆ 1999
8. Sunflower Diary (Boraks-Nemetz, Lillian) ◆ 1999
9. Danger in Disguise (Downie, Mary Alice) ◆ 2001
10. In Search of Klondike Gold (Wilson, Lynda) ◆ 2001
11. The Lenski File (Boraks-Nemetz, Lillian) ◆ 2001
12. Virtual Zone: Titanic's Race to Disaster (Wilson, Lynda) ◆ 2001

ONCE AND FUTURE KING

White, T. H.

PUTNAM ◆ GRADES 7–10 ◆ A/R

ADVENTURE | HISTORICAL

This classic series tells the entire glorious and tragic Arthurian legend. The first novel relates Arthur's life growing up with Kay, his older brother; Sir Ector, his father; and Merlyn, his tutor. The subsequent novels continue to unfold Arthur's life as he discovers that he is King and forms the Knights of the Round Table. Battles for power are fought and won, but Arthur's personal life unravels because of Sir Lancelot and Guinevere. This series is not merely a retelling, for White incorporates humor and fresh insights into the characters as real people with real problems. *The Book of Merlyn* was published separately in 1977, as a final chapter in the story.

1. The Sword in the Stone ◆ 1938
2. The Queen of Air and Darkness ◆ 1939
3. The Ill-Made Knight ◆ 1940
4. The Candle in the Wind ◆ 1958
5. The Book of Merlyn ◆ 1977

ONCE UPON A PROM

Ny, Jeanine Le

POINT ◆ GRADES 9–12

REAL LIFE

It's time for the senior prom and three friends, Jordan, Tara, and Nisha, are eager to go. They have been shopping for dresses and arranging for limos but of course there are problems. Jordan is attracted to a boy who is not her boyfriend. Tara needs to find just the right date. And Nisha's parents won't let her go unless she is escorted by the boy they have chosen. Teen readers of Gossip Girl, Drama!, and I Heart Bikinis will enjoy this series.

1. Dream ◆ 2008
2. Dress ◆ 2008
3. Date ◆ 2008

ONCE UPON A TIME

Various authors

SIMON PULSE ◆ GRADES 6–10

FANTASY

A series of lively fairy tale retellings with an added dollop of romance and set in often unusual situations—*Spirited* during the French and Indian War, *The Night Dance* in the time of King Arthur, and *Water Song* in World War I Belgium.

1. The Storyteller's Daughter: A Retelling of "The Arabian Nights" (Dokey, Cameron) ◆ 2002
2. Beauty Sleep: A Retelling of "Sleeping Beauty" (Dokey, Cameron) ◆ 2002
3. Snow: A Retelling of "Snow White and the Seven Dwarfs" (Lynn, Tracy) ◆ 2003
4. Midnight Pearls: A Retelling of "The Little Mermaid" (Viguie, Debbie) ◆ 2003
5. Sunlight and Shadow: A Retelling of "The Magic Flute" (Dokey, Cameron) ◆ 2004
6. Spirited: A retelling of "Beauty and the Beast" (Holder, Nancy) ◆ 2004
7. Scarlet Moon: A Retelling of "Little Red Riding Hood" (Viguie, Debbie) ◆ 2004
8. The Night Dance: A Retelling of "The Twelve Dancing Princesses" (Weyn, Suzanne) ◆ 2005
9. Water Song: A Retelling of "The Frog Prince" (Weyn, Suzanne) ◆ 2006
10. Golden: A Retelling of "Rapunzel" (Dokey, Cameron) ◆ 2006

11. Before Midnight: A Retelling of "Cinderella" (Dokey, Cameron) ◆ 2007
12. The Rose Bride: A Retelling of "The White Bride and the Black Bride" (Holder, Nancy) ◆ 2007
13. The Crimson Thread: A Retelling of "Rumpelstiltskin" (Weyn, Suzanne) ◆ 2008
14. Belle: A Retelling of "Beauty and the Beast" (Dokey, Cameron) ◆ 2008
15. Wild Orchid: A Retelling of "The Ballad of Mulan" (Dokey, Cameron) ◆ 2009

1-800-WHERE-R-YOU

Cabot, Meg
SIMON & SCHUSTER ◆ GRADES 7–10 ◆ A/R
ADVENTURE

Jessica Mastriana, 16, was a struggling high school student until she walked through a thunderstorm. Before, she was troubled but normal. Now, she is changed. She has psychic powers that bring her to the attention of the government and of others who want her help. She tries unsuccessfully to hide her new abilities and is asked to help find missing children and even solve a murder. The fast-paced action and Jess's strong personality will attract many readers.

1. When Lightning Strikes ◆ 2004
2. Code Name Cassandra ◆ 2004
3. Safe House ◆ 2004
4. Sanctuary ◆ 2004
5. Missing You ◆ 2006

ONE LAST WISH

McDaniel, Lurlene
BANTAM ◆ GRADES 6–9 ◆ A/R
REAL LIFE

Although several of these books feature the same characters, the linking themes are serious illness, death, love, and generosity through the awarding of gifts from the One Last Wish Foundation. In *A Season for Goodbye,* three girls who are facing difficult problems of their own work together to help a 12-year-old with leukemia.

1. A Time to Die ◆ 1992
2. Mourning Song ◆ 1992
3. Mother, Help Me Live ◆ 1992
4. Someone Dies, Someone Lives ◆ 1992

5. Sixteen and Dying ◆ 1992
6. Let Him Live ◆ 1993
7. The Legacy: Making Wishes Come True ◆ 1993
8. Please Don't Die ◆ 1993
9. She Died Too Young ◆ 1994
10. All the Days of Her Life ◆ 1994
11. A Season for Goodbye ◆ 1995
12. Reach for Tomorrow ◆ 1999

ORACLE PROPHECIES

Fisher, Catherine

GREENWILLOW ◆ GRADES 7–10 ◆ A/R

FANTASY

In this intricate fantasy, Mirany has been chosen to be one of the nine young women who serve the Archon of Two Lands, a world threatened by drought and intrigue. The Archons are mortal men who represent the god. Mirany discovers that there is corruption and greed among those who serve the Archon, particularly from the Speaker, who plans to betray the Archon. Mirany begins a quest to find the true heir and thereby thwart the Speaker's plan. Accompanied by Seth, a scribe, and Oblek, a musician, Mirany discovers Alexos, a boy destined to become the next Archon.

1. The Oracle Betrayed ◆ 2004
2. The Sphere of Secrets ◆ 2005
3. Day of the Scarab ◆ 2006

ORACLES OF FIRE *see* Dragons in Our Midst: Oracles of Fire

ORAN TRILOGY

Snyder, Midori

PUFFIN ◆ GRADES 10–12 ◆ A/R

FANTASY

For two hundred years Oran has lived under the rule of the Fire Queen, Zorah. She defeated the other elemental queens and has tried to destroy any child who appeared to be developing powers. Four young women have secretly survived and are preparing to join together and defeat Zorah. Jobber would be the new Fire Queen. Working with Shedwyn (Earth) and Lirrel (Air), she is searching for the woman who will be the Water Queen. Together they will form a Queen's knot and take control of Oran. The Oran Trilogy was originally published as The Queen's Quarter Series in the late 1980s and early 1990s and has been out of print. Puffin reissued the series in 2005.

1. New Moon ◆ 2005
2. Sadar's Keep ◆ 2005
3. Beldan's Fire ◆ 2005

ORION THE HUNTER

Bova, Ben
TOR ◆ GRADES 9–12
SCIENCE FICTION

Adventure, romance, and mythology are interwoven in this well-written saga about Orion the Hunter as he strives for independence from the Creators and a life with his beloved Anya.

1. Orion ◆ 1984
2. Vengeance of Orion ◆ 1988
3. Orion in the Dying Time ◆ 1990
4. Orion and the Conqueror ◆ 1994
5. Orion Among the Stars ◆ 1995

ORMINGAT

Waugh, Sylvia
DELACORTE ◆ GRADES 5–8 ◆ A/R
FANTASY

Aliens from Ormingat living in England are collecting information on Earthlings and their behaviors. Each book in this series features a young person from Ormingat. In *Earthborn,* Nesta Gwynn, 12, learns a secret about her parents. They are aliens who are planning to return to Ormingat, but Nesta does not want to go.

1. Space Race ◆ 2000
2. Earthborn ◆ 2002
3. Who Goes Home ◆ 2004

ORPHAN TRAIN ADVENTURES

Nixon, Joan Lowery
DELACORTE ◆ GRADES 5–8 ◆ A/R
FAMILY LIFE | HISTORICAL

Originally published as a quartet of books, this series has been extended to relate more adventures of the Kelly children. The first book, *A Family Apart,* sets the stage for the series, which takes place in the mid-1800s. When their mother can no longer support them, the six Kelly children are sent from New York City to Missouri on an orphan train. They are placed with different farm families across the Great Plains. The series describes their experiences from the oldest, Frances Mary Kelly, to the youngest, Peaty. In *Caught in the Act,* Michael Patrick Kelly faces cruelty and a harsh life on a Missouri farm; in a later book, he becomes a Union soldier. Though orphan trains did exist, the characters and plots in this series are fictional.

1. A Family Apart ◆ 1987
2. Caught in the Act ◆ 1988
3. In the Face of Danger ◆ 1988
4. A Place to Belong ◆ 1989
5. A Dangerous Promise ◆ 1994
6. Keeping Secrets ◆ 1995
7. Circle of Love ◆ 1997

OUTCAST

Golden, Christopher, and Thomas E. Sniegoski
ALADDIN ◆ GRADES 4–7 ◆ A/R
FANTASY

Timothy is the son of a powerful mage. His father, now deceased, has kept Timothy hidden. Now Timothy has been discovered by Leader, a former apprentice, and he is introduced to the world of magic.

1. The Un-Magician ◆ 2004
2. Dragon Secrets ◆ 2004
3. Ghostfire ◆ 2005
4. Wurm War ◆ 2005

OUTER BANKS TRILOGY

Taylor, Theodore
DOUBLEDAY; HARPERCOLLINS ◆ GRADES 5–8 ◆ A/R
ADVENTURE | HISTORICAL

This adventure trilogy is by the author of *The Cay.* Teetoncey is a frail young girl whom Ben helps rescue from a shipwreck. Many mysteries surround her. Later, as Ben searches for his brother, he discovers that their fates are more closely entwined than he first thought. HarperCollins reissued these books in 1995 with the following titles: *Stranger from the*

Sea: Teetoncey; *Box of Treasures: Teetoncey and Ben O'Neal*; *Into the Wind: The Odyssey of Ben O'Neal*.

1. Teetoncey ◆ 1974
2. Teetoncey and Ben O'Neal ◆ 1975
3. The Odyssey of Ben O'Neal ◆ 1977

THE OUTER LIMITS

Peel, John

TOR KIDS! ◆ GRADES 6–8

FANTASY | HORROR

The books in this series feature different characters in fantastic, even bizarre, situations. In *The Zanti Misfits*, the Zanti have sent their problem creatures to Earth, putting human society in danger of destruction. Deciding what to do with these dangerous misfits is a dilemma—they may destroy Earth, but killing them may bring the wrath of the Zanti. Another book features a character with telekinetic powers, and still another deals with the planet Tarnish, which is ruled by children. Recommend this series to readers who like unusual creatures and surprising plot twists.

1. The Choice ◆ 1997
2. The Zanti Misfits ◆ 1997
3. The Time Shifter ◆ 1997
4. The Lost ◆ 1997
5. The Invaders ◆ 1998
6. The Innocent ◆ 1998
7. The Vanished ◆ 1998
8. The Nightmare ◆ 1998
9. Beware the Metal Children ◆ 1999
10. Alien Invasion from Hollyweird ◆ 1999
11. The Payback ◆ 1999
12. The Change ◆ 1999

OUTERNET

Barlow, Steve

SCHOLASTIC ◆ GRADES 6–9 ◆ A/R

SCIENCE FICTION

Jack Armstrong got just what he wanted for his birthday—a laptop. Of course, it's not new; Jack's father got it from a man at his workplace, a U.S. Air Force base near Cambridge, England. The surprise comes when Jack discovers that his computer is connected to the Outernet, an intergalactic communication network. With his friends Loaf and Merle, Jack faces the evil Tyrant who wants to gain control of the Server.

1. Friend or Foe? ◆ 2002
2. Control ◆ 2002
3. Odyssey ◆ 2002
4. Time Out ◆ 2003
5. The Hunt ◆ 2003
6. Weaver ◆ 2003

OUTLANDER

Gabaldon, Diana

DELACORTE ◆ GRADES 11–12

FANTASY

With World War II over, Claire Randall, a nurse, has finally been reunited with her husband Frank. On a trip to Scotland, Claire walks into a circle of standing stones and travels back in time two hundred years. This is a violent era when women were subservient. Claire's nursing skills earn her a place in the clan; her attractive features and feisty nature earn her a place in Scots warrior James Fraser's bed. This is a lush historical romance that spans generations as Claire leaves the past to bear Jamie's child in the present.

1. Outlander ◆ 1991
2. Dragonfly in Amber ◆ 1992
3. Voyager ◆ 1993
4. Drums of Autumn ◆ 1997
5. The Fiery Cross ◆ 2001
6. A Breath of Snow and Ashes ◆ 2005

OUTRIDERS

Decter, Ed

ALADDIN ◆ GRADES 5–7 ◆ A/R

ADVENTURE

The Outriders are a group of 12-year-old friends who crave adventure and excitement. In *Expedition to Blue Cave,* they uncover a mystery involving stolen antiques. Before they can expose the thieves, Shelby's little sister is kidnapped. In *Expedition to Willow Key,* the friends first find chemical dumping and then alligator poachers. These are fast-paced, somewhat implausible adventure stories.

1. Expedition to Blue Cave ◆ 2007
2. Expedition to Willow Key ◆ 2007
3. Expedition to Pine Hollow ◆ 2007

Oz

Baum, Lyman Frank

MORROW; GREENWILLOW ◆ GRADES 4–8 ◆ A/R

FANTASY

The popular *Wizard of Oz* was only the first of a great many adventures about the land of Oz, which were continued by others after Baum's death. Dorothy returns many times and fights villains; and other children, such as Peter and Betsy Bobbins, find their way to the magical land. The Tin Man and Scarecrow are involved in various battles for control of Oz, but Ozma of Oz is the rightful ruler. All the books share a rich and detailed fantasy laced with satire. The first 15 books were written by L. Frank Baum. Other authors have extended the series. Greenwillow has reissued many of these titles in its Books of Wonder series.

ORIGINAL OZ BOOKS

1. The Wonderful Wizard of Oz ◆ 1900
2. The New Wizard of Oz ◆ 1903
3. The Marvelous Land of Oz ◆ 1904
4. Ozma of Oz ◆ 1907
5. Dorothy and the Wizard of Oz ◆ 1908
6. The Road to Oz ◆ 1909
7. The Emerald City of Oz ◆ 1910
8. The Patchwork Girl of Oz ◆ 1913
9. Tik-Tok of Oz ◆ 1914
10. The Scarecrow of Oz ◆ 1915
11. Rinktink in Oz ◆ 1916
12. The Lost Princess of Oz ◆ 1917
13. The Tin Woodman of Oz ◆ 1918
14. The Magic of Oz ◆ 1919
15. Glinda of Oz ◆ 1920

OZ CONTINUED

1. The Royal Book of Oz (Thompson, Ruth Plumly) ◆ 1921
2. The Cowardly Lion of Oz (Thompson, Ruth Plumly) ◆ 1923
3. Grampa in Oz (Thompson, Ruth Plumly) ◆ 1924
4. The Lost King of Oz (Thompson, Ruth Plumly) ◆ 1925
5. The Hungry Tiger in Oz (Thompson, Ruth Plumly) ◆ 1926
6. The Gnome King of Oz (Thompson, Ruth Plumly) ◆ 1927
7. The Giant Horse of Oz (Thompson, Ruth Plumly) ◆ 1928
8. Jack Pumpkinhead of Oz (Thompson, Ruth Plumly) ◆ 1929
9. The Yellow Knight of Oz (Thompson, Ruth Plumly) ◆ 1930
10. The Pirates in Oz (Thompson, Ruth Plumly) ◆ 1931
11. Purple Prince of Oz (Thompson, Ruth Plumly) ◆ 1932
12. Ojo in Oz (Thompson, Ruth Plumly) ◆ 1933
13. Speedy in Oz (Thompson, Ruth Plumly) ◆ 1934
14. Wishing Horse of Oz (Thompson, Ruth Plumly) ◆ 1935

15. Captain Salt in Oz (Thompson, Ruth Plumly) ◆ 1936
16. Kabumpo in Oz (Thompson, Ruth Plumly) ◆ 1936
17. Handy Mandy in Oz (Thompson, Ruth Plumly) ◆ 1937
18. The Silver Princess in Oz (Thompson, Ruth Plumly) ◆ 1938
19. Ozoplaning with the Wizard of Oz (Thompson, Ruth Plumly) ◆ 1939
20. The Wonder City of Oz (Neill, John R.) ◆ 1940
21. The Scalawagons of Oz (Neill, John R.) ◆ 1941
22. Lucky Bucky in Oz (Neill, John R.) ◆ 1942
23. The Magical Mimics in Oz (Snow, Jack) ◆ 1946
24. The Shaggy Man of Oz (Snow, Jack) ◆ 1949
25. Hidden Valley of Oz (Cosgrove, Rachel) ◆ 1951
26. Merry Go Round in Oz (McGraw, Eloise Jervis) ◆ 1963
27. Yankee in Oz (Thompson, Ruth Plumly) ◆ 1972
28. Autocrats of Oz (Suter, Jon Michael) ◆ 1976
29. Enchanted Island of Oz (Thompson, Ruth Plumly) ◆ 1976
30. Orange Knight of Oz (Suter, Jon Michael) ◆ 1976
31. Forbidden Fountain of Oz (McGraw, Eloise Jervis) ◆ 1980
32. Barnstormer in Oz (Farmer, Philip José) ◆ 1982
33. Return to Oz (Vinge, Joan Dennison) ◆ 1982
34. Dorothy and the Magic Belt (Baum, Roger S.) ◆ 1985
35. Mister Tinker of Oz (Howe, James) ◆ 1985
36. Dorothy of Oz (Baum, Roger S.) ◆ 1989
37. Rewolf of Oz (Baum, Roger S.) ◆ 1990
38. How the Wizard Came to Oz (Abbott, Donald) ◆ 1991
39. SillyOzbuls of Oz (Baum, Roger S.) ◆ 1991
40. The Nome King's Shadow in Oz (Sprague, Gilbert M.) ◆ 1992
41. The SillyOzbul of Oz and the Magic Merry-Go-Round (Baum, Roger S.) ◆ 1992
42. The SillyOzbul of Oz & Toto (Baum, Roger S.) ◆ 1992
43. The Blue Witch of Oz (Shanower, Eric) ◆ 1993
44. The Enchanted Apples of Oz (Shanower, Eric) ◆ 1993
45. The Forgotten Forest of Oz (Shanower, Eric) ◆ 1993
46. The Giant Garden of Oz (Shanower, Eric) ◆ 1993
47. The Magic Chest of Oz (Abbott, Donald) ◆ 1993
48. The Patchwork Bride of Oz (Sprague, Gilbert M.) ◆ 1993
49. Queen Ann in Oz (Carlson, Karyl, and Eric Gjovaag) ◆ 1993
50. Father Goose in Oz (Abbott, Donald) ◆ 1994
51. Christmas in Oz (Hess, Robin) ◆ 1995
52. The Glass Cat of Oz (Hulan, David) ◆ 1995
53. The Magic Dishpan of Oz (Freedman, Jeff) ◆ 1995
54. Masquerade in Oz (Campbell, Bill, and Irwin Terry) ◆ 1995
55. The Runaway in Oz (Neill, John R.) ◆ 1995
56. The Speckled Rose of Oz (Abbott, Donald) ◆ 1995
57. How the Wizard Saved Oz (Abbott, Donald) ◆ 1996
58. The Lavender Bear of Oz (Campbell, Bill) ◆ 1998

PACIFIC CASCADES UNIVERSITY

Various authors

PALISADES PRESS/MULTNOMAH ◆ **GRADES 8–10** ◆ **A/R**

REAL LIFE | VALUES

Follow the adventures of girls as they attend college. Emily is a freshman and has to adjust to her dorm and roommate along with the food and classes. Maddy wants college to inject some stability into her mixed-up life, especially her relationship with her difficult boyfriend. Their faith in God helps them face their challenges.

1. Freshman Blues (Nentwig, Wendy Lee) ◆ 1996
2. Homeward Heart (Johnson, Lissa Halls) ◆ 1996
3. True Identity (Sheahan, Bernie) ◆ 1996
4. Spring Break (Nentwig, Wendy Lee) ◆ 1996
5. Major Changes (Brooks, Jennifer) ◆ 1997
6. Summer Song (Sheahan, Bernie) ◆ 1997
7. Overbooked (Nentwig, Wendy Lee) ◆ 1997

PAGAN CHRONICLES

Jinks, Catherine

CANDLEWICK ◆ **GRADES 6–10** ◆ **A/R**

HISTORICAL

Orphaned Pagan is a spunky 16-year-old squire to the gallant Lord Roland in the first installment in this series set in a realistically presented Middle Ages. He is full of admiration for Lord Roland's bravery and generosity. In the second book, he and his knight have returned to France from a Crusade and are hoping to recruit volunteers for another. By the third book, the two have renounced violence and are in training to become monks, a career that seems ill-suited to Pagan's irrepressible character. Pagan, however, is determined to remain with Roland and occupies himself investigating crimes taking place in the monastery. In the last book, Pagan has become the Archdeacon of Carcassonne and must deal with disaffected Crusaders. The first three books in this series full of adventure and humor are narrated by Pagan and the last by Isidore, his bookish clerk. As the series progresses, the adult subject matter increases.

1. Pagan's Crusade ◆ 2003
2. Pagan in Exile ◆ 2004
3. Pagan's Vows ◆ 2004
4. Pagan's Scribe ◆ 2005

PAGEANT

Bennett, Cherie

BERKLEY ◆ GRADES 7–10

REAL LIFE

Who will be "Miss Teen Spirit"? A popular teen magazine is looking across America to find that special girl. The first four books describe the regional events, giving a behind-the-scenes look at the camaraderie and competition. Teen girls will find these books entertaining.

1. The Southern Girls ◆ 1998
2. The Midwest Girls ◆ 1998
3. The Northeast Girls ◆ 1998
4. The West Coast Girls ◆ 1998
5. The National Pageant ◆ 1998
6. The Winners on the Road ◆ 1999

PANDORA *see* Mythic Misadventures

PANGUR BAN

Sampson, Fay

LION ◆ GRADES 5–8

FANTASY

In ancient Wales, Pangur, a small white cat fleeing from a group of witches and their evil spells, befriends a monk called Niall. In *Pangur Ban,* the cat struggles to rescue Niall and the Princess Finnglas when they encounter a storm at sea and their lives are imperiled by mermaids and monsters. The fight between good and evil continues in later books and in *Finnglas and the Stones of Choosing,* the princess must face seven trials before she can become queen. These books were first published in Britain in the 1980s. An additional volume, *The White Horse Is Running,* is available in Britain.

1. Shape-Shifter: The Naming of Pangur Ban ◆ 2003
2. Pangur Ban: The White Cat ◆ 2003
3. Finnglas of the Horses ◆ 2003
4. Finnglas and the Stones of Choosing ◆ 2003
5. The Serpent of Senargad ◆ 2003

PARTY OF FIVE

Various authors

SIMON & SCHUSTER ◆ GRADES 7–10

REAL LIFE

Following the death of their parents four years ago, the Salinger kids have stayed together. Charlie, the oldest, has taken charge of Claudia, Bailey, Owen, and Julia. In one book, Claudia is attracted to a cute guy named Cliff. Her friend, Jody, tells her she has no chance. That's because Jody wants Cliff for herself. These books reflect some of the episodes from the television program.

1. Too Cool for School: Claudia (Mostow, Debra) ◆ 1997
2. Welcome to My World: Claudia (Winfrey, Elizabeth) ◆ 1997
3. A Boy Friend Is Not a "Boyfriend": Claudia (Costello, Emily) ◆ 1997
4. Everything Changes: Julia (Noonan, Rosalind) ◆ 1997
5. Trouble with Guys: Claudia (Speregen, Devra Newberger) ◆ 1997
6. You Can't Choose Your Family: Claudia (Tamar, Erika) ◆ 1997
7. On My Own: Bailey (Stine, Megan) ◆ 1997
8. Don't Say You Love Me: Sarah (Noonan, Rosalind) ◆ 1998
9. Breaking the Rules: Bailey (Stine, Megan) ◆ 1998
10. Nothing Lasts Forever: Julia (Levine, Michael) ◆ 1998
11. One Step Too Far: Bailey (Stine, Megan) ◆ 1998
12. My Ex-Best Friend: Claudia (Tamar, Erika) ◆ 1998

PARTY ROOM TRILOGY

Burke, Morgan

SIMON PULSE ◆ GRADES 9–12 ◆ A/R

REAL LIFE | MYSTERY

On the Upper East Side of Manhattan, the kids from Talcott Prep School hang out at the Party Room drinking, dancing, and doing drugs. After Kirsten Sawyer and her best friend Samantha Byrne, both 17, have been partying there one night, Samantha leaves with a stranger and is found murdered in Central Park. Kirsten is afraid that the Prep School Killer will come after her, which leads her to an increased use of alcohol and drugs. When the killer is caught and arrested, Kirsten believes she is safe . . . until there are more murders.

1. Get It Started ◆ 2005
2. After Hours ◆ 2005
3. Last Call ◆ 2005

PARVANA *see* The Breadwinner Trilogy

PASSAGES

McCusker, Paul

TOMMY NELSON/FOCUS ON THE FAMILY ◆ GRADES 6–10 ◆ A/R

VALUES

Modern-day children slip through to another world—Marus. Using their religious knowledge they help the inhabitants deal with problems. The books retell Biblical stories in this new context and present values including faith, repentance, and salvation.

1. Darien's Rise ◆ 1999
2. Arin's Judgment ◆ 1999
3. Annison's Risk ◆ 1999
4. Glennall's Betrayal ◆ 2000
5. Draven's Defiance ◆ 2000
6. Fendar's Legacy ◆ 2000

PAXTON CHEERLEADERS

Hall, Katy

MINSTREL/POCKET BOOKS ◆ GRADES 6–8

REAL LIFE | RECREATION

Patti wants to be one of the Paxton cheerleaders. She has been practicing with her friend Tara for the tryouts, but Tara can't do all the moves. Will Patti stick with her friend or find a way to get on the team on her own? This is the sort of dilemma found in this series. Lauren and Cassie have to deal with not always being the best while Patti has to resist being influenced by a new girl. School concerns, worries about boys, and team spirit are issues that will appeal to young teen readers.

1. Go for It, Patti! ◆ 1994
2. Three Cheers for You, Cassie! ◆ 1994
3. Winning Isn't Everything, Lauren! 1994 ◆ 1994
4. We Did It, Tara! ◆ 1995
5. We're in This Together, Patti! ◆ 1995
6. Nobody's Perfect, Cassie! ◆ 1995

PAYTON SKKY

Moore, Stephanie Perry

MOODY PRESS ◆ GRADES 9–12 ◆ A/R

REAL LIFE | VALUES

Payton Skky is beautiful, popular, and dating a great guy. Her values are tested when he pressures her to have sex. And, as an African American, Payton faces prejudice and racism. She relies on her faith to guide her. The books follow Payton into her early years at college. The Perry Skky Jr. books feature a boy in similar situations.

1. Staying Pure ◆ 2000
2. Sober Faith ◆ 2001
3. Saved Race ◆ 2001
4. Sweetest Gift ◆ 2001
5. Surrendered Heart ◆ 2002

P.C. HAWKE MYSTERIES

Zindel, Paul

HYPERION/VOLO ◆ GRADES 5–8 ◆ A/R

MYSTERY

P.C. Hawke and his friend Mackenzie Riggs solve mysteries. In one book, their friend is accused of the murder of a biologist at the Natural History Museum. The investigation involves a necklace, hypnosis, and a tarantula. In another book, P.C. and Mac travel to Monaco and investigate the murder of a guest at a conference.

1. The Scream Museum ◆ 2001
2. The Surfing Corpse ◆ 2001
3. The E-Mail Murders ◆ 2001
4. The Lethal Gorilla ◆ 2001
5. The Square Root of Murder ◆ 2002
6. Death on the Amazon ◆ 2002
7. The Gourmet Zombie ◆ 2002
8. The Phantom of 86th Street ◆ 2002
9. The Houdini Whodunit ◆ 2002
10. Death by CB ◆ 2003
11. The Petrified Parrot ◆ 2003

PELLINOR

Croggon, Alison

CANDLEWICK ◆ GRADES 7–12 ◆ A/R

FANTASY

When the saga begins, Maerad, 16, is a slave in a remote mountain village. She escapes with the help of Bard Cadvan, a man who believes that Maerad is destined to defeat the dark power of the Nameless One. Cadvan becomes her tutor, helping her develop her own magical powers and find the ancient Treesong. As the final confrontation approaches, Maerad is joined by her brother Hem in the fight against darkness. Readers of intricate fantasies such as the Lord of the Rings saga will appreciate this series, as will fans of Tamora Pierce and Robin McKinley.

1. The Naming ◆ 2005
2. The Riddle ◆ 2007
3. The Crow ◆ 2007
4. The Singing ◆ 2009

PELLUCIDAR

Burroughs, Edgar Rice

BALLANTINE ◆ GRADES 7–12

ADVENTURE | FANTASY

Pellucidar is a land under the earth's crest populated with dinosaurs, saber-toothed tigers, and other extinct animals, and lit by the earth's molten core. There are humans too, but they are the slaves of intelligent reptiles called the Mahars. The discoverers of this world—David Innes and Abner Perry—work to free these Stone Age humans in a series of exciting adventures.

1. At the Earth's Core ◆ 1922
2. Pellucidar ◆ 1923
3. Tanar of Pellucidar ◆ 1930
4. Tarzan at the Earth's Core ◆ 1930
5. Back to the Stone Age ◆ 1937
6. Land of Terror ◆ 1944
7. Savage Pellucidar ◆ 1963

PENDRAGON

MacHale, D. J.

ALADDIN ◆ GRADES 5–8 ◆ A/R

FANTASY

Bobby Pendragon, 14, seems normal, but he's not. He is going to save the world. First, by traveling to an alternate dimension, Denduron. Later, he continues his role as a Traveler and strives to save the land of Halla from the evil Saint Dane.

1. The Merchant of Death ◆ 2002
2. The Lost City of Faar ◆ 2003
3. The Never War ◆ 2003
4. The Reality Bug ◆ 2003
5. Black Water ◆ 2004
6. The Rivers of Zadaa ◆ 2005
7. The Quillan Games ◆ 2006
8. The Pilgrims of Rayne ◆ 2007
9. Raven Rise ◆ 2008

PERCY JACKSON AND THE OLYMPIANS

Riordan, Rick

MIRAMAX/HYPERION ◆ GRADES 5–9 ◆ A/R

FANTASY

Perseus Jackson, 12, has always been different, always in the middle of trouble. At school, his troubles are growing. One of his teachers turns into a monster—literally. And his best friend is revealed to be a satyr. Finally, Percy learns the secret. He is the son of Poseidon who had a liaison with a human—Percy's mother. As Poseidon's son, Percy is in danger. His mother appears to have been killed protecting him. Percy is sent to Camp Half-Blood to learn about his powers and prepare for the tasks that await him. In *The Battle of the Labyrinth,* Percy is in high school facing danger in Daedalus's Labyrinth. Many readers who loved the Harry Potter books have been drawn to this series.

1. The Lightning Thief ◆ 2005
2. The Sea of Monsters ◆ 2006
3. The Titan's Curse ◆ 2007
4. The Battle of the Labyrinth ◆ 2008
5. The Last Olympian ◆ 2009

PERN *see also* Acorna

PERN

McCaffrey, Anne

BALLANTINE DEL REY ◆ GRADES 10–12 ◆ A/R

SCIENCE FICTION

From the first settlement on the planet of Pern, the colonists have lived in a world of dragons and the dreaded Thread, which falls from the sky to destroy everything it touches.

1. Moreta, Dragonlady of Pern ◆ 1983
2. Nerilka's Story ◆ 1986
3. Dragonsdawn ◆ 1988
4. Renegades of Pern ◆ 1989
5. All the Weyrs of Pern ◆ 1991
6. Chronicles of Pern: First Fall ◆ 1993
7. The Dolphins of Pern ◆ 1994
8. Dragonseye ◆ 1997
9. The Masterharper of Pern ◆ 1998
10. The Skies of Pern ◆ 2001
11. Dragon's Kin (McCaffrey, Anne, with Todd McCaffrey) ◆ 2004

DRAGONRIDERS OF PERN

1. Dragonflight ◆ 1968
2. Dragonquest ◆ 1971
3. The White Dragon ◆ 1978

PERN: THE HARPER-HALL TRILOGY

McCaffrey, Anne

SIMON & SCHUSTER ◆ GRADES 10–12 ◆ A/R

FANTASY | SCIENCE FICTION

Menolly runs away when her parents refuse to let her sing or become a Harper. She finds a new home with a family of fire lizards. In the second book, she studies with the Masterharper, learns about music and about herself, and makes a friend, Piemur.

1. Dragonsong ◆ 2003
2. Dragonsinger ◆ 2003
3. Dragondrums ◆ 2003

PERRY SKKY JR.

Moore, Stephanie Perry

DAFINA ◆ GRADES 9–12

REAL LIFE | VALUES

Perry Skky Jr. seems to have it all. He is smart, popular, and the star of the football team. As a high school senior, he has the attention of many girls, but he has chosen Tori. He wants to become intimate with her but Tori is not ready. Both of them know that they should wait until after they are married, but Perry is torn between his beliefs and his desires. As the series progresses, Perry faces more temptations, especially when he begins college. As an African American male, Perry also experiences racism. His faith and commitment to God guide his choices. The Payton Skky books feature a girl in similar situations.

1. Prime Choice ◆ 2007
2. Pressing Hard ◆ 2007
3. Problem Solved ◆ 2007
4. Prayed Up ◆ 2008
5. Promise Kept ◆ 2008

PETE THE CAT

Kehret, Peg, and Pete the Cat

DUTTON ◆ GRADES 4–7 ◆ A/R

MYSTERY

Moving to a new neighborhood has been difficult for 12-year-old Alex. He is adjusting to his new school, but the kids there are not very friendly. And the boy who just moved in next door, Rocky, is downright rude. Then street signs are stolen and houses are set on fire. Alex wants to find out who is behind these destructive acts. Aiding Alex is his cat, Pete, who can fully understand humans although they cannot interpret his meows. Pete's perspective is presented in italics, which allows the reader to get inside his head. The mixture of mystery and Pete's "cat's-eye view" of the events is very enjoyable and could even attract reluctant readers. Pete is also given credit as a coauthor of these books.

1. The Stranger Next Door ◆ 2002
2. Spy Cat ◆ 2003
3. Trapped! ◆ 2008

PETER AND THE STARCATCHERS

Barry, Dave, and Ridley Pearson

HYPERION ◆ GRADES 4–8 ◆ A/R

FANTASY | ADVENTURE

This series follows the adventures of a boy named Peter before he became Peter Pan. All of the familiar characters are there, including the pirate Black Stache (aka Captain Hook). In the first book, Peter and a gang of orphan boys have been sent to crew for the cruel pirate Black Stache on his ship *Never Land*. Also on the ship is Molly Aster, 14, who belongs to a secret society of Starcatchers. This group tries to find and protect "starstuff," a magical substance that falls from the heavens. When Peter, Molly, and Peter's gang find a missing trunk of "starstuff," the chase is on. This is an action-filled series with lots of adventure. Barry and Pearson also feature many of these characters in the Never Land series. Visit peterandthestarcatchers.com for more about the books.

1. Peter and the Starcatchers ◆ 2004
2. Peter and the Shadow Thieves ◆ 2006
3. Peter and the Secret of Rundoon ◆ 2007

PETRA AND CALDER

Balliet, Blue

SCHOLASTIC ◆ GRADES 5–8 ◆ A/R

MYSTERY

In the first book, a Vermeer painting has been stolen and Petra and Calder, both 11, become involved in the mystery. Throughout the book there are clues, codes, and cryptic letters that involve the reader in the solution. Reminiscent of *From the Mixed-Up Files of Mrs. Basil E. Frankweiler,* this series's characters use their creativity and problem-solving skills to expose the thieves. Recommend the Sammy Keyes mysteries to readers who have enjoyed these books.

1. Chasing Vermeer ◆ 2004
2. The Wright 3 ◆ 2006
3. The Calder Game ◆ 2008

PETTICOAT PARTY

Karr, Kathleen

HARPERCOLLINS ◆ GRADES 5–8 ◆ A/R

HISTORICAL

Independence, Missouri, 1845. Twelve wagons head west for Oregon. In one wagon are Mr. and Mrs. Brown and their daughters Amelia and Phoebe. There is an accident and ten of the men are injured or killed. Now the women must take charge or the group will not survive. When the series begins, Phoebe is 12. After reaching Oregon when she is 15, she gets caught up in the gold rush and goes to California.

1. Go West, Young Women ◆ 1996
2. Phoebe's Folly ◆ 1996
3. Oregon, Sweet Oregon ◆ 1998
4. Gold-Rush Phoebe ◆ 1998

PHANTOM VALLEY

Beach, Lynn

ALADDIN ◆ GRADES 7–9

FANTASY

Jason McCormack, who is blind, releases an evil spirit that has been trapped in a cave. Jason's seeing-eye dog, Erroll, tries to protect Jason from the danger.

1. The Evil One ◆ 1991
2. The Dark ◆ 1991
3. Scream of the Cat ◆ 1992
4. Stranger in the Mirror ◆ 1992
5. The Spell ◆ 1992
6. Dead Man's Secret ◆ 1992
7. In the Mummy's Tomb ◆ 1992
8. The Headless Ghost ◆ 1992
9. Curse of the Claw ◆ 1993

PHILIP HALL

Greene, Bette

DIAL; HARPERCOLLINS ◆ GRADES 4–7

REAL LIFE

Beth Lambert lives in a small town in Arkansas. She and her girlfriends are in a group called the Pretty Penny Club. But her best friend is a boy, Philip Hall. This series shows the experiences of African American children living in rural settings.

1. Philip Hall Likes Me, I Reckon Maybe ◆ 1974
2. Get On Out of Here, Philip Hall ◆ 1981
3. I've Already Forgotten Your Name, Philip Hall ◆ 2004

PINE HOLLOW *see* Saddle Club: Pine Hollow

PIRATE HUNTER

Strickland, Brad, and Thomas E. Fuller

ALADDIN ◆ GRADES 5–8 ◆ A/R

ADVENTURE

Davy Shea, 12, joins his uncle Patch and Captain William Hunter on their ship, the *Aurora* as they search for the evil pirate Jack Steele. Although they appear to be pirates, too, they are really secret agents on a mission to break the control of the pirates in the Caribbean. With plenty of high seas action, this should appeal to fans of other pirate adventures, like the Jack Sparrow books.

1. Mutiny! ◆ 2002
2. The Guns of Tortuga ◆ 2003
3. Heart of Steele ◆ 2003

PIT DRAGON TRILOGY

Yolen, Jane

HARCOURT ◆ GRADES 6–8 ◆ A/R

ADVENTURE | FANTASY

On a distant planet, a thousand years in the future, fighting pit dragons provide the basis for a people's way of life. Jakkin Stewart gains his freedom by training his dragon, Heart's Blood, to win in the pits. Along the way, he gains the respect and love of Akki and crusades for the destiny of his planet, Austar IV.

1. Dragon's Blood ◆ 1982
2. Heart's Blood ◆ 1984
3. A Sending of Dragons ◆ 1987

PLATINUM TEEN

Juwell, and Precious

PRECIOUSTYMES ENTERTAINMENT ◆ GRADES 10–12

REAL LIFE

Featuring African American teens in an urban environment, each book is told by one of the characters. In *The Ab-solute Truth,* Abdul tells his story. He lives with his parents and younger brother Manny in an apartment above the small store they own. His older brother, Tyrone, was a probation officer who was killed by an ex-con two years earlier. Abdul is a Muslim and he is street smart, although he takes risks such as selling weed to earn money for clothes and a car. His story revolves around his friends, especially his girl Porsha, and basketball, until he gets caught by undercover cops. He learns that Porsha is pregnant and gives her money for an abortion; then he finds out he is not the father. Abdul takes his father's gun for a confrontation with the boy who has been taunting him (and who got Porsha pregnant). These books are short (100 to 125 pages) and the plot moves quickly. The narrators use contemporary language but no profanity. Issues of sexuality, drugs, and violence are prevalent. Part of the urban lit genre, these books will interest readers of Kimani Tru.

1. Dymond in the Tough ◆ 2005
2. The Ab-solute Truth ◆ 2005
3. Runaway ◆ 2006

PLATT FAMILY

Levitin, Sonia
ATHENEUM ◆ GRADES 6–9 ◆ A/R
FAMILY LIFE | HISTORICAL | REAL LIFE

In 1938, the Platts—a Jewish family—escape from Nazi Germany. Their goal is to reach America but the journey is filled with separations, uncertainty, and danger. Once they arrive in America in the 1940s, they must adjust to different customs and traditions.

1. Journey to America ◆ 1986
2. Silver Days ◆ 1992
3. Annie's Promise ◆ 1996

POPULAR

Krulik, Nancy
HYPERION ◆ GRADES 7–10
REAL LIFE

A group of high school students and their ups and downs are the focus here. In one book, Sugar and Josh use a hidden camera to spy on the girls. What they hear is honest and surprising. These books connect with a television series that had a brief broadcast period.

1. Round One ◆ 2000
2. Boys! Boys! Boys! ◆ 2000
3. From the Mouths of Babes ◆ 2000
4. Wherefore Art Thou . . . Josh? ◆ 2001

PRAIRIE LEGACY

Oke, Janette
BETHANY HOUSE ◆ GRADES 9–12 ◆ A/R
REAL LIFE | VALUES

Virginia Simpson is eager to be on her own. Of course, her faith and her family are important to her, but she wants to make her own choices. She begins to spend time with a new friend who encourages her to disobey her family. When a boy drowns, Virginia must face her own role in the tragedy. The series follows Virginia through her graduation from high school and, later, her marriage. Oke's Love Comes Softly series for adults describes the lives of Virginia's grandparents on the prairie.

1. The Tender Years ◆ 1997
2. A Searching Heart ◆ 1998
3. A Quiet Strength ◆ 1999
4. Like Gold Refined ◆ 2000

PRAIRIE RIVER

Gregory, Kristiana

SCHOLASTIC ◆ GRADES 4–7 ◆ A/R

HISTORICAL | REAL LIFE

After Nessa Clemens, 14, runs away from the orphanage, she travels to Prairie River, Kansas. Against her wishes, she had been engaged to marry an older man. In Prairie River, she finds work as a schoolteacher and hopes to escape her past. In the third book, a man arrives who knows about her past and Nessa hopes the information will not cause the townspeople to turn against her. Albert, her best friend from the orphanage, arrives in the fourth book and Nessa finds the situation more awkward than she expected.

1. A Journey of Faith ◆ 2003
2. A Grateful Harvest ◆ 2003
3. Winter Tidings ◆ 2004
4. Hope Springs Eternal ◆ 2005

THE PRESIDENT'S DAUGHTER

White, Ellen Emerson

FEIWEL AND FRIENDS ◆ GRADES 9–12

REAL LIFE

Meg Powers is 16 when her mother, a senator from Massachusetts, begins her campaign for the presidency. Before the campaign, Meg was worried about school, boys, and dating. Now she must deal with the attention of the press and the Secret Service. After her mother is elected, Meg is abducted and brutally mistreated by terrorists. This series was originally published in the 1980s by Avon and has been reissued by Feiwel and Friends with a fourth book added in 2007.

1. The President's Daughter ◆ 1984
2. White House Autumn ◆ 1985
3. Long Live the Queen ◆ 1989
4. Long May She Reign ◆ 2007

PRETTY FREEKIN SCARY

Flesh, Chris P.

GROSSET & DUNLAP ◆ GRADES 5–8 ◆ A/R

HUMOR

Freekin is in love with Lilly but he has one big problem. He's dead . . . and decaying. (Yes, that's two problems.) Meanwhile, Pretty wants Freekin for herself, so once Freekin and Lilly are a couple, Pretty tries to break them up. Visit the Web site www.prettyfreekinscary.com for more creepy fun.

1. You Smell Dead ◆ 2007
2. Me So Pretty! ◆ 2007
3. The Mystery of the Mystery Meat ◆ 2008
4. Been There, Crossed Over ◆ 2008

PRINCE TRILOGY *see* Sword of the Spirits

PRINCESS DIARIES

Cabot, Meg

HARPERCOLLINS ◆ GRADES 7–10 ◆ A/R

HUMOR

Mia Thermopolis is in ninth grade when her father reveals a secret. He is the prince of Genovia . . . and Mia is the crown princess! In addition to tackling the usual teenage problems and pining for a relationship with Michael, Mia must prepare for her future responsibilities. This series has been made into movies and there are many other related materials including a calendar and stationery. Two companion books give girls tips about what it takes to be a princess: *Perfect Princess* and *Princess Lessons*.

1. The Princess Diaries ◆ 2000
2. Princess in the Spotlight ◆ 2001
3. Princess in Love ◆ 2003
4. Princess in Waiting ◆ 2003
5. The Princess Project ◆ 2003
6. Princess in Pink ◆ 2004
7. The Princess Present ◆ 2004
8. Princess in Training ◆ 2005
9. Sweet 16 Princess ◆ 2006
10. Valentine Pricess ◆ 2006
11. Princess on the Brink ◆ 2007
12. Princess Mia ◆ 2008
13. Forever Princess ◆ 2009

THE PRINCESS SCHOOL

Mason, Jane B.

SCHOLASTIC ◆ GRADES 4–7 ◆ A/R

HUMOR

Familiar folktale females experience the difficulties of learning to be a princess. Elements from the classic stories about Ella, Rapunzel, Snow, and Rose are woven into these funny new versions. For example, Ella's fairy godmother is at a convention, so she'll have to make it on her own.

1. If the Shoe Fits ◆ 2004
2. Who's the Fairest? ◆ 2004
3. Let Down Your Hair ◆ 2004
4. Beauty Is a Beast ◆ 2005
5. Princess Charming ◆ 2005
6. Apple-y Ever After ◆ 2005
7. Thorn in Her Side ◆ 2006

PRINTERS DEVIL TRILOGY

Bajoria, Paul

LITTLE, BROWN ◆ GRADES 6–9 ◆ A/R

HISTORICAL | ADVENTURE | MYSTERY

In the first book, 12-year-old orphan Mog is a printer's apprentice in 19th-century London. Mog becomes embroiled in mystery and intrigue surrounding a smuggling and dope trafficking ring. In the process, the reader discovers that Mog is a girl who has been masquerading as a boy, and that Mog has a twin, Nick. In the second and third books, Mog and Nick investigate mysteries in the English countryside and in India. These are fast-paced stories full of danger and of period details.

1. The Printer's Devil ◆ 2005
2. The God of Mischief ◆ 2007
3. The City of Spirits ◆ 2007 (UK); forthcoming in US

PRISCILLA HUTCHINS

McDevitt, Jack

HARPERCOLLINS ◆ GRADES 9–12

SCIENCE FICTION

Priscilla Hutchins, a starship pilot, and archaeologist Richard Wald travel to a distant planet to examine its potential for colonization and the mysterious ruins found there. Priscilla's adventures continue in the books that follow. She investigates alien signals in *Chindi* and struggles to prevent the destruction of a planet in *Deepsix*.

1. The Engines of God ◆ 1994
2. Deepsix ◆ 2001
3. Chindi ◆ 2002
4. Omega ◆ 2003
5. Odyssey ◆ 2006
6. Cauldron ◆ 2007

PRIVATE

Brian, Kate

SIMON PULSE ◆ GRADES 9–12 ◆ A/R

REAL LIFE

Reed Brennan, a sophomore, has transferred to the exclusive Easton Academy. Reed is on a scholarship and does not fit in with the rich, often self-centered girls at the school. She is desperate to fit in and hopes to be invited to live in the "invitation only" dorm for the "Billings girls." When she is invited, she is so aware of her precarious status that she ignores cruel and dangerous behavior by the other girls. As the series progresses, Reed becomes involved in a mystery as her former boyfriend is killed and her current boyfriend is charged. Later, Reed gains power among the girls at the school. Parties, lost virginity, jealousy, hazing, and more are all part of this soap opera-like series for teens. *Last Christmas* (2008) is a prequel. The A-List series and the Gossip Girl books are comparable series.

1. Private ◆ 2006
2. Invitation Only ◆ 2006
3. Untouchable ◆ 2006
4. Confessions ◆ 2007
5. Inner Circle ◆ 2007
6. Legacy ◆ 2008
7. Ambition ◆ 2008
8. Revelation ◆ 2008

PROBABILITY

Kress, Nancy

TOR ◆ GRADES 10–12

SCIENCE FICTION

In the far future, humans can travel across the universe. In *Probability Moon,* members of a "research" expedition to an alien planet must hide their real intent—finding a weapon against the Fallers. The conflict with the Fallers continues in the next two books.

1. Probability Moon ◆ 2000
2. Probability Sun ◆ 2001
3. Probability Space ◆ 2002

PROJECT FASHION

Oliver, Jasmine

SIMON PULSE ◆ GRADES 8–10 ◆ A/R

REAL LIFE

Three girls, Marina, Frankie, and Sinead, are beginning fashion school in London. Their projects include designing clothes, jewelry, and shoes but they are also busy with their friendship, boys, and part-time jobs to make ends meet. The Violet books and The Interns are similar series.

1. Gucci Girls ◆ 2007
2. Armani Angels ◆ 2007
3. Prada Princesses ◆ 2007

PROMISE OF ZION

Elmer, Robert

BETHANY HOUSE ◆ GRADES 6–9 ◆ A/R

HISTORICAL

Dov Zalinski has survived World War II but fears his parents perished in the concentration camps. His parents had hoped to migrate to Palestine and Dov now begins the dangerous journey across war-ravaged countries. With Emily Parkinson, the daughter of a British major, Dov reaches Palestine and the two become involved in the political turmoil there.

1. Promise Breaker ◆ 2000
2. Peace Rebel ◆ 2001
3. Refugee Treasure ◆ 2001
4. Brother Enemy ◆ 2001
5. Freedom Trap ◆ 2002
6. True Betrayer ◆ 2002

PROTECTOR OF THE SMALL

Pierce, Tamora

RANDOM HOUSE ◆ GRADES 5–8 ◆ A/R

FANTASY

Keladry of Mindelan, 10, is training to be a page, an opportunity that has only been available to males. As a girl, she faces special challenges. She succeeds and wins the respect of the other pages. At age 18, Kel becomes a knight and is given an assignment to help save her homeland, Tortall.

1. First Test ◆ 1999
2. Page ◆ 2000
3. Squire ◆ 2001
4. Lady Knight ◆ 2002

PROWLERS

Golden, Christopher
SIMON & SCHUSTER ◆ GRADES 8–12

HORROR

Jack Dwyer, 19, searches for the Prowlers—werewolves that killed his best friend, Artie. With Molly Hatcher, Jack goes after the pack. Jack and Molly and their friends are aided at times by those in Ghostland, including Artie. Their efforts are hampered by the Prowlers' ability to appear as humans.

1. Prowlers ◆ 2001
2. Laws of Nature ◆ 2001
3. Predator and Prey ◆ 2001
4. Wild Things ◆ 2002

PRYDAIN CHRONICLES

Alexander, Lloyd
DELL ◆ GRADES 5–8 ◆ A/R

FANTASY

Taran, a foundling who has no known parents, is Assistant Pig-Keeper for Hen Wen, an oracular pig who is kept in a safe, quiet place by Dallben the wizard. The country is Prydain, a fantasy land loosely based on Welsh legends. Taran dreams of adventure and longs to serve with Gwydion, a warrior of the House of Don. When Hen Wen runs away, Taran gives chase and runs into the warrior's life of which he dreamed. He meets a young enchantress named Eilonwy, and the two of them and many other friends fight against the Death Lord, who would enslave the whole land. They are finally victorious, and the House of Don decides to go to a perfect land. When Taran is invited to go with them, he decides instead to stay and take his rightful place as High King of Prydain. *The High King* won the Newbery Medal. A volume of short stories about Prydain, *The Foundling, and Other Tales of Prydain* was published in 1973.

1. The Book of Three ◆ 1964

2. The Black Cauldron ◆ 1965
3. The Castle of Llyr ◆ 1966
4. Taran Wanderer ◆ 1967
5. The High King ◆ 1968

PSION

Vinge, Joan D.
WARNER ◆ GRADES 9–12
SCIENCE FICTION

In a distant future, a slum child named Cat learns to use his telepathic powers. The government then exploits him, setting him against ruthless enemies. The sequels are more violent than the first book in the series and may be suitable only for older teens.

1. Psion ◆ 1982
2. Catspaw ◆ 1988
3. Dreamfall ◆ 1996

PURE DEAD MAGIC

Gliori, Debi
KNOPF ◆ GRADES 5–8 ◆ A/R
FANTASY

In a Scottish castle, the Strega-Borgia children are in danger. Their father has been kidnapped and their new nanny is unusual. In the second book, their castle, StregaSchloss, is being repaired and Titus, 12, Pandora, 10, and baby Damp have to move. Like the Unfortunate Events books (Snicket) and Eddie Dickens (Ardagh), this series is dark and humorous.

1. Pure Dead Magic ◆ 2001
2. Pure Dead Wicked ◆ 2002
3. Pure Dead Brilliant ◆ 2003
4. Pure Dead Trouble ◆ 2005
5. Pure Dead Batty ◆ 2006
6. Pure Dead Frozen ◆ 2007

PYRATES

Archer, Chris
SCHOLASTIC ◆ GRADES 5–7 ◆ A/R
FANTASY

George has always wondered about his family's heritage. Is he really descended from the famous pirate Captain Kidd? When George and his friends discover tunnels and an underground city, they face curses and creatures seeking to protect the buried treasure.

1. Secret City ◆ 2003
2. Eye of Eternity ◆ 2003
3. Dead Man's Chest ◆ 2003
4. Last Clue ◆ 2003

QUANTUM PROPHECY

Carroll, Michael

PHILOMEL ◆ GRADES 6–9 ◆ A/R

SCIENCE FICTION

It is the tenth anniversary of the extinction of the superhumans after an intense battle between the superheroes and the supervillians. As Danny and Colin, both 13, are celebrating they realize that each is developing extraordinary powers, as is Colin's cousin Renata. The three teens are in danger from those who want the superhumans extinct and also from those who want to exploit their powers. Set in England, this series is full of adventure and will appeal to fans of Alex Rider and The Gatekeepers.

1. The Awakening ◆ 2006
2. The Gathering ◆ 2008
3. The Reckoning ◆ 2009

QUEEN GEEKS

Preble, Laura

BERKELEY JAM ◆ GRADES 8–10

REAL LIFE

At Green Pines High School, Shelby Chapelle, 15, is a geek. When tall, tattooed Becca Gallagher arrives, Shelby has found a friend. The girls form the Queen Geek Social Club and they look for other girls to include. In the first book, they are freshmen; in the second, they are sophomores. Their interests expand to include boys, dances, and romance.

1. The Queen Geek Social Club ◆ 2006
2. Queen Geeks in Love ◆ 2007
3. Prom Queen Geeks ◆ 2008

QUILT TRILOGY

Rinaldi, Ann

SCHOLASTIC ◆ GRADES 6–9 ◆ A/R

FAMILY LIFE | HISTORICAL

Hannah's life has always been focused on her family. She cared for her siblings after the death of their mother. Now her siblings are older and her father is home from his sea voyages. Hannah begins to think about her future. This trilogy spans several generations of strong female characters.

1. A Stitch in Time ◆ 1994
2. Broken Days ◆ 1995
3. The Blue Door ◆ 1996

RACING TO FREEDOM TRILOGY

Hart, Alison

PEACHTREE ◆ GRADES 5–8 ◆ A/R

HISTORICAL

During the Civil War, Gabriel, 12, is a slave on a Kentucky plantation caring for the Thoroughbred horses of his owner, Master Giles. There are renegade bands of soldiers attacking plantations for food, supplies, and horses. Gabriel saves Master Giles's Thoroughbreds and is rewarded with his freedom and a job as a jockey. As the trilogy continues, Gabriel develops his skills as a jockey and trainer. He joins his father, a free man in the Union Army, and experiences the horrors of battle. Issues of racism, freedom, slavery, conflict, and bravery are examined in this series, making it a good choice for discussions.

1. Gabriel's Horses ◆ 2007
2. Gabriel's Triumph ◆ 2007
3. Gabriel's Journey ◆ 2008

RAISE THE FLAG

Rue, Nancy N.

WATERBROOK PRESS ◆ GRADES 7–10

REAL LIFE | VALUES

Six girls at King High School in Reno, Nevada, gather each day for prayer meetings. They are known as the "Flagpole girls." Tobey, a preacher's child, takes the leadership role. The teens confront serious problems such as Shannon's anorexia and a teacher's sexual abuse of Angelica. The girls' Christian values guide their decisions.

1. Don't Count on Homecoming Queen ◆ 1998
2. "B" Is for Bad at Getting Into Harvard ◆ 1998
3. I Only Binge on Holy Hungers ◆ 1998
4. Do I Have to Paint You a Picture ◆ 1998
5. Friends Don't Let Friends Date Jason ◆ 1999
6. When Is Perfect, Perfect Enough? ◆ 1999

RAISIN RODRIGUEZ

Goldschmidt, Judy

RAZORBILL ◆ **GRADES 6–9** ◆ **A/R**

REAL LIFE

After her mother remarries, Raisin Rodriguez, 13, moves from California to Philadelphia to live with her stepfather's family. In her blog to her friends in California, Raisin is angry and obnoxious, referring to her stepfather Horace as Horse Ass. She is equally critical of her new school and her seventh-grade classmates. Raisin faces a lot of criticism when kids at her school see her blog. In the second book, Rachel blogs about her plans for her first kiss. In the third book, Rachel spends winter break in California with her father and realizes that she is not as close to her BFFs as she was before the move.

1. The Secret Blog of Raisin Rodriguez ◆ 2005
2. Raisin Rodriguez and the Big-Time Smooch ◆ 2005
3. Will the Real Raisin Rodriguez Please Stand Up? ◆ 2007

RAMA

Clarke, Arthur C.

BANTAM ◆ **GRADES 10–12** ◆ **A/R**

SCIENCE FICTION

In 2130, a strange object enters our solar system. The crew sent to investigate finds a hollow cylindrical vessel that appears to have been made by intelligent life. In *Rama II*, a similar space ship arrives and three explorers remain on it when it leaves. *The Garden of Rama* records the 13 years the three humans spend on the space ship. The second and third books were written by Clarke and Gentry Lee. The first book won the Hugo, Nebula, and Campbell awards.

1. Rendezvous with Rama ◆ 1973
2. Rama II ◆ 1989
3. The Garden of Rama ◆ 1991
4. Rama Revealed ◆ 1993

RANGER'S APPRENTICE

Flanagan, John

PHILOMEL ◆ GRADES 5–9 ◆ A/R

FANTASY

On Choosing Day, Will, 15, is disheartened when he is not selected for Battleschool. Instead, Will is to train as a Ranger and serve as an apprentice to Ranger Halt. As Will begins his training, the evil magical forces of Morgarath are planning an invasion. Will is included in a mission to stop the invaders. As the series progresses, Will and Evanlyn (a princess in disguise) are captured by the Skandians, raiders from the north country, and Ranger Halt leads a team to rescue them. Filled with invaders, magic, creatures, and battles, this series mirrors many other epic good versus evil series such as the Lord of the Rings.

1. The Ruins of Gorlan ◆ 2005
2. The Burning Bridge ◆ 2006
3. The Icebound Land ◆ 2007
4. The Battle for Skandia ◆ 2008
5. The Sorcerer of the North ◆ 2008

RATHA QUARTET

Bell, Clare E.

SIMON & SCHUSTER ◆ GRADES 7–12 ◆ A/R

ANIMAL FANTASY

Ratha, the leader of an intelligent tribe of prehistoric cats, deals with physical and emotional challenges, including the reappearance of a daughter she tried to kill, in this series of thoughtful novels.

1. Ratha's Creature ◆ 1983
2. Clan Ground ◆ 1984
3. Ratha and Thistle-Chaser ◆ 1990
4. Ratha's Challenge ◆ 1994
5. Ratha's Courage ◆ 2008

RAVENSCLIFF

Huntington, Geoffrey

REGAN BOOKS ◆ GRADES 7–10 ◆ A/R

FANTASY

Devon March, 14, realizes that he has special powers and he knows that there are evil forces lurking around him, hoping to drag him into their Hellhole. Devon goes to live in a mansion, Ravenscliff. There he learns that he is a sorcerer of the Order of the Nightwing. Even at Ravenscliff the demons pursue him. Devon discovers that there is a Hellhole controlled by the Madman and that the mansion is built right over it.

1. Sorcerers of the Nightwing ◆ 2002
2. Demon Witch ◆ 2003

THE REAL DEAL

Kaye, Amy

SMOOCH ◆ GRADES 7–10 ◆ A/R

REAL LIFE

Claire's successful appearance on a reality television show about high school has led to a spin-off show. Now the cameras will focus on her as she appears in a Broadway musical. It's exciting and stressful, putting a strain on Claire's relationship with her newly discovered older half-sister Tina (a secret from her father's past). It also endangers Claire's budding romance with Jeb, another member of the production.

1. Focus on This ◆ 2003
2. Unscripted ◆ 2004

RECLUCE

Modesitt, L. E.

TOR ◆ GRADES 10–12 ◆ A/R

FANTASY

Good and evil. Order and chaos. Recluce is a land that has achieved perfect order. Lerris has the chance to become an order-master but he must accept responsibility and prove his devotion to order. While he strives to reach his destiny, Lerris must escape the forces of the evil wizard Antonin. The saga of Recluce spans generations. *The Towers of the Sunset* is a prequel and describes the island kingdom.

1. The Magic of Recluce ◆ 1991
2. The Towers of the Sunset ◆ 1993
3. The Magic Engineer ◆ 1995
4. The Order War ◆ 1996
5. The Death of Chaos ◆ 1996
6. Fall of Angels ◆ 1997
7. The Chaos Balance ◆ 1998
8. The White Order ◆ 1999
9. Colors of Chaos ◆ 2000
10. Magi'i of Cyador ◆ 2001
11. Scion of Cyador ◆ 2001
12. Wellspring of Chaos ◆ 2004

13. Ordermaster ◆ 2005
14. Natural Ordermage ◆ 2007
15. Mage-Guard of Hamor ◆ 2008

RED RIVER: RED RIVER OF THE NORTH

Snelling, Lauraine

BETHANY HOUSE ◆ GRADES 9–12 ◆ A/R

REAL LIFE | VALUES

The Bjorklund family has left Norway and settled in the Dakota Territory. Life there is a struggle. Their prairie homestead is isolated and the climate is harsh. This series follows the hardships of the family, the expanding settlement, and the arrival of other family members and friends. Faith and the support of God are important elements in this series.

1. An Untamed Land ◆ 1996
2. A New Day Rising ◆ 1996
3. A Land to Call Home ◆ 1997
4. The Reapers' Song ◆ 1998
5. Tender Mercies ◆ 1999
6. A Blessing in Disguise ◆ 1999

RED RIVER: RETURN TO RED RIVER

Snelling, Lauraine

BETHANY HOUSE ◆ GRADES 9–12 ◆ A/R

REAL LIFE | VALUES

Thorliff Bjorklund is at college studying writing. Back home, his relationship with Anji is crumbling. As the series progresses, Thorliff gets a job with a newspaper but he returns home when a disaster strikes. As in the earlier series, Red River of the North, faith and the support of God are important elements.

1. A Dream to Follow ◆ 2001
2. Believing the Dream ◆ 2002
3. More than a Dream ◆ 2003

RED ROCK MYSTERIES

Jenkins, Jerry B., and Chris Fabry

TYNDALE KIDS ◆ GRADES 5–8 ◆ A/R

MYSTERY

Sports, mysteries, and faith are the focus in this series featuring 13-year-old twins Ashley and Bryce Timberline. In *Double Fault,* the twins attend a tennis camp at the local country club and Bryce is accused of vandalism. While trying to clear his name, the twins also find out more about the plane crash that killed their father.

1. Haunted Waters ◆ 2005
2. Stolen Secrets ◆ 2005
3. Missing Pieces ◆ 2005
4. Wild Rescue ◆ 2005
5. Grave Shadows ◆ 2005
6. Phantom Writer ◆ 2005
7. Double Fault ◆ 2005
8. Canyon Echoes ◆ 2005
9. Instant Menace ◆ 2006
10. Escaping Darkness ◆ 2006
11. Windy City Danger ◆ 2006
12. Hollywood Hold Up ◆ 2006
13. Hidden Riches ◆ 2006
14. Wind Chill ◆ 2006
15. Dead End ◆ 2006

REDWALL

Jacques, Brian

PHILOMEL ◆ GRADES 4–8 ◆ A/R

ADVENTURE | ANIMAL FANTASY

Redwall Abbey is the focal point for the mice and other creatures who live in Mossflower Woods. In the first book, *Redwall,* an army of rats tries to conquer the abbey and the defending mice must find the lost sword of Martin the Warrior to save themselves and their beloved abbey. Subsequent titles introduce a changing cast of heroes, heroines, and evildoers who interact in an epic saga full of conspiracies, adventures and heroics. *The Great Redwall Feast* is a colorfully illustrated companion book directed toward a younger audience about the secret preparations by the Redwall creatures for a feast in honor of the Abbott. *A Redwall Winter's Tale* and *The Redwall Cookbook* are additional picture books directed at younger readers. And there is a *Redwall* graphic novel (2007). The books can also be read following events in chronological order: *Lord Brocktree, Martin The Warrior, Mossflower, The Legend of Luke, Outcast of Redwall, Mariel of Redwall, The Bellmaker, Salamandastron, Redwall, Mattimeo, The Pearls of Lutra, The Long Patrol, Marlfox, The Taggerung, Triss, Loamhedge, Rakkety Tam, High Rhulain, Eulalia!,* and *Doomwyte.*

1. Redwall ◆ 1986
2. Mossflower ◆ 1988
3. Mattimeo ◆ 1989
4. Mariel of Redwall ◆ 1991

5. Salamandastron ◆ 1992
6. Martin the Warrior ◆ 1993
7. The Bellmaker ◆ 1994
8. Outcast of Redwall ◆ 1995
9. The Pearls of Lutra ◆ 1996
10. The Long Patrol ◆ 1997
11. Marlfox ◆ 1998
12. The Legend of Luke ◆ 1999
13. Lord Brocktree ◆ 2000
14. The Taggerung ◆ 2001
15. Triss ◆ 2002
16. Loamhedge ◆ 2003
17. Rakkety Tam ◆ 2004
18. High Rhulain ◆ 2005
19. Eulalia! ◆ 2007
20. Doomwyte ◆ 2008

REEL KIDS ADVENTURES

Gustaveson, Dave

YOUTH WITH A MISSION PUBLISHING ◆ GRADES 5–7

ADVENTURE | VALUES

Jeff Caldwell, 15, is interested in the Media Club at his new high school. The club has a mission—to spread a Christian message to other kids at home and around the world. In order to travel with the club, Jeff's parents insist that his 13-year-old sister Mindy be included. This causes some tension for Jeff as well as some scary moments that result from Mindy's impetuous actions. Quickly paced with lots of dialogue, this will appeal to readers who like action and discussions of values.

1. The Missing Video ◆ 1993
2. Mystery at Smokey Mountain ◆ 1994
3. The Stolen Necklace ◆ 1994
4. The Mysterious Case ◆ 1995
5. The Amazon Stranger ◆ 1995
6. The Dangerous Voyage ◆ 1995
7. The Lost Diary ◆ 1996
8. The Forbidden Road ◆ 1996
9. The Danger Zone ◆ 1997

REGENERATION

Singleton, Linda Joy

BERKLEY ◆ GRADES 8–10

SCIENCE FICTION

Five teens have been cloned in an experiment. Now the scientist in charge of the experiment has decided that it is a failure and the clones should die. In this series, the teens try to survive.

1. Regeneration ◆ 2000
2. The Search ◆ 2000
3. The Truth ◆ 2000
4. The Imposter ◆ 2000
5. The Killer ◆ 2001

REMNANTS

Applegate, K. A.
SCHOLASTIC ◆ GRADES 5–9 ◆ A/R

SCIENCE FICTION

It is 2011. Earth will soon be gone, destroyed by a collision with an asteroid. A group of people are brought together and launched into space in a tube. They travel for five hundred years and awake in a strange world. There are complex adventures as the survivors face dangers from the new environment and from each other.

1. The Mayflower Project ◆ 2001
2. Destination Unknown ◆ 2001
3. Then ◆ 2001
4. Nowhere Land ◆ 2002
5. Mutation ◆ 2002
6. Breakdown ◆ 2002
7. Isolation ◆ 2002
8. Mother, May I? ◆ 2002
9. No Place like Home ◆ 2002
10. Lost and Found ◆ 2002
11. Dream Storm ◆ 2003
12. Aftermath ◆ 2003
13. Survival ◆ 2003
14. Begin Again ◆ 2003

REPLICA

Kaye, Marilyn
BANTAM ◆ GRADES 6–9 ◆ A/R

SCIENCE FICTION

Amy Candler, 12, is working on an autobiography assignment. Her mother is vague about her family's history so Amy digs deeper. She then discovers that she is one of 13 clones—all named Amy. The project that created her now wants to control her and the other Amys.

1. Amy, Number Seven ◆ 1998
2. Pursuing Amy ◆ 1999
3. Another Amy ◆ 1999
4. Perfect Girls ◆ 1999
5. Secret Clique ◆ 1999
6. And the Two Shall Meet ◆ 1999
7. The Best of the Best ◆ 1999
8. Mystery Mother ◆ 1999
9. The Fever ◆ 2000
10. Ice Cold ◆ 2000
11. Lucky Thirteen ◆ 2000
12. In Search of Andy ◆ 2000
13. The Substitute ◆ 2000
14. The Beginning ◆ 2000
15. Transformation ◆ 2000
16. Happy Birthday, Dear Amy ◆ 2001
17. Missing Pieces ◆ 2001
18. Return of the Perfect Girls ◆ 2001
19. Dreamcrusher ◆ 2001
20. Like Father, Like Son ◆ 2001
21. Virtual Amy ◆ 2001
22. All About Andy ◆ 2002
23. The War of the Clones ◆ 2002
24. Amy, On Her Own ◆ 2002

REPLICA: THE PLAGUE TRILOGY

Kaye, Marilyn

BANTAM ◆ GRADES 6–9

SCIENCE FICTION

When a plague threatens the present, Amy journeys back in time to find a way to control the disease. When she returns to the present, she is injected into an infected human to investigate the infectious bacteria up close. The final book takes Amy on an adventure in the future.

1. Rewind ◆ 2002
2. Play ◆ 2002
3. Fast Forward ◆ 2002

REX MUNDI

Nelson, Arvid

DARK HORSE ◆ GRADES 10–12

FANTASY | ADVENTURE

With a setting that features an alternate Europe, this series follows Master Physician Julien Sauniere as he investigates a murder and searches for the Holy Grail. It is 1933 and feudal warlords still rule Europe. There are sorcerers, magic, and monsters. Catholics battle against Islam. At the center of the schemes is the Duke of Lorraine, a descendent of Christ who is determined to unite and rule Europe. The illustrations by Juan Ferreyra are lush and realistic.

1. The Guardian of the Temple ◆ 2004
2. The River Underground ◆ 2005
3. The Lost Kings ◆ 2006
4. Crown and Sword ◆ 2007
5. The Valley at the End of the World ◆ 2008

THE RHIANNA CHRONICLES

Luckett, Dave

SCHOLASTIC ◆ GRADES 4–7 ◆ A/R

FANTASY

Rhianna Wildwood is the daughter of an ordinary blacksmith, but she has extraordinary powers. She has a spellcaster, which is connected to its twin at the Office of the Chancellor of Wizardly College in Avalon. In Book Three, Rhianna helps the Queen deal with Wild Magic at the Castle of Avalon. Originally published in Australia, this series features magical events and a spunky female main character who will be attractive to girls.

1. The Girl, the Dragon, and the Wild Magic: Book One of the Rhianna Chronicles ◆ 2003
2. The Girl, the Apprentice, and the Dogs of Iron: Book Two of the Rhianna Chronicles ◆ 2004
3. The Girl, the Queen, and the Castle: Book Three of the Rhianna Chronicles ◆ 2004

RICHARD STEELE TRILOGY

Cann, Kate

SIMON & SCHUSTER ◆ GRADES 9–12 ◆ A/R

REAL LIFE

Richard Steele is pleased when he gets a job as a graphic designer. He hopes his new prosperity will make him more attractive to Portia. In the second book, his friend Bonny moves into his apartment, and in the third, Rich realizes Bonny has grown very important to him. Fans of British series such as the Confessions of Georgia Nicolson will particularly enjoy this.

1. Hard Cash ◆ 2003

2. Shacked Up ◆ 2004
3. Speeding ◆ 2004

RIOT BROTHERS

Amato, Mary

HOLIDAY HOUSE ◆ GRADES 4–7 ◆ A/R

HUMOR

Does putting underpants on your head make you laugh so hard the milk comes out your nose? If so, these are the books for you. In the first book, Wilbur, grade five, and Orville, grade three, have three adventures: they foil a bank robber, search for treasure, and build a catapult. There are numerous cartoon-style illustrations to support the antics. Fans of Captain Underpants will enjoy these books as will reluctant readers.

1. Snarf Attack, Underfoodle, and the Secret of Life: The Riot Brothers Tell All ◆ 2004
2. Drooling and Dangerous: The Riot Brothers Return! ◆ 2006
3. Stinky and Successful: The Riot Brothers Never Stop ◆ 2007
4. Take the Mummy and Run: The Riot Brothers Are on a Roll ◆ 2009

RIVERWORLD SAGA

Farmer, Philip José

BALLANTINE ◆ GRADES 10–12

SCIENCE FICTION

All the humans who ever lived find themselves resurrected and living on the banks of a giant river. But why? Efforts to find out form the center of the series as a motley crew of characters, ranging from Mark Twain to Sir Richard Burton to Genghis Khan, explore their world and its origins. Confrontations erupt as characters from different eras come together and disagree.

1. To Your Scattered Bodies Go ◆ 1971
2. The Fabulous Riverboat ◆ 1971
3. The Dark Design ◆ 1977
4. The Magic Labyrinth ◆ 1980
5. Gods of Riverworld ◆ 1983
6. River of Eternity ◆ 1983

ROLLER COASTER TYCOON

Various authors

GROSSET & DUNLAP ◆ GRADES 4–7

ADVENTURE

Based on a popular video game, these books use the "Choose Your Own Adventure" format to involve readers in decisions about characters in different amusement parks. In the first book, Marty and Megnolia inherit money and build their own park. Other books feature a haunted park and a park that may be controlled by aliens. Fans of the video game and fans of interactive reading will enjoy these books.

1. Sudden Turn (Breaux, Shane) ◆ 2002
2. Sabotage! (Breaux, Shane) ◆ 2002
3. The Great Coaster Contest (West, Tracey) ◆ 2003
4. Kidnapped! (Gorman, Larry Mike) ◆ 2003
5. Haunted Park (Noll, Katherine) ◆ 2003
6. Spaced Out! (Weiss, Bobbi J. G., and David M. Weiss) ◆ 2003

ROMA SUB ROSA

Saylor, Steven

ST. MARTIN'S ◆ GRADES 10–12

HISTORICAL | MYSTERY

Gordianus the Finder is a detective in Rome in the first century B.C. He must investigate within the conspiracies and intrigues of Roman society. In one book, he looks into the murder of a woman who knew too many secrets. In another, he searches for his son, Meto. This series combines historical information with exciting mysteries. The books are listed here in chronological/historical order.

1. Roman Blood ◆ 1991
2. The House of the Vestals ◆ 1997
3. A Gladiator Dies Only Once ◆ 2005
4. Arms of Nemesis ◆ 1992
5. Catalina's Riddle ◆ 1993
6. The Venus Throw ◆ 1996
7. A Murder on the Appian Way ◆ 1996
8. Rubicon ◆ 1999
9. Last Seen in Massilia ◆ 2000
10. A Mist of Prophecies ◆ 2002
11. The Judgment of Caesar ◆ 2004
12. The Triumph of Caesar ◆ 2008

ROMAN MYSTERIES

Lawrence, Caroline

ROARING BROOK; PUFFIN ◆ GRADES 5–8 ◆ A/R

HISTORICAL | MYSTERY

Set in the Roman Empire of the first century A.D., this series features mysteries along with information about the social and political events of the era. Flavia Gemina solves mysteries along with her friends Lupus (a beggar), Jonathan and Miriam (her Christian neighbors), and Nubia (an African slave). In *The Charioteer of Delphi,* the friends search for a missing racehorse and try to discover who is working to sabotage the chariot races at the Circus Maximus. This series has had different publishers—the dates for books vary depending on the edition.

1. The Thieves of Ostia ◆ 2002
2. The Secrets of Vesuvius ◆ 2002
3. The Pirates of Pompeii ◆ 2004
4. The Assassins of Rome ◆ 2005
5. The Dolphins of Laurentum ◆ 2005
6. The Twelve Tasks of Flavia Gemina ◆ 2004
7. The Enemies of Jupiter ◆ 2005
8. The Gladiators from Capua ◆ 2006
9. The Colossus of Rhodes ◆ 2006
10. The Fugitive from Corinth ◆ 2006
11. The Sirens of Surrentum ◆ 2007
12. The Charioteer of Delphi ◆ 2007

ROMEO CRUMB *see* The Nine Lives of Romeo Crumb

ROOKIES

Freeman, Mark

BALLANTINE ◆ GRADES 7–10 ◆ A/R

RECREATION

Major league scouts visit the Rosemont Rockets baseball players. Glen "Scrapper" Mitchell goes to play in Chicago. Dave "DT" Green becomes a rookie power hitter for Boston. Roberto "Magic" Ramirez pitches for Los Angeles. As the series ends, DT and Magic face each other in the World Series.

1. Play Ball! ◆ 1989
2. Squeeze Play ◆ 1989
3. Spring Training ◆ 1989
4. Big-League Break ◆ 1989
5. Play-Off Pressure ◆ 1989
6. Series Showdown ◆ 1989

ROOSEVELT HIGH SCHOOL

Velasquez, Gloria

PIÑATA ◆ GRADES 9–12 ◆ A/R

FAMILY LIFE | REAL LIFE

The problems of students at Roosevelt High School in Laguna, California, are featured in this series. Maya copes with her parents' divorce. African American Ankiza begins to date Hunter, who is white. She must deal with the disapproval of her friends and family. In *Teen Angel,* Celia, 15, becomes pregnant and realizes that Nicky is no longer interested in her. The students seek guidance from the school counselor, Dr. Sandra Martinez.

1. Juanita Fights the School Board ◆ 1994
2. Maya's Divided World ◆ 1995
3. Tommy Stands Alone ◆ 1997
4. Rina's Family Secret ◆ 1998
5. Ankiza ◆ 2001
6. Teen Angel ◆ 2003
7. Tyrone's Betrayal ◆ 2006

ROSWELL HIGH

Metz, Melinda

POCKET BOOKS ◆ GRADES 7–10 ◆ A/R

SCIENCE FICTION

Max, Isabel, and Michael have a secret. They are aliens, hatched from pods following the crash of their space ship in Roswell, New Mexico. Now they are attending Roswell High and trying to fit in. But as they interact with other teens, their secret may be discovered.

1. The Outsider ◆ 1999
2. The Wild One ◆ 1999
3. The Seeker ◆ 2000
4. The Watcher ◆ 2000
5. The Intruder ◆ 2000
6. The Stowaway ◆ 2000
7. The Vanished ◆ 2000
8. The Rebel ◆ 2000
9. The Dark One ◆ 2000
10. The Salvation ◆ 2000

NEW ROSWELL SERIES

These books were written for adults but are also read by teens.

1. No Good Deed (Smith, Dean Wesley, and Kristine K. Rusch) ◆ 2001
2. Loose Ends (Fox, Greg) ◆ 2001
3. Shades (Odom, Mel) ◆ 2002
4. Skeletons in the Closet (Mangels, Andy) ◆ 2002
5. Dreamwalk (Ruditis, Paul) ◆ 2002
6. Little Green Men (Smith, Dean Wesley, and Kristine K. Rusch) ◆ 2002
7. Quarantine (Burns, Laura J.) ◆ 2003
8. A New Beginning (Ryan, Kevin, and Jason Katims) ◆ 2003
9. Nightscape (Ryan, Kevin, and Jason Katims) ◆ 2003
10. Pursuit (Mangels, Andy, and Michael A. Martin) ◆ 2003
11. Turnabout (Mangels, Andy, and Michael A. Martin) ◆ 2003

ROWAN AND NINA *see* "Hour" books

ROWAN HOOD

Springer, Nancy

PHILOMEL; PUTNAM ◆ GRADES 6–9 ◆ A/R

ADVENTURE | FANTASY

In the first book, 13-year-old Rosemary sets off on a search for her father, Robin Hood. She disguises herself as a boy and adopts the name of Rowan. Subsequent novels feature young people who join Rowan's band and have adventures and support each other through problems. In *Lionclaw,* Lionel learns to stand up to his father, Lord Lionclaw. In *Outlaw Princess of Sherwood,* a young girl seeking to avoid an arranged marriage hides in the forest.

1. Rowan Hood: Outlaw Girl of Sherwood Forest ◆ 2001
2. Lion Claw: A Tale of Rowan Hood ◆ 2002
3. Outlaw Princess of Sherwood: A Tale of Rowan Hood ◆ 2003
4. Wild Boy: A Tale of Rowan Hood ◆ 2004
5. Rowan Hood Returns: The Final Chapter ◆ 2005

ROXY GIRLS *see* Luna Bay

ROYAL BALLET SCHOOL DIARIES

Moss, Alexandra

GROSSET & DUNLAP ◆ GRADES 4–7 ◆ A/R

REAL LIFE

Ellie Brown, 11, has loved ballet since she was four years old. Now she is in London, auditioning for the Royal Ballet School. Although she wants to be accepted at the school, she worries about her mother in America. Since the death of her father, there is no one to care for her mother, who is ill. Ellie must choose between going home or following her dream. As the series progresses, Ellie matures and, eventually, faces more dilemmas including *Boys or Ballet?*.

1. Ellie's Chance to Dance ◆ 2005
2. Lauren's Leap of Faith ◆ 2005
3. Isabelle's Perfect Performance ◆ 2005
4. Sophie's Flight of Fancy ◆ 2005
5. Kate's Special Secret ◆ 2005
6. Grace's Show of Strength ◆ 2006
7. New Girl ◆ 2006
8. Boys or Ballet? ◆ 2006

ROYAL DIARIES

Various authors

SCHOLASTIC ◆ GRADES 3–7 ◆ A/R

HISTORICAL

Readers are introduced to different eras in history through these fictionalized diaries. Each book features events from the childhood or adolescence of a famous female. The books include historical notes, documents, maps, genealogy, and illustrations. Fans of Dear America would gain a new perspective on world history from these books.

1. Cleopatra VII: Daughter of the Nile, Egypt, 57 B.C. (Gregory, Kristiana) ◆ 1999
2. Elizabeth I: Red Rose of the House of Tudor, England, 1544 (Lasky, Kathryn) ◆ 1999
3. Marie Antoinette: Princess of Versailles, Austria-France, 1769 (Lasky, Kathryn) ◆ 2000
4. Isabel: Jewel of Castilla, Spain, 1466 (Meyer, Carolyn) ◆ 2000
5. Nzingha: Warrior Queen of Matamba, Angola, Africa, 1595 (McKissack, Patricia C.) ◆ 2000
6. Anastasia: The Last Grand Duchess, Russia, 1914 (Meyer, Carolyn) ◆ 2000
7. Kaiulani: The People's Princess, Hawaii, 1889 (White, Ellen Emerson) ◆ 2001
8. Lady of Ch'iao Kuo: Warrior of the South, Southern China, A.D. 531 (Yep, Laurence) ◆ 2001
9. Victoria: May Blossom of Britannia, England, 1829 (Kirwan, Anna) ◆ 2001
10. Mary: Queen of Scots, Queen Without a Country, France 1553 (Lasky, Kathryn) ◆ 2002
11. Sondok: Princess of the Moon and Stars, Korea, A.D. 595 (Holman, Sheri) ◆ 2002

12. Jahanara: Princess of Princesses, India, 1627 (Lasky, Kathryn) ◆ 2002
13. Eleanor: Crown Jewel of Aquitaine, France, 1136 (Lasky, Kathryn) ◆ 2002
14. Elisabeth of Austria: The Princess Bride, Austria-Hungary, 1853 (Denenberg, Barry) ◆ 2003
15. Kristina: The Girl King, Sweden, 1638 (Meyer, Carolyn) ◆ 2003
16. Weetamoo: Heart of the Pocassets, Massachusetts, 1653 (Smith, Patricia Clark) ◆ 2003
17. Lady of Palenque: Flower of Bacal, Mesoamerica, A.D. 749 (Kirwan, Anna) ◆ 2004
18. Kazunomiya: Prisoner of Heaven, Japan, 1858 (Lasky, Kathryn) ◆ 2004
19. Catherine: The Great Journey, Russia, 1743 (Gregory, Kristiana) ◆ 2005
20. Anacaona, Golden Flower: Haiti, 1490 (Danticat, Edwidge) ◆ 2005

ROYAL PAVILIONS

Chaikin, Linda

BETHANY HOUSE ◆ GRADES 9–12

HISTORICAL

In the time of the Crusades, Tancred Redwan is a rebel who rescues Helena, a courageous Byzantine heiress. Once restored to her family, Helena is to marry a Muslim prince. Tancred again comes to her aid, taking her to his family's castle.

1. Swords and Scimitars ◆ 1996
2. Golden Palaces ◆ 1996
3. Behind the Veil ◆ 1998

RPM

Fabry, Chris

TYNDALE HOUSE ◆ GRADES 5–8 ◆ A/R

REAL LIFE | VALUES

Jamie Maxwell has grown up around auto racing. Her father is a successful NASCAR driver and Jamie dreams of being the first female to win the cup. Tim Carhardt is recovering from a harrowing crash. His confidence has been shaken and he is drifting. Both Jamie and Tim find that their faith is tested as they strive to reach their goals.

1. Blind Spot ◆ 2007
2. Over the Wall ◆ 2007

3. Overdrive ◆ 2008
4. Checkered Flag ◆ 2008

RUIN MIST: THE KINGDOMS AND THE ELVES OF THE REACHES

Stanek, Robert

REAGENT PRESS ◆ GRADES 6–9

FANTASY

Adrina is a princess whose kingdom is threatened; Seth is a warrior elf on a journey to the land of Man; Vilmos is a boy with a magical future. Keeper Martin, head of the Lore Keepers, chronicles the adventures of these three heroes. In one book, they prevent the end of the Kingdom Alliance and they save Quashan'. The events in this series are from Stanek's fantasy series for adults, Ruin Mist Chronicles.

1. Keeper Martin's Tales, Book 1 ◆ 2002
2. Keeper Martin's Tales, Book 2 ◆ 2002
3. Keeper Martin's Tales, Book 3 ◆ 2002
4. Keeper Martin's Tales, Book 4 ◆ 2003

RUIN MIST CHRONICLES

Stanek, Robert

REAGENT PRESS ◆ GRADES 9–12

FANTASY

After the war, the kingdoms were divided. Darkness has fallen over the mortal world. The kings have proclaimed that all magic must be destroyed so that the world can be restored. Princess Adrina must fight for her kingdom while Vilmos studies to be a mage. This series is for adults and older teens and has been reissued in a series for a younger readers, Ruin Mist: The Kingdoms and the Elves of the Reaches.

1. Keeper Martin's Tale ◆ 2002
2. Elf Queen's Quest ◆ 2002
3. Kingdom Alliance ◆ 2003
4. Fields of Honor ◆ 2005
5. Mark of the Dragon ◆ 2005

RUIN MIST TALES

1. The Elf Queen and the King, Book 1 ◆ 2002
2. The Elf Queen and the King, Book 2 ◆ 2002

SADDLE CLUB: PINE HOLLOW

Bryant, Bonnie

BANTAM ◆ GRADES 6–8 ◆ A/R

REAL LIFE

The friends from the Saddle Club series are now in high school. Stevie, Lisa, and Carole are busy with their individual activities as they begin dating, driving, and working. They still love horses and enjoy being together at Pine Hollow stables. The events in this series are more serious. For example, Stevie is involved in an accident that seriously injures another girl, Callie. Several books deal with Callie's injuries, anger, and recovery. Fans of books about horses, school, and boys will want to read this series.

1. The Long Ride ◆ 1998
2. The Trail Home ◆ 1998
3. Reining In ◆ 1998
4. Changing Leads ◆ 1999
5. Conformation Faults ◆ 1999
6. Shying at Trouble ◆ 1999
7. Penalty Points ◆ 1999
8. Course of Action ◆ 1999
9. Riding to Win ◆ 1999
10. Ground Training ◆ 2000
11. Cross-Ties ◆ 2000
12. Back in the Saddle ◆ 2000
13. High Stakes ◆ 2000
14. Headstrong ◆ 2000
15. Setting the Pace ◆ 2000
16. Track Record ◆ 2001
17. Full Gallop ◆ 2001

SADDLE ISLAND

Siamon, Sharon

WALRUS BOOKS ◆ GRADES 5–8 ◆ A/R

REAL LIFE

Kelsie MacKay loves horses. On the eastern shore of Nova Scotia, Kelsie rescues a horse, Caspar, whose owner, Hank Harefield, plans to auction him off. Caspar is a difficult horse, but Kelsie plans to care for him and protect him. Along with her brother Andy she creates a sanctuary—Saddle Island—for unwanted, mistreated horses. Fans of the Mustang Mountain books will want to read these books, too.

1. Gallop to the Sea ◆ 2006

2. Secrets in the Sand ◆ 2006
3. Race to the Rescue ◆ 2007

SADDLES, STARS, AND STRIPES

Kent, Deborah

KINGFISHER ◆ GRADES 4–7 ◆ A/R

HISTORICAL

Horses, history and intrepid female main characters are the focus of this series. In one book, Lexie's brother was a rider for the Pony Express but he has been accused of theft. Lexie, 15, tries to clear his name. Other books take place during the gold rush, the Civil War, and the Revolutionary War. This would be a good choice for middle school reluctant readers.

1. Blackwater Creek ◆ 2005
2. Chance of a Lifetime ◆ 2005
3. Riding the Pony Express ◆ 2006
4. On the Edge of Revolution ◆ 2006

THE SAFE-KEEPER'S SECRET

Shinn, Sharon

VIKING ◆ GRADES 7–12 ◆ A/R

FANTASY

In *The Safe-Keeper's Secret,* Fiona expects to be a Safe-Keeper like her mother Damiana. The Safe-Keeper listens to the secrets of others and never reveals them. When she is 15, Fiona leaves the village to study herbs and healing. Reed, who has been like a brother to her but is really a foundling, also leaves to learn from a merchant. When they return, Damiana is dying and she reveals an important secret about their past. Subsequent books feature different main characters in this fantasy medieval world.

1. The Safe-Keeper's Secret ◆ 2004
2. The Truth-Teller's Tale ◆ 2005
3. The Dream-Maker's Magic ◆ 2006

SAGA OF THE SKOLIAN EMPIRE

Asaro, Catherine

TOR ◆ GRADES 10–12

SCIENCE FICTION

Romance and science fiction are intertwined in this series set in the distant future with side trips to an alternate contemporary Earth. The Skolian Empire and the Traders are longstanding rivals. The Skolians have telepathic abilities and the Traders derive pleasure from pain. In the first book, Soz, a potential leader of the Skolian Empire, meets and falls in love with the Trader heir. Soz faces difficult decisions about the future of her people. Other books feature different characters and interstellar intrigues. *The Quantum Rose* won the Nebula Award for Best Novel. The two *Triad* books provide some history.

1. Primary Inversion ◆ 1995
2. Catch the Lightning ◆ 1996
3. The Last Hawk ◆ 1997
4. The Radiant Seas ◆ 1998
5. Ascendant Sun ◆ 2000
6. The Quantum Rose ◆ 2000
7. Spherical Harmonic ◆ 2001
8. The Moon's Shadow ◆ 2003
9. Skyfall ◆ 2003
10. Schism: Part One of Triad ◆ 2004
11. The Final Key: Part Two of Triad ◆ 2005
12. The Ruby Dice ◆ 2008

THE SAGAS OF DARREN SHAN *see* Cirque du Freak

SAILOR MOON NOVELS

Takeuchi, Naoko

TOKYOPOP ◆ GRADES 4–7

FANTASY

Serena meets a magical cat, Luna, and is given superpowers, becoming Sailor Moon. These novels connect to other TokyoPop manga about this popular character.

1. A Scout Is Born ◆ 1999
2. The Power of Love ◆ 1999
3. Mercury Rising ◆ 1999
4. Mars Attacks! ◆ 2000
5. Eternal Sleep ◆ 2000
6. Scouts on Film ◆ 2000
7. Cel Mates ◆ 2000
8. Diamonds Not Forever ◆ 2000

SALLY LOCKHART TRILOGY

Pullman, Philip

KNOPF ◆ GRADES 9–12 ◆ A/R

HISTORICAL | MYSTERY

Sally Lockhart, 16, lives in London during the Victorian era. Her first mystery is to find out who killed her father and why. She encounters many characters from the darker side of London. As the mystery evolves, Sally's search for a missing ruby places her in great danger. *The Tin Princess* (1994) is a related book that features characters from the Sally Lockhart trilogy.

1. The Ruby in the Smoke ◆ 1985
2. The Shadow in the North ◆ 1988
3. The Tiger in the Well ◆ 1990

SAM AND STEPHANIE

Oliver, Andrew

ADAMS-POMEROY ◆ GRADES 4–7 ◆ A/R

MYSTERY

Adventurous 12-year-olds Sam and Stephanie encounter danger when they investigate the disappearance of an elderly man in their small Wisconsin town in the first book in the series. Subsequent mysteries also require determination and courage from the young sleuths.

1. If Photos Could Talk ◆ 2005
2. Haunted Hill ◆ 2006
3. Scrambled ◆ 2007

SAM GRIBLEY *see* My Side of the Mountain

SAMMY KEYES

Van Draanen, Wendelin

KNOPF ◆ GRADES 5–8 ◆ A/R

MYSTERY

Sammy Keyes is in seventh grade. She lives with her grandmother in an apartment. While playing with some binoculars, she observes a thief at work. Unfortunately, the thief sees her, too. Now she has real problems. Other books have mysteries at Halloween and Christmas. In one book, she helps her actress mother when she is suspected of murdering a rival for an acting part.

1. Sammy Keyes and the Hotel Thief ◆ 1998
2. Sammy Keyes and the Skeleton Man ◆ 1998
3. Sammy Keyes and the Sisters of Mercy ◆ 1999
4. Sammy Keyes and the Runaway Elf ◆ 1999
5. Sammy Keyes and the Curse of Moustache Mary ◆ 2000
6. Sammy Keyes and the Hollywood Mummy ◆ 2001
7. Sammy Keyes and the Search for Snake Eyes ◆ 2002
8. Sammy Keyes and the Art of Deception ◆ 2003
9. Sammy Keyes and the Psycho Kitty Queen ◆ 2004
10. Sammy Keyes and the Dead Giveaway ◆ 2005
11. Sammy Keyes and the Wild Things ◆ 2007
12. Sammy Keyes and the Cold Hard Cash ◆ 2008

SAMURAI CAT

Rogers, Mark E.

TOR; INFINITY ◆ GRADES 10–12

ANIMAL FANTASY

Puns and satire fill these highly illustrated stories about Miaowara Tomokato and his sidekick Shiro, felines who will take on anyone—from King Arthur and his knights to Genghis Khan to characters from science fiction.

1. The Adventures of Samurai Cat ◆ 1984
2. More Adventures of Samurai Cat ◆ 1986
3. Samurai Cat in the Real World ◆ 1989
4. Samurai Cat Goes to the Movies ◆ 1994
5. Samurai Cat Goes to Hell ◆ 1998
6. Sword of the Samurai Cat ◆ 2003

SAMURAI GIRL

Asai, Carrie

SIMON & SCHUSTER ◆ GRADES 6–10 ◆ A/R

FANTASY

As a baby, Heaven was adopted by the Kogo family whose patriarch is a Japanese crime boss. Now, at age 17, she is to be married to the son of a colleague of her adoptive father so that two Japanese families come together. Her wedding is interrupted by a man claiming to be her brother. Heaven watches as he is brutally murdered. She escapes from her family and studies to be a samurai, hoping to find her true identity and avenge her brother's death.

1. The Book of the Sword ◆ 2003
2. The Book of the Shadow ◆ 2003

3. The Book of the Pearl ◆ 2003
4. The Book of the Wind ◆ 2003
5. The Book of the Flame ◆ 2004
6. The Book of the Heart ◆ 2004

SAMURAI MYSTERIES *see* The Ghost in the Tokaido Inn

SANDY LANE STABLES

Various authors

EDC PUBLISHING ◆ GRADES 5–8 ◆ A/R

REAL LIFE

Horses and riding are featured in this series that includes show jumping, competitions, and horses being mistreated. The series was originally published in Britain.

1. A Horse for the Summer (Bates, Michelle) ◆ 1996
2. The Runaway Pony (Leigh, Susannah) ◆ 1996
3. Strangers at the Stables (Bates, Michelle) ◆ 1996
4. The Midnight Horse (Bates, Michelle) ◆ 1998
5. Dream Pony (Leigh, Susannah) ◆ 1998
6. Ride by Moonlight (Bates, Michelle) ◆ 1998
7. Horse in Danger (Bates, Michelle) ◆ 1998
8. The Perfect Pony (Bates, Michelle) ◆ 1999
9. Racing Vacation (Bates, Michelle) ◆ 2000

SARAH'S JOURNEY

Luttrell, Wanda

CHARIOT VICTOR PUBLISHING ◆ GRADES 10–12 ◆ A/R

HISTORICAL | VALUES

Sarah is 12 at the start of this series and the Revolutionary War is beginning. With her family, she moves from Kentucky to Williamsburg, but there is hardship as her brother leaves to fight against the British. Eventually, Sarah returns to Kentucky to open a school in a rural area. Throughout her struggles, she asks God for guidance.

1. Home on Stoney Creek ◆ 1995
2. Stranger in Williamsburg ◆ 1995
3. Reunion in Kentucky ◆ 1995
4. Whispers in Williamsburg ◆ 1997
5. Shadows on Stoney Creek ◆ 1997

SARDINE IN OUTER SPACE

Guibert, Emmanuel, and Joan Sfar

ROARING BROOK ◆ GRADES 4–7

SCIENCE FICTION

A comic book space fantasy in which an independent-minded, redheaded young girl named Sardine enlists the help of her piratical Uncle Yellow Shoulder to foil the villainous plans of the slow-witted Supermuscleman. Originally published in France.

1. Sardine in Outer Space 1 ◆ 2006
2. Sardine in Outer Space 2 ◆ 2006
3. Sardine in Outer Space 3 ◆ 2007
4. Sardine in Outer Space 4 ◆ 2007
5. Sardine in Outer Space 5 ◆ 2008
6. Sardine in Outer Space 6 ◆ 2008

S.A.S.S. *see* Students Across the Seven Seas

SAVED BY THE BELL

Cruise, Beth

ALADDIN ◆ GRADES 6–8 ◆ A/R

ADVENTURE

Different characters appear in the books in this series, which is linked to the television program of the same name. Some of the books feature original characters of the television show; others introduce new classmates. The focus throughout the books is on conflicts that will be familiar to teens—dating, grades, responsibilities, romance, and even social and political issues. These books will appeal especially to teenage girls.

1. Bayside Madness ◆ 1992
2. Zack Strikes Back ◆ 1992
3. California Scheming ◆ 1992
4. Girls' Night Out ◆ 1992
5. Zack's Last Scam ◆ 1992
6. Class Trip Chaos ◆ 1992
7. That Old Zack Magic ◆ 1993
8. Impeach Screech! ◆ 1993
9. One Wild Weekend ◆ 1993
10. Kelly's Hero ◆ 1993
11. Don't Tell a Soul ◆ 1994
12. Computer Confusion ◆ 1994
13. Silver Spurs ◆ 1994
14. Best Friend's Girl ◆ 1994

15. Zack in Action ◆ 1994
16. Operation: Clean Sweep ◆ 1994
17. Scene One, Take Two ◆ 1995
18. Fireside Manners ◆ 1995
19. Picture Perfect ◆ 1995
20. Surf's Up ◆ 1995
21. Screech in Love ◆ 1995
22. Ex-Zack-Ly ◆ 1995
23. Standing Room Only ◆ 1996

SAVED BY THE BELL: THE NEW CLASS

1. Trouble Ahead ◆ 1994
2. Spilling the Beans ◆ 1994
3. Going, Going, Gone! ◆ 1995
4. Breaking the Rules ◆ 1995
5. Spreading the Word ◆ 1995
6. Lights, Camera, Action! ◆ 1995
7. May the Best Team Win ◆ 1995
8. It's the Thought That Counts ◆ 1995
9. Finders, Keepers ◆ 1995
10. Franken-Bobby! ◆ 1995

SAVED BY THE BELL: THE COLLEGE YEARS

1. Freshman Frenzy ◆ 1994
2. Zack Zeroes In ◆ 1994
3. Exit, Stage Right ◆ 1994
4. Mistletoe Magic ◆ 1994

SCREECH OWLS

MacGregor, Roy
McCLELLAND & STEWART ◆ GRADES 4–7
MYSTERY | SPORTS

The Screech Owls are a Canadian high school hockey team. They frequently travel to competitions and often find themselves in the center of puzzling mysteries. Friendship, team rivalry, sportsmanship, and adventure are all part of these books, in addition to some great hockey.

1. Mystery at Lake Placid ◆ 1995
2. The Night They Stole the Stanley Cup ◆ 1995
3. The Screech Owls' Northern Adventure ◆ 1996
4. Murder at Hockey Camp ◆ 1997
5. Kidnapped in Sweden ◆ 1997
6. Terror in Florida ◆ 1997
7. The Quebec City Crisis ◆ 1998
8. The Screech Owls' Home Loss ◆ 1998
9. Nightmare in Nagano ◆ 1998

10. Danger in Dinosaur Valley ◆ 1999
11. The Ghost of the Stanley Cup ◆ 2000
12. The West Coast Murders ◆ 2000
13. Sudden Death in New York City ◆ 2000
14. Horror on River Road ◆ 2001
15. Death Down Under ◆ 2001
16. Power Play in Washington ◆ 2001
17. The Secret of the Deep Woods ◆ 2003
18. Murder at the Winter Games ◆ 2004
19. Attack on the Tower of London ◆ 2004
20. The Screech Owls' Reunion ◆ 2004

SEAFORT SAGA

Feintuch, David
ASPECT ◆ GRADES 9–12
SCIENCE FICTION

This military science fiction saga follows the exploits of Nicholas Seafort. His colonial adventures take him across the stars as he serves as captain, then commander, and even Secretary General—the global executive of Earth. He faces intergalactic dangers and is involved in numerous battles. In his later years, he is the commandant of the Naval Academy, where he must prepare young cadets to face alien invaders.

1. Midshipman's Hope ◆ 1994
2. Prisoner's Hope ◆ 1995
3. Challenger's Hope ◆ 1995
4. Fisherman's Hope ◆ 1996
5. Voices of Hope ◆ 1996
6. Patriarch's Hope ◆ 2000
7. Children of Hope ◆ 2001

SEBASTIAN BARTH

Howe, James
AVON ◆ GRADES 5–7 ◆ A/R
MYSTERY

Sebastian Barth lives in rural Connecticut, where he has a weekly radio show. He becomes involved in solving mysteries as he looks for scoops for the show. He is friends with Alex, the police chief, who helps him out. In *Dew Drop Dead*, he and his friends Corrie and David befriend a homeless man when Corrie's father, a minister, begins a ministry to the homeless. At the same time, the children find a body in an abandoned inn. Clues seem to point to the homeless man, but police work determines that the man died of exposure and the confused homeless man hid the body. Other mysteries are about poisoning in the school cafeteria, and a famous actress in danger.

1. What Eric Knew ◆ 1985
2. Stage Fright ◆ 1986
3. Eat Your Poison, Dear ◆ 1986
4. Dew Drop Dead ◆ 1990

SECRET AGENT MJJ

Jefferies, Marc John, and Danny Hirsch
BIG SMILE ◆ GRADES 4–7
ADVENTURE

At the age of 13, African American Marc John Jefferies is already a Hollywood star when a call comes asking him to serve the cause of good against evil. His codename is Boogieman and his sidekick is Scooter Brosnan. In *The Volcano,* Boogieman has to leave a film set to tackle a volcano that is threatening disaster—is this a natural event?

1. The Missing Princess ◆ 2005
2. The Secret Portrait ◆ 2005
3. The Volcano ◆ 2005
4. The Fountain of Youth ◆ 2006
5. The Pirates of Marathon ◆ 2006
6. The Sun King ◆ 2006

SECRET CIRCLE

Smith, L. J.
HARPERCOLLINS ◆ GRADES 7–10
FANTASY

Cassie joins a coven of young witches in the town of New Salem and endangers everyone when she seeks to attract Adam, the coven leader. In *The Captive,* there is a struggle for power within the coven, and in *The Power,* good and evil battle each other.

1. The Initiation ◆ 1992
2. The Captive ◆ 1992
3. The Power ◆ 1992

THE SECRET COUNTRY TRILOGY

Dean, Pamela

PENGUIN ◆ GRADES 7–10

FANTASY

For years, five cousins have played a game called "The Secret." It is a game they created involving witches, unicorns, magical events, and another world. Then their game becomes a reality. They are in the Secret Country and to save this magical place they must face three challenges. These books were originally published in the 1980s and have been reissued.

1. The Secret Country ◆ 2003
2. The Hidden Land ◆ 2003
3. The Whim of the Dragon ◆ 2003

SECRET REFUGE

Snelling, Lauraine

BETHANY HOUSE ◆ GRADES 9–12 ◆ A/R

FAMILY LIFE | HISTORICAL | VALUES

On her family's plantation in Kentucky, Jesselynn Highwood is preparing to escape the dangers of the Civil War. With her younger brother and the family's Thoroughbred horses, she begins a journey to Missouri. Her sister, Louisa, is involved in smuggling supplies to a hospital in Richmond, Virginia. Strong family values are woven into this historical fiction series.

1. Daughter of Twin Oaks ◆ 2000
2. Sisters of the Confederacy ◆ 2000
3. The Long Way Home ◆ 2001

SECRET TEXTS

Lisle, Holly

WARNER ◆ GRADES 11–12

FANTASY

This complex and fast-paced series features Kait Galweigh, a young diplomat who has a dark secret. If she and her companions can destroy the Mirror of Souls, they may save the people they care for.

1. Diplomacy of Wolves ◆ 1998
2. Vengeance of Dragons ◆ 1999
3. Courage of Falcons ◆ 2000

SECRET WORLD OF ALEX MACK

Various authors

MINSTREL/POCKET BOOKS ◆ GRADES 5–8

ADVENTURE | FANTASY

Alex Mack was just an ordinary teenager until she was drenched with a strange chemical. Now she can move objects with her mind and change shapes by morphing into a liquid form. Alex and her friends—Ray Alvarado, Robyn Russo, Nicole Wilson, and boyfriend Hunter Reeves—get involved in adventures such as capturing a pet-napping ring. Alex also has to worry about keeping her special powers a secret; especially when she gets sick on a trip to New York and can't control her ability to become liquid. Readers who like the popular Nickelodeon television program will enjoy following the familiar characters in these adventures.

1. Alex, You're Glowing! (Gallagher, Diana G.) ◆ 1995
2. Bet You Can't! (Gallagher, Diana G.) ◆ 1995
3. Bad News Babysitting! (Lipman, Ken) ◆ 1995
4. Witch Hunt! (Gallagher, Diana G.) ◆ 1995
5. Mistaken Identity! (Gallagher, Diana G.) ◆ 1996
6. Cleanup Catastrophe! (Dubowski, Cathy East) ◆ 1996
7. Take a Hike! (Dubowski, Cathy East) ◆ 1996
8. Go for the Gold! (Gallagher, Diana G.) ◆ 1996
9. Poison in Paradise! (Gallagher, Diana G.) ◆ 1996
10. Zappy Holidays! (Super Edition) (Gallagher, Diana G.) ◆ 1996
11. Junkyard Jitters! (Barnes-Svarney, Patricia) ◆ 1997
12. Frozen Stiff! (Gallagher, Diana G.) ◆ 1997
13. I Spy! (Peel, John) ◆ 1997
14. High Flyer! (Barnes-Svarney, Patricia) ◆ 1997
15. Milady Alex! (Gallagher, Diana G.) ◆ 1997
16. Father-Daughter Disaster! (Emery, Clayton) ◆ 1997
17. Bonjour, Alex! (Dubowski, Cathy East) ◆ 1997
18. Close Encounters! (Weiss, David Cody, and Bobbi J. G. Weiss) ◆ 1997
19. Hocus Pocus! (Locke, Joseph) ◆ 1997
20. Halloween Invaders! (Vornholt, John) ◆ 1997
21. Truth Trap! (Dubowski, Cathy East) ◆ 1997
22. New Year's Revolution! (Gallagher, Diana G.) ◆ 1997
23. Lost in Vegas! (Peel, John) ◆ 1998
24. Computer Crunch! (Barnes-Svarney, Patricia) ◆ 1998
25. In Hot Pursuit! (Odom, Mel) ◆ 1998
26. Canine Caper! (Gallagher, Diana G.) ◆ 1998
27. Civil War in Paradise! (Stone, Bonnie D.) ◆ 1998
28. Pool Party Panic! (Mitchell, V. E.) ◆ 1998
29. Sink or Swim! (Dubowski, Cathy East) ◆ 1998
30. Gold Rush Fever! (Gallagher, Diana G.) ◆ 1998

31. New York Nightmare! (Pass, Erica) ◆ 1998
32. Haunted House Hijinks! (Vornholt, John) ◆ 1998
33. Lights Camera Action (Garton, Ray) ◆ 1998
34. Paradise Lost, Paradise Regained! (Gallagher, Diana G.) ◆ 1998

THE SEEKER CHRONICLES

James, Betsy

DUTTON; ATHENEUM ◆ GRADES 9–12

FANTASY

Kat, 16, lives in Upslope, a town with rigid rules and expectations for women. Kat's mother was Hillborn and Kat faces exclusion for her mixed heritage. She is torn between her desire to be obedient and her rebellious nature. When she finds Nall, a wounded Rig (seal-man), she helps him recover and eventually falls in love with him. As the series progresses, Kat leaves her home to live with relatives from her mother's family. Later, she returns and reconnects with Nall. Together they travel across the sea to Nall's homeland hoping to find a way to stop the escalating violence on the mainland.

1. Long Night Dance ◆ 1989
2. Dark Heart ◆ 1992
3. Listening at the Gate ◆ 2006

THE SEER

Singleton, Linda Joy

LLEWELLYN ◆ GRADES 6–10

MYSTERY | HORROR

Sabine has psychic abilities that get her in trouble. In the first book, she tries to hide her power but her spirit guide, Opal, is insistent as Sabine foresees danger for a classmate. In the second book, Sabine and a goth friend are seeking a remedy for Sabine's grandmother when they become distracted by Sabine's visions of an unhappy ghost. Reluctant readers will find these books compelling.

1. Don't Die Dragonfly ◆ 2004
2. Last Dance ◆ 2005
3. Witch Ball ◆ 2006
4. Sword Play ◆ 2006
5. Fatal Charm ◆ 2007

SEPTIMUS HEAP

Sage, Angie

HARPERCOLLINS ◆ GRADES 5–8 ◆ A/R

FANTASY

Jenna has been raised by Silas Heap whose own son Septimus (the seventh son of a seventh son) was taken away at birth and is presumed to be dead. Jenna, 10, learns she is a princess and that she is in danger from the assassins of the Supreme Commander. Along with several companions, she escapes from the assassins only to be pursued by the agents of Necromancer DomDaniel. As the series progresses, Septimus Heap is revealed to be alive and serving as Apprentice to the ExtraOrdinary Wizard. Time travel, quests, ghosts, Darke Magyk and more are sure to appeal to fantasy fans.

1. Magyk ◆ 2005
2. Flyte ◆ 2006
3. Physik ◆ 2007
4. Queste ◆ 2008

A SERIES OF UNFORTUNATE EVENTS

Snicket, Lemony

HARPERCOLLINS ◆ GRADES 3–7 ◆ A/R

FANTASY

The lives of the Baudelaire children are full of woe. Their parents perished in a fire, leaving Violet, Klaus, and Sunny at the mercy of the villainous Count Olaf. Just when you think they may find happiness, it is snatched away. The books in this droll series include many side comments and dire predictions. Read them at your own peril. There are related items including boxed sets of books, posters, puzzles, postcards, calendars, and *Lemony Snicket: The Unauthorized Autobiography*. *The Beatrice Letters* (2006) is a (fictional) collection of letters between Lemony Snicket and the elusive Beatrice, offering insight into the author and his series.

1. The Bad Beginning: Book the First ◆ 1999
2. The Reptile Room: Book the Second ◆ 1999
3. The Wide Window: Book the Third ◆ 2000
4. The Miserable Mill: Book the Fourth ◆ 2000
5. The Austere Academy: Book the Fifth ◆ 2000
6. The Ersatz Elevator: Book the Sixth ◆ 2001
7. The Vile Village: Book the Seventh ◆ 2001

8. The Hostile Hospital: Book the Eighth ◆ 2001
9. The Carnivorous Carnival: Book the Ninth ◆ 2002
10. The Slippery Slope: Book the Tenth ◆ 2003
11. The Grim Grotto: Book the Eleventh ◆ 2004
12. The Penultimate Peril: Book the Twelfth ◆ 2005
13. The End—Too Dreadful to Picture: Book the Thirteenth ◆ 2006

SEVEN DEADLY SINS

Wasserman, Robin
SIMON PULSE ◆ **GRADES 10–12** ◆ **A/R**
REAL LIFE

Haven High in Grace, California, is full of teen angst and issues. Harper Grace, whose family founded the town, is popular and predatory. In the first book, Harper has set her sights on another girl's boyfriend. Her popularity is threatened by new girl Kaia, who is willing to use sex to get what she wants. Then there's Kane, the self-centered bad-boy, and Mr. Powell, the hot new teacher. Reviewers have called this series "Desperate Housewives" for teens. Girls who like Gossip Girls, Starlet, and A-List books will be attracted to this series.

1. Lust ◆ 2005
2. Envy ◆ 2005
3. Pride ◆ 2006
4. Wrath ◆ 2006
5. Sloth ◆ 2006
6. Gluttony ◆ 2007
7. Greed ◆ 2007

SEVENS

Wallens, Scott
PUFFIN ◆ **GRADES 6–12** ◆ **A/R**
REAL LIFE

Seven teens have problems ranging from life in a wheelchair to homosexuality to an obsession with good grades. These seven were all involved in a terrible experience in their pasts. This suspenseful series, which takes place over the course of seven weeks, introduces each character and his or her problems, building to a cliff-hanger ending.

1. Shattered: Week 1 ◆ 2002
2. Exposed: Week 2 ◆ 2002
3. Pushed: Week 3 ◆ 2002
4. Meltdown: Week 4 ◆ 2002
5. Torn: Week 5 ◆ 2002

6. Betrayal: Week 6 ◆ 2002
7. Redemption: Week 7 ◆ 2002

7TH HEAVEN

Various authors

RANDOM HOUSE ◆ GRADES 4–7

FAMILY LIFE | VALUES

The Camden family—characters from the popular television series—have further adventures in these books. Readers will enjoy more stories about Rev. and Mrs. Camden and their children and their friends. In one book, Ruthie wins a trip to Hollywood. In another, Lucy and Mary have a survival adventure in New York City. Family values and a commitment to faith infuse these novels. There are related items including a scrapbook and background information about the cast.

1. Nobody's Perfect (Christie, Amanda) ◆ 1999
2. Mary's Story (Christie, Amanda) ◆ 1999
3. Matt's Story (Christie, Amanda) ◆ 1999
4. Middle Sister (Clark, Catherine) ◆ 2000
5. Mr. Nice Guy (Christie, Amanda) ◆ 2000
6. Rivals (Cerasini, Marc) ◆ 2000
7. The Perfect Plan (Christie, Amanda) ◆ 2000
8. Secrets (Christie, Amanda) ◆ 2000
9. The New Me (Christie, Amanda) ◆ 2000
10. Sister Trouble (Christie, Amanda) ◆ 2001
11. Learning the Ropes (Thomas, Jim) ◆ 2001
12. Drive You Crazy (Cerasini, Marc) ◆ 2001
13. Camp Camden (Christie, Amanda) ◆ 2001
14. Lucy's Angel (Christie, Amanda) ◆ 2001
15. Winter Ball (Christie, Amanda) ◆ 2002
16. Dude Ranch (Christie, Amanda) ◆ 2002
17. Sisters Through the Seasons (Christie, Amanda, and Marc Cerasini) ◆ 2002
18. Mary's Rescue (Christie, Amanda) ◆ 2003
19. Wedding Memories (Christie, Amanda) ◆ 2004
20. The East-West Contest (Christie, Amanda) ◆ 2004

THE SEVENTH TOWER

Nix, Garth

SCHOLASTIC ◆ GRADES 6–9 ◆ A/R

FANTASY

Tal lives among the Chosen in the Dark World. He needs a sunstone to maintain his status. When he fails to steal one, he is expelled to the world of the Underfolk. There he joins the rebels and, with Milla, participates in a struggle to combat the evil forces.

1. The Fall ◆ 2000
2. Castle ◆ 2000
3. Aenir ◆ 2001
4. Above the Veil ◆ 2001
5. Into Battle ◆ 2001
6. The Violet Keystone ◆ 2001

SEVENWATERS

Marillier, Juliet

TOR ◆ GRADES 10–12 ◆ A/R

FANTASY

In the first installment of this fantasy trilogy based on Celtic legend, Sorcha must rescue her six brothers from a spell cast by a sorceress. Evil is again in evidence in the *Son of the Shadows,* which features Sorcha's daughter Liadan, who has the power to heal. *Heir to Sevenwaters* (2008) is a new addition to the series, which was being reissued with new covers.

1. Daughter of the Forest ◆ 2000
2. Son of the Shadows ◆ 2001
3. Child of the Prophecy ◆ 2002
4. Heir to Sevenwaters ◆ 2008

SHADOW CHILDREN

Haddix, Margaret Peterson

SIMON & SCHUSTER ◆ GRADES 5–8 ◆ A/R

FANTASY | SCIENCE FICTION

Luke, 12, is a third child in a future society that allows only two children. He must remain hidden. His family is victimized by "the Barons," the elite group of their society. Luke discovers a secret in the Baron house next door—another "shadow child." The series follows Luke and other third-born children as they struggle with being outcasts.

1. Among the Hidden ◆ 1998
2. Among the Imposters ◆ 2001
3. Among the Betrayed ◆ 2003
4. Among the Barons ◆ 2003
5. Among the Brave ◆ 2004
6. Among the Enemy ◆ 2005
7. Among the Free ◆ 2006

THE SHAKESPEARE STEALER

Blackwood, Gary L.
DUTTON ◆ **GRADES 5–8** ◆ **A/R**
HISTORICAL

In London in 1601, Widge is a 14-year-old orphan boy whose master sends him to steal an unpublished play—Hamlet. Instead of stealing the manuscript, Widge becomes an acting apprentice. He has many adventures with Shakespeare's company of actors.

1. The Shakespeare Stealer ◆ 1998
2. Shakespeare's Scribe ◆ 2000
3. Shakespeare's Spy ◆ 2003

THE SHAMER CHRONICLES

Kaaberbol, Lene
HOLT ◆ **GRADES 6–8**
FANTASY

Like her mother, 10-year-old Dina is a Shamer—she can look into people's eyes and see their shameful secrets. Naturally, this does not make her popular and Dina is not proud of her gift. But in the first book, she must use her abilities to rescue her mother and an innocent boy after her mother refuses to abuse her position. This prompts Dina to rethink her own role. Dina grows a little older with each book and the narrative often switches between Dina and her half-brother Davin. These are well-written, exciting books full of traditional elements of fantasy.

1. The Shamer's Daughter ◆ 2004
2. The Shamer's Signet ◆ 2005
3. The Serpent Gift ◆ 2006
4. The Shamer's War ◆ 2006

SHANNARA

Brooks, Terry
BALLANTINE ◆ **GRADES 10–12** ◆ **A/R**
FANTASY

The Druid Allanon needs Brin Ohmsford's skill with the magical wish-song. The Ildatch, an ancient source of evil, is protected by dense dangerous plants but Brin's wishsong can tame them. There are many classic fantasy elements in this trilogy including magic, creatures, quests, and a struggle between good and evil. This is the first Shannara series and originally was a trilogy, but an additional prequel describes some of the events that provide the foundation for the later struggles. A companion volume is *The Heritage of Shannara* (2001), written by Brooks and Teresa Patterson.

1. The Sword of Shannara ◆ 1977
2. The Elfstones of Shannara ◆ 1982
3. The Wishsong of Shannara ◆ 1985
4. First King of Shannara ◆ 1996

SHANNARA: HERITAGE OF SHANNARA

Brooks, Terry

BALLANTINE ◆ GRADES 10–12 ◆ A/R

FANTASY

There are new threats to the Four Lands. The ghost of Druid Allanon calls for three descendants from the Ohmsfords (heroes of the first Shannara trilogy) to face the dangers from the mysterious Shadowen. A companion volume is *The Heritage of Shannara* (2001), written by Brooks and Teresa Patterson.

1. The Scions of Shannara ◆ 1990
2. The Druid of Shannara ◆ 1991
3. The Elf Queen of Shannara ◆ 1992
4. The Talismans of Shannara ◆ 1993

SHANNARA: HIGH DRUID OF SHANNARA

Brooks, Terry

BALLANTINE ◆ GRADES 10–12 ◆ A/R

FANTASY

In the face of great danger, Penderrin Ohmsford embarks on a quest for the limb of a tree that holds the key to his imprisoned aunt's freedom and the chance of peace in the Four Lands.

1. Jarka Ruus ◆ 2003
2. Tanequil ◆ 2004
3. Straken ◆ 2005

SHANNARA: THE SWORD OF SHANNARA

Brooks, Terry

BALLANTINE ◆ GRADES 6–12 ◆ A/R

FANTASY

The three books in this "series" are really just the first Shannara book published in three installments to be accessible to younger readers. A companion volume is *The Heritage of Shannara* (2001), written by Brooks and Teresa Patterson.

1. The Secret of the Sword ◆ 2003
2. The Druid's Keep ◆ 2003
3. In the Shadow of the Warlock ◆ 2003

SHANNARA: THE VOYAGE OF THE JERLE SHANNARA

Brooks, Terry

BALLANTINE ◆ GRADES 10–12 ◆ A/R

FANTASY

The Shannara adventures continue. Walker Boh is the last Druid. He leads a group that includes elves, Rovers, shapeshifters, and other creatures, against Antrax, an evil artificial intelligence. Once Antrax is defeated, the group faces new challenges, including the death of Walker Boh.

1. Ilse Witch ◆ 2000
2. Antrax ◆ 2001
3. Morgawr ◆ 2002

SHIMMER AND THORN

Yep, Laurence

HARPERCOLLINS ◆ GRADES 5–8 ◆ A/R

FANTASY

The Dragon Princess Shimmer is in exile. She teams up with a human boy, Thorn, to try to restore her Dragon Clan's home. Shimmer, Monkey, and other companions become prisoners of the Boneless King and Pomfret the dragon. They must escape and go into battle to save Thorn.

1. Dragon of the Lost Sea ◆ 1982
2. Dragon Steel ◆ 1985
3. Dragon Cauldron ◆ 1991
4. Dragon War ◆ 1992

SHOPAHOLIC

Kinsella, Sophie

DELTA; DIAL ◆ GRADES 10–12

REAL LIFE

Rebecca Bloomwood, 25, has it all. Clothes, a wonderful flat (this series is from Britain), a great career, and a HUGE pile of bills. She is attracted to Luke Brandon, who is very rich, but she knows she must control her spending and debt in order to have a chance with him. In true romantic fiction style, Becky gets Luke, loses Luke and her job, gets a job at Barneys, marries Luke, and shops some more. This is an adult series that teen girls have discovered and list among their favorites.

1. Confessions of a Shopaholic ◆ 2001
2. Shopaholic Takes Manhattan ◆ 2002
3. Shopaholic Ties the Knot ◆ 2003
4. Shopaholic and Sister ◆ 2004
5. Shopaholic and Baby ◆ 2007

SIDEKICKS

Danko, Dan, and Tom Mason

LITTLE, BROWN ◆ GRADES 5–8 ◆ A/R

HUMOR

Guy Martin is a normal 13-year-old . . . except when he is "Speedy," the world's fastest boy and member of a team of apprentice superheroes that helps to defend the world against evil. Sadly, Guy's work as sidekick to Pumpkin Pete (who has the powers of a pumpkin) is less than inspiring. In the third book, Speedy tries to save the beautiful Prudence from the Mole Master, hoping Pumpkin Pete will help rather than hinder for a change. With cartoon illustrations by Barry Gott, these books feature lots of young teen humor and should appeal to fans of Captain Underpants.

1. Sidekicks ◆ 2003
2. Operation Squish! ◆ 2003
3. Attack of the Mole Master ◆ 2004
4. The Candy Man Cometh ◆ 2004
5. The Brotherhood of Rotten Babysitters ◆ 2005
6. Invasion of the Evil Teachers from Planet Buttface ◆ 2005

SIERRA JENSEN

Gunn, Robin Jones

FOCUS ON THE FAMILY; BETHANY HOUSE ◆ GRADES 6–8 ◆ A/R

FAMILY LIFE | VALUES

Sierra lives with her sister Tawni, two younger brothers, and their parents and grandmother. Theirs is an upper-middle-class lifestyle, and Sierra is a casual teenager with a natural approach to life. This puts her in conflict with Tawni, whom Sierra believes always acts as if she is on display. On a mission trip to England, Sierra makes friends with some older teens and meets an interesting boy. He is much older but she eventually dates him.

1. Only You—Sierra ◆ 1995
2. In Your Dreams ◆ 1996
3. Don't You Wish ◆ 1996
4. Close Your Eyes ◆ 1996
5. Without a Doubt ◆ 1997
6. With This Ring ◆ 1997
7. Open Your Heart ◆ 1997
8. Time Will Tell ◆ 1998
9. Now Picture This ◆ 1998
10. Hold on Tight ◆ 1998
11. Closer Than Ever ◆ 1999
12. Take My Hand ◆ 1999

SIGMUND BROUWER'S SPORTS MYSTERY *see* Sports Mystery

SILVER BLADES

Lowell, Melissa
BANTAM ◆ GRADES 4–7 ◆ A/R
REAL LIFE | RECREATION

Four girls who dream of going to the Olympics practice and compete at an exclusive skating club, the Silver Blades. The series starts with Nikki's arrival in Seneca Hills. She meets Jill, Tori, and Danielle and begins to practice for her Silver Blades tryout. She also meets other girls from school, is invited to join in their activities, and becomes interested in a handsome hockey player. In the end, she realizes that skating is really what she wants to do most. Each of the four girls stars in subsequent books. Tori deals with her demanding mother, Jill moves to Colorado, and Danielle lands a starring role in an ice show. Lots of skating technicalities are a natural part of the stories. In the Olympic trilogy, Silver Blades Gold Medal Dreams, Tori overcomes the odds and gets the chance to compete in the Winter Games.

1. Breaking the Ice ◆ 1993
2. In the Spotlight ◆ 1993
3. The Competition ◆ 1994
4. Going for the Gold ◆ 1994
5. The Perfect Pair ◆ 1994
6. Skating Camp ◆ 1994
7. The Ice Princess ◆ 1995
8. Rumors at the Rink ◆ 1995
9. Spring Break ◆ 1995

10. Center Ice ◆ 1995
11. A Surprise Twist ◆ 1995
12. The Winning Spirit ◆ 1995
13. The Big Audition ◆ 1995
14. Nutcracker on Ice ◆ 1995
15. A New Move ◆ 1996
16. Ice Magic ◆ 1996
17. A Leap Ahead ◆ 1996
18. More Than Friends ◆ 1996
19. Natalia Comes to America ◆ 1997
20. The One Way to Win ◆ 1997
21. Rival Roomates ◆ 1997
22. Double Dare ◆ 1998
23. Wanted: One Perfect Boy ◆ 1998

SILVER BLADES GOLD MEDAL DREAMS

1. On the Edge ◆ 1997
2. Now or Never ◆ 1997
3. Chance of a Lifetime ◆ 1998

SILVER BLADES SUPER EDITIONS

1. Rinkside Romance ◆ 1996
2. Wedding Secrets ◆ 1996

SILVER CREEK RIDERS

Kincaid, Beth

JOVE BOOKS ◆ GRADES 6–8
REAL LIFE | RECREATION

Four friends—Melissa, Jenna, Katie, and Sharon—all love horses. After they meet at the Silver Creek riding camp, they find ways to keep in touch and help each other. At camp, they help Melissa as she learns to deal with a tragic accident and her fear of riding again. In another book, Katie meets Matt and it looks like love—except that Katie is attracted to Matt's horse (at first). During the Autumn Horse Show, Melissa helps a horse that is being mistreated. The audience for these books is primarily horse-crazy girls, who will also enjoy the Saddle Club books.

1. Back in the Saddle ◆ 1994
2. True Romance ◆ 1994
3. Winning ◆ 1995

SILVER SEQUENCE

McNish, Cliff

CAROLRHODA ◆ GRADES 5–9 ◆ A/R

SCIENCE FICTION | FANTASY

An evil force is threatening the world and six children are key to its survival. The six are mysteriously drawn to a refuse dump where they develop special skills and powers. Milo turns silver and becomes the protector. Thomas becomes a healer while Emily and Freda can move swiftly on all fours. Helen is a psychic and Walter grows to be a giant. As the series progresses, the six are joined by other children as they face an unknown creature called "The Roar." The plot is presented from the point of view of different characters. Readers who have enjoyed Madeleine L'Engle's Time Fantasy series will appreciate this complex story.

1. The Silver Child ◆ 2005
2. Silver City ◆ 2006
3. Silver World ◆ 2007

SILVERSKIN LEGACY

Whittemore, Jo

LLEWELLYN ◆ GRADES 5–8

FANTASY

Junior high students Ainsley and Megan are spying on their neighbor Mr. Niksrevlis when they find themselves transported to the land of Arylon. There they learn that Mr. Niksrevlis is a king of the Silverskin family and protector of a magical relic that can open portals to other worlds. In the second book, Ainsley and Megan are preparing to return to their own world when Ainsley falls ill. Can Megan find a cure in time? These books are full of magic and adventure.

1. Escape from Arylon ◆ 2006
2. Curse of Arastold ◆ 2006
3. Onaj's Horn ◆ 2007

SILVERWING

Oppel, Kenneth

EOS ◆ GRADES 5–8

ANIMAL FANTASY

A bat named Shade is the runt of the Silverwing colony, and he has strange ideas about sunlight. Shade becomes separated from the rest of the colony during its migration and, with the help of Marina, a bat cast out of her own community, tries to rejoin his flock and save them from evil cannibal bats. In the second book, Shade sets out to find his father and again must confront danger. Full of bat facts and lore, this series also provides plenty of action and a touch of romance. *Darkwing* is a stand-alone fantasy, set millions of years before this series, about the ancestors of bats.

1. Silverwing ◆ 1997
2. Sunwing ◆ 2000
3. Firewing ◆ 2003

SIRIUS MYSTERIES

Wood, Beverley, and Chris Wood
POLESTAR ◆ GRADES 5–9 ◆ A/R
MYSTERY | FANTASY | ADVENTURE

Jeff is still mourning the loss of his dog Buddy when he goes on a cruise to Alaska with his parents. There he finds a statue of a dog and is transported back in time to the 1930s where he meets the bull terrier Patsy Ann and helps to solve a mystery at sea. In the second volume, Patsy Ann lures 14-year-old Jack back to 1935 Juneau, where he identifies the real perpetrator of a crime. These books weave history and humor into the stories.

1. Dogstar ◆ 1997
2. Jack's Knife ◆ 2003
3. The Golden Boy ◆ 2006

SISTERHOOD OF THE TRAVELING PANTS

Brashares, Ann
DELACORTE ◆ GRADES 6–9 ◆ A/R
REAL LIFE

Four friends—Lena, Tibby, Bridget, and Carmen—are upset about spending the summer vacation apart. A pair of jeans that Carmen bought at a secondhand store turns out to be the way the girls stay in touch. They take turns wearing the pants (no one keeps them more than one week) and they each write about their adventures with the pants. There are ten rules governing the pants, ending with "Pants=love. Love your pals. Love yourself."

1. The Sisterhood of the Traveling Pants ◆ 2001
2. The Second Summer of the Sisterhood ◆ 2003
3. Girls in Pants: The Third Summer of the Sisterhood ◆ 2005
4. Forever in Blue: The Fourth Summer of the Sisterhood ◆ 2007

SISTERS

Kaye, Marilyn

GULLIVER BOOKS / HARCOURT BRACE JOVANOVICH ◆ GRADES 6–8

FAMILY LIFE | REAL LIFE

Each book in this series is devoted to one of the four Gray sisters, each of whom has a very distinct personality. Lydia, the baby of the family, is a dreamer and content being a child; Daphne is the sensitive poet; Cassie is the self-centered beauty; Lydia, the eldest at 14, is a leader who is always taking on an important cause. Readers may find that they relate strongly to one of the sisters or maybe to individual qualities of each girl. While the individual stories stand on their own, reading the series provides the reader with a stronger sense of the individual personalities that make up a family.

1. Phoebe ◆ 1987
2. Daphne ◆ 1987
3. Cassie ◆ 1987
4. Lydia ◆ 1987
5. A Friend like Phoebe ◆ 1989

SISTERS OF ISIS

Ewing, Lynne

HYPERION ◆ GRADES 8–10

FANTASY

Meri, Sudi, and Dalila are three 15-year-old girls who live in Washington, D.C. They discover they are descendants of Egyptian pharoahs and not only have magical powers but also great responsibilities. They must protect the world from evil.

1. The Summoning ◆ 2007
2. Divine One ◆ 2007
3. Enchantress ◆ 2007
4. The Haunting ◆ 2008

THE SIXTH SENSE: SECRETS FROM BEYOND

Benjamin, David

SCHOLASTIC ◆ GRADES 5–7

FANTASY

Cole Sear has special powers. He sees and can communicate with the dead. There are secrets that the dead want Cole to share. These secrets will help solve mysteries surrounding their deaths. The popularity of the movie adds to the interest in these books.

1. Survivor ◆ 2000
2. Runaway ◆ 2001
3. Hangman ◆ 2001

SKINNER FAMILY *see* The Great Skinner

SLAPSHOTS

Korman, Gordon

SCHOLASTIC ◆ GRADES 5–8 ◆ A/R

RECREATION

Hockey action is featured in this series. The Stars from Mars face a variety of opponents including the dreaded Oilers. Will the Stars win the trophy cup?

1. The Stars from Mars ◆ 1999
2. All-Mars All-Stars ◆ 1999
3. The Face-Off Phony ◆ 2000
4. Cup Crazy ◆ 2000

SLAYERS

Kanzaka, Hajime

TOKYOPOP ◆ GRADES 7–10

FANTASY

This series of books takes the popular Slayers manga comic series and expands the adventure. In one volume, Lina, a teenage sorceress, finds some stolen money and decides to keep some of it . . . actually, most of it. The people who stole the money are not amused. In another book, Lina and Gourry fight a magical battle in Atlas City. Each book includes several full-color manga illustration pages and many black-and-white pages, too.

1. Volume 1 ◆ 2004
2. Volume 2 ◆ 2004
3. Volume 3 ◆ 2005
4. Volume 4 ◆ 2005
5. Volume 5 ◆ 2005
6. Volume 6 ◆ 2005
7. Volume 7 ◆ 2008
8. Volume 8 ◆ 2008

SLIMEBALLS

Gross, U. B.

RANDOM HOUSE ◆ GRADES 5–7

HUMOR

Two of the books in this series feature Gus, his friend Polly, and the class dullard Ray. Gus plans to win the science fair with his collection of unusual molds. The books are full of gross humor and weird characters. A wacko school nurse is fired and returns in another book as a crazed bus driver. The characters often behave in ways that will appeal to the middle school sense of humor—food fights, slime attacks, and rodents that take over a home.

1. Fun Gus and Polly Pus ◆ 1996
2. Fun Gus Slimes the Bus ◆ 1997
3. The Slithers Buy a Boa ◆ 1997

SMALLVILLE

Various authors

LITTLE, BROWN ◆ GRADES 7–10

FANTASY

Smallville is the hometown of Clark Kent. This book series (and the television series) describe his life as a teenager. He does mundane things, like helping Lana Lang with the high school play. He also faces sinister circumstances and individuals, such as a being that kills by taking your breath away. There is another series of Smallville books for adults.

1. Arrival (Teitelbaum, Michael) ◆ 2002
2. See No Evil (Bennett, Cherie, and Jeff Gottesfeld) ◆ 2002
3. Flight (Bennett, Cherie, and Jeff Gottesfeld) ◆ 2002
4. Animal Rage (Weiss, David Cody, and Bobbi J. G. Weiss) ◆ 2003
5. Speed (Bennett, Cherie, and Jeff Gottesfeld) ◆ 2003
6. Buried Secrets (Colon, Suzan) ◆ 2003
7. Runaway (Colon, Suzan) ◆ 2003
8. Greed (Bennett, Cherie, and Jeff Gottesfeld) ◆ 2003
9. Temptation (Colon, Suzan) ◆ 2004
10. Sparks (Bennett, Cherie, and Jeff Gottesfeld) ◆ 2004

SO LITTLE TIME *see* Mary-Kate and Ashley: So Little Time

SO WEIRD

Various authors

HYPERION ◆ GRADES 4–7

FANTASY

Fi experiences supernatural events. She helps the restless soul of a boy find peace. She uses her computer talents to find the sender of strange e-mails. Her friends Jack and Clu help her investigate these paranormal events.

1. Family Reunion (Dubowski, Cathy East) ◆ 2000
2. Shelter (Mantell, Paul) ◆ 2000
3. Escape (Rees, Elizabeth M.) ◆ 2000
4. Strangeling (Dubowski, Cathy East) ◆ 2000
5. Web Sight (Pollack, Pam) ◆ 2000

SOCK MONKEY

Millionaire, Tony

DARK HORSE ◆ GRADES 6–12

FANTASY

Sock Monkey came from the jungles of Borneo. Now he lives in Massachusetts with a little girl named Ann-Louise. His presence brings both delight and fear. These graphic novels may be enjoyed by a younger audience, although some reviewers place them with YAs.

1. The Adventures of Tony Millionaire's Sock Monkey ◆ 2000
2. Sock Monkey: A Children's Book ◆ 2001
3. Sock Monkey: The Glass Doorknob ◆ 2002
4. Sock Monkey: Uncle Gabby ◆ 2004
5. That Darn Yarn ◆ 2005
6. The Inches Incident ◆ 2007

SONG OF THE LIONESS QUARTET

Pierce, Tamora

ATHENEUM ◆ GRADES 6–9 ◆ A/R

FANTASY

Alanna, 11, disguises herself as a boy to become a page and, later, a knight. She is a strong and skillful warrior who serves Prince Jonathan (who knows her secret). Her magical powers help protect the Prince from the evil sorcerer. Originally published in the 1980s, this series was reissued in the 1990s. *The Immortals* is set in the same world. *Trickster's Choice* (2003) is the first book in the Lioness Quartet, about Alanna's daughter, Alianne.

1. Alanna: The First Adventure ◆ 1983
2. In the Hand of the Goddess ◆ 1984
3. The Woman Who Rides Like a Man ◆ 1986
4. Lioness Rampant ◆ 1988

DAUGHTER OF THE LIONESS

Aliane, 16, the intelligent and rebellious daughter of Alanna the Lioness, manages to outwit the trickster god Kyprioth. In the second book, Aly is at the center of a rebellion against colonial rulers.

1. Trickster's Choice ◆ 2003
2. Trickster's Queen ◆ 2004

SONS OF THE DARK

Ewing, Lynne

HYPERION ◆ GRADES 8–12 ◆ A/R

FANTASY

Four gorgeous and immortal teens with magical powers escape slavery in the parallel universe of Nefandus and must deal with life in modern Los Angeles before fulfilling their destinies. First they must learn to trust each other and to exploit their own powers.

1. Barbarian ◆ 2004
2. Escape ◆ 2004
3. Outcast ◆ 2005
4. Night Sun ◆ 2005

SOOKAN BAK

Choi, Sook Nyul

HOUGHTON MIFFLIN ◆ GRADES 5–8 ◆ A/R

FAMILY LIFE | HISTORICAL

In the first book of this trilogy, *Year of Impossible Goodbyes,* Sookan Bak is 10. It is the 1940s and she and her family are enduring the occupation of their homeland in northern Korea. When the country is divided at the end of the war, the family emigrates to the south, hoping for a better life. *Echoes of the White Giraffe* describes Sookan's life in Pusan and her growing friendship with Junho, a boy she knows from the church choir. In the final book, Sookan is in college in the United States, where she is challenged by a new language, a different culture, and the death of her mother.

1. Year of Impossible Goodbyes ◆ 1991
2. Echoes of the White Giraffe ◆ 1993
3. Gathering of Pearls ◆ 1994

SPACE ABOVE AND BEYOND

Various authors
HARPERCOLLINS ◆ GRADES 5–8
SCIENCE FICTION

In 2063, an Earth space station has been destroyed by aliens and now Earth is in danger. Lieutenants Vansen, West, and Hawke are thrown together to accomplish a dangerous mission and face the Artificial Intelligence (AI) creatures. There are encounters on Mars, a mutiny in space, and an electromagnetic lightning storm. Fans of Star Trek and Deep Space Nine will enjoy these books.

1. The Aliens Approach (Royce, Easton) ◆ 1996
2. Dark Side of the Sun (Anastasio, Dina) ◆ 1996
3. Mutiny (Royce, Easton) ◆ 1996
4. The Enemy (Anastasio, Dina) ◆ 1996
5. Demolition Winter (Telep, Peter) ◆ 1997

SPECIALISTS

Greenland, Shannon
SPEAK ◆ GRADES 8–10 ◆ A/R
ADVENTURE

Kelly James is a computer whiz. When David, a cute college student, asks her to help him hack into a government computer. She is successful but she is caught and recruited into a secret government agency of undercover teen agents. (David is one, too). Now known as Gigi, she searches for a missing toxin (in *Down to the Wire*) and hides out as a cheerleader (in *The Winning Element*). The Cherub series also features undercover teens.

1. Model Spy ◆ 2007
2. Down to the Wire ◆ 2007
3. The Winning Element ◆ 2008
4. Native Tongue ◆ 2008

SPEED RACER

Wheeler, Chase

PENGUIN ◆ GRADES 4–8

REAL LIFE

Speed Racer is a talented young racing driver, son of an automobile engineer who has created a Mach 5 car with James Bond-style features. Speed hopes to become an international champion and often gets into dangerous situations. He remains close to his family and has a steady girlfriend, Trixie. *Go, Speed Racer, Go* (2008) is for younger readers and focuses on Speed's youth.

1. The Great Plan ◆ 2008
2. Challenge of the Masked Racer ◆ 2008
3. The Secret Engine ◆ 2008
4. Race Against the Mammoth Car ◆ 2008
5. The Most Dangerous Race ◆ 2008
6. Race for Revenge ◆ 2008

SPELL CASTERS

Warriner, Holly

ALADDIN ◆ GRADES 5–8 ◆ A/R

FANTASY

Lucinda is a witch who is conflicted about her powers. Her evil grandmother and her sinister cousin Rafe push her to fulfill her destiny. Lucinda's friendship with Sally and her everyday school activities provide a backdrop for spells, seances, and witchcraft.

1. Witch at the Door ◆ 1998
2. Full Moon Magic ◆ 1998
3. Witches' Brew ◆ 1998
4. Julian's Jinx ◆ 1998
5. Witches on Ice ◆ 1999
6. Phoebe's Fortune ◆ 1999

THE SPELLSONG CYCLE

Modesitt, L. E.

TOR ◆ GRADES 9–12

FANTASY

In this unusual series based on the power of music, Anna Marshall, a singer and music teacher from the Midwest, is transported to a world where songs bear the power of magic. Her talents win her a position as regent of the kingdom of Defalk. In the fourth book, Anna dies and the peace she has negotiated is threatened by Sea Priests who use magical drumming as a weapon. Anna's foster daughter and successor, Secca, must test her own powers against this new danger.

1. The Soprano Sorceress ◆ 1997
2. The Spellsong War ◆ 1998
3. Darksong Rising ◆ 1999
4. The Shadow Sorceress ◆ 2001
5. Shadowsinger ◆ 2002

SPINETINGLERS

Coffin, M. T.

AVON ◆ GRADES 6–8

HORROR

Suppose you went to class and your teacher was a bug. When you tried to tell others about it, you realized ahat there were bugs everywhere. In fact, everyone in town is a bug. This is just one weird scenario in the Spinetingler series. There are spooky libraries (*Check It Out—and Die!*), scary schools (*Don't Go to the Principal's Office*), and spooky television (*The Monster Channel*). Bizarre creatures, zombie dogs, cursed cheerleaders, lizard people, and freaks inhabit the books, which also include cliff-hanging plot twists and breathtaking encounters. There are also humorous moments, which you would expect from an author named M. T. Coffin who claims to live in Tombstone with children named Phillip A. Coffin and Carrie A. Coffin. Fans of Goosebumps will take to these books.

1. The Substitute Creature ◆ 1995
2. Billy Baker's Dog Won't Stay Buried ◆ 1995
3. My Teacher's a Bug ◆ 1995
4. Where Have All the Parents Gone? ◆ 1995
5. Check It Out—and Die! ◆ 1995
6. Simon Says, "Croak!" ◆ 1995
7. Snow Day ◆ 1996
8. Don't Go to the Principal's Office ◆ 1996
9. Step on a Crack ◆ 1996
10. The Dead Kid Did It ◆ 1996
11. Fly by Night ◆ 1996
12. Killer Computer ◆ 1996
13. Pet Store ◆ 1996
14. Blood Red Eightball ◆ 1996
15. Escape from the Haunted Mountain ◆ 1996
16. We Wish You a Scary Christmas ◆ 1996
17. The Monster Channel ◆ 1997
18. Mirror, Mirror ◆ 1997
19. Boogey's Back for Blood ◆ 1997
20. Lights, Camera, Die! ◆ 1997

21. Camp Crocodile ◆ 1997
22. Student Exchange ◆ 1997
23. Gimme Back My Brain ◆ 1997
24. Your Turn—to Scream! ◆ 1997
25. The Curse of the Cheerleaders ◆ 1997
26. Wear and Scare ◆ 1997
27. Lizard People ◆ 1997
28. Circus F.R.E.A.K.S. ◆ 1997
29. My Dentist Is a Vampire ◆ 1998
30. Saber-Toothed Tiger ◆ 1998

SPIRIT OF THE GAME

Hafer, Todd

ZONDERKIDZ ◆ GRADES 5–8 ◆ A/R

VALUES | REAL LIFE | RECREATION

In each book of this series Cody Martin, 13, is involved in a sport and in different circumstances that test his faith and commitment to God. In *Goal-Line Stand,* Cody competes with his best friend for a position on the football team. In *Ultimate Challenge,* Cody, now 14, is adjusting to a new stepmother who is expecting a baby. Cody feels unsettled at home and then his best friend tells him he is moving. Cody prepares for the Ultimate Athlete competition while he copes with the changes in his life.

1. Goal-Line Stand ◆ 2004
2. Full-Court Press ◆ 2004
3. Second Wind ◆ 2004
4. Stealing Home ◆ 2004
5. Cody's Varsity Rush ◆ 2005
6. Three-Point Play ◆ 2005
7. Split Decision ◆ 2005
8. Ultimate Challenge ◆ 2005

SPOOKSVILLE

Pike, Christopher

POCKET BOOKS ◆ GRADES 5–8 ◆ A/R

HORROR

Springville seems like an ordinary town, but a closer look reveals strange things going on. Cindy Mackey finds this out when her brother Neil is kidnapped by a ghost. Adam Freeman knows things are different. One of his best friends is Watch, a creature who has returned from the dead. Cindy, Adam, Watch, and their friends Sally Wilcox and Bryce Poole confront howling ghosts, aliens, witches, wicked cats, killer crabs, vampires, and other demons as they try to survive in a very strange town.

This series will be a hit with readers who enjoy Goosebumps, Fear Street, and Buffy the Vampire Slayer.

1. The Secret Path ◆ 1995
2. The Howling Ghost ◆ 1995
3. The Haunted Cave ◆ 1995
4. Aliens in the Sky ◆ 1996
5. The Cold People ◆ 1996
6. The Witch's Revenge ◆ 1996
7. The Dark Corner ◆ 1996
8. The Little People ◆ 1996
9. The Wishing Stone ◆ 1996
10. The Wicked Cat ◆ 1996
11. The Deadly Past ◆ 1996
12. The Hidden Beast ◆ 1996
13. The Creature in the Teacher ◆ 1996
14. The Evil House ◆ 1997
15. Invasion of the No-Ones ◆ 1997
16. Time Terror ◆ 1997
17. The Thing in the Closet ◆ 1997
18. Attack of the Killer Crabs ◆ 1997
19. Night of the Vampire ◆ 1997
20. The Dangerous Quest ◆ 1998
21. The Living Dead ◆ 1998
22. The Creepy Creature ◆ 1998
23. Phone Fear ◆ 1998
24. The Witch's Gift ◆ 1999

SPORTS MYSTERY

Brouwer, Sigmund
TOMMY NELSON ◆ GRADES 9–12 ◆ A/R
MYSTERY | RECREATION

In the first book, Matt, 16, investigates the disappearance of the top scorer of his soccer team. These books have the appeal of sports action and mysteries. Soccer, football, basketball, and stock car racing are among the featured sports.

1. Maverick Mania ◆ 1998
2. Tiger Heat ◆ 1998
3. Cobra Threat ◆ 1998
4. Titan Clash ◆ 1998
5. Scarlet Thunder ◆ 1998
6. Hurricane Power ◆ 1999

SPY FORCE

Abela, Deborah

SIMON & SCHUSTER ◆ GRADES 4–7 ◆ A/R

ADVENTURE

Maxine Remy, 11, is bored and hostile, resenting everything about her life. While visiting her aunt and uncle in Pennsylvania, she discovers her uncle's Matter Transporter. Max convinces a friend, Linden, to join her in the transporter and they travel to London where they are kidnapped by a villain who wants the transporter. After they escape, they find out about a secret agency of spies. In the second book, Max and Linden are asked to join Spy Force. They join forces with another young spy, Ella. The trio goes undercover in a candy factory. Their mission—to stop the evil Mr. Blue from using food to control the minds of children.

1. Mission: in Search of the Time and Space Machine ◆ 2005
2. Mission: Spy Force Revealed ◆ 2005
3. Mission: The Nightmare Vortex ◆ 2005
4. Mission: Hollywood ◆ 2006

SPY GIRLS

Cage, Elizabeth

POCKET BOOKS ◆ GRADES 7–10

ADVENTURE | MYSTERY

A secret agency, the Tower, has chosen three teenage girls to be spies. Caylin, Jo, and Theresa deal with dangers including terrorist plots, a missing ballerina, an international conspiracy, and more. Teens will enjoy these hip, savvy girls who travel around the world and solve crimes.

1. License to Thrill ◆ 1998
2. Live and Let Spy ◆ 1998
3. Nobody Does It Better ◆ 1999
4. Spy Girls Are Forever ◆ 1999
5. Dial 'V' for Vengeance ◆ 1999
6. If Looks Could Kill ◆ 1999

SPY HIGH

Butcher, A. J.

LITTLE, BROWN ◆ GRADES 9–12 ◆ A/R

ADVENTURE

In 2060 Deveraux Academy is no ordinary high school. Yes, there are regular classes, but then there are also lessons in martial arts, electronic eavesdropping, and shock suits. The team of six teens, called the Bond team, is trained to infiltrate evil organizations and combat terrorism.

1. Spy High Mission One ◆ 2004
2. Spy High Mission Two: Chaos Rising ◆ 2004
3. Spy High Mission Three: The Serpent Scenario ◆ 2004
4. Spy High Mission Four: The Paranoia Plot ◆ 2004
5. Spy High Mission Five: Blood Relations ◆ 2005
6. Spy High Mission Six: The Annihilation Agenda ◆ 2005

SPYBOY

Various authors

DARK HORSE ◆ GRADES 10–12

ADVENTURE

Alex Fleming seems to be an ordinary teenager. He goes to high school, worries about dating and bullies, and is an international super spy. A spy!!! Yes, Alex is developing his latent talents for intrigue. He trains in the martial arts and is learning to use high-tech gadgets. Alex's ordinary life is not ordinary anymore.

1. The Deadly Gourmet Affair (David, Peter, Pop Mhan, and Norman Lee) ◆ 2001
2. Trial and Terror (David, Peter, Pop Mhan, and Norman Lee) ◆ 2001
3. Bet Your Life (David, Peter, Carlos Meglia, Pop Mhan, and Norman Lee) ◆ 2001
4. Undercover, Underwear! (David, Peter, Pop Mhan, Norman Lee, and Sunny Lee) ◆ 2002
5. Spy-School Confidential (David, Peter, Pop Mhan, and Norman Lee) ◆ 2003
6. The M.A.N.G.A. Affair (David, Peter, Pop Mhan, and Norman Lee) ◆ 2003
7. Young Justice (David, Peter, Pop Mhan, Norman Lee, Jamie Mendoza, and Todd Nauck) ◆ 2003
8. Final Exam (David, Peter, Pop Mhan, Norman Lee, and Dan Jackson) ◆ 2005

THE SQUIRE'S TALE *see* The Denizens of Camelot

STAR POWER

Hapka, Cathy

ALADDIN ◆ GRADES 6–8 ◆ A/R

REAL LIFE

Tween girls should enjoy this flashy series about a 14-year-old pop star. Fame comes quickly and easily to Star Calloway, but there are problems too. Her family has been missing for two years. Still, Star focuses on her career, her competitors, and her adoring fans.

1. Supernova ◆ 2004
2. Always Dreamin' ◆ 2004
3. Never Give Up ◆ 2004
4. Together We Can Do It ◆ 2004
5. Blast from the Past ◆ 2004
6. Someday, Some Way ◆ 2005
7. Over the Top ◆ 2005
8. Star Bright ◆ 2005

STAR SISTERZ

Various authors

WIZARDS OF THE COAST ◆ GRADES 4–7

REAL LIFE

For tween girls, this is a lighthearted series about a group of friends who receive mysterious messages that influence their actions. The series is connected to a game in which girls collect charms.

1. Nova Rocks! (Emesse, Tea) ◆ 2005
2. Carmen Dives In (Johns, Linda) ◆ 2005
3. Bright Lights for Bella (Perez, Lana) ◆ 2005
4. Rani and the Fashion Divas (Banerjee, Anjali) ◆ 2005
5. Nova and the Charmed Three (Emesse, Tea) ◆ 2006
6. Yumi Talks the Talk (Emesse, Tea) ◆ 2006
7. Carmen's Crystal Ball (Johns, Linda) ◆ 2006
8. Bella Goes Hollywood (Perez, Lana) ◆ 2006
9. Maya Made Over (Green, Debra) ◆ 2007
10. Rani and the Wedding Ghost (Banerjee, Anjali) ◆ 2008

STAR TREK: DEEP SPACE NINE

Various authors

POCKET BOOKS ◆ GRADES 4–8 ◆ A/R

ADVENTURE | SCIENCE FICTION

Fans of the television series *Deep Space Nine* will enjoy reading adventures featuring their favorite characters. Young Jake Sisko and his Ferengi friend Nog are involved in time travel, attending Starfleet Academy's summer space camp, and even a field trip through the Worm Hole. They meet unusual creatures and are often in situations that threaten the future of the world. Jake's father, Commander Benjamin Sisko, supervises the Deep Space Nine space station with the assistance of security officer Odo and first officer Major Kira Nerys. Other characters from the show, including Miles and Keiko O'Brien and the Ferengi businessman Quark, appear in the books. There is lots of action and imaginative situations that should attract science fiction fans.

1. The Star Ghost (Strickland, Brad) ◆ 1994
2. Stowaways (Strickland, Brad) ◆ 1994
3. Prisoners of Peace (Peel, John) ◆ 1994
4. The Pet (Gilden, Mel, and Ted Pedersen) ◆ 1994
5. Arcade (Gallagher, Diana G.) ◆ 1995
6. Field Trip (Peel, John) ◆ 1995
7. Gypsy World (Pedersen, Ted, and John Peel) ◆ 1996
8. Highest Score (Antilles, Kem) ◆ 1996
9. Cardassian Imps (Gilden, Mel) ◆ 1997
10. Space Camp (Pedersen, Ted, and John Peel) ◆ 1997
11. Day of Honor: Honor Bound (Gallagher, Diana G.) ◆ 1997
12. Trapped in Time (Pedersen, Ted) ◆ 1998

STAR TREK: ENTERPRISE

Various authors

POCKET BOOKS ◆ GRADES 5–10

ADVENTURE | SCIENCE FICTION

The television series *Star Trek: Enterprise* ran from 2001 to 2005. The adventures on this show preceded those of the original *Star Trek*. Jonathan Archer commands the *Enterprise,* Earth's first Warp 5 starship. On board is an intergalactic crew including T'Pol, a Vulcan, and Phlox, a Denobulan. The books issued through 2004 paralleled episodes of the television program. A relaunch of new titles began in 2006.

1. By The Book (Smith, Dean Wesley, and Kristine Kathryn Rusch) ◆ 2002
2. What Price Honor (Stern, Dave) ◆ 2002
3. Surak's Soul (Dillard, J. M.) ◆ 2003

4. The Expanse (Dillard, J. M., Rick Berman, and Brannon Braga) ◆ 2003
5. Daedalus: Part ! of 2 (Stern, Dave) ◆ 2003
6. Daedalus's Children: Part 2 of 2 (Stern, Dave) ◆ 2004
7. Shockwave (Ruditis, Paul) ◆ 2004
8. Rosetta (Stern, Dave) ◆ 2006
9. Last Full Measure (Martin, Michael A., and Andy Mangels) ◆ 2006
10. The Good That Men Do (Martin, Michael A., and Andy Mangels) ◆ 2007
11. Broken Bow (Carey, Diane) ◆ 2007
12. Kobayashi Maru (Martin, Michael A., and Andy Mangels) ◆ 2008

STAR TREK: I. K. S. GORKON

DeCandido, Keith R. A.

POCKET BOOKS ◆ GRADES 5–10

ADVENTURE | SCIENCE FICTION

The books in this series follow the adventures of a Klingon Defense Force vessel *I. K. S. Gorkon*. Commanded by Captain Klag, its mission is to search for new civilizations and conquer them. Captain Klag does act with humanity and compassion and is, at times, operating outside the expectations of the Klingon Empire.

1. A Good Day to Die ◆ 2003
2. Honor Bound ◆ 2003
3. Enemy Territory ◆ 2005

STAR TREK: S. C. E.

Various authors

SIMON & SCHUSTER ◆ GRADES 5–10

ADVENTURE | SCIENCE FICTION

The original books about the Starfleet Corp of Engineers (S. C. E.) were issued between 2000 and 2006. The books in this new series are omnibus editions with each title presenting at least four books from the originals. For example, in *Have Tech Will Travel* there are four books from 2002: *The Belly of the Beast, Fatal Error, Hard Crash,* and *Interphase, Part 1*— each by a different author. The books describe the adventures of Captain David Gold, first officer Commander Sonya Gomez, and the crew of the *U.S.S. da Vinci* as they deal with alien attacks, ships trapped in interphase, subspace accelerators, and more. At Starfleet Headquarters they are supported by the S. C. E. under the direction of Captain Montgomery Scott.

1. Have Tech, Will Travel (DeCandido, Keith R. A., et al.) ◆ 2002

2. Miracle Workers (DeCandido, Keith R. A., et al.) ◆ 2002
3. Some Assembly Required (Brodeur, Gret, et al.) ◆ 2003
4. No Surrender (Collins, Mike, et al.) ◆ 2004
5. Foundations (Ward, Dayton, and Kevin Dilmore) ◆ 2005
6. Wildfire (DeCandido, Keith R. A., et al.) ◆ 2005
7. Breakdown (DeCandido, Keith R. A., et al.) ◆ 2006
8. Aftermath (Bennett, Christopher L., et al.) ◆ 2006
9. Grand Designs (Ward, Dayton, et al.) ◆ 2007
10. Creative Couplings (Mack, David) ◆ 2007

STAR TREK: STARFLEET ACADEMY

Various authors

POCKET BOOKS ◆ GRADES 4–8 ◆ A/R

ADVENTURE | SCIENCE FICTION

Many fans of science fiction series want to know everything about the characters. These fans are often so enthralled with the series that publishers and media producers provide numerous spin-offs and related activities (computer games, Web sites, conventions, and so forth). *Star Trek* fans are among the most loyal and intense. The ongoing popularity of the television series, along with every related item, is a testament to that. This series examines the early lives and training of key characters: James T. Kirk, Spock, and Leonard McCoy. Their adventures at the Starfleet Academy include escaping from space pirates and saving earthquake victims on the planet Playamar. Fans will especially enjoy *Crisis on Vulcan,* in which Spock meet young Christopher Pike (who was the captain in the *Star Trek* pilot program).

1. Crisis on Vulcan (Strickland, Brad, and Barbara Strickland) ◆ 1996
2. Aftershock (Vornholt, John) ◆ 1996
3. Cadet Kirk (Carey, Diane L.) ◆ 1996

STAR TREK: THE NEXT GENERATION: STARFLEET ACADEMY

Various authors

POCKET BOOKS ◆ GRADES 4–8 ◆ A/R

ADVENTURE | SCIENCE FICTION

Focusing on the early years of the crew of the *U.S.S. Enterprise,* this series features the Starfleet Academy training experiences of familiar characters including Picard, Worf, Geordi, and Data. In *Deceptions,* Data participates in a research investigation of ancient ruins on the planet Arunu. When the communications system is sabotaged, Data must use his powers as an android to rescue his friends. In *Survival,* Worf and several Starfleet cadets work with a group of Klingon cadets to escape from the evil of an alien force. This series will interest fans of the television programs and movies as well as readers who like fast-paced adventures.

1. Worf's First Adventure (David, Peter) ◆ 1993
2. Line of Fire (David, Peter) ◆ 1993
3. Survival (David, Peter) ◆ 1993
4. Capture the Flag (Vornholt, John) ◆ 1994
5. Atlantis Station (Mitchell, V. E.) ◆ 1994
6. Mystery of the Missing Crew (Friedman, Michael J.) ◆ 1995
7. Secret of the Lizard People (Friedman, Michael J.) ◆ 1995
8. Starfall (Strickland, Brad, and Barbara Strickland) ◆ 1995
9. Nova Command (Strickland, Brad, and Barbara Strickland) ◆ 1995
10. Loyalties (Barnes-Svarney, Patricia) ◆ 1996
11. Crossfire (Vornholt, John) ◆ 1996
12. Breakaway (Weiss, Bobbi J. G., and David Cody Weiss) ◆ 1997
13. The Haunted Starship (Ferguson, Brad, and Kathi Ferguson) ◆ 1997
14. Deceptions (Weiss, Bobbi J. G., and David Cody Weiss) ◆ 1998

STAR TREK: VOYAGER: STARFLEET ACADEMY

Various authors

POCKET BOOKS ◆ GRADES 4–8 ◆ A/R

ADVENTURE | SCIENCE FICTION

The *Voyager* series (on television and in these books) revolves around Kathryn Janeway, daughter of Vice Admiral Edward Janeway. At the Starfleet Academy, Kathryn wants to step out from the shadow of her successful father and establish her own credentials. These adventures put her in situations involving alien animals and an outer-space quarantine that could prove deadly. There is lots of action in these books, which should be appealing to fans of the show and of science fiction. The creatures and outer-space setting may attract reluctant readers.

1. Lifeline (Weiss, Bobbi J. G., and David Cody Weiss) ◆ 1997
2. The Chance Factor (Gallagher, Diana G., and Martin R. Burke) ◆ 1997
3. Quarantine (Barnes-Svarney, Patricia) ◆ 1997

STAR WARS: A NEW HOPE—MANGA

Lucas, George

DARK HORSE ◆ GRADES 5–10

SCIENCE FICTION

The drawings for this series are by Hisao Tamaki. The events parallel Episode IV, which was the original *Star Wars* movie.

1. Manga #1 ◆ 1998
2. Manga #2 ◆ 1998
3. Manga #3 ◆ 1998
4. Manga #4 ◆ 1998

STAR WARS: BOBA FETT

Various authors

SCHOLASTIC ◆ GRADES 5–9 ◆ A/R

SCIENCE FICTION

Boba Fett learned to be a bounty hunter by accompanying his father Jango Fett on his bounty hunting missions. After Jango is killed, Boba is on his own. He is pursued by his father's enemies—especially Count Dooku, who cheated his father. Boba knows Count Dooku's secret—that he built the clone army. Working for Jabba the Hutt, Boba travels the galaxy as a young bounty hunter.

1. The Fight to Survive (Bisson, Terry) ◆ 2002
2. Crossfire (Bisson, Terry) ◆ 2002
3. Maze of Deception (Hand, Elizabeth) ◆ 2003
4. Hunted (Hand, Elizabeth) ◆ 2003
5. A New Threat (Hand, Elizabeth) ◆ 2004
6. Pursuit (Hand, Elizabeth) ◆ 2004

STAR WARS: EPISODE I THE PHANTOM MENACE—MANGA

Lucas, George

DARK HORSE ◆ GRADES 5–10

SCIENCE FICTION

The drawings for this series are by Kia Asamiya. The story parallels the *Phantom Menace* film.

1. Manga #1 ◆ 1999
2. Manga #2 ◆ 2000

STAR WARS: JEDI APPRENTICE

Various authors

SCHOLASTIC ◆ GRADES 6–8

ADVENTURE | SCIENCE FICTION

Follow the early years of Obi-Wan Kenobi. As a boy, Obi-Wan was destined to be a farmer but the force drew him to Qui-Gon Jinn, who might allow him to become a Padawan, a future Jedi Knight. This series explores the relationship that develops between the two as they travel across the universe facing the forces of evil.

1. The Rising Force (Wolverton, Dave) ◆ 1999
2. The Dark Rival (Watson, Jude) ◆ 1999
3. The Hidden Past (Watson, Jude) ◆ 1999
4. The Mark of the Crown (Watson, Jude) ◆ 1999
5. The Defenders of the Dead (Watson, Jude) ◆ 1999
6. The Uncertain Path (Watson, Jude) ◆ 2000
7. The Captive Temple (Watson, Jude) ◆ 2000
8. The Day of Reckoning (Watson, Jude) ◆ 2000
9. The Fight for Truth (Watson, Jude) ◆ 2000
10. The Shattered Peace (Watson, Jude) ◆ 2000
11. The Deadly Hunter (Watson, Jude) ◆ 2000
12. The Evil Experiment (Watson, Jude) ◆ 2001
13. The Dangerous Rescue (Watson, Jude) ◆ 2001
14. The Ties that Bind (Watson, Jude) ◆ 2001
15. The Death of Hope (Watson, Jude) ◆ 2001
16. The Call to Vengeance (Watson, Jude) ◆ 2001
17. The Only Witness (Watson, Jude) ◆ 2002
18. The Threat Within (Watson, Jude) ◆ 2002

STAR WARS: JEDI QUEST

Watson, Jude

SCHOLASTIC ◆ GRADES 5–9 ◆ A/R

SCIENCE FICTION

Obi-Wan Kenobi feels the power in young Anakin Skywalker. He also senses Anakin's restlessness. As Obi-Wan trains Anakin in the ways of the Jedi, the two travel the galaxy and confront evil—often trying to outwit the powerful Granta Omega. The events in this series take place between Episode I and Episode II.

1. The Way of the Apprentice ◆ 2002
2. The Trail of the Jedi ◆ 2002
3. The Dangerous Games ◆ 2002
4. The Master of Disguise ◆ 2002
5. The School of Fear ◆ 2003
6. The Shadow Trap ◆ 2003
7. The Moment of Truth ◆ 2003
8. The Changing of the Guard ◆ 2004
9. The False Peace ◆ 2004
10. The Final Showdown ◆ 2004

STAR WARS: THE EMPIRE STRIKES BACK—MANGA

Lucas, George

DARK HORSE ◆ GRADES 5–10

SCIENCE FICTION

The drawings for this series are by Toshiki Kudo. The action parallels the second *Star Wars* movie.

1. Manga #1 ◆ 1999
2. Manga #2 ◆ 1999
3. Manga #3 ◆ 1999
4. Manga #4 ◆ 1999

STAR WARS: THE LAST OF THE JEDI

Watson, Jude

SCHOLASTIC ◆ GRADES 5–9 ◆ A/R

SCIENCE FICTION

After the return of the Empire in Episode III, Obi-Wan Kenobi is on Tatooine protecting Luke Skywalker. Luke's father, Anakin, has embraced the dark side and become Darth Vader. With most of the Jedi destroyed, Obi-Wan gets word that his former apprentice, Ferus Olin, is still alive. Obi-Wan leaves Luke to find Ferus, who then begins a mission to find other Jedi and bring them together. To accomplish this, Ferus faces the Emperor and must choose between the Jedi and the dark side.

1. The Desperate Mission ◆ 2005
2. Dark Warning ◆ 2005
3. Underworld ◆ 2005
4. Death on Naboo ◆ 2006
5. Tangled Web ◆ 2006
6. Return of the Dark Side ◆ 2006
7. Secret Weapon ◆ 2007
8. Against the Empire ◆ 2007
9. Master of Deception ◆ 2007
10. Reckoning ◆ 2008

STAR WARS: THE RETURN OF THE JEDI—MANGA

Lucas, George

DARK HORSE ◆ GRADES 5–10

SCIENCE FICTION

The drawings for this series are by Shin-ichi Hiromoto. The action parallels the third *Star Wars* movie, in which Han Solo is encased in carbonite by Jabba the Hutt.

1. Manga #1 ◆ 1999
2. Manga #2 ◆ 1999
3. Manga #3 ◆ 1999
4. Manga #4 ◆ 1999

STAR WARS EPISODE 1: JOURNALS

Various authors

SCHOLASTIC ◆ GRADES 4–8 ◆ A/R

ADVENTURE | SCIENCE FICTION

First-person journal entries reveal entertaining insight into the youths of favorite characters, with discussion of early challenges and accomplishments.

1. Anakin Skywalker (Strasser, Todd) ◆ 1999
2. Queen Amidala (Watson, Jude) ◆ 1999
3. Darth Maul (Watson, Jude) ◆ 2000

STAR WARS GALAXY OF FEAR

Whitman, John

BANTAM ◆ GRADES 4–8 ◆ A/R

ADVENTURE | SCIENCE FICTION

Tash Arranda, 13, and her brother Zak, 12, travel through space encountering creatures and circumstances that threaten the security of space communities. In *Spore,* the two children and their Uncle Hoole visit a mining community that has released an ancient, evil force. *Clones* features a visit to a remote planet that is inhabited by familiar characters who turn out to be clones. Readers who enjoy *Star Wars* will like these adventures, many of which include appearances by characters from the movies, including Luke Skywalker and Darth Vader. These are exciting adventures with gruesome creatures that link the horror genre to science fiction.

1. Eaten Alive ◆ 1997
2. City of the Dead ◆ 1997
3. Planet Plague ◆ 1997
4. The Nightmare Machine ◆ 1997
5. Ghost of the Jedi ◆ 1997
6. Army of Terror ◆ 1997
7. The Brain Spiders ◆ 1997
8. The Swarm ◆ 1998
9. Spore ◆ 1998

10. The Doomsday Ship ◆ 1998
11. Clones ◆ 1998
12. The Hunger ◆ 1998

STAR WARS JUNIOR JEDI KNIGHTS

Various authors

BERKLEY ◆ GRADES 4–8 ◆ A/R

ADVENTURE | SCIENCE FICTION

Anakin Solo is the youngest son of Leia Organa Solo and Han Solo. In this series, Anakin attends Luke Skywalker's Jedi Academy, where he makes friends with a child of the Sand People named Tahiri. The friends go through a rigorous training program and become involved in many exciting adventures. In one book, they search the abandoned fortress of Darth Vader for Obi-Wan Kenobi's lightsaber. In another, they travel to the distant moon of Yavin 8 and try to break the curse of the Golden Globe. Readers who enjoy science fiction, especially those who like the *Star Wars* films, will be attracted to this series. The familiar characters and exciting situations should appeal to reluctant readers.

1. The Golden Globe (Richardson, Nancy) ◆ 1995
2. Lyric's World (Richardson, Nancy) ◆ 1996
3. Promises (Richardson, Nancy) ◆ 1996
4. Anakin's Quest (Moesta, Rebecca) ◆ 1997
5. Vader's Fortress (Moesta, Rebecca) ◆ 1997
6. Kenobi's Blade (Moesta, Rebecca) ◆ 1997

STAR WARS YOUNG JEDI KNIGHTS

Anderson, Kevin J., and Rebecca Moesta

BERKLEY ◆ GRADES 4–8 ◆ A/R

ADVENTURE | SCIENCE FICTION

Jacen and Jaina are the twin children of Han Solo and Princess Leia. They are the future of the New Republic and are being trained in the powers of the Force. In one book, the twins help Anja Gallandro, who had planned to destroy their family but has become their friend. In another, Lando Calrissian takes the twins and Anja on a vacation that turns deadly. Encounters with the Dark Side and adventures across the galaxy should attract fans of Star Wars and science fiction.

1. Heirs of the Force ◆ 1995
2. Shadow Academy ◆ 1995
3. The Lost Ones ◆ 1995
4. Lightsabers ◆ 1996
5. Darkest Knight ◆ 1996

6. Jedi Under Siege ◆ 1997
7. Shards of Alderaan ◆ 1997
8. Diversity Alliance ◆ 1997
9. Delusions of Grandeur ◆ 1997
10. Jedi Bounty ◆ 1997
11. The Emperor's Plague ◆ 1998
12. Return to Ord Mantell ◆ 1998
13. Trouble on Cloud City ◆ 1998
14. Crisis at Crystal Reef ◆ 1998

STARCATCHERS *see* Peter and the Starcatchers

STARFLEET ACADEMY *see* Star Trek: Starfleet Academy

STARLET

Reisfeld, Randi
HYPERION ◆ GRADES 9–12
REAL LIFE

Jacey Chandliss won as "America's Next Top Actress" on the *Generation Next* reality show. Now she cannot escape the spotlight . . . or the rumors and slights that are being posted on a blog about her. Is one of her friends the blogger? As the series progresses, Jacey becomes more successful as an actress. Unfortunately, the tabloids scrutinize her every move, including her romantic interest in two actors. Fans of the Gossip Girl and It Girl books will love this series.

1. Starlet ◆ 2007
2. Everyone Who's Anyone ◆ 2007
3. All Access ◆ 2007

STARRING IN... *see* Mary-Kate and Ashley Starring In . . .

STERLING FAMILY

Johnston, Norma
ATHENEUM ◆ GRADES 6–8
FAMILY LIFE | HISTORICAL

These tales about the Sterlings and the Albrights are based on stories the author heard, while growing up in New Jersey, about her relatives living in Yonkers and the Bronx at the turn of the century. The first four books center on teenager Tish Sterling and the problems she and her family are coping with: Her mother is having yet another baby, her older sister marries a man with a child from a previous marriage, her grandfather dies, and the family business is in trouble. The last two books center on a child of the next generation, Saranne Albright, who experiences problems similar to her Aunt Tish's and is particularly distracted by the antics of her troubled friend Paul Hodge. The thoughtful perspectives presented by the two girls help readers to recognize similarities between their own situations and those of girls who grew up in the early part of the last century.

1. The Keeping Days ◆ 1973
2. Glory in the Flower ◆ 1974
3. A Mustard Seed of Magic ◆ 1977
4. The Sanctuary Tree ◆ 1977
5. A Nice Girl Like You ◆ 1980
6. Myself and I ◆ 1981

THE STONEHEART TRILOGY

Fletcher, Charile

HYPERION ◆ GRADES 5–9 ◆ A/R

FANTASY

At the Natural History Museum in London, George, 12, damages a dragon statue and is transported to a parallel world where the statues have come to life and are at war. Because of his attack on the dragon statue, George is being pursued and searches for the stoneheart, the key to his release. He is befriended by Edie, a girl with secret powers, and by the Gunner, a statue of a World War I soldier. As the series progresses, the three face many enemies, including the Grid Man, the Minotaur, and the Walker. And George is being destroyed from within as three veins—marble, bronze, and stone—grow out of his hand toward his heart.

1. The Stoneheart ◆ 2007
2. The Ironhand ◆ 2008
3. Silvertongue ◆ 2009

STORIES FROM EAST HIGH *see* High School Musical Stories from East High

STORY GIRL

Montgomery, L. M., and Barbara Davoll, adapt.

ZONDERKIDZ ◆ GRADES 5–7

HISTORICAL | VALUES

Based on stories by L. M. Montgomery, these books set on Prince Edward Island at the turn of the 20th century feature Sara Stanley, a girl with a gift for telling stories with a Christian message. In the first book, two boys—the King cousins—visit relatives on Prince Edward Island and learn about church, raise funds for a school library, and hear a good story or two. In *Winter on the Island,* the cousins and their friends celebrate Christmas, make New Year's resolutions, start up a newspaper, and experience a blizzard.

1. The King Cousins ◆ 2004
2. Measles, Mischief, and Mishaps ◆ 2004
3. Summer Shenanigans ◆ 2004
4. Dreams, Schemes, and Mysteries ◆ 2004
5. Winter on the Island ◆ 2005
6. Wedding Wishes and Woes ◆ 2005
7. Midnight Madness and Mayhem ◆ 2005
8. Winds of Change ◆ 2005

STRAVAGANZA

Hoffman, Mary

BLOOMSBURY ◆ GRADES 7–10 ◆ A/R

FANTASY

Featuring time travel and an alternate world, Talia—based on Renaissance Italy—the Stravaganza series follows the adventures of teens who leave their modern-day problems behind them and become embroiled in the intrigues of another place and time. In *City of Masks,* Lucien is transported to Bellezza (based on 16th-century Venice) and meets other Stravaganti—time travelers. Lucian becomes Luciano, an apprentice to a scholar, and is caught up in the conflict between the Duchessa and the di Chimici family.

1. City of Masks ◆ 2002
2. City of Stars ◆ 2003
3. City of Flowers ◆ 2005
4. City of Secrets ◆ 2008

THE STRONGBOW SAGA

Roberts, Judson

HARPERTEEN ◆ GRADES 9–12

HISTORICAL

At the beginning of the series, 14-year-old Halfdan, son of a Danish chieftain and an Irish noblewoman, is living as a slave in 9th-century Denmark. His mother manages to secure his release, and Halfdan goes on to become a brave warrior and talented craftsman. These books, which include a lot of historical detail, are narrated by Halfdan, who, although he is determined to avenge his brother's death, dislikes violence and tries to protect the innocent.

1. Viking Warrior ◆ 2006
2. Dragons from the Sea ◆ 2007
3. The Road to Vengeance ◆ 2008

THE STUART QUARTET

Yolen, Jane, and Robert J. Harris
PHILOMEL ◆ GRADES 6–12
HISTORICAL

In the first volume of this quartet about Scotland, orphan Nicola Ambruzzi is a court jester who attracts the attention of the young Mary Queen of Scots and accompanies her as she flees France and returns to Scotland. The first-person narrative, based on the life of a woman called La Jardiniere, is full of rich historical and social detail. *Girl in a Cage* tells the story of Marjorie, the 11-year-old daughter of King Robert the Bruce, who in 1306 is captured by the English and kept in a cage, where she shows courage and pragmatism. The third book features Duncan, a 14-year-old epileptic who takes part in the battle of Culloden in 1746, fighting on the side of Bonnie Prince Charlie.

1. The Queen's Own Fool: A Novel of Mary Queen of Scots ◆ 2000
2. Girl in a Cage ◆ 2002
3. Prince Across the Water ◆ 2004
4. The Rogues ◆ 2007

STUDENTS ACROSS THE SEVEN SEAS

Various authors
SPEAK ◆ GRADES 8–12 ◆ A/R
REAL LIFE | ROMANCE

Combining travel and romance, these light reads follow American students' progress on trips abroad. Sixteen-year-old Abby learns about independence and her own worth when she is in London for the summer, far from her controlling parents. High school junior Kelly takes things too far when she is first in Rome but her interest in art gets her back on track in *Getting the Boot*.

1. Westminster Abby (Ostow, Micol) ◆ 2005
2. Getting the Boot (Strauss, Peggy Guthart) ◆ 2005

3. Spain or Shine (Jellen, Michelle) ◆ 2005
4. Pardon My French (Hapka, Cathy) ◆ 2005
5. The Sound of Munich (Nelson, Suzanne Marie) ◆ 2006
6. Now and Zen (Gerber, Linda C.) ◆ 2006
7. Heart and Salsa (Nelson, Suzanne Marie) ◆ 2006
8. Swede Dreams (Apelqvist, Eva) ◆ 2007
9. The Finnish Line (Gerber, Linda C.) ◆ 2007
10. When Irish Guys are Smiling (Supplee, Suzanne) ◆ 2008
11. French Kissmas (Hapka, Cathy) ◆ 2008

STUDY

Snyder, Maria V.
MIRA BOOKS ◆ GRADES 10–12
FANTASY

In *Poison Study* readers are introduced to Yelena Zaltana. To avoid being executed, Yelena has become the food taster for the Commander. Ironically, this will only delay her death as his food is being poisoned. Yelena's magical powers begin to emerge and she attracts the attention of others in Ixia, including Valek, the head of security. After the overthrow of the govenment, Yelena returns home to Sitia and enters the Magician's Citadel. As her magical powers grow, so do the threats on her life. Throughout the series, Yelena's romance with Valek intensifies. In *Fire Study,* Yelena is now a Soulfinder and she begins a dangerous mission hoping to prevent a war.

1. Poison Study ◆ 2005
2. Magic Study ◆ 2007
3. Fire Study ◆ 2008

SUDDENLY SUPERNATURAL

Kimmel, Elizabeth Cody
LITTLE, BROWN ◆ GRADES 5–8 ◆ A/R
FANTASY

Kat Roberts is starting a new school and she wants to fit in. That has been a challenge because Kat's mother is a medium—she sees the spirits of the dead. Now Kat realizes that she sees spirits, too. In fact, there is a spirit at her school that needs Kat's help.

1. School Spirit ◆ 2008
2. Scaredy Kat ◆ 2009
3. Unhappy Medium ◆ 2009

SUMMER

Applegate, K. A.
SIMON & SCHUSTER ◆ GRADES 7–10

REAL LIFE

Summer is visiting the Florida Keys from Minnesota. She is attracted to three boys with very different personalities and she remembers her boyfriend back home. She returns to Minnesota and becomes engaged to Seth, but visiting Florida again throws her right into Austin's arms. Teens will find these quick, satisfying romantic reads.

1. June Dreams ◆ 1995
2. July's Promise ◆ 1995
3. August Magic ◆ 1995
4. Sand, Surf and Secrets ◆ 1996
5. Rays, Romance and Rivalry ◆ 1996
6. Beaches, Boys and Betrayal ◆ 1996

SUMMER BOYS

Abbott, Hailey
SCHOLASTIC ◆ GRADES 10–12 ◆ A/R

ROMANCE | REAL LIFE

Three cousins vacation at their family's beach house in Maine. There are cute boys everywhere and the girls are determined to date and find romance. Ella is attracted to her older sister's boyfriend. Jamie hooks up with the wrong guy. And suddenly Beth sees her friend George as more than just a friend. As the series progresses, issues include smoking, alcohol, and discussions of sexuality. In *Last Summer,* the girls are preparing to go to college. This series could attract fans of The Sisterhood of the Traveling Pants books.

1. Summer Boys ◆ 2004
2. Summer Boys 2 ◆ 2005
3. After Summer ◆ 2006
4. Last Summer ◆ 2007

THE SUMMER OF MAGIC QUARTET

Spalding, Andrea
ORCA ◆ GRADES 4–7

FANTASY

Canadians Chantel and Adam find a magic talisman soon after they arrive in England to visit their cousins. They become embroiled in a struggle between an ancient White Horse Wise One and an evil dragon. There is time travel and telepathic communication. The saga of the pending divorce of the children's parents adds a real-life element to this fantasy full of historical detail.

1. The White Horse Talisman ◆ 2002
2. Dance of the Stones ◆ 2003
3. Heart of the Hill ◆ 2005
4. Behind the Sorcerer's Cloak ◆ 2006

SUMMER SHARE

Various authors

SIMON & SCHUSTER ◆ GRADES 10–12

REAL LIFE

Sharing houses for the summer—on the beach at Laguna or in the Hollywood Hills, these teenagers surf, laze on the beach, party at night, have romances, and keep secrets from each other.

1. CC (Cape Cod) (Reisfeld, Randi) ◆ 2005
2. LB (Laguna Beach) (Thacker, Nola) ◆ 2005
3. Partiers Preferred (Reisfeld, Randi) ◆ 2007
4. Shirt and Shoes Not Required (Strasser, Todd) ◆ 2007

SUMMERHILL SECRETS

Lewis, Beverly

BETHANY HOUSE ◆ GRADES 6–8 ◆ A/R

VALUES

Merry Hanson, 13, lives in Amish country and early adventures in this series involve her Amish friend, Rachel Zook. In one book, they hide a girl who is being abused at home. Lissa stays with an Amish family and finds the strength to face her problems. Prayer, faith, and family help Merry face each new challenge.

1. Whispers Down the Lane ◆ 1994
2. Secret in the Willows ◆ 1994
3. Catch a Falling Star ◆ 1995
4. Night of the Fireflies ◆ 1995
5. A Cry in the Dark ◆ 1996
6. House of Secrets ◆ 1996
7. Echoes in the Wind ◆ 1997
8. Hide Behind the Moon ◆ 1998
9. Windows on the Hill ◆ 1999
10. Shadows Beyond the Gate ◆ 2000

SUMMIT HIGH

Tullos, Matt

BROADMAN & HOLMAN ◆ GRADES 7–10

REAL LIFE | VALUES

Teens at Summit High find strength in their values. In one book, Justin seeks to help his friends realize the power of religion, but he is rejected. His faith in Christ sustains him. In another book, Kandi deals with racism.

1. Wrong Turn in the Fast Lane ◆ 1998
2. Processing the Computer Conspiracy ◆ 1998
3. Wild Lies and Secret Truth ◆ 1999
4. Deleting the Net Threat ◆ 1999
5. Dangerous Decisions and Hidden Choices ◆ 1999
6. Friends to the End ◆ 1999

SUNSET ISLAND

Bennett, Cherie

BERKLEY ◆ GRADES 6–9

REAL LIFE

While working as au pairs on Sunset Island for the summer, Emma, Carrie, and Samantha find romance and adventure. Related series are Sunset After Dark and Club Sunset Island.

1. Sunset Island ◆ 1991
2. Sunset Kiss ◆ 1991
3. Sunset Dreams ◆ 1991
4. Sunset Farewell ◆ 1991
5. Sunset Reunion ◆ 1991
6. Sunset Secrets ◆ 1992
7. Sunset Heat ◆ 1992
8. Sunset Promises ◆ 1992
9. Sunset Scandal ◆ 1992
10. Sunset Whispers ◆ 1992
11. Sunset Paradise ◆ 1992
12. Sunset Surf ◆ 1993
13. Sunset Deceptions ◆ 1993
14. Sunset on the Road ◆ 1993
15. Sunset Embrace ◆ 1993
16. Sunset Wishes ◆ 1993
17. Sunset Touch ◆ 1993
18. Sunset Wedding ◆ 1993
19. Sunset Glitter ◆ 1994

20. Sunset Stranger ◆ 1994
21. Sunset Heart ◆ 1994
22. Sunset Revenge ◆ 1994
23. Sunset Sensation ◆ 1994
24. Sunset Magic ◆ 1994
25. Sunset Illusions ◆ 1994
26. Sunset Fire ◆ 1994
27. Sunset Fantasy ◆ 1994
28. Sunset Passion ◆ 1994
29. Sunset Love ◆ 1995
30. Sunset Fling ◆ 1995
31. Sunset Tears ◆ 1995
32. Sunset Spirit ◆ 1995
33. Sunset Holiday ◆ 1995
34. Sunset Forever ◆ 1997

CLUB SUNSET ISLAND

1. Too Many Boys ◆ 1994
2. Dixie's First Kiss ◆ 1994
3. Tori's Crush ◆ 1994

SUNSET AFTER DARK

1. Sunset After Dark ◆ 1993
2. Sunset After Midnight ◆ 1993
3. Sunset After Hours ◆ 1993

SUPER GOOFBALLS

Hannan, Peter
HARPERCOLLINS ◆ GRADES 4–8 ◆ A/R

HUMOR

To help pay the bills, the main character (Amazing Techno Dude) and his grandmother (Bodacious Backwards Woman) have taken in eight roommates, each extremely goofy and each a sort of superhero. Life at 1313 Thirteenth Street is crazier than ever. In *Goofballs in Paradise,* the gang goes on vacation and confronts the supervillain Mondo Grumpo. With short chapters and zany action, this may appeal to reluctant readers as well as to fans of Dav Pilkey books.

1. That Stinking Feeling ◆ 2007
2. Goofballs in Paradise ◆ 2007
3. Super Underwear . . . and Beyond ◆ 2007
4. Attack of the 50-Foot Alien Creep-oids ◆ 2007
5. Doomed in Dreamland ◆ 2008
6. Battle of the Brain-Sucking Robots ◆ 2008

SURVIVAL!

Duey, Kathleen, and Karen A. Bale

ALADDIN ◆ GRADES 5–8 ◆ A/R

ADVENTURE | HISTORICAL

The sinking of the *Titanic,* the San Francisco earthquake, the Colorado blizzard—imagine that you are there. The Survival! series places young characters in the middle of exciting, even dangerous situations. In 1850, twins Jess and Will find themselves stranded in Death Valley. In 1871, the Chicago Fire places Nate Cooper and Julie Flynn in great danger from the chaotic crowds and the spreading inferno. Dramatic events are woven into the historical context, which should attract readers who want stories with adventure and courageous characters.

1. Titanic: April 14, 1912 ◆ 1998
2. Earthquake: San Francisco, 1906 ◆ 1998
3. Blizzard: Estes Park, Colorado, 1886 ◆ 1998
4. Fire: Chicago, 1871 ◆ 1998
5. Flood: Mississippi, 1927 ◆ 1998
6. Stranded: Death Valley, Circa 1850 ◆ 1998
7. Cave-in: Pennsylvania, 1880s ◆ 1998
8. Train Wreck: Kansas, 1892 ◆ 1999
9. Hurricane: Open Seas, 1784 ◆ 1999
10. Forest Fire: Hinckley, Minnesota, 1894 ◆ 1999
11. Swamp: Bayou Teche, Louisiana, 1851 ◆ 1999

SWALLOWS AND AMAZONS

Ransome, Arthur

GODINE ◆ GRADES 6–8

ADVENTURE

The first volume in this series introduces readers to an imaginative group of children. John, Susan, Titty, and Roger Walker are allowed to sail their small boat *Swallow* to an island and camp there without their parents. They meet up here with Nancy and Peggy Blackett, who also enjoy a large amount of freedom in their boat *Amazon.* The six youngsters become embroiled in an adventure involving a stolen book. They finally solve the crime and move onto similar nautical adventures in subsequent novels. The books have been reissued many times over the years.

1. Swallows and Amazons ◆ 1930
2. Swallowdale ◆ 1931
3. Peter Duck ◆ 1932
4. Winter Holiday ◆ 1933
5. Coot Club ◆ 1934
6. Pigeon Post ◆ 1936

7. We Didn't Mean to Go to Sea ◆ 1937
8. Secret Water ◆ 1939
9. The Big Six ◆ 1940
10. Missee Lee ◆ 1941
11. The Picts and the Martyrs ◆ 1943
12. Great Northern? ◆ 1947

SWAMPLAND TRILOGY

Martin, S. R.

SCHOLASTIC ◆ GRADES 7–10

FANTASY

Marvin thinks the new neighbors are strange. They look like creatures from the nearby swamp . . . they are creatures from the swamp! In the third book, Marvin's brother Zac enters a terrifying world of darkness. The fast pace should appeal to reluctant readers.

1. Swampland ◆ 2000
2. Tankworld ◆ 2000
3. Endsville ◆ 2000

SWEEP

Tiernan, Cate

PENGUIN ◆ GRADES 8–10 ◆ A/R

FANTASY

High school junior Morgan, who has always felt inferior to her friend Bree, is attracted to Cal and to his Wiccan rituals and beliefs. As the series progresses, Morgan discovers that she is in fact a hereditary witch and becomes an important member of the coven and eventually the most powerful witch of her generation, active in the battle against evil.

1. Book of Shadows ◆ 2001
2. The Coven ◆ 2001
3. Blood Witch ◆ 2001
4. Dark Magick ◆ 2001
5. Awakening ◆ 2001
6. Spellbound ◆ 2001
7. The Calling ◆ 2001
8. Changeling ◆ 2001
9. Strife ◆ 2002
10. Seeker ◆ 2002
11. Legacy ◆ 2002
12. Eclipse ◆ 2002

13. Reckoning ◆ 2002
14. Full Circle ◆ 2002

SWEEP SUPER SPECIAL

1. Night's Child ◆ 2003

SWEET DREAMS

Various authors

BANTAM DOUBLEDAY DELL ◆ GRADES 7–9

REAL LIFE

Teen romance is the focus of this slightly old-fashioned, long-running series that deals with themes including dating, popularity, and friendship.

1. P.S. I Love You (Conklin, Barbara P.) ◆ 1981
2. The Popularity Plan (Vernon, Rosemary) ◆ 1981
3. Laurie's Song (Brand, Debra) ◆ 1981
4. Princess Amy (Pollowitz, Melinda) ◆ 1981
5. Little Sister (Green, Yvonne) ◆ 1981
6. California Girl (Quin-Harkin, Janet) ◆ 1981
7. Green Eyes (Rand, Suzanne) ◆ 1982
8. The Thoroughbred (Campbell, Joanna) ◆ 1982
9. Cover Girl (Green, Yvonne) ◆ 1982
10. Love Match (Quin-Harkin, Janet) ◆ 1982
11. The Problem with Love (Vernon, Rosemary) ◆ 1982
12. Night of the Prom (Spector, Debra) ◆ 1982
13. The Summer Jenny Fell in Love (Vernon, Rosemary) ◆ 1982
14. Dance of Love (Saal, Jocelyn) ◆ 1982
15. Thinking of You (Noble, Jeanette) ◆ 1982
16. How Do You Say Goodbye? (Burman, Margaret) ◆ 1982
17. Ask Annie (Rand, Suzanne) ◆ 1982
18. Ten-Boy Summer (Quin-Harkin, Janet) ◆ 1982
19. Love Song (Park, Anne) ◆ 1982
20. The Popularity Summer (Vernon, Rosemary) ◆ 1982
21. All's Fair in Love (Andrews, Jeanne) ◆ 1982
22. Secret Identity (Campbell, Joanna) ◆ 1982
23. Falling in Love Again (Conklin, Barbara P.) ◆ 1983
24. The Trouble with Charlie (Ellen, Jaye) ◆ 1983
25. Her Secret Self (Willot, Rhondi) ◆ 1983
26. It Must Be Magic (Woodruff, Marian) ◆ 1983
27. Too Young for Love (Maravel, Gailanne) ◆ 1983
28. Trusting Hearts (Saal, Jocelyn) ◆ 1983
29. Never Love a Cowboy (Dukore, Jesse) ◆ 1983
30. Little White Lies (Fisher, Lois I.) ◆ 1983
31. Too Close for Comfort (Spector, Debra) ◆ 1983
32. Daydreamer (Quin-Harkin, Janet) ◆ 1983
33. Dear Amanda (Vernon, Rosemary) ◆ 1983

34. Country Girl (Pollowitz, Melinda) ◆ 1983
35. Forbidden Love (Woodruff, Marian) ◆ 1983
36. Summer Dreams (Conklin, Barbara P.) ◆ 1983
37. Portrait of Love (Noble, Jeanette) ◆ 1983
38. Running Mates (Saal, Jocelyn) ◆ 1983
39. First Love (Spector, Debra) ◆ 1983
40. Secrets (Aaron, Anna) ◆ 1983
41. The Truth About Me and Bobby V. (Johns, Janetta) ◆ 1983
42. The Perfect Match (Woodruff, Marian) ◆ 1983
43. Tender Loving Care (Park, Anne) ◆ 1983
44. Long Distance Love (Dukore, Jesse) ◆ 1983
45. Dream Prom (Burman, Margaret) ◆ 1983
46. On Thin Ice (Saal, Jocelyn) ◆ 1983
47. Te Amo Means I Love You (Kent, Deborah) ◆ 1983
48. Dial L for Love (Woodruff, Marian) ◆ 1983
49. Too Much to Lose (Rand, Suzanne) ◆ 1983
50. Lights, Camera, Love (Maravel, Gailanne) ◆ 1983
51. Magic Moments (Spector, Debra) ◆ 1983
52. Love Notes (Campbell, Joanna) ◆ 1983
53. Ghost of a Chance (Quin-Harkin, Janet) ◆ 1983
54. I Can't Forget You (Fisher, Lois I.) ◆ 1983
55. Spotlight on Love (Pines, Nancy) ◆ 1984
56. Campfire Nights (Cowan, Dale) ◆ 1984
57. On Her Own (Rand, Suzanne) ◆ 1984
58. Rhythm of Love (Foster, Stephanie) ◆ 1984
59. Please Say Yes (Crawford, Alice O.) ◆ 1984
60. Summer Breezes (Blake, Susan) ◆ 1984
61. Exchange of Hearts (Quin-Harkin, Janet) ◆ 1984
62. Just like the Movies (Rand, Suzanne) ◆ 1984
63. Kiss Me, Creep (Woodruff, Marian) ◆ 1984
64. Love in the Fast Lane (Vernon, Rosemary) ◆ 1984
65. The Two of Us (Quin-Harkin, Janet) ◆ 1984
66. Love Times Two (Foster, Stephanie) ◆ 1984
67. I Believe in You (Conklin, Barbara P.) ◆ 1984
68. Lovebirds (Quin-Harkin, Janet) ◆ 1984
69. Call Me Beautiful (Blair, Shannon) ◆ 1984
70. Special Someone (Fields, Terri) ◆ 1984
71. Too Many Boys (Dickenson, Celia) ◆ 1984
72. Goodbye Forever (Conklin, Barbara P.) ◆ 1984
73. Language of Love (Vernon, Rosemary) ◆ 1984
74. Don't Forget Me (Gregory, Diana) ◆ 1984
75. First Summer Love (Foster, Stephanie) ◆ 1984
76. Three Cheers for Love (Rand, Suzanne) ◆ 1984
77. Ten-Speed Summer (Kent, Deborah) ◆ 1984
78. Never Say No (Capron, Jean F.) ◆ 1984
79. Star Struck! (Blair, Shannon) ◆ 1984
80. A Shot at Love (Jarnow, Jill) ◆ 1984
81. Secret Admirer (Spector, Debra) ◆ 1984
82. Hey, Good Looking! (Polcover, Jane) ◆ 1984

83. Love by the Book (Park, Anne) ◆ 1985
84. The Last Word (Blake, Susan) ◆ 1985
85. The Boy She Left Behind (Rand, Suzanne) ◆ 1985
86. Questions of Love (Vernon, Rosemary) ◆ 1985
87. Programmed for Love (Crane, Stephen) ◆ 1985
88. Wrong Kind of Boy (Blair, Shannon) ◆ 1985
89. 101 Ways to Meet Mr. Right (Quin-Harkin, Janet) ◆ 1985
90. Two's a Crowd (Gregory, Diana) ◆ 1985
91. The Love Hunt (Green, Yvonne) ◆ 1985
92. Kiss and Tell (Blair, Shannon) ◆ 1985
93. The Great Boy Chase (Quin-Harkin, Janet) ◆ 1985
94. Second Chances (Levinson, Nancy) ◆ 1985
95. No Strings Attached (Hehl, Eileen) ◆ 1985
96. First, Last and Always (Conklin, Barbara P.) ◆ 1985
97. Dancing in the Dark (Ross, Carolyn) ◆ 1985
98. Love in the Air (Conklin, Barbara P.) ◆ 1985
99. Follow that Boy (Quin-Harkin, Janet) ◆ 1985
100. One Boy Too Many (Caudell, Marian) ◆ 1985
101. Wrong for Each Other (Quin-Harkin, Janet) ◆ 1986
102. Hearts Don't Lie (Fields, Terri) ◆ 1986
103. Cross My Heart (Gregory, Diana) ◆ 1986
104. Playing for Keeps (Stevens, Janice) ◆ 1986
105. The Perfect Boy (Hapgood, Elizabeth R.) ◆ 1986
106. Mission: Love (Makris, Kathryn) ◆ 1986
107. If You Love Me (Steiner, Barbara) ◆ 1986
108. One of the Boys (Jarnow, Jill) ◆ 1986
109. No More Boys (White, Charlotte) ◆ 1986
110. Playing Games (Hehl, Eileen) ◆ 1986
111. Stolen Kisses (Reynolds, Elizabeth) ◆ 1986
112. Listen to Your Heart (Caudell, Marian) ◆ 1986
113. Private Eyes (Winfield, Julia) ◆ 1986
114. Just the Way You Are (Boies, Janice) ◆ 1986
115. Promise Me Love (Redish, Jane) ◆ 1986
116. Heartbreak Hill (MacBain, Carol) ◆ 1986
117. The Other Me (Fields, Terri) ◆ 1986
118. Heart to Heart (Curtis, Stefanie) ◆ 1987
119. Star-Crossed Love (Cadwallader, Sharon) ◆ 1987
120. Mr. Wonderful (Michaels, Fran) ◆ 1987
121. Only Make-Believe (Winfield, Julia) ◆ 1987
122. A Song for Linda (Daley, Dee) ◆ 1987
123. Love in the Wings (Smiley, Virginia) ◆ 1987
124. More than Friends (Boies, Janice) ◆ 1987
125. Parade of Hearts (Beecham, Jahnna) ◆ 1987
126. Here's My Heart (Curtis, Stefanie) ◆ 1987
127. My Best Enemy (Quin-Harkin, Janet) ◆ 1987
128. One Boy at a Time (Fields, Terri) ◆ 1987
129. A Vote for Love (Gregory, Diana) ◆ 1987
130. Dance with Me (Beecham, Jahnna) ◆ 1987
131. Hand-Me-Down Heart (Schultz, Mary) ◆ 1987

132. Winner Takes All (Lykken, Laurie) ◆ 1987
133. Playing the Field (Hehl, Eileen) ◆ 1987
134. Past Perfect (Michaels, Fran) ◆ 1987
135. Geared for Romance (Wyeth, Sharon Dennis) ◆ 1987
136. Stand by for Love (MacBain, Carol) ◆ 1987
137. Rocky Romance (Wyeth, Sharon Dennis) ◆ 1987
138. Heart and Soul (Boies, Janice) ◆ 1987
139. The Right Combination (Beecham, Jahnna) ◆ 1987
140. Love Detour (Curtis, Stefanie) ◆ 1988
141. Winter Dreams (Conklin, Barbara P.) ◆ 1988
142. Lifeguard Summer (Jarnow, Jill) ◆ 1988
143. Crazy for You (Beecham, Jahnna) ◆ 1988
144. Priceless Love (Lykken, Laurie) ◆ 1988
145. This Time for Real (Gorman, Susan) ◆ 1988
146. Gifts from the Heart (Simbal, Joanne) ◆ 1988
147. Trust in Love (Finney, Shan) ◆ 1988
148. Riddles of Love (Baer, Judy) ◆ 1988
149. Practice Makes Perfect (Beecham, Jahnna) ◆ 1988
150. Summer Secrets (Blake, Susan) ◆ 1988
151. Fortunes of Love (Schultz, Mary) ◆ 1988
152. Cross-Country Match (Richards, Ann) ◆ 1988
153. The Perfect Catch (Lykken, Laurie) ◆ 1988
154. Love Lines (Grimes, Francis Hurley) ◆ 1988
155. The Game of Love (Gorman, Susan) ◆ 1988
156. Two Boys Too Many (Bloss, Janet Adele) ◆ 1988
157. Mr. Perfect (Curtis, Stefanie) ◆ 1988
158. Crossed Signals (Boies, Janice) ◆ 1988
159. Long Shot (Simbal, Joanne) ◆ 1988
160. Blue Ribbon Romance (Smiley, Virginia) ◆ 1988
161. My Perfect Valentine (Baker, Susan) ◆ 1988
162. Trading Hearts (Blake, Susan) ◆ 1989
163. My Dream Guy (Cassidy, Carla Bracale) ◆ 1989
164. Playing to Win (Boies, Janice) ◆ 1989
165. A Brush with Love (St. Pierre, Stephanie) ◆ 1989
166. Three's a Crowd (Dale, Allison) ◆ 1989
167. Working at Love (Baer, Judy) ◆ 1989
168. Dream Date (Cassidy, Carla Bracale) ◆ 1989
169. Golden Girl (Ballard, Jane) ◆ 1991
170. Rock 'n' Roll Sweetheart (Lykken, Laurie) ◆ 1991
171. Acting on Impulse (Wallach, Susan Jo) ◆ 1991
172. Sun Kissed (St. Pierre, Stephanie) ◆ 1991
173. Music from the Heart (Laskin, Pamela L.) ◆ 1991
174. Love on Strike (Boies, Janice) ◆ 1991
175. Puppy Love (Cassidy, Carla Bracale) ◆ 1991
176. Wrong-Way Romance (South, Sherri Cobb) ◆ 1991
177. The Truth About Love (Lykken, Laurie) ◆ 1991
178. Project Boyfriend (St. Pierre, Stephanie) ◆ 1991
179. Racing Hearts (Sloate, Susan) ◆ 1991
180. Opposites Attract (Singleton, Linda Joy) ◆ 1991

181. Time Out for Love (O'Connell, June) ◆ 1991
182. Down with Love (Cassidy, Carla Bracale) ◆ 1991
183. The Real Thing (McHugh, Elisabet) ◆ 1991
184. Too Good to Be True (Kirby, Susan) ◆ 1991
185. Focus on Love (Anson, Mandy) ◆ 1991
186. That Certain Feeling (South, Sherri Cobb) ◆ 1991
187. Fair-Weather Love (Cassidy, Carla Bracale) ◆ 1991
188. Play Me a Love Song (Headapohl, Bette) ◆ 1991
189. Cheating Heart (Lykken, Laurie) ◆ 1991
190. Almost Perfect (Singleton, Linda Joy) ◆ 1992
191. Backstage Romance (Kroeger, Kelly) ◆ 1992
192. The Cinderella Game (South, Sherri Cobb) ◆ 1992
193. Love on the Upbeat (O'Connell, June) ◆ 1992
194. Lucky in Love (Hehl, Eileen) ◆ 1992
195. Comedy of Errors (Crawford, Diane M.) ◆ 1992
196. Clashing Hearts (Jenner, Caryn) ◆ 1992
197. The News Is Love (Phelps, Lauren M.) ◆ 1992
198. Partners in Love (Kirby, Susan) ◆ 1992
199. Wings of Love (Wolfe, Anne Herron) ◆ 1992
200. Love to Spare (Singleton, Linda Joy) ◆ 1992
201. His and Hers (O'Connell, June) ◆ 1992
202. Love on Wheels (Jones, Sandy) ◆ 1993
203. Lessons in Love (Headapohl, Bette) ◆ 1993
204. Picture Perfect Romance (Cooper, J. B.) ◆ 1993
205. Cowboy Kisses (Crawford, Diane M.) ◆ 1993
206. Moonlight Melody (Watts, Alycyn) ◆ 1993
207. My Secret Heart (Kirby, Susan) ◆ 1993
208. Romance on the Run (Hastings, Catt) ◆ 1993
209. Weekend Romance (Teeters, Peggy) ◆ 1993
210. Oh, Promise Me (Lykken, Laurie) ◆ 1993
211. Dreamskate (Cash, Angela) ◆ 1993
212. Highland Hearts (Hayes, Maggie) ◆ 1994
213. Finders Keepers (Washburn, Jan) ◆ 1994
214. Don't Bet on Love (South, Sherri Cobb) ◆ 1994
215. Deep in My Heart (Singleton, Linda Joy) ◆ 1994
216. Careless Whispers (Voeller, Sydell) ◆ 1994
217. Head over Heels (Sloate, Susan) ◆ 1994
218. Face Up to Love (Danner, Nikki) ◆ 1994
219. Heartstrings (Wilson, Barbara) ◆ 1994
220. My Funny Guy (Santori, Helen) ◆ 1994
221. A Little More to Love (Erlbach, Arlene) ◆ 1994
222. Fool for Love (Jones, Sandy) ◆ 1994
223. Heartthrob (Schuler, Betty J.) ◆ 1994
224. Boyfriend Blues (Phelps, Lauren M.) ◆ 1995
225. Recipe for Love (Emburg, Kate) ◆ 1995
226. Aloha Love (Kremer, Marcie) ◆ 1995
227. Dreamboat (Singleton, Linda Joy) ◆ 1995
228. Blame It on Love (South, Sherri Cobb) ◆ 1995
229. Rich in Romance (Cash, Angela) ◆ 1995

230. Happily Ever After (Hehl, Eileen) ◆ 1995
231. Love Notes (Maxwell, Janet) ◆ 1995
232. The Love Line (Kroeger, Kelly) ◆ 1995
233. Follow Your Heart (Headapohl, Bette) ◆ 1995

SWEET DREAMS SPECIALS

1. My Secret Love (Quin-Harkin, Janet) ◆ 1986
2. A Change of Heart (Blake, Susan) ◆ 1986
3. Searching for Love (Warren, Andrea) ◆ 1986
4. Taking the Lead (Kent, Deborah) ◆ 1987
5. Never Say Goodbye (Quin-Harkin, Janet) ◆ 1987
6. A Chance to Love (Foster, Stephanie) ◆ 1988

SWEET DREAMS: ON OUR OWN

Quin-Harkin, Janet
BANTAM DOUBLEDAY DELL ◆ GRADES 7–9
REAL LIFE

Friends Jill and Toni have finished high school and are in college in this series. In the first book, Jill must cope with a difficult roommate, the newness of life on campus, and the absence of her friend Toni. In the second book, Toni is attending the local community college. She has a rocky start but then settles into her studies, friendship, and apartment.

1. The Graduates ◆ 1986
2. The Trouble with Toni ◆ 1986
3. Out of Love ◆ 1986
4. Old Friends, New Friends ◆ 1986
5. Growing Pains ◆ 1986
6. Best Friends Forever ◆ 1986

SWEET 16

Various authors
HARPERCOLLINS ◆ GRADES 7–10 ◆ A/R
REAL LIFE

As their sixteenth birthdays approach, teens from different areas of the country get ready to celebrate. In most cases, the unexpected happens and the characters are often caught in their own lies and deceptions. Lucy decides to develop a new persona for her new school. Julia and Maggie meet at the license bureau and decide to switch places.

1. Julia (Metz, Melinda) ◆ 2000
2. Lucy (Barondes, Jessica) ◆ 2000
3. Kari (Bray, Libba) ◆ 2000

4. Trent (Parker, Daniel) ◆ 2000
5. Marisa (Pittel, Jamie) ◆ 2000
6. Sunny and Matt (Metz, Melinda) ◆ 2000

SWEET 16 (MARY-KATE AND ASHLEY)
see Mary-Kate and Ashley Sweet 16

SWEET VALLEY HIGH

Pascal, Francine, creator
BANTAM ◆ **GRADES 7–10** ◆ **A/R**
REAL LIFE

This series of more than 140 titles follows the lives of popular twins Jessica and Elizabeth Wakefield. Their exploits at Sweet Valley High School in California include falling in and out of love, making and losing friends, traveling, modeling, having fun, and sometimes finding themselves in dangerous situations.

1. Double Love ◆ 1983
2. Secrets ◆ 1983
3. Playing with Fire ◆ 1983
4. Power Play ◆ 1983
5. All Night Long ◆ 1984
6. Dangerous Love ◆ 1984
7. Dear Sister ◆ 1984
8. Heartbreaker ◆ 1984
9. Racing Hearts ◆ 1984
10. Wrong Kind of Girl ◆ 1984
11. Too Good to be True ◆ 1984
12. When Love Dies ◆ 1984
13. Kidnapped! ◆ 1984
14. Deceptions ◆ 1984
15. Promises ◆ 1984
16. Rags to Riches ◆ 1985
17. Love Letters ◆ 1985
18. Head over Heels ◆ 1985
19. Showdown ◆ 1985
20. Crash Landing! ◆ 1985
21. Runaway ◆ 1985
22. Too Much in Love ◆ 1985
23. Say Goodbye ◆ 1985
24. Memories ◆ 1985
25. Nowhere to Run ◆ 1986
26. Hostage! ◆ 1986
27. Lovestruck ◆ 1986
28. Alone in the Crowd ◆ 1986

29. Bitter Rivals ◆ 1986
30. Jealous Lies ◆ 1986
31. Taking Sides ◆ 1986
32. The New Jessica ◆ 1986
33. Starting Over ◆ 1987
34. Forbidden Love ◆ 1987
35. Out of Control ◆ 1987
36. Last Chance ◆ 1987
37. Rumors ◆ 1987
38. Leaving Home ◆ 1987
39. Secret Admirer ◆ 1987
40. On the Edge ◆ 1987
41. Outcast ◆ 1987
42. Caught in the Middle ◆ 1988
43. Hard Choices ◆ 1988
44. Pretenses ◆ 1988
45. Family Secrets ◆ 1988
46. Decisions ◆ 1988
47. Troublemaker ◆ 1988
48. Slam Book Fever ◆ 1988
49. Playing for Keeps ◆ 1988
50. Out of Reach ◆ 1988
51. Against the Odds ◆ 1988
52. White Lies ◆ 1989
53. Second Chance ◆ 1989
54. Two-Boy Weekend ◆ 1989
55. Perfect Shot ◆ 1989
56. Lost at Sea ◆ 1989
57. Teacher Crush ◆ 1989
58. Broken-Hearted ◆ 1989
59. In Love Again ◆ 1989
60. That Fatal Night ◆ 1989
61. Boy Trouble ◆ 1990
62. Who's Who? ◆ 1990
63. The New Elizabeth ◆ 1990
64. The Ghost of Tricia Martin ◆ 1990
65. Trouble at Home ◆ 1990
66. Who's to Blame? ◆ 1990
67. The Parent Plot ◆ 1990
68. The Love Bet ◆ 1990
69. Friend Against Friend ◆ 1990
70. Ms. Quarterback ◆ 1990
71. Starring Jessica! ◆ 1991
72. Rock Star's Girl ◆ 1991
73. Regina's Legacy ◆ 1991
74. The Perfect Girl ◆ 1991
75. Amy's True Love ◆ 1991
76. Miss Teen Sweet Valley ◆ 1991
77. Cheating to Win ◆ 1991

78. The Dating Game ◆ 1991
79. The Long-Lost Brother ◆ 1991
80. The Girl They Both Loved ◆ 1991
81. Rosa's Lie ◆ 1992
82. Kidnapped by the Cult ◆ 1992
83. Steven's Bride ◆ 1992
84. The Stolen Diary ◆ 1992
85. Soap Star ◆ 1992
86. Jessica Against Bruce ◆ 1992
87. My Best Friend's Boyfriend ◆ 1993
88. Love Letters for Sale ◆ 1993
89. Elizabeth Betrayed ◆ 1993
90. Don't Go Home with John ◆ 1993
91. In Love with a Prince ◆ 1993
92. She's Not What She Seems ◆ 1993
93. Stepsisters ◆ 1993
94. Are We in Love? ◆ 1993
95. The Morning After ◆ 1993
96. The Arrest ◆ 1993
97. The Verdict ◆ 1993
98. The Wedding ◆ 1993
99. Beware the Babysitter ◆ 1993
100. The Evil Twin ◆ 1993
101. The Boyfriend War ◆ 1994
102. Almost Married ◆ 1994
103. Operation Love Match ◆ 1994
104. Love and Death in London ◆ 1994
105. A Date with a Werewolf ◆ 1994
106. Beware the Wolfman ◆ 1994
107. Jessica's Secret Love ◆ 1994
108. Left at the Altar ◆ 1994
109. Double-Crossed ◆ 1994
110. Death Threat ◆ 1994
111. A Deadly Christmas ◆ 1994
112. Jessica Quits the Squad ◆ 1995
113. The Pom-Pom Wars ◆ 1995
114. "V" for Victory ◆ 1995
115. The Treasure of Death Valley ◆ 1995
116. Nightmare in Death Valley ◆ 1995
117. Jessica the Genius ◆ 1996
118. College Weekend ◆ 1996
119. Jessica's Older Guy ◆ 1996
120. In Love with the Enemy ◆ 1996
121. The High School War ◆ 1996
122. A Kiss Before Dying ◆ 1996
123. Elizabeth's Rival ◆ 1996
124. Meet Me at Midnight ◆ 1996
125. Camp Killer ◆ 1996

126. Tall, Dark, and Deadly ◆ 1996
127. Dance of Death ◆ 1996
128. Kiss of a Killer ◆ 1996
129. Cover Girls ◆ 1997
130. Model Flirt ◆ 1997
131. Fashion Victim ◆ 1997
132. Once Upon a Time ◆ 1997
133. To Catch a Thief ◆ 1997
134. Happily Ever After ◆ 1997
135. Lila's New Flame ◆ 1997
136. Too Hot to Handle ◆ 1997
137. Fight Fire with Fire ◆ 1997
138. What Jessica Wants ◆ 1998
139. Elizabeth Is Mine ◆ 1998
140. Please Forgive Me ◆ 1998
141. A Picture-Perfect Prom ◆ 1998
142. The Big Night ◆ 1998
143. Party Weekend! ◆ 1998

Sweet Valley High Magna Editions

1. The Wakefields of Sweet Valley ◆ 1991
2. The Wakefield Legacy: The Untold Story ◆ 1992
3. A Night to Remember ◆ 1993
4. The Evil Twin ◆ 1993
5. Elizabeth's Secret Diary ◆ 1994
6. Jessica's Secret Diary ◆ 1994
7. Return of the Evil Twin ◆ 1995
8. Elizabeth's Secret Diary Volume II ◆ 1996
9. Jessica's Secret Diary Volume II ◆ 1996
10. The Fowlers of Sweet Valley ◆ 1996
11. The Patmans of Sweet Valley ◆ 1997
12. Elizabeth's Secret Diary Volume III ◆ 1997
13. Jessica's Secret Diary Volume III ◆ 1997

Sweet Valley High Super Editions

1. Perfect Summer ◆ 1985
2. Special Christmas ◆ 1985
3. Spring Break ◆ 1986
4. Malibu Summer ◆ 1986
5. Winter Carnival ◆ 1986
6. Spring Fever ◆ 1987
7. Falling for Lucas ◆ 1996
8. Jessica Takes Manhattan ◆ 1997
9. Mystery Date ◆ 1998
10. Last Wish ◆ 1998
11. Earthquake ◆ 1998
12. Aftershock ◆ 1998

SWEET VALLEY HIGH SUPER STARS

1. Lila's Story ◆ 1989
2. Bruce's Story ◆ 1990
3. Enid's Story ◆ 1990
4. Olivia's Story ◆ 1991
5. Todd's Story ◆ 1992

SWEET VALLEY HIGH SUPER THRILLERS

1. Double Jeopardy ◆ 1987
2. On the Run ◆ 1988
3. No Place to Hide ◆ 1988
4. Deadly Summer ◆ 1989
5. Murder on the Line ◆ 1992
6. Beware the Wolfman ◆ 1994
7. A Deadly Christmas ◆ 1994
8. Murder in Paradise ◆ 1995
9. A Stranger in the House ◆ 1995
10. A Killer on Board ◆ 1995
11. "R" for Revenge ◆ 1997

SWEET VALLEY HIGH SENIOR YEAR

Pascal, Francine, creator

BANTAM ◆ GRADES 7–10 ◆ A/R

REAL LIFE

An earthquake disrupts home and school life for Jessica and Elizabeth as they start their senior year at high school.

1. Can't Stay Away ◆ 1999
2. Say It to My Face ◆ 1999
3. So Cool ◆ 1999
4. I've Got a Secret ◆ 1999
5. If You Only Knew ◆ 1999
6. Your Basic Nightmare ◆ 1999
7. Boy Meets Girl ◆ 1999
8. Maria Who? ◆ 1999
9. The One That Got Away ◆ 1999
10. Broken Angel ◆ 1999
11. Take Me On ◆ 1999
12. Bad Girl ◆ 1999
13. All About Love ◆ 1999
14. Split Decision ◆ 2000
15. On My Own ◆ 2000
16. Three Girls and a Guy ◆ 2000
17. Backstabber ◆ 2000
18. As if I Care ◆ 2000

19. It's My Life ◆ 2000
20. Nothing Is Forever ◆ 2000
21. The It Guy ◆ 2000
22. So Not Me ◆ 2000
23. Falling Apart ◆ 2000
24. Never Let Go ◆ 2000
25. Straight Up ◆ 2001
26. Too Late ◆ 2001
27. Playing Dirty ◆ 2001
28. Meant to Be ◆ 2001
29. Where We Belong ◆ 2001
30. Close to You ◆ 2001
31. Stay or Go ◆ 2001
32. Road Trip ◆ 2001
33. Me, Me, Me ◆ 2001
34. Troublemaker ◆ 2001
35. Control Freak ◆ 2001
36. Tearing Me Apart ◆ 2001
37. Be Mine ◆ 2002
38. Get a Clue ◆ 2002
39. Best of Enemies ◆ 2002
40. Never Give Up ◆ 2002
41. He's Back ◆ 2002
42. Touch and Go ◆ 2002
43. It Takes Two ◆ 2002
44. Cruise Control ◆ 2002
45. Tia in the Middle ◆ 2002
46. Prom Night ◆ 2002
47. Senior Cut Day ◆ 2002
48. Sweet 18 ◆ 2003

SWEET VALLEY JUNIOR HIGH

Pascal, Francine, creator

BANTAM ◆ GRADES 6–8 ◆ A/R

REAL LIFE

Twins Jessica and Elizabeth have differing expectations—and experiences—when they move from middle school to junior high.

1. Get Real ◆ 1999
2. One 2 Many ◆ 1999
3. Soulmates ◆ 1999
4. The Cool Crowd ◆ 1999
5. Boy. Friend. ◆ 1999
6. Lacey's Crush ◆ 1999
7. How to Ruin a Friendship ◆ 1999
8. Cheating on Anna ◆ 1999

9. Too Popular ◆ 1999
10. Twin Switch ◆ 1999
11. Got a Problem? ◆ 2000
12. Third Wheel ◆ 2000
13. Three Days, Two Nights ◆ 2000
14. My Perfect Guy ◆ 2000
15. Hands Off! ◆ 2000
16. Keepin' It Real ◆ 2000
17. Whatever ◆ 2000
18. True Blue ◆ 2000
19. She Loves Me . . . Not ◆ 2000
20. Wild Child ◆ 2000
21. I'm So Outta Here ◆ 2000
22. What You Don't Know ◆ 2000
23. Invisible Me ◆ 2000
24. Clueless ◆ 2000
25. Drama Queen ◆ 2001
26. No More Mr. Nice Guy ◆ 2001
27. She's Back ◆ 2001
28. Dance Fever ◆ 2001
29. He's the One ◆ 2001
30. Too Many Good-Byes ◆ 2001

SWEET VALLEY TWINS

Pascal, Francine, creator
BANTAM ◆ GRADES 6–8 ◆ A/R
FAMILY LIFE | REAL LIFE

Jessica and Elizabeth Wakefield are identical twins who, though close and usually supportive of each other, are also individuals with their own friends, interests, and abilities. In the first title of this popular paperback series, the twins start middle school. Each of the more than 100 subsequent titles deals with typical situations and predicaments that young teens may encounter in school and at home. Occasional titles, such as *Cammi's Crush,* feature other students at Sweet Valley Middle School who are friends of Jessica and Elizabeth.

1. Best Friends ◆ 1986
2. Teacher's Pet ◆ 1986
3. Haunted House ◆ 1986
4. Choosing Sides ◆ 1986
5. Sneaking Out ◆ 1987
6. New Girl ◆ 1987
7. Three's a Crowd ◆ 1987
8. First Place ◆ 1987
9. Against the Rules ◆ 1987
10. One of the Gang ◆ 1987

11. Buried Treasure ◆ 1987
12. Keeping Secrets ◆ 1987
13. Stretching the Truth ◆ 1987
14. Tug of War ◆ 1987
15. Older Boy ◆ 1988
16. Second Best ◆ 1988
17. Boys Against Girls ◆ 1988
18. Center of Attention ◆ 1988
19. Bully ◆ 1988
20. Playing Hooky ◆ 1988
21. Left Behind ◆ 1988
22. Out of Place ◆ 1988
23. Claim to Fame ◆ 1988
24. Jumping to Conclusions ◆ 1988
25. Standing Out ◆ 1989
26. Taking Charge ◆ 1989
27. Teamwork ◆ 1989
28. April Fool! ◆ 1989
29. Jessica and the Brat Attack ◆ 1989
30. Princess Elizabeth ◆ 1989
31. Jessica's Bad Idea ◆ 1989
32. Jessica on Stage ◆ 1989
33. Elizabeth's New Hero ◆ 1989
34. Jessica's the Rock Star ◆ 1989
35. Amy's Pen Pal ◆ 1990
36. Mary Is Missing ◆ 1990
37. War Between the Twins ◆ 1990
38. Lois Strikes Back ◆ 1990
39. Jessica and the Money Mix-Up ◆ 1990
40. Danny Means Trouble ◆ 1990
41. Twins Get Caught ◆ 1990
42. Jessica's Secret ◆ 1990
43. Elizabeth's First Kiss ◆ 1990
44. Amy Moves In ◆ 1991
45. Lucy Takes the Reins ◆ 1991
46. Mademoiselle Jessica ◆ 1991
47. Jessica's New Look ◆ 1991
48. Mansy Miller Fights Back ◆ 1991
49. Twins' Little Sister ◆ 1991
50. Jessica and the Secret Star ◆ 1991
51. Elizabeth the Impossible ◆ 1991
52. Booster Boycott ◆ 1991
53. The Slime that Ate Sweet Valley ◆ 1991
54. Big Party Weekend ◆ 1991
55. Brooke and Her Rock Star Mom ◆ 1991
56. The Wakefields Strike It Rich ◆ 1991
57. Steven's in Love ◆ 1992
58. Elizabeth and the Orphans ◆ 1992
59. Barnyard Battle ◆ 1992

60. Ciao, Sweet Valley ◆ 1992
61. Jessica the Nerd ◆ 1992
62. Sarah's Dad and Sophia's Mom ◆ 1992
63. Poor Lila ◆ 1992
64. Charm School Mystery ◆ 1992
65. Patty's Last Dance ◆ 1993
66. Great Boyfriend Switch ◆ 1993
67. Jessica the Thief ◆ 1993
68. Middle School Gets Married ◆ 1993
69. Won't Someone Help Anna? ◆ 1993
70. Psychic Sisters ◆ 1993
71. Jessica Saves the Trees ◆ 1993
72. Love Potion ◆ 1993
73. Lila's Music Video ◆ 1993
74. Elizabeth the Hero ◆ 1993
75. Jessica and the Earthquake ◆ 1994
76. Yours for a Day ◆ 1994
77. Todd Runs Away ◆ 1994
78. Steven and the Zombie ◆ 1994
79. Jessica's Blind Date ◆ 1994
80. Gossip War ◆ 1994
81. Robbery at the Mall ◆ 1994
82. Steven's Enemy ◆ 1994
83. Amy's Secret Sister ◆ 1994
84. Romeo and Two Juliets ◆ 1995
85. Elizabeth the Seventh Grader ◆ 1995
86. It Can't Happen Here ◆ 1995
87. Mother-Daughter Switch ◆ 1995
88. Steven Gets Even ◆ 1995
89. Jessica's Cookie Disaster ◆ 1995
90. Cousin War ◆ 1996
91. Deadly Voyage ◆ 1996
92. Escape from Terror Island ◆ 1996
93. Incredible Madame Jessica ◆ 1996
94. Don't Talk to Brian ◆ 1996
95. Battle of the Cheerleaders ◆ 1996
96. Elizabeth the Spy ◆ 1996
97. Too Scared to Sleep ◆ 1996
98. Beast Is Watching You ◆ 1996
99. Beast Must Die ◆ 1996
100. If I Die Before I Wake ◆ 1996
101. Twins in Love ◆ 1996
102. Mysterious Doctor Q ◆ 1996
103. Elizabeth Solves It All ◆ 1996
104. Big Brother's in Love Again ◆ 1997
105. Jessica's Lucky Millions ◆ 1997
106. Breakfast of Enemies ◆ 1997
107. The Twins Hit Hollywood ◆ 1997
108. Cammi's Crush ◆ 1997

109. Don't Go in the Basement ◆ 1997
110. Pumpkin Fever ◆ 1997
111. Sisters at War ◆ 1997
112. If Looks Could Kill ◆ 1997
113. The Boyfriend Game ◆ 1998
114. The Boyfriend Mess ◆ 1998
115. Happy Mother's Day, Lila ◆ 1998
116. Jessica Takes Charge ◆ 1998
117. Down with Queen Janet! ◆ 1998
118. No Escape! ◆ 1998

SWEET VALLEY TWINS MAGNA EDITIONS

1. The Magic Christmas ◆ 1992
2. A Christmas Without Elizabeth ◆ 1994
3. BIG for Christmas ◆ 1994

SWEET VALLEY TWINS SUPER CHILLER EDITIONS

Pascal, Francine, creator
BANTAM ◆ GRADES 6–8 ◆ A/R
HORROR

Ghosts, curses, masks that change one's character, and other scary situations are featured in this series. The books are written by Jamie Suzanne.

1. The Christmas Ghost ◆ 1989
2. The Ghost in the Graveyard ◆ 1990
3. The Carnival Ghost ◆ 1990
4. The Ghost in the Bell Tower ◆ 1992
5. The Curse of the Ruby Necklace ◆ 1993
6. The Curse of the Golden Heart ◆ 1994
7. The Haunted Burial Ground ◆ 1994
8. The Secret of the Magic Pen ◆ 1995
9. Evil Elizabeth ◆ 1995

SWEET VALLEY TWINS SUPER EDITIONS

Pascal, Francine, creator
BANTAM ◆ GRADES 6–8 ◆ A/R
REAL LIFE

This paperback series is a spinoff of the Sweet Valley Twins and Friends series. In these books, identical twins Jessica and Elizabeth Wakefield venture away from their home turf, Sweet Valley Middle School, and become involved with extracurricular activities such as volunteering at the zoo, going on a camping trip, and taking a vacation to Paris.

1. The Class Trip ◆ 1988
2. Holiday Mischief ◆ 1998
3. The Big Camp Secret ◆ 1989
4. The Unicorns Go Hawaiian ◆ 1991
5. Lila's Secret Valentine ◆ 1995
6. The Twins Take Paris ◆ 1996
7. Jessica's Animal Instincts ◆ 1996
8. Jessica's First Kiss ◆ 1997
9. The Twins Go to College ◆ 1997
10. The Year Without Christmas ◆ 1997
11. Jessica's No Angel ◆ 1998
12. Goodbye, Middle School ◆ 1998

SWEET VALLEY UNIVERSITY

Pascal, Francine, creator
BANTAM ◆ GRADES 7–10 ◆ A/R
REAL LIFE

Twins Jessica and Elizabeth Wakefield of the Sweet Valley series are off to college. As they get older, they are involved in more grown-up relationships and adventures, and even face life-and-death situations. Fans of the other Sweet Valley books will enjoy following the collegiate exploits of the two girls.

1. College Girls ◆ 1993
2. Love, Lies, and Jessica Wakefield ◆ 1993
3. What Your Parents Don't Know ◆ 1994
4. Anything for Love ◆ 1994
5. Married Woman ◆ 1994
6. Love of Her Life ◆ 1994
7. Good-Bye to Love ◆ 1994
8. Home for Christmas ◆ 1994
9. Sorority Scandal ◆ 1995
10. No Means No ◆ 1995
11. Take Back the Night ◆ 1995
12. College Cruise ◆ 1995
13. SS Heartbreak ◆ 1995
14. Shipboard Wedding ◆ 1995
15. Behind Closed Doors ◆ 1995
16. The Other Woman ◆ 1995
17. Deadly Attraction ◆ 1995
18. Billie's Secret ◆ 1996

19. Broken Promises, Shattered Dreams ◆ 1996
20. Here Comes the Bride ◆ 1996
21. For the Love of Ryan ◆ 1996
22. Elizabeth's Summer Love ◆ 1996
23. Sweet Kiss of Summer ◆ 1996
24. His Secret Past ◆ 1996
25. Busted! ◆ 1996
26. The Trial of Jessica Wakefield ◆ 1996
27. Elizabeth and Todd Forever ◆ 1997
28. Elizabeth's Heartbreak ◆ 1997
29. One Last Kiss ◆ 1997
30. Beauty and the Beach ◆ 1997
31. The Truth About Ryan ◆ 1997
32. The Boys of Summer ◆ 1997
33. Out of the Picture ◆ 1997
34. Spy Girl ◆ 1997
35. Undercover Angels ◆ 1997
36. Have You Heard About Elizabeth ◆ 1997
37. Breaking Away ◆ 1998
38. Good-Bye, Elizabeth ◆ 1998
39. Elizabeth Loves New York ◆ 1998
40. Private Jessica ◆ 1998
41. Escape to New York ◆ 1998
42. Sneaking In ◆ 1998
43. The Price of Love ◆ 1998
44. Love Me Always ◆ 1998
45. Don't Let Go ◆ 1999
46. I'll Never Love Again ◆ 1999
47. You're Not My Sister ◆ 1999
48. No Rules ◆ 1999
49. Stranded ◆ 1999
50. Summer of Love ◆ 1999
51. Living Together ◆ 2000
52. Fooling Around ◆ 2000
53. Truth or Dare ◆ 2000
54. Rush Week ◆ 2000
55. The First Time ◆ 2000
56. Dropping Out ◆ 2000
57. Who Knew? ◆ 2000
58. The Dreaded Ex ◆ 2000
59. Elizabeth in Love ◆ 2000
60. Secret Love Diaries: Elizabeth ◆ 2000
61. Secret Love Diaries: Jessica ◆ 2000
62. Secret Love Diaries: Sam ◆ 2000
63. Secret Love Diaries: Chloe ◆ 2000

SWEET VALLEY UNIVERSITY: ELIZABETH

Pascal, Francine, creator

BANTAM ◆ GRADES 7–10 ◆ A/R

REAL LIFE

After quarreling with her sister Jessica, Elizabeth Wakefield decides not to return to Sweet Valley University and sets off for England. There she meets an attractive young aristocrat.

1. University, Interrupted ◆ 2001
2. London Calling ◆ 2001
3. Royal Pain ◆ 2001
4. Downstairs, Upstairs ◆ 2001
5. Max's Choice ◆ 2001
6. I Need You ◆ 2001

SWEET VALLEY UNIVERSITY THRILLER EDITIONS

Pascal, Francine, creator

BANTAM ◆ GRADES 7–10 ◆ A/R

HORROR | REAL LIFE

Companions to the Sweet Valley High University series, these mystery-thriller books are page-turners, with Sweet Valley University students investigating murders, being threatened by stalkers, and foiling other evil plots.

1. Wanted for Murder ◆ 1995
2. He's Watching You ◆ 1995
3. Kiss of the Vampire ◆ 1995
4. The House of Death ◆ 1995
5. Running for Her Life ◆ 1996
6. The Roommate ◆ 1996
7. What Winston Saw ◆ 1997
8. Dead Before Dawn ◆ 1997
9. Killer at Sea ◆ 1997
10. Channel X ◆ 1997
11. Love and Murder ◆ 1998
12. Don't Answer the Phone ◆ 1998
13. CyberStalker: The Return of William White, Part I ◆ 1998
14. Deadly Terror: The Return of William White, Part II ◆ 1999
15. Loving the Enemy ◆ 1999
16. Killer Party ◆ 1999
17. Very Bad Things ◆ 2000
18. Face It ◆ 2000

SWITCHERS

Thompson, Kate

HYPERION ◆ GRADES 6–9 ◆ A/R

FANTASY

Tess and Kevin are Switchers and can adopt the form of animals at will. In the face of an oncoming Ice Age, they use these powers to defeat the monsters who are responsible. In the second book, Tess must decide her future. Among the choices is immortality—as either a vampire or a phoenix. The decision is harder than she expected.

1. Switchers ◆ 1998
2. Midnight's Choice ◆ 1998
3. Wild Blood ◆ 1999

SWORD DANCER SAGA

Roberson, Jennifer

DAW BOOKS ◆ GRADES 10–12

FANTASY

Del is a sword master from the North. Tiger is a skillful warrior from the South. They join together to face danger and to understand Tiger's past. Tiger realizes that he must find his homeland and learn about his destiny. As the series progresses, so does the romance between Del and Tiger.

1. Sword-Dancer ◆ 1986
2. Sword-Singer ◆ 1988
3. Sword-Maker ◆ 1989
4. Sword-Breaker ◆ 1991
5. Sword-Born ◆ 1998
6. Sword-Sworn ◆ 2002

SWORD OF SHADOWS

Jones, J. V.

WARNER; TOR ◆ GRADES 10–12

FANTASY

An epic fantasy set in a subarctic landscape into which evil is intruding. Details from history, mythology, and religion add to the atmosphere. Lovers Raif and Ash face many challenges in their quest to find the Fortress of Black Ice and seek to March are separated after she is kidnapped, and he must choose between attempting her rescue and completing his quest to find the Fortress of Black Ice.

1. A Cavern of Black Ice ◆ 1999
2. A Fortress of Grey Ice ◆ 2000
3. A Sword from Red Ice ◆ 2005

SWORD OF THE SPIRITS

Christopher, John

ALADDIN ◆ GRADES 5–8

ADVENTURE | SCIENCE FICTION

Post-apocalyptic England is the setting of this trilogy. It is a world of warriors, dwarfs, mutants and seers. Luke Perry, the future ruler, is thrown into chaos as he finds out that his world is not as it seems. He must hide after his father is murdered and his half-brother takes the throne. Continuous action, drama, and intrigue create a satisfying read for fans of science fiction.

1. The Prince in Waiting ◆ 1970
2. Beyond the Burning Lands ◆ 1971
3. The Sword of the Spirits ◆ 1972

SYLVIE CYCLE

Townley, Roderick

ATHENEUM ◆ GRADES 5–9 ◆ A/R

FANTASY

Sylvie, 12, is a storybook princess who lives out her life in the pages of a fairy tale book. Her life has been dictated by her Readers. Now Sylvie has a goal—to accomplish one Great Good Thing. She transcends the text of her book and sets off on her own adventures, even saving the actual book she lives in. In the second book, Sylvie and the other characters are uploaded to the internet for more adventures.

1. The Great Good Thing ◆ 2001
2. Into the Labyrinth ◆ 2002
3. The Constellation of Sylvie ◆ 2005

T*WITCHES

Gilmour, H. B., and Randi Reisfeld

SCHOLASTIC ◆ GRADES 6–9 ◆ A/R

FANTASY

Cam and Alex are identical twin sisters who have never known each other. They have been separated since birth and meet accidentally. They work together to solve the mystery of their past and to deal with strange circumstances. As the series progresses, an evil warlock, Thantos, wants to destroy them

1. The Power of Two ◆ 2001
2. Building a Mystery ◆ 2001
3. Seeing Is Deceiving ◆ 2001
4. Dead Wrong ◆ 2002
5. Don't Think Twice ◆ 2002
6. Double Jeopardy ◆ 2002
7. Kindred Spirits ◆ 2003
8. The Witch Hunters ◆ 2003
9. Split Decision ◆ 2004
10. Destiny's Twins ◆ 2004

TAG AND WALKER *see* Walker and Tag

TAKE IT TO THE XTREME

Withers, Pam

WALRUS ◆ GRADES 6–9 ◆ A/R

ADVENTURE

In the first book, Jake, 15, works for an adventure tour service. On a whitewater rafting trip, one of the adult guides is injured. Jake has to overcome his animosity toward another boy, Peter, so they can work together to get help. In the second book, Jake and Peter are now best friends and junior guides for Sam's Adventure Tours. In this book, there is a mountain rescue after a helicopter crash and an avalanche. There is a lot of action and excitement, making this a consideration for reluctant readers.

1. Raging River ◆ 2003
2. Peak Survival ◆ 2003
3. Adrenalin Rush ◆ 2004
4. Skater Stuntboys ◆ 2005
5. Surf Zone ◆ 2005
6. Vertical Limits ◆ 2006
7. Dirt Bike Daredevils ◆ 2006
8. Wake's Edge ◆ 2007
9. BMX Tunnel Run ◆ 2007
10. Mountainbike Maniacs ◆ 2008

TALENT

Dean, Zoey

RAZORBILL ◆ GRADES 8–10

REAL LIFE

When Emily arrives at Bel Air Middle School from Iowa, Kristy "Mac" Armstrong is intrigued. Mac's mother is a talent agent and Mac feels that Emily has potential. With her friends Marisol and Dee, Mac decides to make Emily "a star." This series features gossipy girls, fashion, parties, and Hollywood—all of the elements for successful chick lit. Pair this with Zoey Dean's A List series.

1. Talent ◆ 2008
2. Star Power ◆ 2008
3. Almost Famous ◆ 2009

TALES FROM THE CRYPT GRAPHIC NOVELS

Various authors

PAPERCUTZ ◆ GRADES 10–12

HORROR

The classic horror comics from the 1950s have been updated and reformatted into graphic novels. Each volume features several stories by different authors; for example, there are four stories in *Ghouls Gone Wild*. Zombies, creepy cemeteries, the Crypt-Keeper, and more will attract fans of horror fiction.

1. Ghouls Gone Wild (McGregor, Don, and Mark Bilgrey) ◆ 2007
2. Can You Fear Me Now? (Kleid, Neil, and Stefan Petrucha) ◆ 2007
3. Zombielicious (Todd, Mort, et al.) ◆ 2008
4. Crypt-Keeping It Real (Van Lente, Fred, et al.) ◆ 2008
5. Yabba Dabba Voodoo (Van Lente, Fred, et al.) ◆ 2008

TALES FROM THE ODYSSEY

Osborne, Mary Pope

HYPERION ◆ GRADES 4–8 ◆ A/R

FANTASY

Homer's *Odyssey* is retold in this series. At the end of the Trojan War, Odysseus and his men begin the dangerous journey home. They encounter all the familiar mythical creatures including Cyclops, Circe, and Aeolus.

1. The One-Eyed Giant ◆ 2002
2. The Land of the Dead ◆ 2003
3. Sirens and Sea Monsters ◆ 2003
4. The Gray-Eyed Goddess ◆ 2003
5. Return to Ithaca ◆ 2004
6. The Final Battle ◆ 2004

TALES OF ALVIN MAKER

Card, Orson Scott

T. DOHERTY/TOR ◆ GRADES 8–10 ◆ A/R

FANTASY

This series takes place on the American frontier in the 19th century. The
author creates an alternative history with magical creatures. Alvin is the
seventh son of a seventh son and is developing the powers of a mage. He
faces the evil of the Unmaker using folk magic and the help of others,
including a guardian angel. Alvin's love, Peggy, has the gift to see the
future.

1. Seventh Son ◆ 1987
2. Red Prophet ◆ 1988
3. Prentice Alvin ◆ 1989
4. Alvin Journeyman ◆ 1995
5. Heartfire ◆ 1998
6. The Crystal City: A Tale of Alvin Maker ◆ 2003

TALES OF GOM IN THE LEGENDS OF ULM

Chetwin, Grace

LOTHROP, LEE & SHEPARD; BRADBURY BOOKS ◆ GRADES 6–8

FANTASY

Fantasy lovers will enjoy this series full of mountain lore, wizardry, and
adventure. Gom, a mountain boy growing up in the land of Ulm, has
many unusual talents. In the first book, his mother has disappeared, leaving a mysterious stone rune with Gom. This leads to his first great challenge. In the second book, he tries to return the rune to his mother while
being pursued by evil forces that also want it. In the third book, he finds
his mother and begins to learn about wizardry and other worlds.

1. Gom on Windy Mountain ◆ 1986
2. The Riddle and the Rune ◆ 1987
3. The Crystal Stair ◆ 1988
4. The Starstone ◆ 1989

TALES OF TERROR

Bradman, Tony

EGMONT ◆ GRADES 4–7

HORROR

Horror is the unifying theme in this series of British imports that take ordinary situations and give them scary twists. In *Final Cut,* Billy Gibson finds himself in a horror movie and must decide which side will win. In *Voodoo Child,* Megan hopes a voodoo doll will get rid of her father's girl-friend. Bold illustrations add a sinister touch.

1. Deadly Game ◆ 2004
2. Final Cut ◆ 2004
3. Voodoo Child ◆ 2004

TALES OF THE FROG PRINCESS

Baker, E. D.

BLOOMSBURY ◆ GRADES 4–7 ◆ A/R

FANTASY | HUMOR

Princess Emeralda, 14, kisses Eadric, a frog. In a twist on the usual tale, she turns into a frog. Emeralda and Eadric work together to try to undo the spell. Thus begins this series of twisted tales.

1. The Frog Princess ◆ 2002
2. Dragon's Breath ◆ 2003
3. Once Upon a Curse ◆ 2004
4. No Place for Magic ◆ 2006
5. The Salamander Spell ◆ 2007

TALES OF THE NINE CHARMS

Farber, Erica, and J. R. Sansevere

DELACORTE ◆ GRADES 6–9 ◆ A/R

FANTASY

When Walker Crane falls into a fountain, he enters another world. There he teams up with Niko and Aurora to face the Dragons of the Dark. Zoe, 13, and Lila, 11, enter the adventure in later books.

1. Circle of Three ◆ 2000
2. The Secret in the Stones ◆ 2001
3. Islands of the Black Moon ◆ 2002

TALES OF THE OTORI

Hearn, Lian

RIVERHEAD BOOKS ◆ GRADES 10–12 ◆ A/R

FANTASY

In an imagined feudal Japan, young Takeo becomes the ward of Lord Otori. Takeo discovers his supernatural abilities and joins the group of assassins known as The Tribe. As Takeo becomes immersed in the mysteries of The Tribe, his beloved Kaede returns to her homeland. Their separation strengthens their commitment and they reunite and secretly marry. Now they must prepare for war in their respective kingdoms.

1. Across the Nightingale Floor ◆ 2002
2. Grass for His Pillow ◆ 2003
3. Brilliance of the Moon ◆ 2004

TARRAGON ISLAND

Tate, Nikki

SONO NIS PRESS ◆ GRADES 6–8

FAMILY LIFE | REAL LIFE

Heather Blake's family has moved from Toronto to small, isolated Tarragon Island in British Columbia. Heather misses her friends, shopping, and her writing group. She is beginning to adjust when she must face a family tragedy. Her new friends on the island help her cope.

1. Tarragon Island ◆ 1999
2. No Cafes in Narnia ◆ 2000
3. Trouble on Tarragon Island ◆ 2005

TARTAN MAGIC TRILOGY

Yolen, Jane

HARCOURT ◆ GRADES 4–7 ◆ A/R

FANTASY

American twins Jennifer and Peter find Scotland to be a place full of magic in this series full of ghosts, local lore, adventure, and suspense. In the last book, they visit a graveyard and become embroiled in a 300-year-old feud between former lovers.

1. The Wizard's Map ◆ 1999
2. The Pictish Child ◆ 1999
3. The Bagpiper's Ghost ◆ 2002

TEEN ANGELS

Bennett, Cherie, and Jeff Gottesfeld

AVON ◆ GRADES 9–12

FANTASY

In the first book, Cisco is training to become an angel by trying to help a self-destructive rock star. Later, teen angel Nicole tries to help Cisco's sister Shelby who is distraught over Cisco's death.

1. Heaven Can't Wait ◆ 1996
2. Love Never Dies ◆ 1996
3. Angel Kisses ◆ 1996
4. Heaven Help Us ◆ 1996
5. Nightmare in Heaven ◆ 1996
6. Love Without End ◆ 1996

10TH GRADE SOCIAL CLIMBER

Mechling, Lauren, and Laura Moser

GRAPHIA/HOUGHTON MIFFLIN ◆ GRADES 10–12 ◆ A/R

REAL LIFE

As this series begins, Mimi Shulman, 15, is the new girl at the Baldwin School in New York City. She is clearly an outsider among the rich and selfish girls and she is determined to be accepted by the most popular group. She records her efforts and observations in a diary, which eventually becomes public and makes her even more of an outsider. She repairs her relationships in the second book and travels to Berlin and London in the third. Adult language, alcohol, divorced parents with new partners, and other contemporary teen issues will attract the fans of Gossip Girl and It Girl books.

1. The Rise and Fall of a 10th-Grade Social Climber ◆ 2005
2. All Q, No A: More Tales of a 10th-Grade Social Climber ◆ 2006
3. Foreign Exposure: The Social Climber Abroad ◆ 2007

THAT'S SO RAVEN

TOKYOPOP ◆ GRADES 6–8

FANTASY

Raven is a teen with her own Disney Channel show—"That's So Raven." She has a special power—she can see into the future. Even though she has this gift, she often misinterprets her visions, creating chaos and fun. This cine-manga series is sure to appeal to fans of the television show.

1. That's So Raven ◆ 2004

2. The Trouble with Boys ◆ 2004
3. Smother Dearest ◆ 2005

THOROUGHBRED

Campbell, Joanna, creator
HARPERCOLLINS ◆ GRADES 4–7 ◆ A/R
REAL LIFE | RECREATION

Eighteen-year-old jockey Samantha McLean and her middle school-aged adopted sister live at Whitebrook, a Thoroughbred breeding and training farm in Kentucky. In addition to typical problems with school, friends, boyfriends, and parents, the girls handle the pressures of riding and racing. Girls who like horses will enjoy this series about what it's like to live on a horse farm.

1. A Horse Called Wonder ◆ 1991
2. Wonder's Promise ◆ 1991
3. Wonder's First Race ◆ 1991
4. Wonder's Victory ◆ 1991
5. Ashleigh's Dream ◆ 1993
6. Wonder's Yearling ◆ 1993
7. Samantha's Pride ◆ 1993
8. Sierra's Steeplechase ◆ 1993
9. Pride's Challenge ◆ 1994
10. Pride's Last Race ◆ 1994
11. Wonder's Sister ◆ 1994
12. Shining's Orphan ◆ 1994
13. Cindy's Runaway Colt ◆ 1995
14. Cindy's Glory ◆ 1995
15. Glory's Triumph ◆ 1995
16. Glory in Danger ◆ 1996
17. Ashleigh's Farewell ◆ 1996
18. Glory's Rival ◆ 1997
19. Cindy's Heartbreak ◆ 1997
20. Champion's Spirit ◆ 1997
21. Wonder's Champion ◆ 1997
22. Arabian Challenge ◆ 1997
23. Cindy's Honor ◆ 1997
24. The Horse of Her Dreams ◆ 1997
25. Melanie's Treasure ◆ 1998
26. Sterling's Second Chance ◆ 1998
27. Christina's Courage ◆ 1998
28. Camp Saddlebrook ◆ 1998
29. Melanie's Last Ride ◆ 1998
30. Dylan's Choice ◆ 1998
31. A Home for Melanie ◆ 1998
32. Cassidy's Secret ◆ 1999

33. Racing Parker ◆ 1999
34. On the Track ◆ 1999
35. Dead Heat ◆ 1999
36. Without Wonder ◆ 1999
37. Star in Danger ◆ 1999
38. Down to the Wire ◆ 1999
39. Living Legend ◆ 2000
40. Ultimate Risk ◆ 2000
41. Close Call ◆ 2000
42. Bad Luck Filly ◆ 2000
43. Fallen Star ◆ 2000
44. Perfect Image ◆ 2000
45. Star's Chance ◆ 2001
46. Racing Image ◆ 2001
47. Cindy's Desert Adventure ◆ 2001
48. Cindy's Bold Start ◆ 2001
49. Rising Star ◆ 2001
50. Team Player ◆ 2001
51. Distance Runner ◆ 2001
52. Perfect Challenge ◆ 2002
53. Derby Fever ◆ 2002
54. Cindy's Last Hope ◆ 2002
55. Great Expectations ◆ 2002
56. Hoofprints in the Snow ◆ 2002
57. Faith in a Long Shot ◆ 2003
58. Christina's Shining Star ◆ 2003
59. Star's Inspiration ◆ 2003
60. Taking the Reins ◆ 2003
61. Parker's Passion ◆ 2003
62. Unbridled Fury ◆ 2003
63. Starstruck ◆ 2004
64. The Price of Fame ◆ 2004
65. Bridal Dreams ◆ 2004
66. Samantha's Irish Luck ◆ 2004
67. Breaking the Fall ◆ 2004
68. Kaitlin's Wild Ride ◆ 2004
69. Melanie's Double Jinx ◆ 2004
70. Allie's Legacy ◆ 2005
71. Calamity Jinx ◆ 2005
72. Legacy's Gift ◆ 2005

THOROUGHBRED SUPER EDITIONS

1. Ashleigh's Christmas Miracle (Campbell, Joanna) ◆ 1994
2. Ashleigh's Diary (Campbell, Joanna) ◆ 1995
3. Ashleigh's Hope (Campbell, Joanna) ◆ 1996
4. Samantha's Journey (Campbell, Joanna, and Karen Bentley) ◆ 1997

THOROUGHBRED: ASHLEIGH

Campbell, Joanna

HARPERCOLLINS ◆ **GRADES 4–7** ◆ **A/R**

REAL LIFE | **RECREATION**

Before the Thoroughbred series, Ashleigh Griffen lived at her family's farm in Kentucky. This series begins when Ashleigh helps an abused horse, Lightning, back to health. When the humane society tells her that there is now a home for Lightning, Ashleigh is upset. She tries to find a way to keep Lightning. Girls who like horse stories will enjoy this series.

1. Lightning's Last Hope ◆ 1998
2. A Horse for Christmas ◆ 1998
3. Waiting for Stardust ◆ 1999
4. Goodbye, Midnight Wanderer ◆ 1999
5. The Forbidden Stallion ◆ 1999
6. A Dangerous Ride ◆ 1999
7. Derby Day ◆ 1999
8. The Lost Foal ◆ 2000
9. Holiday Homecoming ◆ 2000
10. Derby Dreams ◆ 2001
11. Ashleigh's Promise ◆ 2001
12. Winter Race Camp ◆ 2002
13. The Prize ◆ 2002
14. Ashleigh's Western Challenge ◆ 2002
15. Stardust's Foal ◆ 2003

THOROUGHBRED: ASHLEIGH'S COLLECTION

Campbell, Joanna

HARPERCOLLINS ◆ **GRADES 4–7** ◆ **A/R**

REAL LIFE | **RECREATION**

Here are three of Ashleigh's favorite stories. In the first book, Susan has fallen and worries about riding again. Then a mistreated horse, Evening Star, comes to the stable and begins to trust Susan. Can she overcome her fear and help Star? Fans of horse stories will enjoy this collection.

1. Star of Shadowbrook Farm ◆ 1998
2. The Forgotten Filly ◆ 1998
3. Battlecry Forever! ◆ 1998

THE THOUSAND CULTURES

Barnes, John

TOM DOHERTY ASSOCIATES ◆ GRADES 9–12

SCIENCE FICTION

A new form of travel provides contact between two formerly isolated planets: Nou Occitan, a world in which the arts are revered, and Caledony, where the arts are regarded with disdain. The first book deals with this clash of cultures. In *Earth Made of Glass,* Giraut—former ambassador to Caledony—and Margaret Leones work to bring peace to the planet of Briand.

1. A Million Open Doors ◆ 1992
2. Earth Made of Glass ◆ 1998
3. The Merchants of Souls ◆ 2001
4. The Armies of Memory ◆ 2006

THREE GIRLS IN THE CITY

Betancourt, Jeanne

SCHOLASTIC ◆ GRADES 6–9 ◆ A/R

REAL LIFE

At a summer photography class in New York City, three 13-year old girls meet and become friends. Carolyn is timid and her Wyoming background has not prepared her for such a big city. Joy is privileged and willful. Maya is from Harlem and is proud of her African American heritage.

1. Self-Portrait ◆ 2003
2. Exposed ◆ 2003
3. Black and White ◆ 2004
4. Close-Up ◆ 2004

THREE INVESTIGATORS

Various authors

RANDOM HOUSE ◆ GRADES 5–7 ◆ A/R

ADVENTURE | MYSTERY

Jupiter Jones and his friends Pete and Bob form the Three Investigators and operate out of a secret office in the junkyard owned by Jupiter's aunt and uncle. Jupiter is a young Sherlock Holmes, never missing anything and coming to conclusions that astonish his friends and nearly always turn out to be right. The mysteries are fairly complicated, and the solutions depend on historic or scientific knowledge. Jupiter, as the First

Investigator, supplies the brains, and Pete, stronger and more athletic, is the Second Investigator. Bob is in charge of research and records. Boys who like the Hardy Boys will find more depth and realism in the Three Investigators.

1. The Secret of Terror Castle (Arthur, Robert) ◆ 1964
2. The Mystery of the Stuttering Parrot (Arthur, Robert) ◆ 1964
3. The Mystery of the Whispering Mummy (Arthur, Robert) ◆ 1965
4. The Mystery of the Green Ghost (Arthur, Robert) ◆ 1965
5. The Mystery of the Vanishing Treasure (Arthur, Robert) ◆ 1966
6. The Secret of Skeleton Island (Arthur, Robert) ◆ 1966
7. The Mystery of the Fiery Eye (Arthur, Robert) ◆ 1967
8. The Mystery of the Silver Spider (Arthur, Robert) ◆ 1967
9. The Mystery of the Screaming Clock (Arthur, Robert) ◆ 1968
10. The Mystery of the Moaning Cave (Arden, William) ◆ 1968
11. The Mystery of the Talking Skull (Arthur, Robert) ◆ 1969
12. The Mystery of the Laughing Shadow (Arden, William) ◆ 1969
13. The Secret of the Crooked Cat (Arden, William) ◆ 1970
14. The Mystery of the Coughing Dragon (West, Nick) ◆ 1970
15. The Mystery of the Flaming Footprints (Carey, M. V.) ◆ 1971
16. The Mystery of the Nervous Lion (West, Nick) ◆ 1971
17. The Mystery of the Singing Serpent (Carey, M. V.) ◆ 1972
18. The Mystery of the Shrinking House (Arden, William) ◆ 1972
19. The Secret of Phantom Lake (Arden, William) ◆ 1973
20. The Mystery of Monster Mountain (Carey, M. V.) ◆ 1973
21. The Secret of the Haunted Mirror (Carey, M. V.) ◆ 1974
22. The Mystery of the Dead Man's Riddle (Arden, William) ◆ 1974
23. The Mystery of the Invisible Dog (Carey, M. V.) ◆ 1975
24. The Mystery of Death Trap Mine (Carey, M. V.) ◆ 1976
25. The Mystery of the Dancing Devil (Arden, William) ◆ 1976
26. The Mystery of the Headless Horse (Arden, William) ◆ 1977
27. The Mystery of the Magic Circle (Carey, M. V.) ◆ 1978
28. The Mystery of the Deadly Double (Arden, William) ◆ 1978
29. The Mystery of the Sinister Scarecrow (Carey, M. V.) ◆ 1979
30. The Secret of Shark Reef (Arden, William) ◆ 1979
31. The Mystery of the Scar-Faced Beggar (Carey, M. V.) ◆ 1981
32. The Mystery of the Blazing Cliffs (Carey, M. V.) ◆ 1981
33. The Mystery of the Purple Pirate (Arden, William) ◆ 1982
34. The Mystery of the Wandering Caveman (Carey, M. V.) ◆ 1982
35. The Mystery of the Kidnapped Whale (Brandel, Marc) ◆ 1983
36. The Mystery of the Missing Mermaid (Carey, M. V.) ◆ 1983
37. The Mystery of the Two-Toed Pigeon (Brandel, Marc) ◆ 1984
38. The Mystery of the Smashing Glass (Arden, William) ◆ 1984
39. The Mystery of the Trail of Terror (Carey, M. V.) ◆ 1984
40. The Mystery of the Rogues' Reunion (Brandel, Marc) ◆ 1985
41. The Mystery of the Creep-Show Crooks (Carey, M. V.) ◆ 1985
42. The Mystery of Wrecker's Rock (Arden, William) ◆ 1986
43. The Mystery of the Cranky Collector (Carey, M. V.) ◆ 1986
44. The Case of the Savage Statue (Carey, M. V.) ◆ 1987

THREE INVESTIGATORS CRIMEBUSTERS

1. Hot Wheels (Arden, William) ◆ 1989
2. Murder to Go (Stine, Megan, and H. William Stine) ◆ 1989
3. Rough Stuff (Stone, G. H.) ◆ 1989
4. Funny Business (McCay, William) ◆ 1989
5. An Ear for Danger (Brandel, Marc) ◆ 1989
6. Thriller Diller (Stine, Megan, and H. William Stine) ◆ 1989
7. Reel Trouble (Stone, G. H.) ◆ 1989
8. Shoot the Works (McCay, William) ◆ 1990
9. Foul Play (Lerangis, Peter) ◆ 1990
10. Long Shot (Stine, Megan, and H. William Stine) ◆ 1990
11. Fatal Error (Stone, G. H.) ◆ 1990

TIFFANY ACHING ADVENTURES *see* Discworld

TIGER AND DEL *see* Sword Dancer Saga

TIGER'S APPRENTICE

Yep, Laurence
SCHOLASTIC ◆ GRADES 6–9 ◆ A/R
FANTASY

In San Francisco, eighth-grader Tom has been learning magic from his
Chinese grandmother. On her death, Tom must take over the defense of
a mysterious coral rose that is being sought by the evil Kung Kung. Chinese mythology is woven into this exciting fantasy.

1. The Tiger's Apprentice ◆ 2003
2. Tiger's Blood ◆ 2005
3. Tiger Magic ◆ 2006

TILLERMAN CYCLE

Voigt, Cynthia
ATHENEUM ◆ GRADES 5–8 ◆ A/R
FAMILY LIFE

Two of the books in this outstanding series have won awards: *Dicey's
Song,* a Newbery, and *A Solitary Blue,* a Newbery Honor. In *Homecoming,* the four Tillerman children are abandoned by their mother, and it is
up to 13-year-old Dicey to get them safely to their grandmother's house,
far away on Chesapeake Bay. *Dicey's Song* continues the story, with their
adjustment to living with Gram. The rest of the titles are continuations

of the story and companion titles about other people with whom the Tillermans come in contact.

1. Homecoming ◆ 1981
2. Dicey's Song ◆ 1982
3. A Solitary Blue ◆ 1983
4. The Runner ◆ 1985
5. Come a Stranger ◆ 1986
6. Sons from Afar ◆ 1987
7. Seventeen Against the Dealer ◆ 1989

TIME FANTASY SERIES

L'Engle, Madeleine

FARRAR, STRAUS & GIROUX; DELL ◆ GRADES 4–8 ◆ A/R

ADVENTURE | FANTASY

The four books in this fantasy series feature different members of the Murry family in the classic struggle between good and evil in the universe. *A Wrinkle in Time,* which won the Newbery Medal, chronicles Meg Murry's efforts to find her father, overcome the forces of darkness that are threatening the Earth, and recognize her own limitations and strengths. In doing these things, Meg, her brother Charles Wallace, and a friend, Calvin, travel through space and time to rescue Mr. Murry from the evil It. Later books focus on different members of the family as the struggle continues. Readers will be challenged by the intricate plot devices, including time travel and elements of classic literary tales. In all the books, there are complex issues of values, beliefs, and a connection with spiritual powers in the battle against cruelty, injustice, and intolerance.

1. A Wrinkle in Time ◆ 1962
2. A Wind in the Door ◆ 1973
3. A Swiftly Tilting Planet ◆ 1978
4. Many Waters ◆ 1986

TIME TRAVEL MYSTERIES

Reiss, Kathryn

HARCOURT ◆ GRADES 5–9 ◆ A/R

MYSTERY

In *Dreadful Sorry* teenager Molly Teague is haunted by visions of a girl who disappeared more than 80 years ago. Molly hopes to escape the dreams by visiting her father and new stepmother in Maine. Instead, the dreams become even more vivid. What do they mean? Who is Clementine? And what does Molly's boyfriend have to do with the mystery? Other books in the series feature different characters in mysterious time travel situations.

1. Time Windows ◆ 1991
2. Dreadful Sorry ◆ 1993
3. Pale Phoenix ◆ 1994
4. PaperQuake ◆ 1998
5. Paint By Magic ◆ 2002

TIME TRAVEL QUARTET

Cooney, Caroline B.

BANTAM DOUBLEDAY DELL ◆ GRADES 6–10 ◆ A/R

FANTASY

In the first book, Annie Lockwood travels back to 1895, falls in love with Hiram Stratton Jr., and becomes involved in a murder. In the second of these stories of ill-timed romance, Annie returns to the 1890s and works to free Strat from an insane asylum. *Prisoner of Time* features Strat's sister Devonny and Annie's brother Tod. And in *For All Time,* Annie overshoots Strat's time and ends up in ancient Egypt.

1. Both Sides of Time ◆ 1995
2. Out of Time ◆ 1995
3. Prisoner of Time ◆ 1998
4. For All Time ◆ 2001

THE TIME TRAVELERS *see* Gideon the Cutpurse

TIME TRILOGY

Anderson, Margaret J.

KNOPF ◆ GRADES 5–8

FANTASY

In this science fantasy trilogy, Jennifer and Robert discover that they can slip through the Circle of Stones and travel through time to the year 2179. There they come upon a peaceful society trying to protect itself from a barbaric mechanized society. As the trilogy progresses, these people who refuse to meet violence with violence struggle to protect their community.

1. In the Keep of Time ◆ 1977
2. In the Circle of Time ◆ 1979
3. The Mists of Time ◆ 1984

TIME ZONE HIGH

Strasser, Todd

SIMON & SCHUSTER ◆ GRADES 7–10 ◆ A/R

REAL LIFE

These entertaining books, set at a high school on the West Coast, concentrate mainly on romantic attachments. In *How I Spent My Life on Earth,* a rumor has spread that an asteroid is headed for Earth, and the students spend a night confronting impending doom and examining their relationships.

1. How I Changed My Life ◆ 1995
2. How I Created My Perfect Prom Date ◆ 1998
3. How I Spent My Last Night on Earth ◆ 1998

TIMEJUMPERS

Valentine, James

ALADDIN ◆ GRADES 5–8

FANTASY

Theo lives way in the future. When his TimeMaster JumpMan Pro malfunctions, he is stranded in the 21st century. Gen and Jules are in high school; Theo's appearance interrupts a tender moment between them. Theo has broken the first rule of TimeJumping by interfering with the past. Can these three teens find a way to return Theo to his own time? Originally published as Jumpman.

1. The Past Is Gone ◆ 2007
2. The Present Never Happens ◆ 2007
3. The Future Is Unknown ◆ 2007

TIMETRIPPER

Petrucha, Stefan

RAZORBILL ◆ GRADES 8–11 ◆ A/R

SCIENCE FICTION

After the death of his father, Harry Keller, who is in high school, begins having visions of the past and the future. Then, his mental abilities expand and he is able to enter an alternate universe that he calls "A Time" where time can be altered. There are monsters (Quirks) and other humans in "A Time"—many with plans to create chaos in real time. Harry tries to understand his role in this time-bending world.

1. Yestermorrow ◆ 2006
2. InRage ◆ 2006
3. Blindsighted ◆ 2006
4. FutureImperfect ◆ 2007

TODAYSGIRLS.COM

Various authors

THOMAS NELSON ◆ GRADES 6–9 ◆ A/R

REAL LIFE | VALUES

Six high school girls have a Web site with a private chat room. In the first book, a stranger crashes the chat room and threatens Amber. In the second book, Jamie faces a dilemma when the painting that wins an art scholarship for her is not really her painting. Faith and values play important roles in this series.

1. Stranger Online (Smith, Carol) ◆ 1997
2. Portrait of Lies (Mackall, Dandi Daley) ◆ 2000
3. Tangled Web (Holl, Kristi) ◆ 2000
4. R U 4 Real? (Peacock, Nancy) ◆ 2000
5. Luv@First Site (Kindig, Tess Eileen) ◆ 2000
6. Chat Freak (Holl, Kristi) ◆ 2000
7. N 2 Deep (Knowlton, Laurie Lazzaro) ◆ 2001
8. Please Reply! (Mackall, Dandi Daley) ◆ 2001
9. 4Give & 4Get (Holl, Kristi) ◆ 2001
10. Power Drive (Peacock, Nancy) ◆ 2001
11. Unpredictable (Kindig, Tess Eileen) ◆ 2001
12. Fun E-Farm (Wiseman, Heather) ◆ 2001

TOM CLANCY'S NET FORCE *see* Net Force

TOM SWIFT

Appleton, Victor

SIMON & SCHUSTER ◆ GRADES 7–8

ADVENTURE | FANTASY

Mutant sea creatures, a cyborg kick boxer, and microbots are just some of the creatures that this updated Tom Swift and his friends battle to protect our world. In *Mutant Beach,* Tom faces a giant squid and a 50-foot shark, which could be the result of his research into growth hormones. Tom battles those who are out to blame him while he tries to find out who is really responsible. *Fire Biker* features Tom and his sister Sandra. They have invented a jet-powered cycle and a suit that makes the wearer invisible, but their inventions have been stolen and now the whole world is in danger. These are action-packed books with the kinds of creatures and suspense that will attract the readers of R. L. Stine's series as well as readers who like the adventure of *Star Trek* and *Star Wars*.

1. The Black Dragon ◆ 1991
2. The Negative Zone ◆ 1991
3. Cyborg Kickboxer ◆ 1991
4. The DNA Disaster ◆ 1991
5. Monster Machine ◆ 1991
6. Aquatech Warriors ◆ 1991
7. Moonstalker ◆ 1992
8. The Microbots ◆ 1992
9. Fire Biker ◆ 1992
10. Mind Games ◆ 1992
11. Mutant Beach ◆ 1992
12. Death Quake ◆ 1993
13. Quantum Force ◆ 1993

TOM SWIFT YOUNG INVENTOR

Appleton, Victor
ALADDIN ◆ GRADES 5–9 ◆ A/R
ADVENTURE | FANTASY

Updated scenarios and fast action will introduce new readers to the exploits of Tom Swift. In *Into the Abyss,* Tom's father is testing his underwater exploration vehicle but becomes lost during a storm. It is up to Tom to rescue him. In *The Robot Olympics,* an anti-science group threatens to disrupt a national science competition. Tom's sister, Sandy, figures in some of the adventures, including *The Space Hotel,* in which the two investigate a mysterious disappearance.

1. Into the Abyss ◆ 2006
2. The Robot Olympics ◆ 2006
3. The Space Hotel ◆ 2006
4. Rocket Racers ◆ 2007
5. On Top of the World ◆ 2007
6. Under the Radar ◆ 2007

TOMORROW

Marsden, John
HOUGHTON MIFFLIN ◆ GRADES 8–12 ◆ A/R
ADVENTURE

A group of Australian teens return from a camping trip to find that their country has been invaded and their families imprisoned. Ellie and her friends survive in the countryside and use guerrilla tactics against the enemy. In *A Killing Frost,* they tackle a containership. In *Burning for Revenge,* they become separated from a group of New Zealand rescuers and attack an airfield.

1. Tomorrow, When the War Began ◆ 1995
2. The Dead of Night ◆ 1997
3. A Killing Frost ◆ 1998
4. Darkness, Be My Friend ◆ 1999
5. Burning for Revenge ◆ 2000
6. The Night Is for Hunting ◆ 2001
7. The Other Side of Dawn ◆ 2002

TOUCHSTONE TRILOGY

Augarde, Steve

RANDOM HOUSE ◆ GRADES 8–12

FANTASY

In *The Various,* Meg, 11, is visiting her uncle on his farm, areas of which are to be sold to developers. Following a mysterious voice, Meg enters the old barn and encounters Pegs, a winged horse. Pegs is one of the Various, a community of fairies who are struggling to keep their homeland. Meg joins with them to try to stop her uncle from selling their territory. *Celadine* is a prequel set during World War I in which another.

1. The Various ◆ 2004
2. Celadine ◆ 2006
3. Winter Wood ◆ 2009

TRACES: LUKE HARDING, FORENSIC INVESTIGATOR

Ross, Malcolm

KINGFISHER ◆ GRADES 6–9 ◆ A/R

MYSTERY

In London, Luke Harding, 16, is a forensic investigator. With his robot Malc (Mobile Aid to Law and Crime) he investigates crimes, including the murder of a classmate. This series could attract fans of the Alex Rider books.

1. Framed! ◆ 2005
2. Lost Bullet ◆ 2005
3. Roll Call ◆ 2006
4. Double Check ◆ 2006
5. Final Lap ◆ 2006
6. Blood Brother ◆ 2008

TRAIL OF THREAD

Hubalek, Linda K.
BUTTERFIELD BOOKS ◆ GRADES 7–10
HISTORICAL

Pioneer women in the mid-19th century are featured in this atmospheric historical fiction series. In the first book, Deborah Pieratt writes letters describing her family's journey from Kentucky to the Territory of Kansas. Carefully researched details of the experiences on a wagon train and descriptions of quilting patterns make for absorbing reading.

1. Trail of Thread: A Woman's Westward Journey ◆ 1995
2. Thimble of Soil: A Woman's Quest for Land ◆ 1996
3. Stitch of Courage: A Woman's Fight for Freedom ◆ 1996

TRAILBLAZERS

Jackson, Dave, and Neta Jackson
BETHANY HOUSE ◆ GRADES 4–7 ◆ A/R
HISTORICAL | VALUES

Christian heroes from every era of American history are featured in stories based on their lives. Each book focuses on an ordinary child whose life has been changed. A young slave girl is helped to escape by Harriet Tubman after hearing stories about this Moses who helped her people by following the Northern Star. A young orphan boy meets Peter Cartwright, one of the circuit-riding preachers, and is helped to find his mother, who was taken away by Indians. Celeste Key is a turn-of-the-century child whose family is harassed by the Ku Klux Klan. They move to Florida, and Celeste enters a school started by Mary McLeod Bethune. Each story is followed by information about the historical figure featured.

1. Kidnapped by River Rats: William and Catherine Booth ◆ 1991
2. The Queen's Smuggler: William Tyndale ◆ 1991
3. Spy for the Night Riders: Martin Luther ◆ 1992
4. The Hidden Jewel: Amy Carmichael ◆ 1992
5. Escape from the Slave Traders: David Livingston ◆ 1992
6. The Chimney Sweep's Ransom: John Wesley ◆ 1992
7. Imprisoned in the Golden City: Adoniram and Ann Judson ◆ 1993
8. The Bandit of Ashley Downs: George Mueller ◆ 1993
9. Shanghaied to China: Hudson Taylor ◆ 1993
10. Listen for the Whippoorwill: Harriet Tubman ◆ 1993
11. Attack in the Rye Grass: Narcissa and Marcus Whitman ◆ 1994
12. Trial by Poison: Mary Slessor ◆ 1994
13. Flight of the Fugitives: Gladys Aylward ◆ 1994
14. The Betrayer's Fortune: Menno Simons ◆ 1994
15. Abandoned on the Wild Frontier: Peter Cartwright ◆ 1995

16. Danger on the Flying Trapeze: Dwight L. Moody ◆ 1995
17. The Runaway's Revenge: John Newton ◆ 1995
18. The Thieves of Tyburn Square: Elizabeth Fry ◆ 1995
19. Quest for the Lost Prince: Samuel Morris ◆ 1996
20. The Warrior's Challenge: David Zeisberger ◆ 1996
21. The Drummer Boy's Battle: Florence Nightingale ◆ 1996
22. Traitor in the Tower: John Bunyan ◆ 1996
23. Defeat of the Ghost Riders: Mary Bethune ◆ 1997
24. The Fate of the Yellow Woodbee: Nate Saint ◆ 1997
25. The Gold Miner's Rescue: Sheldon Jackson ◆ 1998
26. The Mayflower Secret: Governor William Bradford ◆ 1998
27. Assassins in the Cathedral: Festo Kivengere ◆ 1999
28. Mask of the Wolf Boy: Jonathan and Rosalind Goforth ◆ 1999
29. Race for the Record: Joy Ridderhof ◆ 1999
30. Ambushed in Jaguar Swamp: Barbrooke Grubb ◆ 1999
31. The Forty-Acre Swindle: George Washington Carver ◆ 2000
32. Hostage on the Nighthawk: William Penn ◆ 2000
33. Journey to the End of the Earth: William Seymour ◆ 2000
34. Drawn by a China Moon: Lottie Moon ◆ 2000
35. Sinking the Dayspring: John G. Paton ◆ 2001
36. Roundup of the Street Rovers: Charles Loring Brace ◆ 2001
37. Blinded by the Shining Path: Romulo Saune ◆ 2002
38. Risking the Forbidden Game: Maude Cary ◆ 2002
39. Exiled to the Red River: Chief Spokane Garry ◆ 2003
40. Caught in the Rebel Camp: Frederick Douglass ◆ 2003

TRASH

Bennett, Cherie, and Jeff Gottesfeld
BERKLEY ◆ GRADES 8–12
REAL LIFE

Six teens are summer interns on a new reality talk show. The antics onscreen are outrageous while behind the scenes the interns have their own problems. A show about mass murders may reveal Chelsea's secret. Lisha is being stalked. Sky's best friend is dating the woman he wants. The first book in the series has been reissued with the title *Hot Trash*.

1. Trash ◆ 1997
2. Love, Lies and Video ◆ 1997
3. Good Girls, Bad Boys ◆ 1997
4. Dirty Big Secrets ◆ 1997
5. The Evil Twin ◆ 1997
6. Truth or Scare ◆ 1998

TRAVELING PANTS *see* Sisterhood of the Traveling Pants

TRIGUN MAXIMUM

Nightow, Yasuhiro

DARK HORSE ◆ **GRADES 8–12**

FANTASY

The original popular Trigun manga is continued in this series. Vash the Stampede, a super-gunslinger, is back with a bounty on his head. He moves from one violent conflict to another, confronting evil villains including Gray the Ninelives. Fans of action and manga will want to see these books.

1. The Hero Returns ◆ 2004
2. Death Blue ◆ 2004
3. His Life as a . . . ◆ 2004
4. Bottom of the Dark ◆ 2005
5. Break Out ◆ 2005
6. The Gunslinger ◆ 2005
7. Happy Days ◆ 2005
8. Silent Ruin ◆ 2006
9. LR ◆ 2006
10. Wolfwood ◆ 2006
11. Zero Hour ◆ 2007
12. The Gunslinger ◆ 2008

TRIPODS

Christopher, John

MACMILLAN ◆ **GRADES 5–8** ◆ **A/R**

SCIENCE FICTION

Aliens have taken over the Earth, and every Earth boy receives a cap at age 13 so the aliens can control his thoughts. The aliens take the form of huge metal tripods, and no one knows if that is their real form or if they are just machines that aliens use. Will, Henry, and Jean Paul escape to the White Mountains and find a colony of free men. Jean Paul, Will, and a German boy named Fritz are sent on a mission to the city of the aliens to learn their ways, and Will barely escapes with his life. The aliens are completely defeated as a result of what Fritz and Will are able to learn. *When the Tripods Came* is a prequel to the series, and readers may want to read it first.

1. The White Mountains ◆ 1967
2. The City of Gold and Lead ◆ 1967
3. The Pool of Fire ◆ 1968
4. When the Tripods Came ◆ 1988

TROLL KING

Vornholt, John

ALADDIN ◆ GRADES 4–7 ◆ A/R

FANTASY

The land of Bonespittle is ruled by the evil sorcerer Stygius Rex. The lowly trolls are oppressed—forced to work as laborers. One troll, Rollo, tries to change the plight of the trolls by leading them in a rebellion. Ogres, fairies, elves, gnomes, and other creatures add to the excitement in this fantasy series.

1. The Troll King ◆ 2002
2. The Troll Queen ◆ 2003
3. The Troll Treasure ◆ 2003

TROLL TRILOGY

Langrish, Katherine

EOS ◆ GRADES 5–8 ◆ A/R

FANTASY

After the death of his father, Peer Ulfsson is taken to live with his despicable twin uncles, who plan to give Peer to the Troll King to serve as a slave to the king's son. Aided by Hilde, a farm girl who lives nearby, Peer outwits his uncles, sending them to the Troll kingdom instead. In *Troll Blood,* Peer and Hilde, whose relationship is developing beyond friendship, voyage on a haunted Viking ship to Vinland. Nordic mythology is woven into this series.

1. Troll Fell ◆ 2004
2. Troll Mill ◆ 2006
3. Troll Blood ◆ 2008

TROLLTOWN *see* The Word and the Void

TROUBLESHOOTERS

Brockmann, Suzanne

BALLANTINE ◆ GRADES 11–12

REAL LIFE

A Navy SEAL Troubleshooter squad trained to deal with terrorists is the focus of this series of thrillers full of romance, mystery, and suspense. For mature readers.

1. The Unsung Hero ◆ 2000
2. The Defiant Hero ◆ 2001
3. Over the Edge ◆ 2001
4. Out of Control ◆ 2002
5. Into the Night ◆ 2002
6. Gone Too Far ◆ 2003
7. Flashpoint ◆ 2004
8. Hot Target ◆ 2004
9. Breaking Point ◆ 2005
10. Into the Storm ◆ 2006
11. Force of Nature ◆ 2007
12. All Through the Night ◆ 2007
13. Into the Fire ◆ 2008

TRUE COLORS

Carlson, Melody
THINK BOOKS ◆ GRADES 9–12 ◆ A/R
REAL LIFE | VALUES

Teen issues like drug abuse, sexuality, body image, and peer pressure are featured in this series. In *Dark Blue,* Jordan is busy making new friends while her "old" friend Kara feels left out. She finds strength in her faith in God. In other books, Emily feels pressured to be thin while Ruth reacts to her difficult home situation by cutting herself. There are questions that accompany the books, making them a choice for group discussions of values and faith.

1. Dark Blue: Color Me Lonely ◆ 2004
2. Deep Green: Color Me Jealous ◆ 2004
3. Torch Red: Color Me Torn ◆ 2004
4. Pitch Black: Color Me Lost ◆ 2004
5. Burnt Orange: Color Me Wasted ◆ 2005
6. Fool's Gold: Color Me Consumed ◆ 2005
7. Blade Silver: Color Me Scarred ◆ 2005
8. Bitter Rose: Color Me Crushed ◆ 2006
9. Faded Denim: Color Me Trapped ◆ 2006
10. Bright Purple: Color Me Confused ◆ 2006
11. Moon White: Color Me Enchanted ◆ 2007
12. Harsh Pink: Color Me Burned ◆ 2007

TRUE-TO-LIFE *see* Hamilton High

TRUTH OR DARE

Hopkins, Cathy

SIMON & SCHUSTER ◆ GRADES 7–10 ◆ A/R

REAL LIFE

Everyone knows the game Truth or Dare. Cat has played the game but cannot face the results. How can she tell her boyfriend that it is over? Her friend, Becca, is no help. In the second book, the two girls compete for the title of Pop Princess. These books were originally published in England.

1. White Lies and Barefaced Truths ◆ 2004
2. The Princess of Pop ◆ 2004
3. Teen Queens and Has-Beens ◆ 2004
4. Starstruck ◆ 2005
5. Double Dare ◆ 2006
6. Midsummer Meltdown ◆ 2006
7. Love Lottery ◆ 2006
8. All Mates Together ◆ 2007

THE TUCKET ADVENTURES

Paulsen, Gary

DELACORTE ◆ GRADES 5–8 ◆ A/R

ADVENTURE | HISTORICAL

Francis Tucket is 14 when this series begins. While heading west on the Oregon Trail, Francis is separated from his family and captured by Pawnees. He is aided by Mr. Grimes, who teaches him survival skills but also gives him a look at the violent ways of a frontiersman. Francis leaves Mr. Grimes and searches for his family only to encounter more ruthless outlaws. This is a gritty series that does not romanticize the difficulties of life on the frontier. With lots of action, this should appeal to boys and perhaps to reluctant readers.

1. Mr. Tucket ◆ 1994
2. Call Me Francis Tucket ◆ 1995
3. Tucket's Ride ◆ 1997
4. Tucket's Gold ◆ 1999
5. Tucket's Home ◆ 2000

TURNING SEVENTEEN

Various authors

PARACHUTE PRESS ◆ GRADES 7–10 ◆ A/R

REAL LIFE

Four friends—Kerri, Jessica, Erin, and Maya—experience a variety of teenage anxieties. For example, Kerri wins a bet when she gets a date with Matt. Unfortunately, Matt finds out. This series is presented in cooperation with *Seventeen* magazine.

1. Any Guy You Want (Noonan, Rosalind) ◆ 2000
2. More than This (Straub, Wendy Corsi) ◆ 2000
3. For Real (Roberts, Christa) ◆ 2000
4. Show Me Love (Craft, Elizabeth) ◆ 2000
5. Can't Let Go (Noonan, Rosalind) ◆ 2000
6. This Boy Is Mine (Straub, Wendy Corsi) ◆ 2001
7. Secrets and Lies (Roberts, Christa) ◆ 2001
8. We Have to Talk (Craft, Elizabeth) ◆ 2001
9. Just Trust Me (Noonan, Rosalind) ◆ 2001
10. Reality Check (Carroll, Jacqueline) ◆ 2001

THE TWILIGHT SAGA

Meyer, Stephenie

LITTLE, BROWN ◆ GRADES 9–12 ◆ A/R

HORROR

Vampires, forbidden love, danger—this series has it all. Bella, 17, lives with her father near Seattle, Washington. At school she is attracted to Edward who she discovers is a vampire. Their romance grows but Edward knows that he must leave Bella. Even though Edward and his family hunt wildlife, not humans, he still fears for her safety. Lonely and depressed, Bella develops a relationship with Jacob but soon learns that he has a secret too. Like other vampire series (Buffy and Angel), this is extremely popular and the release of the fourth book in August 2008 was a media event. Readers may also enjoy the House of Night series. A film of the first book was in production in fall 2008.

1. Twilight ◆ 2005
2. New Moon ◆ 2006
3. Eclipse ◆ 2007
4. Breaking Dawn ◆ 2008

TWISTED JOURNEYS

Various authors

LERNER ◆ GRADES 4–8

HORROR | ADVENTURE

Like the Choose-Your-Own-Adventure books, this graphic novel series lets readers create their own stories. Popular topics including pirates, time travel, and zombies add to the appeal and could also attract reluctant readers.

1. Captured by Pirates (Fontes, Justine) ◆ 2007
2. Escape from Pyramid X (Jolley, Dan) ◆ 2007
3. Terror in Ghost Mansion (Storrie, Paul D.) ◆ 2007
4. The Treasure of Mount Fate (Limke, Jeff) ◆ 2007
5. Nightmare on Zombie Island (Storrie, Paul D.) ◆ 2008
6. The Time Travel Trap (Jolley, Dan) ◆ 2008
7. Vampire Hunt (Jolley, Dan) ◆ 2008
8. Alien Incident on Planet J (Jolley, Dan) ◆ 2008

TWO OF A KIND *see* Mary-Kate and Ashley: Two of a Kind

2099

Peel, John

SCHOLASTIC ◆ GRADES 5–8 ◆ A/R

SCIENCE FICTION

It is 2099 and 14-year-old Tristan Connor has been working to stop the dangerous actions of Devon, only to discover that Devon is his clone. With the help of a policewoman and an Underworld crook, Tristan must stop the doomsday virus that Devon has released. With cliff-hanging endings, the books do not stand alone. The action comes to a dramatic conclusion in *Firestorm.* Fans of futuristic novels and computers will enjoy the cyber-action.

1. Doomsday ◆ 1999
2. Betrayal ◆ 1999
3. Traitor ◆ 2000
4. Revolution ◆ 2000
5. Meltdown ◆ 2000
6. Firestorm ◆ 2000

2001

Clarke, Arthur C.

NAL; BALLANTINE ◆ GRADES 9–12 ◆ A/R

SCIENCE FICTION

The computer named Hal plays a starring role in *2001,* an allegorical story about the history and future of mankind. In *2010,* scientists race to recover the information from the deserted *2001* space ship. Humans continue to search for the secret of the strange monolith in the succeeding volumes.

1. 2001: A Space Odyssey ◆ 1968
2. 2010: Odyssey Two ◆ 1982
3. 2061: Odyssey Three ◆ 1988
4. 3001: The Final Odyssey ◆ 1997

UGLIES

Westerfeld, Scott

SIMON PULSE ◆ GRADES 9–12 ◆ A/R

SCIENCE FICTION

In this futuristic world, when you turn sixteen you undergo an operation and are made "pretty." Tally Youngblood is eager for her sixteenth birthday; she is tired of being ugly. Tally meets Shay, another ugly, who questions the society's program and encourages Tally to escape to the Smoke, a community of those who refuse to conform. When Shay runs away, Tally is told to find her or remain ugly. Ethical dilemmas are explored as Tally becomes a pretty but still questions the constraints of her society. Tally's story concludes with the third book. In *Extras,* there are new social expectations and Aya Fuse, 15, is confronted with choices about gadgets, gossip, and popularity.

1. Uglies ◆ 2005
2. Pretties ◆ 2005
3. Specials ◆ 2006
4. Extras ◆ 2007

UNCLE STINKY *see* The Adventures of Uncle Stinky

UNCOMMON HEROES

Henderson, Dee

MULTNOMAH ◆ GRADES 10–12

REAL LIFE | VALUES

This series about Navy SEALs combines suspense and romance with Christian values and strong female characters. *True Valor* features a feisty combat pilot named Gracie Yates whose plane crashes behind enemy lines in Iraq. She is rescued by an air force major with whom she has a long but chaste history.

1. True Devotion ◆ 2000
2. True Valor ◆ 2002

3. True Honor ◆ 2002
4. True Courage ◆ 2004

UNDERCOVER GIRL

Harris, Christine

SCHOLASTIC ◆ GRADES 5–7 ◆ A/R

MYSTERY

Jesse Sharp is a kid, an orphan, and a spy. Trained by C2, a secret spy organization, Jesse goes undercover to solve mysteries and expose the bad guys. In one book, she thwarts a kidnapping; in another, she must find a bomb before it explodes. Along with the mysteries there are questions about the actual purpose of C2. Is it a legitimate spy agency or does it have a hidden agenda?

1. Secrets ◆ 2005
2. Fugitive ◆ 2006
3. Nightmare ◆ 2006
4. Danger ◆ 2007
5. Twisted ◆ 2007

THE UNDERLAND CHRONICLES

Collins, Suzanne

SCHOLASTIC ◆ GRADES 4–8 ◆ A/R

FANTASY

Gregor, 11, and his sister Boots, 2, enter the Underland and encounter unusual humans along with giant cockroaches, spiders, rats, and bats. Gregor discovers that the humans are captives and that one of them is his father. The second book follows Gregor's return to the Underland to fulfill a prophecy, and Gregor later battles a terrible plague, defends the residents of the Underland, and must confront his own dark side.

1. Gregor the Overlander ◆ 2003
2. Gregor and the Prophecy of Bane ◆ 2004
3. Gregor and the Curse of the Warmbloods ◆ 2005
4. Gregor and the Marks of Secret ◆ 2006
5. Gregor and the Code of Claw ◆ 2007

UNDERWHERE

Hale, Bruce

HARPERCOLLINS ◆ GRADES 4–7 ◆ A/R

HUMOR

Zeke discovers that there is a world under ours . . . a world where the creatures wear underwear outside their clothes. Along with his twin sister Stephanie and their neighbor Hector, Zeke enters Underwhere and is proclaimed the prince. Zeke used to be an ordinary kid. Now he faces zombies, pirates, sea serpents, and more. The book shifts from text to extended pages in a graphic novel format, which should appeal to many kids.

1. Prince of Underwhere ◆ 2008
2. Pirates of Underwhere ◆ 2008
3. Flyboy of Underwhere ◆ 2008

UNICORN

Lee, Tanith

MACMILLAN; TOR ◆ GRADES 7–12 ◆ A/R

FANTASY

Tanaquil, the daughter of a sorceress, makes a unicorn from strange golden bones. and the unicorn lures her away to a seaside city and a perfect world. In the second book, Tanaquil meets her half-sister, who has a golden unicorn that must be mended. Despite her misgivings, Tanaquil brings it to life and discovers that it is not only a beast of war but provides entry to a world whose purpose is war.

1. Black Unicorn ◆ 1991
2. Gold Unicorn ◆ 1994
3. Red Unicorn ◆ 1997

UNICORN CHRONICLES

Coville, Bruce

SCHOLASTIC ◆ GRADES 5–8 ◆ A/R

FANTASY

A magic amulet allows Cara Hunter to enter the land of Luster. Cara's grandmother gave her the amulet and a message for the unicorn Queen. In Luster, Cara is accompanied on her journey by Lightfoot, an adolescent unicorn. Along the way they face danger from delvers, dragons, and a woman named Beloved, who hates unicorns and seeks to destroy them.

1. Into the Land of the Unicorns ◆ 1994
2. Song of the Wanderer ◆ 1999
3. Dark Whispers ◆ 2008

UNIVERSITY HOSPITAL

Bennett, Cherie

BERKLEY ◆ GRADES 7–10

REAL LIFE

After graduating from high school, five teens hope to enter medical school. A summer program at a hospital may earn them a scholarship. They are connected but still competitive. Tristan and Summer begin a romantic relationship but Zoey finds out. Teens will find the romance and medical details fascinating.

1. University Hospital ◆ 1999
2. Condition Critical ◆ 1999
3. Crisis Point ◆ 2000
4. Heart Trauma ◆ 2000
5. Prognosis: Heartbreak ◆ 2002

UNSEEN

Cusick, Richie Tankersley

PUFFIN ◆ GRADES 10–12 ◆ A/R

HORROR

Lucy feels she is being followed. Running through a cemetery, she encounters a nearly dead girl, who transfers her psychic powers to Lucy just before dying. Now, Lucy's visions and her sense of impending doom grow. Her only confidante is the dead girl's brother, Byron. When Lucy and Byron are in a car crash and Byron is killed, Lucy knows she is alone and in ever-increasing danger.

1. It Begins ◆ 2005
2. Rest in Peace ◆ 2005
3. Blood Brothers ◆ 2006
4. Sin and Salvation ◆ 2006

USAGI YOJIMBO

Sakai, Stan

FANTAGRAPHICS BOOKS; DARK HORSE ◆ GRADES 5–8

FANTASY

Usagi Yojimbo is a ronin—a samurai without a master. He is also a rabbit. Usagi wanders across feudal Japan sometimes serving as a bodyguard. His adventures follow Japanese traditions and incorporate many Japanese legends. The first seven books were published by Fantagraphics Books; there have been many editions and the dates reflect the dates on amazon.com for currently available books. Beginning with the eighth book, the publisher is Dark Horse.

1. The Ronin ◆ 1987
2. Circles ◆ 1996
3. Gen's Story ◆ 1997
4. Shades of Death ◆ 1997
5. The Dragon Bellow Conspiracy ◆ 1998
6. Daisho ◆ 1998
7. The Brink of Life and Death ◆ 1998
8. Seasons ◆ 1999
9. Grasscutter ◆ 1999
10. Grey Shadows ◆ 2000
11. Demon Mask ◆ 2001
12. Lone Goat and Kid ◆ 2001
13. Grasscutter II: Journey to Atsuta Shrine ◆ 2002
14. Samurai ◆ 2002
15. The Wanderer's Road ◆ 2002
16. The Shrouded Moon ◆ 2003
17. Duel at Kitanoji ◆ 2003
18. Travels with Jotaro ◆ 2004
19. Fathers and Sons ◆ 2005
20. Glimpses of Death ◆ 2006
21. The Mother of Mountains ◆ 2007

VALDEMAR: GRYPHON TRILOGY

Lackey, Mercedes

DAW ◆ GRADES 7–12 ◆ A/R

FANTASY

Prehistoric Valdemar is the setting for this series that provides background information for three other series—Mage Wars, Magic Winds, and Mage Storms. The city of White Gryphon is threatened and the combined efforts of humans and gryphons are needed to defeat the evil.

1. The Black Gryphon ◆ 1994
2. The White Gryphon ◆ 1995
3. The Silver Gryphon ◆ 1996

VALDEMAR: MAGE STORMS

Lackey, Mercedes

DAW ◆ GRADES 7–12 ◆ A/R

FANTASY

This series follows the events in the Mage Wars and Magic Wind series. Also set in Valdemar, it focuses on two young adults—Karal and An'de-sha. As they realize their talents, they join with others to face the mage storms. Eventually, they come to understand that the storms are linked to events in the prehistory of Valdemar. These events are described in the Gryphon Trilogy.

1. Storm Warning ◆ 1994
2. Storm Rising ◆ 1995
3. Storm Breaking ◆ 1996

VALDEMAR: MAGE WARS

Lackey, Mercedes
DAW ◆ GRADES 7–12 ◆ A/R
FANTASY

Vanyel discovers his destiny—first at the High Court of Valdemar and later as a Herald-Mage. With his Companion, Yfandes, he faces the dark magic. The adventures continue with the series Magic Winds, and Mage Storms. The Gryphon Trilogy provides background information on the magical events in Valdemar.

1. Magic's Pawn ◆ 1989
2. Magic's Promise ◆ 1990
3. Magic's Price ◆ 1990

VALDEMAR: MAGE WINDS

Lackey, Mercedes
DAW ◆ GRADES 7–12 ◆ A/R
FANTASY

Valdemar is a magical land. Elspeth Herald must develop her magical powers to become the mage needed to face the coming dangers. This series comes after the events in Mage Wars and before those in Mage Storms. The prequel series is the Gryphon Trilogy.

1. Winds of Fate ◆ 1991
2. Winds of Change ◆ 1992
3. Winds of Fury ◆ 1993

VALDEMAR: MAGEWORLDS

Doyle, Debra, and James D. MacDonald

TOR ◆ GRADES 6–9

FANTASY

This series follows years of turmoil between the Republic and the Mageworlds. Battles, intrigue, royal feuds, supernatural powers, creatures, and more are found in these books, which one review called a space opera (like an intergalactic soap opera). In one book, Beka seeks to avenge her mother's assassination. In another, the adventure focuses on the body of a starship captain that was found on his broken-down ship. Two prequels, the fourth and seventh books, provide background information on the conflict and the early warriors.

1. The Price of the Stars ◆ 1993
2. Starpilot's Grave ◆ 1993
3. By Honor Betray'd ◆ 1994
4. The Gathering Flame: The Prequel to Mageworlds ◆ 1995
5. The Long Hunt ◆ 1996
6. A Working of Stars ◆ 2002
7. The Stars Asunder: A New Novel of the Mageworlds ◆ 2003

VAMPIRATES

Somper, Justin

LITTLE, BROWN ◆ GRADES 6–9 ◆ A/R

FANTASY | HORROR

After their father's death, twins Connor and Grace Tempest, 14, run away to sea and are separated by a storm. A pirate ship rescues Connor while Grace is rescued by Vampirates. Each twin becomes involved in the way of life on the ships and, when they are reunited, the twins have different perspectives on their rescuers. Connor continues his involvement with pirates, even attending the Pirate Academy. Grace remembers her Vampirate protector Lorcan, who became blind keeping her safe. The fast-paced action in this series will attract reluctant readers.

1. Demons of the Ocean ◆ 2006
2. Tide of Terror ◆ 2007
3. Blood Captain ◆ 2008

VAMPIRE ACADEMY

Mead, Rachael

RAZORBILL ◆ GRADES 11–12 ◆ A/R

HORROR

St. Vladimir's Academy is a training ground for vampires and their body-guards. Lissa is a Moroi Vampire Princess who, with her best friend Rose, has been sent to St. Vlad's. Rose is half-human and half-vampire and she is to be Lissa's guard. There is plenty of vampire lore here along with typical teen issues of sexuality and peer pressure. In the second book, the winter break ski trip in Idaho is threatened by the evil Strigoi, the most dangerous of the vampires.

1. Vampire Academy ◆ 2007
2. Frostbite ◆ 2008
3. Shadow Kiss ◆ 2008

VAMPIRE DIARIES

Smith, L. J.

HARPERCOLLINS ◆ GRADES 7–10

FANTASY | HORROR

Elena finds herself drawn to Stefan when she meets him at school. She later finds out that he and his brother are vampires and the series follows Elena's attraction to both brothers and her own conversion into a vampire. The books were reissued in 1999.

1. The Awakening ◆ 1991
2. The Struggle ◆ 1991
3. The Fury ◆ 1991
4. Dark Reunion ◆ 1991

VAMPIRE KISSES

Schreiber, Ellen

HARPERTEEN ◆ GRADES 7–10 ◆ A/R

HORROR

Raven is a goth girl who wants to meet a vampire. In her community, at home, and at school, she is an outsider, often the target of bullies. Raven wants to know more about Alexander, the son of the new residents of the town's old mansion. It turns out that he is a vampire. In the second book, Alexander has left town and Raven tries to find him. Together they face Jagger, an evil vampire who plans to bite Raven. Later, Jagger's equally evil twin Luna brings more danger to Raven. This is not as intense as many other vampire series such as House of Night (Cast) and the Twilight Saga (Meyer).

1. Vampire Kisses ◆ 2003
2. Kissing Coffins ◆ 2005
3. Vampireville ◆ 2006
4. Dance with a Vampire ◆ 2007
5. The Coffin Club ◆ 2008

THE VAMPIRE'S PROMISE

Cooney, Caroline B.

SCHOLASTIC ◆ GRADES 6–8 ◆ A/R

HORROR

Teenagers with ordinary concerns find themselves involved with vampires. In *Fatal Bargain,* six teenagers decide to have a party in an old abandoned house and meet a hungry vampire who declares that one of them will be his victim. They need to decide which one it will be. After some failed escape attempts, and encounters with various people who stumble on the scene, they all escape, only to confront the monster again.

1. Deadly Offer ◆ 1991
2. Evil Returns ◆ 1992
3. Fatal Bargain ◆ 1993

THE VARIOUS *see* Touchstone Trilogy

VESPER HOLLY

Alexander, Lloyd

DUTTON ◆ GRADES 5–7 ◆ A/R

ADVENTURE | HUMOR

Vesper is the teenage daughter of a deceased famous scholar and adventurer. Her father's best friend, Brinnie, and his wife, Mary, have become Vesper's guardians, and together they travel the world from one adventure to another. The evil Dr. Helvitius is their arch enemy, always coming up with some evil scheme against innocent people. In Central America, he is building a canal that will ruin the land of the Indian people. In Europe, he is planning for a small country to be annexed by its neighbors. Vesper and Brinnie are always one step ahead of him, with the help of various friends they collect along the way. Brinnie's pompous behavior supplies humor, while Vesper is an exciting heroine.

1. The Illyrian Adventure ◆ 1986
2. The El Dorado Adventure ◆ 1987

3. The Drackenberg Adventure ◆ 1988
4. The Jedera Adventure ◆ 1989
5. The Philadelphia Adventure ◆ 1990
6. The Xanadu Adventure ◆ 2005

VET VOLUNTEERS *see* Wild at Heart

VICKY AUSTIN

L'Engle, Madeleine

FARRAR, STRAUS & GIROUX; BANTAM DOUBLEDAY DELL ◆ GRADES 4–7 ◆ A/R

FAMILY LIFE | MYSTERY | REAL LIFE

In *Meet the Austins,* Vicky is 12 and her family is faced with taking in a spoiled orphan girl. The father, a country doctor, is offered a position in New York, where they become involved in an international plot. On a cross-country camping trip, they meet a spoiled rich boy who takes a liking to Vicky. The Austins spend summers in their grandfather's house on an island off the East Coast. Here Vicky befriends a boy who is doing research on dolphins and discovers that she has a real affinity for the animals. This series tackles issues of life and death, faith and cynicism, and shows a loving family dealing intelligently with problems. A simple Christmas story, *The Twenty-Four Days Before Christmas* (1964), is a prequel written on a much easier level than the rest of the series.

1. Meet the Austins ◆ 1960
2. The Moon by Night ◆ 1963
3. The Young Unicorns ◆ 1968
4. A Ring of Endless Light ◆ 1980
5. Troubling a Star ◆ 1994

VICTORIAN TALES OF LONDON

Blackwell, Lawana

BETHANY HOUSE ◆ GRADES 9–12 ◆ A/R

HISTORICAL | VALUES

This series features teenage girls who are searching for true love while maintaining their virtue and values in Victorian London. In *The Maiden of Mayfair,* Sarah Matthews was raised as an orphan in the Foundling Home for Girls. A rich widow suspects that Sarah may be her granddaughter. She takes her into her own home and Sarah must adjust to the manners of London society, which provide a backdrop for these rags to riches sagas.

1. The Maiden of Mayfair ◆ 2001
2. Catherine's Heart ◆ 2002
3. Leading Lady ◆ 2004

THE VIKING

Tebbetts, Christopher

PUFFIN ◆ GRADES 6–8 ◆ A/R

FANTASY

Zack Gilman, 14, is tailgating with his father at a Minnesota Vikings game when he gets lost in a snowstorm. He travels to the time of the real Vikings (whose traits and appearance remind Zack of people in the present, including a boy who has bullied him). Zack becomes involved in the quest for Yggdrasil's Chest and in solving the Prophecy of the Lost Boy.

1. Viking Pride ◆ 2003
2. Quest for Faith ◆ 2003
3. Land of the Dead ◆ 2003
4. Hammer of the Gods ◆ 2003

VIKING QUEST

Johnson, Lois Walfrid

MOODY ◆ GRADES 5–8 ◆ A/R

HISTORICAL | VALUES

Set in Ireland and Norway in the 10th century, this series features Briana "Bree" O'Toole and her brother Devin. After being abducted by Vikings from their home in Ireland, the two are separated and face different challenges. Bree serves as a slave but manages to escape from her captors. The Viking leader, Mikkel, pursues her, believing she has also taken a bag of coins. Bree and Devin find courage and solace in their faith in God.

1. Raiders from the Sea ◆ 2003
2. Mystery of the Silver Coins ◆ 2003
3. The Invisible Friend ◆ 2004
4. Heart of Courage ◆ 2005
5. Raider's Promise ◆ 2006

VIOLET

Walker, Melissa

BERKLEY ◆ GRADES 8–10

REAL LIFE

Violet Greenfield goes from gawky high school girl to high-fashion runway model in New York City and around the world. It isn't all glamorous fun as Violet leaves behind her friends and learns about the work that goes with modeling. Still, there is a lot of attention, including from guys like Paulo. But what about her old friend Roger? Violet faces issues about her body image and her identity in this series.

1. Violet on the Runway ◆ 2007
2. Violet by Design ◆ 2007
3. Violet in Private ◆ 2008

VIRTUAL REALITY

Kritlow, William

THOMAS NELSON ◆ GRADES 7–10

FANTASY

In a virtual reality chamber, Kelly and her brother Tim must use their computer skills and their faith to solve problems. In one book, they try to rescue the president and his son from an alternate, hostile virtual reality.

1. A Race Against Time ◆ 1995
2. The Deadly Maze ◆ 1995
3. Backfire ◆ 1995

VIRTUAL WORLD CHRONOLOGS

Skurzynski, Gloria

SIMON & SCHUSTER; ATHENEUM ◆ GRADES 6–9 ◆ A/R

SCIENCE FICTION

Corgan, 14, has been genetically engineered to be the best player of any electronic game. The Council has been preparing him to represent them in a virtual war. Along with his partners Sharla and Brig, he succeeds in winning the confrontation, although Brig dies. In *Clones,* Sharla has secretly produced four clones of Brig even though the Council only allows one. One of the clones, Brigand, is determined to kill Corgan and defeat the Council.

1. Virtual War ◆ 1997
2. The Clones ◆ 2002
3. The Revolt ◆ 2005
4. The Choice ◆ 2006

VISITORS

Philbrick, Rodman, and Lynn Harnett

SCHOLASTIC ◆ GRADES 5–8 ◆ A/R

SCIENCE FICTION

When Nick and his twin sister Jessie investigate a strange glow above the hills, their lives are changed. Brain-stealing aliens have invaded Earth. With their friend Frasier, they try to destroy the aliens' energy source. When Jessie is captured by the aliens, Nick and Frasier must get help from another alien to save her.

1. Strange Invaders ◆ 1997
2. Things ◆ 1997
3. Brain Stealers ◆ 1997

VIVI HARTMAN

Feder, Harriet K.

LERNER ◆ GRADES 6–10 ◆ A/R

MYSTERY

Vivi Hartman is a lively and intelligent teenage daughter of a rabbi. In *Mystery of the Kaifeng Scroll,* she uses her linguistic talents to track down her mother when she goes missing in Turkey. At a funeral on a Seneca reservation in *Death on Sacred Ground,* she learns that a murder may have taken place.

1. Mystery in Miami Beach ◆ 1992
2. Mystery of the Kaifeng Scroll ◆ 1995
3. Death on Sacred Ground ◆ 2001

VOYAGE OF THE BASSET

Various authors

RANDOM HOUSE ◆ GRADES 4–7 ◆ A/R

FANTASY

The Voyage of the Basset is a magical series for dreamers. In each book, children encounter opportunities to use their imaginations. In the first book, two children are transported from their home in Victorian England to a realm of fairies and beasts. There, Hope and Apollo are given tasks that involve centaurs and Pegasus. In another book, Thor's hammer has been stolen and the Basset is sent to find a human to help recover it. This series is based on an oversized, profusely illustrated fantasy *Voyage of the Basset* by James C. Christensen.

1. Islands in the Sky (Lee, Tanith) ◆ 1999
2. The Raven Queen (Windling, Terri, and Ellen Steiber) ◆ 1999
3. Journey to Otherwhere (Smith, Sherwood) ◆ 2000
4. Thor's Hammer (Shetterly, Will) ◆ 2000
5. Fire Bird (Zambreno, Mary Frances) ◆ 2001

WAKARA OF EAGLE LODGE

Shands, Linda

REVELL ◆ GRADES 6–9

REAL LIFE | VALUES

After her mother's death in a car accident, Wakara Sheridan, 15, tries to help at her family's lodge. Wakara is skeptical about the faith shown by some of the employees of Eagle Lodge, but her beliefs change when she escapes a forest fire. In the third book, Wakara explores her Native American heritage (she is also part Irish) and she faces another test of her faith.

1. Wild Fire ◆ 2001
2. Blind Fury ◆ 2001
3. White Water ◆ 2001

WALKER AND TAG

Vick, Helen H.

HARBINGER HOUSE ◆ GRADES 6–9 ◆ A/R

FANTASY

Walker, 15, is a Hopi Indian boy who travels 800 years back in time to the world of the Sinagua culture. A younger white boy, Tag, inadvertently travels along with him. Walker becomes involved with the people and agrees to lead them to a new home.

1. Walker of Time ◆ 1993
2. Walker's Journey Home ◆ 1995
3. Tag Against Time ◆ 1996

WARCRAFT, THE SUNWELL TRILOGY

Knaak, Richard A.

TOKYOPOP ◆ GRADES 7–10

FANTASY

An action-packed manga version of the popular video game featuring Kalec, a blue dragon who can adopt a human form, and Anveena, a beautiful young maiden. Kalec and Anveena join forces in a race to find the Sunwell, a magical power source, before Dar'Khan can seize it. The attractive illustrations are by Jae-Hwan Kim. Also available in a Kaplan SAT/ACT Vocabulary Building version that includes an index of more than 300 words and definitions.

1. Dragon Hunt ◆ 2005
2. Shadows of Ice ◆ 2006
3. Ghostlands ◆ 2007

WARRIORS

Hunter, Erin
HARPERCOLLINS ◆ GRADES 5–9 ◆ A/R
FANTASY

A house cat named Rusty has lived in comfort with Twolegs but leaves to enter the world of the wildcat clans. A world with four different clans—ThunderClan, ShadowClan, WindClan, and RiverClan. Rusty becomes an apprentice named Firepaw. After he proves himself, he beecomes a warrior cat in training named Fireheart. He begins a quest to be a true warrior.

1. Into the Wild ◆ 2003
2. Fire and Ice ◆ 2003
3. Forest of Secrets ◆ 2003
4. Rising Storm ◆ 2004
5. A Dangerous Path ◆ 2004
6. The Darkest Hour ◆ 2004

WARRIORS: POWER OF THREE

Hunter, Erin
HARPERCOLLINS ◆ GRADES 5–9 ◆ A/R
FANTASY

This series follows the events in Warriors: The New Prophecy. Three Thunderclan kits—Hollypaw, Jaypaw, and Lionpaw—are descendants of Firestar and each has a gift. There are dark days approaching and these three will be challenged to protect the future of the Clans. As they develop their talents they also confront their own demons and they go on a quest to the mountains, seeking to understand their destiny.

1. The Sight ◆ 2007
2. Dark River ◆ 2007
3. Outcast ◆ 2008

  4. Eclipse ◆ 2008
  5. Long Shadows ◆ 2008

WARRIORS: THE NEW PROPHECY

Hunter, Erin

HARPERCOLLINS ◆ GRADES 5–9 ◆ A/R

FANTASY

A new generation of feline warriors faces more challenges to the clans. Humans ("Twolegs") are destroying the habitats of the cats. Six cats, children of the original warriors, join together to save the clans, eventually realizing that salvation lies in finding a new home.

  1. Midnight ◆ 2005
  2. Moonrise ◆ 2005
  3. Dawn ◆ 2006
  4. Starlight ◆ 2006
  5. Twilight ◆ 2006
  6. Sunset ◆ 2007

WATCHERS

Lerangis, Peter

SCHOLASTIC ◆ GRADES 5–8 ◆ A/R

FANTASY

Each book features a different character in a supernatural adventure. In *Last Stop,* David's father disappeared six months ago. While riding the subrail, David is surprised when the train makes an unexpected stop at an abandoned station. As David looks at the platform, he is convinced that he sees his father. In *Rewind,* Adam's video camera can rewind reality. The action is fast-paced and will hold the interest of reluctant readers.

  1. Last Stop ◆ 1998
  2. Rewind ◆ 1998
  3. I. D. ◆ 1998
  4. War ◆ 1999
  5. Island ◆ 1999
  6. Lab 6 ◆ 1999

WATCHERS AT THE WELL

Chalker, Jack L.

BALLANTINE ◆ GRADES 10–12

FANTASY

The Well World is a place where beings experience strange transformations. Space wanderer Nathan Brazil has become the guardian of the Well of Souls. He knows powerful secrets but has grown weary of his responsibilities. When danger threatens the Well World, Nathan and Mavra Chang work to protect the future of the world. This trilogy stands alone but there are other Well World novels dating back into the late 1970s.

1. Echoes of the Well of Souls: A Well World Novel ◆ 1993
2. Shadow of the Well of Souls: A Well World Novel ◆ 1994
3. Gods of the Well of Souls: A Well World Novel ◆ 1995

WATCHER'S QUEST

Buffie, Margaret

KIDS CAN PRESS ◆ GRADES 7–10 ◆ A/R

FANTASY

What begins as a modern family story set in Manitoba quickly develops into an intricate fantasy with roots in Celtic mythology. Emma has been raised as a human but is really an alien, a Watcher. Emma has kept watch over her alien sister, Summer, a changeling and the queen of Argadnel. Emma joins with another Watcher, Tom, to find her mother's true daughter, Ailla. The two compete with aliens in a game to win Ailla. The relationship between Tom and Emma grows when they search for the four Wands—Earth, Wind, Water, and Fire.

1. The Watcher ◆ 2002
2. The Seeker ◆ 2002
3. The Finder ◆ 2004

WATCHING ALICE

Parker, Daniel, and Lee Miller

PUTNAM ◆ GRADES 7–10 ◆ A/R

REAL LIFE

Tom Sinclair is 16 and he wants to begin a new life in New York City. He meets Alice Brown and is deeply attracted to her; then she disappears. Alice's diary and some mysterious e-mail messages help direct his search for her. Tom finds that his own past may have something to do with the disappearance.

1. Break the Surface ◆ 2004
2. Walk on Water ◆ 2004
3. Seek the Prophet ◆ 2004
4. Find the Miracle ◆ 2005

WATER

Dalkey, Kara

AVON ◆ GRADES 7–10 ◆ A/R

FANTASY

Romance and adventure are interwoven into these rich fantasies featuring a 16-year-old mermyd called Nia who lives in Atlantis. Nia has ambitions that are thwarted and she comes to realize that their government is rife with intrigue and plots. In the second book, Nia becomes involved with a "dry-lander," and in the final book of the trilogy, Nia and Corwin hold the key to the survival of her city.

1. Ascension ◆ 2002
2. Reunion ◆ 2002
3. Transformation ◆ 2002

WAVE WALKERS

Meyer, Kai

ALADDIN ◆ GRADES 6–9 ◆ A/R

FANTASY

The world is facing destruction from the forces of the evil Maelstrom. Two 14-year-old "polliwogs"—humans who can walk on water—may be the keys to salvation. Jolly, a girl who was raised by pirates, and Munk team up and face their destiny. The floating city of Aelenium is the focus of the Maelstrom's attack and the teens must find a way to close the underwater gate.

1. Pirate Curse ◆ 2006
2. Pirate Emperor ◆ 2007
3. Pirate Wars ◆ 2008

THE WEDDING PLANNER'S DAUGHTER

Paratore, Coleen Murtagh

SIMON & SCHUSTER ◆ GRADES 5–9 ◆ A/R

REAL LIFE │ FAMILY LIFE

Willa Havisham's mother is a wedding planner and, for now, the two of them are living in Cape Cod with Willa's grandmother. In the first book, Willa is 12. She wants to stay in one place, make friends, and lead a normal tween/teen life. With her mom dating her English teacher, Willa may just get her wish. As the series progresses, Willa's mother remarries and becomes pregnant. Willa grows up, too—she is 14 in the third book. Her interests and issues change as she deals with her mother's miscarriage and her own disappointments and achievements. Willa loves to read and there are quotes and comments about books throughout the series.

1. The Wedding Planner's Daughter ◆ 2005
2. The Cupid Chronicles ◆ 2006
3. Willa by Heart ◆ 2008

WEETZIE BAT SAGA

Block, Francesca Lia

HARPERCOLLINS ◆ GRADES 10–12 ◆ A/R

REAL LIFE

Set in Los Angeles, these books describe the struggles, anxieties, joys, and hopes of a group of friends. Weetzie is 23 and she loves the glamour and romance of Hollywood movies. She meets Dirk, a gay man looking for love. They each find companions and move in together. Witch Baby joins the group and struggles to find her place. Two books issued in 2004 combine the earlier volumes. *Beautiful Boys* includes *Missing Angel Juan* and *Baby Be-Bop,* both featuring male heroes; *Goat Girls* includes *Witch Baby* and *Cherokee Bat and the Goat Guys,* both with female protagonists' point of views.

1. Weetzie Bat ◆ 1989
2. Witch Baby ◆ 1991
3. Cherokee Bat and the Goat Guys ◆ 1992
4. Missing Angel Juan ◆ 1993
5. Baby Be-Bop ◆ 1995

WELL OF SOULS *see* Watchers at the Well

WEREWOLF CHRONICLES

Philbrick, W. Rodman, and Lynn Harnett

SCHOLASTIC ◆ GRADES 5–8

HORROR

Fox Hollow looks like an ordinary town, but there is something very frightening in the woods. Only the wolf-boy knows the secret, and only he can save the town. The wolf-boy, who is later called Gruff, was raised by wolves, who protected him and fed him after he was abandoned. Now a danger has entered the woods: the werewolves. They want Gruff to join them, and, even though he tries to resist, their powers are beginning to affect him. His efforts to keep Fox Hollow from the werewolves put him into even more danger. Gruff may be able to save the town only by becoming a werewolf himself.

1. Night Creature ◆ 1996
2. Children of the Wolf ◆ 1996
3. The Wereing ◆ 1996

THE WESSEX PAPERS

Parker, Daniel

AVON ◆ GRADES 9–12 ◆ A/R

MYSTERY

Wessex Academy is a private school for privileged students, who get up to a variety of pranks and rebellions. Sunday and her friend Fred uncover a blackmail plot and their efforts to expose the perpetrators continue throughout the three books.

1. Trust Falls ◆ 2002
2. Fallout ◆ 2002
3. Outsmart ◆ 2002

WEST CREEK MIDDLE SCHOOL *see* Losers, Inc.

WESTMARK

Alexander, Lloyd

BANTAM DOUBLEDAY DELL ◆ GRADES 5–7 ◆ A/R

ADVENTURE | FANTASY

This series is set in a world much like our own in the late Renaissance. Theo is a printer's helper who is embroiled in a revolt against a corrupt government. When his master is killed, he falls in with the scheming Count and with Mickle, a poor girl with an amazing talent for ventriloquism. They meet up with a group of revolutionaries led by the charismatic Florian, who wants to do away with the monarchy altogether. Mickle and Theo fall in love, and she is revealed to be the king's long-lost daughter. She and Theo plan to marry, and the next two books in this trilogy concern their struggles against enemies in and out of Westmark.

1. Westmark ◆ 1981
2. The Kestrel ◆ 1982
3. The Beggar Queen ◆ 1984

WHAT IF . . .

Ruckdeschel, Liz, and Sara James

DELACORTE ◆ GRADES 7–10

REAL LIFE

Like the Choose Your Own Adventure books, this series is interactive and you "Choose Your Destiny." As the series begins, Haley Miller is 15. Readers make choices to lead her through common teen issues. Peer pressure, relationships, parties and dances, homework and grades, alcohol, drugs, and dating are among the situations that Haley and the reader face.

1. What If . . . Everyone Knew Your Name ◆ 2006
2. What If . . . All the Boys Wanted You ◆ 2006
3. What If . . . You Broke All the Rules ◆ 2007
4. What If . . . Everyone Was Doing It ◆ 2007
5. What If . . . All the Rumors Were True ◆ 2008
6. What If . . . Your Past Came Back to Haunt You ◆ 2008

THE WHEEL OF TIME

Jordan, Robert

TOR ◆ GRADES 10–12 ◆ A/R

FANTASY

The Third Age is the Age of Prophecy. A peaceful world is threatened by the Dark One. Rand al'Thor is chosen to revisit the heritage (and madness) of the Dragon on a quest to find the magical elements to rescue the world from evil. *New Spring* (2004) is a prequel.

1. The Eye of the World ◆ 1990
2. The Great Hunt ◆ 1990
3. The Dragon Reborn ◆ 1991
4. The Shadow Rising ◆ 1992
5. The Fires of Heaven ◆ 1993
6. Lord of Chaos ◆ 1994
7. A Crown of Swords ◆ 1996
8. The Path of Daggers ◆ 1998
9. Winter's Heart ◆ 2000
10. Crossroads of Twilight ◆ 2003
11. Knife of Dreams ◆ 2005

THE WHEEL OF TIME (RELATED BOOKS)

Jordan, Robert

STARSCAPE ◆ GRADES 7–10 ◆ A/R

FANTASY

These books from the original series are revised to be accessible to a younger audience.

1. From the Two Rivers: The Eye of the World, Book One ◆ 2002
2. To the Blight: Part Two of The Eye of the World ◆ 2002
3. The Hunt Begins: The Great Hunt, Part 1 ◆ 2003
4. New Threads in the Pattern: The Great Hunt, Part 2 ◆ 2003

WHISPERING BROOK

Bender, Carrie

HERALD PRESS ◆ GRADES 6–9

FAMILY LIFE | REAL LIFE

The Petersheims are a large Amish family living on several farms in Lancaster County, Pennsylvania. These books focus on the struggles of different family members. In *Hemlock Hill Hideaway,* Omar and his sister work on the farm and make a home for a difficult child named Dannie. These stories provide insights into the Amish world.

1. Whispering Brook Farm ◆ 1999
2. Summerville Days ◆ 1999
3. Hemlock Hill Hideaway ◆ 2000
4. Chestnut Ridge Acres ◆ 2001
5. Woodland Dell's Secret ◆ 2002
6. Timber Lane Cove ◆ 2003

WHITE MANE KIDS

Various authors

WHITE MANE PUBLISHING ◆ GRADES 6–10

HISTORICAL

All of these books feature characters caught up in the Civil War. In *Ghosts of Vicksburg,* Jamie Carswell is fighting in Mississippi with the 14th Wisconsin regiment. Jamie used to visit his cousins there, but their home has been destroyed. His cousins are in Vicksburg and face more destruction, which leads Jamie to question his role in the conflict. These are fast-paced books that should interest fans of this era.

1. The Secret of the Lion's Head (Hall, Beverly B.) ◆ 1995
2. The Night Riders of Harper's Ferry (Ernst, Kathleen) ◆ 1996
3. Broken Drum (Hemingway, Edith Morris) ◆ 1996
4. Brothers at War (Blair, Margaret Whitman) ◆ 1996
5. The Bravest Girl in Sharpsburg (Ernst, Kathleen) ◆ 1997
6. Shenandoah Autumn (Joslyn, Mauriel) ◆ 1998
7. House of Spies: Danger in Civil War Washington (Blair, Margaret Whitman) ◆ 1999
8. Rebel Hart (Hemingway, Edith Morris) ◆ 1999
9. Retreat from Gettysburg (Ernst, Kathleen) ◆ 2000
10. Freedom Calls (Sawyer, Kem Knapp) ◆ 2001
11. Hayfoot, Strawfoot: The Bucktail Recruits (Robertson, William P.) ◆ 2001
12. The Bucktails' Shenandoah March (Robertson, William P.) ◆ 2002
13. Ghosts of Vicksburg (Ernst, Kathleen) ◆ 2003
14. The Bucktails' Antietam Trials (Robertson, William P.) ◆ 2004
15. Anybody's Hero: The Battle of Old Men and Young Boys (Haislip, Phyllis Hall) ◆ 2004
16. The Battling Bucktails at Fredericksburg (Robertson, William P.) ◆ 2004
17. The Sand Castle: Blockade Running and the Battle of Fort Fisher (Blair, Margaret Whitman) ◆ 2004

WHY ME?

Kent, Deborah
SIMON & SCHUSTER ◆ GRADES 6–9 ◆ A/R
REAL LIFE

Teens coping with illness and injury are the focus of this trilogy featuring unrelated characters. In the first book, 15-year-old Chloe comes down with lupus and retreats from her everyday life and her boyfriend. In *Living with a Secret,* Cassie tries to hide her diabetes. And in *Don't Cry for Yesterday,* Amber's spinal cord is severed when the car driven by her date crashes. Fans of Lurlene McDaniel will enjoy these stories.

1. The Courage to Live ◆ 2001
2. Living with a Secret ◆ 2001
3. Don't Cry for Yesterday ◆ 2002

WICKED

Holder, Nancy, and Debbie Viguie
SIMON & SCHUSTER ◆ GRADES 9–12 ◆ A/R
FANTASY

When her parents die, 16-year-old Holly Cathers goes to live with her twin cousins Amanda and Nicole and their mother. Holly soon discovers that she and her cousins have magical powers. Her life becomes more complicated when she falls in love with Jer Deveraux, whose family are warlocks with a longstanding grudge against her own relatives. As the series progresses, Holly and her cousins must rescue each other, Jer, and relatives from dangerous situations.

1. Witch ◆ 2002
2. Curse ◆ 2002
3. Legacy ◆ 2003
4. Spellbound ◆ 2003

WICKED DEAD

Petrucha, Stefan, and Thomas Pendleton
HARPERTEEN ◆ GRADES 10–12 ◆ A/R
HORROR

Four dead girls are trapped in an abandoned orphanage. Daphne, Shirley, Mary, and Anne tell stories often involving violence and death. The ghost girls are always aware that the "Headmistress" is nearby. In *Lurker,* Mandy connects with a hunky guy on the Internet. Mandy is cautious, remembering that a classmate was brutally killed; still, this guy seems so hot. Like the books of Christopher Pike and R. L. Stine, there are surprises and cliffhangers that will leave the reader breathless. There is an official Web site at wickeddead.com.

1. Lurker ◆ 2007
2. Torn ◆ 2007
3. Snared ◆ 2008
4. Crush ◆ 2008
5. Prey ◆ 2008
6. Skin ◆ 2008

WILD AT HEART

Anderson, Laurie Halse
PLEASANT COMPANY ◆ GRADES 4–7 ◆ A/R
REAL LIFE

Animal lovers will love this series. At the Wild at Heart Animal Clinic, animals are cared for and protected. Maggie, 13, lives with her grandmother who is a vet at the clinic. She resents having to train some new volunteers but she appreciates their help when animals are found in abusive situations. Issues such as animal testing and cruelty to pets are explored. In 2007 and 2008, this series was being re-released with new covers under the series title Vet Volunteers.

1. Fight for Life: Book 1: Maggie ◆ 2000
2. Homeless: Book 2: Sunita ◆ 2000
3. Trickster: Book 3: David ◆ 2000
4. Manatee Blues: Book 4: Brenna ◆ 2000
5. Say Good-Bye: Book 5: Zoe ◆ 2001
6. Storm Rescue: Book 6: Sunita ◆ 2001
7. Teacher's Pet: Book 7: Maggie ◆ 2001
8. Trapped: Book 8: Brenna ◆ 2001
9. Fear of Falling: Book 9: David ◆ 2001
10. Time to Fly: Book 10: Zoe ◆ 2002
11. Masks: Book 11: Sunita ◆ 2002
12. End of the Race: Book 12: Maggie ◆ 2003

WILD ROSE INN

Armstrong, Jennifer
BANTAM ◆ GRADES 6–10
FAMILY LIFE | HISTORICAL

This series follows six generations of young women who have ties to an inn in Marblehead, Massachusetts. In the first book, Bridie comes from Scotland to join her parents in the New World and discovers that she must hide her beliefs in the Puritan community. In the second book, Ann is torn between love for her country and her attraction for a British sailor.

1. Bridie of the Wild Rose Inn, 1695 ◆ 1994
2. Ann of the Wild Rose Inn, 1774 ◆ 1994
3. Emily of the Wild Rose Inn, 1858 ◆ 1994
4. Laura of the Wild Rose Inn, 1898 ◆ 1994
5. Claire of the Wild Rose Inn, 1928 ◆ 1994
6. Grace of the Wild Rose Inn, 1944 ◆ 1994

WILLY FREEMAN *see* Arabus Family Saga

WIMPY KID *see* Diary of a Wimpy Kid

THE WIND OF FIRE

Nicholson, William

HYPERION ◆ **GRADES 5–8** ◆ **A/R**

FANTASY

Twins Kestrel and Bowman, born into the regimented society of Amaranth, rebel against the focus on work and order and set off on a quest to find the voice of the Wind Singer, believing this will free their people, the Manth. In the third book, the siblings lead the Manth on a dangerous journey to a new homeland.

1. The Wind Singer: An Adventure ◆ 2001
2. Slaves of the Mastery ◆ 2001
3. Firesong ◆ 2002

WINDS OF LIGHT

Brouwer, Sigmund

VICTOR BOOKS ◆ **GRADES 6–8** ◆ **A/R**

FANTASY | HISTORICAL | VALUES

As an orphan in the 1300s, Thomas must search for his rightful place. Leaving the monks who raised him, Thomas struggles to regain Magnus, an English manor that has been taken from its owners. He encounters a dangerous conspiracy and he comes to realize that it is God's power, not his own anger and violence, that will restore the manor. Thomas's efforts are aided by Katherine, who loves him, and by Sir William, who had escaped the brutality of the conquest of Magnus. Once established as Thomas of Magnus, there are other tests to Thomas's faith. Evil within the leadership of the church threatens Thomas. He is enticed by a group of sorcerers to abandon his faith and enter their false world. The drama of this historical fiction series is supported by the dedication to Christian values.

1. Wings of an Angel ◆ 1992
2. Barbarians from the Isle ◆ 1992
3. Legend of Burning Water ◆ 1992
4. The Forsaken Crusade ◆ 1992
5. A City of Dreams ◆ 1993
6. Merlin's Destiny ◆ 1993
7. The Jester's Quest ◆ 1994
8. Dance of Darkness ◆ 1997

WINNIE PERRY

Myracle, Lauren

DUTTON ◆ GRADES 4–7 ◆ A/R

REAL LIFE

As Winnie Perry celebrates her eleventh birthday (in *Eleven*), she begins a month-by-month account of her life. She makes a new friend (Dinah) and becomes distant from her former best friend (Amanda). The book ends (and the second book begins) as she turns twelve. As Winnie matures, so do the situations that she confronts, including getting her period, her first bra, entering junior high, and her first romance. The books are told in Winnie's voice and tween readers will relate to her everyday struggles and successes.

1. Eleven ◆ 2004
2. Twelve ◆ 2007
3. Thirteen ◆ 2008

WINNIE THE HORSE GENTLER

Mackall, Dandi Daley

TYNDALE KIDS ◆ GRADES 4–8 ◆ A/R

REAL LIFE | VALUES

Although Winnie, 12, can connect with horses, she struggles in her relationships with people. The death of her mother two years ago has left Winnie hurt and afraid. Her father can't seem to settle down and Winnie and her sister have moved five times. Now Winnie has the chance to buy a horse, but her father wants to move again. Winnie's work with horses allows her to open up to God's love and she begins to place her trust in Him.

1. Wild Thing ◆ 2002
2. Eager Star ◆ 2002
3. Bold Beauty ◆ 2002
4. Midnight Mystery ◆ 2002
5. Unhappy Appy ◆ 2003
6. Gift Horse ◆ 2003
7. Friendly Foal ◆ 2004
8. Buckskin Bandit ◆ 2004

WINNING SEASON

Wallace, Rich

VIKING ◆ GRADES 4–7 ◆ A/R

RECREATION

Sports fans, get ready. Here's a new series of books featuring popular sports. In the first book, Manny wants to play football but, because he is small, he spends a lot of time on the bench. Manny hopes to prove that he deserves to play. Basketball is featured in the second book. Jared is a great player with a bad temper. Later books in this quick-read series feature other middle-school boys facing a variety of sports challenges.

1. The Roar of the Crowd ◆ 2004
2. Technical Foul ◆ 2004
3. Fast Company ◆ 2005
4. Double Fake ◆ 2005
5. Emergency Quarterback ◆ 2005
6. Southpaw ◆ 2006
7. Dunk Under Pressure ◆ 2006
8. Takedown ◆ 2006
9. Curveball ◆ 2007
10. Second-String Center ◆ 2007

WISE CHILD

Furlong, Monica

RANDOM HOUSE ◆ GRADES 6–8 ◆ A/R

FANTASY

After the death of her grandmother, Wise Child (who has been abandoned by her parents) struggles to survive in the poverty of her village. She is befriended by Juniper, a witch, who trains her in magic, herbs, and healing. As the series progresses, Wise Child and Juniper are threatened by Wise Child's evil aunt, Meroot, and they begin a quest to Juniper's home kingdom in Cornwall. *Juniper* is a prequel and, sequentially, comes first.

1. Juniper ◆ 1991
2. Wise Child ◆ 1987
3. Colman ◆ 2004

WITCH

McClymer, Kelly

SIMON & SCHUSTER ◆ GRADES 6–9 ◆ A/R

FANTASY

Prudence has it all. She's smart and popular. She's a cheerleader. She is also half witch and half mortal. Now her family is leaving Beverly Hills and moving to Salem, Massachusetts, so Prudence and her brother can attend St. Agatha's Day School for Witches. Prudence starts in the remedial class and has a tutor to help her work on her magic skills. As this series progresses, Prudence improves as a witch—even making the cheer squad—and she develops romantic attachments.

1. The Salem Witch Tryouts ◆ 2006
2. Competition's a Witch ◆ 2007
3. She's a Witch Girl ◆ 2007

WITCH

Naylor, Phyllis Reynolds

DELACORTE ◆ GRADES 5–7 ◆ A/R

HORROR

Lynn is convinced that her neighbor, Mrs. Tuggle, is a witch; but when she and her best friend Mouse try to convince people, no one will listen. Readers will want to keep turning the pages in this suspenseful series as Mrs. Tuggle is overcome, only to return in another form and another way.

1. Witch's Sister ◆ 1975
2. Witch Water ◆ 1977
3. The Witch Herself ◆ 1978
4. The Witch's Eye ◆ 1990
5. Witch Weed ◆ 1992
6. The Witch Returns ◆ 1992

W.I.T.C.H.—ADVENTURES

Kaaberbol, Lene, adapter

HYPERION ◆ GRADES 5–8

FANTASY

Each of these books features one of the W.I.T.C.H. girls and their elemental talents. Irma represents water; Taranee, fire; Cornelia, earth; Hay Lin, air; and Will holds an amulet that allows all the elements to meet and work together. In *The Cruel Empress,* Hay Lin finds a lantern that serves as a portal to a city imprisoned by the Cruel Empress.

1. When Lightning Strikes ◆ 2004
2. Heartbreak Island ◆ 2005
3. Stolen Spring ◆ 2005
4. The Cruel Empress ◆ 2005

W.I.T.C.H.—CHAPTER BOOKS

Various adapters

HYPERION/VOLO ◆ GRADES 5–8 ◆ A/R

FANTASY

Will, Irma, Taranee, Cornelia, and Hay Lin have secret magical powers. They join together to fight the evil of Prince Phobos. Meanwhile, they go to middle school, do homework, and have ups and downs with their friends.

1. The Power of Five (Lenhard, Elizabeth) ◆ 2004
2. The Disappearance (Lenhard, Elizabeth) ◆ 2004
3. Finding Meridian (Lenhard, Elizabeth) ◆ 2004
4. The Fire of Friendship (Lenhard, Elizabeth) ◆ 2004
5. The Last Tear (Lenhard, Elizabeth) ◆ 2004
6. Illusions and Lies (Lenhard, Elizabeth) ◆ 2004
7. The Light of Meridian (Komorn, Julie) ◆ 2004
8. Out of the Dark (Komorn, Julie) ◆ 2004
9. The Four Dragons (Lenhard, Elizabeth) ◆ 2004
10. A Bridge Between Worlds (Lenhard, Elizabeth) ◆ 2004
11. The Crown of Light (Lenhard, Elizabeth) ◆ 2004
12. The Return of a Queen (Lenhard, Elizabeth) ◆ 2005
13. A Different Path (Lenhard, Elizabeth) ◆ 2005
14. Worlds Apart (Egan, Kate) ◆ 2005
15. The Courage to Choose (Egan, Kate) ◆ 2005
16. Path of Revenge (Egan, Kate) ◆ 2005
17. The Darkest Dream (Egan, Kate) ◆ 2005
18. Keeping Hope (Egan, Kate) ◆ 2005
19. The Other Truth (Alfonsi, Alice) ◆ 2006
20. Whispers of Doubt (Alfonsi, Alice) ◆ 2006
21. A Weakened Heart (Alfonsi, Alice) ◆ 2006
22. A Choice Is Made (Alfonsi, Alice) ◆ 2006
23. Farewell to Move (Alfonsi, Alice) ◆ 2006
24. Trust Your Heart (Alfonsi, Alice) ◆ 2006
25. Enchanted Waters (Alfonsi, Alice) ◆ 2006
26. Friends Forever (Alfonsi, Alice) ◆ 2006

W.I.T.C.H.—GRAPHIC NOVELS

Author Not Available

HYPERION ◆ GRADES 5–8

FANTASY

The five girls from the W.I.T.C.H. books are featured in these graphic novels. Will, Irma, Taranee, Cornelia, and Hay Lin work as a team to fight evil and protect the Veil—the boundary between good and evil. Full-color art will attract many readers.

1. The Power of Friendship ◆ 2005
2. Meridian Magic ◆ 2005
3. The Revealing ◆ 2005
4. Between Light and Dark ◆ 2006
5. Legends Revealed ◆ 2006
6. Forces of Change ◆ 2006
7. Under Pressure ◆ 2007
8. An Unexpected Return ◆ 2007

WITCH CHILD

Rees, Celia

CANDLEWICK ◆ GRADES 8–12 ◆ A/R

FANTASY

In 1659, Mary Newbury, 14, watched as her grandmother was hung for being a witch. Mary must hide her own skills as a healer or she will suffer the same fate. She leaves England and journeys to America but she faces the suspicion of the villagers there, especially the minister who condemned her grandmother. Mary's story is told through journal entries that capture the dramatic action. The second book is set in modern times as Agnes Herne explores her connection to Mary and to her Native American beliefs.

1. Witch Child ◆ 2002
2. Sorceress ◆ 2003

WITCH SEASON

Mariotte, Jeff

SIMON & SCHUSTER ◆ GRADES 9–12 ◆ A/R

FANTASY

Kerry's summer job is at a posh resort in California. She shares a residence with other teens working there. Daniel Blessing, a young man with a mysterious past, arrives and Kerry is attracted to him. However, his past catches up with him in the form of Season Howe, a witch. Daniel is killed and Kerry struggles to understand the evil that destroyed him.

1. Summer ◆ 2004
2. Fall ◆ 2004
3. Winter ◆ 2005
4. Spring ◆ 2005

A WIZARD IN RHYME

Stasheff, Christopher

BALLANTINE ◆ GRADES 10–12

FANTASY

Matt is transported to a land called Merovence while reading a poem. There he helps Princess Alisande to regain her throne and is instrumental in removing other threats, including that of a ruthless khan in *The Crusading Wizard*.

> 1. Her Majesty's Wizard ◆ 1986
> 2. The Oathbound Wizard ◆ 1993
> 3. The Witch Doctor ◆ 1994
> 4. The Secular Wizard ◆ 1994
> 5. My Son the Wizard ◆ 1997
> 6. The Haunted Wizard ◆ 2000
> 7. The Crusading Wizard ◆ 2000
> 8. The Feline Wizard ◆ 2000
> 9. A Wizard in a Feud ◆ 2001

WIZARD OF OZ *see* Oz

WIZARDRY

Cook, Rick

BAEN ◆ GRADES 7–12

FANTASY

Wiz Zumwalt, a computer programmer and wizard, finds his high-tech skills in demand. He programs demons, battles dark forces, and is kidnapped by dragons.

> 1. Wizard's Bane ◆ 1989
> 2. Wizardry Compiled ◆ 1990
> 3. Wizardry Cursed ◆ 1991

WIZARDRY

Duane, Diane

HARCOURT ◆ GRADES 5–8 ◆ A/R

ADVENTURE | FANTASY

Nita is a 13-year-old girl tormented by bullies because she chooses not to fight back. While hiding in the local library, she discovers a book of instructions in the ancient art of wizardry. She meets Kit, a boy who is also a beginning wizard, and together they go on their first quest: to find the book that holds the key to preserving the universe. In the companion books, Nita and Kit go on other adventures: becoming whales to conquer the evil Lone Power in the deepest part of the Atlantic Ocean, cloning a computer and helping Nita's sister travel through several worlds in outer space, and becoming entangled in a magic battle in Ireland. With the popularity of fantasy books, this series has been reissued and expanded.

1. So You Want to be a Wizard ◆ 1983
2. Deep Wizardry ◆ 1985
3. High Wizardry ◆ 1989
4. A Wizard Abroad ◆ 1993
5. The Wizard's Dilemma ◆ 2001
6. A Wizard Alone ◆ 2002
7. Wizard's Holiday ◆ 2003
8. Wizards at War ◆ 2005

WODAN'S CHILDREN

Paxson, Diana L.

MORROW ◆ GRADES 10–12

FANTASY

The story of Siegfried and Brunhilde is retold in this trilogy set on the Rhine in the fifth century.

1. The Wolf and the Raven ◆ 1993
2. The Dragons of the Rhine ◆ 1995
3. The Lord of Horses ◆ 1996

WOLFBAY WINGS

Brooks, Bruce

HARPERCOLLINS ◆ GRADES 4–8 ◆ A/R

REAL LIFE | RECREATION

The Wolfbay Wings are a Squirt A ice hockey team that has become very successful. Unfortunately, a new coach and new players make the future uncertain. Each book in this series features a different player. Dixon "Woodsie" Woods is 11 years old and is worried about the team's prospects. William Fowler, "Billy," is only 10, and he is bothered by his teammates, Coach Cooper, and his overbearing father. There are statistics about the featured player on the back of each book and a tear-out sports card in the front. With lots of details about hockey and ample action, this should be a good choice for sports fans.

1. Woodsie ◆ 1997
2. Zip ◆ 1997

3. Cody ◆ 1997

4. Boot ◆ 1998

5. Prince ◆ 1998

6. Shark ◆ 1998

7. Billy ◆ 1998

8. Dooby ◆ 1998

9. Reed ◆ 1998

10. Subtle ◆ 1999

11. Barry ◆ 1999

12. Woodsie, Again ◆ 1999

WOLVES CHRONICLES

Aiken, Joan

DELACORTE; BANTAM ◆ GRADES 4–8 ◆ A/R

ADVENTURE | FANTASY

High melodrama and an "unhistorical" setting mark this loosely connected series. In the England of this alternate world, King James III rules, Hanoverians are constantly plotting to put Prince George on the throne, and packs of vicious wolves menace the countryside. The Wolves Chronicles begin with the story of two little girls who are left in the care of an evil woman who schemes to take their inheritance. The girls are rescued by the mysterious orphan boy Simon, who later in the series is revealed to be a duke. Simon befriends a Cockney girl, Dido, whose parents are evil Hanoverians, and the rest of the series is about their adventures, by themselves and with other friends, as they defend the true king.

1. The Wolves of Willoughby Chase ◆ 1963

2. Black Hearts in Battersea ◆ 1964

3. Nightbirds on Nantucket ◆ 1966

4. The Whispering Mountain ◆ 1968

5. The Cuckoo Tree ◆ 1971

6. The Stolen Lake ◆ 1981

7. Dido and Pa ◆ 1986

8. Is Underground ◆ 1993

9. Cold Shoulder Road ◆ 1996

10. Dangerous Games ◆ 2000

11. Midwinter Nightingale ◆ 2003

12. Witch of Clatteringshaws ◆ 2005

THE WORD AND THE VOID

Brooks, Terry

BALLANTINE DEL REY ◆ **GRADES 10–12** ◆ **A/R**

FANTASY

Nest Freemark, a 14-year-old with inherited magical powers, finds herself in the middle of a struggle between Knight of the Word John Ross and a force known as the Void. By the last book in the trilogy, Nest is 29 and she and John must fight evil once more.

1. Running with the Demon ◆ 1997
2. A Knight of the Word ◆ 1998
3. Angel Fire East ◆ 1999

WORLD WAR

Turtledove, Harry

BALLANTINE DEL REY ◆ **GRADES 9–12**

SCIENCE FICTION

In the midst of World War II, lizard-like aliens invade Earth. They seek total control. Their arrival adds to the general turmoil, and strange alliances are created. This series is linked to Turtledove's later Colonization series, in which the aliens' colonization fleet turns up.

1. World War: In the Balance ◆ 1994
2. World War: Tilting the Balance ◆ 1995
3. World War: Upsetting the Balance ◆ 1996
4. World War: Striking the Balance ◆ 1996

WORLDWEAVERS

Alexander, Alma

EOS ◆ **GRADES 7–10** ◆ **A/R**

FANTASY

Thea is the seventh child of parents who were both seventh children and she is expected to develop powerful magical abilities. When she does not, she is sent to Grandma Spider, who helps her realize her gift as a world-weaver—one who can weave dreams and stories. Thea goes to the Wand-less Academy for more training, a school that depends on computers and is supposed to be protected from spells. In *Spellspam,* someone is using the computers to send emails that attack the opener.

1. Gift of the Unmage ◆ 2007
2. Spellspam ◆ 2008
3. Cybermage ◆ 2009

WORMLING

Jenkins, Jerry B., and Chris Fabry

TYNDALE HOUSE ◆ GRADES 5–8 ◆ A/R

FANTASY

Owen Reeder has always seemed ordinary. Then he enters another world—the Lowlands—and joins with Watcher in the search for the King's son. Facing many threats, including the evil Dragon, Owen accepts his role as the Wormling. Christian imagery and beliefs permeate this series for middle school readers.

1. The Book of the King ◆ 2007
2. The Sword of the Wormling ◆ 2007
3. The Changeling ◆ 2007
4. The Minions of Time ◆ 2008
5. The Author's Blood ◆ 2008

WREN

Smith, Sherwood

HARCOURT ◆ GRADES 4–7 ◆ A/R

ADVENTURE | FANTASY

While living in an orphanage, Wren's friend Tess finds out that she is really Princess Teressa. This discovery changes the lives of both girls permanently. Along with their friends Tyron and Prince Connor, they battle the evil forces of King Andreus. The four friends learn to master the power of magic and use it only for the greater good.

1. Wren to the Rescue ◆ 1990
2. Wren's Quest ◆ 1993
3. Wren's War ◆ 1995

WRIGHT AND WONG

Burns, Laura J., and Melinda Metz

RAZORBILL; PENGUIN ◆ GRADES 5–8 ◆ A/R

MYSTERY

Lively seventh-grade extrovert Agatha Wong and her friend Orville Wright, who has Asperger's syndrome and greatly prefers peace and quiet, are close despite their differences, and together they investigate mysteries.

    1. The Case of the Prank That Stank ◆ 2005
    2. The Case of the Nana-napper ◆ 2005
    3. The Case of the Trail Mix-up ◆ 2005
    4. The Case of the Slippery Soap Star ◆ 2006

X FILES

Various authors
HARPERCOLLINS ◆ GRADES 5–10 ◆ A/R
FANTASY | HORROR

Terror in the forest, dying teenagers, a serial killer, a dead alligator man at the circus, and extraterrestrial entities—these are just a few of the problems investigated by Agents Mulder and Scully. Fans of the television program will flock to this series, which is based on teleplays of specific episodes. Like the show, these books are gritty and grim, with enough twists in the plot to leave you wondering what is really true. There are many different X Files books, including ones for young adult and adult readers.

X FILES (GRADES 5–8)

    1. X Marks the Spot (Martin, Les) ◆ 1995
    2. Darkness Falls (Martin, Les) ◆ 1995
    3. Tiger, Tiger (Martin, Les) ◆ 1995
    4. Squeeze (Steiber, Ellen) ◆ 1996
    5. Humbug (Martin, Les) ◆ 1996
    6. Shapes (Steiber, Ellen) ◆ 1996
    7. Fear (Martin, Les) ◆ 1996
    8. Voltage (Royce, Easton) ◆ 1996
    9. E.B.E. (Martin, Les) ◆ 1996
  10. Die Bug Die (Martin, Les) ◆ 1997
  11. Ghost in the Machine (Martin, Les) ◆ 1997

X FILES (GRADES 7–10)

    1. The Calusari (Nix, Garth) ◆ 1997
    2. Eve (Steiber, Ellen) ◆ 1997
    3. Bad Sign (Easton, Royce) ◆ 1997
    4. Our Town (Elfman, Eric) ◆ 1997
    5. Empathy (Steiber, Ellen) ◆ 1997
    6. Fresh Bones (Martin, Les) ◆ 1997
    7. Control (Owens, Everett) ◆ 1997
    8. The Host (Martin, Les) ◆ 1997
    9. Hungry Ghosts (Steiber, Ellen) ◆ 1998

10. Dark Matter (Easton, Royce) ◆ 1999
11. Howlers (Owens, Everett) ◆ 1999
12. Grotesque (Steiber, Ellen) ◆ 1999
13. Quarantine (Martin, Les) ◆ 1999
14. Regeneration (Owens, Everett) ◆ 1999
15. Haunted (Steiber, Ellen) ◆ 2000
16. Miracle Man (Bisson, Terry) ◆ 2000

X GAMES XTREME MYSTERIES

Hill, Laban C.
HYPERION ◆ GRADES 4–8
MYSTERY | RECREATION

Fans of the X Games (on ESPN) will enjoy these fast-paced mysteries with in-line skating, snowboarding, wakeboarding, snow mountain biking and other extreme sports. In one mystery, Jamil and his friends are at a mystery party and they investigate the theft of plans for a new wakeboard. In another book, Kevin is almost lost in a man-made avalanche. Other books feature Nat and Wall, who are also part of the Xtreme detectives. Merging sports action with mysteries could attract reluctant readers.

1. Crossed Tracks ◆ 1998
2. Deep Powder, Deep Trouble ◆ 1998
3. Rocked Out: A Summer X Games Special ◆ 1998
4. Half Pipe Rip-Off ◆ 1998
5. Lost Wake ◆ 1998
6. Out of Line ◆ 1998
7. Spiked Snow: A Winter X Games Special ◆ 1999
8. Totally Snowed ◆ 1999

XANTH SAGA

Anthony, Piers
BALLANTINE; TOR ◆ GRADES 10–12 ◆ A/R
FANTASY

Xanth is a magic world where nearly everyone—including ogres, gargoyles, and centaurs—has a special talent. The population of this world has varied adventures and embarks on assorted quests. These books for adults are popular with strong teen readers.

1. A Spell for Chameleon ◆ 1977
2. The Source of Magic ◆ 1979
3. Castle Roogna ◆ 1979
4. Centaur Aisle ◆ 1981
5. Ogre, Ogre ◆ 1982

6. Night Mare ◆ 1982
7. Dragon on a Pedestal ◆ 1983
8. Crewel Lye: A Caustic Yarn ◆ 1985
9. Golem in the Gears ◆ 1986
10. Vale of the Vole ◆ 1987
11. Heaven Cent ◆ 1988
12. Man from Mundania ◆ 1989
13. Isle of View ◆ 1990
14. Question Quest ◆ 1991
15. The Color of Her Panties ◆ 1992
16. Demons Don't Dream ◆ 1993
17. Harpy Thyme ◆ 1994
18. Geis of the Gargoyle ◆ 1995
19. Roc and a Hard Place ◆ 1995
20. Yon Ill Wind ◆ 1996
21. Faun and Games ◆ 1997
22. Zombie Lover ◆ 1998
23. Xone of Contention ◆ 1999
24. The Dastard ◆ 2000
25. Swell Foop ◆ 2001
26. Up in a Heaval ◆ 2002
27. Cube Route ◆ 2003
28. Currant Events ◆ 2004
29. Pet Peeve ◆ 2005
30. Stork Naked ◆ 2006
31. Air Apparent ◆ 2007
32. Two to the Fifth ◆ 2008

XANTHE AND XAVIER *see* "Hour" books

XYZ TRILOGY

Rivers, Karen
RAINCOAST ◆ GRADES 8–10
FANTASY

In each book of this series, ordinary teens develop supernatural powers. Xenos, 17, discovers he can fly; Yale finds she can become invisible; and Zara can read the thoughts of others. While the stories are not linked, teens will be intrigued by the dilemmas in them. Each teen must choose how to use his or her new powers. Yale has always been ignored by the other kids. Now that she can walk among them and listen to their secrets, will she use the information against them?

1. X in Flight ◆ 2007
2. Y in the Shadows ◆ 2008
3. What Z Sees ◆ 2008

YORK TRILOGY

Naylor, Phyllis Reynolds

ATHENEUM; ALADDIN ◆ GRADES 8–10 ◆ A/R

FANTASY

Dan Roberts, 15, is enjoying a vacation in York, England, but he is troubled by his parents' behavior. Why did they take this trip in the middle of the school year? Why are their moods so unpredictable? These questions are overwhelmed by strange experiences that seem to be connected with some mysterious gypsies. Dan travels to the past to try to understand why he is being haunted.

1. Shadows on the Wall ◆ 2001
2. Faces in the Water ◆ 2002
3. Footprints at the Window ◆ 2003

THE YOUNG AMERICANS

Various authors

WHITE MANE PUBLISHING ◆ GRADES 6–8

HISTORICAL

The Civil War comes to life in these well-researched, exciting books. In *Save the Colors,* Charley Olson, 12, joins the First Minnesota Regiment as a drummer boy. His initial battle experience is at First Manassas (Bull Run) and it is frightening. Charley must maintain the cadence for the troops but he is totally unprotected. Readers will gain insight into the impact of war on individuals.

1. Rose at Bull Run: Romance and Realities of First Bull Run (Sappey, Maureen Stack) ◆ 1998
2. Yankee Spy: A Union Girl in Richmond During the Pennisular Campaign (Sappey, Maureen Stack) ◆ 1998
3. Dreams of Ships, Dreams of Julia: At Sea with the Monitor and the Merrimac, Virginia, 1862 (Sappey, Maureen Stack) ◆ 1998
4. Powder Monkey: Battle Between the Merrimac and the Cumberland, Congress, and Monitor, 1862 (Campbell, Carole R.) ◆ 1999
5. Save the Colors: A Civil War Battle Cry (Reisberg, Joanne A.) ◆ 2001

YOUNG BOND

Higson, Charlie

MIRAMAX ◆ GRADES 5–9 ◆ A/R

MYSTERY | ADVENTURE

Before he was 007, he was James Bond, a student at Eton who seemed to attract mysteries and intrigue. In *Blood Fever*, James, 13, is on summer vacation visiting his cousin Victor on the island of Sardinia. There is a theft, a conspiracy, a kidnapping, and a mysterious millionaire. Can James rescue the kidnapped girl and stop the villain? This is an exciting series with many twists and turns.

1. Silverfin ◆ 2005
2. Blood Fever ◆ 2006
3. Double or Die ◆ 2008
4. Hurricane Gold ◆ 2009

YOUNG FOUNDERS

Massie, Elizabeth

TOR ◆ GRADES 8–10 ◆ A/R

HISTORICAL

Each book in this series features a different era in the history of the United States of America. In *1870: Not With Our Blood,* Patrick O'Neill's father dies at Gettysburg and his mother moves the family to New Jersey. Working in the mills is harsh and dangerous and Patrick is drawn to write for a newspaper that exposes the conditions in the factories. Other books examine life at Jamestown, during the American Revolutionary War, and during the Civil War. This series was reissued in 2007.

1. 1870: Not With Our Blood ◆ 2000
2. 1609: Winter of the Dead ◆ 2000
3. 1776: Son of Liberty ◆ 2000
4. 1863: A House Divided ◆ 2000

YOUNG HEROES

Yolen, Jane, and Robert J. Harris

HARPERCOLLINS ◆ GRADES 4–7 ◆ A/R

FANTASY

Tales from mythology are brought to life in spirited renditions that look at heroes' younger years. In the first book, a 13-year-old Odysseus is captured by pirates and joins young prisoners Penelope and Helen in exciting adventures. Twelve-year-old Atalanta and her best friend, a bear, join in the hunt for the creature that killed her father in the third book.

1. Odysseus in the Serpent Maze ◆ 2001
2. Hippolyta and the Curse of the Amazons ◆ 2002
3. Atalanta and the Arcadian Beast ◆ 2003
4. Jason and the Gorgon's Blood ◆ 2004

YOUNG INDIANA JONES CHRONICLES: CHOOSE YOUR OWN ADVENTURE

Brightfield, Richard

BANTAM ◆ GRADES 5–8

ADVENTURE | FANTASY

The series uses the popular Choose Your Own Adventure format in which readers turn to different pages based on what they want to happen. For example, if you decide to go to the party, turn to page 45; if you want to stay in the dorm, turn to page 51. These books feature the popular character of Indiana Jones when he is a young man and place him at the center of events around the world. The popularity of the character and the format should attract reluctant readers.

1. The Valley of the Kings ◆ 1992
2. South of the Border ◆ 1992
3. Revolution in Russia ◆ 1992
4. Masters of the Louvre ◆ 1993
5. African Safari ◆ 1993
6. Behind the Great Wall ◆ 1993
7. The Roaring Twenties ◆ 1993
8. The Irish Rebellion ◆ 1993

YOUNG JEDI KNIGHTS *see* Star Wars Young Jedi Knights

YOUNG ROYALS

Meyer, Carolyn

HARCOURT ◆ GRADES 6–9 ◆ A/R

HISTORICAL

This series looks at the dramatic youths of four royal women of the 16th century: Queen Mary I, Queen Elizabeth I, Anne Boleyn, and Catherine of Aragon.

1. Mary, Bloody Mary ◆ 1999
2. Beware, Princess Elizabeth ◆ 2001
3. Doomed Queen Anne ◆ 2002
4. Patience, Princess Catherine ◆ 2004

THE YOUNG UNDERGROUND

Elmer, Robert

BETHANY HOUSE ◆ GRADES 5–8 ◆ A/R

HISTORICAL

Peter and Elise Andersen are 11-year-old twins involved in the Resistance in Denmark during World War II. They help their Jewish friend, Henrik, escape to Sweden and then help an injured RAF pilot. By the end of the series, the twins are 14 and try to stop a plot against a group of Jews traveling to Israel.

1. A Way Through the Sea ◆ 1994
2. Beyond the River ◆ 1994
3. Into the Flames ◆ 1995
4. Far From the Storm ◆ 1995
5. Chasing the Wind ◆ 1996
6. A Light in the Castle ◆ 1996
7. Follow the Star ◆ 1996
8. Touch the Sky ◆ 1997

YOU'RE THE ONE

Lantz, Francess

ALADDIN ◆ GRADES 6–9 ◆ A/R

REAL LIFE

In *A Royal Kiss,* Samantha, 14, meets a prince and they fall in love. They manage to stay out of the limelight until the press finds out about their relationship. Just when it looks as if Samantha will lose Prince Sebastian, her mother comes to the rescue. Fans of improbable "girl gets the great guy" romances will enjoy this series.

1. Sing Me a Love Song ◆ 2000
2. A Royal Kiss ◆ 2000
3. Lights, Camera, Love! ◆ 2000

YURT

Brittain, C. Dale

SIMON & SCHUSTER ◆ GRADES 9–12

FANTASY

Daimbert is the wizard to the King of Yurt. As such, he faces all manner of unusual situations. There's a plague of horned rabbits, a zombie creature, a blue djinn, black magic, and more. Readers who like humor and fantasy will enjoy these books.

1. A Bad Spell in Yurt ◆ 1991
2. The Wood Nymph and the Cranky Saint ◆ 1993
3. Mage Quest ◆ 1993
4. The Witch and the Cathedral ◆ 1995
5. Daughter of Magic ◆ 1996
6. Is This Apocalypse Necessary? ◆ 2000

ZACK FREEMAN *see* Butt Wars

ZENDA

Petti, Ken, and John Amodeo
GROSSET & DUNLAP ◆ GRADES 4–7 ◆ A/R
FANTASY

On Azureblue, gazing balls reveal 13 messages that tell the destiny of each child. Unfortunately for Zenda, the balls are not used until a child is 12 ½ years old. But Zenda can't wait. When she takes her gazing ball too soon, it breaks. Now she must recover the 13 pieces.

1. Zenda and the Gazing Ball ◆ 2004
2. A New Dimension ◆ 2004
3. The Crystal Planet ◆ 2004
4. Lost on Aquaria ◆ 2004
5. The Impossible Butterfly ◆ 2004
6. A Test of Mirrors ◆ 2004
7. The Astral Summer ◆ 2005
8. A Light from Within ◆ 2005
9. Trapped in Time ◆ 2008

ZODIAC GIRLS

Hopkins, Cathy
KINGFISHER ◆ GRADES 6–9 ◆ A/R
REAL LIFE

Do know your astrological sign? Each book in this series features a girl with a different sign—Gemma is a Gemini; Danu is a Sagittarius. Each girl has problems—Gemma is at a new boarding school while Danu has gone from being a good student to one who is struggling. And each girl becomes a Zodiac Girl—for one month, her planets will allign and she will receive help with her problems from unexpected sources, like Greek gods and goddesses in everyday roles, such as Venus as a beautician. This is fun fiction from the author of the Mates, Dates books.

1. From Geek to Goddess ◆ 2007
2. Recipe for Rebellion ◆ 2007
3. Discount Diva ◆ 2007
4. Brat Princess ◆ 2007
5. Star Child ◆ 2008

ZOEY 101

Various authors

SCHOLASTIC ◆ GRADES 5–7 ◆ A/R

REAL LIFE

Zoey 101 was a television series on Nickelodeon. This series parallels some of the episodes in the program. In *Girls Got Game!*, Zoey arrives at Pacific Coast Academy, a boarding school that is accepting girls for the first time. Zoey is in Room 101 and she meets her new roommate, finds a new group of friends, and tries out for the basketball team. Many books feature opportunities for the girls to socialize with boys—a beach party, spring break, and the election for class president. This should be popular with tween readers.

1. Girls Got Game! (Mason, Jane B., and Sarah Hines Stephens) ◆ 2005
2. Dramarama (Mason, Jane B., and Sarah Hines Stephens) ◆ 2005
3. Pranks for Nothing! (Reisfeld, Randi) ◆ 2006
4. Beach Party (Mason, Jane B.) ◆ 2006
5. Back to Normal (Mason, Jane B.) ◆ 2006
6. Spring Break-Up (Mason, Jane B.) ◆ 2006
7. Lights Out! (Simpson, Fiona) ◆ 2006
8. Girls vs. Boys (Mason, Jane B., and Sarah Hines Stephens) ◆ 2007
9. A Quinn in Need (Mason, Jane B.) ◆ 2007
10. The Curse of PCA (Mason, Jane B., and Sarah Hines Stephens) ◆ 2007

ZORRO GRAPHIC NOVELS

McGregor, Don

PAPERCUTZ ◆ GRADES 6–10

ADVENTURE

The popular legend of Zorro continues in these graphic novels, which tie in with the Antonio Banderas motion picture. With the beautiful but scarred Eulalia Bandini, Zorro is on the run from Captain Monasterio. Lots of action and color illustrations with sharp angles will attract reluctant readers.

1. Scars! ◆ 2005
2. Drownings! ◆ 2006
3. Vultures! ◆ 2006

APPENDIXES
AND
INDEXES

BOOKS FOR BOYS

These series were selected for their appeal to boys.

Adam Pelko
Adventures of a Young Sailor
Alden All Stars
Alex Rider
Animorphs
Animorphs: Alternamorphs
Animorphs: Animorph Chronicles
Animorphs: Megamorphs
Anthony Monday
Avatar: The Earth Kingdom
  Chronicles
Avatar: The Last Airbender
Avatar Graphic Novels
Baseball Card Adventures
Bingo Brown
Black Book (Diary of a Teenage
  Stud)
Black Stallion
Blue Avenger
Blue-Eyed Son Trilogy
Brian Robeson
Bruno and Boots
Butt Wars
CHERUB
Chip Hilton Sports Series
Chronicles of Courage
Cirque du Freak
Concrete
The Contender
Danny Watts
The Diamond Brothers
Danger Boy
Diary of a Wimpy Kid
Don't Get Caught
Don't Touch That Remote!
Drift X
Everest
Extreme Team
Fear Street
Fear Street: Fear Street
  Cheerleaders

Fear Street: Fear Street Sagas
Fear Street: Fear Street Seniors
Fear Street: Fear Street Super
  Chillers
Fear Street: Ghosts of Fear Street
Fear Street: 99 Fear Street
Fireball
The Gatekeepers
Goosebumps
Goosebumps: Give Yourself
  Goosebumps
Goosebumps Graphix
Goosebumps Horrorland
Goosebumps Series 2000
Gordy Smith
Graveyard School
Guy Strang
Hardy Boys
Hardy Boys Casefiles
Hardy Boys, Undercover Brothers
Hardy Boys, Undercover Brothers:
  Graphic Novels
He-Man Women Haters Club
Help! I'm Trapped
High Seas Trilogy
Hover Car Racer
Impact Zone
Jack Henry
James Budd
The Jersey
Joey Pigza
Johnny Dixon
Journey of Allen Strange
Jumper
Lewis Barnavelt
M. T. Anderson's Thrilling Tales
The Magickers
Mars Year One
Matt Christopher's Sports Stories
Mike Pillsbury
Misery Guts

Misfits, Inc.
Mummy Chronicles
My Side of the Mountain
Mystic Knights of Tir Na Nog
Nancy Drew and the Hardy Boys
  Super Mysteries
NASCAR Pole Position
  Adventures
Net Force
NFL Monday Night Football Club
Norby
Nose
Outcast
Outernet
Pendragon
Perry Skky Jr.
Richard Steele Trilogy
Riot Brothers
Rookies
Slapshots
Slimeballs
Sports Mystery
SpyBoy
Sword of the Spirits
Take It to the Xtreme
Tales of Gom in the Legends of
  Ulm
Three Investigators
Tom Swift
Tom Swift, Young Inventor
Tripods
The Tucket Adventures
Underwhere
The Viking
Walker and Tag
White Mane Kids
Winning Season
Wolfbay Wings
X Games Xtreme Mysteries
The Young Americans
Young Bond

BOOKS FOR GIRLS

These series were selected for their appeal to girls.

A-List
Abby's South Seas Adventures
Al (Alexandra)
Alice
The Alphabetical Hookup List
  Trilogy
Amelia
American Dreams (Avon)
American Girls: Girls of Many
  Lands
American Girls: History Mysteries
Angels Unlimited
The Ashleys
Au Pairs
Avalon 1: Web of Magic
Avalon 2: Quest for Magic
Avonlea
Babes
Baby-Sitters Club
Baby-Sitters Club Friends Forever
Baby-Sitters Club Graphic Novels
Baby-Sitters Club Mysteries
Baby-Sitters Club Portrait
  Collection
Baby-Sitters Club Super Specials
Bad Girls
Beacon Street Girls
Black Stallion: Young Black
  Stallion
Boston Jane
Bratz
Brides of Wildcat County
Brio Girls
The Broadway Ballplayers
B.Y. Times
California Diaries
Camp Confidential
Celebutantes
Cheer Squad
Cheer Usa!
Cheerleaders

Cheetah Girls
Chestnut Hill
Chicks with Sticks
Christy
Christy Miller
Christy Miller: Christy and Todd:
  The College Years
Class Secrets
Clearwater Crossing
Clique
Clueless
The Complicated Life of Claudia
  Cristina Cortez
Confessions of a Teen Nanny
Confessions of a Teenage Drama
  Queen
Confessions of Georgia Nicolson
Date Him or Dump Him?
Dear Dumb Diary
Del Rio Bay Clique
Diary of a Crush
Diary of a Teenage Girl
The Divas
The Double Dutch Club
Egerton Hall Novels
The Elliott Cousins
Enchanted Hearts
Fab 5
Fabulous Five
The Fashion-Forward Adventures
  of Imogene
Fat Glenda
Flirt
Friends for a Season
The Friendship Ring
From the Files of Madison Finn
Generation Girl
Gilmore Girls
Girl
The Girls Quartet
Girls R.U.L.E.

Goddesses
Golden Filly Series
Gossip Girl
Heart Beats
Heartland
High School Musical Stories from
  East High
Holly's Heart
Hollywood Sisters
Hotlanta
How I Survived Middle School
I "Heart" Bikinis
Inside Girl
Internet Girls
Interns
The It Girl
Jennie McGrady Mysteries
Jessica Darling
Julep O'Toole
Kimani Tru
Kyla May Miss. Behaves
LBD (Les Bambinos Dangereuses)
Liberty Letters
Life at Sixteen
Lizzie McGuire
Lizzie McGuire Mysteries
Lizzie McGuire (Tokyopop)
Love Stories
Love Stories: Brothers Trilogy
Love Stories: His. Hers. Theirs
Love Stories: Prom Trilogy
Love Stories: Super Editions
Love Stories: Year Abroad
Love Trilogy
Ludell
Luna Bay
The Luxe
Magic in Manhattan
Maizon
Making Out
Making Waves

Mary-Kate and Ashley: Adventures of Mary-Kate and Ashley
Mary-Kate and Ashley: Graduation Summer
Mary-Kate and Ashley: So Little Time
Mary-Kate and Ashley: Two of a Kind
Mary-Kate and Ashley in Action
Mary-Kate and Ashley Starring In . . .
Mary-Kate and Ashley Sweet 16
Mates, Dates, and. . .
Mirror Image
Moesha
Mustang Mountain
Nancy Drew
Nancy Drew: Girl Detective
Nancy Drew and the Hardy Boys Super Mysteries
Nancy Drew Files
Nancy Drew Graphic Novels
Nancy Drew on Campus
Nannies
No Secrets: The Story of a Girl Band
Non-Blonde Cheerleader
Not Just Proms and Parties
Once Upon a Prom
1-800-Where-R-You
Pacific Cascades University
Pageant
Paxton Cheerleaders
Payton Skky

Princess Diaries
Private
Project Fashion
The Real Deal
The Rhianna Chronicles
Royal Ballet School Diaries
Saddle Club: Pine Hollow
Saddle Island
Saddles, Stars, and Stripes
Sandy Lane Stables
Secret Refuge
Seven Deadly Sins
Shopaholic
Silver Creek Riders
Sisterhood of the Traveling Pants
Sisters
Sisters of Isis
Spy Girls
Star Power
Star Sisterz
Starlet
Sterling Family
Students Across the Seven Seas
Summer
Summer Boys
Summer Share
Sunset Island
Sweet Dreams
Sweet Dreams: On Our Own
Sweet 16
Sweet Valley High
Sweet Valley High Senior Year
Sweet Valley Junior High

Sweet Valley Twins
Sweet Valley Twins Super Chiller Editions
Sweet Valley Twins Super Editions
Sweet Valley University
Sweet Valley University: Elizabeth
Sweet Valley University Thriller Editions
T*Witches
Talent
Tarragon Island
Teen Angels
10th Grade Social Climber
Thoroughbred
Thoroughbred: Ashleigh
Thoroughbred: Ashleigh's Collection
Three Girls in the City
True Colors
Truth or Dare
Turning Seventeen
The Twilight Saga
Uglies
Undercover Girl
Violet
The Wedding Planner's Daughter
Wild at Heart
Winnie Perry
W.I.T.C.H.—Adventures
W.I.T.C.H.—Chapter Books
W.I.T.C.H.—Graphic Novels
You're the One
Zodiac Girls
Zoey 101

BOOKS FOR RELUCTANT READERS

These series were selected as those that would have the most appeal to reluctant readers.

Adventures of Daniel Boom aka
  Loud Boy
The Adventures of Uncle Stinky
Akiko
Alden All Stars
Alex Rider
Alexander Cold and Nadia Santos
Angel
Angel (Graphic Novels)
Angels Unlimited
Animorphs
Animorphs: Alternamorphs
Animorphs: Animorph Chronicles
Animorphs: Megamorphs
Are You Afraid of the Dark?
Baby-Sitter
Baby-Sitters Club
Baby-Sitters Club Friends Forever
Baby-Sitters Club Graphic Novels
Baby-Sitters Club Mysteries
Baby-Sitters Club Portrait
  Collection
Baby-Sitters Club Super Specials
Beacon Street Girls
Beverly Hills, 90210
Bionicle Adventures
Bionicle Chronicles
Bionicle Legends
Bloodwater Mysteries
Bluford High
Bone Chillers
Bratz
Bratz! Clued In
Bratz! Lil' Bratz
Brian Robeson
Bruno and Boots
Buffy the Vampire Slayer
  (Archway/Pocket)
Buffy the Vampire Slayer (Dark
  Horse)

Buffy the Vampire Slayer: Buffy
  and Angel
Buffy the Vampire Slayer: Buffy
  and Angel: The Unseen Trilogy
Buffy the Vampire Slayer: Stake
  Your Destiny
Buffy the Vampire Slayer: The
  Angel Chronicles
Buffy the Vampire Slayer: The
  Gatekeeper Trilogy
Buffy the Vampire Slayer: The Lost
  Slayer Serial Novel
Buffy the Vampire Slayer: The
  Willow Files
Buffy the Vampire Slayer: The
  Xander Years
Buffy the Vampire Slayer: Wicked
  Willow
Butt Wars
@CAFE
California Diaries
Captain Underpants
Charmed
Cheetah Girls
Choose Your Own Adventure
Choose Your Own Nightmare
Choose Your Own Star Wars
  Adventures
Clique
Clueless
The Complicated Life of Claudia
  Cristina Cortez
The Contender
Danger.com
Dear Dumb Diary
Diary of a Wimpy Kid
Dinoverse
Dogtown Ghetto
Don't Get Caught
Don't Touch That Remote!
Drama!
Drama Club

Eerie Indiana
Elsie Edwards
Everest
The Extraordinary Adventures of
  Ordinary Boy
Extreme Team
Fabulous Five
Fear Street
Fear Street: Fear Street
  Cheerleaders
Fear Street: Fear Street Sagas
Fear Street: Fear Street Seniors
Fear Street: Fear Street Super
  Chillers
Fear Street: Ghosts of Fear Street
Fear Street: 99 Fear Street
Fearless
Ferret Chronicles
Fiendly Corners
Fingerprints
Gilmore Girls
Goosebumps
Goosebumps: Give Yourself
  Goosebumps
Goosebumps Graphix
Goosebumps Horrorland
Goosebumps Series 2000
Graveyard School
The Grosse Adventures
Hardy Boys, Undercover Brothers
Hardy Boys, Undercover Brothers:
  Graphic Novels
Have a Nice Life
He-Man Women Haters Club
Hear No Evil
Help! I'm Trapped
High School Musical Stories from
  East High
"Hour" Books
House of Horrors
Internet Girls
Island

It's Happy Bunny
Jackie Chan Adventures
The Jersey
Joey Pigza
Journey of Allen Strange
Just . . .
Kim Possible (Chapter Books)
Kim Possible (TokyoPop)
Kimani Tru
Klooz
A Knight's Story
Lightning on Ice
Lily Quench
Live from Brentwood High
Lizzie McGuire
Lizzie McGuire Mysteries
Lizzie McGuire (TokyoPop)
Magic Pickle Graphic Novels
Mars Year One
Mates, Dates, and . . .
The Midnight Library
Mike Pillsbury
Missing Persons
Mysteries in Our National Parks
Nancy Drew: Girl Detective
Nancy Drew Graphic Novels
NASCAR Pole Position
    Adventures
NFL Monday Night Football Club
Nightmare Hall
Nightmare Room
Nightmare Room Thrillogy
Nightmares! How Will Yours End?
Nose
On the Run
1-800-Where-R-You

Platinum Teen
Pretty Freekin Scary
Princess Diaries
Riot Brothers
Saddles, Stars, and Stripes
Sardine in Outer Space
Sebastian Barth
Secret World of Alex Mack
The Seer
Sidekicks
Slapshots
Slimeballs
Smallville
Sons of the Dark
Spinetinglers
Spooksville
Star Trek: Deep Space Nine
Star Trek: Enterprise
Star Trek: I. K. S. Gorkon
Star Trek: S. C. E.
Star Trek: Starfleet Academy
Star Trek: The Next Generation:
    Starfleet Academy
Star Trek: Voyager: Starfleet
    Academy
Star Wars: A New Hope—Manga
Star Wars: Boba Fett
Star Wars: Episode I The Phantom
    Menace—Manga
Star Wars: Jedi Apprentice
Star Wars: Jedi Quest
Star Wars: The Empire Strikes
    Back—Manga
Star Wars: The Last of the Jedi
Star Wars: The Return of the
    Jedi—Manga
Star Wars Episode 1: Journals

Star Wars Galaxy of Fear
Star Wars Junior Jedi Knights
Star Wars Young Jedi Knights
Students Across the Seven Seas
Summer Boys
Super Goofballs
Survival!
Swampland Trilogy
Sweep
Take It to the Xtreme
Tales from the Crypt Graphic
    Novels
Tales of Terror
Thoroughbred
Thoroughbred: Ashleigh
Thoroughbred: Ashleigh's
    Collection
TodaysGirls.com
Tom Swift, Young Inventor
Trigun Maximum
The Tucket Adventures
Twisted Journeys
Underwhere
Vampirates
Watchers
What If . . .
White Mane Kids
Wild at Heart
Winning Season
Wolfbay Wings
X Files
X Games Xtreme Mysteries
The Young Americans
Young Bond
Young Indiana Jones Chronicles:
    Choose Your Own Adventure
Zorro Graphic Novels

AUTHOR INDEX

Authors are listed with the series to which they contributed. Series are listed in alphabetical order in the main section of this book.

A

Aaron, Anna
  Sweet Dreams
Abbey, Lynn
  Magic: The Gathering—
    Artifacts Cycle
Abbott, Donald
  Oz
Abbott, Hailey
  Summer Boys
Abbott, Tony
  Don't Touch That Remote!
Abela, Deborah
  Spy Force
Abrahams, Peter
  Echo Falls Mystery
Abrams, J. J.
  Alias
Abrams, Liesa
  Love Stories
Adams, Douglas
  Hitchhiker's Trilogy
Adina, Shelley
  All About Us Novels
Aiken, Joan
  Wolves Chronicles
Aks, Patricia
  Cheerleaders
Albert, Susan Wittig
  China Bayles Mystery
Alexander, Alma
  Worldweavers
Alexander, Heather
  Mary-Kate and Ashley:
    Adventures of Mary-Kate and
    Ashley
Alexander, Lloyd
  Prydain Chronicles
  Vesper Holly
  Westmark
Alexander, Nina
  Love Stories

Mary-Kate and Ashley:
    Adventures of Mary-Kate and
    Ashley
Alexander, Wilma E.
  On Time's Wing
Alexandra, Belinda
  Charmed
Alfonsi, Alice
  High School Musical Stories
    from East High
  Lizzie McGuire
  W.I.T.C.H.—Chapter Books
Algozin, Bruce
  Dungeons and Dragons: Endless
    Quest
Alirez, Ben
  Bluford High
Allen, Roger MacBride
  David Brin's Out of Time
  Isaac Asimov's Caliban
Allende, Isabel
  Alexander Cold and Nadia
    Santos
Allison, Jennifer
  Gilda Joyce
Amato, Mary
  Riot Brothers
Amodeo, John
  Zenda
Anastasio, Dina
  Space Above and Beyond
Anders, C. J.
  Dawson's Creek
Anderson, Jodi Lynn
  May Bird
Anderson, Kevin J.
  Crystal Doors
  Dragonflight
  Star Wars Young Jedi Knights
Anderson, Laurie Halse
  Wild at Heart
Anderson, Louis
  Dungeons and Dragons: Endless
    Quest

Anderson, M. T.
  M. T. Anderson's Thrilling
    Tales
Anderson, Margaret J.
  Time Trilogy
Andrews, Jeanne
  Sweet Dreams
Andrews, Michael
  Dungeons and Dragons: Endless
    Quest
Andrews, V. C.
  Dollanganger
Anson, Mandy
  Sweet Dreams
Anthony, David
  Knightscares
Anthony, Piers
  Xanth Saga
Antilles, Kem
  Dungeons and Dragons: Endless
    Quest
  Star Trek: Deep Space Nine
Apelqvist, Eva
  Students Across the Seven Seas
Appel, Allen
  Alex Balfour
Applegate, K. A.
  Animorphs
  Animorphs: Alternamorphs
  Animorphs: Animorph
    Chronicles
  Animorphs: Megamorphs
  EverWorld
  Love Stories
  Love Stories: Super Editions
  Making Out
  Making Waves
  Remnants
  Summer
Appleton, Victor
  Tom Swift
  Tom Swift Young Inventor
Aragones, Sergio
  The Groo
Archer, Chris
  Mindwarp

Pyrates

Arden, William
Three Investigators

Armstrong, Jennifer
Dear Mr. President
Fire-Us Trilogy
Wild Rose Inn

Arthur, Robert
Three Investigators

Asai, Carrie
Samurai Girl

Asaro, Catherine
Saga of the Skolian Empire

Ashby, R. S.
Jackie Chan Adventures

Ashton, Victoria
Confessions of a Teen Nanny

Asim, Jabari
Jamestown's American Portraits

Asimov, Isaac
Foundation
I, Robot
Norby

Asimov, Janet
Norby

Askegren, Pierce
Alias

Asprin, Robert
Myth Adventures

Atwater-Rhodes, Amelia
Den of Shadows
Kiesha'ra

Auerbach, Annie
The Grosse Adventures

Augarde, Steve
Touchstone Trilogy

Ayres, Katherine
American Girls: History
Mysteries

B

Bach, Richard
Ferret Chronicles

Bader, Bonnie
Mary-Kate and Ashley:
Adventures of Mary-Kate and
Ashley

Baer, Judy
Live from Brentwood High
Sweet Dreams

Baglio, Ben M.
Choose Your Own Adventure

Bajoria, Paul
Printers Devil Trilogy

Baker, E. D.
Tales of the Frog Princess

Baker, Jennifer
Class Secrets

Clueless
Dawson's Creek
Enchanted Hearts

Baker, Richard
Dungeons and Dragons:
Forgotten Realms—The Last
Mythal

Baker, Susan
Sweet Dreams

Bale, Karen A.
Survival!

Ballard, Jane
Sweet Dreams

Balliet, Blue
Petra and Calder

Banerjee, Anjali
Dungeons and Dragons:
Knights of the Silver Dragon
Star Sisterz

Banim, Lisa
Lizzie McGuire Mysteries
Mary-Kate and Ashley: Two of a
Kind

Banks, Iain M.
The Culture

Banscherus, J.
Klooz

Barham, Lisa
The Fashion-Forward
Adventures of Imogene

Barlow, Steve
Outernet

Barnes, John
The Thousand Cultures

Barnes-Svarney, Patricia
Secret World of Alex Mack
Star Trek: The Next
Generation: Starfleet
Academy
Star Trek: Voyager: Starfleet
Academy

Baron, Nick
Dungeons and Dragons: Endless
Quest

Barondes, Jessica
Sweet 16

Barron, T. A.
The Great Tree of Avalon
Heartlight
The Lost Years of Merlin

Barry, Dave
Never Land
Peter and the Starcatchers

Bates, Michelle
Sandy Lane Stables

Batson, Wayne Thomas
The Door Within Trilogy

Baum, Lyman Frank
Oz

Baum, Roger S.
Oz

Beach, Lynn
Phantom Valley

Bear, Greg
Foundation

Becker, Eve
Abracadabra

Beckett, Jim
Choose Your Own Adventure

Bee, Coach Clair
Chip Hilton Sports Series

Beecham, Jahnna
Sweet Dreams

Beechen, Adam
American Dreams

Beechwood, Beth
High School Musical Stories
from East High

Bell, Clare E.
Ratha Quartet

Bell, Hilari
Farsala Trilogy

Bellairs, John
Anthony Monday
Johnny Dixon
Lewis Barnavelt

Benary-Isbert, Margot
Lechow Family

Bender, Carrie
Whispering Brook

Benford, Gregory
Foundation

Benjamin, David
The Sixth Sense: Secrets from
Beyond

Bennett, Cherie
Enchanted Hearts
Mirror Image
Pageant
Smallville
Sunset Island
Teen Angels
Trash
University Hospital

Bennett, Christopher L.
Star Trek: S. C. E.

Bennett, Holly
The Bonemender

Bentley, Karen
Thoroughbred

Benton, Jim
Dear Dumb Diary
It's Happy Bunny

Benz, Derek
Grey Griffins

Berman, Ron
Dream Series

Bernard, Elizabeth
Love Stories

Betancourt, Jeanne
Cheer USA!

Byers, Richard Lee
  Are You Afraid of the Dark?

Byrd, Sandra
  Friends for a Season

Byrne, John
  Hellboy

C

Cabot, Meg
  The Mediator
  1-800-Where-R-You
  Princess Diaries

Cadnum, Michael
  The Book of the Lion

Cadwallader, Sharon
  American Dreams
  Sweet Dreams

Cage, Elizabeth
  Spy Girls

Calhoun, Mary
  Katie John

Calhoun, T. B.
  NASCAR Pole Position
    Adventures

Campbell, Bill
  Oz

Campbell, Carole R.
  The Young Americans

Campbell, Gaetz Dayle
  On Time's Wing

Campbell, Joanna
  Sweet Dreams
  Thoroughbred
  Thoroughbred: Ashleigh
  Thoroughbred: Ashleigh's
    Collection

Campbell, Joanna, creator
  Thoroughbred

Campbell, Tonie
  Dream Series

Canavan, Trudi
  The Black Magician Trilogy

Cann, Kate
  Hard Cash
  Love Trilogy
  Richard Steele Trilogy

Capron, Jean F.
  Sweet Dreams

Card, Orson Scott
  Ender Wiggin
  Homecoming Saga
  Tales of Alvin Maker

Carey, Diane L.
  Distress Call 911
  Star Trek: Enterprise
  Star Trek: Starfleet Academy

Carey, M. V.
  Three Investigators

Carlson, Dale Bick
  James Budd

Carlson, Karyl
  Oz

Carlson, Melody
  Carter House Girls
  Degrees of Betrayal
  Degrees of Guilt
  Diary of a Teenage Girl
  FaithGirlz: Girls of 622 Harbor
    View
  Notes From a Spinning Planet
  True Colors

Carr, Mike
  Dungeons and Dragons: Endless
    Quest

Carroll, Jacqueline
  Jackie Chan Adventures
  Turning Seventeen

Carroll, Michael
  Quantum Prophecy

Carter, Cassandra
  Kimani Tru

Casanova, Mary
  American Girls: Girls of Many
    Lands

Cascone, A. G.
  Deadtime Stories

Cash, Angela
  Sweet Dreams

Cassidy, Carla Bracale
  Sweet Dreams

Cast, Kristin
  House of Night

Cast, P. C.
  House of Night

Cates, Emily
  Haunting with Louisa

Caudell, Marian
  Sweet Dreams

Cerasini, Marc
  Kim Possible (Chapter Books)
  7th Heaven
  7th Heaven

Chadwick, Paul
  Concrete

Chaikin, Linda
  Royal Pavilions

Chaikin, Miriam
  Molly

Chalker, Jack L.
  Watchers at the Well

Chandler, Elizabeth
  Dark Secrets
  Love Stories
  Love Stories: Super Editions

Charbonnet, Gabrielle
  American Gold Gymnasts

Chase, Paula
  Del Rio Bay Clique

Chaykin, Howard
  Chronicles of Conan

Cheng, Terrence
  Art Encounters

Cherryh, C. J.
  Alliance-Union
  Foreigner

Chester, Kate
  Hear No Evil

Chetwin, Grace
  Tales of Gom in the Legends of
    Ulm

Chima, Cinda Williams
  The Heir

Choi, Sook Nyul
  Sookan Bak

Christie, Amanda
  7th Heaven

Christopher, John
  Fireball
  Sword of the Spirits
  Tripods

Christopher, Matt
  Extreme Team
  Matt Christopher's Sports
    Stories

Ciencin, Denise
  Angel
  Buffy the Vampire Slayer

Ciencin, Scott
  Angel
  Angel
  Buffy the Vampire Slayer
  Charmed
  Charmed
  Dinotopia
  Dinoverse
  Jurassic Park Adventures
  Kim Possible: Pick a Villain
  The Lurker Files

Clancy, Tom
  Net Force

Clark, Catherine
  Gilmore Girls
  Love Stories
  7th Heaven

Clarke, Arthur C.
  Rama
  2001

Clarke, Nicole
  Flirt

Clement-Moore, Rosemary
  Maggie Quinn: Girl vs. Evil

Cling, Jacqueline
  Kim Possible: Pick a Villain

Cofer, Judith Ortiz
  First Person Fiction

Coffin, M. T.
  Spinetinglers

Cohen, Alice E.
  Are You Afraid of the Dark?

Royal Diaries
Dent, Grace
  LBD (Les Bambinos
    Dangereuses)
Derby, Kathleen
  Are You Afraid of the Dark?
Devine, L.
  Drama High
DeWeese, Gene
  Dinotopia
Dhami, Narinder
  Babes
Dickenson, Celia
  Sweet Dreams
Dickinson, Peter
  The Kin
Dicks, Terrance
  Baker Street Irregulars
Dillard, J. M.
  Star Trek: Enterprise
Dilmore, Kevin
  Star Trek: S. C. E.
DiMartino, Michael Dante
  Avatar Graphic Novels
Dionne, Wanda
  American Dreams
Divakaruni, Chitra Banerjee
  American Girls: Girls of Many
    Lands
Dixon, Franklin W.
  Hardy Boys
  Hardy Boys Casefiles
  Hardy Boys, Undercover
    Brothers
  Hardy Boys, Undercover
    Brothers Murder House
    Trilogy
D'Lacey, Chris
  Dragon
Doder, Joshua
  Grk
Dokey, Cameron
  Angel
  Buffy the Vampire Slayer
  Charmed
  Charmed
  Enchanted Hearts
  Love Stories
  Mary-Kate and Ashley:
    Graduation Summer
  Once Upon a Time
Donovan, Dale and Johns
  Dungeons and Dragons:
    Knights of the Silver Dragon
Doolittle, June
  Mary-Kate and Ashley:
    Adventures of Mary-Kate and
    Ashley
Dower, Laura
  From the Files of Madison Finn

Downie, Mary Alice
  On Time's Wing
Dowswell, Paul
  Adventures of a Young Sailor
Doyle, Bill
  Crime Through Time
Doyle, Debra
  Valdemar: Mageworlds
Doyle, Patrick
  Edgar Font's Hunt for a House
    to Haunt
Doyon, Stephanie
  Love Stories
  On the Road
Drake, Emily
  The Magickers
Draper, Sharon M.
  Hazelwood High
Duane, Diane
  Wizardry
Dubowski, Cathy East
  Gilmore Girls
  Journey of Allen Strange
  Luna Bay
  Mary-Kate and Ashley:
    Adventures of Mary-Kate and
    Ashley
  Mary-Kate and Ashley: Two of a
    Kind
  Secret World of Alex Mack
  So Weird
Duck, Phillip Thomas
  Kimani Tru
Duey, Kathleen
  Survival!
Dukore, Jesse
  Sweet Dreams
Dunbar, Fiona
  Lulu Baker
Duncan, David
  A Handful of Men
  Man of His Word
Dunkle, Clare B.
  Hollow Kingdom
DuPrau, Jeanne
  City of Ember
Durgin, Doranna
  Angel

E

Easton, Royce
  X Files
Eddings, David
  The Belgariad
  Malloreon
Egan, Kate
  W.I.T.C.H.—Chapter Books

Eisenberg, Lisa
  Mary-Kate and Ashley:
    Adventures of Mary-Kate and
    Ashley
Elfman, Eric
  X Files
Ellen, Jaye
  Sweet Dreams
Elliott, Greg
  Charmed
Ellis, Carol
  Cheerleaders
  Mary-Kate and Ashley:
    Adventures of Mary-Kate and
    Ashley
Ellis, Deborah
  Art Encounters
  The Breadwinner Trilogy
Elmer, Robert
  Promise of Zion
  The Young Underground
Emburg, Kate
  Love Stories
  Sweet Dreams
Emery, Clayton
  Are You Afraid of the Dark?
  Magic: The Gathering—Magic
    Legends Cycle
  Secret World of Alex Mack
Emesse, Tea
  Star Sisterz
Erdrich, Louise
  Omakayas
Erlbach, Arlene
  Sweet Dreams
Ernst, Kathleen
  American Girls: History
    Mysteries
  White Mane Kids
Espenson, Jane
  Buffy the Vampire Slayer
Espinosa, Rod
  Neotopia
Estes, Rose
  Dungeons and Dragons: Endless
    Quest
Evanier, Mark
  The Groo
Ewing, Lynne
  Daughters of the Moon
  Sisters of Isis
  Sons of the Dark

F

Fabry, Chris
  Red Rock Mysteries
  RPM
  Wormling

Gikow, Louise
  Mary-Kate and Ashley: Two of a
    Kind
Gilden, Mel
  Beverly Hills, 90210
  Cybersurfers
  Star Trek: Deep Space Nine
Gilligan, Alison
  Choose Your Own Adventure
Gilligan, Shannon
  Choose Your Own Adventure
Gilman, Laura Anne
  Buffy the Vampire Slayer
  Grail Quest
Gilmore, Ford Lytle
  Hollow
Gilmour, H. B.
  Clueless
  T*Witches
Givner, Joan
  Ellen Fremedon
Gjovaag, Eric
  Oz
Gleitzman, Morris
  Misery Guts
Gliori, Debi
  Pure Dead Magic
Glut, Don
  Dinotopia
Godbersen, Anna
  The Luxe
Goddard, Drew
  Buffy the Vampire Slayer
Golden, Christopher
  Angel (Graphic Novels)
  Body of Evidence
  Buffy the Vampire Slayer
  Buffy the Vampire Slayer
  Buffy the Vampire Slayer: Buffy
    and Angel
  Buffy the Vampire Slayer: The
    Gatekeeper Trilogy
  Buffy the Vampire Slayer: The
    Gatekeeper Trilogy
  Buffy the Vampire Slayer: The
    Lost Slayer Serial Novel
  Buffy the Vampire Slayer: The
    Lost Slayer Serial Novel
  Choose Your Own Star Wars
    Adventures
  Hollow
  Outcast
  Prowlers
Golding, Julia
  Cat Royal Adventures
  The Companions Quartet
Goldman, Leslie
  Bratz: Clued In!
  Lizzie McGuire
Goldschmidt, Judy
  Raisin Rodriguez

Goodman, Deborah Lerne
  Choose Your Own Adventure
Goodman, Julius
  Choose Your Own Adventure
Gorman, Larry Mike
  Roller Coaster Tycoon
Gorman, Susan
  Sweet Dreams
Gottesfeld, Jeff
  Mirror Image
  Smallville
  Teen Angels
  Trash
Gould, Steven
  Jumper
Grace, N. B
  High School Musical Stories
    from East High
Grace, N. B.
  High School Musical Stories
    from East High
Grace, N. B. and Beechwood
  High School Musical Stories
    from East High
Graf, Mike
  Adventures with the Parkers
Graham, Denise R.
  Dungeons and Dragons:
    Knights of the Silver Dragon
Grant, K. M.
  de Granville Trilogy
Graver, Fred
  Choose Your Own Adventure
Graves, Damien
  The Midnight Library
Gray, Luli
  Falcon
Green, Debra
  Star Sisterz
Green, Yvonne
  Sweet Dreams
Greene, Bette
  Philip Hall
Greene, Constance C.
  Al (Alexandra)
Greene, Gretchen
  Love Stories: His. Hers. Theirs
Greenland, Shannon
  Specialists
Gregory, Deborah
  Cheetah Girls
Gregory, Diana
  Sweet Dreams
Gregory, Kristiana
  Prairie River
  Royal Diaries
Griffiths, Andy
  Butt Wars
  Just . . .

Griggs, Terry
  Cat's Eye Corner
Grimes, Francis Hurley
  Sweet Dreams
Gross, U. B.
  Slimeballs
Grubb, Jeff
  Magic: The Gathering—
    Artifacts Cycle
  Magic: The Gathering—Ice Age
    Cycle
Guibert, Emmanuel
  Sardine in Outer Space
Guilford, J. D.
  Kimani Tru
Gunn, Robin Jones
  Christy Miller
  Christy Miller: Christy and
    Todd: The College Years
  Sierra Jensen
Gustaveson, Dave
  Reel Kids Adventures
Gutman, Dan
  Baseball Card Adventures

H

Haddix, Margaret Peterson
  Shadow Children
Hafer, Todd
  Spirit of the Game
Haft, Erin
  Love Stories
Hahn, Mary Downing
  Gordy Smith
Haislip, Phyllis Hall
  White Mane Kids
Hale, Bruce
  Chet Gecko Mysteries
  Underwhere
Hale, Shannon
  Goose Girl
Halecroft, David
  Alden All Stars
Hall, Beverly B.
  White Mane Kids
Hall, Katy
  Paxton Cheerleaders
Hallowell, Tommy
  Alden All Stars
Hamilton, Virginia
  Justice Trilogy
Hampton, Bill
  Choose Your Own Adventure
Hand, Elizabeth
  Star Wars: Boba Fett
Hand, Jimmie
  Dream Series

Hanna, Steven
  Alias
Hannan, Peter
  Super Goofballs
Hantman, Clea
  Goddesses
Hapgood, Elizabeth R.
  Sweet Dreams
Hapka, Cathy
  Alias
  Bionicle Chronicles
  Dinotopia
  High School Musical Stories
    from East High
  Star Power
  Students Across the Seven Seas
Haptie, Charlotte
  The Karmidee
Harnett, Lynn
  Visitors
  Werewolf Chronicles
Harris, Christine
  Undercover Girl
Harris, Deborah Turner
  The Adept
Harris, Robert J.
  The Stuart Quartet
  Young Heroes
Harrison, Emma
  Alias
  Alias
  Charmed
  Charmed
  Everwood
  Mary-Kate and Ashley:
    Graduation Summer
Harrison, Lisi
  Clique
Harry, Miranda
  Love Stories
Hart, Alison
  American Girls: History
    Mysteries
  Racing to Freedom Trilogy
Hastings, Catt
  Sweet Dreams
Hautala, Rick
  Body of Evidence
Hautman, Pete
  Bloodwater Mysteries
Haworth-Attard, Barbara
  On Time's Wing
Hawthorne, Rachel
  Love Stories: His. Hers. Theirs
  Love Stories: Year Abroad
Hayden
  Kimani Tru
Hayes, Maggie
  Sweet Dreams
Haynes, Betsy
  Bone Chillers

Fabulous Five
Headapohl, Bette
  Sweet Dreams
Hearn, Lian
  Tales of the Otori
Heckerling, Amy
  Clueless
Hehl, Eileen
  Sweet Dreams
Hemingway, Edith Morris
  White Mane Kids
Henderson, Alice
  Buffy the Vampire Slayer: Stake
    Your Destiny
Henderson, Dee
  Uncommon Heroes
Henderson, Holly E.
  Dawson's Creek
Hendry, Diana
  Harvey Angell Trilogy
Hennesy, Carolyn
  Mythic Misadventures
Henry, Emma
  Love Stories: His. Hers. Theirs
Hermes, Patricia
  My Side of the Story
Herndon, Cory J.
  Magic: The Gathering—
    Mirrodin Cycle
  Magic: The Gathering—Ravnica
    Cycle
Herndon, Cory J. and McGough
  Magic: The Gathering—Lorwyn
    Cycle
  Magic: The Gathering—
    Shadowmoor Cycle
Hess, Robin
  Oz
Higson, Charlie
  Young Bond
Hildick, E. W.
  Ghost Squad
Hill, Kirkpatrick
  American Girls: Girls of Many
    Lands
Hill, Laban C.
  Art Encounters
  Choose Your Own Adventure
  Choose Your Own Nightmare
  X Games Xtreme Mysteries
Hill, Stuart
  The Icemark Chronicles
Hillman, Craig
  Love Stories: Super Editions
Hirano, Kohta
  Hellsing
Hirsch, Danny
  Secret Agent MJJ
Hirschfeld, Robert
  Choose Your Own Nightmare

Matt Christopher's Sports
    Stories
Ho, Minfong
  First Person Fiction
Hodgman, Ann
  Choose Your Own Adventure
Hoeye, Michael
  Hermux Tantamoq Adventures
Hoffman, Mary
  Stravaganza
Hoh, Diane
  Cheerleaders
  Med Center
  Nightmare Hall
Holder, Nancy
  Angel
  Buffy the Vampire Slayer
  Buffy the Vampire Slayer
  Buffy the Vampire Slayer: Buffy
    and Angel
  Buffy the Vampire Slayer: Buffy
    and Angel: The Unseen
    Trilogy
  Buffy the Vampire Slayer: Buffy
    and Angel: The Unseen
    Trilogy
  Buffy the Vampire Slayer: Stake
    Your Destiny
  Buffy the Vampire Slayer: The
    Angel Chronicles
  Buffy the Vampire Slayer: The
    Gatekeeper Trilogy
  Buffy the Vampire Slayer: The
    Gatekeeper Trilogy
  Once Upon a Time
  Wicked
Holder, Nancy, and Jeff Mariotte
  Angel
Holdstock, Robert
  Merlin Codex
Holl, Kristi
  TodaysGirls.com
Holm, Jennifer L.
  Boston Jane
Holman, Sheri
  Royal Diaries
Holohan, Maureen
  The Broadway Ballplayers
Hoobler, Dorothy
  The Ghost in the Tokaido Inn
Hoobler, Thomas
  The Ghost in the Tokaido Inn
Hopkins, Cathy
  Mates, Dates, and . . .
  Truth or Dare
  Zodiac Girls
Horowitz, Anthony
  Alex Rider
  The Diamond Brothers
  The Gatekeepers
Howard, Robert E.
  Chronicles of Conan

Millner, Denene
  Hotlanta
Mills, Bart
  Beverly Hills, 90210
Mills, Claudia
  Losers, Inc.
Minsky, Terri
  Lizzie McGuire (TokyoPop)
Minter, J.
  Inside Girl
  The Insiders
Mitchell, Mark
  Are You Afraid of the Dark?
Mitchell, V. E.
  Are You Afraid of the Dark?
  Secret World of Alex Mack
  Star Trek: The Next
    Generation: Starfleet
    Academy
Miyazaki, Hayao
  Howl's Moving Castle (Graphic
    Novels)
Mlynowski, Sarah
  Magic in Manhattan
Modesitt, L. E.
  Recluce
  The Spellsong Cycle
Moesta, Rebecca
  Buffy the Vampire Slayer
  Crystal Doors
  Star Wars Junior Jedi Knights
  Star Wars Young Jedi Knights
Montgomery, Anson
  Choose Your Own Adventure
Montgomery, L. M.
  Story Girl
Montgomery, Lucy Maud
  Avonlea
Montgomery, R. A.
  Choose Your Own Adventure
  Choose Your Own Nightmare
Montgomery, Ramsey
  Choose Your Own Adventure
Montgomery, Raymond
  Choose Your Own Adventure
Montgomery, Richard
  Choose Your Own Adventure
Moore, James A.
  Buffy the Vampire Slayer
Moore, Leslie
  House of Horrors
Moore, Roger E.
  Dungeons and Dragons: Endless
    Quest
Moore, Stephanie Perry
  Payton Skky
  Perry Skky Jr.
Moore, Vance
  Magic: The Gathering—
    Masquerade Cycle

Magic: The Gathering—
    Odyssey Cycle
Morgan, Melissa
  Camp Confidential
Morris, Gerald
  The Denizens of Camelot
Morris, Gilbert
  Bonnets and Bugles
  Daystar Voyages
Morris, Susan J.
  Magic: The Gathering—
    Shadowmoor Cycle
Morse, Scott
  Magic Pickle Graphic Novels
Mortenson, R. K.
  Landon Snow
Moser, Laura
  10th Grade Social Climber
Moss, Alexandra
  Royal Ballet School Diaries
Moss, Marissa
  Amelia
Mostow, Debra
  Party of Five
Mountain, Robert
  Choose Your Own Adventure
Muchamore, Robert
  Cherub
Mueller, Kate
  Choose Your Own Adventure
Muldrow, Diane
  Dish
Mull, Brandon
  Fablehaven
Murphy, Shirley Rousseau
  Joe Grey Mysteries
Murphy, T. M.
  Belltown Mystery
Murray, Victoria Christopher
  The Divas
Myers, Bill
  Forbidden Doors
Myracle, Lauren
  Internet Girls
  Winnie Perry

N

Namm, Diane
  Love Stories
Navarro, Yvonne
  Buffy the Vampire Slayer
  Buffy the Vampire Slayer: The
    Willow Files
  Buffy the Vampire Slayer: The
    Willow Files
  Buffy the Vampire Slayer:
    Wicked Willow

Buffy the Vampire Slayer:
    Wicked Willow
Naylor, Phyllis Reynolds
  Alice
  Bessledorf Hotel
  Club of Mysteries
  Witch
  York Trilogy
Neill, John R.
  Oz
Nelson, Arvid
  Rex Mundi
Nelson, Suzanne Marie
  Students Across the Seven Seas
Nentwig, Wendy Lee
  Pacific Cascades University
Nesbit, Jeffrey Asher
  Degrees of Betrayal
Newman, Marc
  Choose Your Own Adventure
Nicholson, Wes
  Dungeons and Dragons: Endless
    Quest
Nicholson, William
  Noble Warriors
  The Wind of Fire
Nicieza, Fabian
  Buffy the Vampire Slayer
Nightow, Yasuhiro
  Trigun Maximum
Niles, Douglas
  Dungeons and Dragons: Endless
    Quest
Nimmo, Jenny
  Children of the Red King
  Gwyn Griffiths Trilogy
Nix, Garth
  Abhorsen
  Keys to the Kingdom
  The Seventh Tower
  X Files
Nixon, Joan Lowery
  Orphan Train Adventures
Noble, Jeanette
  Sweet Dreams
Nodelman, Perry
  The Minds Series
Noll, Katherine
  Aly and AJ's Rock 'n' Roll
    Mysteries
  Roller Coaster Tycoon
Noonan, Rosalind
  Charmed
  Party of Five
  Turning Seventeen
Norby, Lisa
  Cheerleaders
Norfleet, Celeste O.
  Kimani Tru

Perelman, Helen
  High School Musical Stories
    from East High
Peretti, Frank
  Cooper Kids
Perez, Lana
  Dungeons and Dragons:
    Knights of the Silver Dragon
  Star Sisterz
Perl, Lila
  Fat Glenda
Perlberg, Deborah
  Mary-Kate and Ashley:
    Adventures of Mary-Kate and
    Ashley
Pete the Cat
  Pete the Cat
Peters, Stephanie True
  Matt Christopher's Sports
    Stories
Petrie, Doug
  Buffy the Vampire Slayer
Petrucha, Stefan
  Nancy Drew Graphic Novels
  Tales from the Crypt Graphic
    Novels
  Timetripper
  Wicked Dead
Petti, Ken
  Zenda
Peyton, K. M.
  Flambards
Pfeffer, Susan Beth
  Jamestown's American Portraits
Phelps, Lauren M.
  Sweet Dreams
Philbrick, W. Rodman
  House on Cherry Street
  Visitors
  Werewolf Chronicles
Pieczenik, Steve
  Net Force
Pielichaty, Helena
  Girls of Avenue Z
Pierce, Meredith Ann
  Darkangel Trilogy
  Firebringer Trilogy
Pierce, Tamora
  Beka Cooper
  Circle of Magic
  Circle of Magic: The Circle
    Opens
  Immortals
  Protector of the Small
  Song of the Lioness Quartet
Pike, Christopher
  Cheerleaders
  The Last Vampire
  Spooksville
Pilkey, Dav
  Captain Underpants

Pines, Nancy
  Sweet Dreams
Pini, Richard
  ElfQuest
Pini, Wendy
  ElfQuest
Pinkney, Andrea Davis
  Dear Mr. President
Pittel, Jamie
  Sweet 16
Ploog, Mike
  Chronicles of Conan
Plummer, Rachel
  Dungeons and Dragons:
    Knights of the Silver Dragon
Polcover, Jane
  Sweet Dreams
Pollack, Pam
  So Weird
Pollotta, Nick
  Dungeons and Dragons: Endless
    Quest
Pollowitz, Melinda
  Sweet Dreams
Ponti, James
  Journey of Allen Strange
Pratchett, Terry
  Bromeliad
  Discworld
  Johnny Maxwell
Preble, Laura
  Queen Geeks
Precious
  Platinum Teen
Preiss, Pauline
  Mary-Kate and Ashley:
    Adventures of Mary-Kate and
    Ashley
Presser, Arlynn
  Love Stories
Prior, Natalie Jane
  Lily Quench
Pullman, Philip
  His Dark Materials
  Sally Lockhart Trilogy

Q

Quin-Harkin, Janet
  Enchanted Hearts
  Love Stories
  Sweet Dreams
  Sweet Dreams: On Our Own

R

Rabb, M. E.
  Missing Persons

Rabe, Jean
  Dungeons and Dragons: Endless
    Quest
Raine, Allison
  Love Stories: Super Editions
Rand, Suzanne
  Sweet Dreams
Randall, David
  In the Shadow of the Bear
Ransom, Candice F.
  Dungeons and Dragons:
    Knights of the Silver Dragon
  Kobie Roberts
Ransome, Arthur
  Swallows and Amazons
Reding, Jaclyn
  Highland Heroes
Redish, Jane
  Sweet Dreams
Reece, Colleen L.
  Juli Scott Super Sleuth
Reed, Teresa
  Moesha
Rees, Celia
  Celia Rees Supernatural Trilogy
  Witch Child
Rees, Douglas
  Art Encounters
Rees, Elizabeth M.
  American Dreams
  Art Encounters
  Heart Beats
  The Jersey
  So Weird
Reeve, Philip
  The Hungry City Chronicles
Reichman, Justin
  Dream Series
Reilly, Matthew
  Hover Car Racer
Reinsmith, Richard
  Dungeons and Dragons: Endless
    Quest
Reisberg, Joanne A.
  The Young Americans
Reisfeld, Randi
  Clueless
  Love Stories
  Starlet
  Summer Share
  T*Witches
  Zoey 101
Reiss, Kathryn
  American Girls: History
    Mysteries
  Time Travel Mysteries
Rennison, Louise
  Confessions of Georgia Nicolson
Resnick, Michael D.
  Art Encounters

Scrimger, Richard
  Nose
Seidman, David L.
  Are You Afraid of the Dark?
Selman, Matty
  The Jersey
Sewell, Earl
  Kimani Tru
Sfar, Joan
  Sardine in Outer Space
Shahan, Sherry
  Eerie Indiana
Shan, Darren
  Cirque du Freak
  Demonata
Shands, Linda
  Wakara of Eagle Lodge
Shanower, Eric
  Age of Bronze
  Oz
Shaw, Deirdre
  American Dreams
Sheahan, Bernie
  Pacific Cascades University
Sheldon, Dyan
  Confessions of a Teenage Drama
    Queen
Sherman, Josepha
  Buffy the Vampire Slayer
  Dungeons and Dragons: Endless
    Quest
Shetterly, Will
  Voyage of the Basset
Shinn, Sharon
  The Safe-Keeper's Secret
Shusterman, Neal
  Dark Fusion
Siamon, Sharon
  Mustang Mountain
  Saddle Island
Sieberetz, Barbara
  Dawson's Creek
Siegman, Meryl
  Choose Your Own Adventure
Silverberg, Robert
  Dragonflight
  The Majipoor Cycle
Simbal, Joanne
  Sweet Dreams
Simon, Barbara Brooks
  I Am American
Simon, Morris
  Dungeons and Dragons: Endless
    Quest
Simpson, Fiona
  Zoey 101
Simpson, Robert
  Mystic Knights of Tir Na Nog
Sinclair, Jay
  The Jersey

Sinclair, Stephanie
  Love Stories
Singletary, Mabel Elizabeth
  The Double Dutch Club
Singleton, Linda Joy
  Cheer Squad
  Regeneration
  The Seer
  Sweet Dreams
Skurnick, Elizabeth
  Alias
  Love Stories: His. Hers. Theirs
Skurzynski, Gloria
  Mysteries in Our National Parks
  Virtual World Chronologs
Skye, Obert
  Leven Thumps
Slack, David
  Jackie Chan Adventures
Slade, Arthur G.
  Northern Frights
Sloan, Holly Goldberg
  Dream Series
Sloate, Susan
  Sweet Dreams
Smiley, Virginia
  Sweet Dreams
Smith, Carol
  TodaysGirls.com
Smith, Dean Wesley
  Roswell High
Smith, Dean Wesley and Rusch
  Star Trek: Enterprise
Smith, Jeff
  Bone
Smith, K. T.
  Beverly Hills, 90210
Smith, L. J.
  Dark Visions
  Forbidden Game
  Night World
  Secret Circle
  Vampire Diaries
Smith, Patricia Clark
  Royal Diaries
Smith, Sherwood
  Voyage of the Basset
  Wren
Smith, Susan
  Best Friends
Snelling, Lauraine
  Golden Filly Series
  High Hurdles
  Red River: Red River of the
    North
  Red River: Return to Red River
  Secret Refuge
Snicket, Lemony
  A Series of Unfortunate Events

Sniegoski, Tom
  Angel
  The Brimstone Network
  Buffy the Vampire Slayer: Buffy
    and Angel
  The Fallen
  Outcast
Snow, Jack
  Oz
Snyder, Maria V.
  Study
Snyder, Midori
  Dinotopia
  Oran Trilogy
Soesbee, Ree
  Dungeons and Dragons:
    Knights of the Silver Dragon
Solitaire, Jenna
  Daughter of Destiny
Somper, Justin
  Vampirates
Somtow, S. P.
  Dragonflight
Son, John
  First Person Fiction
Sook, Ryan
  Buffy the Vampire Slayer
Sorenson, Jody
  Cheerleaders
Sorrells, Walter
  Flight 29 Down
South, Sherri Cobb
  Sweet Dreams
Spalding, Andrea
  The Summer of Magic Quartet
Spector, Debra
  Sweet Dreams
Speregen, Devra Newberger
  Party of Five
Sprague, Gilbert M.
  Oz
Springer, Nancy
  Enola Holmes
  Rowan Hood
Stableford, Brian
  Emortality
Stackpole, Michael A.
  Age of Discovery Trilogy
  DragonCrown War Cycle
Stainer, M. L.
  Lyon Saga
Stanek, Robert
  Ruin Mist: The Kingdoms and
    the Elves of the Reaches
  Ruin Mist Chronicles
Stanley, Carol
  Cheerleaders
Stasheff, Christopher
  A Wizard in Rhyme

Z

Zach, Cheryl
  American Dreams
  Dear Diary
  Life at Sixteen

Love Stories: Super Editions
Mind over Matter
Zahn, Timothy
  Dragonback
Zambreno, Mary Frances
  Voyage of the Basset

Zeinert, Karen
  Jamestown's American Portraits
Zimmerman, Zoe
  Love Stories: Brothers Trilogy
Zindel, Paul
  P.C. Hawke Mysteries

TITLE INDEX

The series in which the title appears is shown in parentheses following the title. Series are listed in alphabetical order in the main section of this book.

A

The A-List (A-List)

Aaron Let's Go (Making Out)

The Ab-solute Truth (Platinum Teen)

Abandoned (Jennie McGrady Mysteries)

Abandoned on the Wild Frontier (Trailblazers)

Abby and the Best Kid Ever (Baby-Sitters Club)

Abby and the Mystery Baby (Baby-Sitters Club Mysteries)

Abby and the Notorious Neighbor (Baby-Sitters Club Mysteries)

Abby and the Secret Society (Baby-Sitters Club Mysteries)

Abby in Wonderland (Baby-Sitters Club)

Abby the Bad Sport (Baby-Sitters Club)

Abby's Book (Baby-Sitters Club Portrait Collection)

Abby's Lucky Thirteen (Baby-Sitters Club)

Abby's Twin (Baby-Sitters Club)

Abby's Un-Valentine (Baby-Sitters Club)

Abduction (Kidnapped)

Abhorsen (Abhorsen)

Abner and Me (Baseball Card Adventures)

The Abominable Snow Monster (Graveyard School)

Abominable Snowman (Choose Your Own Adventure)

The Abominable Snowman of Pasadena (Goosebumps)

Above the Veil (The Seventh Tower)

Abracadeath (Hardy Boys, Undercover Brothers: Graphic Novels)

Abraham Lincoln (Dear Mr. President)

The Absolute (Animorphs)

Absolute Zero (Hardy Boys Casefiles)

Accessory to the Crime (Bratz: Clued In!)

Accidental Dreams (The Lily Adventures)

Accidentally Fabulous (The Fashion-Forward Adventures of Imogene)

Achieving Personal Perfection (Clueless)

Achingly Alice (Alice)

Acorna (Acorna)

Acorna's People (Acorna)

Acorna's Quest (Acorna)

Acorna's Rebels (Acorna)

Acorna's Search (Acorna)

Acorna's Triumph (Acorna)

Acorna's World (Acorna)

Across the Nightingale Floor (Tales of the Otori)

Across the Steel River (Across the Steel River)

Acting on Impulse (Sweet Dreams)

Acting Up (Cheerleaders)

Acting Up (Hardy Boys Casefiles)

Action! (Nancy Drew: Girl Detective)

The Adept (The Adept)

Adrenalin Rush (Take It to the Xtreme)

The Adventurer (Highland Heroes)

The Adventures of Captain Underpants (Captain Underpants)

The Adventures of Samurai Cat (Samurai Cat)

The Adventures of the Blue Avenger (Blue Avenger)

The Adventures of Tony Millionaire's Sock Monkey (Sock Monkey)

Aenir (The Seventh Tower)

Aerie (The Fallen)

African Safari (Young Indiana Jones Chronicles: Choose Your Own Adventure)

After Hours (Party Room Trilogy)

After School Ghost Hunter (Klooz)

After Summer (Summer Boys)

After the Storm (Heartland)

The Aftermath (Asteroid Wars)

Aftermath (Remnants)

Aftermath (Star Trek: S. C. E.)

Aftershock (Mindwarp)

Aftershock (Star Trek: Starfleet Academy)

Aftershock (Sweet Valley High)

Against All Odds (Hardy Boys Casefiles)

Against the Empire (Star Wars: The Last of the Jedi)

Against the Odds (Sweet Valley High)

Against the Rules (Nancy Drew Files)

Against the Rules (Sweet Valley Twins)

Agent Out (Fearless FBI)

The Agony of Alice (Alice)

Air Apparent (Xanth Saga)

Air Ferrets Aloft (Ferret Chronicles)

Aisha Goes Wild (Making Out)

Aisling (Indigo)

The Akhenaten Adventure (Children of the Lamp)

Akiko (Akiko)

Akiko: The Training Master (Akiko)

Akiko and the Alpha Centauri 5000 (Akiko)

Akiko and the Great Wall of Trudd (Akiko)

Akiko and the Intergalactic Zoo (Akiko)

Akiko and the Journey to Toog (Akiko)

Akiko and the Missing Misp (Akiko)

Akiko in the Castle of Alia Rellapor (Akiko)

Akiko in the Sprubly Islands (Akiko)

Akiko on the Planet Smoo (Akiko)

Alanna (Song of the Lioness Quartet)

The Alaskan Adventure (Hardy Boys)

The Alchemist's Cat (Deptford Histories)

Alex Ryan, Stop That (Losers, Inc.)

Alex, You're Glowing! (Secret World of Alex Mack)

Alexandra the Great (Al (Alexandra))

Alex's Challenge (Camp Confidential)

Alice Alone (Alice)

Alice in April (Alice)

Alice In-Between (Alice)

Alice in Blunderland (Alice)

Alice in Lace (Alice)

Alice in Rapture, Sort of (Alice)

Alice in the Know (Alice)

Alice on Her Way (Alice)

Alice on the Outside (Alice)

Alice the Brave (Alice)

Alicia (Clique)

The Alien (Animorphs)

Alien Blood (Mindwarp)

Alien, Go Home! (Choose Your Own Adventure)

Alien Incident on Planet J (Twisted Journeys)

Alien Invasion from Hollyweird (The Outer Limits)

Alien Scream (Mindwarp)

Alien Terror (Mindwarp)

Alien Vacation (Journey of Allen Strange)

The Aliens Approach (Space Above and Beyond)

Aliens Ate My Homework (Alien Adventures)

Aliens in the Sky (Spooksville)

Aliens Stole My Body (Alien Adventures)

All About Andy (Replica)

All About Love (Sweet Valley High Senior Year)

All Access (Starlet)

All But Alice (Alice)

All-Day Nightmare (Goosebumps: Give Yourself Goosebumps)

All For Texas (Jamestown's American Portraits)

All I Want Is Everything (Gossip Girl)

All-Mars All-Stars (Slapshots)

All Mates Together (Truth or Dare)

The All-New Amelia (Amelia)

The All-New Amelia (Amelia)

The All-New Mallory Pike (Baby-Sitters Club)

All Night Long (Nannies)

All Night Long (Sweet Valley High)

All-Night Mall Party! (Bratz)

All-Night Party (Fear Street)

All or Nothing (Cheerleaders)

All or Nothing (Chestnut Hill)

All Over It (Lizzie McGuire)

All Q, No A (10th Grade Social Climber)

All Shook Up (From the Files of Madison Finn)

All-Star Pride (Lightning on Ice)

All That (Love Stories: Super Editions)

All that Glitters (Avalon 1: Web of Magic)

All that Glitters (From the Files of Madison Finn)

All That Glitters (Inside Girl)

All That Glitters (Mary-Kate and Ashley Sweet 16)

All the Days of Her Life (One Last Wish)

All the King's Horses (Horsefeathers)

All the Way (Cheerleaders)

All the Weyrs of Pern (Pern)

All Through the Night (Troubleshooters)

Allie's Legacy (Thoroughbred)

Allies of the Night (Cirque du Freak)

All's Fair in Love (Sweet Dreams)

All's Fairy in Love and War (Avalon 2: Quest for Magic)

Almost Alice (Alice)

Almost Famous (Talent)

Almost Married (Sweet Valley High)

Almost Perfect (Sweet Dreams)

Almost Ten and a Half (Kobie Roberts)

Aloha, Baby-Sitters! (Baby-Sitters Club Super Specials)

Aloha Love (Sweet Dreams)

Alone (Fearless)

Alone in Snakebite Canyon (Goosebumps: Give Yourself Goosebumps)

Alone in the Crowd (Sweet Valley High)

Along Came a Spider (Deadtime Stories)

The Alphabetical Hookup List A–J (The Alphabetical Hookup List Trilogy)

The Alphabetical Hookup List K–Q (The Alphabetical Hookup List Trilogy)

The Alphabetical Hookup List R–Z (The Alphabetical Hookup List Trilogy)

Al's Blind Date (Al (Alexandra))

Alvin Journeyman (Tales of Alvin Maker)

Always Dreamin' (Star Power)

Always Loving Zoey (Making Out)

Always There (Heartland)

Am I the Princess or the Frog? (Dear Dumb Diary)

Amalia (California Diaries)

Amalia, Diary Three (California Diaries)

Amalia, Diary Two (California Diaries)

The Amazing Maurice and His Educated Rodents (Discworld)

The Amazon Stranger (Reel Kids Adventures)

The Amber Spyglass (His Dark Materials)

Ambition (Private)

Ambush at Amboseli (Anika Scott)

Ambushed in Jaguar Swamp (Trailblazers)

Amelia Hits the Road (Amelia)

Amelia Lends a Hand (Amelia)

Amelia Takes Command (Amelia)

Amelia Works it Out (Amelia)

Amelia Writes Again (Amelia)

Amelia's 5th-Grade Notebook (Amelia)

Amelia's Are-We-There-Yet Longest Ever Car Trip (Amelia)

Amelia's Best Year Ever (Amelia)

Amelia's Book of Notes and Note Passing (Amelia)

Arin's Judgment (Passages)

The Ark (Lechow Family)

Ark Angel (Alex Rider)

Armani Angels (Project Fashion)

The Armies of Memory (The Thousand Cultures)

The Arms of Hercules (Book of the Gods)

Arms of Nemesis (Roma Sub Rosa)

Army of Terror (Star Wars Galaxy of Fear)

Around the World with the Lil' Bratz (Bratz: Lil' Bratz)

The Arrest (Sweet Valley High)

The Arrival (Animorphs)

The Arrival (Journey of Allen Strange)

Arrival (Smallville)

Artemis Fowl (Artemis Fowl)

As Ever, Gordy (Gordy Smith)

As I Am (Love Stories)

As if I Care (Sweet Valley High Senior Year)

As Puck Would Have It (Charmed)

As You Wish (Christy Miller: Christy and Todd: The College Years)

Ascendance (The DemonWars)

Ascendant Sun (Saga of the Skolian Empire)

Ascension (Water)

Ashes of Victory (Honor Harrington)

Ashleigh's Christmas Miracle (Thoroughbred)

Ashleigh's Diary (Thoroughbred)

Ashleigh's Dream (Thoroughbred)

Ashleigh's Farewell (Thoroughbred)

Ashleigh's Hope (Thoroughbred)

Ashleigh's Promise (Thoroughbred: Ashleigh)

Ashleigh's Western Challenge (Thoroughbred: Ashleigh)

Ashley's Lost Angel (Forever Angels)

Ask Annie (Sweet Dreams)

Assassin (Lady Grace Mysteries)

Assassin's Blade (Magic: The Gathering—Magic Legends Cycle Two)

Assassins in the Cathedral (Trailblazers)

The Assassins of Rome (Roman Mysteries)

The Astral Summer (Zenda)

At All Costs (Honor Harrington)

At All Costs (Nancy Drew and the Hardy Boys Super Mysteries)

At First Sight (Love Stories)

At the Crossing Places (Arthur Trilogy)

At the Earth's Core (Pellucidar)

Atalanta and the Arcadian Beast (Young Heroes)

Atlantis Station (Star Trek: The Next Generation: Starfleet Academy)

The Attack (Animorphs)

Attack in the Rye Grass (Trailblazers)

Attack of Apollyon (Left Behind—The Kids)

The Attack of the Aqua Apes (Fear Street: Ghosts of Fear Street)

Attack of the Beastly Baby-Sitter (Goosebumps: Give Yourself Goosebumps)

Attack of the Denebian Starship (Daystar Voyages)

Attack of the Fiend (Last Apprentice)

Attack of the 50-Foot Alien Creepoids (Super Goofballs)

Attack of the Graveyard Ghouls (Goosebumps Series 2000)

Attack of the Jack-O'-Lanterns (Goosebumps)

Attack of the Killer Ants (Bone Chillers)

Attack of the Killer Bebes (Kim Possible (Chapter Books))

Attack of the Killer Crabs (Spooksville)

Attack of the Living Mask (Choose Your Own Nightmare)

Attack of the Mole Master (Sidekicks)

Attack of the Mutant (Goosebumps)

Attack of the Two-Ton Tomatoes (Eerie Indiana)

Attack of the Vampire Worms (Fear Street: Ghosts of Fear Street)

Attack of the Video Villains (Hardy Boys)

Attack on Petra (Left Behind—The Kids)

Attack on the Tower of London (Screech Owls)

Atticus of Rome, 30 B.C. (The Life and Times)

Attitude (Making Waves)

The Au Pairs (Au Pairs)

Audacious (Brides of Wildcat County)

August (Countdown)

August Magic (Summer)

Aunt Weird (House of Horrors)

The Austere Academy (A Series of Unfortunate Events)

The Author's Blood (Wormling)

Autocrats of Oz (Oz)

Autumn (Miki Falls)

Autumnal (Angel (Graphic Novels))

Autumnal (Buffy the Vampire Slayer)

AutumnQuest (DragonSpawn Cycle)

Avatar (Angel)

Avatar (Indigo)

Avenger (Danny Watts)

Awakening (Lily Dale)

The Awakening (Quantum Prophecy)

Awakening (Sweep)

The Awakening (Vampire Diaries)

The Awakening Evil (Fear Street: Fear Street Sagas)

Aware of the Wolf (Knightscares)

Away Laughing on a Fast Camel (Confessions of Georgia Nicolson)

B

"B" Is for Bad at Getting Into Harvard (Raise the Flag)

Babe and Me (Baseball Card Adventures)

Babes in Boyland (Clueless)

Babes in the Woods (He-Man Women Haters Club)

The Baby Angel (Forever Angels)

Baby Be-Bop (Weetzie Bat Saga)

Baby Help (Hamilton High)

The Baby-Sitter (Baby-Sitter)

The Baby-Sitter Burglaries (Nancy Drew)

The Baby-Sitter II (Baby-Sitter)

The Baby-Sitter III (Baby-Sitter)

The Baby-Sitter IV (Baby-Sitter)

Baby-Sitters at Shadow Lake (Baby-Sitters Club Super Specials)

Baby-Sitters Beware (Baby-Sitters Club Mysteries)

Baby-Sitters' Christmas Chiller (Baby-Sitters Club Mysteries)

The Beast of Baskerville (Deadtime Stories)

The Beast under the Wizard's Bridge (Lewis Barnavelt)

Beastly Tales (Fear Street: Ghosts of Fear Street)

A Beautiful Place on Yonge Street (Harper Winslow)

Beautiful Stranger (A-List)

Beauty and the Beach (Sweet Valley University)

Beauty Is a Beast (The Princess School)

Beauty Sleep (Once Upon a Time)

Beauty Sleepover Bash! (Bratz: Lil' Bratz)

Bec (Demonata)

Because I'm Worth It (Gossip Girl)

The Becoming (Daughters of the Moon)

Becoming Me (Diary of a Teenage Girl)

Been There, Crossed Over (Pretty Freekin Scary)

Before Gaia (Fearless)

Before Midnight (Once Upon a Time)

The Beggar Queen (Westmark)

Begin Again (Remnants)

The Beginning (Animorphs)

The Beginning (Replica)

Behind Closed Doors (Sweet Valley University)

Behind His Back (Love Stories)

Behind the Curtain (Echo Falls Mystery)

Behind the Great Wall (Young Indiana Jones Chronicles: Choose Your Own Adventure)

Behind the Mountains (First Person Fiction)

Behind-the-Scenes Secrets (Bratz: Clued In!)

Behind the Sorcerer's Cloak (The Summer of Magic Quartet)

Behind the Veil (Royal Pavilions)

Behind the Wheel (Choose Your Own Adventure)

Beldan's Fire (Oran Trilogy)

Believing (Lily Dale)

Believing the Dream (Red River: Return to Red River)

Belinda's Obsession (Not Just Proms and Parties)

The Bell, the Book, and the Spellbinder (Johnny Dixon)

Bella Goes Hollywood (Star Sisterz)

Belle (Once Upon a Time)

The Bellmaker (Redwall)

Ben Takes a Chance (Making Out)

Benched! (Alden All Stars)

Bending the Rules (Generation Girl)

Ben's in Love (Making Out)

Bernie and the Bessledorf Ghost (Bessledorf Hotel)

Bernie Magruder and the Bats in the Belfry (Bessledorf Hotel)

Bernie Magruder and the Bus Station Blow Up (Bessledorf Hotel)

Bernie Magruder and the Case of the Big Stink (Bessledorf Hotel)

Bernie Magruder and the Disappearing Bodies (Bessledorf Hotel)

Bernie Magruder and the Drive-Thru Funeral Parlor (Bessledorf Hotel)

Bernie Magruder and the Haunted Hotel (Bessledorf Hotel)

Bernie Magruder and the Parachute Peril (Bessledorf Hotel)

Bernie Magruder and the Pirate's Treasure (Bessledorf Hotel)

Berserker (Berserker)

Berserker: Blue Death (Berserker)

The Berserker Attack (Berserker)

Berserker Base (Berserker)

Berserker Kill (Berserker)

Berserker Lies (Berserker)

Berserker Man (Berserker)

Berserker Prime (Berserker)

The Berserker Throne (Berserker)

Berserker Wars (Berserker)

Berserkers (Berserker)

Berserker's Planet (Berserker)

Berserker's Star (Berserker)

Best (Boy)friend Forever (Camp Confidential)

Best Dressed (Lizzie McGuire)

The Best Friend (Fear Street)

The Best Friend 2 (Fear Street)

Best Friend, Worst Enemy (Holly's Heart)

Best Friends (Sweet Valley Twins)

Best Friends for Never (Clique)

Best Friends Forever (Mary-Kate and Ashley: So Little Time)

Best Friends Forever (Sweet Dreams: On Our Own)

Best Friend's Girl (Saved by the Bell)

Best of Enemies (Nancy Drew and the Hardy Boys Super Mysteries)

Best of Enemies (Sweet Valley High Senior Year)

The Best of the Best (Replica)

Bet You Can't! (Secret World of Alex Mack)

Bet Your Life (SpyBoy)

The Betrayal (Fear Street: Fear Street Sagas)

Betrayal (2099)

Betrayal: Lady Grace Mysteries, From the Daybookes of Lady Grace Cavendish; Book the Second (Lady Grace Mysteries)

Betrayal: Part One (Age of Bronze)

Betrayal: Week 6 (Sevens)

Betrayal at Cross Creek (American Girls: History Mysteries)

Betrayed (Cheerleaders)

Betrayed (Fearless)

Betrayed (Fingerprints)

Betrayed (House of Night)

Betrayed (Jennie McGrady Mysteries)

Betrayed By Love (Nancy Drew Files)

Betrayed! (Crime Through Time)

The Betrayer's Fortune (Trailblazers)

Bettypalooza (Clueless)

Between Light and Dark (W.I.T.C.H.—Graphic Novels)

Between Madison and Palmetto (Maizon)

Between Worlds (Charmed)

Beverly Hills Brontosaurus (Dinoverse)

Beverly Hills, 90210 (Beverly Hills, 90210)

Beware Dawn! (Baby-Sitters Club Mysteries)

Beware of the Purple Peanut Butter (Goosebumps: Give Yourself Goosebumps)

Beware, Princess Elizabeth (Young Royals)

Beware the Babysitter (Sweet Valley High)

Beware the Bohrok (Bionicle Chronicles)

Beware the Fish! (Bruno and Boots)

Beware the Metal Children (The Outer Limits)

Beware the Shopping Mall! (Bone Chillers)

Blood Brother (Traces: Luke Harding, Forensic Investigator)

Blood Brothers (Unseen)

Blood Captain (Vampirates)

Blood Fever (Young Bond)

Blood Is Thicker (Bluford High)

Blood Money (Hardy Boys Casefiles)

Blood of Carthage (Buffy the Vampire Slayer)

Blood on the Handle (Choose Your Own Adventure)

Blood Red Eightball (Spinetinglers)

Blood Red Horse (de Granville Trilogy)

Blood Relations (Blue-Eyed Son Trilogy)

Blood Relations (Hardy Boys Casefiles)

Blood Sport (Hardy Boys Casefiles)

Blood Tide (Never Land)

Blood Witch (Sweep)

Blooded (Buffy the Vampire Slayer)

Bloodhound (Beka Cooper)

Bloodlines (Magic: The Gathering—Artifacts Cycle)

Bloodroot (China Bayles Mystery)

Bloody Jack (Bloody Jack Adventures)

The Blossom Angel (Forever Angels)

Blossom Culp and the Sleep of Death (Blossom Culp)

A Blossom Promise (The Blossom Family)

The Blossoms and the Green Phantom (The Blossom Family)

The Blossoms Meet the Vulture Lady (The Blossom Family)

Blown Away (Hardy Boys Casefiles)

Blown Away (Hardy Boys, Undercover Brothers)

blowtorch@psycho.com (Bone Chillers)

Blue Avenger and the Theory of Everything (Blue Avenger)

Blue Avenger Cracks the Code (Blue Avenger)

Blue Bloods (Blue Bloods)

The Blue Djinn of Babylon (Children of the Lamp)

The Blue Door (Quilt Trilogy)

Blue Girl (Glory)

Blue Is for Nightmares (Blue Is for Nightmares)

Blue Moon (Circle of Three)

Blue Moon (Life at Sixteen)

Blue Noon (Midnighters)

Blue Ribbon Romance (Sweet Dreams)

The Blue Sword (Damar Chronicles)

The Blue Witch of Oz (Oz)

The Bluebeard Room (Nancy Drew)

BMX Tunnel Run (Take It to the Xtreme)

Board Games (Luna Bay)

Board to Death (Hardy Boys, Undercover Brothers: Graphic Novels)

Boardwalk Bust (Hardy Boys, Undercover Brothers)

The Bodies in the Bessledorf Hotel (Bessledorf Hotel)

Body Bags (Body of Evidence)

Body Check (Matt Christopher's Sports Stories)

Body Lines (Heart Beats)

Body Switchers from Outer Space (Fear Street: Ghosts of Fear Street)

Boiling Point (Dish)

Bold Beauty (Winnie the Horse Gentler)

Bollywood Babes (Babes)

The Bomb in the Bessledorf Bus Depot (Bessledorf Hotel)

Bombay Boomerang (Hardy Boys)

Bon Voyage, Christie & Company (Christie & Company)

The Bonemender (The Bonemender)

The Bonemender's Choice (The Bonemender)

The Bonemender's Oath (The Bonemender)

Bonjour, Alex! (Secret World of Alex Mack)

Bonjour, Wildcats (High School Musical Stories from East High)

Boo Year's Eve (Graveyard School)

Boogey's Back for Blood (Spinetinglers)

The Book of Air (The Dragon Quartet)

Book of Earth (Diadem)

The Book of Earth (The Dragon Quartet)

The Book of Fire (The Dragon Quartet)

The Book of Fours (Buffy the Vampire Slayer)

Book of Horrors (Nightmare Hall)

Book of Magic (Diadem)

The Book of Merlyn (Once and Future King)

Book of Names (Diadem)

Book of Nightmares (Diadem)

Book of Shadows (Sweep)

Book of Signs (Diadem)

Book of the Dead (Angel)

The Book of the Flame (Samurai Girl)

The Book of the Heart (Samurai Girl)

The Book of the King (Wormling)

The Book of the Lion (The Book of the Lion)

The Book of the Pearl (Samurai Girl)

The Book of the Shadow (Samurai Girl)

The Book of the Sword (The Darkest Age)

The Book of the Sword (Samurai Girl)

The Book of the Wind (Samurai Girl)

The Book of Three (Charmed)

The Book of Three (Prydain Chronicles)

Book of Thunder (Diadem)

The Book of Water (The Dragon Quartet)

Booster Boycott (Sweet Valley Twins)

Boot (Wolfbay Wings)

The Borderline Case (Hardy Boys Casefiles)

Born of Elven Blood (Dragonflight)

Bornstone's Elixir (Akiko Graphic Novels)

Boston Jane (Boston Jane)

Boston Jane: The Claim (Boston Jane)

Boston Jane: Wilderness Days (Boston Jane)

Both Sides of Time (Time Travel Quartet)

Bottom of the Dark (Trigun Maximum)

Bounty Hunters (Left Behind—The Kids)

A Boy at War (Adam Pelko)

Boy Crazy (Mary-Kate and Ashley: So Little Time)

Boy-Crazy Stacey (Baby-Sitters Club)

Boy. Friend. (Sweet Valley Junior High)

The Buccaneers (High Seas Trilogy)

Buckskin Bandit (Winnie the Horse Gentler)

The Bucktails' Antietam Trials (White Mane Kids)

The Bucktails' Shenandoah March (White Mane Kids)

Budding Star (Angels Unlimited)

Bueno Nacho (Kim Possible (Chapter Books))

Bueno Nacho and Tick Tick Tick (Kim Possible (TokyoPop))

Bugged Out! (Choose Your Own Nightmare)

The Bugman Lives! (Fear Street: Ghosts of Fear Street)

Building a Mystery (T*Witches)

The Bully (Bluford High)

Bully (Sweet Valley Twins)

The Bully Coach (American Gold Gymnasts)

The Bungalow Mystery (Nancy Drew)

Bureau of Lost (Eerie Indiana)

Buried Alive (Distress Call 911)

Buried Alive: A Mystery in Denali National Park (Mysteries in Our National Parks)

Buried in Time (Nancy Drew and the Hardy Boys Super Mysteries)

Buried Secrets (Nancy Drew Files)

Buried Secrets (Smallville)

Buried Treasure (Sweet Valley Twins)

Burn (Making Waves)

Burned (Hardy Boys, Undercover Brothers)

The Burning (Fear Street: Fear Street Sagas)

The Burning (Guardians of Ga'Hoole)

The Burning: The Unseen Trilogy Book 1 (Buffy the Vampire Slayer: Buffy and Angel: The Unseen Trilogy)

Burning Bones (Body of Evidence)

The Burning Bridge (Ranger's Apprentice)

Burning for Revenge (Tomorrow)

The Burning Questions of Bingo Brown (Bingo Brown)

Burnt Orange (True Colors)

Burying the Sun (Angel on the Square)

Busted! (Left Behind—The Kids)

Busted! (Sweet Valley University)

But What About Me? (Hamilton High)

Butt Wars! (Butt Wars)

Buying Time (On the Road)

Buzzard's Feast (Against the Odds)

Buzzer Basket (Chip Hilton Sports Series)

By Balloon to the Sahara (Choose Your Own Adventure)

By Honor Betray'd (Valdemar: Mageworlds)

By The Book (Star Trek: Enterprise)

Bye-Bye-Boy Friend (Mary-Kate and Ashley: Two of a Kind)

C

Cabin Six Plays Cupid (Camp Sunnyside)

Caddy Ever After (Casson Family)

Cadet Kirk (Star Trek: Starfleet Academy)

Calamity Jinx (Thoroughbred)

A Calculus of Angels (The Age of Unreason)

The Calder Game (Petra and Calder)

California Crazy (Holly's Heart)

California Dreaming (A-List)

California Dreams (Mary-Kate and Ashley Sweet 16)

California Girl (Sweet Dreams)

California Girls! (Baby-Sitters Club Super Specials)

California Gold (Abby's South Seas Adventures)

California Scheming (Saved by the Bell)

Call for Courage (Golden Filly Series)

Call Me Beautiful (Sweet Dreams)

Call Me Francis Tucket (The Tucket Adventures)

Call Me María (First Person Fiction)

The Call of Earth (Homecoming Saga)

The Call to Vengeance (Star Wars: Jedi Apprentice)

The Calling (Sweep)

Calling All Boys (Mary-Kate and Ashley: Two of a Kind)

Calling All Creeps! (Goosebumps)

Calling on Dragons (Enchanted Forest Chronicles)

Calling the Shots (Angels Unlimited)

Calm Before the Storm (Dawson's Creek)

The Calusari (X Files)

The Camelot Spell (Grail Quest)

Cammi's Crush (Sweet Valley Twins)

Camp Camden (7th Heaven)

Camp Can't (The Complicated Life of Claudia Cristina Cortez)

Camp Confessions (Cheer Squad)

Camp Crocodile (Spinetinglers)

Camp Dracula (Graveyard School)

Camp Fear Ghouls (Fear Street: Ghosts of Fear Street)

Camp Killer (Sweet Valley High)

Camp Nowhere (Nightmare Room)

Camp Out (Fear Street)

Camp Rock 'n' Roll (Mary-Kate and Ashley: Two of a Kind)

Camp Saddlebrook (Thoroughbred)

Camp Spaghetti (Camp Sunnyside)

Camp Zombie (Camp Zombie)

Camp Zombie: The Lake's Revenge (Camp Zombie)

Camp Zombie: The Second Summer (Camp Zombie)

Campaign Chaos (Generation Girl)

Campaign of Crime (Hardy Boys Casefiles)

The Campfire Crush (Date Him or Dump Him?)

Campfire Nights (Sweet Dreams)

Campus Exposures (Nancy Drew on Campus)

Can Adults Become Human? (Dear Dumb Diary)

Can of Worms (Mike Pillsbury)

Can You Fear Me Now? (Tales from the Crypt Graphic Novels)

Can You Get an F in Lunch? (How I Survived Middle School)

The Candle in the Wind (Once and Future King)

Candles (On Time's Wing)

Candles, Cake, Celebrate! (Mary-Kate and Ashley: Two of a Kind)

The Candlestone (Dragons in Our Midst)

The Candy Man Cometh (Sidekicks)

Canine Caper! (Secret World of Alex Mack)

The Cannibals (The Curse of the Jolly Stone Trilogy)

The Case of the Fagin File (Baker Street Irregulars)

The Case of the Firecrackers (Chinatown Mystery)

The Case of the Flapper 'Napper (Mary-Kate and Ashley: Adventures of Mary-Kate and Ashley)

The Case of the Floating Crime (Nancy Drew)

The Case of the Flying Phantom (Mary-Kate and Ashley: Adventures of Mary-Kate and Ashley)

The Case of the Fun House Mystery (Mary-Kate and Ashley: Adventures of Mary-Kate and Ashley)

The Case of the Game Show Mystery (Mary-Kate and Ashley: Adventures of Mary-Kate and Ashley)

The Case of the Ghost Grabbers (Baker Street Irregulars)

The Case of the Giggling Ghost (Mary-Kate and Ashley: Adventures of Mary-Kate and Ashley)

The Case of the Goblin Pearls (Chinatown Mystery)

The Case of the Golden Slipper (Mary-Kate and Ashley: Adventures of Mary-Kate and Ashley)

The Case of the Great Elephant Escape (Mary-Kate and Ashley: Adventures of Mary-Kate and Ashley)

The Case of the Green Ghost (Mary-Kate and Ashley: Adventures of Mary-Kate and Ashley)

The Case of the Haunted Camp (Mary-Kate and Ashley: Adventures of Mary-Kate and Ashley)

The Case of the Haunted Holiday (Baker Street Irregulars)

The Case of the Haunted Maze (Mary-Kate and Ashley: Adventures of Mary-Kate and Ashley)

The Case of the Hidden Holiday Riddle (Mary-Kate and Ashley: Adventures of Mary-Kate and Ashley)

The Case of the High Seas Secret (Mary-Kate and Ashley: Adventures of Mary-Kate and Ashley)

The Case of the Hollywood Who-Done-It (Mary-Kate and Ashley: Adventures of Mary-Kate and Ashley)

The Case of the Hotel Who-Done-It (Mary-Kate and Ashley: Adventures of Mary-Kate and Ashley)

The Case of the Icy Igloo Inn (Mary-Kate and Ashley: Adventures of Mary-Kate and Ashley)

The Case of the Jingle Bell Jinx (Mary-Kate and Ashley: Adventures of Mary-Kate and Ashley)

Case of the Kate Haters (Lizzie McGuire Mysteries)

The Case of the Left-handed Lady (Enola Holmes)

The Case of the Lion Dance (Chinatown Mystery)

The Case of the Logical I Ranch (Mary-Kate and Ashley: Adventures of Mary-Kate and Ashley)

The Case of the Lost Song (Nancy Drew)

The Case of the Mall Mystery (Mary-Kate and Ashley: Adventures of Mary-Kate and Ashley)

The Case of the Missing Marquess (Enola Holmes)

The Case of the Missing Masterpiece (Baker Street Irregulars)

The Case of the Missing Mummy (Mary-Kate and Ashley: Adventures of Mary-Kate and Ashley)

Case of the Missing She-Geek (Lizzie McGuire Mysteries)

The Case of the Mystery Cruise (Mary-Kate and Ashley: Adventures of Mary-Kate and Ashley)

The Case of the Nana-napper (Wright and Wong)

The Case of the Nutcracker Ballet (Mary-Kate and Ashley: Adventures of Mary-Kate and Ashley)

The Case of the Peculiar Pink Fan (Enola Holmes)

The Case of the Photo Finish (Nancy Drew)

The Case of the Prank That Stank (Wright and Wong)

The Case of the Psychic's Vision (Hardy Boys)

The Case of the Rising Stars (Nancy Drew)

The Case of the Rock and Roll Mystery (Mary-Kate and Ashley: Adventures of Mary-Kate and Ashley)

The Case of the Rock Star's Secret (Mary-Kate and Ashley: Adventures of Mary-Kate and Ashley)

The Case of the Safecracker's Secret (Nancy Drew)

The Case of the Savage Statue (Three Investigators)

The Case of the Screaming Scarecrow (Mary-Kate and Ashley: Adventures of Mary-Kate and Ashley)

The Case of the Sea World Adventure (Mary-Kate and Ashley: Adventures of Mary-Kate and Ashley)

The Case of the Shark Encounter (Mary-Kate and Ashley: Adventures of Mary-Kate and Ashley)

The Case of the Silk King (Choose Your Own Adventure)

The Case of the Slam Dunk Mystery (Mary-Kate and Ashley: Adventures of Mary-Kate and Ashley)

The Case of the Slippery Soap Star (Wright and Wong)

The Case of the Summer Camp Caper (Mary-Kate and Ashley: Adventures of Mary-Kate and Ashley)

The Case of the Sundae Surprise (Mary-Kate and Ashley: Adventures of Mary-Kate and Ashley)

The Case of the Surfing Secret (Mary-Kate and Ashley: Adventures of Mary-Kate and Ashley)

The Case of the Surprise Call (Mary-Kate and Ashley: Adventures of Mary-Kate and Ashley)

The Case of the Tattooed Cat (Mary-Kate and Ashley: Adventures of Mary-Kate and Ashley)

The Case of the Trail Mix-up (Wright and Wong)

The Case of the Twin Teddy Bears (Nancy Drew)

The Case of the 202 Clues (Mary-Kate and Ashley: Adventures of Mary-Kate and Ashley)

Challenge at Second Base (Matt Christopher's's Sports Stories)

The Challenge Box (Circle of Three)

Challenge of the Masked Racer (Speed Racer)

Challenger's Hope (Seafort Saga)

Chamber of Fear (Fear Street: Fear Street Sagas)

The Chameleon Wore Chartreuse (Chet Gecko Mysteries)

Champion's Spirit (Thoroughbred)

Champion's Trial (Magic: The Gathering—Magic Legends Cycle Two)

Championship Ball (Chip Hilton Sports Series)

Championship Summer (Alden All Stars)

The Chance Factor (Star Trek: Voyager: Starfleet Academy)

The Chance of a Lifetime (Cassie Perkins)

Chance of a Lifetime (Saddles, Stars, and Stripes)

Chance of a Lifetime (Silver Blades)

A Chance to Love (Sweet Dreams)

Chandlefort (In the Shadow of the Bear)

The Change (Animorphs)

The Change (The Outer Limits)

A Change of Heart (Sweet Dreams)

Change of Plans (Everwood)

Changeling (Sweep)

The Changeling (Wormling)

Changeling Diapers (Journey of Allen Strange)

Changeling Places (Charmed)

Changing Leads (Saddle Club: Pine Hollow)

Changing Loves (Cheerleaders)

The Changing of the Guard (Star Wars: Jedi Quest)

Changing Times (B.Y. Times)

Channel X (Sweet Valley University Thriller Editions)

The Chaos Balance (Recluce)

Chaos Bleeds (Buffy the Vampire Slayer)

The Charioteer of Delphi (Roman Mysteries)

Charlie Bone and the Beast (Children of the Red King)

Charlie Bone and the Castle of Mirrors (Children of the Red King)

Charlie Bone and the Hidden King (Children of the Red King)

Charlie Bone and the Invisible Boy (Children of the Red King)

Charlie Bone and the Shadow (Children of the Red King)

Charlie Bone and the Time Twister (Children of the Red King)

Charlotte in Paris (Beacon Street Girls)

Charm School Mystery (Sweet Valley Twins)

Charmed Again (Charmed)

The Charmed Bracelet (Nancy Drew Graphic Novels)

Charmed Forces (Camp Confidential)

Charmed Life (Chrestomanci)

Charmed Thirds (Jessica Darling)

Chase (Fearless)

The Chase (Forbidden Game)

The Chase for the Mystery Twister (Hardy Boys)

Chasing the Falconers (On the Run)

Chasing the King (Dream Series)

Chasing the Wind (The Young Underground)

Chasing Vermeer (Petra and Calder)

Chat Freak (TodaysGirls.com)

Cheat Sheet (How I Survived Middle School)

The Cheater (Fear Street)

Cheating (Cheerleaders)

The Cheating Heart (Nancy Drew Files)

Cheating Heart (Sweet Dreams)

Cheating on Anna (Sweet Valley Junior High)

Cheating to Win (Sweet Valley High)

Check It Out—and Die! (Spinetinglers)

Checkered Flag (RPM)

Checkout Time at the Dead-End Hotel (Goosebumps: Give Yourself Goosebumps)

Chelsea's Ride (Not Just Proms and Parties)

Cher and Cher Alike (Clueless)

Cher Goes Enviro-Mental (Clueless)

Cher Negotiates New York (Clueless)

Cherokee Bat and the Goat Guys (Weetzie Bat Saga)

Cher's Frantically Romantic Assignment (Clueless)

Cher's Furiously Fit Workout (Clueless)

Cher's Guide to . . . Whatever (Clueless)

The Chessmen of Doom (Johnny Dixon)

Chestnut Ridge Acres (Whispering Brook)

The Chestnut Soldier (Gwyn Griffiths Trilogy)

Chicken Chicken (Goosebumps)

Chicks with Sticks (Chicks with Sticks)

Chicks with Sticks: Knit Two Together (Chicks with Sticks)

Chicks with Sticks: Knitwise (Chicks with Sticks)

The Chief (The Contender)

Chief Honor (Lightning on Ice)

Child of an Ancient City (Dragonflight)

Child of the Dark Prophecy (The Great Tree of Avalon)

Child of the Hunt (Buffy the Vampire Slayer)

Child of the Owl (Golden Mountain Chronicles)

Child of the Prophecy (Sevenwaters)

Childhood's End (Oh My Goddess!)

Children of Fear (Fear Street: Fear Street Sagas)

The Children of Green Knowe (Green Knowe)

Children of Hope (Seafort Saga)

Children of the Mind (Ender Wiggin)

Children of the Wolf (Werewolf Chronicles)

The Children's Crusade (Books of Magic)

Chile Death (China Bayles Mystery)

Chill (Making Waves)

The Chimera's Curse (The Companions Quartet)

The Chimney Sweep's Ransom (Trailblazers)

Chindi (Priscilla Hutchins)

Chinese Dragons (Choose Your Own Adventure)

The Chocolate-Covered Contest (Nancy Drew)

The Chocolate Lover (Missing Persons)

Claudia and the Perfect Boy (Baby-Sitters Club)

Claudia and the Phantom Phone Calls (Baby-Sitters Club)

Claudia and the Recipe for Danger (Baby-Sitters Club Mysteries)

Claudia and the Sad Good-bye (Baby-Sitters Club)

Claudia and the Terrible Truth (Baby-Sitters Club)

Claudia and the World's Cutest Baby (Baby-Sitters Club)

Claudia Gets Her Guy (Baby-Sitters Club Friends Forever)

Claudia Kishi, Live from WSTO! (Baby-Sitters Club)

Claudia Kishi, Middle School Dropout (Baby-Sitters Club)

Claudia Makes Up Her Mind (Baby-Sitters Club)

Claudia, Queen of the Seventh Grade (Baby-Sitters Club)

Claudia's—Freind—Friend (Baby-Sitters Club)

Claudia's Big Party (Baby-Sitters Club)

Claudia's Book (Baby-Sitters Club Portrait Collection)

Claw of the Dragon (Dungeons and Dragons: Endless Quest)

Claws and Effect (Mrs. Murphy)

Clean Sweep (Hardy Boys Casefiles)

Cleanup Catastrophe! (Secret World of Alex Mack)

Cleopatra VII (Royal Diaries)

Cliff-Hanger (Hardy Boys Casefiles)

Cliff Hanger (Mysteries in Our National Parks)

The Climb (Everest)

The Clique (Clique)

Cloak and Dagger (Net Force)

Cloned (Kim Possible: Pick a Villain)

Clones (Star Wars Galaxy of Fear)

The Clones (Virtual World Chronologs)

Close Call (Golden Filly Series)

Close Call (Thoroughbred)

Close Encounters (Nancy Drew: Girl Detective)

Close Encounters! (Secret World of Alex Mack)

Close Kin (Hollow Kingdom)

Close Out (Impact Zone)

Close Quarters (Alias)

Close Quarters (High Hurdles)

Close to the Ground (Angel)

Close to You (Sweet Valley High Senior Year)

Close-Up (Three Girls in the City)

Close Up and Personal (Flirt)

Close Your Eyes (Sierra Jensen)

Closer than Ever (Mary-Kate and Ashley: Two of a Kind)

Closer Than Ever (Sierra Jensen)

Clovermead (In the Shadow of the Bear)

A Club in Montmartre (Art Encounters)

Clue in the Ancient Disguise (Nancy Drew)

The Clue in the Antique Trunk (Nancy Drew)

The Clue in the Camera (Nancy Drew)

The Clue in the Crossword Cypher (Nancy Drew)

The Clue in the Crumbling Wall (Nancy Drew)

The Clue in the Diary (Nancy Drew)

The Clue in the Embers (Hardy Boys)

The Clue in the Jewel Box (Nancy Drew)

The Clue in the Old Album (Nancy Drew)

The Clue in the Old Stagecoach (Nancy Drew)

The Clue of the Black Keys (Nancy Drew)

The Clue of the Broken Blade (Hardy Boys)

The Clue of the Broken Locket (Nancy Drew)

The Clue of the Dancing Puppet (Nancy Drew)

The Clue of the Gold Doubloons (Nancy Drew)

The Clue of the Hissing Serpent (Hardy Boys)

The Clue of the Leaning Chimney (Nancy Drew)

The Clue of the Linoleum Lederhosen (M. T. Anderson's Thrilling Tales)

Clue of the Screeching Owl (Hardy Boys)

The Clue of the Tapping Heels (Nancy Drew)

The Clue of the Velvet Mask (Nancy Drew)

The Clue of the Whistling Bagpipes (Nancy Drew)

The Clue on the Crystal Dove (Nancy Drew)

The Clue on the Silver Screen (Nancy Drew)

Clueless (Sweet Valley Junior High)

Clueless: A Novel (Clueless)

The Clues Challenge (Nancy Drew)

Clues in the Car Wash (Klooz)

Clutch Hitter! (Chip Hilton Sports Series)

The Coalition of Lions (Arthurian-Aksumite Cycle)

Cobra Connection (Choose Your Own Adventure)

The Cobra King of Kathmandu (Children of the Lamp)

Cobra Threat (Sports Mystery)

Code Name Cassandra (1-800-Where-R-You)

Cody (Wolfbay Wings)

Cody's Varsity Rush (Spirit of the Game)

The Coffin (Nightmare Hall)

The Coffin Club (Vampire Kisses)

Cohen! (The O.C.)

Cold as Ice (Nancy Drew Files)

Cold Case (Net Force)

The Cold Cash Caper (Hardy Boys)

Cold Fire (Circle of Magic: The Circle Opens)

The Cold People (Spooksville)

Cold Shoulder Road (Wolves Chronicles)

Cold Sweat (Hardy Boys Casefiles)

Collateral Damage (Alias)

College Bound (Beverly Hills, 90210)

College Cruise (Sweet Valley University)

College Girls (Sweet Valley University)

College Weekend (Fear Street)

College Weekend (Sweet Valley High)

Collision Course (Hardy Boys Casefiles)

Colman (Wise Child)

Colonization (Colonization)

Colonization: Down to Earth (Colonization)

Colonization: Homeward Bound (Colonization)

Colonization: Second Contact (Colonization)

A Crime for Christmas (Nancy Drew and the Hardy Boys Super Mysteries)

Crime in the Cards (Hardy Boys)

Crime in the Kennel (Hardy Boys)

Crime in the Queen's Court (Nancy Drew)

The Crime Lab Case (Nancy Drew)

The Crimson Flame (Hardy Boys)

The Crimson Spell (Charmed)

The Crimson Thread (Once Upon a Time)

Crisis at Crystal Reef (Star Wars Young Jedi Knights)

Crisis on Vulcan (Star Trek: Starfleet Academy)

Crisis Point (University Hospital)

The Crisscross Crime (Hardy Boys)

The Crisscross Shadow (Hardy Boys)

The Crooked Bannister (Nancy Drew)

Cross-Country Crime (Hardy Boys)

Cross-Country Gallop (Horseshoes)

Cross-Country Match (Sweet Dreams)

Cross My Heart (Sweet Dreams)

Cross Our Hearts (Mary-Kate and Ashley Sweet 16)

Cross-Ties (Saddle Club: Pine Hollow)

Crosscurrents (Nancy Drew Files)

Crossed Signals (Sweet Dreams)

Crossed Tracks (X Games Xtreme Mysteries)

Crossfire (Star Trek: The Next Generation: Starfleet Academy)

Crossfire (Star Wars: Boba Fett)

Crossings (Buffy the Vampire Slayer)

Crossroads of Twilight (The Wheel of Time)

Croutons for Breakfast (Brio Girls)

The Crow (Pellinor)

Crown and Sword (Rex Mundi)

The Crown of Dalemark (Dalemark Quartet)

Crown of Horns (Bone)

The Crown of Light (W.I.T.C.H.—Chapter Books)

A Crown of Swords (The Wheel of Time)

The Crowning Terror (Hardy Boys Casefiles)

The Cruel Empress (W.I.T.C.H.—Adventures)

Cruise Control (Sweet Valley High Senior Year)

Crunch Time (High School Musical Stories from East High)

Crusade of the Flaming Sword (Hardy Boys)

The Crusading Wizard (A Wizard in Rhyme)

Crush (Wicked Dead)

Crushing on You (Love Stories)

A Cry in the Dark (Summerhill Secrets)

Cry of the Cat (Goosebumps Series 2000)

The Cry of the Icemark (The Icemark Chronicles)

Cry of the Wolf (Avalon 1: Web of Magic)

Crypt-Keeping It Real (Tales from the Crypt Graphic Novels)

The Crystal City (Tales of Alvin Maker)

Crystal Doors (Crystal Doors)

Crystal Doors: Ocean Realm (Crystal Doors)

Crystal Doors: Sky Realm (Crystal Doors)

Crystal Mask (Echorium Sequence)

The Crystal Planet (Zenda)

The Crystal Prison (Deptford Mice)

The Crystal Stair (Tales of Gom in the Legends of Ulm)

Cube Route (Xanth Saga)

Cuchifrita, Ballerina (Cheetah Girls)

The Cuckoo Clock of Doom (Goosebumps)

The Cuckoo Tree (Wolves Chronicles)

Cult of Crime (Hardy Boys Casefiles)

Cup Crazy (Slapshots)

Cupcake (Gingerbread)

Cupid Cakes (Lulu Baker)

The Cupid Chronicles (The Wedding Planner's Daughter)

Currant Events (Xanth Saga)

The Curse (Forbidden Doors)

Curse (Wicked)

Curse of Arastold (Silverskin Legacy)

The Curse of Arkady (The Magickers)

Curse of Batterslea Hall (Choose Your Own Adventure)

The Curse of Camp Cold Lake (Goosebumps)

The Curse of PCA (Zoey 101)

Curse of the Bane (Last Apprentice)

The Curse of the Black Cat (Nancy Drew)

The Curse of the Blue Figurine (Johnny Dixon)

Curse of the Blue Tattoo (Bloody Jack Adventures)

The Curse of the Cave Creatures (Goosebumps: Give Yourself Goosebumps)

The Curse of the Cheerleaders (Spinetinglers)

Curse of the Claw (Phantom Valley)

The Curse of the Creeping Coffin (Goosebumps: Give Yourself Goosebumps)

The Curse of the Gloamglozer (Edge Chronicles)

The Curse of the Golden Heart (Sweet Valley Twins Super Chiller Editions)

The Curse of the Golden Skull and Other Stories (Chronicles of Conan)

The Curse of the Idol's Eye (Mind over Matter)

Curse of the Lost Grove (Dungeons and Dragons: Knights of the Silver Dragon)

Curse of the Mummy's Tomb (Goosebumps)

The Curse of the Nile (Mummy Chronicles)

The Curse of the Ruby Necklace (Sweet Valley Twins Super Chiller Editions)

Cursed (Buffy the Vampire Slayer: Buffy and Angel)

Curveball (Winning Season)

Cut Back (Impact Zone)

The Cutting Edge (A Handful of Men)

Cutting Edge (Nancy Drew Files)

Cyber Scare (Deadtime Stories)

Cybercops and Flame Wars (Cybersurfers)

CyberHacker (Choose Your Own Adventure)

Cybermage (Worldweavers)

Cyberspace Cowboy (Cybersurfers)

Cyberspace Warrior (Choose Your Own Adventure)

Cyberspy (Net Force)

CyberStalker (Sweet Valley University Thriller Editions)

Cyborg Kickboxer (Tom Swift)

Cyteen (Alliance-Union)

Czar of Alaska (MacGregor Family Adventure)

D

Daedalus (Star Trek: Enterprise)

Daedalus's Children (Star Trek: Enterprise)

Dagger Magic (The Adept)

Dagger of Doom (Dungeons and Dragons: Knights of the Silver Dragon)

Daggerspell (Deverry)

Daisho (Usagi Yojimbo)

Daisy Chains (Friends for a Season)

Daja's Book (Circle of Magic)

The Dance (Love Stories: Super Editions)

The Dance Dilemma (Date Him or Dump Him?)

Dance Fever (Sweet Valley Junior High)

Dance Magic (Here Comes Heavenly)

Dance of Darkness (Winds of Light)

Dance of Death (Fear Street: Fear Street Sagas)

Dance of Death (Sweet Valley High)

Dance of Love (Sweet Dreams)

The Dance of the Skull and Other Stories (Chronicles of Conan)

Dance of the Stones (The Summer of Magic Quartet)

Dance Till You Die (Nancy Drew Files)

Dance Trap (The Complicated Life of Claudia Cristina Cortez)

Dance with a Vampire (Vampire Kisses)

Dance with Me (American Dreams)

Dance with Me (Sweet Dreams)

Dancin' Divas (Bratz: Lil' Bratz)

Dancing in My Nuddy Pants (Confessions of Georgia Nicolson)

Dancing in the Dark (Sweet Dreams)

The Danger (Dive)

Danger (Undercover Girl)

Danger at Anchor Mine (Choose Your Own Adventure)

Danger at Echo Cliffs (Lassie)

Danger at the Wild West Show (American Girls: History Mysteries)

Danger Down Under (Nancy Drew and the Hardy Boys Super Mysteries)

Danger for Hire (Nancy Drew Files)

Danger in Dinosaur Valley (Screech Owls)

Danger in Disguise (Nancy Drew Files)

Danger in Disguise (On Time's Wing)

Danger in the Extreme (Hardy Boys)

Danger in the Fourth Dimension (Hardy Boys)

Danger on Crab Island (Neptune Adventures)

Danger on Parade (Nancy Drew Files)

Danger on the Air (Hardy Boys)

Danger on the Diamond (Hardy Boys)

Danger on the Flying Trapeze (Trailblazers)

Danger on the Great Lakes (Nancy Drew)

Danger on Thunder Mountain (American Adventure)

Danger on Vampire Trail (Hardy Boys)

Danger Time (Goosebumps: Give Yourself Goosebumps)

Danger Unlimited (Hardy Boys Casefiles)

Danger Zone (Distress Call 911)

Danger Zone (Hardy Boys Casefiles)

The Danger Zone (Reel Kids Adventures)

Dangerous (Brides of Wildcat County)

Dangerous Decisions and Hidden Choices (Summit High)

Dangerous Games (Nancy Drew and the Hardy Boys Super Mysteries)

The Dangerous Games (Star Wars: Jedi Quest)

Dangerous Games (Wolves Chronicles)

Dangerous Love (Sweet Valley High)

Dangerous Loves (Nancy Drew Files)

A Dangerous Path (Warriors)

A Dangerous Plan (Left Behind—The Kids)

Dangerous Plays (Nancy Drew: Girl Detective)

A Dangerous Promise (Orphan Train Adventures)

The Dangerous Quest (Spooksville)

Dangerous Relations (Nancy Drew Files)

The Dangerous Rescue (Star Wars: Jedi Apprentice)

A Dangerous Ride (Thoroughbred: Ashleigh)

The Dangerous Transmission (Hardy Boys)

The Dangerous Voyage (Reel Kids Adventures)

Dangerously Alice (Alice)

Dangers of the Rainbow Nebula (Daystar Voyages)

Danny (Love Stories: Brothers Trilogy)

Danny Means Trouble (Sweet Valley Twins)

Daphne (Sisters)

The Dare (Fear Street)

Dare to Scare (Mary-Kate and Ashley: Two of a Kind)

Daredevil Park (Choose Your Own Adventure)

Daredevils (Hardy Boys)

Darien's Rise (Passages)

The Dark (Phantom Valley)

Dark Angel (Night World)

Dark Ararat (Emortality)

Dark Blue (True Colors)

The Dark Corner (Spooksville)

The Dark Design (Riverworld Saga)

Dark Destiny (Bionicle Legends)

The Dark Ground (Dark Ground Trilogy)

The Dark Hand (Jackie Chan Adventures)

Dark Heart (The Seeker Chronicles)

Dark Horse (Mustang Mountain)

The Dark Is Rising (Dark Is Rising)

Dark Lies (Extreme Zone)

The Dark Lord's Demise (The Archives of Anthropos)

The Dark Mage (Avalon 2: Quest for Magic)

Dark Magick (Sweep)

Dark Matter (X Files)

Dark Mirror (Angel)

Dark Moon (Firebringer Trilogy)

Dark Moon (Nightmare Hall)

Dark of the Moon (On Time's Wing)

The Dark One (Roswell High)

The Dark Portal (Deptford Mice)

Dark Quetzal (Echorium Sequence)

Dark Reunion (Vampire Diaries)

The Dark Rival (Star Wars: Jedi Apprentice)

Dark River (Warriors: Power of Three)

The Dark Secret of Weatherend (Anthony Monday)

Dark Side of the Sun (Space Above and Beyond)

Dark Spell Over Morlandria (Daystar Voyages)

The Dark Stairs (Herculeah Jones)

The Dark Tower (Dark Tower)

Dark Vengeance (Charmed)

Dark Warning (Star Wars: The Last of the Jedi)

Dark Whispers (Unicorn Chronicles)

Darkangel (Darkangel Trilogy)

Darkening Skies (Left Behind—The Kids)

The Darkest Dream (W.I.T.C.H.—Chapter Books)

Darkest Hour (Heartland)

Darkest Hour (The Mediator)

The Darkest Hour (Warriors)

Darkest Knight (Star Wars Young Jedi Knights)

A Darkling Plain (The Hungry City Chronicles)

Darkness, Be My Friend (Tomorrow)

Darkness Before Dawn (Hazelwood High)

Darkness Below (Bionicle Adventures)

Darkness Calls (Hellboy)

Darkness Falls (Hardy Boys Casefiles)

Darkness Falls (X Files)

Darksong Rising (The Spellsong Cycle)

Darkspell (Deverry)

The Darksteel Eye (Magic: The Gathering—Mirrodin Cycle)

Darth Maul (Star Wars Episode 1: Journals)

The Dastard (Xanth Saga)

Date (Once Upon a Prom)

A Date with a Werewolf (Sweet Valley High)

Date with Death (Charmed)

A Date with Deception (Nancy Drew Files)

Dating (Cheerleaders)

Dating Game (Mary-Kate and Ashley: So Little Time)

The Dating Game (Sweet Valley High)

Daughter of Magic (Yurt)

Daughter of the Forest (Sevenwaters)

Daughter of Twin Oaks (Secret Refuge)

Daughters of Darkness (Night World)

Daughters of Silence (Fear Street: Fear Street Sagas)

Dawn (California Diaries)

Dawn (Warriors: The New Prophecy)

Dawn and the Big Sleepover (Baby-Sitters Club)

Dawn and the Disappearing Dogs (Baby-Sitters Club Mysteries)

Dawn and the Halloween Mystery (Baby-Sitters Club Mysteries)

Dawn and the Impossible Three (Baby-Sitters Club)

Dawn and the Older Boy (Baby-Sitters Club)

Dawn and the School Spirit War (Baby-Sitters Club)

Dawn and the Surfer Ghost (Baby-Sitters Club Mysteries)

Dawn and the We Love Kids Club (Baby-Sitters Club)

Dawn and Too Many Baby-Sitters (Baby-Sitters Club)

Dawn and Whitney, Friends Forever (Baby-Sitters Club)

Dawn, Diary Three (California Diaries)

Dawn, Diary Two (California Diaries)

Dawn on the Coast (Baby-Sitters Club)

Dawn Saves the Planet (Baby-Sitters Club)

Dawn Schafer, Undercover Babysitter (Baby-Sitters Club Mysteries)

Dawn Selby, Super Sleuth (Best Friends)

Dawn's Big Date (Baby-Sitters Club)

Dawn's Big Move (Baby-Sitters Club)

Dawn's Book (Baby-Sitters Club Portrait Collection)

Dawn's Family Feud (Baby-Sitters Club)

Dawn's Wicked Stepsister (Baby-Sitters Club)

The Day I Met Him (Love Stories)

The Day My Butt Went Psycho! (Butt Wars)

Day of Honor (Star Trek: Deep Space Nine)

The Day of Reckoning (Star Wars: Jedi Apprentice)

Day of the Dinosaur (Hardy Boys)

The Day of the Djinn Warriors (Children of the Lamp)

Day of the Dragon (Extreme Team)

Day of the Dragon: Super Special (Jackie Chan Adventures)

Day of the Scarab (Oracle Prophecies)

Daydreamer (Sweet Dreams)

Days of Air and Darkness (Deverry)

Days of Blood and Fire (Deverry)

Dayworld (Dayworld)

Dayworld Breakup (Dayworld)

Dayworld Rebel (Dayworld)

Dead and Buried (Hear No Evil)

Dead Before Dawn (Sweet Valley University Thriller Editions)

Dead End (Extreme Zone)

Dead End (Fear Street)

Dead End (Red Rock Mysteries)

Dead Heat (Thoroughbred)

Dead in the Water (Hardy Boys Casefiles)

The Dead Kid Did It (Spinetinglers)

Dead Letter (Herculeah Jones)

The Dead Lifeguard (Fear Street: Fear Street Super Chillers)

Dead Man in Deadwood (Hardy Boys Casefiles)

Dead Man's Bones (China Bayles Mystery)

Dead Man's Chest (Pyrates)

Dead Man's Hand (Danger.com)

Dead Man's Secret (Phantom Valley)

The Demon of River Heights (Nancy Drew Graphic Novels)

The Demon Spirit (The DemonWars)

Demon Thief (Demonata)

Demon Witch (Ravenscliff)

The Demon's Den (Hardy Boys)

Demons Don't Dream (Xanth Saga)

Demons of the Ocean (Vampirates)

Den of Thieves (Cat Royal Adventures)

The Departure (Animorphs)

Depend on Katie John (Katie John)

Deprivation House (Hardy Boys, Undercover Brothers Murder House Trilogy)

Depth Charge (Journey of Allen Strange)

Depths (Concrete)

Derby Day (Thoroughbred: Ashleigh)

Derby Dreams (Thoroughbred: Ashleigh)

Derby Fever (Thoroughbred)

Deryni Checkmate (Chronicles of Deryni)

Deryni Rising (Chronicles of Deryni)

The Desert Thieves (Hardy Boys)

Designs in Crime (Nancy Drew Files)

Desolation Angels (The Big Empty)

Desperate Measures (Jennie McGrady Mysteries)

Desperate Measures (Nancy Drew and the Hardy Boys Super Mysteries)

The Desperate Mission (Star Wars: The Last of the Jedi)

The Desperate Search (American Adventure)

Destination Unknown (Remnants)

Destiny's Twins (T*Witches)

Destroyer (Foreigner)

Detective's Duel (Klooz)

Detour for Emily (Hamilton High)

The Devil in Miss Urd (Oh My Goddess!)

Devil's Breath Volcano (MacGregor Family Adventure)

Dew Drop Dead (Sebastian Barth)

Dial L for Loser (Clique)

Dial L for Love (Sweet Dreams)

Dial 'V' for Vengeance (Spy Girls)

Diamond (The Divas)

The Diamond Champs (Matt Christopher's's Sports Stories)

Diamond Deceit (Nancy Drew Files)

Diamond of Darkhold (City of Ember)

The Diamond of Drury Lane (Cat Royal Adventures)

Diamonds Not Forever (Sailor Moon Novels)

The Diaries (Clearwater Crossing)

Diary of a Mad Mummy (Goosebumps: Give Yourself Goosebumps)

Diary of a Wimpy Kid (Diary of a Wimpy Kid)

Diary of a Wimpy Kid: Rodrick Rules (Diary of a Wimpy Kid)

Diary of a Wimpy Kid: The Last Straw (Diary of a Wimpy Kid)

Dicey's Song (Tillerman Cycle)

Dido and Pa (Wolves Chronicles)

Die Bug Die (X Files)

A Different Path (W.I.T.C.H.—Chapter Books)

Diggers (Bromeliad)

A Dilly of a Death (China Bayles Mystery)

Dinosaur Island (Choose Your Own Adventure)

Dinosaurs Ate My Homework (Dinoverse)

Diplomacy of Wolves (Secret Texts)

Diplomatic Deceit (Hardy Boys Casefiles)

Dirt Bike Daredevils (Take It to the Xtreme)

Dirt Bike Racer (Matt Christopher's's Sports Stories)

Dirt Bike Runaway (Matt Christopher's's Sports Stories)

The Dirt Eaters (Longlight Legacy)

Dirty Big Secrets (Trash)

A Dirty Deed (Across the Steel River)

Dirty Deeds (Hardy Boys Casefiles)

Dirty Jersey (Kimani Tru)

The Disappearance (W.I.T.C.H.—Chapter Books)

Disappeared (Alias)

Disappearing Acts (Herculeah Jones)

The Disappearing Floor (Hardy Boys)

Disaster at Parson's Point (Neptune Adventures)

Disaster for Hire (Hardy Boys Casefiles)

Discount Diva (Zodiac Girls)

Discover the Destroyer (EverWorld)

The Discovery (Animorphs)

The Discovery (Dive)

The Disoriented Express (Nancy Drew Graphic Novels)

Dissension (Magic: The Gathering—Ravnica Cycle)

Distance Runner (Thoroughbred)

Dive Right In (Matt Christopher's's Sports Stories)

The Diversion (Animorphs)

Diversity Alliance (Star Wars Young Jedi Knights)

The Divide (The Divide Trilogy)

Divine Madness (Cherub)

Divine One (Sisters of Isis)

Dixie's First Kiss (Sunset Island)

DJ's Challenge (High Hurdles)

The DNA Disaster (Tom Swift)

Do I Have to Paint You a Picture (Raise the Flag)

The Dog Ate My Homework (Bone Chillers)

A Dog Called Grk (Grk)

Dog Eat Dog (Blue-Eyed Son Trilogy)

Dog Gone Mess (Mary-Kate and Ashley in Action)

Doggone Town (Nancy Drew Graphic Novels)

Dogstar (Sirius Mysteries)

Dollars and Sense (B.Y. Times)

The Dollhouse that Time Forgot (Eerie Indiana)

The Dolphin Trap (Neptune Adventures)

Dolphin Watch (Dinotopia)

The Dolphins of Laurentum (Roman Mysteries)

The Dolphins of Pern (Pern)

Don't Answer the Phone (Sweet Valley University Thriller Editions)

Don't Bet on Love (Sweet Dreams)

Don't Count on Homecoming Queen (Raise the Flag)

Don't Cry for Yesterday (Why Me?)

Don't Die Dragonfly (The Seer)

Don't Eat the Mystery Meat (Graveyard School)

Dragon Moon (Dragon Keeper Trilogy)

Dragon of Doom (Dungeons and Dragons: Endless Quest)

Dragon of the Lost Sea (Dragon of the Lost Sea)

Dragon of the Lost Sea (Shimmer and Thorn)

Dragon on a Pedestal (Xanth Saga)

The Dragon Reborn (The Wheel of Time)

The Dragon Revenant (Deverry)

Dragon Road (Golden Mountain Chronicles)

Dragon Secrets (Outcast)

The Dragon Society (Obsidian Chronicles)

Dragon Steel (Dragon of the Lost Sea)

Dragon Steel (Shimmer and Thorn)

Dragon Sword (Danger Boy)

The Dragon Throne (The Book of the Lion)

Dragon Venom (Obsidian Chronicles)

Dragon War (Dragon of the Lost Sea)

Dragon War (Shimmer and Thorn)

Dragon Weather (Obsidian Chronicles)

Dragondrums (Pern: The Harper-Hall Trilogy)

Dragonflight (Pern)

Dragonfly in Amber (Outlander)

Dragonfly on My Shoulder (Brio Girls)

Dragonquest (Pern)

Dragon's Blood (Pit Dragon Trilogy)

Dragon's Breath (Tales of the Frog Princess)

Dragons' Den (Choose Your Own Adventure)

Dragons from the Sea (The Strongbow Saga)

Dragon's Gate (Golden Mountain Chronicles)

Dragon's Hoard (A Knight's Story)

Dragon's Kin (Pern)

Dragon's Milk (Dragon Chronicles)

Dragon's Nest (Deltora: Dragons of Deltora)

The Dragons of the Rhine (Wodan's Children)

Dragon's Plunder (Dragonflight)

Dragon's Ransom (Dungeons and Dragons: Endless Quest)

Dragonsdawn (Pern)

Dragonseye (Pern)

Dragonsinger (Pern: The Harper-Hall Trilogy)

The Dragonslayer (Bone)

Dragonsong (Pern: The Harper-Hall Trilogy)

Dragonwings (Golden Mountain Chronicles)

Drama Queen (Sweet Valley Junior High)

Dramarama (Zoey 101)

Draugr (Northern Frights)

Draven's Defiance (Passages)

The Drawing of the Three (Dark Tower)

Drawn by a China Moon (Trailblazers)

Dread Locks (Dark Fusion)

Dread Mountain (Deltora: Deltora Quest)

The Dreaded Ex (Sweet Valley University)

The Dreadful Future of Blossom Culp (Blossom Culp)

Dreadful Sorry (Time Travel Mysteries)

Dream (Once Upon a Prom)

Dream a Little Dream (Aloha Cove)

Dream Date (Sweet Dreams)

The Dream Date Debate (Mary-Kate and Ashley: Two of a Kind)

Dream Holiday (Mary-Kate and Ashley Sweet 16)

The Dream-Maker's Magic (The Safe-Keeper's Secret)

Dream On (Clearwater Crossing)

Dream Pony (Sandy Lane Stables)

Dream Prom (Sweet Dreams)

Dream Storm (Remnants)

The Dream Team (Mary-Kate and Ashley in Action)

A Dream to Cherish (Cassie Perkins)

A Dream to Follow (Red River: Return to Red River)

Dreamcrusher (Replica)

Dreamboat (Sweet Dreams)

Dreamfall (Psion)

The Dreaming Place (Dragonflight)

Dreams of Ships, Dreams of Julia (The Young Americans)

Dreams, Schemes, and Mysteries (Story Girl)

Dreamskate (Sweet Dreams)

Dreamwalk (Roswell High)

Dress (Once Upon a Prom)

Dress Reversal (Nancy Drew Graphic Novels)

Dressed to Steal (Nancy Drew: Girl Detective)

Drive You Crazy (7th Heaven)

Drooling and Dangerous (Riot Brothers)

Dropping Out (Sweet Valley University)

Drowned (Hollow)

Drowned Ammet (Dalemark Quartet)

Drowned Wednesday (Keys to the Kingdom)

Drownings! (Zorro Graphic Novels)

The Druid of Shannara (Shannara: Heritage of Shannara)

The Druid's Keep (Shannara: The Sword of Shannara)

The Drum, the Doll, and the Zombie (Johnny Dixon)

Drummer Boy at Bull Run (Bonnets and Bugles)

The Drummer Boy's Battle (Trailblazers)

Drums of Autumn (Outlander)

Duckling Ugly (Dark Fusion)

Ducky (California Diaries)

Ducky, Diary Three (California Diaries)

Ducky, Diary Two (California Diaries)

Dude Ranch (7th Heaven)

Dude Ranch O'Death (Hardy Boys, Undercover Brothers: Graphic Novels)

Dude with a 'Tude (Clueless)

Duel at Kitanoji (Usagi Yojimbo)

Duel Identity (Net Force)

Duel of the Masters (Dungeons and Dragons: Endless Quest)

Duel on the Diamond (Alden All Stars)

Dueling Princes (Calypso Chronicles)

Dugout Jinx (Chip Hilton Sports Series)

The Dummy (Nightmare Hall)

Dumping Princes (Calypso Chronicles)

Dungeon of Doom (Hardy Boys)

Elizabeth the Seventh Grader (Sweet Valley Twins)

Elizabeth the Spy (Sweet Valley Twins)

Elizabeth's First Kiss (Sweet Valley Twins)

Elizabeth's Heartbreak (Sweet Valley University)

Elizabeth's New Hero (Sweet Valley Twins)

Elizabeth's Rival (Sweet Valley High)

Elizabeth's Secret Diary (Sweet Valley High)

Elizabeth's Secret Diary Volume II (Sweet Valley High)

Elizabeth's Secret Diary Volume III (Sweet Valley High)

Elizabeth's Summer Love (Sweet Valley University)

Elkhound (Beka Cooper)

Ellen Fremedon (Ellen Fremedon)

Ellen Fremedon, Journalist (Ellen Fremedon)

Ellen Fremedon, Volunteer (Ellen Fremedon)

Ellie's Chance to Dance (Royal Ballet School Diaries)

The Ellimist Chronicles (Animorphs: Animorph Chronicles)

Eloise (Allie's Ghost Hunter)

Elske (The Kingdom)

The Elusive Heiress (Nancy Drew)

Elysium (Allie's Ghost Hunter)

The Emerald City of Oz (Oz)

The Emerald-Eyed Cat (Nancy Drew)

Emergency Quarterback (Winning Season)

Emily of the Wild Rose Inn, 1858 (Wild Rose Inn)

Emily Windsnap and the Castle in the Mist (Emily Windsnap)

Emily Windsnap and the Monster from the Deep (Emily Windsnap)

Emily's Rebellion (Not Just Proms and Parties)

Empathy (X Files)

Emperor and Clown (Man of His Word)

Emperor Mage (Immortals)

Emperor's Fist (Magic: The Gathering—Magic Legends Cycle Two)

The Emperor's Plague (Star Wars Young Jedi Knights)

The Emperor's Shield (Hardy Boys Casefiles)

Empire of Unreason (The Age of Unreason)

The Empty Kingdom (Arthurian-Aksumite Cycle)

En Garde (Nancy Drew: Girl Detective)

The Enchanted Apples of Oz (Oz)

Enchanted Island of Oz (Oz)

Enchanted Kingdom (Choose Your Own Adventure)

Enchanted Waters (W.I.T.C.H.—Chapter Books)

Enchanters' End Game (The Belgariad)

Enchantress (Sisters of Isis)

The Encounter (Animorphs)

The Encounter (Forbidden Doors)

Encounter at Cold Harbor (Bonnets and Bugles)

The End—Too Dreadful to Picture (A Series of Unfortunate Events)

End Game (The Midnight Library)

End Game (Net Force)

End of Summer (American Dreams)

End of the Race (Wild at Heart)

The End of the Trail (Hardy Boys)

Endangered Species (Angel)

Endangered Species (Hardy Boys Casefiles)

Ender in Exile (Ender Wiggin)

Ender's Game (Ender Wiggin)

Ender's Shadow (Ender Wiggin)

Endless Catacombs (Dungeons and Dragons: Endless Quest)

Endsville (Swampland Trilogy)

Enemies (Hollow)

The Enemies of Jupiter (Roman Mysteries)

The Enemy (Space Above and Beyond)

An Enemy at Green Knowe (Green Knowe)

Enemy in the Fort (American Girls: History Mysteries)

Enemy Match (Nancy Drew)

Enemy Territory (Star Trek: I. K. S. Gorkon)

The Engines of God (Priscilla Hutchins)

Enid's Story (Sweet Valley High)

Enna Burning (Goose Girl)

Enoch's Ghost (Dragons in Our Midst: Oracles of Fire)

Enter . . . the Viper (Jackie Chan Adventures)

Enter the Dark Hand (Jackie Chan Adventures)

Enter the Enchanted (EverWorld)

Entertain the End (EverWorld)

Entrances and Exits (Drama!)

Envy (The Luxe)

Envy (Seven Deadly Sins)

Equal Rites (Discworld)

Eragon (Inheritance)

Eric (Discworld)

Erin and the Movie Star (Camp Sunnyside)

The Ersatz Elevator (A Series of Unfortunate Events)

The Escape (Animorphs)

Escape (Choose Your Own Adventure)

Escape (Fearless)

Escape (Island)

Escape (So Weird)

Escape (Sons of the Dark)

Escape from Arylon (Silverskin Legacy)

Escape from Camp Run-for-Your-Life (Goosebumps: Give Yourself Goosebumps)

Escape from Fear (Mysteries in Our National Parks)

Escape from Horror House (Goosebumps: Give Yourself Goosebumps)

Escape from New Babylon (Left Behind—The Kids)

Escape from Pyramid X (Twisted Journeys)

Escape from Terror Island (Sweet Valley Twins)

Escape from the Carnival of Horrors (Goosebumps: Give Yourself Goosebumps)

Escape from the Carnivale (Never Land)

Escape from the Haunted Mountain (Spinetinglers)

Escape from the Island of Aquarius (Cooper Kids)

Escape From the Red Comet (Daystar Voyages)

Escape from the Slave Traders (Trailblazers)

Escape from Vampire Park (Graveyard School)

Escape from War (My Side of the Story)

Escape of the He-Beast (Fear Street: Ghosts of Fear Street)

Faerie Wars (The Faerie Wars Chronicles)

Faery Lands Forlorn (Man of His Word)

Faina (Alias)

Fair Play (American Dreams)

A Fair to Remember (Camp Confidential)

Fair-Weather Love (Sweet Dreams)

Fairway Phenom (Matt Christopher's's Sports Stories)

Faith in a Long Shot (Thoroughbred)

The Faith Trials, Volume 1 (Buffy the Vampire Slayer)

Fake (Fearless)

The Fake Heir (Nancy Drew Graphic Novels)

The Fake Teacher (Don't Touch That Remote!)

The Fakersville Power Station (Edgar Font's Hunt for a House to Haunt)

Falcondance (Kiesha'ra)

Falcon and the Carousel of Time (Falcon)

Falcon and the Charles Street Witch (Falcon)

Falcon of Abydos (MacGregor Family Adventure)

Falcon's Egg (Falcon)

The Falcon's Malteser (The Diamond Brothers)

The Fall (Cherub)

The Fall (The Seventh Tower)

Fall (Witch Season)

The Fall Musical (Drama Club)

Fall of a Kingdom (Farsala Trilogy)

Fall of Angels (Recluce)

The Fall of the Templar (Grey Griffins)

The Fallen (Bluford High)

The Fallen (The Fallen)

The Fallen (The Nine Lives of Chloe King)

Fallen Star (Thoroughbred)

Falling Apart (Sweet Valley High Senior Year)

Falling for Claire (Making Out)

Falling for Lucas (Sweet Valley High)

Falling for Ryan (Love Stories)

Falling In Like (Camp Confidential)

Falling in Love (Cheerleaders)

Falling in Love Again (Sweet Dreams)

Falling Up (Diary of a Teenage Girl)

Fallout (The Wessex Papers)

False Alarm (Hardy Boys Casefiles)

False Friends (Nancy Drew on Campus)

False Impressions (Nancy Drew Files)

False Memories (Buffy the Vampire Slayer)

False Moves (Nancy Drew Files)

False Notes (Nancy Drew: Girl Detective)

The False Peace (Star Wars: Jedi Quest)

False Pretenses (Nancy Drew Files)

Fame (In the Cards)

The Familiar (Animorphs)

A Family Apart (Orphan Train Adventures)

Family Reunion (So Weird)

Family Secrets (Christy)

Family Secrets (Dear Diary)

Family Secrets (Sweet Valley High)

Fangtastic! (My Sister the Vampire)

Fantasies (Beverly Hills, 90210)

Far (The Freak)

Far From the Storm (The Young Underground)

Faradawn (Fog Mound)

Farewell, Dawn (Baby-Sitters Club)

Farewell, My Lunchbag! (Chet Gecko Mysteries)

Farewell to Move (W.I.T.C.H.— Chapter Books)

Farewell to the Island (Island Trilogy)

Farming Fear (Hardy Boys)

Farthest Reach (Dungeons and Dragons: Forgotten Realms— The Last Mythal)

The Farthest Shore (Earthsea)

Fashion Frenzy (Beacon Street Girls)

Fashion Funk (Bratz: Lil' Bratz)

Fashion Victim (Sweet Valley High)

Fashionistas (Interns)

Fast Break (Hardy Boys Casefiles)

Fast Company (Winning Season)

Fast Food Fight (Mary-Kate and Ashley in Action)

Fast Forward (Replica: The Plague Trilogy)

Fast Forward to Normal (Brio Girls)

Fast Life (Kimani Tru)

Fat Glenda Turns Fourteen (Fat Glenda)

Fat Glenda's Summer Romance (Fat Glenda)

Fatal Attraction (Nancy Drew Files)

Fatal Bargain (The Vampire's Promise)

Fatal Charm (The Seer)

Fatal Error (Three Investigators)

Fatal Ransom (Nancy Drew Files)

The Fate of the Yellow Woodbee (Trailblazers)

Father-Daughter Disaster! (Secret World of Alex Mack)

Father Figure (Alias)

Father Goose in Oz (Oz)

Fathers and Sons (Usagi Yojimbo)

Faun and Games (Xanth Saga)

Fear (Fearless)

Fear (X Files)

Fear Games (Nightmare Room Thrillogy)

Fear of Falling (Wild at Heart)

Fear on Wheels (Hardy Boys)

Fear the Fantastic (EverWorld)

Fearless (Angel)

Fearless (Fearless)

A Feather of Stone (Balefire)

The Feathered Serpent (Julian Escobar)

February (Countdown)

Feeding Frenzy (Hardy Boys, Undercover Brothers)

Feet of Clay (Discworld)

The Feline Wizard (A Wizard in Rhyme)

The Fellowship of the Ring (Lord of the Rings)

Fence Busters (Chip Hilton Sports Series)

Fendar's Legacy (Passages)

Feud (Lady Grace Mysteries)

Feuding (Cheerleaders)

The Fever (Replica)

Field of Dishonor (Honor Harrington)

Field of Screams (Fear Street: Ghosts of Fear Street)

Field Trip (Star Trek: Deep Space Nine)

Fields of Honor (Ruin Mist Chronicles)

The Fiery Cross (Outlander)

Fiery Fullback (Chip Hilton Sports Series)

Flesh and Blood (Hardy Boys Casefiles)

The Flickering Torch Mystery (Hardy Boys)

Flight (Smallville)

Flight into Danger (Hardy Boys Casefiles)

Flight of the Dragon Kyn (Dragon Chronicles)

Flight of the Fugitives (Trailblazers)

Flight of the Phoenix (Mummy Chronicles)

Flight to Freedom (First Person Fiction)

The Flint Island Treehouse (Edgar Font's Hunt for a House to Haunt)

Flirt in the Mirror (Mirror Image)

Flirting (Cheerleaders)

Flirting with Danger (Nancy Drew Files)

Flood (Med Center)

Flood: Mississippi, 1927 (Survival!)

Flowers in the Attic (Dollanganger)

Fly by Night (Spinetinglers)

A Fly Named Alfred (Harper Winslow)

Flyboy of Underwhere (Underwhere)

Flyers (Jurassic Park Adventures)

Flying Blind (Cooper Kids)

Flying High (Angels Unlimited)

Flying High (B.Y. Times)

The Flying Saucer Mystery (Nancy Drew)

Flying Too High (Nancy Drew Files)

Flyte (Septimus Heap)

Focus on Love (Sweet Dreams)

Focus on This (The Real Deal)

Fogging Over (Angels Unlimited)

Follow that Boy (Sweet Dreams)

Follow the Star (The Young Underground)

Follow Your Heart (Sweet Dreams)

Following My Own Footsteps (Gordy Smith)

Food Chain (Buffy the Vampire Slayer)

Fool for Love (Sweet Dreams)

Fooling Around (Sweet Valley University)

Fool's Gold (True Colors)

Football Fugitive (Matt Christopher's's Sports Stories)

Football Double Threat (Matt Christopher's's Sports Stories)

Football Nightmare (Matt Christopher's's Sports Stories)

Footprints at the Window (York Trilogy)

Footprints Under the Window (Hardy Boys)

For All Time (Time Travel Quartet)

For Love or Money (Nancy Drew Files)

For Money and Love (Mob Princess)

For Real (Turning Seventeen)

For the Love of Ryan (Sweet Valley University)

Forbidden Castle (Choose Your Own Adventure)

Forbidden Fountain of Oz (Oz)

Forbidden Love (Sweet Dreams)

Forbidden Love (Sweet Valley High)

The Forbidden Road (Reel Kids Adventures)

Forbidden Secrets (Fear Street: Fear Street Sagas)

The Forbidden Stallion (Thoroughbred: Ashleigh)

Force of Nature (Troubleshooters)

Forces of Change (W.I.T.C.H.— Graphic Novels)

Foreign Exposure (10th Grade Social Climber)

Foreigner (Foreigner)

Forest Fire (Survival!)

Forest of Darkness (Dungeons and Dragons: Endless Quest)

Forest of Fear (Choose Your Own Adventure)

Forest of Secrets (Warriors)

Forest of the Pygmies (Alexander Cold and Nadia Santos)

The Forests of Silence (Deltora: Deltora Quest)

A Forever Friend (Cassie Perkins)

Forever in Blue (Sisterhood of the Traveling Pants)

Forever Princess (Princess Diaries)

Forever Rose (Casson Family)

Forged by Fire (Hazelwood High)

Forget Me Not (Aloha Cove)

Forget Me Not (From the Files of Madison Finn)

Forget Me Not (Glory)

Forget Me Not (Mary-Kate and Ashley Sweet 16)

Forgetting (Cheerleaders)

The Forging of the Blade (Lowthar's Blade)

Forging the Sword (Farsala Trilogy)

The Forgotten (Animorphs)

Forgotten (Jennie McGrady Mysteries)

The Forgotten Angel (Forever Angels)

The Forgotten Filly (Thoroughbred: Ashleigh's Collection)

The Forgotten Forest of Oz (Oz)

The Forgotten Planet (Choose Your Own Adventure)

The Forsaken Crusade (Winds of Light)

Forsaken House (Dungeons and Dragons: Forgotten Realms— The Last Mythal)

Fortress Draconis (DragonCrown War Cycle)

A Fortress of Grey Ice (Sword of Shadows)

The Fortune-Teller's Secret (Nancy Drew)

Fortunes of Love (Sweet Dreams)

The Forty-Acre Swindle (Trailblazers)

Forty Thousand in Gehenna (Alliance-Union)

Forward the Foundation (Foundation)

Foul Play (Hardy Boys Casefiles)

Foul Play (Hardy Boys, Undercover Brothers)

Foul Play (Three Investigators)

Foundation (Foundation)

Foundation and Chaos (Foundation)

Foundation and Earth (Foundation)

Foundation and Empire (Foundation)

Foundations (Star Trek: S. C. E.)

Foundation's Edge (Foundation)

Foundation's Fear (Foundation)

Foundation's Triumph (Foundation)

Fountain of Weird (Eerie Indiana)

The Fountain of Youth (Secret Agent MJJ)

The Fountains of Youth (Emortality)

Four and Twenty Blackbirds (Bardic Voices)

The Four Dorothys (Drama!)

G

Gaal the Conqueror (The Archives of Anthropos)

Gabriel's Horses (Racing to Freedom Trilogy)

Gabriel's Journey (Racing to Freedom Trilogy)

Gabriel's Triumph (Racing to Freedom Trilogy)

Gaia Abducted (Fearless)

Galactic Challenge (Dungeons and Dragons: Endless Quest)

Galilee Man (CyberQuest)

The Gallant Boys of Gettysburg (Bonnets and Bugles)

Gallop to the Sea (Saddle Island)

A Game Called Chaos (Hardy Boys)

The Game of Love (Sweet Dreams)

The Game of Silence (Omakayas)

The Game of Worlds (David Brin's Out of Time)

Game On! (Adventures of Daniel Boom AKA Loud Boy)

Game On! (Kim Possible: Pick a Villain)

Game Plan for Disaster (Hardy Boys)

Gameprey (Net Force)

Gangsters at the Grand Atlantic (American Girls: History Mysteries)

Garden of Evil (Charmed)

The Garden of Rama (Rama)

Garden of Shadows (Dollanganger)

Garden of the Purple Dragon (Dragon Keeper Trilogy)

The Gate of Bones (The Magickers)

Gatekeepers (Dreamhouse Kings)

Gateway to the Gods (EverWorld)

The Gathering (Justice Trilogy)

The Gathering (Quantum Prophecy)

Gathering Blue (The Giver)

The Gathering Dark (Magic: The Gathering—Ice Age Cycle)

The Gathering Flame (Valdemar: Mageworlds)

Gathering of Pearls (Sookan Bak)

Gathering of the Gargoyles (Darkangel Trilogy)

The Gator Ate Her (Graveyard School)

Gator Prey (Against the Odds)

Geared for Romance (Sweet Dreams)

Geis of the Gargoyle (Xanth Saga)

Gemini 7 (Danger.com)

The General (Cherub)

The General's Notorious Widow (Belles of Lordsburg)

The Genius Thieves (Hardy Boys Casefiles)

Gen's Story (Usagi Yojimbo)

Gentle's Holler (Maggie Valley)

The Georgia Dagger (Hardy Boys Casefiles)

Get a Clue! (Lizzie McGuire Mysteries)

Get a Clue (Sweet Valley High Senior Year)

Get a Life (Clearwater Crossing)

Get It Started (Party Room Trilogy)

Get On Out of Here, Philip Hall (Philip Hall)

Get Real (Mary-Kate and Ashley: So Little Time)

Get Real (Sweet Valley Junior High)

Get to Work, Hercules! (Myth-O-Mania)

Get Well Soon, Mallory! (Baby-Sitters Club)

Get Your Vote On! (High School Musical Stories from East High)

Gettin' Hooked (Kimani Tru)

Getting Burned (Nancy Drew: Girl Detective)

Getting Closer (Nancy Drew on Campus)

Getting Even (Cheerleaders)

Getting Even (Molly)

Getting Serious (Cheerleaders)

Getting the Boot (Students Across the Seven Seas)

Getting There (Mary-Kate and Ashley Sweet 16)

The Ghost at Dawn's House (Baby-Sitters Club)

The Ghost at Skeleton Rock (Hardy Boys)

Ghost Beach (Goosebumps)

The Ghost Belonged to Me (Blossom Culp)

Ghost Camp (Goosebumps)

Ghost Circles (Bone)

The Ghost Ferry (Haunting with Louisa)

Ghost Horses (Mysteries in Our National Parks)

Ghost Hunter (Choose Your Own Adventure)

Ghost Hunter (Chronicles of Ancient Darkness)

The Ghost in the Attic (Haunting with Louisa)

The Ghost in the Bell Tower (Sweet Valley Twins Super Chiller Editions)

The Ghost in the Graveyard (Sweet Valley Twins Super Chiller Editions)

Ghost in the Machine (X Files)

Ghost in the Machinery (Nancy Drew Graphic Novels)

Ghost in the Mirror (Goosebumps Series 2000)

The Ghost in the Mirror (Lewis Barnavelt)

The Ghost in the Tokaido Inn (The Ghost in the Tokaido Inn)

Ghost Knight (Deadtime Stories)

Ghost Light on Graveyard Shoal (American Girls: History Mysteries)

The Ghost Next Door (Goosebumps)

Ghost of a Chance (Hardy Boys)

Ghost of a Chance (Sweet Dreams)

The Ghost of Avalanche Mountain (Goldstone Trilogy)

The Ghost of Blackwood Hall (Nancy Drew)

The Ghost of Craven Cove (Nancy Drew)

Ghost of the Jedi (Star Wars Galaxy of Fear)

The Ghost of the Lantern Lady (Nancy Drew)

The Ghost of the Stanley Cup (Screech Owls)

The Ghost of Tricia Martin (Sweet Valley High)

Ghost on the Net (Cybersurfers)

Ghost Riders (Ballad)

Ghost Roads (Buffy the Vampire Slayer: The Gatekeeper Trilogy)

Ghost Soldiers (Invisible Detectives)

The Ghost Sonata (Gilda Joyce)

The Ghost Squad and the Ghoul of Grunberg (Ghost Squad)

The Ghost Squad and the Halloween Conspiracy (Ghost Squad)

The Ghost Squad and the Menace of the Malevs (Ghost Squad)

The Ghost Squad and the Prowling Hermits (Ghost Squad)

The Ghost Squad Breaks Through (Ghost Squad)

The Gold Miner's Rescue (Trailblazers)

Gold Rush Fever! (Secret World of Alex Mack)

Gold-Rush Phoebe (Petticoat Party)

The Gold Train Bandits (American Adventure)

Gold Unicorn (Dragonflight)

Gold Unicorn (Unicorn)

Golden (Once Upon a Time)

The Golden Angel (Forever Angels)

Golden Bees of Tulami (Dogtown Ghetto)

The Golden Boy (Sirius Mysteries)

The Golden Compass (His Dark Materials)

Golden Girl (Sweet Dreams)

Golden Girls (Camp Confidential)

The Golden Globe (Star Wars Junior Jedi Knights)

The Golden Hour ("Hour" books)

Golden Palaces (Royal Pavilions)

The Golden Tree (Guardians of Ga'Hoole)

Goldstone (Goldstone Trilogy)

Golem in the Gears (Xanth Saga)

The Golem's Eye (The Bartimaeus Trilogy)

Gom on Windy Mountain (Tales of Gom in the Legends of Ulm)

Gone (Fearless)

Gone Too Far (Troubleshooters)

Good-Bye, Dressel Hills (Holly's Heart)

Good-Bye, Elizabeth (Sweet Valley University)

Good-Bye Is Not Forever (Aloha Cove)

Good-bye Stacey, Good-bye (Baby-Sitters Club)

Good-Bye to All That (Brio Girls)

Good-Bye to Love (Sweet Valley University)

A Good Day to Die (Star Trek: I. K. S. Gorkon)

Good Girls, Bad Boys (Trash)

Good Intentions (Life at Sixteen)

Good Neighbors (The Floods)

The Good That Men Do (Star Trek: Enterprise)

The Good, the Bad, and the Bunny (It's Happy Bunny)

The Good, the Bad & the Gassy (The Grosse Adventures)

The Good, the Bad, and the Smelly (The Adventures of Uncle Stinky)

Goodbye Forever (Sweet Dreams)

Goodbye, Middle School (Sweet Valley Twins Super Editions)

Goodbye, Midnight Wanderer (Thoroughbred: Ashleigh)

Goodbye, Sweet Prince (Christy)

Goodnight Kiss (Fear Street: Fear Street Super Chillers)

Goodnight Kiss 2 (Fear Street: Fear Street Super Chillers)

Goofballs in Paradise (Super Goofballs)

The Goose Girl (Goose Girl)

Gordo and the Girl and You're a Good Man Lizzie McGuire (Lizzie McGuire (TokyoPop))

The Gorgon's Gaze (The Companions Quartet)

Gossip Girl (Gossip Girl)

Gossip War (Sweet Valley Twins)

Got a Problem? (Sweet Valley Junior High)

The Gourmet Zombie (P.C. Hawke Mysteries)

Grace Notes (FaithGirlz: Blog On)

Grace of the Wild Rose Inn, 1944 (Wild Rose Inn)

Grace Under Pressure (FaithGirlz: Blog On)

Grace's Show of Strength (Royal Ballet School Diaries)

Grace's Twist (Camp Confidential)

The Graduates (Sweet Dreams: On Our Own)

Graduation Day (Baby-Sitters Club Friends Forever)

Graduation Day (Beverly Hills, 90210)

Graduation Day (Fear Street: Fear Street Seniors)

Grampa in Oz (Oz)

Grand Canyon (Adventures with the Parkers)

Grand Canyon Odyssey (Choose Your Own Adventure)

The Grand Crusade (DragonCrown War Cycle)

Grand Designs (Star Trek: S. C. E.)

The Grand Escape (Club of Mysteries)

Grandpa's Monster Movies (Deadtime Stories)

Grasping at Moonbeams (Brio Girls)

Grass for His Pillow (Tales of the Otori)

Grasscutter (Usagi Yojimbo)

Grasscutter II: Journey to Atsuta Shrine (Usagi Yojimbo)

A Grateful Harvest (Prairie River)

Grave Danger (Hardy Boys Casefiles)

Grave Matters (Jennie McGrady Mysteries)

Grave Robbers (Choose Your Own Adventure)

Grave Secrets (Deadtime Stories)

Grave Shadows (Red Rock Mysteries)

The Gray-Eyed Goddess (Tales from the Odyssey)

Great Airport Mystery (Hardy Boys)

A Great and Terrible Beauty (Gemma Doyle)

The Great Boy Chase (Sweet Dreams)

Great Boyfriend Switch (Sweet Valley Twins)

The Great Brain (The Great Brain)

The Great Brain at the Academy (The Great Brain)

The Great Brain Does It Again (The Great Brain)

The Great Brain Is Back (The Great Brain)

The Great Brain Reforms (The Great Brain)

The Great Coaster Contest (Roller Coaster Tycoon)

The Great Cow Race (Bone)

Great Expectations (Thoroughbred)

The Great Good Thing (Sylvie Cycle)

The Great Hunt (The Wheel of Time)

Great Northern? (Swallows and Amazons)

The Great Plan (Speed Racer)

The Great Powers Outage (The Extraordinary Adventures of Ordinary Boy)

The Great Quarterback Switch (Matt Christopher's's Sports Stories)

The Great Race (Net Force)

The Great Skinner Enterprise (The Great Skinner)

The Great Skinner Getaway (The Great Skinner)

H

Happy Holidays, Jessi (Baby-Sitters Club)

Happy Mother's Day, Lila (Sweet Valley Twins)

Hard Cash (Hard Cash)

Hard Cash (Richard Steele Trilogy)

Hard Choices (Sweet Valley High)

Hard Drive to Short (Matt Christopher's's Sports Stories)

Hard Lessons (Black Stallion: Young Black Stallion)

Hard to Get (Nancy Drew on Campus)

Hard to Resist (Love Stories)

Hardcourt Upset (Chip Hilton Sports Series)

A Hardy Day's Night (Hardy Boys, Undercover Brothers: Graphic Novels)

Harpy Thyme (Xanth Saga)

Harry Potter and the Chamber of Secrets (Harry Potter)

Harry Potter and the Deathly Hallows (Harry Potter)

Harry Potter and the Goblet of Fire (Harry Potter)

Harry Potter and the Half-Blood Prince (Harry Potter)

Harry Potter and the Order of the Phoenix (Harry Potter)

Harry Potter and the Prisoner of Azkaban (Harry Potter)

Harry Potter and the Sorcerer's Stone (Harry Potter)

Harsh Pink (True Colors)

The Harvest (Buffy the Vampire Slayer)

Harvey Angell (Harvey Angell Trilogy)

Harvey Angell and the Ghost Child (Harvey Angell Trilogy)

Harvey Angell Beats Time (Harvey Angell Trilogy)

A Hat Full of Sky (Discworld)

Hatchet (Brian Robeson)

Hatchling (Dinotopia)

The Hatchling (Guardians of Ga'Hoole)

Haunted (Angel)

Haunted (Buffy the Vampire Slayer)

Haunted (Fear Street)

Haunted (Fingerprints)

Haunted (Hardy Boys, Undercover Brothers)

Haunted (The Mediator)

Haunted (X Files)

The Haunted Baby (Choose Your Own Nightmare)

The Haunted Bridge (Nancy Drew)

The Haunted Burial Ground (Sweet Valley Twins Super Chiller Editions)

Haunted by Desire (Charmed)

The Haunted Car (Goosebumps Series 2000)

The Haunted Carousel (Nancy Drew)

The Haunted Cave (Spooksville)

The Haunted Dollhouse (Nancy Drew Graphic Novels)

The Haunted Fort (Hardy Boys)

The Haunted Heart (Enchanted Hearts)

Haunted Hill (Sam and Stephanie)

Haunted House (Sweet Valley Twins)

Haunted House Hijinks! (Secret World of Alex Mack)

The Haunted Mask (Goosebumps)

The Haunted Mask II (Goosebumps)

Haunted Park (Roller Coaster Tycoon)

The Haunted School (Goosebumps)

The Haunted Showboat (Nancy Drew)

The Haunted Starship (Star Trek: The Next Generation: Starfleet Academy)

Haunted Waters (Red Rock Mysteries)

The Haunted Wizard (A Wizard in Rhyme)

The Haunting (Forbidden Doors)

The Haunting (House on Cherry Street)

The Haunting (Sisters of Isis)

The Haunting of Drang Island (Northern Frights)

The Haunting of Horse Island (Nancy Drew)

Have a Hot Time, Hades! (Myth-O-Mania)

Have Tech, Will Travel (Star Trek: S. C. E.)

Have to Have It (Nannies)

Have You Heard About Elizabeth (Sweet Valley University)

Have Yourself an Eerie Little Christmas (Eerie Indiana)

Having It All (Cheerleaders)

Hawaii Five-Go! (Luna Bay)

Hawksong (Kiesha'ra)

Hayfoot, Strawfoot (White Mane Kids)

Hayloft Hideout (Lassie)

Hazed (Hardy Boys, Undercover Brothers)

Hazezon (Magic: The Gathering—Magic Legends Cycle)

Head Games (Body of Evidence)

Head over Heels (The Jersey)

Head over Heels (Lizzie McGuire)

Head over Heels (Sweet Dreams)

Head over Heels (Sweet Valley High)

Head to Head (Extreme Team)

The Headless Bicycle Rider (Graveyard School)

The Headless Ghost (Goosebumps)

The Headless Ghost (Phantom Valley)

Headless Halloween (Goosebumps Series 2000)

Heads or Tails (Jack Henry)

Headstrong (Saddle Club: Pine Hollow)

The Healing of Crossroads (Crossroads Trilogy)

The Healing of Texas Jake (Club of Mysteries)

Heart and Salsa (Students Across the Seven Seas)

Heart and Soul (Clearwater Crossing)

Heart and Soul (Sweet Dreams)

Heart Breakers (Luna Bay)

A Heart Full of Hope (Christy Miller)

Heart of Avalon (Avalon 2: Quest for Magic)

Heart of Courage (Viking Quest)

Heart of Danger (Nancy Drew Files)

Heart of Glass (A-List)

Heart of Gold (Chestnut Hill)

Heart of Ice (Nancy Drew Files)

Heart of Steele (Pirate Hunter)

Heart of the Hill (The Summer of Magic Quartet)

Heart of the Hills (American Dreams)

Heart of the Hunter (Fear Street: Fear Street Sagas)

Heart of the Pharaoh (Mummy Chronicles)

Heart to Heart (From the Files of Madison Finn)

High Deryni (Chronicles of Deryni)

High Fashion (Flirt)

High Five! (Lizzie McGuire)

High Flyer! (Secret World of Alex Mack)

The High King (Prydain Chronicles)

The High King's Tomb (The Green Rider)

The High Lord (The Black Magician Trilogy)

High Marks for Malice (Nancy Drew Files)

High Rhulain (Redwall)

High Risk (Nancy Drew: Girl Detective)

High Risk (Nancy Drew Files)

The High School War (Sweet Valley High)

High-Speed Showdown (Hardy Boys)

High Spirits (Charmed)

High Stakes (Nancy Drew and the Hardy Boys Super Mysteries)

High Stakes (Saddle Club: Pine Hollow)

High Survival (Nancy Drew and the Hardy Boys Super Mysteries)

High Tide (Fear Street: Fear Street Super Chillers)

High Wire (Edgar and Ellen)

High Wire (Net Force)

High-Wire Act (Hardy Boys Casefiles)

High Wizardry (Wizardry)

Highest Score (Star Trek: Deep Space Nine)

The Highest Stand (Dream Series)

Highland Hearts (Sweet Dreams)

Highway Robbery (Hardy Boys Casefiles)

Highway to Hell (Maggie Quinn: Girl vs. Evil)

Hijacked! (Choose Your Own Adventure)

Hippolyta and the Curse of the Amazons (Young Heroes)

His and Hers (Sweet Dreams)

His Life as a . . . (Trigun Maximum)

His Other Girlfriend (Love Stories)

His Secret Past (Sweet Valley University)

Hiss Me Deadly (Chet Gecko Mysteries)

Hit and Run (Fabulous Five)

Hit and Run (Misfits, Inc.)

Hit and Run Holiday (Nancy Drew Files)

Hit or Myth (Myth Adventures)

Hit the Beach (From the Files of Madison Finn)

The Hitchhiker's Guide to the Galaxy (Hitchhiker's Trilogy)

Hits and Misses (Nancy Drew and the Hardy Boys Super Mysteries)

Hitting the Slopes (Generation Girl)

The Hockey Machine (Matt Christopher's's Sports Stories)

Hocus-Pocus (Mary-Kate and Ashley: Two of a Kind)

Hocus Pocus! (Secret World of Alex Mack)

Hocus-Pocus Horror (Goosebumps: Give Yourself Goosebumps)

Hogfather (Discworld)

Hold on Tight (The Insiders)

Hold on Tight (Sierra Jensen)

Holding Fast (Heartland)

Holiday Homecoming (Thoroughbred: Ashleigh)

Holiday in the Sun (Mary-Kate and Ashley Starring In . . .)

Holiday Magic (Mary-Kate and Ashley: Two of a Kind)

A Holiday Memory (Heartland)

Holiday Mischief (Sweet Valley Twins Super Editions)

The Hollow Kingdom (Hollow Kingdom)

The Hollower (Angel (Graphic Novels))

Hollywood Hold Up (Red Rock Mysteries)

Hollywood Hook-Up (Moesha)

Hollywood Horror (Nancy Drew and the Hardy Boys Super Mysteries)

Hollywood Noir (Angel)

Home Child (On Time's Wing)

Home for Christmas (Sweet Valley University)

A Home for Melanie (Thoroughbred)

Home Is Where Your Horse Is (Horsefeathers)

Home on Stoney Creek (Sarah's Journey)

Home Run Feud (Chip Hilton Sports Series)

The Homecoming (Black Stallion: Young Black Stallion)

Homecoming (Tillerman Cycle)

Homecoming Queen (Carter House Girls)

Homeless (Wild at Heart)

Homeward Heart (Pacific Cascades University)

Honestly, Katie John! (Katie John)

Honor Among Enemies (Honor Harrington)

Honor Bound (Star Trek: I. K. S. Gorkon)

The Honor of the Queen (Honor Harrington)

Honus and Me (Baseball Card Adventures)

The Hooded Hawk Mystery (Hardy Boys)

Hoofbeats of Danger (American Girls: History Mysteries)

Hoofprints in the Snow (Thoroughbred)

Hoop City (Dream Series)

Hoop Crazy (Chip Hilton Sports Series)

Hope Happens (Clearwater Crossing)

Hope Springs Eternal (Prairie River)

Hoping for Rain (I Am American)

The Horizontal Man (Finnegan Zwake)

The Hork-Bajir Chronicles (Animorphs: Animorph Chronicles)

The Horror (House on Cherry Street)

The Horror at Camp Jellyjam (Goosebumps)

Horror Hotel (Fear Street: Ghosts of Fear Street)

Horror Hotel: The Vampire Checks In (Fear Street: Ghosts of Fear Street)

Horror House (Choose Your Own Adventure)

Horror of High Ridge (Choose Your Own Adventure)

Horror on River Road (Screech Owls)

Horrors of the Black Ring (Goosebumps Series 2000)

The Horse and His Boy (Chronicles of Narnia)

Horse Angels (Horsefeathers)

A Horse Called Raven (Black Stallion: Young Black Stallion)

A Horse Called Wonder (Thoroughbred)

Horse Cents (Horsefeathers)

Hurricane Joe (Hardy Boys, Undercover Brothers)

Hurricane Power (Sports Mystery)

Hurricane Rescue (Neptune Adventures)

Hurting (Cheerleaders)

Hyde and Shriek (Hardy Boys, Undercover Brothers: Graphic Novels)

The Hypersonic Secret (Hardy Boys)

Hyperspace (Choose Your Own Adventure)

I

I Am Not Joey Pigza (Joey Pigza)

I Am Your Evil Twin (Goosebumps Series 2000)

I Believe in You (Sweet Dreams)

I Can See You (The Midnight Library)

I Can't Forget You (Sweet Dreams)

I. D. (Watchers)

I Do (Diary of a Teenage Girl)

I Do (Love Stories)

I Do, Don't I? (Gilmore Girls)

I Do, I Don't and Come Fly with Me (Lizzie McGuire (TokyoPop))

I Heard a Rumor (How I Survived Middle School)

I Know You, Al (Al (Alexandra))

I Left My Sneakers in Dimension X (Alien Adventures)

I Like It Like That (Gossip Girl)

I Live in Your Basement! (Goosebumps)

I Love You, You Idiot (Gilmore Girls)

I Need You (Sweet Valley University: Elizabeth)

I Only Binge on Holy Hungers (Raise the Flag)

I Promise (Christy Miller: Christy and Todd: The College Years)

I, Robot (I, Robot)

I Should Worry, I Should Care (Molly)

I Spy! (Secret World of Alex Mack)

I Want My Sister Back (Mary-Kate and Ashley Sweet 16)

I Was a Non-Blonde Cheerleader (Non-Blonde Cheerleader)

I Was a Sixth-Grade Zombie (Fear Street: Ghosts of Fear Street)

I Was a Teenage T. Rex (Dinoverse)

Ice Cold (Replica)

Ice Cold, by Molly (The Broadway Ballplayers)

The Ice-Cold Case (Hardy Boys)

Ice Magic (Matt Christopher's's Sports Stories)

Ice Magic (Silver Blades)

The Ice Princess (Silver Blades)

The Ice Queen (China Tate)

The Icebound Land (Ranger's Apprentice)

Iced! (Crime Through Time)

Icefire (Dragon)

Identity Theft (Hardy Boys, Undercover Brothers: Graphic Novels)

If Ever I Return, Pretty Peggy-O (Ballad)

If I Die Before I Wake (Sweet Valley Twins)

If I Were Your Boyfriend (Kimani Tru)

If Looks Could Kill (Nancy Drew Files)

If Looks Could Kill (Spy Girls)

If Looks Could Kill (Sweet Valley Twins)

If Only You Knew (Hotlanta)

If Photos Could Talk (Sam and Stephanie)

If the Shoe Fits (The Princess School)

If You Love Me (Sweet Dreams)

If You Loved Me (Hamilton High)

If You Only Knew (The Friendship Ring)

If You Only Knew (Sweet Valley High Senior Year)

I'll Have What He's Having (@CAFE)

The Ill-Made Knight (Once and Future King)

The Ill-Made Mute (The Bitterbynde)

I'll Never Love Again (Sweet Valley University)

Illegal Procedure (Hardy Boys Casefiles)

The Illusion (Animorphs)

Illusions and Lies (W.I.T.C.H.—Chapter Books)

Illusions of Evil (Nancy Drew Files)

The Illyrian Adventure (Vesper Holly)

Ilse Witch (Shannara: The Voyage of the Jerle Shannara)

I'm So Outta Here (Sweet Valley Junior High)

Image (Angel)

Immortal (Buffy the Vampire Slayer)

Immortalis (The DemonWars)

Impeach Screech! (Saved by the Bell)

Impetuous (Brides of Wildcat County)

The Importance of Being Gordo (Lizzie McGuire)

The Impossible Butterfly (Zenda)

The Impossible Journey (Angel on the Square)

The Impossible Lisa Barnes (Anika Scott)

The Imposter (Regeneration)

Impressions (Angel)

Imprisoned in the Golden City (Trailblazers)

In and Out of Love (Nancy Drew on Campus)

In Darkness, Death (The Ghost in the Tokaido Inn)

In Deep Water (American Gold Swimmers)

In Enemy Hands (Honor Harrington)

In Hot Pursuit! (Secret World of Alex Mack)

In Love (Cheerleaders)

In Love Again (Sweet Valley High)

In Love with a Prince (Sweet Valley High)

In Love with the Enemy (Sweet Valley High)

In Miranda, Lizzie Does Not Trust and The Longest Yard (Lizzie McGuire (TokyoPop))

In or Out (In or Out)

In Plane Sight (Hardy Boys)

In Search of Andy (Replica)

In Search of Klondike Gold (On Time's Wing)

In Search of the Black Rose (Nancy Drew)

In Self-Defense (Hardy Boys Casefiles)

In the Belly of the Bloodhound (Bloody Jack Adventures)

In the Circle of Time (Time Trilogy)

In the Club (Celebutantes)

In the Coils of the Snake (Hollow Kingdom)

The Jungle Pyramid (Hardy Boys)

Juniper (Wise Child)

Junkyard Jitters! (Secret World of Alex Mack)

Just Annoying! (Just . . .)

Just Ask (Diary of a Teenage Girl)

Just Between Us (Mary-Kate and Ashley: So Little Time)

Just Disgusting! (Just . . .)

Just Don't Make a Scene, Mum! (Fab 5)

Just Friends (Clearwater Crossing)

Just Jazz (FaithGirlz: Blog On)

Just Joking! (Just . . .)

Just Jump! (The Double Dutch Club)

Just Kidding (Beacon Street Girls)

Just like Lizzie (Lizzie McGuire)

Just like Sisters (Class Secrets)

Just like the Movies (Sweet Dreams)

Just Plain Al (Al (Alexandra))

Just Say Yes (Clearwater Crossing)

Just Shocking! (Just . . .)

Just Stupid! (Just . . .)

Just the Two of Us (Nancy Drew on Campus)

Just the Way You Are (Sweet Dreams)

Just Trust Me (Turning Seventeen)

Just Visiting (From the Files of Madison Finn)

Just Wacky! (Just . . .)

Justice and Her Brothers (Justice Trilogy)

Justin and Nicole (Love Stories: Prom Trilogy)

K

Kabumpo in Oz (Oz)

The Kachina Doll Mystery (Nancy Drew)

Kaitlin's Wild Ride (Thoroughbred)

Kaiulani (Royal Diaries)

Kari (Sweet 16)

Karin's Dilemma (Not Just Proms and Parties)

Kate Finds Love (Making Out)

Kate's Special Secret (Royal Ballet School Diaries)

Kathleen (American Girls: Girls of Many Lands)

Katie John (Katie John)

Katie John and Heathcliff (Katie John)

Katie Steals the Show (Camp Sunnyside)

Katie's Angel (Forever Angels)

Katie's Dating Tips (Fabulous Five)

Kazunomiya (Royal Diaries)

Keep a Lid on It, Pandora! (Myth-O-Mania)

Keep It Real (From the Files of Madison Finn)

Keep Me in Mind (Buffy the Vampire Slayer: Stake Your Destiny)

Keep Out, Claudia! (Baby-Sitters Club)

Keep the Faith (Clearwater Crossing)

Keeper (Dream Series)

Keeper Martin's Tale (Ruin Mist Chronicles)

Keeper Martin's Tales, Book 1 (Ruin Mist: The Kingdoms and the Elves of the Reaches)

Keeper Martin's Tales, Book 2 (Ruin Mist: The Kingdoms and the Elves of the Reaches)

Keeper Martin's Tales, Book 3 (Ruin Mist: The Kingdoms and the Elves of the Reaches)

Keeper Martin's Tales, Book 4 (Ruin Mist: The Kingdoms and the Elves of the Reaches)

Keeper of the Earth (Daughter of Destiny)

Keeper of the Flames (Daughter of Destiny)

Keeper of the Waters (Daughter of Destiny)

Keeper of the Winds (Daughter of Destiny)

The Keepers of the Flame (Fire-Us Trilogy)

The Keeper's Shadow (Longlight Legacy)

Keepin' It Real (Sweet Valley Junior High)

Keepin' It Real: Bratz, the Video (Bratz)

The Keeping Days (Sterling Family)

Keeping Hope (W.I.T.C.H.—Chapter Books)

Keeping It Real (Angels Unlimited)

Keeping It Real (Moesha)

Keeping Secrets (Mary-Kate and Ashley Sweet 16)

Keeping Secrets (Nancy Drew on Campus)

Keeping Secrets (Orphan Train Adventures)

Keeping Secrets (Sweet Valley Twins)

Kelly's Hero (Saved by the Bell)

Kenobi's Blade (Star Wars Junior Jedi Knights)

Kentucky Dreamer (Golden Filly Series)

Kenzie's Story (Degrees of Betrayal)

The Kestrel (Westmark)

Kevin (Love Stories: Brothers Trilogy)

The Key in the Satin Pocket (Nancy Drew)

Key Lardo (Chet Gecko Mysteries)

Key to the Griffon's Lair (Dungeons and Dragons: Knights of the Silver Dragon)

Keysha's Drama (Kimani Tru)

Kickoff to Danger (Hardy Boys)

The Kid from Courage (Dream Series)

The Kid Who Only Hit Homers (Matt Christopher's's Sports Stories)

Kidnapped! (Choose Your Own Adventure)

Kidnapped (Nightmare Hall)

Kidnapped! (Roller Coaster Tycoon)

Kidnapped! (Sweet Valley High)

Kidnapped at the Casino (Hardy Boys, Undercover Brothers)

Kidnapped by River Rats (Trailblazers)

Kidnapped by the Cult (Sweet Valley High)

Kidnapped in Sweden (Screech Owls)

The Kill (Forbidden Game)

Kill Game (Fearless FBI)

Killer (Fearless)

The Killer (Regeneration)

Killer at Sea (Sweet Valley University Thriller Editions)

Killer Clown of Kings County (Bone Chillers)

Killer Computer (Spinetinglers)

Killer Lunch Lady (Al's World)

A Killer on Board (Sweet Valley High)

Killer Party (Sweet Valley University Thriller Editions)

Killer Smile (Concrete)

L

Lacrosse Firestorm (Matt Christopher's's Sports Stories)

Ladies' Choice (He-Man Women Haters Club)

The Ladies of the Lake (Gilda Joyce)

Lady Friday (Keys to the Kingdom)

Lady J (Drama High)

Lady Knight (Protector of the Small)

Lady of Ch'iao Kuo (Royal Diaries)

Lady of Palenque (Royal Diaries)

The Lady of the Sorrows (The Bitterbynde)

Lady with an Alien (Art Encounters)

Lair of the Lich (Dungeons and Dragons: Endless Quest)

Lake of Skulls (A Knight's Story)

The Lake of Souls (Cirque du Freak)

The Lake of Tears (Deltora: Deltora Quest)

Lake Rescue (Beacon Street Girls)

The Lamp from the Warlock's Tomb (Anthony Monday)

The Land (Logan Family)

Land of Loss (EverWorld)

Land of Terror (Pellucidar)

The Land of the Dead (Tales from the Odyssey)

Land of the Dead (The Viking)

A Land to Call Home (Red River: Red River of the North)

Landon Snow and the Auctor's Kingdom (Landon Snow)

Landon Snow and the Auctor's Riddle (Landon Snow)

Landon Snow and the Island of Arcanum (Landon Snow)

Landon Snow and the Shadows of Malus Quidam (Landon Snow)

Landon Snow and the Volucer Dragon (Landon Snow)

The Language of Love (Love Stories)

Language of Love (Sweet Dreams)

Lara Gets Even (Making Out)

Lara Gets Lucky (Making Out)

The Lark and the Wren (Bardic Voices)

The Last Battle (Chronicles of Narnia)

The Last Battle (Dragonmaster)

The Last Battle of the Icemark (The Icemark Chronicles)

Last Breath (Body of Evidence)

Last Breath (Nightmare Hall)

Last Call (Party Room Trilogy)

Last Chance (Fear Street: Fear Street Seniors)

Last Chance (Sweet Valley High)

Last Chance Quarterback (Alden All Stars)

Last Clue (Pyrates)

The Last Continent (Discworld)

Last Dance (Heart Beats)

Last Dance (Nancy Drew Files)

Last Dance (The Seer)

Last Date (Nightmare Hall)

Last Full Measure (Star Trek: Enterprise)

The Last Hawk (Saga of the Skolian Empire)

The Last Hero (Discworld)

The Last Laugh (Hardy Boys Casefiles)

The Last Leap (Hardy Boys Casefiles)

The Last of the Nephilim (Dragons in Our Midst: Oracles of Fire)

The Last of the Sky Pirates (Edge Chronicles)

The Last Olympian (Percy Jackson and the Olympians)

Last Resort (Nancy Drew and the Hardy Boys Super Mysteries)

Last Run (Choose Your Own Adventure)

Last Seen in Massilia (Roma Sub Rosa)

Last Splash (Making Waves)

Last Stop (Watchers)

Last Summer (Summer Boys)

Last Summer with Maizon (Maizon)

The Last Tear (W.I.T.C.H.—Chapter Books)

The Last Vampire (The Last Vampire)

The Last Wars (Ferret Chronicles)

Last Wish (Sweet Valley High)

The Last Word (Sweet Dreams)

Latin Nights (Heart Beats)

Laura of the Wild Rose Inn, 1898 (Wild Rose Inn)

Laura's Secret (Fabulous Five)

Lauren's Leap of Faith (Royal Ballet School Diaries)

Laurie's Song (Sweet Dreams)

The Lavender Bear of Oz (Oz)

Lavender Lies (China Bayles Mystery)

Law of the Jungle (Hardy Boys Casefiles)

Laws of Nature (Prowlers)

The Lazarus Plot (Hardy Boys Casefiles)

LB (Laguna Beach) (Summer Share)

LBD (LBD (Les Bambinos Dangereuses))

LBD: It's a Girl Thing (LBD (Les Bambinos Dangereuses))

LBD: Live and Fabulous! (LBD (Les Bambinos Dangereuses))

Leader of the Pack (Oh My Goddess!)

Leading Lady (Victorian Tales of London)

A Leap Ahead (Silver Blades)

Learning the Ropes (7th Heaven)

Leaving Home (On the Road)

Leaving Home (Sweet Valley High)

Left at the Altar (Sweet Valley High)

Left Behind (Sweet Valley Twins)

Left Out, by Rosie (The Broadway Ballplayers)

Legacy (Journey of Allen Strange)

Legacy (Private)

Legacy (Sweep)

Legacy (Wicked)

The Legacy (One Last Wish)

Legacy of Evil (Bionicle Legends)

Legacy of Lies (Dark Secrets)

Legacy's Gift (Thoroughbred)

The Legend of Annie Murphy (Cooper Kids)

Legend of Burning Water (Winds of Light)

The Legend of Luke (Redwall)

The Legend of Merlin (Charmed)

The Legend of Miner's Creek (Nancy Drew)

The Legend of the Ancient Scroll (Mystic Knights of Tir Na Nog)

The Legend of the Emerald Lady (Nancy Drew)

Legend of the Lost Gold (Nancy Drew)

Legend of the Lost Legend (Goosebumps)

Legend of the Zodiac (Jackie Chan Adventures)

Legends of Metru Nui (Bionicle Adventures)

Legends Revealed (W.I.T.C.H.—Graphic Novels)

Little Lefty (Matt Christopher's's Sports Stories)

Little Magic Shop of Horrors (Deadtime Stories)

Little Miss Stoneybrook . . . and Dawn (Baby-Sitters Club)

A Little More to Love (Sweet Dreams)

Little Myth Marker (Myth Adventures)

The Little People (Spooksville)

Little Pet Shop of Horrors (Bone Chillers)

Little Pet Werewolf (Graveyard School)

Little Red Ink Drinker (The Ink Drinker)

Little School of Horrors (Graveyard School)

Little Sister (Sweet Dreams)

Little Things (Buffy the Vampire Slayer)

Little White Lies (Holly's Heart)

Little White Lies (Mary-Kate and Ashley Sweet 16)

Little White Lies (Sweet Dreams)

Live and Let Spy (Spy Girls)

Live Bait (Fearless FBI)

Live Free, Die Hardy! (Hardy Boys, Undercover Brothers: Graphic Novels)

The Lives of Christopher Chant (Chrestomanci)

The Living Dead (Spooksville)

Living Freight (On Time's Wing)

The Living God (A Handful of Men)

Living It Up (Cheerleaders)

Living Legend (Thoroughbred)

Living on Nothing Atoll (Aloha Cove)

Living Together (Sweet Valley University)

Living with a Secret (Why Me?)

Lizard People (Spinetinglers)

Lizzie at Last (Losers, Inc.)

Lizzie for President (Lizzie McGuire)

Lizzie Goes Wild (Lizzie McGuire)

Lizzie Loves Ethan (Lizzie McGuire)

Lizzie's Nightmare and Sibling Bonding (Lizzie McGuire (TokyoPop))

Loamhedge (Redwall)

Locker 13 (Nightmare Room)

The Lodge of the Lynx (The Adept)

Logan Likes Mary Anne! (Baby-Sitters Club)

Lois Strikes Back (Sweet Valley Twins)

The Loki Wolf (Northern Frights)

London (Love Stories: Year Abroad)

London Calling (Flirt)

London Calling (Sweet Valley University: Elizabeth)

The London Deception (Hardy Boys)

Lone Goat and Kid (Usagi Yojimbo)

Long-Arm Quarterback (Matt Christopher's's Sports Stories)

Long Distance Love (Sweet Dreams)

Long Hot Summer (Dawson's Creek)

Long Hot Summoning (The Keeper's Chronicles)

The Long Hunt (Valdemar: Mageworlds)

Long Live the Queen (The President's Daughter)

The Long-Lost Brother (Sweet Valley High)

Long May She Reign (The President's Daughter)

Long Night Dance (The Seeker Chronicles)

Long Night's Journey (Angel (Graphic Novels))

The Long Patrol (Redwall)

The Long Ride (Saddle Club: Pine Hollow)

Long Shadows (Warriors: Power of Three)

Long Shot (Dream Series)

Long Shot (Sweet Dreams)

Long Shot (Three Investigators)

Long Shot for Paul (Matt Christopher's's Sports Stories)

Long Stretch at First Base (Matt Christopher's's Sports Stories)

The Long Way Around (Dream Series)

The Long Way Home (Buffy the Vampire Slayer)

The Long Way Home (Secret Refuge)

Long Way Home (Buffy the Vampire Slayer: Buffy and Angel: The Unseen Trilogy)

Longhorn Territory (Choose Your Own Adventure)

Look to Windward (The Culture)

Look Who's Playing First Base (Matt Christopher's's Sports Stories)

Looking for Trouble (Camp Sunnyside)

Looking Good (Cheerleaders)

Loose Ends (Roswell High)

Lord Brocktree (Redwall)

Lord Loss (Demonata)

Lord of Chaos (The Wheel of Time)

The Lord of Horses (Wodan's Children)

Lord of the Shadows (Cirque du Freak)

Lord Prestimion (The Majipoor Cycle)

Lord Valentine's Castle (The Majipoor Cycle)

Lords and Ladies (Discworld)

Lorwyn (Magic: The Gathering—Lorwyn Cycle)

Losers, Inc (Losers, Inc.)

Losing the Plot (Angels Unlimited)

Lost (Fearless)

L.O.S.T. (L.O.S.T.)

The Lost (The Outer Limits)

Lost and Found (Bluford High)

Lost and Found (Enchanted Hearts)

Lost and Found (From the Files of Madison Finn)

Lost and Found (Remnants)

Lost at Sea (Abby's South Seas Adventures)

Lost at Sea (Sweet Valley High)

Lost Bullet (Traces: Luke Harding, Forensic Investigator)

Lost City (Dinotopia)

The Lost City of Faar (Pendragon)

The Lost Colony (Artemis Fowl)

The Lost Diary (Reel Kids Adventures)

The Lost Foal (Thoroughbred: Ashleigh)

Lost in Stinkeye Swamp (Goosebumps: Give Yourself Goosebumps)

Lost in the Everglades (Nancy Drew)

Lost in the Fog (Colonial Captives)

Lost in the Gator Swamp (Hardy Boys)

Lost in Vegas! (Secret World of Alex Mack)

Lost Jewels of Nabooti (Choose Your Own Adventure)

M

Mac Attack! (Adventures of Daniel Boom AKA Loud Boy)

Macdonald Hall Goes Hollywood (Bruno and Boots)

Mad Dogs (Cherub)

The Mad Gasser of Bessledorf Street (Bessledorf Hotel)

Mad House (Hardy Boys, Undercover Brothers: Graphic Novels)

Madame Amelia Tells All (Amelia)

Madame President (How I Survived Middle School)

Mademoiselle Jessica (Sweet Valley Twins)

Maeve on the Red Carpet (Beacon Street Girls)

Mage-Guard of Hamor (Recluce)

Mage Quest (Yurt)

Maggie (California Diaries)

Maggie, Diary Two (California Diaries)

Maggie's Door (Nory Ryan)

Maggot Pie (Jiggy McCue)

Maggy, Diary Three (California Diaries)

The Magic and the Healing (Crossroads Trilogy)

Magic Casement (Man of His Word)

The Magic Chest of Oz (Oz)

The Magic Christmas (Sweet Valley Twins)

The Magic Dishpan of Oz (Oz)

The Magic Engineer (Recluce)

The Magic Labyrinth (Riverworld Saga)

Magic Lessons (Magic or Madness Trilogy)

Magic Master (Choose Your Own Adventure)

The Magic Mix-Up (Abracadabra)

Magic Moments (Sweet Dreams)

The Magic of Oz (Oz)

The Magic of Recluce (Recluce)

Magic of the Unicorn (Choose Your Own Adventure)

Magic or Madness (Magic or Madness Trilogy)

Magic Pickle (Magic Pickle Graphic Novels)

Magic Pickle and the Planet of the Grapes (Magic Pickle Graphic Novels)

Magic Pickle vs. the Egg Poacher (Magic Pickle Graphic Novels)

Magic Steps (Circle of Magic: The Circle Opens)

Magic Study (Study)

Magic Train and Grubby Longjohn's Olde Tyme Revue (Lizzie McGuire (TokyoPop))

The Magical Fellowship (Age of Magic Trilogy)

The Magical Mimics in Oz (Oz)

The Magician's Apprentice (Magician Trilogy)

The Magician's Challenge (Magician Trilogy)

The Magician's Company (Magician Trilogy)

Magician's Gambit (The Belgariad)

The Magicians' Guild (The Black Magician Trilogy)

The Magician's Nephew (Chronicles of Narnia)

The Magicians of Caprona (Chrestomanci)

The Magickers (The Magickers)

Magic's Child (Magic or Madness Trilogy)

Magic's Pawn (Valdemar: Mage Wars)

Magic's Price (Valdemar: Mage Wars)

Magic's Promise (Valdemar: Mage Wars)

Magi'i of Cyador (Recluce)

Magyk (Septimus Heap)

Maia of Thebes, 1463 B.C. (The Life and Times)

Maid Mary Anne (Baby-Sitters Club)

The Maiden of Mayfair (Victorian Tales of London)

Maizon at Blue Hill (Maizon)

The Majipoor Chronicles (The Majipoor Cycle)

Major Changes (Pacific Cascades University)

Major Meltdown (Dawson's Creek)

Make Lemonade (Make Lemonade Trilogy)

Make Mine to Go (@CAFE)

Make No Mistake (Nancy Drew Files)

The Makeover Experiment (Mary-Kate and Ashley: So Little Time)

Makeovers by Marcia (Losers, Inc.)

Makeup Shake-Up (Mary-Kate and Ashley in Action)

Makin' It Up! (Bratz: Lil' Bratz)

Making a Splash (Mary-Kate and Ashley: Two of a Kind)

Making Choices (Everwood)

Making It (Cheerleaders)

Making Money (Discworld)

Making Strides (Chestnut Hill)

Making the Saint (Circle of Three)

Making Waves (Angels Unlimited)

Making Waves (Making Waves)

Making Waves (Nancy Drew Files)

Making Waves (On the Road)

Makuta's Revenge (Bionicle Chronicles)

Malibu Summer (Sweet Valley High)

Mall Mania (Fabulous Five)

Malled (Hardy Boys, Undercover Brothers: Graphic Novels)

Mallory and the Dream Horse (Baby-Sitters Club)

Mallory and the Ghost Cat (Baby-Sitters Club Mysteries)

Mallory and the Secret Diary (Baby-Sitters Club)

Mallory and the Trouble with the Twins (Baby-Sitters Club)

Mallory Hates Boys (and Gym) (Baby-Sitters Club)

Mallory on Strike (Baby-Sitters Club)

Mallory Pike, #1 Fan (Baby-Sitters Club)

Mallory's Christmas Wish (Baby-Sitters Club)

The Malted Falcoln (Chet Gecko Mysteries)

A Man Betrayed (Book of Words)

Man from Mundania (Xanth Saga)

Man vs. Beast (Cherub)

Mana's Story (The Kin)

Manatee Blues (Wild at Heart)

Manga #1 (Star Wars: A New Hope—Manga)

Manga #1 (Star Wars: Episode I The Phantom Menace—Manga)

Manga #1 (Star Wars: The Empire Strikes Back—Manga)

Manga #1 (Star Wars: The Return of the Jedi—Manga)

Manga #2 (Star Wars: A New Hope—Manga)

Manga #2 (Star Wars: Episode I The Phantom Menace—Manga)

Manga #2 (Star Wars: The Empire Strikes Back—Manga)

Manga #2 (Star Wars: The Return of the Jedi—Manga)

Manga #3 (Star Wars: A New Hope—Manga)

Manga #3 (Star Wars: The Empire Strikes Back—Manga)

Manga #3 (Star Wars: The Return of the Jedi—Manga)

Manga #4 (Star Wars: A New Hope—Manga)

Manga #4 (Star Wars: The Empire Strikes Back—Manga)

Manga #4 (Star Wars: The Return of the Jedi—Manga)

The M.A.N.G.A. Affair (SpyBoy)

The Mansion in the Mist (Anthony Monday)

Mansy Miller Fights Back (Sweet Valley Twins)

Many Waters (Time Fantasy Series)

Mara Strikes Back! (Oh My Goddess!)

March (Countdown)

Mardi Gras Masquerade (Nancy Drew: Girl Detective)

Mardi Gras Mystery (Choose Your Own Adventure)

Mardi Gras Mystery (Nancy Drew)

Maria Who? (Sweet Valley High Senior Year)

Marie Antoinette (Royal Diaries)

Mariel of Redwall (Redwall)

Marisa (Sweet 16)

Mark of the Beast (Left Behind—The Kids)

The Mark of the Blue Tattoo (Hardy Boys)

The Mark of the Crown (Star Wars: Jedi Apprentice)

Mark of the Dragon (Ruin Mist Chronicles)

Mark of the Yuan-Ti (Dungeons and Dragons: Knights of the Silver Dragon)

The Mark on the Door (Hardy Boys)

Marked (House of Night)

Marlfox (Redwall)

Marooned! (Mars Year One)

Married Woman (Sweet Valley University)

Mars Attacks! (Sailor Moon Novels)

Marsquake! (Mars Year One)

Martial Law (Hardy Boys, Undercover Brothers)

Martin the Warrior (Redwall)

The Marvelous Land of Oz (Oz)

Mary (Royal Diaries)

Mary Anne + 2 Many Babies (Baby-Sitters Club)

Mary Anne and Camp BSC (Baby-Sitters Club)

Mary Anne and Miss Priss (Baby-Sitters Club)

Mary Anne and the Great Romance (Baby-Sitters Club)

Mary Anne and the Haunted Bookstore (Baby-Sitters Club Mysteries)

Mary Anne and the Library Mystery (Baby-Sitters Club Mysteries)

Mary Anne and the Little Princess (Baby-Sitters Club)

Mary Anne and the Memory Garden (Baby-Sitters Club)

Mary Anne and the Music Box Secret (Baby-Sitters Club Mysteries)

Mary Anne and the Playground Fight (Baby-Sitters Club)

Mary Anne and the Search for Tigger (Baby-Sitters Club)

Mary Anne and the Secret in the Attic (Baby-Sitters Club Mysteries)

Mary Anne and the Silent Witness (Baby-Sitters Club Mysteries)

Mary Anne and the Zoo Mystery (Baby-Sitters Club Mysteries)

Mary Anne and Too Many Boys (Baby-Sitters Club)

Mary Anne Breaks the Rules (Baby-Sitters Club)

Mary Anne in the Middle (Baby-Sitters Club)

Mary Anne Misses Logan (Baby-Sitters Club)

Mary Anne Saves the Day (Baby-Sitters Club)

Mary Anne Saves the Day (Baby-Sitters Club Graphic Novels)

Mary Anne to the Rescue (Baby-Sitters Club)

Mary Anne vs. Logan (Baby-Sitters Club)

Mary Anne's Bad Luck Mystery (Baby-Sitters Club)

Mary Anne's Big Breakup (Baby-Sitters Club Friends Forever)

Mary Anne's Book (Baby-Sitters Club Portrait Collection)

Mary Anne's Makeover (Baby-Sitters Club)

Mary Anne's Revenge (Baby-Sitters Club Friends Forever)

Mary, Bloody Mary (Young Royals)

Mary Is Missing (Sweet Valley Twins)

Mary's Rescue (7th Heaven)

Mary's Story (7th Heaven)

Mask of the Wolf Boy (Trailblazers)

The Masked Monkey (Hardy Boys)

Maskerade (Discworld)

Masks (Wild at Heart)

Masquerade (Blue Bloods)

Masquerade in Oz (Oz)

Massie (Clique)

Master and Fool (Book of Words)

Master of Aikido (Choose Your Own Adventure)

Master of Deception (Star Wars: The Last of the Jedi)

The Master of Disguise (Star Wars: Jedi Quest)

Master of Judo (Choose Your Own Adventure)

Master of Karate (Choose Your Own Adventure)

Master of Kendo (Choose Your Own Adventure)

Master of Kung Fu (Choose Your Own Adventure)

Master of Martial Arts (Choose Your Own Adventure)

Master of Tae Kwon Do (Choose Your Own Adventure)

The Masterharper of Pern (Pern)

Masters of Mayhem (Kim Possible: Pick a Villain)

Masters of the Louvre (Young Indiana Jones Chronicles: Choose Your Own Adventure)

Mates, Dates, and Chocolate Cheats (Mates, Dates, and . . .)

Mates, Dates, and Cosmic Kisses (Mates, Dates, and . . .)

Mates, Dates, and Designer Divas (Mates, Dates, and . . .)

Mates, Dates, and Diamond Destiny (Mates, Dates, and . . .)

Mates, Dates, and Great Escapes (Mates, Dates, and . . .)

Mates, Dates, and Inflatable Bras (Mates, Dates, and . . .)

Mates, Dates, and Mad Mistakes (Mates, Dates, and . . .)

Mates, Dates, and Sequin Smiles (Mates, Dates, and . . .)

Mates, Dates, and Sizzling Summers (Mates, Dates, and . . .)

Mates, Dates, and Sleepover Secrets (Mates, Dates, and . . .)

Mates, Dates, and Sole Survivors (Mates, Dates, and . . .)

Mates, Dates, and Tempting Trouble (Mates, Dates, and . . .)

Matter (The Culture)

A Matter of Attitude (Kimani Tru)

A Matter of Trust (Bluford High)

Mattimeo (Redwall)

Matt's Story (7th Heaven)

Maui Mystery (Abby's South Seas Adventures)

Maverick Mania (Sports Mystery)

Max and Jane (Love Stories: Prom Trilogy)

Maximum Challenge (Hardy Boys)

Maximum Security (Cherub)

Max's Choice (Sweet Valley University: Elizabeth)

May (Countdown)

May Bird Among the Stars (May Bird)

May Bird and the Ever After (May Bird)

May Bird, Warrior Princess (May Bird)

May the Best Team Win (Saved by the Bell)

Maya Made Over (Star Sisterz)

Maya's Divided World (Roosevelt High School)

Mayday! (Choose Your Own Adventure)

The Mayflower Project (Remnants)

The Mayflower Secret (Trailblazers)

Mayhem in Miami (Aly and AJ's Rock 'n' Roll Mysteries)

Mayhem in Motion (Hardy Boys Casefiles)

The Maze (Dinotopia)

Maze of Deception (Star Wars: Boba Fett)

Maze of Shadows (Bionicle Adventures)

The Maze of the Beast (Deltora: Deltora Quest)

Me and Fat Glenda (Fat Glenda)

Me and My Little Brain (The Great Brain)

Me, Me, Me (Sweet Valley High Senior Year)

Me So Pretty! (Pretty Freekin Scary)

Mean Streak (Kids from Kennedy Middle School)

Meant to Be (Diary of a Teenage Girl)

Meant to Be (Sweet Valley High Senior Year)

Measle and the Dragodon (Measle)

Measle and the Mallockee (Measle)

Measle and the Wrathmonk (Measle)

Measles, Mischief, and Mishaps (Story Girl)

A Measure of Thanks (Dish)

The Medusa Plague (Dragonlance Defenders of Magic)

Meet Me at Midnight (Sweet Valley High)

Meet the Austins (Vicky Austin)

A Meeting of Minds (The Minds Series)

Meets the Eye (Body of Evidence)

Megan's Ghost (Camp Sunnyside)

Melanie Edwards, Super Kisser (Fabulous Five)

Melanie's Double Jinx (Thoroughbred)

Melanie's Identity Crisis (Fabulous Five)

Melanie's Last Ride (Thoroughbred)

Melanie's Treasure (Thoroughbred)

Melanie's Valentine (Fabulous Five)

Melissa (Fab 5)

Meltdown (Danny Watts)

Meltdown (Mindwarp)

Meltdown (2099)

Meltdown: Week 4 (Sevens)

The Melted Coins (Hardy Boys)

Memories (Sweet Valley High)

The Memory of Earth (Homecoming Saga)

Men at Arms (Discworld)

Menace of Alia Rellapor, Part 1 (Akiko Graphic Novels)

Menace of Alia Rellapor, Part 3 (Akiko Graphic Novels)

Menace of Alia Rellapor, Part 2 (Akiko Graphic Novels)

The Mennyms (Mennyms)

Mennyms Alive (Mennyms)

Mennyms Alone (Mennyms)

Mennyms in the Wilderness (Mennyms)

Mennyms Under Siege (Mennyms)

Mercadian Masques (Magic: The Gathering—Masquerade Cycle)

The Merchant of Death (Pendragon)

Merchanter's Luck (Alliance-Union)

The Merchants of Souls (The Thousand Cultures)

Mercury Rising (Sailor Moon Novels)

Meredith (The Elliott Cousins)

Meridian Magic (W.I.T.C.H.—Graphic Novels)

The Merlin Effect (Heartlight)

Merlin's Destiny (Winds of Light)

Merry Go Round in Oz (Oz)

Merry Meet (Circle of Three)

The Message (Animorphs)

Message in a Bottle (Love Letters)

The Message in the Haunted Mansion (Nancy Drew)

The Message in the Hollow Oak (Nancy Drew)

Messenger (The Giver)

Mick (Blue-Eyed Son Trilogy)

Mickey and Me (Baseball Card Adventures)

The Microbots (Tom Swift)

Middle School Gets Married (Sweet Valley Twins)

Middle Sister (7th Heaven)

Midnight (Warriors: The New Prophecy)

Midnight Diary (Fear Street)

Midnight for Charlie Bone (Children of the Red King)

The Midnight Horse (Sandy Lane Stables)

Midnight Madness and Mayhem (Story Girl)

Midnight Mystery (Winnie the Horse Gentler)

Midnight Over Sanctaphrax (Edge Chronicles)

Midnight Pearls (Once Upon a Time)

Midnight Predator (Den of Shadows)

Midnight Rescue (Christy)

Midnight's Choice (Switchers)

Midshipman's Hope (Seafort Saga)

Midsummer Meltdown (Truth or Dare)

The Midwest Girls (Pageant)

Midwinter Nightingale (Wolves Chronicles)

Milady Alex! (Secret World of Alex Mack)

The Moons of Mirrodin (Magic: The Gathering—Mirrodin Cycle)

The Moon's Shadow (Saga of the Skolian Empire)

Moonstalker (Tom Swift)

The Moonstone Castle Mystery (Nancy Drew)

More Adventures of Samurai Cat (Samurai Cat)

More Adventures of the Great Brain (The Great Brain)

More Minds (The Minds Series)

More than a Dream (Red River: Return to Red River)

More than a Friend (Love Stories)

More Than Friends (Silver Blades)

More than Friends (Sweet Dreams)

More Than This (Clearwater Crossing)

More than This (Turning Seventeen)

More than Words (Beverly Hills, 90210)

Moreta, Dragonlady of Pern (Pern)

Morgain's Revenge (Grail Quest)

Morgawr (Shannara: The Voyage of the Jerle Shannara)

The Morning After (Sweet Valley High)

Morningtide (Magic: The Gathering—Lorwyn Cycle)

Mort (Discworld)

Mortal Engines (The Hungry City Chronicles)

Mortal Fear (Buffy the Vampire Slayer)

Mossflower (Redwall)

The Most Dangerous Race (Speed Racer)

Most Likely to Deceive (Class Secrets)

Most Likely to Die (Nancy Drew Files)

Most Wanted (Danger.com)

Mostly Harmless (Hitchhiker's Trilogy)

Mother-Daughter Switch (Sweet Valley Twins)

Mother, Help Me Live (One Last Wish)

Mother, May I? (Remnants)

The Mother of Mountains (Usagi Yojimbo)

Motocross Madness (Hardy Boys)

Motocross Mania (Choose Your Own Adventure)

Mountain Bike Mania (Matt Christopher's's Sports Stories)

Mountain Biker (Choose Your Own Adventure)

Mountain Light (Golden Mountain Chronicles)

Mountain Madness (Christy)

Mountain of Mirrors (Dungeons and Dragons: Endless Quest)

Mountain Survival (Choose Your Own Adventure)

Mountainbike Maniacs (Take It to the Xtreme)

The Mountains of Majipoor (The Majipoor Cycle)

Mourning Song (One Last Wish)

The Movie Star Angel (Forever Angels)

Moving as One (Heart Beats)

Moving On (Everwood)

Moving Pictures (Discworld)

Moving Target (Nancy Drew Files)

Moving Up (Cheerleaders)

Moving Up (High Hurdles)

Mr. Cheeters Is Missing (Nancy Drew Graphic Novels)

Mr. Nice Guy (7th Heaven)

Mr. Perfect (Sweet Dreams)

Mr. Tucket (The Tucket Adventures)

Mr. Wonderful (Sweet Dreams)

Ms. Quarterback (Sweet Valley High)

The Much-Adored Sandy Shore (Cassie Perkins)

Mud City (The Breadwinner Trilogy)

The Mummy Case (Hardy Boys)

The Mummy, the Will, and the Crypt (Johnny Dixon)

The Mummy Walks (Goosebumps Series 2000)

The Mummy Who Wouldn't Die (Choose Your Own Nightmare)

The Mummy's Curse (Hardy Boys, Undercover Brothers)

The Mummy's Footsteps (Mind over Matter)

Murder at Hockey Camp (Screech Owls)

Murder at Monticello (Mrs. Murphy)

Murder at the Mall (Hardy Boys, Undercover Brothers)

Murder at the Winter Games (Screech Owls)

Murder by Magic (Hardy Boys Casefiles)

Murder House (Hardy Boys, Undercover Brothers Murder House Trilogy)

Murder in Paradise (Sweet Valley High)

Murder in the Holy Place (Left Behind—The Kids)

Murder, My Tweet (Chet Gecko Mysteries)

Murder on Ice (Nancy Drew Files)

A Murder on the Appian Way (Roma Sub Rosa)

Murder on the Fourth of July (Nancy Drew and the Hardy Boys Super Mysteries)

Murder on the Line (Sweet Valley High)

Murder on the Prowl (Mrs. Murphy)

Murder on the Ridge (Across the Steel River)

Murder on the Set (Nancy Drew: Girl Detective)

Murder, She Meowed (Mrs. Murphy)

Murder to Go (Three Investigators)

Muses on the Move (Goddesses)

The Music Festival Mystery (Nancy Drew)

Music from the Heart (Sweet Dreams)

The Music Meltdown (Mary-Kate and Ashley in Action)

A Mustard Seed of Magic (Sterling Family)

Mutant Beach (Tom Swift)

The Mutation (Animorphs)

Mutation (Remnants)

Mutiny! (Pirate Hunter)

Mutiny (Space Above and Beyond)

Mutiny in Space (Choose Your Own Adventure)

My Best Enemy (Sweet Dreams)

My Best Friend Is Invisible (Goosebumps)

My Best Friend's Boyfriend (Mary-Kate and Ashley Sweet 16)

My Best Friend's Boyfriend (Sweet Valley High)

My Best Friend's Girlfriend (Love Stories: Super Editions)

My Bonny Light Horseman (Bloody Jack Adventures)

My Brother, the Ghost (House of Horrors)

My Deadly Valentine (Nancy Drew Files)

The Mystery of the Madman at Cornwall Crag (James Budd)

The Mystery of the Magic Circle (Three Investigators)

The Mystery of the Masked Rider (Nancy Drew)

Mystery of the Maya (Choose Your Own Adventure)

Mystery of the Missing Crew (Star Trek: The Next Generation: Starfleet Academy)

The Mystery of the Missing Mascot (Nancy Drew)

The Mystery of the Missing Mermaid (Three Investigators)

The Mystery of the Missing Millionaires (Nancy Drew)

The Mystery of the Moaning Cave (Three Investigators)

The Mystery of the Moss-Covered Mansion (Nancy Drew)

The Mystery of the Mother Wolf (Nancy Drew)

The Mystery of the Mystery Meat (Pretty Freekin Scary)

The Mystery of the Nervous Lion (Three Investigators)

The Mystery of the 99 Steps (Nancy Drew)

Mystery of the Phantom Gold (American Adventure)

The Mystery of the Purple Pirate (Three Investigators)

The Mystery of the Rogues' Reunion (Three Investigators)

Mystery of the Sacred Stones (Choose Your Own Adventure)

The Mystery of the Samurai Sword (Hardy Boys)

The Mystery of the Scar-Faced Beggar (Three Investigators)

The Mystery of the Screaming Clock (Three Investigators)

Mystery of the Secret Room (Choose Your Own Adventure)

The Mystery of the Shrinking House (Three Investigators)

Mystery of the Silver Coins (Viking Quest)

The Mystery of the Silver Spider (Three Investigators)

The Mystery of the Silver Star (Hardy Boys)

The Mystery of the Singing Serpent (Three Investigators)

The Mystery of the Sinister Scarecrow (Three Investigators)

The Mystery of the Smashing Glass (Three Investigators)

Mystery of the Spiral Bridge (Hardy Boys)

The Mystery of the Stuttering Parrot (Three Investigators)

The Mystery of the Talking Skull (Three Investigators)

The Mystery of the Tolling Bell (Nancy Drew)

The Mystery of the Trail of Terror (Three Investigators)

The Mystery of the Two-Toed Pigeon (Three Investigators)

The Mystery of the Vanishing Treasure (Three Investigators)

The Mystery of the Wandering Caveman (Three Investigators)

Mystery of the Whale Tattoo (Hardy Boys)

The Mystery of the Whispering Mummy (Three Investigators)

Mystery of the Winged Lion (Nancy Drew)

Mystery of the Wizard's Tomb (Dungeons and Dragons: Knights of the Silver Dragon)

Mystery of Ura Senke (Choose Your Own Adventure)

The Mystery of Wrecker's Rock (Three Investigators)

Mystery on Makatunk Island (Hardy Boys)

Mystery on Maui (Nancy Drew)

Mystery on Skull Island (American Girls: History Mysteries)

Mystery on the Menu (Nancy Drew)

Mystery Train (Nancy Drew and the Hardy Boys Super Mysteries)

Mystery with a Dangerous Beat (Hardy Boys)

Mystic Knoll (Charmed)

Mystify the Magician (EverWorld)

Myth Alliances (Myth Adventures)

Myth Conceptions (Myth Adventures)

Myth Directions (Myth Adventures)

M.Y.T.H. Inc. in Action (Myth Adventures)

M.Y.T.H. Inc. Link (Myth Adventures)

Myth-ing Persons (Myth Adventures)

Myth-ion Improbable (Myth Adventures)

Myth-Nomers and Im-Pervections (Myth Adventures)

Myth-taken Identity (Myth Adventures)

Myth-told Tales (Myth Adventures)

N

N 2 Deep (TodaysGirls.com)

Nabbed! (Crime Through Time)

Naked (Fearless)

Naked Eye (Fearless FBI)

The Naked Sun (I, Robot)

Namesakes (Alias)

The Naming (Pellinor)

Nancy's Mysterious Letter (Nancy Drew)

The Nannies (Nannies)

Narrow Walk (Nikki Sheridan)

Nashville Nights (Aly and AJ's Rock 'n' Roll Mysteries)

Nasty the Snowman (Fiendly Corners)

Natalia Comes to America (Silver Blades)

Natalie's Secret (Camp Confidential)

The National Pageant (Pageant)

Native Tongue (Specialists)

Natural Enemies (Nancy Drew Files)

Natural Ordermage (Recluce)

The Navigator (The Navigator Trilogy)

Nechama on Strike (B.Y. Times)

A Necklace of Water (Balefire)

Need for Speed (The Jersey)

Neela (American Girls: Girls of Many Lands)

The Negative Zone (Tom Swift)

Nemesis (Angel)

Nemesis (Indigo)

Nemesis (The Lurker Files)

Nemesis (Magic: The Gathering—Masquerade Cycle)

Neotopia (Neotopia)

Neotopia: The Perilous Winds of Athanon (Neotopia Color Manga No. 2) (Neotopia)

Neotopia (Neotopia)

Nerilka's Story (Pern)

Never Been Kissed (Mary-Kate and Ashley Sweet 16)

Never Do Anything, Ever (Dear Dumb Diary)

The Never-Ending Day (China Tate)

Never Give Up (Star Power)

Nightbirds on Nantucket (Wolves Chronicles)

The Nightmare (The Outer Limits)

Nightmare (Undercover Girl)

The Nightmare Game (Dark Ground Trilogy)

Nightmare in Angel City (Hardy Boys Casefiles)

Nightmare in Death Valley (Sweet Valley High)

Nightmare in Heaven (Teen Angels)

Nightmare in Nagano (Screech Owls)

Nightmare in New Orleans (Nancy Drew and the Hardy Boys Super Mysteries)

Nightmare in 3-D (Fear Street: Ghosts of Fear Street)

The Nightmare Machine (Star Wars Galaxy of Fear)

Nightmare on Planet X (Deadtime Stories)

Nightmare on Zombie Island (Twisted Journeys)

Nightrise (The Gatekeepers)

Night's Child (Sweep)

Nightscape (Roswell High)

Nightshade (China Bayles Mystery)

Nina Shapes Up (Making Out)

Nina Won't Tell (Making Out)

The Nine-Hour Date (Love Stories: His. Hers. Theirs)

The Nine Lives of Romeo Crumb (The Nine Lives of Romeo Crumb)

The Nine Lives of Romeo Crumb: Life One (The Nine Lives of Romeo Crumb)

The Nine Lives of Romeo Crumb: Life Three (The Nine Lives of Romeo Crumb)

The Nine Lives of Romeo Crumb: Life Two (The Nine Lives of Romeo Crumb)

The Ninespire Experiment (Knightscares)

Ninja Avenger (Choose Your Own Adventure)

Ninja Cyborg (Choose Your Own Adventure)

Ninja Master! (Oh My Goddess!)

Ninth Key (The Mediator)

No Answer (Fear Street: Fear Street Seniors)

No Arm in Left Field (Matt Christopher's's Sports Stories)

No Boys Allowed (Camp Sunnyside)

No Cafes in Narnia (Tarragon Island)

No Doubt (Clearwater Crossing)

No Escape! (Sweet Valley Twins)

No Exit (The Big Empty)

No Future for You (Buffy the Vampire Slayer)

No Girly Girls Allowed (The Jersey)

No Good Deed (Roswell High)

No Guarantees (Life at Sixteen)

No Guys Pact (Holly's Heart)

No-Hitter (Chip Hilton Sports Series)

No Laughing Matter (Nancy Drew Files)

No Lifeguard on Duty (Brio Girls)

No Means No (Sweet Valley University)

No Mercy (Hardy Boys Casefiles)

No More Boys (Sweet Dreams)

No More Broken Promises (Cassie Perkins)

No More Mr. Nice Guy (Sweet Valley Junior High)

No More Sad Goodbyes (Hamilton High)

No Place for Magic (Tales of the Frog Princess)

No Place like Home (Remnants)

No Place to Hide (Sweet Valley High)

No Rules (Sweet Valley University)

No Secrets (Beverly Hills, 90210)

No Strings Attached (Nancy Drew)

No Strings Attached (Sweet Dreams)

No Surrender (Star Trek: S. C. E.)

No Survivors (Nightmare Room Thrillogy)

No Time Like Show Time (Hermux Tantamoq Adventures)

No Time to Die (Dark Secrets)

No Way Out (Hardy Boys)

No Way Out (Hardy Boys Casefiles)

No World So Dark (Ghost)

The Nobodies (The Anybodies)

Nobody Does It Better (Gossip Girl)

Nobody Does It Better (Spy Girls)

Nobody's Business (Nancy Drew Files)

Nobody's Perfect (7th Heaven)

Nobody's Perfect, Cassie! (Paxton Cheerleaders)

Nocturne (Indigo)

Nocturnes (Ghost)

Nod's Limbs (Edgar and Ellen)

Noli's Story (The Kin)

Noman (Noble Warriors)

The Nome King's Shadow in Oz (Oz)

A Non-Blonde Cheerleader in Love (Non-Blonde Cheerleader)

Norby and the Court Jester (Norby)

Norby and the Invaders (Norby)

Norby and the Lost Princess (Norby)

Norby and the Oldest Dragon (Norby)

Norby and the Queen's Necklace (Norby)

Norby and the Terrified Taxi (Norby)

Norby and Yobo's Great Adventure (Norby)

Norby Down to Earth (Norby)

Norby Finds a Villain (Norby)

Norby, the Mixed-Up Robot (Norby)

Norby's Other Secret (Norby)

Normal (Fearless)

The Northeast Girls (Pageant)

Nory Ryan's Song (Nory Ryan)

A Nose for Adventure (Nose)

The Nose from Jupiter (Nose)

Noses Are Red (Nose)

Not Forgotten (Angel)

The Not-Just-Anybody Family (The Blossom Family)

Not-So-Simple Life (Diary of a Teenage Girl)

Not That I Care (The Friendship Ring)

Note from the Underground (Buffy the Vampire Slayer)

Notes From a Spinning Planet— Ireland (Notes From a Spinning Planet)

Notes From a Spinning Planet— Mexico (Notes From a Spinning Planet)

Notes From a Spinning Planet— Papua New Guinea (Notes From a Spinning Planet)

Nothin' But Net (Matt Christopher's's Sports Stories)

Nothing Can Keep Us Together (Gossip Girl)

One Real Thing (Clearwater Crossing)

One Smooth Move (Extreme Team)

One Step Too Far (Party of Five)

The One That Got Away (Sweet Valley High Senior Year)

One Twin Too Many (Mary-Kate and Ashley: Two of a Kind)

One 2 Many (Sweet Valley Junior High)

The One Way to Win (Silver Blades)

One Wild Weekend (Saved by the Bell)

Only Human (Missing Link Trilogy)

Only in Your Dreams (Gossip Girl)

Only Make-Believe (Sweet Dreams)

Only the Lonely (From the Files of Madison Finn)

The Only Witness (Star Wars: Jedi Apprentice)

Only You—Sierra (Sierra Jensen)

Only You Can Save Mankind (Johnny Maxwell)

Onslaught (Magic: The Gathering—Onslaught Cycle)

Oops, Doggy, Dog! (Cheetah Girls)

The Ooze (Fear Street: Ghosts of Fear Street)

The Opal Deception (Artemis Fowl)

Open Season (Hardy Boys Casefiles)

Open Your Heart (Sierra Jensen)

Operation (Saved by the Bell)

Operation: Survival (Hardy Boys, Undercover Brothers)

Operation: Titanic (Nancy Drew and the Hardy Boys Super Mysteries)

Operation Evaporation (Mary-Kate and Ashley in Action)

Operation Love Match (Sweet Valley High)

Operation Squish! (Sidekicks)

Opportunity Knocks Twice (Brio Girls)

The Opposite Numbers . . . (Hardy Boys, Undercover Brothers: Graphic Novels)

Opposites Attract (Sweet Dreams)

The Oracle Betrayed (Oracle Prophecies)

Orange Knight of Oz (Oz)

Orchard of the Crescent Moon (Gwyn Griffiths Trilogy)

The Orchid Thief (Nancy Drew: Girl Detective)

The Order War (Recluce)

Ordermaster (Recluce)

Oregon, Sweet Oregon (Petticoat Party)

The Origin (Buffy the Vampire Slayer)

Origins (Missing Link Trilogy)

Orion (Orion the Hunter)

Orion Among the Stars (Orion the Hunter)

Orion and the Conqueror (Orion the Hunter)

Orion in the Dying Time (Orion the Hunter)

Orphans of Chaos (Chronicles of Chaos)

The Orphan's Tent (Dragonflight)

The Other (Animorphs)

The Other Me (Sweet Dreams)

The Other Side of Dawn (Tomorrow)

The Other Side of Summer (Gilmore Girls)

The Other Truth (W.I.T.C.H.—Chapter Books)

The Other Way Round (Anna)

The Other Wind (Earthsea)

The Other Woman (Sweet Valley University)

Otherwise Engaged (Nancy Drew on Campus)

Otto and the Bird Charmers (The Karmidee)

Otto and the Flying Twins (The Karmidee)

Otto in the Time of the Warrior (The Karmidee)

Our Journey West (I Am American)

Our Lips Are Sealed (Mary-Kate and Ashley Starring In . . .)

Our Secret Love (Love Stories)

Our Town (X Files)

Out from Boneville (Bone)

Out of Bounds (Beacon Street Girls)

Out of Bounds (Nancy Drew Files)

Out of Control (Nancy Drew and the Hardy Boys Super Mysteries)

Out of Control (Sweet Valley High)

Out of Control (Troubleshooters)

Out of Line (X Games Xtreme Mysteries)

Out of Love (Sweet Dreams: On Our Own)

Out of My League (Love Stories: Super Editions)

Out of Place (Sweet Valley Twins)

Out of Reach (Sweet Valley High)

Out of the Blue (High Hurdles)

Out of the Dark (W.I.T.C.H.—Chapter Books)

Out of the Darkness (Heartland)

Out of the Deep (Mysteries in Our National Parks)

Out of the Madhouse (Buffy the Vampire Slayer: The Gatekeeper Trilogy)

Out of the Mist (Golden Filly Series)

Out of the Picture (Sweet Valley University)

Out of the Woodwork (Buffy the Vampire Slayer)

Out of Their Minds (The Minds Series)

Out of Time (Mindwarp)

Out of Time (Time Travel Quartet)

Outcast (Chronicles of Ancient Darkness)

The Outcast (Guardians of Ga'Hoole)

Outcast (Sons of the Dark)

Outcast (Sweet Valley High)

Outcast (Warriors: Power of Three)

Outcast of Redwall (Redwall)

Outlander (Outlander)

Outlaw (Magic: The Gathering—Kamigawa Cycle)

Outlaw Gulch (Choose Your Own Adventure)

Outlaw Princess of Sherwood (Rowan Hood)

Outlaw's Gold (CyberQuest)

Outlaws of Sherwood Forest (Choose Your Own Adventure)

The Outlaw's Silver (Hardy Boys)

The Outlaw's Twin Sister (Belles of Lordsburg)

Outrageously Alice (Alice)

The Outsider (The O.C.)

The Outsider (Roswell High)

Outsmart (The Wessex Papers)

Over & Out (Camp Confidential)

Over Sea, Under Stone (Dark Is Rising)

Perfect Getaway (Hardy Boys Casefiles)

The Perfect Gift (Mary-Kate and Ashley: Two of a Kind)

The Perfect Girl (Sweet Valley High)

Perfect Girls (Replica)

The Perfect Horse (Horseshoes)

Perfect Image (Thoroughbred)

Perfect Match (Inside Girl)

The Perfect Match (Sweet Dreams)

The Perfect Pair (Silver Blades)

The Perfect Plan (7th Heaven)

Perfect Planet (Choose Your Own Adventure)

The Perfect Plot (Nancy Drew Files)

The Perfect Pony (Sandy Lane Stables)

Perfect Shot (Sweet Valley High)

Perfect Strangers (Love Letters)

The Perfect Summer (Mary-Kate and Ashley Sweet 16)

Perfect Summer (Sweet Valley High)

Peril in the Bessledorf Parachute Factory (Bessledorf Hotel)

Perilous Seas (Man of His Word)

Perils of Love (Left Behind—The Kids)

Permanent Rose (Casson Family)

The Personal Correspondence of Catherine Clark and Meredith Lyons (Liberty Letters)

The Personal Correspondence of Elizabeth Walton and Abigail Matthews (Liberty Letters)

The Personal Correspondence of Emma Edmunds and Mollie Turner (Liberty Letters)

The Personal Correspondence of Hannah Brown and Sarah Smith (Liberty Letters)

The Pet (Star Trek: Deep Space Nine)

Pet Peeve (Xanth Saga)

Pet Store (Spinetinglers)

Petals on the Wind (Dollanganger)

Peter and the Secret of Rundoon (Peter and the Starcatchers)

Peter and the Shadow Thieves (Peter and the Starcatchers)

Peter and the Starcatchers (Peter and the Starcatchers)

Peter Duck (Swallows and Amazons)

The Petrified Parrot (P.C. Hawke Mysteries)

Pet's Revenge (Edgar and Ellen)

The Phantom (The Last Vampire)

The Phantom Freighter (Hardy Boys)

The Phantom of 86th Street (P.C. Hawke Mysteries)

The Phantom of Pine Hill (Nancy Drew)

Phantom of the Auditorium (Goosebumps)

The Phantom of the Roxy (Mind over Matter)

The Phantom of Venice (Nancy Drew)

Phantom Racer (Oh My Goddess!)

Phantom Submarine (Choose Your Own Adventure)

Phantom Writer (Red Rock Mysteries)

Pharaoh's Tomb (CyberQuest)

The Philadelphia Adventure (Vesper Holly)

Philip Hall Likes Me, I Reckon Maybe (Philip Hall)

Phoebe (Sisters)

Phoebe Who? (Charmed)

Phoebe's Folly (Petticoat Party)

Phoebe's Fortune (Spell Casters)

The Phoenix Equation (Hardy Boys Casefiles)

Phone Fear (Spooksville)

Phone Home, Persephone! (Myth-O-Mania)

Photo Finish (Hover Car Racer)

Physik (Septimus Heap)

Piano Lessons Can Be Murder (Goosebumps)

The Pictish Child (Tartan Magic Trilogy)

The Picts and the Martyrs (Swallows and Amazons)

The Picture of Guilt (Nancy Drew Files)

Picture Perfect (Charmed)

Picture Perfect (From the Files of Madison Finn)

Picture Perfect? (Generation Girl)

Picture Perfect (Saved by the Bell)

The Picture-Perfect Mystery (Nancy Drew)

A Picture-Perfect Prom (Sweet Valley High)

Picture Perfect Romance (Sweet Dreams)

Picture This (Lizzie McGuire)

Pictures of the Night (Egerton Hall Novels)

Pied Piper (Charmed)

Pier Pressure (Luna Bay)

Pigeon Post (Swallows and Amazons)

The Pilgrims of Rayne (Pendragon)

Pillars of Pentegarn (Dungeons and Dragons: Endless Quest)

The Pinhoe Egg (Chrestomanci)

Pirate Curse (Wave Walkers)

Pirate Emperor (Wave Walkers)

Pirate Wars (Wave Walkers)

Pirate's Cross (CyberQuest)

The Pirates in Oz (Oz)

The Pirates of Marathon (Secret Agent MJJ)

The Pirates of Pompeii (Roman Mysteries)

Pirates of Underwhere (Underwhere)

Pirates on the Internet (Cybersurfers)

Pirate's Revenge (Colonial Captives)

Pit of Vipers (Nancy Drew: Girl Detective)

Pitch Black (True Colors)

Pitchers' Duel (Chip Hilton Sports Series)

Pizza Zombies (Fiendly Corners)

A Place in the Heart (Aloha Cove)

A Place to Belong (Orphan Train Adventures)

The Plague (Feather and Bone: The Crow Chronicles)

The Plague (My Side of the Story)

Plainsong for Caitlin (American Dreams)

Planar Chaos (Magic: The Gathering—Time Spiral Cycle)

Planeshift (Magic: The Gathering—Invasion Cycle)

Planeswalker (Magic: The Gathering—Artifacts Cycle)

Planet of Terror (Nightmares! How Will Yours End?)

Planet of the Dragons (Choose Your Own Adventure)

Planet Plague (Star Wars Galaxy of Fear)

Play (Have a Nice Life)

Play (Replica: The Plague Trilogy)

Play Ball! (Rookies)

Play It Again (From the Files of Madison Finn)

Play Me a Love Song (Sweet Dreams)

Play-Off Pressure (Rookies)

Pride's Last Race (Thoroughbred)

Primary Inversion (Saga of the Skolian Empire)

Prime Choice (Perry Skky Jr.)

Prime Evil (Buffy the Vampire Slayer)

Prime Time (Clearwater Crossing)

The Prime-Time Crime (Hardy Boys)

Prime-Time Pitcher (Matt Christopher's's Sports Stories)

Prince (Wolfbay Wings)

Prince Across the Water (The Stuart Quartet)

Prince Caspian (Chronicles of Narnia)

The Prince in Waiting (Sword of the Spirits)

Prince of Underwhere (Underwhere)

Princess Amy (Sweet Dreams)

Princess Charming (The Princess School)

The Princess Club (Christy)

The Princess Diaries (Princess Diaries)

Princess Elizabeth (Sweet Valley Twins)

Princess in Love (Princess Diaries)

Princess in the Spotlight (Princess Diaries)

Princess in Training (Princess Diaries)

Princess in Waiting (Princess Diaries)

Princess Mia (Princess Diaries)

The Princess of Fairwood High (Homeroom)

The Princess of Pop (Truth or Dare)

Princess on the Brink (Princess Diaries)

The Princess Present (Princess Diaries)

The Princess Project (Princess Diaries)

The Princess, the Crone, and the Dung-Cart Knight (The Denizens of Camelot)

The Printer's Devil (Printers Devil Trilogy)

Prison Ship (Adventures of a Young Sailor)

Prisoner of Elderwood (Dungeons and Dragons: Endless Quest)

Prisoner of the Ant People (Choose Your Own Adventure)

Prisoner of Time (Time Travel Quartet)

Prisoner's Hope (Seafort Saga)

Prisoners of Peace (Star Trek: Deep Space Nine)

Prisoners of the Pit (Bionicle Legends)

Private (Private)

Private Eyes (Sweet Dreams)

Private Jessica (Sweet Valley University)

Private Lives (Net Force)

The Prize (Thoroughbred: Ashleigh)

Probability Moon (Probability)

Probability Space (Probability)

Probability Sun (Probability)

Problem Solved (Perry Skky Jr.)

The Problem with Here Is That It's Where I'm From (Dear Dumb Diary)

The Problem with Love (Sweet Dreams)

The Problem with Parents (Camp Sunnyside)

Process of Elimination (Nancy Drew and the Hardy Boys Super Mysteries)

Processing the Computer Conspiracy (Summit High)

Prognosis (University Hospital)

Program for Destruction (Hardy Boys)

Programmed for Love (Sweet Dreams)

Project (FaithGirlz: Girls of 622 Harbor View)

Project: Mystery Bus (FaithGirlz: Girls of 622 Harbor View)

Project: Raising Faith (FaithGirlz: Girls of 622 Harbor View)

Project: Rescue Chelsea (FaithGirlz: Girls of 622 Harbor View)

Project: Runaway (FaithGirlz: Girls of 622 Harbor View)

Project: Secret Admirer (FaithGirlz: Girls of 622 Harbor View)

Project: Ski Trip (FaithGirlz: Girls of 622 Harbor View)

Project: Take Charge (FaithGirlz: Girls of 622 Harbor View)

Project Black Bear (China Tate)

Project Boyfriend (Sweet Dreams)

Project Paris (The Fashion-Forward Adventures of Imogene)

Project UFO (Choose Your Own Adventure)

Prom Date (Fear Street: Fear Street Seniors)

Prom Dates from Hell (Maggie Quinn: Girl vs. Evil)

Prom Night (Sweet Valley High Senior Year)

Prom Princess (Mary-Kate and Ashley: Two of a Kind)

Prom Queen (Fear Street)

Prom Queen Geeks (Queen Geeks)

The Promethian Flame (The Cronus Chronicles)

The Promise (Black Stallion: Young Black Stallion)

A Promise and a Rainbow (The Double Dutch Club)

Promise Breaker (Promise of Zion)

A Promise Is Forever (Christy Miller)

Promise Kept (Perry Skky Jr.)

Promise Me Love (Sweet Dreams)

Promise Me You'll Stop Me (Distress Call 911)

Promises (Star Wars Junior Jedi Knights)

Promises (Sweet Valley High)

Promises, Promises (Beacon Street Girls)

Promises, Promises (Clearwater Crossing)

The Prophecy (Animorphs)

The Prophecy (Daughters of the Moon)

Prophecy (Magic: The Gathering—Masquerade Cycle)

The Prophet of Yonwood (City of Ember)

The Proposal (Animorphs)

The Proposal (Christy)

The Protester's Song (Misfits, Inc.)

Proving It (Cheerleaders)

Prowlers (Prowlers)

P.S. I Loathe You (Clique)

P.S. I Love You (Sweet Dreams)

P.S. I Really Like You (How I Survived Middle School)

P.S. Wish You Were Here (Mary-Kate and Ashley: Two of a Kind)

Psion (Psion)

Psychic Sisters (Sweet Valley Twins)

Ptolemy's Gate (The Bartimaeus Trilogy)

Public Enemies (On the Run)

Ratha's Challenge (Ratha Quartet)

Ratha's Courage (Ratha Quartet)

Ratha's Creature (Ratha Quartet)

The Raven Queen (Voyage of the Basset)

Raven Rise (Pendragon)

Raven's Gate (The Gatekeepers)

Ravinica (Magic: The Gathering—Ravnica Cycle)

Ray and Me (Baseball Card Adventures)

Rays, Romance and Rivalry (Summer)

Re-Vamped! (My Sister the Vampire)

Reach for the Stars (Fame School)

Reach for Tomorrow (One Last Wish)

The Reaction (Animorphs)

Ready? (Love Trilogy)

Ready, Shoot, Score! (Cheer USA!)

Real Fake (Nancy Drew: Girl Detective)

Real Horror (Hardy Boys Casefiles)

The Real Thing (Sweet Dreams)

Reality Bites (Camp Confidential)

The Reality Bug (Pendragon)

Reality Check (Clearwater Crossing)

Reality Check (Turning Seventeen)

The Reality Machine (Choose Your Own Adventure)

Realm of the Reaper (EverWorld)

The Realms of the Gods (Immortals)

Reaper Man (Discworld)

The Reapers' Song (Red River: Red River of the North)

Rebecca's Flame (On Time's Wing)

Rebel (Fearless)

The Rebel (Roswell High)

Rebel Angels (Gemma Doyle)

Rebel Glory (Lightning on Ice)

Rebel Hart (White Mane Kids)

Recipe for Love (Sweet Dreams)

Recipe for Murder (Nancy Drew Files)

Recipe for Rebellion (Zodiac Girls)

A Recipe for Trouble (Dish)

Reckless (The It Girl)

Reckoning (The Fallen)

The Reckoning (Quantum Prophecy)

Reckoning (Star Wars: The Last of the Jedi)

Reckoning (Sweep)

Reckonings (Books of Magic)

The Recruit (Cherub)

Recruited (Alias)

Red Dice (The Last Vampire)

Red-Hot Hightops (Matt Christopher's's Sports Stories)

Red Is for Remembrance (Blue Is for Nightmares)

Red Prophet (Tales of Alvin Maker)

Red Rider's Hood (Dark Fusion)

Red Tide Alert (Neptune Adventures)

Red Unicorn (Dragonflight)

Red Unicorn (Unicorn)

Red Velvet (Friends for a Season)

Red Wolf's Daughter (MythQuest)

The Red Wyvern (Deverry)

Redemption (Angel)

Redemption: Week 7 (Sevens)

Redwall (Redwall)

Reed (Wolfbay Wings)

Reel Thrills (Hardy Boys)

Reel Trouble (Three Investigators)

Reflex (Jumper)

Refugee Treasure (Promise of Zion)

Regeneration (Regeneration)

Regeneration (X Files)

Regina's Legacy (Sweet Valley High)

Regular Guy (Guy Strang)

Rehearsing for Romance (Nancy Drew Files)

Reining In (Saddle Club: Pine Hollow)

The Reluctant Pitcher (Matt Christopher's's Sports Stories)

Reluctantly Alice (Alice)

Remember Me (Dear Diary)

Rendezvous in Rome (Nancy Drew Files)

Rendezvous with Rama (Rama)

Renegades of Pern (Pern)

The 'Rents (Lizzie McGuire)

Replaced (Alias)

The Reptile Room (A Series of Unfortunate Events)

The Rescue (Guardians of Ga'Hoole)

Rescue (Kidnapped)

Rescue Ferrets at Sea (Ferret Chronicles)

Rescue Party (Dinotopia)

The Resistance (Animorphs)

Rest in Peace (Unseen)

Rest in Pieces (House of Horrors)

Rest in Pieces (Mrs. Murphy)

The Restaurant at the End of the Universe (Hitchhiker's Trilogy)

Resurrecting Ravana (Buffy the Vampire Slayer)

Retreat from Gettysburg (White Mane Kids)

The Return (Animorphs)

The Return (Flight 29 Down)

The Return of a Queen (W.I.T.C.H.—Chapter Books)

The Return of Meteor Boy? (The Extraordinary Adventures of Ordinary Boy)

Return of the Dark Side (Star Wars: The Last of the Jedi)

Return of the Evil Twin (Sweet Valley High)

The Return of the Great Brain (The Great Brain)

Return of the Home Run Kid (Matt Christopher's's Sports Stories)

The Return of the King (Lord of the Rings)

Return of the Mummy (Goosebumps)

Return of the Ninja (Choose Your Own Adventure)

Return of the Perfect Girls (Replica)

Return to Atlantis (Choose Your Own Adventure)

Return to Brookmere (Dungeons and Dragons: Endless Quest)

Return to Chaos (Buffy the Vampire Slayer)

Return to Del (Deltora: Deltora Quest)

Return to Foreverware (Eerie Indiana)

Return to Ghost Camp (Goosebumps Series 2000)

Return to Horrorland (Goosebumps Series 2000)

Return to Ithaca (Tales from the Odyssey)

Return to Lost City (Dinotopia)

Return to Ord Mantell (Star Wars Young Jedi Knights)

Return to Oz (Oz)

Return to Terror Tower (Goosebumps: Give Yourself Goosebumps)

Return to the Carnival of Horrors (Goosebumps: Give Yourself Goosebumps)

River Quest (Dinotopia)

River Rats (Hardy Boys Casefiles)

River Secrets (Goose Girl)

The River Underground (Rex Mundi)

Riverboat Ruse (Nancy Drew: Girl Detective)

The Rivers of Zadaa (Pendragon)

The Road Not Taken (Alias)

Road Pirates (Hardy Boys Casefiles)

The Road to Camlann (Arthurian Knights)

The Road to Freedom (Jamestown's American Portraits)

The Road to Memphis (Logan Family)

The Road to Oz (Oz)

The Road to the Majors (Dream Series)

The Road to Vengeance (The Strongbow Saga)

The Road to War (Left Behind—The Kids)

Road Trip (Diary of a Teenage Girl)

Road Trip (Sweet Valley High Senior Year)

The Roar of the Crowd (Winning Season)

The Roaring River Mystery (Hardy Boys)

The Roaring Twenties (Young Indiana Jones Chronicles: Choose Your Own Adventure)

Robbers and Robots (Dungeons and Dragons: Endless Quest)

Robbery at the Mall (Sweet Valley Twins)

The Robin and the Kestrel (Bardic Voices)

The Robot Olympics (Tom Swift Young Inventor)

Robots and Empire (I, Robot)

The Robots of Dawn (I, Robot)

The Robot's Revenge (Hardy Boys)

Roc and a Hard Place (Xanth Saga)

Rock 'n' Roll Sweetheart (Sweet Dreams)

Rock and Roll Mystery (Choose Your Own Adventure)

Rock Jaw, Master of the Eastern Border (Bone)

Rock 'n' Revenge (Hardy Boys Casefiles)

Rock 'n' Roll Renegades (Hardy Boys)

Rock On (Extreme Team)

The Rock Rats (Asteroid Wars)

Rock Star's Girl (Sweet Valley High)

Rocked Out (X Games Xtreme Mysteries)

Rocket Racers (Tom Swift Young Inventor)

Rocky Road (Hardy Boys, Undercover Brothers)

The Rocky Road to Revenge (Hardy Boys)

Rocky Romance (Sweet Dreams)

Rodeo Horse (Mustang Mountain)

Rogue Berserker (Berserker)

The Rogues (The Stuart Quartet)

Rogues in the House and Other Stories (Chronicles of Conan)

Roll Call (Traces: Luke Harding, Forensic Investigator)

Roll of Thunder, Hear My Cry (Logan Family)

Roller Hockey Radicals (Matt Christopher's's Sports Stories)

Roller Hockey Rumble (Extreme Team)

Roller Star (Choose Your Own Adventure)

Rolling Thunder (NASCAR Pole Position Adventures)

Roman Blood (Roma Sub Rosa)

Romance on the Run (Sweet Dreams)

Romantically Correct (Clueless)

Rome (Love Stories: Year Abroad)

Romeo and Ghouliette (Bone Chillers)

Romeo and Two Juliets (Sweet Valley Twins)

The Ronin (Usagi Yojimbo)

Room 13 (Moondog)

The Roommate (Nightmare Hall)

The Roommate (Sweet Valley University Thriller Editions)

Rosa's Lie (Sweet Valley High)

Rose at Bull Run (The Young Americans)

The Rose Bride (Once Upon a Time)

The Rose Queen (Missing Persons)

Rosemary Remembered (China Bayles Mystery)

Rosetta (Star Trek: Enterprise)

The Rosewood Casket (Ballad)

Rough Riding (Hardy Boys Casefiles)

Rough Stuff (Three Investigators)

Roughing It (Distress Call 911)

Round One (Popular)

Roundup of the Street Rovers (Trailblazers)

Rowan Farm (Lechow Family)

Rowan Hood (Rowan Hood)

Rowan Hood Returns (Rowan Hood)

The Royal Book of Oz (Oz)

A Royal Kiss (You're the One)

Royal Pain (Kim Possible (Chapter Books))

Royal Pain (Sweet Valley University: Elizabeth)

Royal Pain and Twin Factor (Kim Possible (TokyoPop))

Royal Revenge (Nancy Drew and the Hardy Boys Super Mysteries)

RSVP (Camp Confidential)

Rubicon (Roma Sub Rosa)

The Ruby Dice (Saga of the Skolian Empire)

The Ruby in the Smoke (Sally Lockhart Trilogy)

The Ruby Raven (Finnegan Zwake)

Rueful Death (China Bayles Mystery)

The Ruins of Gorlan (Ranger's Apprentice)

Ruler of the Realm (The Faerie Wars Chronicles)

The Rumor About Julia (Love Stories)

Rumors (Cheerleaders)

Rumors (The Luxe)

Rumors (Sweet Valley High)

Rumors and I've Got Rhythmic (Lizzie McGuire (TokyoPop))

Rumors at the Rink (Silver Blades)

Run (Fearless)

Run, Billy, Run (Matt Christopher's's Sports Stories)

Run for It (Matt Christopher's's Sports Stories)

Run for Your Life (On Time's Wing)

Runaway (Dear Diary)

The Runaway (Fear Street)

Runaway (Platinum Teen)

Runaway (The Sixth Sense: Secrets from Beyond)

Runaway (Smallville)

Runaway (Sweet Valley High)

The Runaway Bride (Nancy Drew Files)

The Runaway Crisis (Fabulous Five)

The Scarecrow Walks at Midnight (Goosebumps)

Scared Stiff (Al's World)

Scaredy Kat (Suddenly Supernatural)

The Scarlet Macaw Scandal (Nancy Drew: Girl Detective)

Scarlet Moon (Once Upon a Time)

The Scarlet Slipper Mystery (Nancy Drew)

Scarlet Thunder (Sports Mystery)

Scars! (Zorro Graphic Novels)

Scary Birthday to You! (Goosebumps: Give Yourself Goosebumps)

Scary Summer (Goosebumps Graphix)

Scene of the Crime (Choose Your Own Adventure)

Scene of the Crime (Hardy Boys Casefiles)

Scene One, Take Two (Saved by the Bell)

Scent of Danger (Nancy Drew Files)

Scheme Team (Chestnut Hill)

Scheming (Cheerleaders)

Schism (Saga of the Skolian Empire)

School Dance Party (Mary-Kate and Ashley Starring In . . .)

The School of Fear (Star Wars: Jedi Quest)

School Plot (The Floods)

School Spirit (Suddenly Supernatural)

School Time Style (Bratz: Lil' Bratz)

School's Out—Forever (Maximum Ride)

Scion of Cyador (Recluce)

The Scions of Shannara (Shannara: Heritage of Shannara)

Score (Have a Nice Life)

Scorpia (Alex Rider)

Scourge (Magic: The Gathering—Onslaught Cycle)

A Scout Is Born (Sailor Moon Novels)

Scouts on Film (Sailor Moon Novels)

Scrambled (Sam and Stephanie)

Scratch (Flight 29 Down)

Scratch and the Sniffs (He-Man Women Haters Club)

The Scream (Forbidden Doors)

Scream Around the Campfire (Graveyard School)

The Scream Museum (P.C. Hawke Mysteries)

Scream of the Cat (Phantom Valley)

Scream of the Evil Genie (Goosebumps: Give Yourself Goosebumps)

The Scream of the Haunted Mask (Goosebumps Horrorland)

Scream School (Goosebumps Series 2000)

The Scream Tea (Fear Street: Ghosts of Fear Street)

Scream, Team! (Graveyard School)

The Scream Team (Nightmare Hall)

Screamers (Hardy Boys Casefiles)

The Screaming Heart (Fearless)

Screech in Love (Saved by the Bell)

The Screech Owls' Home Loss (Screech Owls)

The Screech Owls' Northern Adventure (Screech Owls)

The Screech Owls' Reunion (Screech Owls)

Sea City, Here We Come! (Baby-Sitters Club Super Specials)

Sea for Yourself (Luna Bay)

Sea Glass (Golden Mountain Chronicles)

The Sea of Monsters (Percy Jackson and the Olympians)

Sea of Suspicion (Nancy Drew Files)

Sea You, Sea Me! (Hardy Boys, Undercover Brothers: Graphic Novels)

Seal Island Scam (Girls R.U.L.E.)

Sealed with a Diss (Clique)

Sealed With a Kiss (Diary of a Crush)

Sealed with a Kiss (Holly's Heart)

Sealed with a Kiss (Mary-Kate and Ashley: Two of a Kind)

Search (Kidnapped)

The Search (Left Behind—The Kids)

The Search (Regeneration)

Search for Aladdin's Lamp (Choose Your Own Adventure)

The Search for Cindy Austin (Nancy Drew)

Search for Safety (Bluford High)

Search for Senna (EverWorld)

The Search for Snout (Alien Adventures)

Search for the Mountain Gorillas (Choose Your Own Adventure)

The Search for the Red Dawn (Chronicles of the Imaginarium Geographica)

The Search for the Silver Persian (Nancy Drew)

The Search for the Snow Leopard (Hardy Boys)

Search the Amazon! (Choose Your Own Adventure)

Searching for Dragons (Enchanted Forest Chronicles)

Searching for Love (Sweet Dreams)

A Searching Heart (Prairie Legacy)

Seaside High (Aloha Cove)

Seaside Mystery (Choose Your Own Adventure)

A Season for Goodbye (One Last Wish)

A Season of Hope (Heartland)

Seasons (Usagi Yojimbo)

Second Best (Life at Sixteen)

Second Best (Sweet Valley Twins)

Second-Best Friend (Holly's Heart)

Second Chance (Drama High)

Second Chance (Left Behind—The Kids)

Second Chance (Sweet Valley High)

Second Chances (Sweet Dreams)

Second Choices (Nikki Sheridan)

Second Evil (Fear Street: Fear Street Cheerleaders)

Second Foundation (Foundation)

Second Helpings (Jessica Darling)

The Second Horror (Fear Street: 99 Fear Street)

Second Sight (Circle of Three)

Second Sight (Mindwarp)

Second-String Center (Winning Season)

The Second Summer of the Sisterhood (Sisterhood of the Traveling Pants)

The Second Summoning (The Keeper's Chronicles)

Second Time's the Charm (Camp Confidential)

Second Wave (Acorna's Children)

Second Wind (Golden Filly Series)

Second Wind (Spirit of the Game)

The Secret (Animorphs)

The Secret (Fear Street: Fear Street Sagas)

Secret (Making Waves)

Secret Admirer (Dear Diary)

Secret Admirer (Fear Street)

Secret Admirer (Sweet Dreams)

Secret Treasure of Tibet (Choose Your Own Adventure)

Secret Vampire (Night World)

Secret Warning (Hardy Boys)

Secret Water (Swallows and Amazons)

Secret Weapon (Star Wars: The Last of the Jedi)

Secrets! (B.Y. Times)

Secrets (Fingerprints)

Secrets (7th Heaven)

Secrets (Sweet Dreams)

Secrets (Sweet Valley High)

Secrets (Undercover Girl)

Secrets and Lies (Turning Seventeen)

Secrets Can Kill (Nancy Drew Files)

Secrets in the Sand (Saddle Island)

Secrets in the Shadows (Bluford High)

The Secrets of Belltown (Belltown Mystery)

The Secrets of Cain's Castle (Belltown Mystery)

The Secrets of Code Z (Belltown Mystery)

The Secrets of Cranberry Beach (Belltown Mystery)

The Secrets of Grim Woods (Lowthar's Blade)

Secrets of New Babylon (Left Behind—The Kids)

The Secrets of Pilgrim Pond (Belltown Mystery)

Secrets of the Nile (Nancy Drew and the Hardy Boys Super Mysteries)

Secrets of the Past (Generation Girl)

The Secrets of the Twisted Cross (Belltown Mystery)

The Secrets of Vesuvius (Roman Mysteries)

Secrets on 26th Street (American Girls: History Mysteries)

The Secular Wizard (A Wizard in Rhyme)

See No Evil (Hardy Boys Casefiles)

See No Evil (Smallville)

Seed of Destruction (Hellboy)

Seeds of Yesterday (Dollanganger)

Seeing Double (Bratz: Clued In!)

Seeing Is Deceiving (T*Witches)

The Seeing Stone (Arthur Trilogy)

Seek the Prophet (Watching Alice)

Seeker (Noble Warriors)

The Seeker (Roswell High)

Seeker (Sweep)

The Seeker (Watcher's Quest)

The Seer (Antrian)

The Seeress of Kell (Malloreon)

Self-Portrait (Three Girls in the City)

The Senator's Other Daughter (Belles of Lordsburg)

A Sending of Dragons (Pit Dragon Trilogy)

Senior Cut Day (Sweet Valley High Senior Year)

Senior Year (Beverly Hills, 90210)

The Separation (Animorphs)

September (Countdown)

Series Showdown (Rookies)

The Serpent Gift (The Shamer Chronicles)

The Serpent of Senargad (Pangur Ban)

The Serpent's Children (Golden Mountain Chronicles)

Serpent's Reach (Alliance-Union)

The Serpent's Tooth Mystery (Hardy Boys)

Servant to Abigail Adams (I Am American)

Setting the Pace (Alden All Stars)

Setting the Pace (High Hurdles)

Setting the Pace (Saddle Club: Pine Hollow)

The Seven (Flight 29 Down)

Seven Crows (Buffy the Vampire Slayer: Buffy and Angel)

The Seven Songs of Merlin (The Lost Years of Merlin)

Seven Spiders Spinning (Hamlet Chronicles)

Seventeen Against the Dealer (Tillerman Cycle)

Seventeen and In-Between (Elsie Edwards)

1776 (Young Founders)

Seventeen Wishes (Christy Miller)

Seventh-Grade Menace (Fabulous Five)

Seventh Grade Rumors (Fabulous Five)

The Seventh Sentinel (Dragonlance Defenders of Magic)

Seventh Son (Tales of Alvin Maker)

Sex (Fearless)

Sex? (Love Trilogy)

Shacked Up (Hard Cash)

Shacked Up (Richard Steele Trilogy)

Shades (Roswell High)

Shades of Death (Usagi Yojimbo)

The Shadewell Shenanigans (The Illmoor Chronicles)

Shadow Academy (Star Wars Young Jedi Knights)

Shadow Beast (Invisible Detectives)

The Shadow Companion (Grail Quest)

Shadow Girl (Nightmare Room)

The Shadow in the North (Sally Lockhart Trilogy)

The Shadow in the Tomb and Other Stories (Chronicles of Conan)

The Shadow Killers (Hardy Boys)

Shadow Kiss (Vampire Academy)

Shadow Man (Danger.com)

Shadow of a Doubt (Nancy Drew Files)

Shadow of Honor (Net Force)

Shadow of the Giant (Ender Wiggin)

Shadow of the Hegemon (Ender Wiggin)

Shadow of the Sphinx (Charmed)

Shadow of the Swastika (Choose Your Own Adventure)

Shadow of the Well of Souls (Watchers at the Well)

Shadow over San Mateo (Golden Filly Series)

Shadow Puppets (Ender Wiggin)

The Shadow Rising (The Wheel of Time)

Shadow Self (Dear Diary)

The Shadow Sorceress (The Spellsong Cycle)

The Shadow Thieves (The Cronus Chronicles)

The Shadow Trap (Star Wars: Jedi Quest)

Shadow Tree (Glory)

Shadowed (Alias)

Shadowgate (Deltora: Dragons of Deltora)

Shadowland (The Mediator)

The Shadowlands (Deltora: Deltora Shadowlands)

Shadowmoor (Magic: The Gathering—Shadowmoor Cycle)

ShadowQueen (L.O.S.T.)

Shadows Beyond the Gate (Summerhill Secrets)

Sign of the Dove (Dragon Chronicles)

Sign of the Dragon (MacGregor Family Adventure)

The Sign of the Falcon (Nancy Drew)

Sign of the Ox (Jackie Chan Adventures)

Sign of the Shapeshifter (Dungeons and Dragons: Knights of the Silver Dragon)

The Sign of the Twisted Candles (Nancy Drew)

Silenced! (Crime Through Time)

The Silent Hand (Fearless)

Silent Night (Fear Street: Fear Street Super Chillers)

Silent Night 3 (Fear Street: Fear Street Super Chillers)

Silent Night 2 (Fear Street: Fear Street Super Chillers)

Silent Ruin (Trigun Maximum)

The Silent Scream (Nightmare Hall)

Silent Superstitions (Christy)

The Silent Suspect (Nancy Drew)

Silent Tears (Life at Sixteen)

The Silent War (Asteroid Wars)

Silent Witness (Jennie McGrady Mysteries)

The SillyOzbul of Oz and the Magic Merry-Go-Round (Oz)

The SillyOzbul of Oz & Toto (Oz)

SillyOzbuls of Oz (Oz)

The Silver Chair (Chronicles of Narnia)

The Silver Child (Silver Sequence)

Silver City (Silver Sequence)

The Silver Cobweb (Nancy Drew)

Silver Days (Platt Family)

The Silver Door (Cat's Eye Corner)

The Silver Gryphon (Valdemar: Gryphon Trilogy)

Silver Is for Secrets (Blue Is for Nightmares)

Silver on the Tree (Dark Is Rising)

The Silver Princess in Oz (Oz)

The Silver Spell (Dungeons and Dragons: Knights of the Silver Dragon)

Silver Spurs (Saved by the Bell)

Silver Wings (Choose Your Own Adventure)

Silver World (Silver Sequence)

Silverfin (Young Bond)

Silvertongue (The Stoneheart Trilogy)

Silverwing (Silverwing)

Simon and Marshall's Excellent Adventure (Eerie Indiana)

Simon Says, "Croak!" (Spinetinglers)

Simon's Dream (Fog Mound)

Simply Alice (Alice)

Sin and Salvation (Unseen)

Sing Me a Love Song (You're the One)

The Singer of All Songs (Chanters of Tremaris Trilogy)

The Singing (Pellinor)

Singing in Seattle (Aly and AJ's Rock 'n' Roll Mysteries)

Singing Sensation (Generation Girl)

The Sinister Omen (Nancy Drew)

Sinister Parade (Nancy Drew Files)

Sinister Signpost (Hardy Boys)

Sink It, Rusty (Matt Christopher's's Sports Stories)

Sink or Swim (From the Files of Madison Finn)

Sink or Swim! (Secret World of Alex Mack)

Sink or Swim and Number One (Kim Possible (TokyoPop))

Sinking the Dayspring (Trailblazers)

Sins of the Father (Buffy the Vampire Slayer)

Sir Thursday (Keys to the Kingdom)

The Siren Song (The Cronus Chronicles)

Sirens and Sea Monsters (Tales from the Odyssey)

The Sirens of Surrentum (Roman Mysteries)

Sister of the South (Deltora: Dragons of Deltora)

Sister Spy (Alias)

Sister Trouble (7th Heaven)

The Sisterhood of the Traveling Pants (Sisterhood of the Traveling Pants)

Sisters at War (Sweet Valley Twins)

Sisters in Crime (Nancy Drew Files)

Sisters of the Confederacy (Secret Refuge)

Sisters Through the Seasons (7th Heaven)

Sitcom School (Don't Touch That Remote!)

Six Haunted Hairdos (Hamlet Chronicles)

Sixteen and Dying (One Last Wish)

1609 (Young Founders)

16 Isn't Always Sweet (Kimani Tru)

Skateboard Champion (Choose Your Own Adventure)

Skateboard Renegades (Matt Christopher's's Sports Stories)

Skateboard Tough (Matt Christopher's's Sports Stories)

Skater Stuntboys (Take It to the Xtreme)

Skating Camp (Silver Blades)

Skeleton Key (Alex Rider)

The Skeleton on the Skateboard (Graveyard School)

Skeletons in the Closet (Roswell High)

The Skeleton's Revenge (Graveyard School)

Ski Trip Trouble (Date Him or Dump Him?)

Ski Weekend (Fear Street)

The Skies of Pern (Pern)

Skin (Wicked Dead)

Skin and Bones (Hardy Boys)

Skin Deep (Alias)

Skin Deep (Body of Evidence)

Skin Deep (Clearwater Crossing)

Skinny Dipping (Au Pairs)

Skipping a Beat (Nancy Drew Files)

Skull in the Birdcage (Knightscares)

Skullduggery (Bloodwater Mysteries)

Sky Blue Frame (Hardy Boys)

Sky Dance (Dinotopia)

Sky High (Hardy Boys Casefiles)

Sky Horse (Mustang Mountain)

Sky-jam! (Choose Your Own Adventure)

The Sky Phantom (Nancy Drew)

Sky Sabotage (Hardy Boys)

Skye's Final Test (Keystone Stables)

Skyfall (Saga of the Skolian Empire)

The Skyfire Puzzle (Hardy Boys)

Slam Book Fever (Sweet Valley High)

Slam Dunk (Matt Christopher's's Sports Stories)

Slam Dunk Sabotage (Hardy Boys)

Sonya and the Chain Letter Gang (Best Friends)

Sonya and the Haunting of Room 16A (Best Friends)

Sonya Begonia and the Eleventh Birthday Blues (Best Friends)

Sooner or Later (Heartland)

Sophie (Fab 5)

Sophie's Flight of Fancy (Royal Ballet School Diaries)

The Soprano Sorceress (The Spellsong Cycle)

The Sorcerer King (Faerie Path)

The Sorcerer of the North (Ranger's Apprentice)

Sorcerers of Majipoor (The Majipoor Cycle)

Sorcerers of the Nightwing (Ravenscliff)

Sorceress (Witch Child)

Sorceress of Darshiva (Malloreon)

Sorority Scandal (Sweet Valley University)

Sorority Sister (Nightmare Hall)

Sorrel (In the Shadow of the Bear)

Soul Eater (Chronicles of Ancient Darkness)

Soul Music (Discworld)

Soul of the Bride (Charmed)

Soul Survivor (Body of Evidence)

Soul Trade (Angel)

Soulmate (Night World)

Soulmates (Sweet Valley Junior High)

The Sound of Munich (Students Across the Seven Seas)

Sound Off! (Adventures of Daniel Boom AKA Loud Boy)

Sour Puss (Mrs. Murphy)

The Source of Magic (Xanth Saga)

Sourcery (Discworld)

South by Southeast (The Diamond Brothers)

South of the Border (Young Indiana Jones Chronicles: Choose Your Own Adventure)

South Pole Sabotage (Choose Your Own Adventure)

Southern Fried Makeover (Clueless)

The Southern Girls (Pageant)

Southpaw (Winning Season)

Space and Beyond (Choose Your Own Adventure)

Space Camp (Star Trek: Deep Space Nine)

The Space Hotel (Tom Swift Young Inventor)

Space Patrol (Choose Your Own Adventure)

Space Race (Ormingat)

Space Vampire (Choose Your Own Adventure)

Spaced Out! (Roller Coaster Tycoon)

Spain or Shine (Students Across the Seven Seas)

Spanish Dagger (China Bayles Mystery)

Spark of Suspicion (Hardy Boys)

Sparks (Smallville)

Speaker for the Dead (Ender Wiggin)

Special Christmas (Sweet Valley High)

Special Someone (Sweet Dreams)

Specials (Uglies)

The Speckled Rose of Oz (Oz)

The Specter from the Magician's Museum (Lewis Barnavelt)

Specter Rising (The Brimstone Network)

Speed (Smallville)

Speed Demon (NASCAR Pole Position Adventures)

Speed Times Five (Hardy Boys)

Speeding (Hard Cash)

Speeding (Richard Steele Trilogy)

Speedy in Oz (Oz)

The Spell (Forbidden Doors)

The Spell (Phantom Valley)

Spell Danger (Here Comes Heavenly)

A Spell for Chameleon (Xanth Saga)

Spell of the Screaming Jokers (Fear Street: Ghosts of Fear Street)

The Spell of the Sorcerer's Skull (Johnny Dixon)

Spell of the Winter Wizard (Dungeons and Dragons: Endless Quest)

Spellbinder (Night World)

Spellbound (Enchanted Hearts)

Spellbound (Sweep)

Spellbound (Wicked)

The Spellcoats (Dalemark Quartet)

Spells and Sleeping Bags (Magic in Manhattan)

Spellspam (Worldweavers)

Spellsinger (Avalon 1: Web of Magic)

The Spellsong War (The Spellsong Cycle)

The Sphere of Secrets (Oracle Prophecies)

Spherical Harmonic (Saga of the Skolian Empire)

The Spider Beside Her (Graveyard School)

The Spider Sapphire Mystery (Nancy Drew)

Spies and Lies (Nancy Drew and the Hardy Boys Super Mysteries)

Spike and Dru (Buffy the Vampire Slayer)

Spike It! (Matt Christopher's Sports Stories)

Spiked! (Hardy Boys Casefiles)

Spiked Snow (X Games Xtreme Mysteries)

Spilling the Beans (Saved by the Bell)

Spin City (Flirt)

Spin It Like That (Kimani Tru)

Spinout (NASCAR Pole Position Adventures)

The Spirit Catchers (Art Encounters)

Spirit of the Wolf (Charmed)

Spirit Song (Cheer Squad)

Spirit Walker (Chronicles of Ancient Darkness)

Spirited (Once Upon a Time)

Splash Party (American Gold Swimmers)

The Splintering of Time (Gideon the Cutpurse)

Split Decision (American Gold Gymnasts)

Split Decision (Spirit of the Game)

Split Decision (Sweet Valley High Senior Year)

Split Decision (T*Witches)

Split Ends (Edgar and Ellen)

Split Image (Journey of Allen Strange)

Splitting (Cheerleaders)

Spore (Star Wars Galaxy of Fear)

Spotlight on Love (Sweet Dreams)

Spreading the Word (Saved by the Bell)

Spring (Miki Falls)

Spring (Witch Season)

Spring Break (Fear Street: Fear Street Seniors)

Spring Break (The O.C.)

Spring Break (Pacific Cascades University)

Starstruck (Thoroughbred)

Starstruck (Truth or Dare)

Start Here (Have a Nice Life)

Starting Over (Cheerleaders)

Starting Over (Sweet Valley High)

Starting with Alice (Alice)

Startled by His Furry Shorts (Confessions of Georgia Nicolson)

Static (Flight 29 Down)

Statue of Liberty Adventure (Choose Your Own Adventure)

Stay Away from the Treehouse (Fear Street: Ghosts of Fear Street)

Stay or Go (Sweet Valley High Senior Year)

Stay Out of the Basement (Goosebumps)

Stay Tuned for Danger (Nancy Drew Files)

Staying Pure (Payton Skky)

Staying Together (Cheerleaders)

Stealing Bradford (Carter House Girls)

Stealing Home (Matt Christopher's Sports Stories)

Stealing Home (Spirit of the Game)

Stealing Princes (Calypso Chronicles)

Stealing Secrets (Cheerleaders)

Step on a Crack (Spinetinglers)

The Stepbrother (Fear Street)

Stepping on the Cracks (Gordy Smith)

The Steps Up the Chimney (Magician's House Quartet)

The Stepsister (Fear Street)

The Stepsister 2 (Fear Street)

Stepsisters (Sweet Valley High)

Sterling's Second Chance (Thoroughbred)

Steven and the Zombie (Sweet Valley Twins)

Steven Gets Even (Sweet Valley Twins)

Steven's Bride (Sweet Valley High)

Steven's Enemy (Sweet Valley Twins)

Steven's in Love (Sweet Valley Twins)

The Sting of the Scorpion (Hardy Boys)

Stink Trek (The Adventures of Uncle Stinky)

Stinky & Stan Blast Off! (The Grosse Adventures)

Stinky and Successful (Riot Brothers)

Stinky Business (Don't Touch That Remote!)

Stirring It Up (Dish)

A Stitch in Time (Quilt Trilogy)

Stitch of Courage (Trail of Thread)

Stock Car Champion (Choose Your Own Adventure)

The Stolen (The Nine Lives of Chloe King)

Stolen Affections (Nancy Drew Files)

The Stolen Bones (Nancy Drew: Girl Detective)

The Stolen Diary (Sweet Valley High)

The Stolen Kiss (Nancy Drew Files)

Stolen Kisses (Love Stories)

Stolen Kisses (Sweet Dreams)

Stolen Kisses, Secrets, and Lies (Mob Princess)

The Stolen Lake (Wolves Chronicles)

The Stolen Necklace (Reel Kids Adventures)

The Stolen Relic (Nancy Drew: Girl Detective)

Stolen Secrets (Red Rock Mysteries)

Stolen Spring (W.I.T.C.H.—Adventures)

The Stone Fey (Damar Chronicles)

The Stone Goddess (First Person Fiction)

Stone Horse (Mustang Mountain)

The Stone Idol (Hardy Boys)

The Stone Light (Dark Reflections Trilogy)

The Stoneheart (The Stoneheart Trilogy)

The Stones of Green Knowe (Green Knowe)

Stop in the Name of Pants (Confessions of Georgia Nicolson)

Stop that Bull, Theseus! (Myth-O-Mania)

Stop the Clock (Nancy Drew: Girl Detective)

Stork Naked (Xanth Saga)

The Storm (Flight 29 Down)

Storm Breaking (Valdemar: Mage Storms)

Storm Clouds (High Hurdles)

Storm of Wings (Dragonmaster)

Storm Rescue (Wild at Heart)

Storm Rising (FaithGirlz: Blog On)

Storm Rising (Valdemar: Mage Storms)

Storm Warning (FaithGirlz: Blog On)

Storm Warning (Valdemar: Mage Storms)

Stormchaser (Edge Chronicles)

Stormbreaker (Alex Rider)

The Story Tree (Akiko Graphic Novels)

The Storyteller's Daughter (Once Upon a Time)

The Stowaway (Roswell High)

The Stowaway Solution (On the Run)

Stowaways (Star Trek: Deep Space Nine)

Straight-A Teacher (Holly's Heart)

Straight Up (Sweet Valley High Senior Year)

Straken (Shannara: High Druid of Shannara)

Stranded (Jennie McGrady Mysteries)

Stranded (Sweet Valley University)

Stranded: Death Valley, Circa 1850 (Survival!)

Stranded in Komura/Moonshopping (Akiko Graphic Novels)

Stranding on Cedar Point (Neptune Adventures)

Strange Armor (Concrete)

Strange Bedfellows and Other Stories (Angel (Graphic Novels))

Strange Brew (Bone Chillers)

The Strange Case of Baby H (American Girls: History Mysteries)

Strange Invaders (Visitors)

Strange Memories (Nancy Drew Files)

Strange Message in the Parchment (Nancy Drew)

Strange Places (Hellboy)

The Strange Power (Dark Visions)

Strange Times at Fairwood High (Homeroom)

Strangeling (So Weird)

The Stranger (Animorphs)

A Stranger at Green Knowe (Green Knowe)

A Stranger in the House (Sweet Valley High)

Stranger in the Mirror (Mirror Image)

Surf Holiday (Mary-Kate and Ashley: So Little Time)

Surf Monkeys (Choose Your Own Adventure)

Surf, Sand, and Secrets (Mary-Kate and Ashley: Two of a Kind)

Surf Zone (Take It to the Xtreme)

The Surfing Corpse (P.C. Hawke Mysteries)

Surf's Up (Saved by the Bell)

Surprise Endings (Christy Miller)

The Surprise Party (Fear Street)

Surprise, Surprise! (Mary-Kate and Ashley: Two of a Kind)

A Surprise Twist (Silver Blades)

Surrendered Heart (Payton Skky)

Surrogates (Angel (Graphic Novels))

Survival (Flight 29 Down)

Survival (Island)

Survival (Remnants)

Survival (Star Trek: The Next Generation: Starfleet Academy)

Survival at Sea (Choose Your Own Adventure)

Survival of the Fittest (Charmed)

Survival of the Fittest (Hardy Boys Casefiles)

Survival Run (Hardy Boys Casefiles)

Survive! (Dinotopia)

Survivor (Jurassic Park Adventures)

Survivor (The Sixth Sense: Secrets from Beyond)

The Suspect in the Smoke (Nancy Drew)

The Suspect Next Door (Nancy Drew Files)

The Suspicion (Animorphs)

Suspicious Identity (The Lily Adventures)

Suth's Story (The Kin)

Swallowdale (Swallows and Amazons)

Swallows and Amazons (Swallows and Amazons)

The Swami's Ring (Nancy Drew)

Swamp (Survival!)

The Swamp Monster (Hardy Boys)

Swampland (Swampland Trilogy)

The Swarm (Star Wars Galaxy of Fear)

Swede Dreams (Students Across the Seven Seas)

Sweet (Making Waves)

Sweet America (Jamestown's American Portraits)

Sweet-and-Sour Summer (Dish)

Sweet and Vicious (In or Out)

Sweet Dreams (Christy Miller)

Sweet 18 (Sweet Valley High Senior Year)

The Sweet Far Thing (Gemma Doyle)

Sweet Kiss of Summer (Sweet Valley University)

Sweet Lil' Nails! (Bratz: Lil' Bratz)

Sweet Myth-tery of Life (Myth Adventures)

Sweet Revenge (Nancy Drew Files)

Sweet Sixteen (Buffy the Vampire Slayer)

Sweet Sixteen (Love Stories: Super Editions)

Sweet 16 Princess (Princess Diaries)

Sweet Talkin' Demon (Charmed)

Sweetest Gift (Payton Skky)

The Sweetest Thing (Inside Girl)

Sweetheart, Evil Heart (Fear Street: Fear Street Seniors)

Swell Foop (Xanth Saga)

Swift Horse (Mustang Mountain)

A Swiftly Tilting Planet (Time Fantasy Series)

Swindled! (Crime Through Time)

Swiss Secrets (Nancy Drew Files)

Switched (Fear Street)

Switched (My Sister the Vampire)

Switchers (Switchers)

Switching Channels (Eerie Indiana)

Switching Goals (Mary-Kate and Ashley Starring In . . .)

The Sword and the Circle (Arthurian Knights)

The Sword Bearer (The Archives of Anthropos)

Sword-Born (Sword Dancer Saga)

Sword-Breaker (Sword Dancer Saga)

Sword-Dancer (Sword Dancer Saga)

A Sword from Red Ice (Sword of Shadows)

The Sword in the Stone (Once and Future King)

Sword-Maker (Sword Dancer Saga)

The Sword of Bedwyr (The Crimson Shadow)

The Sword of Shannara (Shannara)

Sword of the Samurai Cat (Samurai Cat)

The Sword of the Spirits (Sword of the Spirits)

The Sword of the Wormling (Wormling)

Sword Play (The Seer)

Sword-Singer (Sword Dancer Saga)

Sword-Sworn (Sword Dancer Saga)

Swords and Scimitars (Royal Pavilions)

The Swordsheath Scroll (Dragonlance Dwarven Nations Trilogy)

Sworn to Silence (Class Secrets)

Sympathy for the Devil (Oh My Goddess!)

T

Tackle Without a Team (Matt Christopher's Sports Stories)

Tag Against Time (Walker and Tag)

Tagged for Terror (Hardy Boys Casefiles)

The Taggerung (Redwall)

The Tail of Emily Windsnap (Emily Windsnap)

Tail of the Tip-off (Mrs. Murphy)

Tainted Love (Nannies)

Take a Hike! (Secret World of Alex Mack)

Take Back the Night (Sweet Valley University)

Take It Off (The Insiders)

Take Me On (Sweet Valley High Senior Year)

Take My Hand (Sierra Jensen)

Take Off (Impact Zone)

Take the Mummy and Run (Riot Brothers)

Takedown (Matt Christopher's Sports Stories)

Takedown (Winning Season)

Taking a Stand (Generation Girl)

Taking Chances (Heartland)

Taking Chances (On the Road)

Taking Charge! (Generation Girl)

Taking Charge (Sweet Valley Twins)

Taking Over (Cheerleaders)

Taking Risks (Cheerleaders)

Taking Sides (Sweet Valley High)

Taking the Lead (Sweet Dreams)

Taking the Reins (Thoroughbred)

The Tale of Aang (Avatar: The Earth Kingdom Chronicles)

The Tale of Azula (Avatar: The Earth Kingdom Chronicles)

Tempted (The It Girl)

Tempted Champions (Buffy the Vampire Slayer)

Ten-Boy Summer (Sweet Dreams)

Ten Seconds to Play! (Chip Hilton Sports Series)

Ten-Speed Summer (Sweet Dreams)

Tender Loving Care (Sweet Dreams)

Tender Mercies (Red River: Red River of the North)

The Tender Years (Prairie Legacy)

Tennis Ace (Matt Christopher's Sports Stories)

The Tennis Trap (Camp Sunnyside)

The Tenth Power (Chanters of Tremaris Trilogy)

Teresa (The Elliott Cousins)

A Terminal Case of the Uglies (Bone Chillers)

Terminal Shock (Hardy Boys)

Terri and the Shopping Mall Disaster (Best Friends)

Terri the Great (Best Friends)

Terrible Master Urd (Oh My Goddess!)

The Terrible Terri Rumors (Best Friends)

Terrier (Beka Cooper)

Terror (Fearless)

Terror at High Tide (Hardy Boys)

Terror in Australia (Choose Your Own Adventure)

Terror in Florida (Screech Owls)

Terror in Ghost Mansion (Twisted Journeys)

Terror in the Sky (American Adventure)

Terror in the Stadium (Left Behind—The Kids)

Terror in Tiny Town (Deadtime Stories)

Terror Island (Choose Your Own Adventure)

Terror on the Titanic (Choose Your Own Adventure)

Terror on Track (Hardy Boys Casefiles)

Terror Trips (Goosebumps Graphix)

Terrorist Trap (Choose Your Own Adventure)

The Test (Animorphs)

The Test (Dungeons and Dragons: Endless Quest)

The Test Case (Hardy Boys)

A Test of Mirrors (Zenda)

Thanks for Nothing (From the Files of Madison Finn)

That Certain Feeling (Sweet Dreams)

That Darn Yarn (Sock Monkey)

That Fatal Night (Sweet Valley High)

That Old Zack Magic (Saved by the Bell)

That Stinking Feeling (Super Goofballs)

That Was Then (Diary of a Teenage Girl)

That's So Raven (That's So Raven)

That's What's Up! (Del Rio Bay Clique)

Then (Remnants)

Then He Ate My Boy Entrancers (Confessions of Georgia Nicolson)

Theodore Roosevelt (Dear Mr. President)

There's a Ghost in the Boy's Bathroom (Graveyard School)

There's a New Name at School (The Ashleys)

These Our Actors (Buffy the Vampire Slayer)

They Call Me Creature (Nightmare Room)

They Say (Eerie Indiana)

They Wear What Under Their Kilts (Emily Williams)

Thick as Thieves (Hardy Boys Casefiles)

Thicker than Water (Heartland)

The Thief (Attolia)

Thief of Hearts (Body of Evidence)

Thief of Hearts: 1995 (Golden Mountain Chronicles)

Thief of Time (Discworld)

The Thieves of Ostia (Roman Mysteries)

The Thieves of Tyburn Square (Trailblazers)

Thimble of Soil (Trail of Thread)

The Thing in the Closet (Spooksville)

The Thing Under the Bed (Bone Chillers)

Things (Visitors)

Think I'll Just Curl Up and Die (Fab 5)

Think Like a Mountain (Concrete)

Thinking of You (Sweet Dreams)

Third Evil (Fear Street: Fear Street Cheerleaders)

The Third Horror (Fear Street: 99 Fear Street)

Third Planet from Altair (Choose Your Own Adventure)

Third Watch (Acorna's Children)

Third Wheel (Sweet Valley Junior High)

The Thirst (Fear Street: Fear Street Seniors)

Thirteen (Kobie Roberts)

Thirteen (Winnie Perry)

Thirteen Means Magic (Abracadabra)

The Thirteenth Pearl (Nancy Drew)

This Boy Is Mine (Turning Seventeen)

This Can't Be Happening at Macdonald Hall! (Bruno and Boots)

This Full House (Make Lemonade Trilogy)

This Generation of Americans (Jamestown's American Portraits)

This Gum for Hire (Chet Gecko Mysteries)

This Rocks! (The Jersey)

This Side of Evil (Nancy Drew Files)

This Time for Real (Sweet Dreams)

Thomas (Deptford Histories)

Thomas Jefferson (Dear Mr. President)

Thorn in Her Side (The Princess School)

The Thoroughbred (Sweet Dreams)

Thor's Hammer (Voyage of the Basset)

A Thousand Ships (Age of Bronze)

The Thran (Magic: The Gathering—Invasion Cycle)

The Threat (Animorphs)

The Threat Within (Star Wars: Jedi Apprentice)

Three Cheers for Love (Sweet Dreams)

Three Cheers for You, Cassie! (Paxton Cheerleaders)

Three Days, Two Nights (Sweet Valley Junior High)

Three Evil Wishes (Fear Street: Ghosts of Fear Street)

Three Girls and a God (Goddesses)

Three Girls and a Guy (Sweet Valley High Senior Year)

Too Many Boys (Sweet Dreams)

Too Many Counselors (Camp Sunnyside)

Too Many Good-Byes (Sweet Valley Junior High)

Too Many Secrets (Jennie McGrady Mysteries)

Too Many Traitors (Hardy Boys Casefiles)

Too Much in Love (Sweet Valley High)

Too Much Magic (Abracadabra)

Too Much to Lose (Sweet Dreams)

Too Popular (Sweet Valley Junior High)

Too Scared to Sleep (Sweet Valley Twins)

Too Soon for Jeff (Hamilton High)

Too Young for Love (Sweet Dreams)

Top Ten Ways to Die (Hardy Boys, Undercover Brothers)

Top Wing (Matt Christopher's Sports Stories)

Torch Red (True Colors)

Tori's Crush (Sunset Island)

Torn (Wicked Dead)

Torn: Week 5 (Sevens)

Torn Apart (Love Stories)

A Totally Cher Affair (Clueless)

Totally Crushed! (Lizzie McGuire)

Totally Snowed (X Games Xtreme Mysteries)

Touch and Go (Sweet Valley High Senior Year)

Touch the Sky (The Young Underground)

Touchdown for Tommy (Matt Christopher's Sports Stories)

Touchdown Pass (Chip Hilton Sports Series)

Touching Darkness (Midnighters)

Tough Enough (Dawson's Creek)

Tough to Tackle (Matt Christopher's Sports Stories)

Tour of Danger (Nancy Drew and the Hardy Boys Super Mysteries)

Tourist Trap (Edgar and Ellen)

Tournament Crisis (Chip Hilton Sports Series)

The Tower at the End of the World (Lewis Barnavelt)

The Tower of Air (Jimmy Fincher Saga)

Tower of Darkness (Dungeons and Dragons: Endless Quest)

The Tower of Geburah (The Archives of Anthropos)

Tower of the Elephant and Other Stories (Chronicles of Conan)

The Tower Room (Egerton Hall Novels)

The Tower Treasure (Hardy Boys)

The Towers of the Sunset (Recluce)

Toxic Revenge (Hardy Boys Casefiles)

The Toy Shop of Terror (Choose Your Own Nightmare)

Toy Terror (Goosebumps: Give Yourself Goosebumps)

Track of the Bear (Choose Your Own Adventure)

The Track of the Zombie (Hardy Boys)

Track Record (Saddle Club: Pine Hollow)

Trade Wind Danger (Nancy Drew: Girl Detective)

Trading Hearts (Sweet Dreams)

The Tragic School Bus (Graveyard School)

The Trail Home (Saddle Club: Pine Hollow)

Trail of Bones (Danger Boy)

Trail of Lies (Nancy Drew Files)

Trail of Terror (Girls R.U.L.E.)

The Trail of the Jedi (Star Wars: Jedi Quest)

Trail of Thread (Trail of Thread)

Trails of Treachery (Nancy Drew: Girl Detective)

Train Wreck (Survival!)

Training for Trouble (Hardy Boys)

Traitor (Danny Watts)

Traitor (2099)

The Traitor (Golden Mountain Chronicles)

Traitor in the Tower (Trailblazers)

Transcendence (The DemonWars)

Transformation (Replica)

Transformation (Water)

A Trap in Time (Celia Rees Supernatural Trilogy)

Trapped (Fear Street)

Trapped! (Pete the Cat)

Trapped (Wild at Heart)

Trapped at Sea (Hardy Boys)

Trapped at the Bottom of the Sea (Cooper Kids)

Trapped in Bat Wing Hall (Goosebumps: Give Yourself Goosebumps)

Trapped in Time (Star Trek: Deep Space Nine)

Trapped in Time (Zenda)

Trapped in Tiny Town (Deadtime Stories)

Trapped! (Crime Through Time)

Trash (Trash)

Traveler (Oh My Goddess!)

Travels of Thelonious (Fog Mound)

Travels with Jotaro (Usagi Yojimbo)

The Treasure at Dolphin Bay (Hardy Boys)

Treasure at Eagle Mountain (Lassie)

Treasure Diver (Choose Your Own Adventure)

Treasure Hunters (Bone)

The Treasure in the Royal Tower (Nancy Drew)

The Treasure of Alpheus Winterborn (Anthony Monday)

The Treasure of Bessledorf Hill (Bessledorf Hotel)

The Treasure of Death Valley (Sweet Valley High)

The Treasure of Green Knowe (Green Knowe)

The Treasure of Mount Fate (Twisted Journeys)

Treasure of the Onyx Dragon (Choose Your Own Adventure)

Trek Through Tangleroot (Knightscares)

Trent (Sweet 16)

Trial and Terror (Hardy Boys)

Trial and Terror (SpyBoy)

Trial by Fire (Avalon 1: Web of Magic)

Trial by Fire (Bionicle Adventures)

Trial by Fire (Nancy Drew Files)

Trial by Poison (Trailblazers)

The Trial of Jessica Wakefield (Sweet Valley University)

The Trial of Magic (Age of Magic Trilogy)

Trials of Death (Cirque du Freak)

Trick or . . . Trapped (Goosebumps: Give Yourself Goosebumps)

Trick-or-Trouble (Hardy Boys)

Trickery Treat (Charmed)

Tricks of the Trade (Hardy Boys)

Trickster (Wild at Heart)

Trickster's Choice (Song of the Lioness Quartet)

Trickster's Queen (Song of the Lioness Quartet)

The Tunnel Behind the Waterfall (Magician's House Quartet)

Tunnels of Blood (Cirque du Freak)

Turn Up the Heat (High School Musical Stories from East High)

Turnabout (Roswell High)

Turning Up the Heat (Dish)

Turns on a Dime (Goldstone Trilogy)

Tweeb Trouble (Kim Possible: Pick a Villain)

Twelve (Winnie Perry)

The Twelve Tasks of Flavia Gemina (Roman Mysteries)

The 24-Hour War (Dungeons and Dragons: Endless Quest)

24/7 (Love Stories)

2061 (2001)

Twice Upon a Time (Alex Balfour)

Twilight (The Mediator)

Twilight (The Twilight Saga)

Twilight (Warriors: The New Prophecy)

The Twin Dilemma (Nancy Drew)

Twin Switch (Sweet Valley Junior High)

Twins (Fearless)

Twins Get Caught (Sweet Valley Twins)

The Twins Go to College (Sweet Valley Twins Super Editions)

The Twins Hit Hollywood (Sweet Valley Twins)

Twins in Love (Sweet Valley Twins)

Twins in Trouble (B.Y. Times)

Twins' Little Sister (Sweet Valley Twins)

The Twins Take Paris (Sweet Valley Twins Super Editions)

Twist and Shout (Mary-Kate and Ashley: Two of a Kind)

Twist of Fate (Distress Call 911)

Twisted (Fearless)

Twisted (Undercover Girl)

The Twisted Claw (Hardy Boys)

The Twisted Tale of Tiki Island (Goosebumps: Give Yourself Goosebumps)

Two-Boy Weekend (Sweet Valley High)

Two Boys Too Many (Sweet Dreams)

Two for the Road (Mary-Kate and Ashley: Two of a Kind)

Two Hearts (Beverly Hills, 90210)

Two of a Kind (Alias)

The Two of Us (Sweet Dreams)

Two Points for Murder (Nancy Drew Files)

Two Strikes on Johnny (Matt Christopher's Sports Stories)

2001 (2001)

2010 (2001)

Two-Timing Aisha (Making Out)

Two to the Fifth (Xanth Saga)

The Two Towers (Lord of the Rings)

Two's a Crowd (Mary-Kate and Ashley: Two of a Kind)

Two's a Crowd (Sweet Dreams)

Typhoon! (Choose Your Own Adventure)

Typhoon Island (Hardy Boys)

Tyrone's Betrayal (Roosevelt High School)

Tyrone's Story (Degrees of Guilt)

U

Uglies (Uglies)

Ugly Little Monsters (Buffy the Vampire Slayer)

The Ultimate (Animorphs)

Ultimate Challenge (Spirit of the Game)

The Ultimate Challenge (Goosebumps: Give Yourself Goosebumps)

The Ultimate Enemy (Berserker)

The Ultimate Escape (Net Force)

Ultimate Risk (Thoroughbred)

Ultimate Scoring Machine (NFL Monday Night Football Club)

U.N. Adventure (Choose Your Own Adventure)

The Un-Magician (Outcast)

Unbridled Fury (Thoroughbred)

The Uncertain Path (Star Wars: Jedi Apprentice)

Uncivil Acts (Nancy Drew: Girl Detective)

Uncivil War (Hardy Boys Casefiles)

Uncle's Big Surprise (Jackie Chan Adventures)

The Undead (Forbidden Doors)

Under Copp's Hill (American Girls: History Mysteries)

Under Dragon's Wing (Dungeons and Dragons: Endless Quest)

Under His Spell (Nancy Drew Files)

Under Pressure (Everwood)

Under Pressure (W.I.T.C.H.—Graphic Novels)

Under the Big Top (Lassie)

Under the Healing Sign (Crossroads Trilogy)

Under the Jolly Roger (Bloody Jack Adventures)

Under the Magician's Spell (Goosebumps: Give Yourself Goosebumps)

Under the Radar (Tom Swift Young Inventor)

Under Town (Edgar and Ellen)

Undercover Angels (Sweet Valley University)

Undercover Artists (Live from Brentwood High)

Undercover Tailback (Matt Christopher's Sports Stories)

Undercover, Underwear! (SpyBoy)

The Underground (Animorphs)

The Underground (Left Behind—The Kids)

Underground Kingdom (Choose Your Own Adventure)

The Underground Railroad (Choose Your Own Adventure)

Understand the Unknown (EverWorld)

Underworld (Star Wars: The Last of the Jedi)

The Unexpected (Animorphs)

An Unexpected Return (W.I.T.C.H.—Graphic Novels)

Unforgettable (The It Girl)

Unhappy Appy (Winnie the Horse Gentler)

Unhappy Medium (Suddenly Supernatural)

The Unicorns Go Hawaiian (Sweet Valley Twins Super Editions)

Uninvited Guests (Buffy the Vampire Slayer)

University Hospital (University Hospital)

University, Interrupted (Sweet Valley University: Elizabeth)

The Unknown (Animorphs)

Unnatural Selection (Buffy the Vampire Slayer)

Unpredictable (TodaysGirls.com)

Unscripted (The Real Deal)

Unseen Powers (Extreme Zone)

The Unsung Hero (Troubleshooters)

Volume 3: Run, Jonah, Run (Black Book (Diary of a Teenage Stud))

Voodoo Child (Tales of Terror)

Voodoo Moon (Charmed)

The Voodoo Plot (Hardy Boys)

Vote! (The Complicated Life of Claudia Cristina Cortez)

A Vote for Love (Sweet Dreams)

Vote 4 Amelia (Amelia)

Vox (Edge Chronicles)

Voyage of Fear (Bionicle Adventures)

Voyage of Ice (Chronicles of Courage)

Voyage of Midnight (Chronicles of Courage)

Voyage of Plunder (Chronicles of Courage)

Voyage of Slaves (Castaways of the Flying Dutchman)

The Voyage of the Dawn Treader (Chronicles of Narnia)

Voyage to Silvermight (Knightscares)

Voyager (Outlander)

Voyager in Night (Alliance-Union)

Vultures! (Zorro Graphic Novels)

W

The Wailing Siren Mystery (Hardy Boys)

Waiting (Cheerleaders)

Waiting for Stardust (Thoroughbred: Ashleigh)

Waiting in the Wings (Ballet Friends)

Wake the Devil (Hellboy)

The Wakefield Legacy (Sweet Valley High)

The Wakefields of Sweet Valley (Sweet Valley High)

The Wakefields Strike It Rich (Sweet Valley Twins)

Wake's Edge (Take It to the Xtreme)

Walk in Hell (The Great War)

Walk on Water (Watching Alice)

Walker of Time (Walker and Tag)

Walker's Journey Home (Walker and Tag)

The Wanderer's Road (Usagi Yojimbo)

Wanted (Hardy Boys, Undercover Brothers)

Wanted: One Perfect Boy (Silver Blades)

Wanted—Mud Blossom (The Blossom Family)

Wanted for Murder (Sweet Valley University Thriller Editions)

War! (B.Y. Times)

War (Watchers)

War Between the Twins (Sweet Valley Twins)

War Comes to Willy Freeman (Arabus Family Saga)

A War of Gifts (Ender Wiggin)

War of Honor (Honor Harrington)

War of the Black Curtain (Jimmy Fincher Saga)

The War of the Clones (Replica)

War of the Dragon (Left Behind—The Kids)

The War of the Ember (Guardians of Ga'Hoole)

War of the Wardrobes (Mary-Kate and Ashley: Two of a Kind)

War with the Evil Power Master (Choose Your Own Adventure)

War with the Mutant Spider Ants (Choose Your Own Adventure)

Warehouse Rumble (Hardy Boys)

The Warning (Animorphs)

The Warrior Heir (The Heir)

The Warrior's Challenge (Trailblazers)

The Waste Lands (Dark Tower)

Watch Out for Room 13 (Choose Your Own Nightmare)

The Watcher (Roswell High)

The Watcher (Watcher's Quest)

Watcher in the Piney Woods (American Girls: History Mysteries)

Watcher in the Woods (Dreamhouse Kings)

Watching the Roses (Egerton Hall Novels)

Water Around, Earth Below! (Mystic Knights of Tir Na Nog)

The Water Mirror (Dark Reflections Trilogy)

Water Song (Once Upon a Time)

Water Street (Nory Ryan)

The Waterless Sea (Chanters of Tremaris Trilogy)

Wave Good-Bye (Luna Bay)

The Way Back (The O.C.)

The Way of the Apprentice (Star Wars: Jedi Quest)

A Way Through the Sea (The Young Underground)

We Came Through Ellis Island (I Am American)

We Can't Wait! (Mary-Kate and Ashley: Graduation Summer)

We Did It, Tara! (Paxton Cheerleaders)

We Didn't Mean to Go to Sea (Swallows and Amazons)

We Have to Talk (Turning Seventeen)

We Wish You a Scary Christmas (Spinetinglers)

We Wish You an Eerie Christmas (Eerie Indiana)

A Weakened Heart (W.I.T.C.H.—Chapter Books)

The Weakness (Animorphs)

Wear and Scare (Spinetinglers)

Weather or Not (Luna Bay)

Weather the Storm (American Dreams)

Weaver (Outernet)

Web of Horror (Hardy Boys Casefiles)

Web Sight (So Weird)

The Wedding (Sweet Valley High)

The Wedding: An Encounter with Jan van Eyck (Art Encounters)

The Wedding Day Mystery (Nancy Drew)

Wedding Memories (7th Heaven)

The Wedding Planner's Daughter (The Wedding Planner's Daughter)

Wedding Secrets (Silver Blades)

Wedding Wishes and Woes (Story Girl)

Wednesday Witness (Juli Scott Super Sleuth)

The Wee Free Men (Discworld)

Weekend at Poison Lake (Goosebumps: Give Yourself Goosebumps)

Weekend Romance (Sweet Dreams)

Weetamoo (Royal Diaries)

Weetzie Bat (Weetzie Bat Saga)

Weird Science (Fear Street: Ghosts of Fear Street)

Welcome Back, Stacey! (Baby-Sitters Club)

Welcome Home, Mary Anne (Baby-Sitters Club Friends Forever)

Welcome to Alien Inn (Bone Chillers)

Welcome to BSC, Abby (Baby-Sitters Club)

The White Dragon of Sharnu (Daystar Voyages)

The White Gryphon (Valdemar: Gryphon Trilogy)

The White Horse Talisman (The Summer of Magic Quartet)

White House Autumn (The President's Daughter)

White Is for Magic (Blue Is for Nightmares)

White Lies (Sweet Valley High)

White Lies and Barefaced Truths (Truth or Dare)

The White Mountains (Tripods)

The White Order (Recluce)

White Water (Wakara of Eagle Lodge)

White Water Terror (Nancy Drew Files)

Who Are You? (Choose Your Own Adventure)

Who Are You Wit'? (Del Rio Bay Clique)

Who Do You Love? (Love Stories)

Who Framed Alice Prophet? (Eerie Indiana)

Who Goes Home (Ormingat)

Who I Am (Diary of a Teenage Girl)

Who Is Carrie? (Arabus Family Saga)

Who Killed Harlowe Thrombey? (Choose Your Own Adventure)

Who Killed the Homecoming Queen (Fear Street)

Who Knew? (Sweet Valley University)

Who Loves Kate (Making Out)

Who's 'Bout to Bounce? (Cheetah Girls)

Who's Been Sleeping in My Grave? (Fear Street: Ghosts of Fear Street)

Who's Got Spirit? (How I Survived Middle School)

Who's Out to Get Linda (Best Friends)

Who's the Fairest? (The Princess School)

Who's to Blame? (Sweet Valley High)

Who's Who (B.Y. Times)

Who's Who? (Sweet Valley High)

Who's Your Mummy? (Goosebumps Horrorland)

Why I Quit the Baby-Sitter's Club (Bone Chillers)

Why I'm Afraid of Bees (Goosebumps)

Why I'm Not Afraid of Ghosts (Fear Street: Ghosts of Fear Street)

The Wiccan (Forbidden Doors)

Wicked (Fear Street: Fear Street Seniors)

The Wicked Cat (Spooksville)

Wicked for the Weekend (Nancy Drew Files)

Wicked Ways (Nancy Drew Files)

The Wide Window (A Series of Unfortunate Events)

Wild (Making Waves)

Wild Blood (Switchers)

Wild Boy (Rowan Hood)

The Wild Cat Crime (Nancy Drew)

Wild Child (Sweet Valley Junior High)

Wild Fire (Wakara of Eagle Lodge)

Wild Horse (Mustang Mountain)

Wild Lies and Secret Truth (Summit High)

Wild Magic (Immortals)

The Wild One (Roswell High)

Wild Orchid (Once Upon a Time)

Wild Pitch (Alden All Stars)

Wild Pitch (Matt Christopher's Sports Stories)

Wild Rescue (Red Rock Mysteries)

A Wild Ride (Dungeons and Dragons: Endless Quest)

Wild Ride (Extreme Team)

Wild Spirit (Black Stallion: Young Black Stallion)

Wild Thing (Winnie the Horse Gentler)

Wild Things (Prowlers)

Wild Wheels (Hardy Boys Casefiles)

Wildcat Spirit (High School Musical Stories from East High)

Wildfire (Left Behind—The Kids)

Wildfire (Star Trek: S. C. E.)

Will the Real Raisin Rodriguez Please Stand Up? (Raisin Rodriguez)

A Will to Survive (Hardy Boys)

Will Work for Fashion (Bratz)

Willa by Heart (The Wedding Planner's Daughter)

The Willow Files, Volume 1 (Buffy the Vampire Slayer: The Willow Files)

The Willow Files, Volume 2 (Buffy the Vampire Slayer: The Willow Files)

Win, Lose, or Die (Nightmare Hall)

Win, Place, or Die (Nancy Drew Files)

Wind Chill (Red Rock Mysteries)

A Wind in the Door (Time Fantasy Series)

Wind on the River (Jamestown's American Portraits)

The Wind Singer (The Wind of Fire)

Windchaser (Dinotopia)

Windmill Windup (Matt Christopher's Sports Stories)

Windows on the Hill (Summerhill Secrets)

Winds of Change (Story Girl)

Winds of Change (Valdemar: Mage Winds)

Winds of Fate (Valdemar: Mage Winds)

Winds of Fury (Valdemar: Mage Winds)

Windy City Danger (Red Rock Mysteries)

Winging It (Angels Unlimited)

Wingman on Ice (Matt Christopher's Sports Stories)

Wings (Bromeliad)

The Wings of a Falcon (The Kingdom)

Wings of an Angel (Winds of Light)

Wings of Fear (Nancy Drew Files)

Wings of Love (Sweet Dreams)

The Wings of Merlin (The Lost Years of Merlin)

Winner Take All (Hardy Boys Casefiles)

Winner Take All (Mary-Kate and Ashley: Two of a Kind)

Winner Takes All (Sweet Dreams)

Winner Takes the Cake (Dish)

The Winner's Circle (Golden Filly Series)

The Winners on the Road (Pageant)

Winning (Silver Creek Riders)

The Winning Element (Specialists)

Winning Isn't Everything, Lauren! 1994 (Paxton Cheerleaders)

Winning London (Mary-Kate and Ashley Starring In . . .)

The Winning Spirit (Silver Blades)

Wonder's Promise (Thoroughbred)

Wonder's Sister (Thoroughbred)

Wonder's Victory (Thoroughbred)

Wonder's Yearling (Thoroughbred)

Won't Someone Help Anna? (Sweet Valley Twins)

The Wood Nymph and the Cranky Saint (Yurt)

Woodland Dell's Secret (Whispering Brook)

Woodsie (Wolfbay Wings)

Woodsie, Again (Wolfbay Wings)

Woof, There It Is (Cheetah Girls)

Worf's First Adventure (Star Trek: The Next Generation: Starfleet Academy)

Working at Love (Sweet Dreams)

Working Lunch (Dish)

A Working of Stars (Valdemar: Mageworlds)

World Behind the Door (Art Encounters)

World War (World War)

World War: Striking the Balance (World War)

World War: Tilting the Balance (World War)

World War: Upsetting the Balance (World War)

Worlds Apart (Everwood)

Worlds Apart (W.I.T.C.H.—Chapter Books)

The Worm Tunnel (Finnegan Zwake)

Worry Warts (Misery Guts)

Worst Day of Your Life (Choose Your Own Adventure)

Worst Enemies/Best Friends (Beacon Street Girls)

The Worst of Times (Jamestown's American Portraits)

Worth Dying For (Distress Call 911)

Would I Lie to You (Gossip Girl)

Wrath (Seven Deadly Sins)

Wrath of the Bloodeye (Last Apprentice)

The Wrath of the Grinning Ghost (Johnny Dixon)

Wreck and Roll (Hardy Boys)

The Wreckers (High Seas Trilogy)

Wren to the Rescue (Wren)

Wren's Quest (Wren)

Wren's War (Wren)

The Wright 3 (Petra and Calder)

A Wrinkle in Time (Time Fantasy Series)

Writ in Stone (Nancy Drew Graphic Novels)

Write Here, Right Now (Flirt)

The Write Stuff (Love Letters)

Writer Ferrets Chasing the Muse (Ferret Chronicles)

Written in the Stars (Circle of Three)

The Wrong Chemistry (Nancy Drew Files)

Wrong for Each Other (Sweet Dreams)

Wrong Kind of Boy (Sweet Dreams)

Wrong Kind of Girl (Sweet Valley High)

The Wrong Number (Fear Street)

Wrong Number (Oh My Goddess!)

Wrong Number 2 (Fear Street)

Wrong Side of the Law (Hardy Boys Casefiles)

The Wrong Track (Nancy Drew Files)

Wrong Turn in the Fast Lane (Summit High)

Wrong-Way Romance (Sweet Dreams)

Wurm War (Outcast)

Wyrd Sisters (Discworld)

Wyvernhail (Kiesha'ra)

X

X in Flight (XYZ Trilogy)

X Marks the Spot (X Files)

The Xanadu Adventure (Vesper Holly)

The Xander Years, Volume 1 (Buffy the Vampire Slayer: The Xander Years)

The Xander Years, Volume 2 (Buffy the Vampire Slayer: The Xander Years)

Xenocide (Ender Wiggin)

Xone of Contention (Xanth Saga)

Y

Y in the Shadows (XYZ Trilogy)

Yabba Dabba Voodoo (Tales from the Crypt Graphic Novels)

Yanked (David Brin's Out of Time)

Yankee Belles in Dixie (Bonnets and Bugles)

Yankee Blue or Rebel Grey? (I Am American)

Yankee in Oz (Oz)

Yankee Spy (The Young Americans)

The Year Mom Won the Pennant (Matt Christopher's Sports Stories)

The Year My Life Went Down the Loo (Emily Williams)

Year of Impossible Goodbyes (Sookan Bak)

The Year Without Christmas (Sweet Valley Twins Super Editions)

The Yearling (Black Stallion: Young Black Stallion)

The Yellow Feather Mystery (Hardy Boys)

The Yellow Knight of Oz (Oz)

Yellowstone (Adventures with the Parkers)

Yestermorrow (Timetripper)

Yon Ill Wind (Xanth Saga)

Yosemite (Adventures with the Parkers)

You Are a Genius (Choose Your Own Adventure)

You Are a Millionaire (Choose Your Own Adventure)

You Are a Monster (Choose Your Own Adventure)

You Are a Shark (Choose Your Own Adventure)

You Are a Superstar (Choose Your Own Adventure)

You Are an Alien (Choose Your Own Adventure)

You Are Microscopic (Choose Your Own Adventure)

You Can't Choose Your Family (Party of Five)

You Can't Scare Me! (Goosebumps)

You Just Can't Get Enough (Gossip Girl)

You Know You Love Me (Gossip Girl)

You Smell Dead (Pretty Freekin Scary)

The Young Black Stallion (Black Stallion)

Young Justice (SpyBoy)

The Young Unicorns (Vicky Austin)

Your Basic Nightmare (Sweet Valley High Senior Year)

Your Code Name Is Jonah (Choose Your Own Adventure)

Genre/Subject Index

This index gives access by genre (in bold capital letters) and by subject, enabling you to find series by genre and to identify books that deal with specific topcis, such as horses or U.S. history.

ADVENTURE

Abby's South Seas Adventures (5–8)
Adam Pelko (6–10)
Adventures of a Young Sailor (5–8)
Adventures with the Parkers (5–8)
Against the Odds (6–9)
Alex Rider (6–10)
Alexander Cold and Nadia Santos (6–10)
Alias (8–12)
Anika Scott (5–8)
Animorphs (4–8)
Animorphs: Alternamorphs (4–8)
Animorphs: Animorph Chronicles (4–8)
Animorphs: Megamorphs (5–8)
Anthony Monday (5–7)
Black Stallion (5–8)
Bloody Jack Adventures (7–10)
The Bonemender (7–10)
Brian Robeson (4–8)
Buffy the Vampire Slayer (6–10)
Buffy the Vampire Slayer (6–10)
Buffy the Vampire Slayer: Buffy and Angel (6–10)
Buffy the Vampire Slayer: Buffy and Angel: The Unseen Trilogy (6–10)
Buffy the Vampire Slayer: Stake Your Destiny (6–10)
Buffy the Vampire Slayer: The Angel Chronicles (6–10)
Buffy the Vampire Slayer: The Gatekeeper Trilogy (6–10)
Buffy the Vampire Slayer: The Lost Slayer Serial Novel (6–10)
Buffy the Vampire Slayer: The Willow Files (6–10)
Buffy the Vampire Slayer: The Xander Years (6–10)

Buffy the Vampire Slayer: Wicked Willow (6–10)
Cherub (6–10)
Choose Your Own Adventure (4–8)
Choose Your Own Nightmare (4–8)
Choose Your Own Star Wars Adventures (4–8)
Chronicles of Ancient Darkness (5–9)
Chronicles of Courage (6–9)
Chronicles of Elantra (10–12)
Cooper Kids (5–7)
The Curse of the Jolly Stone Trilogy (7–10)
Cybersurfers (6–9)
Damar Chronicles (6–10)
Danger.com (6–9)
Danny Watts (8–10)
Dark Is Rising (4–8)
Diadem (6–8)
Dive (7–10)
Dragon Chronicles (6–9)
The Ellie Chronicles (8–12)
Everest (6–9)
Fablehaven (5–8)
Fearless (8–12)
Fearless FBI (8–12)
Finnegan Zwake (6–9)
Five Ancestors (6–9)
Flight 29 Down (7–10)
The Gatekeepers (5–9)
Girls R.U.L.E. (6–8)
Goosebumps: Give Yourself Goosebumps (4–8)
Grk (5–7)
High Seas Trilogy (6–9)
House of Night (9–12)
Inkheart (5–12)
Island (6–9)
Jackie Chan Adventures (4–8)

Julie of the Wolves (5–8)
Kidnapped (5–8)
A Knight's Story (4–8)
The Life and Times (4–7)
MacGregor Family Adventure (5–8)
Mind over Matter (4–8)
Mindwarp (6–8)
Mustang Mountain (5–8)
Mysteries in Our National Parks (5–8)
Neptune Adventures (4–7)
Never Land (4–7)
Noble Warriors (7–10)
Norby (5–7)
On the Run (5–8)
Once and Future King (7–10)
1-800-Where-R-You (7–10)
Outer Banks Trilogy (5–8)
Outriders (5–7)
Pellucidar (7–12)
Peter and the Starcatchers (4–8)
Pirate Hunter (5–8)
Pit Dragon Trilogy (6–8)
Printers Devil Trilogy (6–9)
Redwall (4–8)
Reel Kids Adventures (5–7)
Rex Mundi (10–12)
Roller Coaster Tycoon (4–7)
Rowan Hood (6–9)
Saved by the Bell (6–8)
Secret Agent MJJ (4–7)
Secret World of Alex Mack (5–8)
Sirius Mysteries (5–9)
Specialists (8–10)
Spy Force (4–7)
Spy Girls (7–10)
Spy High (9–12)
SpyBoy (10–12)
Star Trek: Deep Space Nine (4–8)
Star Trek: Enterprise (5–10)

ADVENTURE (cont.)
Star Trek: I. K. S. Gorkon (5–10)
Star Trek: S. C. E. (5–10)
Star Trek: Starfleet Academy (4–8)
Star Trek: The Next Generation:
  Starfleet Academy (4–8)
Star Trek: Voyager: Starfleet
  Academy (4–8)
Star Wars: Jedi Apprentice (6–8)
Star Wars Episode 1: Journals
  (4–8)
Star Wars Galaxy of Fear (4–8)
Star Wars Junior Jedi Knights
  (4–8)
Star Wars Young Jedi Knights
  (4–8)
Survival! (5–8)
Swallows and Amazons (6–8)
Sword of the Spirits (5–8)
Take It to the Xtreme (6–9)
Three Investigators (5–7)
Time Fantasy Series (4–8)
Tom Swift (7–8)
Tom Swift Young Inventor (5–9)
Tomorrow (8–12)
The Tucket Adventures (5–8)
Twisted Journeys (4–8)
Vesper Holly (5–7)
Westmark (5–7)
Wizardry (5–8)
Wolves Chronicles (4–8)
Wren (4–7)
Young Bond (5–9)
Young Indiana Jones Chronicles:
  Choose Your Own Adventure
  (5–8)
Zorro Graphic Novels (6–10)

Afghanistan
The Breadwinner Trilogy (6–9)

African Americans
Arabus Family Saga (5–8)
Bluford High (9–12)
The Contender (6–8)
Del Rio Bay Clique (7–10)
The Divas (7–10)
Drama High (10–12)
Hazelwood High (7–10)
Hotlanta (7–10)
Journey of Allen Strange (4–7)
Junebug (4–7)
Justice Trilogy (5–8)
Kimani Tru (10–12)
Logan Family (4–7)

Ludell (5–8)
Maizon (6–8)
Moesha (6–8)
Payton Skky (9–12)
Perry Skky Jr. (9–12)
Philip Hall (4–7)
Platinum Teen (10–12)
Racing to Freedom Trilogy (5–8)
Secret Agent MJJ (4–7)

Aliens
Alien Adventures (4–7)
Antrian (6–8)
Bromeliad (6–9)
Journey of Allen Strange (4–7)
Mindwarp (6–8)
Nose (6–8)
Ormingat (5–8)
Space Above and Beyond (5–8)
Tripods (5–8)
Visitors (5–8)

Amish
Summerhill Secrets (6–8)
Whispering Brook (6–9)

Angels
Angels Unlimited (4–7)
Forever Angels (4–7)
Teen Angels (9–12)

ANIMAL FANTASY
Chet Gecko Mysteries (4–7)
Club of Mysteries (4–7)
Deptford Histories (5–8)
Deptford Mice (5–8)
Feather and Bone: The Crow
  Chronicles (5–8)
Ferret Chronicles (7–10)
Fog Mound (4–7)
Guardians of Ga'Hoole (4–8)
Hermux Tantamoq Adventures
  (5–8)
Joe Grey Mysteries (9–12)
Lionboy Trilogy (4–8)
Mistmantle Chronicles (4–7)
The Nine Lives of Romeo Crumb
  (6–8)
Ratha Quartet (7–12)
Redwall (4–8)
Samurai Cat (10–12)
Silverwing (5–8)
Warriors (5–9)
Warriors: Power of Three (5–9)

Warriors: The New Prophecy
  (5–9)

Animals *see also* **specific
kinds of animals (e.g.,
Cats) that may be real
or anthropomorphic**
Ferret Chronicles (7–10)
Wild at Heart (4–7)

Appalachia
Ballad (10–12)

Art
Art Encounters (7–12)
Petra and Calder (5–8)

Arthurian legends
Arthur Trilogy (6–9)
Arthurian-Aksumite Cycle (7–12)
Arthurian Knights (6–8)
The Denizens of Camelot (6–9)
Grail Quest (5–8)
The Great Tree of Avalon (7–12)
The Lost Years of Merlin (6–10)
Merlin Codex (9–12)
Once and Future King (7–10)

Asperger's syndrome
Wright and Wong (5–8)

Australia
Tomorrow (8–12)

Automobile racing
DriftX (9–12)
NASCAR Pole Position
  Adventures (5–8)
RPM (5–8)
Speed Racer (4–8)

Baby-sitting
Baby-Sitter (6–8)
Baby-Sitters Club (4–7)
Baby-Sitters Club Friends Forever
  (4–7)
Baby-Sitters Club Mysteries (4–7)
Baby-Sitters Club Super Specials
  (4–7)

Ballet *see* **Dancing**

Baseball
Baseball Card Adventures (4–8)

FANTASY (cont.)

The Fallen (8–12)
Farsala Trilogy (6–10)
Ferret Chronicles (7–10)
Fingerprints (7–10)
Fire-Us Trilogy (6–12)
Fireball (5–7)
Firebringer Trilogy (7–10)
The Floods (5–7)
Forever Angels (4–7)
The Freak (8–10)
The Gatekeepers (5–9)
Gemma Doyle (9–12)
Ghost Squad (5–8)
Gideon the Cutpurse (5–8)
Goddesses (6–9)
Goldstone Trilogy (5–7)
Goose Girl (6–9)
Grail Quest (5–8)
The Great Tree of Avalon (7–12)
Green Knowe (4–8)
The Green Rider (10–12)
Grey Griffins (5–8)
The Groo (6–12)
Guardians of Ga'Hoole (4–8)
Gwyn Griffiths Trilogy (4–7)
Hamlet Chronicles (4–7)
A Handful of Men (9–12)
Harry Potter (3–9)
Harvey Angell Trilogy (4–7)
Have a Nice Life (9–12)
Heartlight (6–9)
The Heir (8–12)
Help, I'm Trapped (5–8)
Here Comes Heavenly (6–8)
His Dark Materials (7–12)
Hitchhiker's Trilogy (7–12)
Hollow Kingdom (6–9)
Homecoming Saga (9–12)
"Hour" books (5–8)
House on Cherry Street (5–8)
Howl's Moving Castle (6–10)
Howl's Moving Castle (Graphic Novels) (6–10)
The Icemark Chronicles (6–10)
The Illmoor Chronicles (5–9)
Immortals (7–10)
In the Shadow of the Bear (7–12)
Indigo (7–12)
Inheritance (5–12)
The Ink Drinker (4–7)
Inkheart (5–12)
Invisible Detectives (5–9)

Jackie Chan Adventures (4–8)
The Jersey (4–7)
Jiggy McCue (4–7)
Johnny Dixon (5–8)
Johnny Maxwell (5–8)
Jurassic Park Adventures (4–7)
Justice Trilogy (5–8)
The Karmidee (4–7)
The Keeper's Chronicles (7–12)
Keys to the Kingdom (5–8)
Kiesha'ra (7–10)
Kim Possible (Chapter Books) (4–7)
Kim Possible: Pick a Villain (4–7)
Kim Possible (TokyoPop) (4–7)
The Kin (6–9)
The Kingdom (6–10)
Knightscares (6–9)
Landon Snow (5–8)
Left Behind—The Kids (6–10)
Leven Thumps (5–8)
Lewis Barnavelt (5–8)
Lily Dale (8–10)
Lily Quench (4–7)
Lionboy Trilogy (4–8)
Longlight Legacy (6–10)
Lord of the Rings (5–12)
L.O.S.T. (8–10)
The Lost Years of Merlin (6–10)
Lowthar's Blade (5–8)
Lulu Baker (4–7)
The Lurker Files (6–10)
Magic: The Gathering—Artifacts Cycle (9–12)
Magic: The Gathering—Ice Age Cycle (9–12)
Magic: The Gathering—Invasion Cycle (9–12)
Magic: The Gathering—Kamigawa Cycle (9–12)
Magic: The Gathering—Lorwyn Cycle (9–12)
Magic: The Gathering—Magic Legends Cycle (9–12)
Magic: The Gathering—Magic Legends Cycle Two (9–12)
Magic: The Gathering—Masquerade Cycle (9–12)
Magic: The Gathering—Mirrodin Cycle (9–12)
Magic: The Gathering—Odyssey Cycle (9–12)
Magic: The Gathering—Onslaught Cycle (9–12)
Magic: The Gathering—Ravnica Cycle (9–12)

Magic: The Gathering—Shadowmoor Cycle (9–12)
Magic: The Gathering—Time Spiral Cycle (9–12)
Magic in Manhattan (6–9)
Magic or Madness Trilogy (8–11)
Magician Trilogy (4–7)
Magician's House Quartet (5–8)
The Magickers (6–10)
The Majipoor Cycle (10–12)
Malloreon (10–12)
Man of His Word (10–12)
May Bird (5–7)
Measle (4–7)
The Mediator (7–10)
Mennyms (5–8)
Merlin Codex (9–12)
Mike Pillsbury (6–9)
The Minds Series (6–9)
Mindwarp (6–8)
Mirror Image (7–10)
Mummy Chronicles (4–7)
My Sister the Vampire (5–8)
Mystic Knights of Tir Na Nog (5–8)
Myth Adventures (5–8)
Myth-O-Mania (4–7)
Mythic Misadventures (5–8)
MythQuest (4–8)
The Navigator Trilogy (6–10)
Neotopia (6–12)
Never Land (4–7)
NFL Monday Night Football Club (4–7)
The Nine Lives of Chloe King (9–12)
The Nine Lives of Romeo Crumb (6–8)
Noble Warriors (7–10)
Northern Frights (5–8)
Nose (6–8)
Obsidian Chronicles (10–12)
Oh My Goddess! (10–12)
Once Upon a Time (6–10)
Oracle Prophecies (7–10)
Oran Trilogy (10–12)
Ormingat (5–8)
Outcast (4–7)
The Outer Limits (6–8)
Outlander (11–12)
Oz (4–8)
Pangur Ban (5–8)
Pellinor (7–12)
Pellucidar (7–12)
Pendragon (5–8)

Folk and fairy tales

Football

NFL Monday Night Football Club (4–7)

Friendship

Across the Steel River (5–8)
Al (Alexandra) (5–8)
Alden All Stars (4–8)
Baby-Sitters Club (4–7)
Baby-Sitters Club Friends Forever (4–7)
Baby-Sitters Club Super Specials (4–7)
Beacon Street Girls (6–9)
Best Friends (4–7)
Bratz (4–7)
Bratz: Lil' Bratz (4–7)
B.Y. Times (4–8)
@CAFE (7–10)
Camp Confidential (4–7)
Camp Sunnyside (4–7)
Chicks with Sticks (7–10)
Christy Miller (6–8)
The Complicated Life of Claudia Cristina Cortez (5–7)
Confessions of a Teen Nanny (8–12)
Diary of a Wimpy Kid (5–8)
The Double Dutch Club (5–7)
Egerton Hall Novels (9–12)
Elsie Edwards (4–8)
Fabulous Five (6–9)
FaithGirlz: Girls of 622 Harbor View (5–7)
The Friendship Ring (6–9)
The Girls Quartet (6–9)
Girls R.U.L.E. (6–8)
He-Man Women Haters Club (6–9)
In or Out (7–10)
In the Cards (5–8)
The Insiders (9–12)
Kids from Kennedy Middle School (5–7)
LBD (Les Bambinos Dangereuses) (7–10)
Maizon (6–8)
Moesha (6–8)
Molly (4–7)
Paxton Cheerleaders (6–8)
Queen Geeks (8–10)
Reel Kids Adventures (5–7)
Secret World of Alex Mack (5–8)
Silver Blades (4–7)
Silver Creek Riders (6–8)

Sisterhood of the Traveling Pants (6–9)
Sisters (6–8)
Sunset Island (6–9)
Swallows and Amazons (6–8)
Sweet Valley High (7–10)
Sweet Valley High Senior Year (7–10)
Sweet Valley Junior High (6–8)
Sweet Valley Twins (6–8)
Sweet Valley Twins Super Chiller Editions (6–8)
Sweet Valley Twins Super Editions (6–8)
Sweet Valley University (7–10)
Sweet Valley University Thriller Editions (7–10)
Talent (8–10)
Tarragon Island (6–8)
Thoroughbred (4–7)
Three Girls in the City (6–9)
TodaysGirls.com (6–9)
Truth or Dare (7–10)
Turning Seventeen (7–10)
Wolfbay Wings (4–8)
Zodiac Girls (6–9)

Gay/lesbian

Drama! (10–12)

Germany

Lechow Family (5–8)

Ghosts

Allie's Ghost Hunter (6–8)
Blossom Culp (5–7)
Edgar Font's Hunt for a House to Haunt (4–7)
Ghost Squad (5–8)
Gilda Joyce (6–9)
Green Knowe (4–8)
Haunting with Louisa (5–8)
May Bird (5–7)
The Seer (6–10)

Graphic novels/manga

Adventures of Daniel Boom AKA Loud Boy (4–7)
Age of Bronze (9–12)
Akiko (4–7)
Akiko Graphic Novels (4–7)
Akira (8–12)
Angel (Graphic Novels) (8–12)
Astro Boy (8–12)
Avatar Graphic Novels (4–7)

Baby-Sitters Club Graphic Novels (4–7)
Bone (6–10)
Buffy the Vampire Slayer (6–10)
Chronicles of Conan (9–12)
CLAMP School Detectives (4–8)
Concrete (7–10)
Dragon Ball (7–10)
Dragon Ball Z (7–10)
ElfQuest (9–12)
Goosebumps Graphix (4–8)
The Groo (6–12)
The Grosse Adventures (4–7)
Hardy Boys, Undercover Brothers: Graphic Novels (5–9)
Hellboy (10–12)
Hellsing (10–12)
Howl's Moving Castle (Graphic Novels) (6–10)
Kim Possible (Chapter Books) (4–7)
Kim Possible (TokyoPop) (4–7)
Lizzie McGuire (TokyoPop) (4–7)
Magic Pickle Graphic Novels (5–8)
Miki Falls (7–12)
Nancy Drew Graphic Novels (4–8)
Neotopia (6–12)
Oh My Goddess! (10–12)
Rex Mundi (10–12)
Sailor Moon Novels (4–7)
Sardine in Outer Space (4–7)
Slayers (7–10)
Sock Monkey (6–12)
SpyBoy (10–12)
Star Wars: A New Hope—Manga (5–10)
Star Wars: Episode I The Phantom Menace—Manga (5–10)
Star Wars: The Empire Strikes Back—Manga (5–10)
Star Wars: The Return of the Jedi—Manga (5–10)
That's So Raven (6–8)
Trigun Maximum (8–12)
Twisted Journeys (4–8)
Usagi Yojimbo (5–8)
Warcraft, the Sunwell Trilogy (7–10)
Zorro Graphic Novels (6–10)

HISTORICAL

Across the Steel River (5–8)
Adventures of a Young Sailor (5–8)
Age of Bronze (9–12)
The Age of Unreason (10–12)

HORROR (cont.)

Last Apprentice (5–8)
The Last Vampire (9–12)
Maggie Quinn: Girl vs. Evil (9–12)
The Midnight Library (5–8)
Midnighters (6–10)
Mindwarp (6–8)
Moondog (10–12)
Night World (9–12)
Nightmare Hall (6–9)
Nightmare Room (4–7)
Nightmare Room Thrillogy (4–7)
Nightmares! How Will Yours End? (4–7)
The Outer Limits (6–8)
Prowlers (8–12)
The Seer (6–10)
Spinetinglers (6–8)
Spooksville (5–8)
Sweet Valley Twins Super Chiller Editions (6–8)
Sweet Valley University Thriller Editions (7–10)
Tales from the Crypt Graphic Novels (10–12)
Tales of Terror (4–7)
The Twilight Saga (9–12)
Twisted Journeys (4–8)
Unseen (10–12)
Vampirates (6–9)
Vampire Academy (11–12)
Vampire Diaries (7–10)
Vampire Kisses (7–10)
The Vampire's Promise (6–8)
Werewolf Chronicles (5–8)
Wicked Dead (10–12)
Witch (5–7)
X Files (5–10)

Horses

Black Stallion (5–8)
Black Stallion: Young Black Stallion (5–8)
Chestnut Hill (4–7)
Golden Filly Series (6–9)
Heartland (4–7)
High Hurdles (4–7)
Horsefeathers (7–10)
Horseshoes (5–7)
Keystone Stables (5–8)
Mustang Mountain (5–8)
Racing to Freedom Trilogy (5–8)
Saddle Club: Pine Hollow (6–8)
Saddle Island (5–8)

Saddles, Stars, and Stripes (4–7)
Sandy Lane Stables (5–8)
Secret Refuge (9–12)
Silver Creek Riders (6–8)
Thoroughbred (4–7)
Thoroughbred: Ashleigh (4–7)
Thoroughbred: Ashleigh's Collection (4–7)
Winnie the Horse Gentler (4–8)

Hospitals

Med Center (6–8)

HUMOR

Adventures of Daniel Boom AKA Loud Boy (4–7)
The Adventures of Uncle Stinky (4–7)
Alice (5–8)
Alien Adventures (4–7)
Al's World (4–8)
Annabel Andrews (5–7)
Bad Girls (6–9)
Bessledorf Hotel (5–7)
Bingo Brown (4–7)
Black Book (Diary of a Teenage Stud) (8–12)
The Blossom Family (4–7)
Bone Chillers (5–8)
Bratz (4–7)
Bratz: Clued In! (4–7)
Bratz: Lil' Bratz (4–7)
Bruno and Boots (6–8)
Butt Wars (5–8)
Captain Underpants (3–8)
Confessions of Georgia Nicolson (7–10)
Dear Dumb Diary (5–8)
The Diamond Brothers (5–8)
Diary of a Wimpy Kid (5–8)
Discworld (6–12)
Edgar and Ellen (4–7)
The Extraordinary Adventures of Ordinary Boy (4–7)
The Fairy Godmother (7–12)
The Floods (5–7)
Girl (7–10)
Goddesses (6–9)
The Great Brain (5–7)
The Great Skinner (4–7)
The Groo (6–12)
The Grosse Adventures (4–7)
Have a Nice Life (9–12)
Help, I'm Trapped (5–8)

Herculeah Jones (5–7)
The Illmoor Chronicles (5–9)
It's Happy Bunny (7–10)
Jack Henry (5–8)
Jessica Darling (10–12)
Jiggy McCue (4–7)
Johnny Maxwell (5–8)
Just . . . (5–8)
Kyla May Miss. Behaves (4–7)
M. T. Anderson's Thrilling Tales (4–7)
Magic Pickle Graphic Novels (5–8)
Myth-O-Mania (4–7)
Nose (6–8)
Pretty Freekin Scary (5–8)
Princess Diaries (7–10)
The Princess School (4–7)
Riot Brothers (4–7)
Sidekicks (5–8)
Slimeballs (5–7)
Super Goofballs (4–8)
Tales of the Frog Princess (4–7)
Underwhere (4–7)
Vesper Holly (5–7)

Ice hockey

Lightning on Ice (8–10)
Screech Owls (4–7)
Slapshots (5–8)
Wolfbay Wings (4–8)

Ice skating

Silver Blades (4–7)

Illness

Why Me? (6–9)

Immigration

First Person Fiction (6–10)
Platt Family (6–9)

Ireland

Chronicles of Faerie (8–12)

Japan

The Ghost in the Tokaido Inn (7–9)
Tales of the Otori (10–12)

Japanese Americans

Adam Pelko (6–10)

Jewish life

Anna (4–8)
B.Y. Times (4–8)

Media tie-in (cont.)

Buffy the Vampire Slayer: The Xander Years (6–10)

Buffy the Vampire Slayer: Wicked Willow (6–10)

Charmed (7–12)

Choose Your Own Star Wars Adventures (4–8)

Christy (5–8)

Clueless (6–9)

Dawson's Creek (7–12)

Dinotopia (6–9)

Eerie Indiana (5–8)

Everwood (7–12)

Flight 29 Down (7–10)

Gilmore Girls (7–10)

Harry Potter (3–9)

High School Musical Stories from East High (4–8)

Howl's Moving Castle (6–10)

Howl's Moving Castle (Graphic Novels) (6–10)

Inheritance (5–12)

Jackie Chan Adventures (4–8)

Jumper (10–12)

Jurassic Park Adventures (4–7)

Kim Possible (Chapter Books) (4–7)

Kim Possible (TokyoPop) (4–7)

Lizzie McGuire (4–7)

Lizzie McGuire Mysteries (4–7)

Lizzie McGuire (TokyoPop) (4–7)

Lord of the Rings (5–12)

Mary-Kate and Ashley: Adventures of Mary-Kate and Ashley (4–7)

Mary-Kate and Ashley: So Little Time (4–7)

Mary-Kate and Ashley: Two of a Kind (4–7)

Mary-Kate and Ashley in Action (4–7)

Mary-Kate and Ashley Starring In . . . (4–7)

Mary-Kate and Ashley Sweet 16 (4–7)

Moesha (6–8)

Mystic Knights of Tir Na Nog (5–8)

MythQuest (4–8)

The O.C. (10–12)

Party of Five (7–10)

Saved by the Bell (6–8)

Secret World of Alex Mack (5–8)

7th Heaven (4–7)

The Sixth Sense: Secrets from Beyond (5–7)

Smallville (7–10)

Speed Racer (4–8)

Star Trek: Deep Space Nine (4–8)

Star Trek: Enterprise (5–10)

Star Trek: I. K. S. Gorkon (5–10)

Star Trek: S. C. E. (5–10)

Star Trek: Starfleet Academy (4–8)

Star Trek: The Next Generation: Starfleet Academy (4–8)

Star Trek: Voyager: Starfleet Academy (4–8)

Star Wars: A New Hope—Manga (5–10)

Star Wars: Episode I The Phantom Menace—Manga (5–10)

Star Wars: Jedi Apprentice (6–8)

Star Wars: The Empire Strikes Back—Manga (5–10)

Star Wars: The Return of the Jedi—Manga (5–10)

Star Wars Episode 1: Journals (4–8)

Star Wars Galaxy of Fear (4–8)

Star Wars Junior Jedi Knights (4–8)

Star Wars Young Jedi Knights (4–8)

That's So Raven (6–8)

The Twilight Saga (9–12)

X Files (5–10)

Zoey 101 (5–7)

Mermaids and mermen

Emily Windsnap (4–7)

Mexican Americans

Dogtown Ghetto (6–8)

Mexico

Julian Escobar (6–8)

Mice

Deptford Histories (5–8)

Deptford Mice (5–8)

Redwall (4–8)

Missing children

Janie (6–9)

Money

Hard Cash (9–12)

Shopaholic (10–12)

Monsters and creatures

Alien Adventures (4–7)

Animorphs (4–8)

Animorphs: Alternamorphs (4–8)

Animorphs: Animorph Chronicles (4–8)

Animorphs: Megamorphs (5–8)

Are You Afraid of the Dark? (5–8)

Bone Chillers (5–8)

Camp Zombie (5–7)

Choose Your Own Nightmare (4–8)

Deadtime Stories (4–7)

Eerie Indiana (5–8)

EverWorld (7–12)

Fiendly Corners (5–8)

Goosebumps (4–8)

Goosebumps: Give Yourself Goosebumps (4–8)

Goosebumps Horrorland (4–8)

Goosebumps Series 2000 (4–8)

House of Horrors (5–7)

Magician Trilogy (4–7)

Mind over Matter (4–8)

Mindwarp (6–8)

Pretty Freekin Scary (5–8)

Spinetinglers (6–8)

Spooksville (5–8)

Star Wars Galaxy of Fear (4–8)

Swampland Trilogy (7–10)

Tales from the Odyssey (4–8)

Tom Swift (7–8)

Werewolf Chronicles (5–8)

Mountain climbing

Everest (6–9)

Multicultural

American Girls: Girls of Many Lands (4–8)

Cheetah Girls (6–9)

Daughters of the Moon (9–12)

Dish (4–7)

The Double Dutch Club (5–7)

Music

Aly and AJ's Rock 'n' Roll Mysteries (6–9)

Bardic Voices (10–12)

Cheetah Girls (6–9)

The Divas (7–10)

Echorium Sequence (6–9)

Fame School (6–8)

The Spellsong Cycle (9–12)

Star Power (6–8)

Pirates (cont.)

Peter and the Starcatchers (4–8)

Pirate Hunter (5–8)

Wave Walkers (6–9)

Prehistoric peoples

Chronicles of Ancient Darkness (5–9)

Princesses

Goose Girl (6–9)

The Minds Series (6–9)

Princess Diaries (7–10)

The Princess School (4–7)

REAL LIFE

A-List (9–12)

Al (Alexandra) (5–8)

Alden All Stars (4–8)

Aloha Cove (7–10)

The Alphabetical Hookup List Trilogy (9–12)

Aly and AJ's Rock 'n' Roll Mysteries (6–9)

Amelia (4–8)

American Dreams (8–10)

American Girls: Girls of Many Lands (4–8)

Anika Scott (5–8)

The Ashleys (8–10)

Au Pairs (9–12)

Avonlea (5–8)

Babes (5–7)

Baby-Sitters Club (4–7)

Baby-Sitters Club Friends Forever (4–7)

Baby-Sitters Club Graphic Novels (4–7)

Baby-Sitters Club Mysteries (4–7)

Baby-Sitters Club Portrait Collection (4–7)

Baby-Sitters Club Super Specials (4–7)

Bad Girls (6–9)

Ballet Friends (4–7)

Beacon Street Girls (6–9)

Best Friends (4–7)

Beverly Hills, 90210 (7–10)

Bingo Brown (4–7)

Black Book (Diary of a Teenage Stud) (8–12)

Black Stallion: Young Black Stallion (5–8)

Blue Avenger (7–10)

Blue-Eyed Son Trilogy (7–10)

Bluford High (9–12)

Bratz (4–7)

Bratz: Clued In! (4–7)

Bratz: Lil' Bratz (4–7)

The Breadwinner Trilogy (6–9)

Brian Robeson (4–8)

Brides of Wildcat County (7–10)

Brio Girls (6–10)

B.Y. Times (4–8)

@CAFE (7–10)

California Diaries (6–8)

Calypso Chronicles (7–10)

Camp Confidential (4–7)

Camp Sunnyside (4–7)

Carter House Girls (8–10)

Cassie Perkins (4–7)

Celebutantes (7–10)

Cheer Squad (6–8)

Cheer USA! (6–9)

Cheetah Girls (6–9)

Chestnut Hill (4–7)

Chicks with Sticks (7–10)

China Tate (5–8)

Christy (5–8)

Christy Miller (6–8)

Christy Miller: Christy and Todd: The College Years (9–12)

Class Secrets (6–10)

Clearwater Crossing (6–9)

Clique (6–9)

Clueless (6–9)

The Complicated Life of Claudia Cristina Cortez (5–7)

Confessions of a Teen Nanny (8–12)

Confessions of a Teenage Drama Queen (7–10)

Confessions of Georgia Nicolson (7–10)

The Contender (6–8)

Date Him or Dump Him? (6–9)

Dawson's Creek (7–12)

Dear Diary (7–12)

Dear Dumb Diary (5–8)

Degrees of Guilt (7–10)

Del Rio Bay Clique (7–10)

Diary of a Crush (8–11)

Diary of a Teenage Girl (9–12)

Diary of a Wimpy Kid (5–8)

Dish (4–7)

Distress Call 911 (7–10)

The Divas (7–10)

Dogtown Ghetto (6–8)

Don't Get Caught (6–9)

Don't Touch That Remote! (5–7)

The Double Dutch Club (5–7)

Drama! (10–12)

Drama Club (9–12)

Drama High (10–12)

DriftX (9–12)

Egerton Hall Novels (9–12)

Ellen Fremedon (5–7)

The Elliott Cousins (7–8)

Elsie Edwards (4–8)

Emily Williams (10–12)

Everwood (7–12)

Fab 5 (7–10)

Fabulous Five (6–9)

FaithGirlz: Blog On (7–10)

FaithGirlz: Girls of 622 Harbor View (5–7)

Fame School (6–8)

The Fashion-Forward Adventures of Imogene (6–10)

Fat Glenda (4–8)

First Person Fiction (6–10)

Flicka (5–8)

Flirt (7–10)

Friends for a Season (5–8)

The Friendship Ring (6–9)

From the Files of Madison Finn (6–8)

Generation Girl (7–10)

Gingerbread (10–12)

Girl (7–10)

Girls of Avenue Z (5–7)

The Girls Quartet (6–9)

Girls R.U.L.E. (6–8)

Glory (6–9)

Golden Filly Series (6–9)

Goldstone Trilogy (5–7)

Gossip Girl (9–12)

The Great Brain (5–7)

Guy Strang (5–8)

Hamilton High (8–12)

Hard Cash (9–12)

Harper Winslow (6–9)

Hazelwood High (7–10)

He-Man Women Haters Club (6–9)

Heart Beats (7–8)

Heartland (4–7)

High Hurdles (4–7)

High School Musical Stories from East High (4–8)

Holly's Heart (6–9)

Hollywood Sisters (5–8)

Homeroom (7–10)

REAL LIFE (cont.)

Three Girls in the City (6–9)
Time Zone High (7–10)
TodaysGirls.com (6–9)
Trash (8–12)
Troubleshooters (11–12)
True Colors (9–12)
Truth or Dare (7–10)
Turning Seventeen (7–10)
Uncommon Heroes (10–12)
University Hospital (7–10)
Vicky Austin (4–7)
Violet (8–10)
Wakara of Eagle Lodge (6–9)
Watching Alice (7–10)
The Wedding Planner's Daughter
 (5–9)
Weetzie Bat Saga (10–12)
What If . . . (7–10)
Whispering Brook (6–9)
Why Me? (6–9)
Wild at Heart (4–7)
Winnie Perry (4–7)
Winnie the Horse Gentler (4–8)
Wolfbay Wings (4–8)
You're the One (6–9)
Zodiac Girls (6–9)
Zoey 101 (5–7)

RECREATION

Alden All Stars (4–8)
American Gold Gymnasts (4–7)
American Gold Swimmers (4–7)
Baseball Card Adventures (4–8)
The Broadway Ballplayers (4–7)
Cheer Squad (6–8)
Cheer USA! (6–9)
Cheerleaders (7–9)
Chip Hilton Sports Series (5–8)
Dream Series (6–12)
Extreme Team (4–7)
Horseshoes (5–7)
Impact Zone (7–12)
Lightning on Ice (8–10)
Matt Christopher's Sports Stories
 (3–7)
NASCAR Pole Position
 Adventures (5–8)
NFL Monday Night Football Club
 (4–7)
Paxton Cheerleaders (6–8)
Rookies (7–10)
Silver Blades (4–7)

Silver Creek Riders (6–8)
Slapshots (5–8)
Spirit of the Game (5–8)
Sports Mystery (9–12)
Thoroughbred (4–7)
Thoroughbred: Ashleigh (4–7)
Thoroughbred: Ashleigh's
 Collection (4–7)
Winning Season (4–7)
Wolfbay Wings (4–8)
X Games Xtreme Mysteries (4–8)

Robots

Eager (6–9)
I, Robot (10–12)
Isaac Asimov's Caliban (9–12)
Norby (5–7)
Traces: Luke Harding, Forensic
 Investigator (6–9)

Romance

The Alphabetical Hookup List
 Trilogy (9–12)
American Dreams (9–12)
Black Book (Diary of a Teenage
 Stud) (8–12)
Brides of Wildcat County (7–10)
@CAFE (7–10)
Christy (5–8)
Christy Miller (6–8)
Christy Miller: Christy and Todd:
 The College Years (9–12)
Confessions of Georgia Nicolson
 (7–10)
The Elliott Cousins (7–8)
Enchanted Hearts (7–12)
Flambards (7–8)
The Girls Quartet (6–9)
Heart Beats (7–8)
Highland Heroes (11–12)
Holly's Heart (6–9)
Impact Zone (7–12)
Live from Brentwood High (6–9)
Love Letters (7–10)
Love Stories (7–10)
Love Stories: Brothers Trilogy
 (7–10)
Love Stories: His. Hers. Theirs
 (7–10)
Love Stories: Prom Trilogy (7–10)
Love Stories: Super Editions
 (7–10)
Love Stories: Year Abroad (7–10)
Love Trilogy (10–12)
Making Out (8–12)

Making Waves (9–12)
Miki Falls (7–12)
The Minds Series (6–9)
Night World (9–12)
Once Upon a Time (6–10)
Outlander (11–12)
Payton Skky (9–12)
Richard Steele Trilogy (9–12)
Saved by the Bell (6–8)
Secret Circle (7–10)
Students Across the Seven Seas
 (8–12)
Summer (7–10)
Summer Boys (10–12)
Summer Share (10–12)
Sunset Island (6–9)
Sweet Dreams (7–9)
Sweet Dreams: On Our Own
 (7–9)
Sweet Valley High (7–10)
Sweet Valley High Senior Year
 (7–10)
Sweet Valley University (7–10)
Sweet Valley University: Elizabeth
 (7–10)
Time Zone High (7–10)
Troubleshooters (11–12)
Truth or Dare (7–10)
Turning Seventeen (7–10)
Uncommon Heroes (10–12)
University Hospital (7–10)
Vampire Diaries (7–10)
Victorian Tales of London (9–12)
Water (7–10)
Wild Rose Inn (6–10)
You're the One (6–9)

Rome

The Life and Times (4–7)
Roma Sub Rosa (10–12)

Russia

Angel on the Square (6–9)

School stories

All About Us Novels (8–10)
Bad Girls (6–9)
Best Friends (4–7)
Bingo Brown (4–7)
Bluford High (9–12)
Bruno and Boots (6–8)
B.Y. Times (4–8)
Calypso Chronicles (7–10)
Christie & Company (5–7)
Christy (5–8)

Class Secrets (6–10)
Clearwater Crossing (6–9)
Clique (6–9)
The Complicated Life of Claudia Cristina Cortez (5–7)
Confessions of a Teenage Drama Queen (7–10)
Dear Dumb Diary (5–8)
Del Rio Bay Clique (7–10)
Diary of a Wimpy Kid (5–8)
Don't Get Caught (6–9)
Don't Touch That Remote! (5–7)
Drama Club (9–12)
Drama High (10–12)
Egerton Hall Novels (9–12)
Fabulous Five (6–9)
Fame School (6–8)
From the Files of Madison Finn (6–8)
Generation Girl (7–10)
Harper Winslow (6–9)
Help, I'm Trapped (5–8)
High School Musical Stories from East High (4–8)
Homeroom (7–10)
How I Survived Middle School (4–7)
In or Out (7–10)
In the Cards (5–8)
Internet Girls (10–12)
The It Girl (9–12)
Jessica Darling (10–12)
Kids from Kennedy Middle School (5–7)
Kimani Tru (10–12)
Lizzie McGuire (4–7)
Lizzie McGuire Mysteries (4–7)
Lizzie McGuire (TokyoPop) (4–7)
Losers, Inc. (4–7)
Miki Falls (7–12)
Non-Blonde Cheerleader (8–12)
Once Upon a Prom (9–12)
Popular (7–10)
Private (9–12)
Queen Geeks (8–10)
Roosevelt High School (9–12)
Roswell High (7–10)
Saved by the Bell (6–8)
The Seer (6–10)
Seven Deadly Sins (10–12)
Slimeballs (5–7)
Summit High (7–10)
Sweet Valley High (7–10)
Sweet Valley High Senior Year (7–10)

Sweet Valley Junior High (6–8)
Sweet Valley Twins (6–8)
Sweet Valley Twins Super Editions (6–8)
Sweet Valley University (7–10)
Sweet Valley University: Elizabeth (7–10)
Sweet Valley University Thriller Editions (7–10)
Time Zone High (7–10)
University Hospital (7–10)
Vampire Academy (11–12)
The Wessex Papers (9–12)
Witch (6–9)
Zoey 101 (5–7)

SCIENCE FICTION

Acorna (10–12)
Acorna's Children (10–12)
Alien Adventures (4–7)
Alliance-Union (10–12)
Animorphs (4–8)
Animorphs: Alternamorphs (4–8)
Animorphs: Animorph Chronicles (4–8)
Animorphs: Megamorphs (5–8)
Antrian (6–8)
Asteroid Wars (10–12)
Berserker (9–12)
The Big Empty (7–10)
Choose Your Own Star Wars Adventures (4–8)
City of Ember (6–8)
Colonization (9–12)
The Culture (11–12)
Daystar Voyages (6–9)
Dayworld (10–12)
Dragonback (7–10)
Eager (6–9)
Emortality (9–12)
Ender Wiggin (9–12)
Foreigner (10–12)
Foundation (10–12)
The Giver (6–10)
The Great War (10–12)
Heartlight (6–9)
Homecoming Saga (9–12)
Honor Harrington (9–12)
Hover Car Racer (6–9)
The Hungry City Chronicles (7–10)
I, Robot (10–12)
Isaac Asimov's Caliban (9–12)
Jimmy Fincher Saga (7–10)

Johnny Maxwell (5–8)
Journey of Allen Strange (4–7)
Jumper (10–12)
Justice Trilogy (5–8)
The Lighthouse Trilogy (6–9)
Magician Trilogy (4–7)
The Majipoor Cycle (10–12)
Mars Year One (5–8)
Maximum Ride (7–10)
Midnighters (6–10)
Missing Link Trilogy (6–9)
Norby (5–7)
Orion the Hunter (9–12)
Outernet (6–9)
Pern (10–12)
Pern: The Harper-Hall Trilogy (10–12)
Priscilla Hutchins (9–12)
Probability (10–12)
Psion (9–12)
Quantum Prophecy (6–9)
Rama (10–12)
Regeneration (8–10)
Remnants (5–9)
Replica (6–9)
Replica: The Plague Trilogy (6–9)
Riverworld Saga (10–12)
Roswell High (7–10)
Saga of the Skolian Empire (10–12)
Sardine in Outer Space (4–7)
Seafort Saga (9–12)
Shadow Children (5–8)
Silver Sequence (5–9)
Space Above and Beyond (5–8)
Star Trek: Deep Space Nine (4–8)
Star Trek: Enterprise (5–10)
Star Trek: I. K. S. Gorkon (5–10)
Star Trek: S. C. E. (5–10)
Star Trek: Starfleet Academy (4–8)
Star Trek: The Next Generation: Starfleet Academy (4–8)
Star Trek: Voyager: Starfleet Academy (4–8)
Star Wars: A New Hope—Manga (5–10)
Star Wars: Boba Fett (5–9)
Star Wars: Episode I The Phantom Menace—Manga (5–10)
Star Wars: Jedi Apprentice (6–8)
Star Wars: Jedi Quest (5–9)
Star Wars: The Empire Strikes Back—Manga (5–10)
Star Wars: The Last of the Jedi (5–9)

SCIENCE FICTION
(cont.)

Star Wars: The Return of the Jedi—Manga (5–10)

Star Wars Episode 1: Journals (4–8)

Star Wars Galaxy of Fear (4–8)

Star Wars Junior Jedi Knights (4–8)

Star Wars Young Jedi Knights (4–8)

Sword of the Spirits (5–8)

The Thousand Cultures (9–12)

Timetripper (8–11)

Tripods (5–8)

2099 (5–8)

2001 (9–12)

Uglies (9–12)

Virtual World Chronologs (6–9)

Visitors (5–8)

World War (9–12)

Scotland
Horseshoes (5–7)

The Stuart Quartet (6–12)

Tartan Magic Trilogy (4–7)

Sea stories *see also* Boats and ships
Adventures of a Young Sailor (5–8)

Shopping
Shopaholic (10–12)

Slavery
Arabus Family Saga (5–8)

Racing to Freedom Trilogy (5–8)

Space and space ships *see also* Aliens
Antrian (6–8)

Choose Your Own Star Wars Adventures (4–8)

Norby (5–7)

Star Trek: Deep Space Nine (4–8)

Star Trek: Starfleet Academy (4–8)

Star Trek: The Next Generation: Starfleet Academy (4–8)

Star Trek: Voyager: Starfleet Academy (4–8)

Star Wars: A New Hope—Manga (5–10)

Star Wars: Episode I The Phantom Menace—Manga (5–10)

Star Wars: Jedi Apprentice (6–8)

Star Wars: The Empire Strikes Back—Manga (5–10)

Star Wars: The Return of the Jedi—Manga (5–10)

Star Wars Episode 1: Journals (4–8)

Star Wars Galaxy of Fear (4–8)

Star Wars Junior Jedi Knights (4–8)

Star Wars Young Jedi Knights (4–8)

2001 (9–12)

Spies and spying
Alex Rider (6–10)

Alias (8–12)

Cherub (6–10)

Secret Agent MJJ (4–7)

Specialists (8–10)

Spy Force (4–7)

Spy Girls (7–10)

Spy High (9–12)

SpyBoy (10–12)

Undercover Girl (5–7)

Sports *see also* specific sports (e.g., Baseball, Basketball)
Alden All Stars (4–8)

American Gold Gymnasts (4–7)

The Broadway Ballplayers (4–7)

Chip Hilton Sports Series (5–8)

Dream Series (6–12)

Extreme Team (4–7)

Hover Car Racer (6–9)

The Jersey (4–7)

Matt Christopher's Sports Stories (3–7)

Screech Owls (4–7)

Spirit of the Game (5–8)

Sports Mystery (9–12)

Winning Season (4–7)

X Games Xtreme Mysteries (4–8)

Supernatural *see also* Ghosts, Monsters and creatures
Angel (7–12)

Angel (Graphic Novels) (8–12)

Bardic Voices (10–12)

Blossom Culp (5–7)

Blue Bloods (9–12)

The Bonemender (7–10)

The Brimstone Network (6–9)

Buffy the Vampire Slayer (6–10)

Buffy the Vampire Slayer (6–10)

Buffy the Vampire Slayer: Buffy and Angel (6–10)

Buffy the Vampire Slayer: Buffy and Angel: The Unseen Trilogy (6–10)

Buffy the Vampire Slayer: Stake Your Destiny (6–10)

Buffy the Vampire Slayer: The Angel Chronicles (6–10)

Buffy the Vampire Slayer: The Gatekeeper Trilogy (6–10)

Buffy the Vampire Slayer: The Lost Slayer Serial Novel (6–10)

Buffy the Vampire Slayer: The Willow Files (6–10)

Buffy the Vampire Slayer: The Xander Years (6–10)

Buffy the Vampire Slayer: Wicked Willow (6–10)

Celia Rees Supernatural Trilogy (6–8)

Charmed (7–12)

Cirque du Freak (6–9)

CLAMP School Detectives (4–8)

Dark Is Rising (4–8)

Dark Secrets (7–10)

Dark Tower (9–12)

Darkangel Trilogy (6–10)

Daughter of Destiny (9–12)

Demonata (9–12)

Den of Shadows (7–10)

Dragonflight (7–10)

Enchanted Hearts (7–12)

Forbidden Doors (7–9)

Forbidden Game (7–10)

Gemma Doyle (9–12)

Ghost (10–12)

Goldstone Trilogy (5–7)

Goosebumps Horrorland (4–8)

Hellsing (10–12)

Hollow (7–10)

House of Night (9–12)

House on Cherry Street (5–8)

The Ink Drinker (4–7)

Johnny Maxwell (5–8)

Kiesha'ra (7–10)

Last Apprentice (5–8)

The Last Vampire (9–12)

Lily Quench (4–7)

Maggie Quinn: Girl vs. Evil (9–12)

The Mediator (7–10)

Midnighters (6–10)

Mind over Matter (4–8)

Moondog (10–12)

My Sister the Vampire (5–8)

ABOUT THE AUTHORS

REBECCA L. THOMAS is an elementary school librarian, Shaker Heights City Schools, Ohio. She is the author of numerous reference books, including *Across Cultures* (Libraries Unlimited, 2007) and the recent supplement to the 7th edition of *A to Zoo* (Libraries Unlimited, 2008).

CATHERINE BARR is editor of the Libraries Unlimited Children's and Young Adult Literature Reference series and author or coauthor of other Libraries Unlimited titles including *High/Low Handbook* and the Best Books series (*Best Books for Children, Best Books for Middle School and Junior High Readers, Best Books for High School Readers,* and *Best New Media*).